# SKETCHES
## OF THE
# NATURAL HISTORY OF CEYLON

AN ELEPHANT CORRAL.

# SKETCHES
## OF THE
# NATURAL HISTORY OF CEYLON

## WITH
## NARRATIVES AND ANECDOTES

ILLUSTRATIVE OF THE HABITS AND INSTINCTS OF THE
**MAMMALIA, BIRDS, REPTILES, FISHES, INSECTS,**
INCLUDING A MONOGRAPH OF

# THE ELEPHANT

AND A DESCRIPTION OF THE MODES OF CAPTURING AND TRAINING IT
WITH ENGRAVINGS FROM ORIGINAL DRAWINGS


## J. EMERSON TENNENT



GYAN

*Published by*

Gyan Publishing House
5, Ansari Road
Daryaganj, New Delhi-110002
Phone: 011-47034999, 9811692060
E-mail: books@gyanbooks.com

*Distribution Network*
gyanbooks.com
India, USA, Canada, UK, Australia, France



ISBN : 978-81-212-4031-4 (PB)
First Published, 1861

2nd Impression 2020

*Printed at:* Gyan Press, Delhi.



**Sketches of the Natural History of Ceylon**
Author: J. Emerson Tennent

# SKETCHES

OF THE

# NATURAL HISTORY OF CEYLON

WITH

NARRATIVES AND ANECDOTES

Illustrative of the Habits and Instincts of the

MAMMALIA, BIRDS, REPTILES, FISHES, INSECTS, &c.

INCLUDING A MONOGRAPH OF

THE ELEPHANT

AND A DESCRIPTION OF THE MODES OF CAPTURING AND TRAINING IT

WITH ENGRAVINGS FROM ORIGINAL DRAWINGS

BY

SIR J. EMERSON TENNENT, K.C.S. LL.D. &c.

Author of

"Ceylon, an Account of the Island, Physical, Historical, and Topographical" &c. &c.

LONDON

LONGMAN, GREEN, LONGMAN, AND ROBERTS

1861

# INTRODUCTION.

A CONSIDERABLE portion of the contents of the present volume formed the zoological section of a much more comprehensive work recently published, on the history and present condition of Ceylon.[1] But its inclusion there was a matter of difficulty; for to have altogether omitted the chapters on Natural History would have impaired the completeness of the plan on which I had attempted to describe the island; whilst to insert them as they here appear, without curtailment, would have encroached unduly on the space required for other essential topics. In this dilemma, I was obliged to adopt the alternative of so condensing the matter as to bring the whole within the prescribed proportions.

But this operation necessarily diminished the general interest of the subjects treated, as well by the omission of incidents which would otherwise have been retained, as by the exclusion of anecdotes calculated to illustrate the habits and instincts of the animals described.

[1] *Ceylon: An Account of the Island, Physical, Historical, and Topographical; with Notices of its Natural History, Antiquities, and Productions.* By Sir JAMES EMERSON TENNENT, K.C.S., LL.D., &c. Illustrated by Maps, Plans, and Drawings. 2 vols. 8vo. Longman and Co., 1859.

A suggestion to re-publish these sections in an independent form has afforded an opportunity for repairing some of these defects by revising the entire, restoring omitted passages, and introducing fresh materials collected in Ceylon; the additional matter occupying a very large portion of the present volume.

I have been enabled, at the same time, to avail myself of the corrections and communications of scientific friends; and thus to compensate, in some degree for what is still incomplete, by increased accuracy in minute particulars.

In the Introduction to the First Edition of the original work I alluded, in the following terms, to that portion of it which is now reproduced in an extended form :—

"Regarding the *fauna* of Ceylon, little has been published in any collective form, with the exception of a volume by Dr. KELAART entitled *Prodromus Faunæ Zeilanicæ;* several valuable papers by Mr. EDGAR L. LAYARD in the *Annals and Magazine of Natural History* for 1852 and 1853 ; and some very imperfect lists appended to PRIDHAM'S compiled account of the island.[1] KNOX, in the charming narrative of his captivity, published in the reign of Charles II., has devoted a chapter to the animals of Ceylon, and Dr. DAVY has described some of the reptiles: but with these exceptions the subject is almost untouched in works relating to the colony. Yet a more than ordinary interest attaches to

[1] *An Historical, Political, and Statistical Account of Ceylon and its Dependencies,* by C. PRIDHAM, Esq. 2 vols. 8vo. London, 1849.

the inquiry, since Ceylon, instead of presenting, as is generally assumed, an identity between its *fauna* and that of Southern India, exhibits a remarkable diversity, taken in connection with the limited area over which the animals included in it are distributed. The island, in fact, may be regarded as the centre of a geographical circle, possessing within itself forms, whose allied species radiate far into the temperate regions of the north, as well as into Africa, Australia, and the isles of the Eastern Archipelago.

"In the chapters that I have devoted to its elucidation, I have endeavoured to interest others in the subject, by describing my own observations and impressions, with fidelity, and with as much accuracy as may be expected from a person possessing, as I do, no greater knowledge of zoology and the other physical sciences than is ordinarily possessed by any educated gentleman. It was my good fortune, however, in my journeys to have the companionship of friends familiar with many branches of natural science: the late Dr. Gardner, Mr. Edgar L. Layard, an accomplished zoologist, Dr. Templeton, and others; and I was thus enabled to collect on the spot many interesting facts relative to the structure and habits of the numerous tribes. These, chastened by the corrections of my fellow-travellers, and established by the examination of collections made in the colony, and by subsequent comparison with specimens contained in museums at home, I have ventured to submit as faithful outlines of the *fauna* of Ceylon.

"The sections descriptive of the several classes are accompanied by lists, prepared with the assistance of scientific friends, showing the extent to which each particular branch had been investigated by naturalists, up to the period of my departure from Ceylon at the close of 1849. These, besides their inherent interest, will, I trust, stimulate others to engage in the same pursuit, by exhibiting chasms, which it remains for future industry and research to fill up;—and the study of the zoology of Ceylon may thus serve as a preparative for that of Continental India, embracing, as the former does, much that is common to both, as well as possessing a *fauna* peculiar to the island, that in itself will amply repay more extended scrutiny.

"From these lists have been excluded all species regarding the authenticity of which reasonable doubts could be entertained[1], and of some of them, a very few have been printed in *italics*, in order to denote the desirability of more minute comparison with well-determined specimens in the great national depositories before finally incorporating them with the Singhalese catalogues.

"In the labour of collecting and verifying the facts embodied in these sections, I cannot too warmly express my thanks for the aid I have received from gentlemen interested in similar studies in Ceylon: from

[1] An exception occurs in the list of shells, prepared by Mr. Sylvanus Hanley, in which some whose localities are doubtful have been admitted for reasons adduced. (See p. 387.)

Dr. Kelaart[1] and Mr. Edgar L. Layard, as well as from officers of the Ceylon Civil Service; the Hon. Gerald C. Talbot, Mr. C. R. Buller, Mr. Mercer, Mr. Morris, Mr. Whiting, Major Skinner, and Mr. Mitford.

"Before venturing to commit these chapters of my work to the press, I have had the advantage of having portions of them read by Professor Huxley, Mr. Moore, of the East India House Museum; Mr. R. Patterson, F.R.S., author of the *Introduction to Zoology;* and by Mr. Adam White, of the British Museum; to each of whom I am exceedingly indebted for the care they have bestowed. In an especial degree I have to acknowledge the kindness of Dr. J. E. Gray, F.R.S., for valuable additions and corrections in the list of the Ceylon Reptilia; and to Professor Faraday for some notes on the nature and qualities of the "Serpent Stone,"[2] submitted to him.

"The extent to which my observations on *the Elephant* have been carried, requires some explanation. The existing notices of this noble creature are chiefly devoted to its habits and capabilities *in captivity;* and very few works, with which I am acquainted, contain illustrations of its instincts and functions when wild in its native woods. Opportunities for observing the latter, and for collecting facts in connection with them, are abundant in Ceylon; and from the moment of my

[1] It is with deep regret that I have to record the death of this accomplished gentleman, which occurred in 1860.

[2] See p. 312.

arrival, I profited by every occasion afforded to me for observing the elephant in a state of nature, and obtaining from hunters and natives correct information as to its œconomy and disposition. Anecdotes in connection with this subject, I received from some of the most experienced residents in the island; amongst others, from Major SKINNER, Captain PHILIP PAYNE GALLWEY, Mr. FAIRHOLME, Mr. CRIPPS, and Mr. MORRIS. Nor can I omit to express my acknowledgments to Professor OWEN, of the British Museum, to whom this portion of my manuscript was submitted previous to its committal to the press."

To the foregoing observations I have little to add beyond my acknowledgment to Dr. ALBERT GÜNTHER, of the British Museum, for the communication of important facts in illustration of the ichthyology of Ceylon, as well as of the reptiles of the island.

Mr. BLYTH, of the Calcutta Museum, has carefully revised the Catalogue of Birds, and supplied me with much useful information in regard to their geographical distribution. To his experienced scrutiny is due the perfected state in which the list is now presented. It will be seen, however, from the italicised names still retained, that inquiry is far from being exhausted.

Mr. THWAITES, the able Director of the Royal Botanic Gardens at Peradenia, near Kandy, has forwarded to me many valuable observations, not only in connection with the botany, but the zoology of the mountain region. The latter I have here embodied in their appropriate places, and those relating to plants and vegetation will appear in a future edition of my large work.

To M. Nietner, of Colombo, I am likewise indebted for many particulars regarding Singhalese Entomology, a department to which his attention has been given, with equal earnestness and success.

Through the Hon. Richard Morgan, acting Senior Puisne Judge of the Supreme Court at Colombo, I have received from his Interpreter, M. D. de Silva Gooneratne Modliar, a Singhalese gentleman of learning and observation, many important notes, of which I have largely availed myself, in relation to the wild animals, and the folk-lore and superstitions of the natives in connection with them.

Of the latter I have inserted numerous examples; in the conviction that, notwithstanding their obvious errors in many instances, these popular legends and traditions occasionally embody traces of actual observation, and may contain hints and materials deserving of minuter inquiry.

I wish distinctly to disclaim offering the present volume as a compendium of the Natural History of Ceylon. I present it merely as a "mémoire pour servir," materials to assist some future inquirer in the formation of a more detailed and systematic account of the *fauna* of the island. My design has been to point out to others the extreme richness and variety of the field, the facility of exploring it, and the charms and attractions of the undertaking. I am eager to show

how much remains to do by exhibiting the little that has as yet been done.

The departments of *Mammalia* and *Birds* are the only two which can be said to have as yet undergone tolerably close investigation; although even in these it is probable that large additions still remain to be made to the ascertained species. But, independently of forms and specific characteristics, the more interesting inquiry into habits and instincts is still open for observation and remark; and for the investigation of these no country can possibly afford more inviting opportunities than Ceylon.

Concerning the *Reptilia* a considerable amount of information has been amassed. The Batrachians and smaller Lizards have, I apprehend, been imperfectly investigated; but the Tortoises are well known, and the Serpents, from the fearful interest attaching to the race, and stimulating their destruction, have been so vigilantly pursued, that there is reason to believe that few, if any, varieties exist which have not been carefully examined. In a very large collection, made by Mr. CHARLES REGINALD BULLER during many years' residence in Kandy, and recently submitted by him to Dr. Günther, only one single specimen proved to be new or previously unknown to belong to the island.

Of the *Ichthyology* of Ceylon I am obliged to speak in very different terms; for although the materials are abundant almost to profusion, little has yet been done to bring them under thoroughly scientific scrutiny. In the following pages I have alluded to the large collection of examples of Fishes sent home by officers of the Medical Staff, and which still remain unopened, in the Fort Pitt Museum at Chatham; but I am not without hope that these may shortly undergo comparison with the drawings which exist of each, and that this branch of the island *fauna* may at last attract the attention to which its richness so eminently entitles it.

In the department of Entomology much has already been achieved; but an extended area still invites future explorers; and one which the Notes of Mr. Walker prefixed to the List of Insects in this volume, show to be of extraordinary interest, from the unexpected convergence in Ceylon of characteristics heretofore supposed to have been kept distinct by the broad lines of geographical distribution.

Relative to the inferior classes of *Invertebrata* very little has as yet been ascertained. The Mollusca, especially the lacustrine and fluviatile, have been most imperfectly investigated; and of the land-shells, a large proportion have yet to be submitted to scientific examination.

The same may be said of the *Arachnida* and *Crustacea*. The jungle is frequented by spiders, *phalangia*[1], and acarids, of which nothing is known with certainty; and the sea-shore and sands have been equally overlooked, so far as concerns the infinite variety of lobsters, crayfish, crabs, and all their minor congeners. The

[1] Commonly called "harvest-men."

*polypi*, *echini*, *asterias*, and other *radiata* of the coast, as well as the *acalephæ* of the deeper waters, have shared the same neglect; and literally nothing has been done to collect and classify the infusoriæ and minuter zoophytes, the labours of Dr. Kelaart amongst the Diatomaceæ being the solitary exception.

Nothing is so likely to act as a stimulant to future research as an accurate conception of what has already been achieved. With equal terseness and truth Dr. Johnson has observed that the traveller who would bring back knowledge from any country must carry knowledge with him at setting out; and I am not without hope that the demonstration I now venture to offer, of the little that has already been done for zoology in Ceylon, may serve to inspire others with a desire to resume and complete the inquiry.

J. EMERSON TENNENT.

London: November 1st, 1861.

# CONTENTS.

## CHAPTER I.

### MAMMALIA.

## CHAP. IV.

### THE ELEPHANT.

*Elephant Shooting.*



## CHAP. V.

### THE ELEPHANT.

*An Elephant Corral.*



## CHAP. VI.

### THE ELEPHANT.

*The Captives.*

## CHAP. XI.

### MOLLUSCA, RADIATA, AND ACALEPHÆ.



## CHAP. XII.

### INSECTS.



## CHAP. XIII.

### ARACHNIDÆ, MYRIOPODA, CRUSTACEA, ETC.

# LIST OF ILLUSTRATIONS.

ERRATUM.

Page 104. for "THEORALDUS" read "THEOBALDUS."

*Errata.*

In List of Illustrations, p. xxiii. line 12, for *Ceatophora* read *Ceratophora.*
P. 433, note, *for* Fœciloptera *read* Pœciloptera.

# THE

# NATURAL HISTORY OF CEYLON

# CHAPTER I.

## MAMMALIA.

WITH the exception of the Mammalia and Birds, the fauna of Ceylon has, up to the present, failed to receive that systematic attention to which its richness and variety most amply entitle it. The Singhalese themselves, habitually indolent, and singularly unobservant of nature and her operations, are at the same time restrained from the study of natural history by the tenet of their religion which forbids the taking of life under any circumstances. From the nature of their avocations, the majority of the European residents, engaged in planting and commerce, are discouraged by want of leisure from cultivating the taste; and it is to be regretted that, with few exceptions, the civil servants of the government, whose position and duties would have afforded them influence and extended opportunities for successful investigation, have never seen the importance of encouraging such studies.

The first effective impulse to the cultivation of natural science in Ceylon, was communicated by Dr. Davy when connected with the medical staff[1] of the army from 1816 to 1820, and his example stimulated some of the assistant-surgeons of Her Majesty's forces to make col-

[1] DR. DAVY, brother to the illustrious Sir Humphry Davy, published, in 1821, his *Account of the Interior of Ceylon and its Inhabitants*, which contains the earliest notice of the Natural History of the island, and especially of its ophidian reptiles.

lections in illustration of the productions of the colony. Of these the late Dr. Kinnis was one of the most energetic and successful. He was seconded by Dr. Templeton of the Royal Artillery, who engaged assiduously in the investigation of various orders, and commenced an interchange of specimens with Mr. Blyth [1], the distinguished naturalist and curator of the Calcutta Museum. The birds and rarer vertebrata of the island were thus compared with their peninsular congeners, and a tolerable knowledge of those belonging to the island, so far as regards the higher classes of animals, has been the result. The example so set was perseveringly followed by Mr. E. L. Layard and the late Dr. Kelaart, and infinite credit is due to Mr. Blyth for the zealous and untiring energy with which he has devoted his attention and leisure to the identification of the specimens forwarded from Ceylon, and to their description in the Calcutta Journal. To him, and to the gentlemen I have named, we are mainly indebted for whatever accurate knowledge we now possess of the zoology of the colony.

The mammalia, birds, and reptiles received their first scientific description in an able work published in 1852 by Dr. Kelaart of the army medical staff [2], which is by far the most valuable that has yet appeared on the Singhalese fauna. Co-operating with him, Mr. Layard has supplied a fund of information especially in ornithology and conchology. The zoophytes and crustacea have I believe been partially investigated by Professor Harvey, who visited Ceylon in 1852, and more re-

[1] *Journ. Asiat. Soc. Bengal*, vol. xv. p. 280, 314.

[2] *Prodromus Faunæ Zeylanicæ; being Contributions to the Zoology of Ceylon*, by F. KELAART, Esq., M.D., F.L.S., &c. &c. 2 vols. Colombo and London, 1852.

CEYLON MONKEYS.

1. *Presbytes cephalopterus.*
2. *P. Thersites.*
3. *P. Priamus.*
4. *Macacus pileatus.*

cently by Professor Schmarda, of the University of Prague. From the united labours of these gentlemen and others interested in the same pursuits, we may hope at an early day to obtain such a knowledge of the zoology of Ceylon as will to some extent compensate for the long indifference of the government officers.

I. QUADRUMANA. 1. *Monkeys.*—To a stranger in the tropics, among the most attractive creatures in the forests are the troops of *monkeys* that career in ceaseless chase among the loftiest trees. In Ceylon there are five species, four of which belong to one group, the Wanderoos, and the other is the little graceful grimacing *rilawa* [1], which is the universal pet and favourite of both natives and Europeans. The Tamil conjurors teach it to dance, and in their wanderings carry it from village to village, clad in a grotesque dress, to exhibit its lively performances. It does not object to smoke tobacco. The Wanderoo is too grave and melancholy to be trained to these drolleries.

KNOX, in his captivating account of the island, gives an accurate description of both; the Rilawas, with "no beards, white faces, and long hair on the top of their heads, which parteth and hangeth down like a man's, and which do a deal of mischief to the corn, and are so impudent that they will come into their gardens and eat such fruit as grows there. And the Wanderoos, some

[1] *Macacus pileatus*, Shaw and Desmarest. The "bonneted Macaque" is common in the south and west; it is replaced on the neighbouring coast of the Peninsula of India by the Toque, *M. radiatus*, which closely resembles it in size, habit, and form, and in the peculiar appearance occasioned by the hairs radiating from the crown of the head. A spectacled monkey is *said* to inhabit the low country near to Bintenne; but I have never seen one brought thence. A paper by Dr. TEMPLETON, in the *Mag. Nat. Hist.* n. s. xiv. p. 361, contains some interesting facts relative to the Rilawa of Ceylon.

as large as our English spaniel dogs, of a darkish grey colour, and black faces with great white beards round from ear to ear, which makes them show just like old men. This sort does but little mischief, keeping in the woods, eating only leaves and buds of trees, but when they are catched they will eat anything."[1]

KNOX, whose experience during his long captivity was confined almost exclusively to the hill country around Kandy, spoke in all probability of one large and comparatively powerful species, *Presbytes ursinus*, which inhabits the lofty forests, and which, as well as another of the same group, *P. Thersites*, was, till recently, unknown to European naturalists. The Singhalese word *Ouandura* has a generic sense, and being in every respect the equivalent for our own term of "monkey," it necessarily comprehends the low country species, as well as those which inhabit other parts of the island. In point of fact, there are no less than four animals in the island, each of which is entitled to the name of "wanderoo."[2] Each separate species has appropriated

[1] KNOX, *Historical Relation of Ceylon, an Island in the East Indies.*—P. i. ch. vi. p. 25. Fol. Lond. 1681. See an account of his captivity in SIR J. EMERSON TENNENT'S *Ceylon*, etc., Vol. II. p. 66 n.

[2] Down to a very late period, a large and somewhat repulsive-looking monkey, common to the Malabar coast, the Silenus veter, *Linn.*, was, from the circumstance of his possessing a "great white beard," incorrectly assumed to be the "wanderoo" of Ceylon, described by KNOX; and under that usurped name it has figured in every author from Buffon to the present time. Specimens of the true Singhalese species were, however, received in Europe; but in the absence of information in this country as to their actual habitat, they were described, first by Zimmerman, on the continent, under the name of *Leucoprymnus cephalopterus*, and subsequently by Mr. E. Bennett, under that of *Semnopithecus Nestor* (*Proc. Zool. Soc.* pt. i. p. 67 : 1833); the generic and specific characters being on this occasion most carefully pointed out by that eminent naturalist. Eleven years later Dr. Templeton forwarded to the Zoological Society a description, accompanied by drawings, of the wanderoo of the western maritime districts of Ceylon, and noticed the fact that the wanderoo of authors (*S. veter*) was not to be found

to itself a different district of the wooded country, and seldom encroaches on the domain of its neighbours.

1. Of the four species found in Ceylon, the most numerous in the island, and the one best known in Europe, is the Wanderoo of the low country, the *P. cephalopterus* of Zimmerman.[1] Although common in the southern and western provinces, it is never found at a higher elevation than 1300 feet. It is an active and intelligent creature, little larger than the common bonneted Macaque, and far from being so mischievous as others of the monkeys in the island. In captivity it is remarkable for the gravity of its demeanour and for an air of melancholy in its expression and movements which are completely in character with its snowy beard and venerable aspect. In disposition it is gentle and confiding, sensible in the highest degree of kindness, and eager for endearing attention, uttering a low plaintive cry when its sympathies are excited. It is particularly cleanly in its habits when domesticated, and spends much of its time in trimming its fur, and carefully divesting its hair of particles of dust.

Those which I kept at my house near Colombo were chiefly fed upon plantains and bananas, but for nothing did they evince a greater partiality than the rose-coloured flowers of the red hibiscus (H. *rosa-*

in the island except as an introduced species in the custody of the Arab horse-dealers, who visit the port of Colombo at stated periods. Mr. Waterhouse, at the meeting (*Proc. Zool. Soc.* p. 1: 1844) at which this communication was read, recognised the identity of the subject of Dr. Templeton's description with that already laid before them by Mr. Bennett; and from this period the species in question was believed to truly represent the wanderoo of Knox. The later discovery, however, of the *P. ursinus* by Dr. Kelaart, in the mountains amongst which we are assured that Knox spent so many years of captivity, reopens the question, but at the same time appears to me clearly to demonstrate that in this latter we have in reality the animal to which his narrative refers.

[1] Leucoprymnus Nestor, *Bennett.*

*sinensis*). These they devoured with unequivocal gusto; they likewise relished the leaves of many other trees, and even the bark of a few of the more succulent ones. A hint might possibly be taken from this circumstance for improving the regimen of monkeys in menageries, by the occasional admixture of a few fresh leaves and flowers with their solid and substantial dietary.

A white monkey, taken between Ambepusse and Kornegalle, where they are said to be numerous, was brought to me to Colombo. Except in colour, it had all the characteristics of *Presbytes cephalopterus.* So striking was its whiteness that it might have been conjectured to be an albino, but for the circumstance that its eyes and face were black. I have heard that white monkeys have been seen near the Ridi-galle Wihara in Seven Korles and also at Tangalle; but I never saw another specimen. The natives say they are not uncommon, and KNOX that they are "milk-white both in body and face; but of this sort there is not such plenty."[1] The Rev. R. SPENCE HARDY mentions, in his learned work on *Eastern Monachism,* that on the occasion of his visit to the great temple of Dambool, he encountered a troop of white monkeys on the rock in which it is situated — which were, doubtless, a variety of the Wanderoo.[2] PLINY was aware of the fact that white monkeys are occasionally found in India.[3]

When observed in their native wilds, a party of twenty or thirty of these creatures is generally busily engaged in the search for berries and buds. They are seldom to be seen on the ground, except when

[1] KNOX, pt. i. c. vi. p. 25.
[2] *Eastern Monachism,* c. xix. p. 204.
[3] PLINY, Nat. Hist. l. viii. c. xxxii.

they may have descended to recover seeds or fruit which have fallen at the foot of their favourite trees. When disturbed, their leaps are prodigious: but, generally speaking, their progress is made not so much by *leaping* as by swinging from branch to branch, using their powerful arms alternately; and when baffled by distance, flinging themselves obliquely so as to catch the lower boughs of an opposite tree, the momentum acquired by their descent being sufficient to cause a rebound of the branch, that carries them upwards again, till they can grasp a higher and more distant one, and thus continue their headlong flight. In these perilous achievements, wonder is excited less by the surpassing agility of these little creatures, frequently encumbered as they are by their young, which cling to them in their career, than by the quickness of their eye and the unerring accuracy with which they seem almost to calculate the angle at which a descent will enable them to cover a given distance, and the recoil to attain a higher altitude.

2. The low country Wanderoo is replaced in the hills by the larger species, *P. ursinus*, which inhabits the mountain zone. The natives, who designate the latter the *Maha* or Great Wanderoo, to distinguish it from the *Kaloo*, or black one, with which they are familiar, describe it as much wilder and more powerful than its congener of the lowland forests. It is rarely seen by Europeans, this portion of the country having till very recently been but partially opened; and even now it is difficult to observe its habits, as it seldom approaches the few roads which wind through these deep solitudes. At early morning, ere the day begins to dawn, its loud and peculiar howl, which consists of a quick repetition

of the sounds *how how!* may be frequently heard in the mountain jungles, and forms one of the characteristic noises of these lofty situations. It was first captured by Dr. Kelaart in the woods near Nuera-ellia, and from its peculiar appearance it has been named *P. ursinus* by Mr. Blyth.[1]

3. The *P. Thersites,* which is chiefly distinguished from the others by wanting the head tuft, is so rare that it was for some time doubtful whether the single specimen procured by Dr. Templeton from the Nuera-kalawa, west of Trincomalie, and on which Mr. Blyth conferred this new name, was in reality native; but the occurrence of a second, since identified by Dr. Kelaart, has established its existence as a separate species. Like the common wanderoo, the one obtained by Dr. Templeton was partial to fresh vegetables, plantains, and fruit; but he ate freely boiled rice, beans, and gram. He was fond of being noticed and petted, stretching out his limbs in succession to be scratched, drawing himself up so that his ribs might be reached by the finger, closing his eyes during the operation, and evincing his satisfaction by grimaces irresistibly ludicrous.

4. The *P. Priamus* inhabits the northern and eastern provinces, and the wooded hills which occur in these portions of the island. In appearance it differs both in size and in colour from the common wanderoo, being larger and more inclined to grey; and in habits it is much less reserved. At Jaffna, and in other parts of the island where the population is comparatively nu-

[1] Mr. Blyth quotes as authority for this trivial name a passage from MAJOR FORBES' *Eleven Years in Ceylon;* and I can vouch for the graphic accuracy of the remark. —"A species of very large monkey, that passed some distance before me, when resting on all fours, looked so like a Ceylon bear, that I nearly took him for one."

merous, these monkeys become so familiarised with the presence of man as to exhibit the utmost daring and indifference. A flock of them will take possession of a Palmyra palm; and so effectually can they crouch and conceal themselves among the leaves that, on the slightest alarm, the whole party becomes invisible in an instant. The presence of a dog, however, excites such an irrepressible curiosity that, in order to watch his movements, they never fail to betray themselves. They may be frequently seen congregated on the roof of a native hut: and, some years ago, the child of a European clergyman stationed near Jaffna having been left on the ground by the nurse, was so teased and bitten by them as to cause its death.

The Singhalese have the impression that the remains of a monkey are never to be found in the forest; a belief which they have embodied in the proverb that "he who has seen a white crow, the nest of a paddi bird, a straight coco-nut tree, or a dead monkey, is certain to live for ever." This piece of folk-lore has evidently reached Ceylon from India, where it is believed that persons dwelling on the spot where a hanumân monkey, *Semnopithecus entellus*, has been killed, will die, that even its bones are unlucky, and that no house erected where they are hid under ground can prosper. Hence when a dwelling is to be built, it is one of the employments of the Jyotish philosophers to ascertain by their science that none such are concealed; and Buchanan observes that "it is, perhaps, owing to this fear of ill-luck that no native will acknowledge his having seen a dead hanumân." [1]

[1] BUCHANAN'S *Survey of Bhagulpoor*, p. 142. At Gibraltar it is believed that the body of a *dead monkey* has never been found on the rock.

The only other quadrumanous animal found in Ceylon is the little loris[1], which, from its sluggish movements, nocturnal habits, and consequent inaction during the day, has acquired the name of the "Ceylon Sloth."

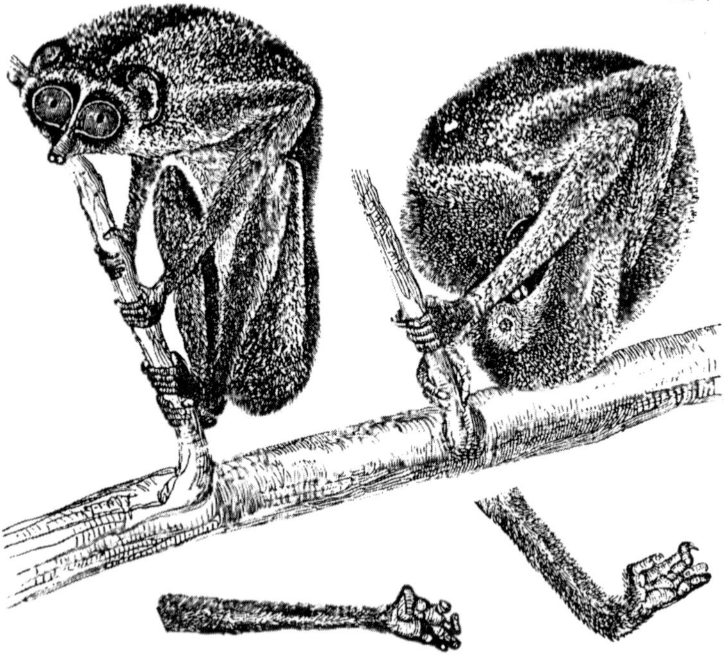

THE LORIS.

There are two varieties in the island; one of the ordinary fulvous brown, and another larger, whose fur is entirely black. A specimen of the former was sent to me from Chilaw, on the western coast, and lived for some time at Colombo, feeding on rice, fruit, and vegetables. It was partial to ants and other insects, and was always eager for milk or the bone of a fowl. The naturally slow motion of its limbs enables the loris to

[1] Loris gracilis, *Geof.*

approach its prey so stealthily that it seizes birds before they can be alarmed by its presence. The natives assert that it has been known to strangle the pea-fowl at night, to feast on the brain. During the day the one which I kept was usually asleep in the strange position represented on the last page; its perch firmly grasped with both hands, its back curved into a ball of soft fur, and its head hidden deep between its legs. The singularly-large and intense eyes of the loris have attracted the attention of the Singhalese, who capture the creature for the purpose of extracting them as charms and love-potions, and this they are said to effect by holding the little animal to the fire till its eyeballs burst. Its Tamil name is *thavangu*, or "thin-bodied;" and hence a deformed child or an emaciated person has acquired in the Tamil districts the same epithet. The light-coloured variety of the loris in Ceylon has a spot on its forehead, somewhat resembling the *namam*, or mark worn by the worshippers of Vishnu; and, from this peculiarity, it is distinguished as the *Nama-thavangu.*[1]

II. CHEIROPTERA. *Bats.*—The multitude of *bats* is one of the features of the evening landscape; they abound in every cave and subterranean passage, in the tunnels on the highways, in the galleries of the fortifications, in the roofs of the bungalows, and the ruins of every temple and building. At sunset they are seen issuing from their diurnal retreats to roam through the twilight in search of crepuscular insects, and as night approaches and the lights in the rooms attract the night-flying lepidoptera, the bats sweep round the dinner-table and

[1] There is an interesting notice of the Loris of Ceylon by Dr. TEMPLETON, in the *Mag. Nat. Hist.* 1844, ch. xiv. p. 362.

carry off their tiny prey within the glitter of the lamps. Including the frugivorous section about sixteen species have been identified in Ceylon; and remarkable varieties of two of these are peculiar to the island. The colours of some of them are as brilliant as the plumage of a bird, bright yellow, deep orange, and a rich ferruginous brown inclining to red.[1]

But of all the bats, the most conspicuous from its size and numbers, and the most interesting from its habits, is the rousette of Ceylon[2];—the "flying fox," as it is called by Europeans, from the similarity to that animal in its head and ears, its bright eyes, and intelligent little face. In its aspect it has nothing of the disagreeable and repulsive look so common amongst the ordinary vespertilionidæ; it likewise differs from them in the want of the nose-leaf, as well as of the tail. In the absence of the latter, its flight is directed by means of a membrane attached to the inner side of each of the hind legs, and kept distended at the lower extremity by a projecting bone, just as a fore-and-aft sail is distended by a "gaff."

In size the body measures from ten to twelve inches in length, but the arms are prolonged, and especially the metacarpal bones and phalanges of the four fingers over which the leathery wings are distended, till the alar expanse measures between four and five feet. Whilst the function of these metamorphosed limbs in sustaining flight entitles them to the designation of "wings," they are endowed with another faculty, the existence of

[1] Rhinolophus affinis? *var.* rubidus, *Kelaart.*

Hipposideros murinus, *var.* fulvus, *Kelaart.*

Hipposideros speoris, *var.* aureus, *Kelaart.*

Kerivoula picta, *Pallas.*

Scotophilus Heathii, *Horsf.*

[2] Pteropus Edwardsii, *Geoff.*

FLYING FOXES.

*Pteropus Edwardsii.*

which essentially distinguishes them from the feathery wings of a bird, and vindicates the appropriateness of the term *Cheiro-ptera*[1], or "winged hands," by which the bats are designated. Over the entire surface of the thin membrane of which they are formed, sentient nerves of the utmost delicacy are distributed, by means of which the animal is enabled during the darkness to direct its motions with security, avoiding objects against contact with which at such times its eyes and other senses would be insufficient to protect it.[2] Spallanzani ascertained the perfection of this faculty by a series of cruel experiments, by which he demonstrated that bats, even after their eyes had been destroyed, and their external organs of smell and hearing obliterated, were still enabled to direct their flight with unhesitating confidence, avoiding even threads suspended to intercept them. But after ascertaining the fact, Spallanzani was slow to arrive at its origin; and ascribed the surprising power to the existence of some sixth supplementary sense, the enjoyment of which was withheld from other animals. Cuvier, however, dissipated the obscurity by showing the seat of this extraordinary endowment to be in the wings, the superficies of which retains the exquisite sensitiveness to touch that is inherent in the palms of the human hand and the extremities of the fingers, as well as in the feet of some of the mammalia.[3] The face and head of the *Pteropus* are covered with brownish-grey hairs, the neck and chest are dark ferruginous grey, and the rest of the body brown, inclining to black.

[1] χεὶρ, the "hand," and πτερὸν, a "wing."

[2] See BELL *On the Hand*, ch. iii. p. 70.

[3] See article on *Cheiroptera*, in TODD'S *Cyclopædia of Anatomy and Physiology*, vol. i. p. 599.

These active and energetic creatures, though chiefly frugivorous, are to some extent insectivorous also, as attested by their teeth [1], as well as by their habits. They feed, amongst other things, on the guava, the plantain, the rose-apple, and the fruit of the various fig-trees. Flying foxes are abundant in all the maritime districts, especially at the season when the *pulum-imbul*[2], one of the silk-cotton trees, is putting forth its flower-buds, of which they are singularly fond. By day they suspend themselves from the highest branches, hanging by the claws of the hind legs, with the head turned upwards, and pressing the chin against the breast. At sunset taking wing, they hover, with a murmuring sound occasioned by the beating of their broad membranous wings, around the fruit trees, on which they feed till morning, when they resume their pensile attitude as before.

A favourite resort of these bats is to the lofty india-rubber trees, which on one side overhang the Botanic Gardens of Paradenia in the vicinity of Kandy. Thither for some years past, they have congregated, chiefly in the autumn, taking their departure when the figs of the *ficus elastica* are consumed. Here they hang in such prodigious numbers, that frequently, large branches give way beneath their accumulated weight. Every forenoon, generally between the hours of 9 and 11 A. M., they take to wing, apparently for exercise, and possibly to sun their wings and fur, and dry them after the dews of the early morning. On these occasions, their numbers are quite surprising, flying in clouds as thick as

[1] Those which I have examined have four minute incisors in each jaw, with two canines and a very minute pointed tooth behind each canine. They have six molars in the upper jaw and ten in the lower, longitudinally grooved, and with a cutting edge directed backwards.

[2] Eriodendron Orientale, *Stead.*

bees or midges. After these recreations, they hurry back to their favourite trees, chattering and screaming like monkeys, and always wrangling and contending angrily for the most shady and comfortable places in which to hang for the rest of the day protected from the sun. The branches they resort to soon become almost divested of leaves, these being stripped off by the action of the bats, attaching and detaching themselves by means of their hooked feet. At sunset, they fly off to their feeding-grounds, probably at a considerable distance, as it requires a large area to furnish sufficient food for such multitudes.

In all its movements and attitudes, the action of the *Pteropus* is highly interesting. If placed upon the ground, it is almost helpless, none of its limbs being calculated for progressive motion; it drags itself along by means of the hook attached to each of its extended thumbs, pushing at the same time with those of its hind feet. Its natural position is exclusively pensile; it moves laterally from branch to branch with great ease, by using each foot alternately, and climbs, when necessary, by means of its claws.

When at rest, or asleep, the disposition of the limbs is most curious. At such times it suspends itself by one foot only, bringing the other close to its side, and thus it is enabled to wrap itself in the ample folds of its wings, which envelop it like a mantle, leaving only its upturned head uncovered. Its fur is thus protected from damp and rain, and to some extent its body is sheltered from the sun.

As it collects its food by means of its mouth, either when on the wing, or when suspended within reach of it, the flying-fox is always more or less liable to have the spoil wrested from it by its intrusive companions, before it can make good its way to some secure retreat in which to devour it unmolested. In such conflicts they bite viciously, tear each other with their hooks, and scream incessantly, till, taking to flight, the persecuted one reaches some place of safety, where he hangs by one foot, and grasping the fruit he has secured in the claws and opposable thumb of the other, he hastily reduces it to lumps, with which he stuffs his cheek pouches till they become distended like those of a monkey; then suspended in safety, he commences to chew and suck the pieces, rejecting the refuse with his tongue.

To drink, which it does by lapping, the *Pteropus* suspends itself head downwards from a branch above the water.

Insects, caterpillars, birds' eggs, and young birds are devoured by them; and the Singhalese say that the flying-fox will even attack a tree snake. It is killed by the natives for the sake of its flesh, which, I have been told by a gentleman who has eaten of it, resembles that of the hare.[1] It is strongly attracted to the coconut trees during the period when toddy is drawn for distillation, and exhibits, it is said, at such times, symptoms resembling intoxication.

Neither the flying-fox, nor any other bat that I know of in Ceylon, ever hybernates.

There are several varieties (one of them peculiar to the island) of the horse-shoe-headed *Rhinolophus*, with the strange leaf-like appendage erected on the extremity of the nose.

[1] In Western India the native Portuguese eat the flying-fox, and pronounce it delicate, and far from disagreeable in flavour.

It has been suggested that the insectivorous bats, though nocturnal, are deficient in that keen vision characteristic of animals which take their prey by night.

RHINOLOPHUS.

I doubt whether this conjecture be well founded; it certainly does not apply to the *Pteropus* and the other frugivorous species, in which the faculty of sight is singularly clear. As regards the others, it is possible that in their peculiar œconomy some additional power may be required to act in concert with that of vision, as in insects, touch is superadded, in its most sensitive development, to that of sight. It is probable that the noseleaf, which forms an extended screen stretched behind the nostrils in some of the bats, may be intended by nature to facilitate the collection and conduction of odours, just as the vast expansion of the shell of the ear in the same family is designed to assist in the collection of sounds—and thus to supplement their vision when in pursuit of prey in the dusk by the superior sensitiveness of the organs of hearing and smell.

One tiny little bat, not much larger than the humble

bee [1], and of a glossy black colour, is sometimes to be seen about Colombo. It is so familiar and gentle that it will alight on the cloth during dinner, and manifests so little alarm that it seldom makes any effort to escape before a wine glass can be inverted to secure it.

Although not strictly in order, this seems not an inappropriate place to notice one of the most curious peculiarities connected with the bats — their singular parasite, the Nycteribia.[2] On cursory observation this creature appears to have neither head, antennæ, eyes, nor mouth ; and the earlier observers of its structure satisfied themselves that the place of the latter was supplied by a cylindrical sucker, which, being placed between the shoulders, the insect had no option but to turn on its back to feed. Another anomaly was thought to compensate for this apparent inconvenience ; — its three pairs of legs, armed with claws, are so arranged that they seem to be equally distributed over its upper and under sides, the creature being thus enabled to use them like hands, and to grasp the strong hairs above it while extracting its nourishment.

It moves, in fact, by rolling itself rapidly along, rotating like a wheel on the extremities of its spokes, or like the clown in a pantomime, hurling himself forward on hands and feet alternately. Its celerity is so great that Colonel Montague, who was one of the first to describe it minutely [3], says its speed exceeds that of any

[1] It is a *very* small Singhalese variety of Scotophilus Coromandelicus, *F. Cuv.*

[2] This extraordinary creature had formerly been discovered only on a few European bats. Joinville figured one which he found on the large roussette (the flying-fox), and says he had seen another on a bat of the same family. Dr. Templeton observed them in Ceylon in great abundance on the fur of the *Scotophilus Coromandelicus,* and they will, no doubt, be found on many others.

[3] Celeripes vespertilionis, *Mont. Lin. Trans.* xi. p. 11.

known insect, and as its joints are so flexible as to yield in every direction (like what mechanics call a "ball and socket"), its motions are exceedingly grotesque as it tumbles through the fur of the bat.

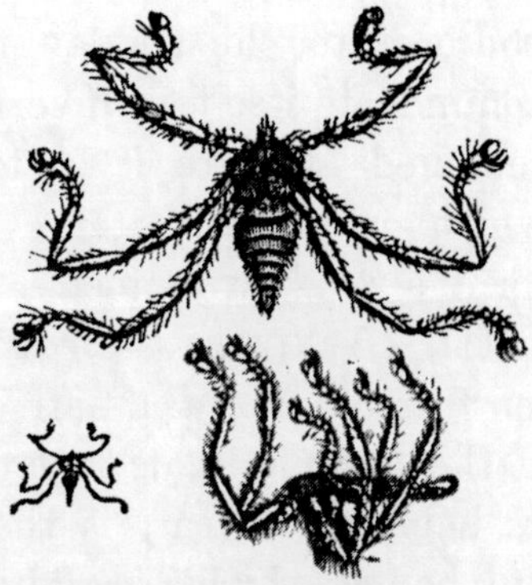
NYCTERIBIA.

To enable it to attain its marvellous velocity, each foot is armed with two sharp hooks, with elastic opposable pads, so that the hair can not only be rapidly seized and firmly held, but as quickly disengaged, as the creature whirls away in its headlong career.

The insects to which it bears the nearest affinity, are the *Hippoboscidæ*, or "spider flies," that infest birds and horses; but, unlike them, the Nycteribia is unable to fly.

Its strangest peculiarity, and that which gave rise to the belief that it was headless, is its faculty when at rest of throwing back its head and pressing it close between its shoulders till the under side becomes uppermost, not a vestige of head being discernible where we would naturally look for it, and the whole seeming but a casual inequality on its back.

On closer examination this apparent tubercle is found to have a leathery attachment like a flexible neck, and by a sudden jerk the little creature is enabled to project it forward into its normal position, when it is discovered to be furnished with a mouth, antennæ, and four eyes, two on each side.

The organisation of such an insect is a marvellous adaptation of physical form to special circumstances. As the nycteribia has to make its way through fur and hairs, its feet are furnished with prehensile hooks that almost convert them into hands; and being obliged to conform to the sudden flights of its patron, and accommodate itself to inverted positions, all attitudes are rendered alike to it by the arrangement of its limbs, which enables it, after every possible gyration, to find itself always on its feet.

III. CARNIVORA.—*Bears.*—Of the *carnivora*, the one most dreaded by the natives of Ceylon, and the only one of the larger animals that makes the depths of the forest its habitual retreat, is the bear [1], attracted chiefly by the honey which is found in the hollow trees and clefts of the rocks. Occasionally spots of fresh earth are observed which have been turned up by the bears in search of some favourite root. They feed also on the termites and ants. A friend of mine traversing the forest, near Jaffna, at early dawn, had his attention attracted by the growling of a bear, that was seated upon a lofty branch, thrusting portions of a red-ants' nest into his mouth with one paw, whilst with the other he endeavoured to clear his eyebrows and lips of the angry inmates, which bit and tortured him in their rage. The Ceylon bear is found in the low and dry districts of the northern and south-eastern coast, and is seldom met with on the mountains or the moist and damp plains of the west. It is furnished with a bushy tuft of hair on the back, between the shoulders, by which the young are accustomed to cling till sufficiently strong to provide for their own safety. During a severe drought that prevailed in the northern province in 1850, the district of Caretchy was so infested by bears that the

[1] Prochilus labiatus, *Blainville.*

Oriental custom of the women resorting to the wells was altogether suspended, as it was a common occurrence to find one of these animals in the water, unable to climb up the yielding and slippery soil, down which its thirst had impelled it to slide during the night.

Although the structure of the bear shows him to be naturally omnivorous, he rarely preys upon flesh in

INDIAN BEAR.

Ceylon, and his solitary habits whilst in search of honey and fruits render him timid and retiring. Hence he evinces alarm on the approach of man or other animals, and, unable to make a rapid retreat, his panic, rather than any vicious disposition, leads him to become an assailant in self-defence. But so furious are his assaults under such circumstances that the Singhalese have a terror of his attack greater than that created by any other beast of the forest. If not armed with a gun, a native, in the places where bears abound, usually carries a light axe, called "kodelly," with which to strike them on the head. The bear, on the other hand, always aims at the face, and, if successful in prostrating his victim, usually commences by assailing the eyes. I have met numerous individuals on our journeys who exhibited frightful scars from such encounters, the white seams of their wounds contrasting hideously with the dark colour of the rest of their bodies.

The Veddahs in Bintenne, whose principal stores consist of honey, live in dread of the bears, because, attracted by the perfume, they will not hesitate to attack their rude dwellings, when allured by this irresistible temptation. The Post-office runners, who always travel by night, are frequently exposed to danger from these animals, especially along the coast from Putlam to Aripo, where they are found in considerable numbers; and, to guard against surprise, they are accustomed to carry flambeaux, to give warning to the bears, and enable them to shuffle out of the path.[1]

[1] Amongst the Singhalese there is a belief that certain charms are efficacious in protecting them from the violence of bears, and those whose avocations expose them to encounters of this kind are accustomed to carry a talisman either attached to their neck or enveloped in the folds of their luxuriant hair. A friend of mine, writing of an adventure which occurred at Anarajapoora, thus describes an occasion on which a Moor, who attended him, was somewhat rudely disabused of his belief in the efficacy of charms upon bears:—"Desiring to change the position of a herd of deer, the Moorman (with his charm) was sent across some swampy land to disturb them. As he was proceeding, we saw him suddenly turn from an old tree and run back with all speed, his hair becoming unfastened and like his clothes streaming in the wind. It soon became evident that he was flying from some terrific object, for he had thrown down his gun, and, in his panic, he was taking the shortest line towards us, which lay across a swamp covered with sedge and rushes that greatly impeded his progress, and prevented us approaching him, or seeing what was the cause of his flight. Missing his steps from one hard spot to another he repeatedly fell into the water, but he rose and resumed his flight. I advanced as far as the sods would bear my weight,

Leopards[1] are the only formidable members of the tiger race in Ceylon[2], and they are neither very numerous nor very dangerous, as they seldom attack man. By the Europeans, the Ceylon leopard is erroneously called a *cheetah*, but the true "cheetah" (*felis jubata*), the hunting leopard of India, does not exist in the island.[3]

There is a rare variety of the leopard which has been found in various parts of the island, in which the skin, instead of being spotted, is of a uniform black.[4] Leopards frequent the vicinity of pasture lands in quest of the deer and other peaceful animals which resort to them; and the villagers often complain of the destruc-

but to go further was impracticable. Just within ball-range there was an open space, and, as the man gained it, I saw that he was pursued by a bear and two cubs. As the person of the fugitive covered the bear, it was impossible to fire without risk. At last he fell exhausted, and the bear being close upon him, I discharged both barrels. The first broke the bear's shoulder, but this only made her more savage, and rising on her hind legs she advanced with ferocious growls, when the second barrel, though I do not think it took effect, served to frighten her, for turning round she retreated, followed by the cubs. Some natives then waded through the mud to the Moorman, who was just exhausted, and would have been drowned but that he fell with his head upon a tuft of grass: the poor man was unable to speak, and for several weeks his intellect seemed confused. The adventure sufficed to satisfy him that he could not again depend upon a charm to protect him from bears, though he always insisted that but for its having fallen from his hair where he had fastened it under his turban, the bear would not have ventured to attack him."

[1] Felis pardus, *Linn.* What is called a leopard, or a cheetah, in Ceylon, is in reality the true panther.

[2] A belief is prevalent at Trincomalie that a Bengal tiger inhabits the jungle in its vicinity; and the story runs that it escaped from the wreck of a vessel on which it had been embarked for England. Officers of the Government state positively that they have more than once come on it whilst hunting; and one gentleman of the Royal Engineers, who had seen it, assured me that he could not be mistaken as to its being a tiger of India, and one of the largest description.

[3] Mr. BAKER, in his *Eight Years in Ceylon*, has stated that there are two species of leopard in the island, one of which he implies is the Indian cheetah. But although he specifies discrepancies in size, weight, and marking between the varieties which he has examined, his data are not sufficient to identify any of them with the true *felis jubata*.

[4] F. melas, *Peron* and *Leseur*.

tion of their cattle by these formidable marauders. In relation to them, the natives have a curious but firm

LEOPARD AND CHEETAH.

conviction that when a bullock is killed by a leopard, and, in expiring, falls so that *its right side is undermost*, the leopard will not return to devour it. I have been told by English sportsmen (some of whom share in the popular belief), that sometimes, when they have proposed to watch by the carcase of a bullock recently killed by a leopard, in the hope of shooting the spoiler on his return in search of his prey, the native owner of the slaughtered animal, though earnestly desiring to be avenged, has assured them that it would be in vain, as, the beast having fallen on its right side, the leopard would not return.

The Singhalese hunt them for the sake of their extremely beautiful skins, but prefer taking them in traps and pitfalls, and occasionally in spring cages formed of poles driven firmly into the ground, within which a kid is generally fastened as a bait; the door being held open by a sapling bent down by the united force of several men, and so arranged as to act as a spring, to which a noose is ingeniously attached, formed of plaited deer's hide. The cries of the kid attract the leopard, which being tempted to enter, is enclosed by the liberation of the spring, and grasped firmly round the body by the noose.

Like the other carnivora, leopards are timid and cowardly in the presence of man, never intruding on him voluntarily, and making a hasty retreat when approached. Instances have, however, occurred of individuals having been slain by them; and it is believed, that, having once tasted human blood, they, like the tiger, acquire an habitual relish for it. A peon, on duty by night at the court-house of Anarajapoora, was some years ago carried off by a leopard from a table in the verandah on which he had laid down his head to sleep. At Batticaloa a "cheetah" in two instances in succession was known to carry off men placed on a stage erected in a tree to drive away elephants from rice-land: but such cases are rare, and, as compared with their dread of the bear, the natives of Ceylon entertain but slight apprehensions of the "cheetah." It is, however, the dread of sportsmen, whose dogs when beating in the jungle are especially exposed to its attacks: and I am aware of an instance in which a party having tied their dogs to the tent-pole for security, and fallen asleep round them, a leopard sprang into the tent and carried off a dog from the midst of its slumbering masters. On one occasion being in the mountains near Kandy, a messenger despatched to me through the jungle excused his delay by stating that a "cheetah" had seated itself in the only practicable path, and remained quietly licking its fore paws and rubbing them over its face, till he was forced to drive it, with stones, into the forest.

Leopards are strongly attracted by the peculiar odour which accompanies small-pox. The reluctance of the natives to submit themselves or their children to vaccination exposes the island to frightful visitations of this disease; and in the villages in the interior it is usual on such occasions to erect huts in the jungle to serve as temporary hospitals. Towards these the leopards are certain to be allured; and the medical officers are obliged to resort to increased precautions in consequence. This fact is connected with a curious native superstition. Amongst the avenging scourges sent direct from the gods, the Singhalese regard both the ravages of the leopard, and the visitation of the small-pox. The latter they call *par excellence* "*maha ledda*," the great "sickness;" they look upon it as a special manifestation of *devidosay*, "the displeasure of the gods;" and the attraction of the cheetahs to the bed of the sufferer they attribute to the same indignant agency. A few years ago, the capua, or demon-priest of a "dewale," at Oggalbodda, a village near Caltura, when suffering under small-pox, was devoured by a cheetah, and his fate was regarded by those of an opposite faith as a special judgment from heaven.

Such is the awe inspired by this belief in connection with the small-pox, that a person afflicted with it is always approached as one in immediate communication with the deity; his attendants address him as "my lord," and "your lordship," and exhaust on him the whole series of honorific epithets in which their language abounds for approaching personages of the most exalted rank. At evening and morning, a lamp is lighted before him, and invoked with prayers to protect his family from the dire calamity which has befallen himself. And after his recovery, his former associates refrain from communication with him until a ceremony shall have been performed by the capua, called *awasara-pandema*, or "the offering of lights for permission," the object of which is to entreat permission of the deity to regard him as freed from the divine displeasure, with liberty to his friends to renew their intercourse as before.

Major SKINNER, who for upwards of forty years has had occasionally to live for long periods in the interior, occupied in the prosecution of surveys and the construction of roads, is strongly of opinion that the disposition of the leopard towards man is essentially pacific, and that, when discovered, its natural impulse is to effect its escape. In illustration of this I insert an extract from one of his letters, which describes an adventure highly characteristic of this instinctive timidity:—

"On the occasion of one of my visits to Adam's Peak, in the prosecution of my military reconnoissances of the mountain zone, I fixed on a pretty little patena (*i. e.*, meadow) in the midst of an extensive and dense forest in the southern segment of the Peak Range, as a favourable spot for operations. It would have been difficult, after descending from the cone of the peak, to have found one's way to this point, in the midst of so vast a wilderness of trees, had not long experience assured me that good game tracks would be found leading to it, and by one of them I reached it. It was in the afternoon, just after one of those tropical sunshowers that decorate every branch and blade with pendant brilliants, and the little patena was covered with game, either driven to the open space by the drippings from the leaves or tempted by the freshness of the pasture: there were several pairs of elk, the bearded antlered male contrasting finely with his mate; and other varieties of game in a profusion not to be found in any place frequented by man. It was some time before I would allow them to be disturbed by the rude fall of the axe, in our necessity to establish our bivouac for the night, and they were so unaccustomed to danger that it was long before they took alarm at our noises.

"The following morning, anxious to gain a height for my observations in time to avail myself of the clear atmosphere of sunrise, I started off by myself through the jungle, leaving orders for my men, with my surveying instruments, to follow my track by the notches which I cut in the bark of the trees. On leaving the plain, I availed myself of a fine wide game track which lay in my direction, and had gone, perhaps, half a mile from the camp, when I was startled by a slight rustling in the nilloo [1] to my right, and in another instant, by the spring of a magnificent leopard, which, in a bound of full eight feet in height over the lower brushwood, lighted at my feet within eighteen inches of the spot whereon I stood, and lay in a crouching position, his fiery gleaming eyes fixed on me.

[1] A species of one of the suffruticose *Acanthaceæ* (Strobilanthes), which grows abundantly in the mountain ranges of Ceylon.

"The predicament was not a pleasant one. I had no weapon of defence, and with one spring or blow of his paw the beast could have annihilated me. To move I knew would only encourage his attack. It occurred to me at the moment that I had heard of the power of man's eye over wild animals, and accordingly I fixed my gaze as intently as the agitation of such a moment enabled me on his eyes: we stared at each other for some seconds, when, to my inexpressible joy, the beast turned and bounded down the straight open path before me. This scene occurred just at that period of the morning when the grazing animals retired from the open patena to the cool shade of the forest: doubtless, the leopard had taken my approach for that of a deer, or some such animal. And if his spring had been at a quadruped instead of a biped, his distance was so well measured, that it must have landed him on the neck of a deer, an elk, or a buffalo; as it was, one pace more would have done for me. A bear would not have let his victim off so easily."

Notwithstanding the unequalled agility of the monkey, it falls a prey, and not unfrequently, to the leopard. The latter, on approaching a tree on which a troop of monkeys have taken shelter, causes an instant and fearful excitement, which they manifest by loud and continued screams, and incessant restless leaps from branch to branch. The leopard meanwhile walks round and round the tree, with his eyes firmly fixed upon his victims, till at last exhausted by terror, and prostrated by vain exertions to escape, one or more falls a prey to his voracity. So rivetted is the attention of both during the struggle, that a sportsman, on one occasion, attracted by the noise, was enabled to approach within an uncomfortable distance of the leopard, before he discovered the cause of the unusual dismay amongst the monkeys overhead.

It is said, but I have never been able personally to verify the fact, that the leopard of Ceylon exhibits a peculiarity in being unable entirely to retract its claws within their sheaths.

There is another piece of curious folk lore, in connexion with the leopard. The natives assert that it devours the *kaolin* clay called by them *kiri-mattie*[1] in a very peculiar way. They say that the cheetah places it in lumps beside him, and then gazes intently on the sun, till on turning his eyes on the clay, every piece appears of a red colour like flesh, when he instantly devours it.

They likewise allege that the female cheetah never produces more than one litter of whelps.

Of the *lesser feline species*, the number and variety in Ceylon is inferior to those of India. The Palm-cat[2] lurks by day among the fronds of the coco-nut palms, and by night makes destructive forays on the fowls of the villagers; and, in order to suck the blood of its victim, inflicts a wound so small as to be almost imperceptible. The glossy genette[3], the "*Civet*" of Europeans, is common in the northern province, where the Tamils confine it in cages for the sake of its musk, which they collect from the wooden bars on which it rubs itself. Edrisi, the Moorish geographer, writing in the twelfth century, enumerates musk as one of the productions then exported from Ceylon.[4]

[1] See Sir J. E. TENNENT'S *Ceylon*, vol. i. p. 31.

[2] Paradoxurus typus, *F. Cuv.*

[3] Viverra Indica, *Geoffr.*, *Hodgs.*

[4] EDRISI, *Géogr.* sec. vii. Jauberts's translation, t. ii. p. 72. In connexion with cats, a Singhalese gentleman has described to me a

*Dogs.*—There is no native wild dog in Ceylon, but every village and town is haunted by mongrels of European descent, that are known by the generic description of *Pariahs.* They are a miserable race, lean, wretched, and mangy, acknowledged by no owners, living on the garbage of the streets and sewers, and if spoken to unexpectedly, they shrink with an almost involuntary cry. Yet in these persecuted outcasts there survives that germ of instinctive affection which binds the dog to the human race, and a gentle word, even a look of compassionate kindness, is sufficient foundation for a lasting attachment.

The Singhalese, from their religious aversion to taking away life in any form, permit the increase of these desolate creatures till in the hot season they become so numerous as to be a nuisance; and the only expedient hitherto devised by the civil government to reduce their numbers, is once in each year to offer a reward for their destruction, when the Tamils and Malays pursue them in the streets with clubs (guns being forbidden by the police for fear of accidents), and the unresisting dogs are beaten to death on the side-paths and door-steps where they had been taught to resort for food. Lord Torrington, during his government of Ceylon, attempted the more civilised experiment of putting some check on their numbers, by imposing a dog-tax, the effect of which would have been to lead to the drowning of puppies; whereas there is reason to believe that dogs

plant in Ceylon, called *Cuppa-may-niya* by the natives; by which he says cats are so enchanted, that they play with it as they would with a captured mouse; throwing it into the air, watching it till it falls, and crouching to see if it will move. It would be worth inquiring into the truth of this; and the explanation of the attraction.

are at present *bred* by the horse-keepers to be killed for sake of the reward.

The Pariahs of Colombo exhibit something of the same instinct, by which the dogs in other eastern cities partition the towns into districts, each apportioned to a separate pack, by whom it is jealously guarded from the encroachments of all intruders. Travellers at Cairo and Constantinople are often startled at night by the racket occasioned by the demonstrations made by the rightful possessors of a locality in repelling its invasion by some straggling wanderer. At Alexandria, in 1844, the dogs had multiplied to such an inconvenient extent, that Mehemet Ali, to abate the nuisance, caused them to be shipped in boats and conveyed to one of the islands at the mouth of the Nile. But the streets, thus deprived of their habitual patroles, were speedily infested by dogs from the suburbs, in such numbers that the evil became greater than before, and in the following year, the legitimate denizens were recalled from their exile in the Delta, and speedily drove back the intruders within their original boundary. May not this disposition of the dog be referable to the impulse by which, in a state of nature, each pack appropriates its own hunting-fields within a particular area? and may not the impulse which, even in a state of domestication, they still manifest to attack a passing dog upon the road, be a remnant of this localised instinct, and a concomitant dislike of intrusion?

*Jackal.*—The Jackal[1] in the low country of Ceylon hunts thus in packs, headed by a leader, and these audacious prowlers have been seen to assault and pull

[1] Canis Aureus, *Linn.*

down a deer. The small number of hares in the districts they infest is ascribed to their depredations. In the legends of the natives, and in the literature of the Buddhists, the jackal in Ceylon is as essentially the type of cunning as the fox is the emblem of craft and adroitness in the traditions of Europe. In fact, it is more than doubtful whether the jackal of the East be not the creature alluded to, in the various passages of the Sacred Writings which make allusion to the artfulness and subtlety of the "fox."

These faculties they display in a high degree in their hunting expeditions, especially in the northern portions of the island, where they are found in the greatest numbers. In these districts, where the wide sandy plains are thinly covered with brushwood, the face of the country is diversified by patches of thick jungle and detached groups of trees, that form insulated groves and topes. At dusk, or after nightfall, a pack of jackals, having watched a hare or a small deer take refuge in one of these retreats, immediately surround it on all sides; and having stationed a few to watch the path by which the game entered, the leader commences the attack by raising the unearthly cry peculiar to their race, and which resembles the sound *okkay!* loudly and rapidly repeated. The whole party then rush into the jungle, and drive out the victim, which generally falls into the ambush previously laid to entrap it.

A native gentleman [1], who had favourable opportunities of observing the movements of these animals, informed me, that when a jackal has brought down his game and killed it, his first impulse is to hide it in the nearest jungle, whence he issues with an air of easy indifference

[1] Mr. D. de Silva Gooneratné.

to observe whether anything more powerful than himself may be at hand, from which he might encounter the risk of being despoiled of his capture. If the coast be clear, he returns to the concealed carcase, and carries it away, followed by his companions. But if a man be in sight, or any other animal to be avoided, my informant has seen the jackal seize a coco-nut husk in his mouth, or any similar substance, and fly at full speed, as if eager to carry off his pretended prize, returning for the real booty at some more convenient season.

They are subject to hydrophobia, and instances are frequent in Ceylon of cattle being bitten by them and dying in consequence.

An excrescence is sometimes found on the head of the jackal, consisting of a small horny cone about half an inch in length, and concealed by a tuft of hair. This the natives call *narric-comboo;* and they aver that this "Jackal's Horn" only grows on the head of the

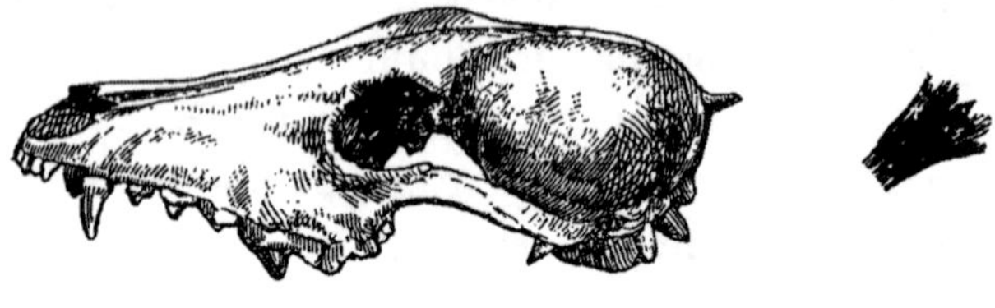

JACKAL'S SKULL AND HORN.

leader of the pack.[1] Both the Singhalese and the Tamils regard it as a talisman, and believe that its for-

[1] In the Museum of the College of Surgeons, London (No. 4362 A), there is a cranium of a jackal which exhibits this strange osseous process on the super-occipital; and I have placed along with it a specimen of the horny sheath, which was presented to me by Mr. Lavalliere, the late district judge of Kandy.

tunate possessor can command by its instrumentality the realisation of every wish, and that if stolen or lost by him, it will invariably return of its own accord. Those who have jewels to conceal rest in perfect security if along with them they can deposit a narri-comboo, fully convinced that its presence is an effectual safeguard against robbers.

One fabulous virtue ascribed to the *narric-comboo* by the Singhalese is absurdly characteristic of their passion for litigation, as well as of their perceptions of the "glorious uncertainty of the law." It is the popular belief that the fortunate discoverer of a jackal's horn becomes thereby invincible in every lawsuit, and must irresistibly triumph over every opponent. A gentleman connected with the Supreme Court of Colombo has repeated to me a circumstance, within his own knowledge, of a plaintiff who, after numerous defeats, eventually succeeded against his opponent by the timely acquisition of this invaluable charm. Before the final hearing of the cause, the mysterious horn was duly exhibited to his friends; and the consequence was, that the adverse witnesses, appalled by the belief that no one could possibly give judgment against a person so endowed, suddenly modified their previous evidence, and secured an unforeseen victory for the happy owner of the *narric-comboo!*

*The Mongoos.*—Of the Mongoos or Ichneumon four species have been described; and one, that frequents the hills near Neuera-ellia[1], is so remarkable from its bushy

[1] *Herpestes vitticollis.* Mr. W. ELLIOTT, in his *Catalogue of Mammalia found in the Southern Maharata Country*, Madras, 1840, says, that "One specimen of this Herpestes was procured by accident in the Ghât forests in 1829, and is now deposited in the British Museum; it is very rare, inhabiting only the thickest woods, and its habits are very little known," p. 9. In Ceylon it is comparatively common.

fur, that the invalid soldiers in the sanatarium there, to whom it is familiar, have given it the name of the "Ceylon Badger."

I have found universally that the natives of Ceylon attach no credit to the European story of the Mongoos (*H. griseus*) resorting to some plant, which no one has yet succeeded in identifying, as an antidote against the

HERPESTES VITTICOLLIS.

bite of the venomous serpents on which it preys. There is no doubt that, in its conflicts with the cobra de capello and other poisonous snakes, which it attacks with as little hesitation as the harmless ones, it may be seen occasionally to retreat, and even to retire into the jungle, and, it is added, to eat some vegetable; but a gentleman, who has been a frequent observer of its exploits, assures me that most usually the herb it resorted to was grass; and if this were not at hand, almost any other plant that grew near seemed equally acceptable. Hence has probably arisen the long list of plants, such as the *Ophioxylon serpentinum* and *Ophiorhiza mungos*, the *Aristolochia Indica*, the *Mimosa octandria*, and others, each of which has been asserted to be the ichneumon's specific; whilst their multiplicity is demonstrative of the non-existence of any one in particular on which the animal relies as an antidote. Were there any truth in the tale as regards the mongoos, it would be difficult to understand why creatures, such as the secretary bird and the falcon, and others, which equally destroy serpents, should be left defenceless, and the ichneumon alone provided with a prophylactic. Besides, were the ichneumon inspired by that courage which would result from the consciousness of security, it would be so indifferent to the bite of the serpent that we might conclude that, both in its approaches and its assault, it would be utterly careless as to the precise mode of its attack. Such, however, is far from being the case; and next to its audacity, nothing can be more surprising than the adroitness with which it escapes the spring of the snake under a due sense of danger, and the cunning with which it makes its arrangements to leap upon the back and fasten its teeth in the head of the cobra. It is this display of instinctive ingenuity that Lucan[1] celebrates where he paints the ichneumon diverting the attention of the asp, by the motion of his bushy tail, and then seizing it in the midst of its confusion:—

> "Aspidas ut Pharias caudâ solertior hostis
> Ludit, et iratas incertâ provocat umbrâ:

[1] The passage in Lucan is a versification of the same narrative related by Pliny, lib. viii. ch. 53; and Ælian, lib. iii. ch. 22.

> Obliquusque caput vanas serpentis in auras
> Effusæ toto comprendit guttura morsu
> Letiferam citra saniem; tunc irrita pestis
> Exprimitur, faucesque fluunt pereunte veneno."
> *Pharsalia*, lib. iv. v. 729.

The mystery of the mongoos and its antidote has been referred to the supposition that there may be some peculiarity in its organisation which renders it *proof against* the poison of the serpent. It remains for future investigation to determine how far this conjecture is founded in truth; and whether in the blood of the mongoos there exists any element or quality which acts as a prophylactic. Such exceptional provisions are not without precedent in the animal œconomy: the hornbill feeds with impunity on the deadly fruit of the strychnos; the milky juice of some species of euphorbia, which is harmless to oxen, is invariably fatal to the zebra; and the tsetse fly, the pest of South Africa, whose bite is mortal to the ox, the dog, and the horse, is harmless to man and the untamed creatures of the forest.[1]

The Singhalese distinguish one species of mongoos, which they designate "*Hotambeya*," and which they assert never preys upon serpents. A writer in the *Ceylon Miscellany* mentions, that they are often to be seen "crossing rivers and frequently mud-brooks near Chilaw; the adjacent thickets affording them shelter, and their food consisting of aquatic reptiles, crabs, and mollusca."[2]

[1] Dr. LIVINGSTONE, *Tour in S. Africa*, p. 80. Is it a fact that, in America, pigs extirpate the rattlesnakes with impunity?

[2] This is possibly the "musbilai" or mouse-cat of Behar, which preys upon birds and fish. Can it be the Urva of the Nepalese (*Urva cancrivora*, Hodgson), which Mr. Hodgson describes as dwelling in bur-

IV. RODENTIA. *Squirrels.*—Smaller animals in great numbers enliven the forests and lowland plains with

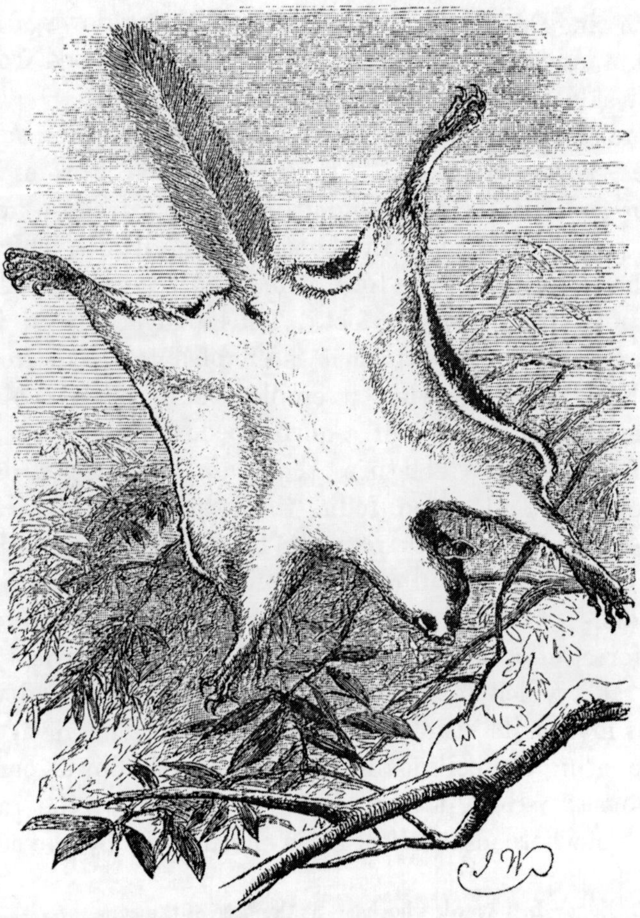

FLYING SQUIRREL.

their graceful movements. Squirrels[1], of which there are a great variety, make their shrill metallic call heard

rows, and being carnivorous and ranivorous?—Vide *Journn. As. Soc. Beng.* vol. vi. p. 56.

[1] Of two kinds which frequent the mountains, one which is peculiar to Ceylon was discovered

at early morning in the woods; and when sounding their note of warning on the approach of a civet or a tree-snake, the ears tingle with the loud trill of defiance, which rings as clear and rapid as the running down of an alarum, and is instantly caught up and re-echoed from every side by their terrified playmates.

One of the largest, belonging to a closely allied sub-genus, is known as the "Flying Squirrel,"[1] from its being assisted, in its prodigious leaps from tree to tree, by a parachute formed by the skin of the flanks, which, on the extension of the limbs front and rear, is laterally expanded from foot to foot. Thus buoyed up in its descent, the spring which it is enabled to make from one lofty tree to another resembles the flight of a bird rather than the bound of a quadruped.

Of these pretty creatures there are two species, one common to Ceylon and India, the other (*Sciuropterus Layardii*, Kelaart) is peculiar to the island, and by far the most beautiful of the family.

*Rats.*—Among the multifarious inhabitants to which the forest affords at once a home and provender is the tree rat[2], which forms its nest on the branches, and by turns makes its visits to the dwellings of the natives, frequenting the ceilings in preference to the lower parts of houses. Here it is incessantly followed by the rat-snake[3], whose domestication is encouraged by the ser-

by Mr. Edgar L. Layard, who has done me the honour to call it the *Sciurus Tennentii*. Its dimensions are large, measuring upwards of two feet from head to tail. It is distinguished from the *S. macrurus* by the predominant black colour of the upper surface of the body, with the exception of a rusty spot at the base of the ears.

[1] Pteromys oral., *Tickel.* P. petaurista, *Pallas.*

[2] There are two species of the tree rat in Ceylon: M. rufescens, *Gray;* (M. flavescens, *Elliot;*) and Mus nemoralis, *Blyth.*

[3] Coryphodon Blumenbachii, *Merr.*

vants, in consideration of its services in destroying vermin. I had one day an opportunity of surprising a snake that had just seized on a rat of this description, and of covering it suddenly with a glass shade, before it had time to swallow its prey. The serpent, appeared stunned by its own capture, and allowed the rat to escape from its jaws, which cowered at one side of the glass in the most pitiable state of trembling terror. The two were left alone for some moments, and on my return to them the snake was as before in the same attitude of sullen stupor. On setting them at liberty, the rat bounded towards the nearest fence; but quick as lightning it was followed by its pursuer, which seized it before it could gain the hedge, through which I saw the snake glide with its victim in its jaws. In parts of the central province, at Oovah and Bintenne, the house-rat is eaten as a common article of food. The Singhalese believe it and the mouse to be liable to hydrophobia.

Another indigenous variety of the rat is that which made its appearance for the first time in the coffee plantations on the Kandyan hills in the year 1847; and in such swarms does it continue to infest them, at intervals, that as many as a thousand have been killed in a single day on one estate. In order to reach the buds and blossoms of the coffee, it cuts such of the slender branches as would not sustain its weight, and feeds on them when fallen to the ground; and so delicate and sharp are its incisors, that the twigs thus destroyed are detached by as clean a cut as if severed with a knife.

The coffee-rat[1] is an insular variety of the *Mus hirsutus* of W. Elliot, found in Southern India. They in-

[1] Golunda Ellioti, *Gray*.

habit the forests, making their nests among the roots of the trees, and feeding, in the season, on the ripe seeds of the nilloo. Like the lemmings of Norway and Lapland,

COFFEE RAT.

they migrate in vast numbers on the occurrence of a scarcity of their ordinary food. The Malabar coolies are so fond of their flesh, that they evince a preference for those districts in which the coffee plantations are subject to their incursions, where they fry the rats in coco-nut oil, or convert them into curry.

*Bandicoot.* — Another favourite article of food with the coolies is the pig-rat or Bandicoot [1], which attains on those hills the weight of two or three pounds, and grows to nearly the length of two feet. As it feeds on grain and roots, its flesh is said to be delicate, and much resembling young pork.

[1] Mus bandicota, *Beckst.* The English term bandicoot is a corruption of the Telinga name *pandikoku*, literally *pig-rat.*

Its nests, when rifled, are frequently found to contain considerable quantities of rice, stored up against the dry season.

BANDICOOT

*Porcupine.*—The Porcupine[1] is another of the *rodentia* which has drawn down upon itself the hostility of the planters, from its destruction of the young coconut palms, to which it is a pernicious and persevering, but withal so crafty, a visitor, that it is with difficulty any trap can be so disguised, or any bait made so alluring, as to lead to its capture. The usual expedient in Ceylon is to place some of its favourite food at the extremity of a trench, so narrow as to prevent the porcupine turning, whilst the direction of his quills effectually bars his retreat backwards. On a newly planted coconut tope, at Hang-welle, within a few miles of Colombo,

[1] Hystrix leucurus, *Sykes.*

I have heard of as many as twenty-seven being thus captured in a single night; but such success is rare. The more ordinary expedient is to smoke them out by burning straw at the apertures of their burrows. At Ootacamund, on the continent of the Dekkan, spring-guns have been used with great success by the Superintendent of the Horticultural Gardens; placing them so as to sweep the runs of the porcupines. The flesh is esteemed a delicacy in Ceylon, and in consistency, colour, and flavour it very much resembles young pork.

V. EDENTATA. *Pengolin.*—Of the *Edentata* the only example in Ceylon is the scaly ant-eater, called by the Singhalese, Caballaya, but usually known by its Malay name of *Pengolin*[1], a word indicative of its faculty, when alarmed, of "rolling itself up" into a compact ball, by bending its head towards its stomach, arching its back into a circle, and securing all by a powerful fold of its mail-covered tail. The feet of the pengolin are armed with powerful claws, which in walking they double in, like the ant-eater of Brazil. These they use in extracting their favourite food from ant-hills and decaying wood. When at liberty, they burrow in the dry ground to a depth of seven or eight feet, where they reside in pairs, and produce annually one or two young.[2]

Of two specimens which I kept alive at different times, one, about two feet in length, from the vicinity of Kandy, was a gentle and affectionate creature, which,

[1] Manis pentadactyla, *Linn.*

[2] I am assured that there is a hedge-hog in Ceylon; but as I have never seen it, I cannot tell whether it belongs to either of the two species known in India (*Erinaceus mentalis* and *E. collaris*)—nor can I vouch for its existence there at all. But the fact was told to me, in connexion with the statement, that its favourite dwelling is in the same burrow with the pengolin. The popular belief in this is attested by a Singhalese proverb, in relation to an intrusive personage; the import of which is that he is like "*a hedge-hog in the den of a pengolin.*"

after wandering over the house in search of ants, would attract attention to its wants by climbing up my knee, laying hold of my leg with its prehensile tail. The other, more than double that length, was caught in the jungle near Chilaw, and brought to me in Colombo. I had always understood that the pengolin was unable to climb trees; but the one last mentioned frequently as-

THE PENGOLIN.

cended a tree in my garden, in search of ants; and this it effected by means of its hooked feet, aided by an oblique grasp of the tail. The ants it seized by extending its round and glutinous tongue along their tracks; and in the stomach of one which was opened after death, I found a quantity of small stones and gravel, which had been taken to facilitate digestion. In both specimens in my possession the scales of the back were a cream-coloured white, with a tinge of red in that which came from Chilaw, probably acquired by the insinuation of the Cabook dust which abounds along the western coast of the island.

Of the habits of the pengolin I found that very little was known by the natives, who regard it with aversion, one name given to it being the "Negombo Devil." Those kept by me were, generally speaking, quiet during the day, and grew restless and active as evening and night approached. Both had been taken near rocks, in the hollows of which they had their dwelling, but owing to their slow power of motion, they were unable to reach their hiding place when overtaken. When frightened, they rolled themselves instantly into a rounded ball; and such was the powerful force of muscle, that the strength of a man was insufficient to uncoil it. In reconnoitring they made important use of the tail, resting upon it and their hind legs, and holding themselves nearly erect, to command a view of their object. The strength of this powerful limb will be perceived from the accompanying drawing of

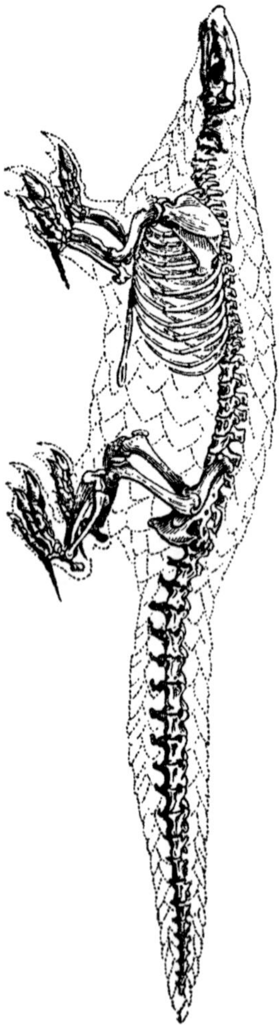

SKELETON OF PENGOLIN.

the skeleton of the Manis; in which it will be seen that the tail is equal in length to all the rest of the body, whilst the vertebræ which compose it are stronger by far than those of the back.

From the size and position of the bones of the leg, the pengolin is endued with prodigious power; and its faculty of exerting this vertically, was displayed in overturning heavy cases, by insinuating itself under them, between the supports, by which it is customary in Ceylon to raise trunks a few inches above the floor, in order to prevent the attacks of white ants.

VI. RUMINANTIA. *The Gaur.*—Besides the deer, and some varieties of the humped ox, that have been introduced from the opposite continent of India, Ceylon has probably but one other indigenous bovine *ruminant*, the buffalo.[1] There is a tradition that the gaur, found in the extremity of the Indian peninsula, was at one period a native of the Kandyan Mountains; but as Knox speaks of one which in his time "was kept among the king's creatures" at Kandy[2], and his account of it tallies with that of the *Bos Gaurus* of Hindustan, it would appear even then to have been a rarity. A place between Neuera-ellia and Adam's Peak bears the name of "Gowra-ellia," and it is not impossible that the animal may yet be discovered in some of the imperfectly explored regions of the island.[3] I have heard of an instance in which a very old Kandyan, residing in the mountains near the Horton Plains, asserted that when young he had seen what he believed to have been a gaur, and he described it as between an elk and a buffalo in size,

[1] Bubalus buffelus, *Gray*.

[2] KNOX, *Historical Relation of Ceylon, &c.*, A.D. 1681. Book i. c. 6.

[3] KELAART, *Fauna Zeylan.*, p. 87.

dark brown in colour, and very scantily provided with hair.

*Oxen.*—Oxen are used by the peasantry both in ploughing and in tempering the mud in the wet paddi fields before sowing the rice; and when the harvest is reaped they "tread out the corn," after the immemorial custom of the East. The wealth of the native chiefs and landed proprietors frequently consists in their herds of bullocks, which they hire out to their dependents during the seasons for agricultural labour; and as they already supply them with land to be tilled, and lend the seed which is to crop it, the further contribution of this portion of the labour serves to render the dependence of the peasantry on the chiefs and headmen complete.

The cows are often worked as well as the oxen; and as the calves are always permitted to suck them, milk is an article which the traveller can rarely hope to procure in a Kandyan village. From their constant exposure at all seasons, the cattle in Ceylon, both those employed in agriculture and those on the roads, are subject to devastating murrains, that sweep them away by thousands. So frequent is the recurrence of these calamities, and so extended their ravages, that they exercise a serious influence upon the commercial interests of the colony, by reducing the facilities of agriculture, and augmenting the cost of carriage during the most critical periods of the coffee harvest.

A similar disorder, probably peripneumonia, frequently carries off the cattle in Assam and other hill countries on the continent of India; and there, as in Ceylon, the inflammatory symptoms in the lungs and throat, and the internal derangement and external eruptive appearances, seem to indicate that the disease is a feverish influenza, attributable to neglect and exposure in a moist and variable climate; and that its prevention might be hoped for, and the cattle preserved, by the simple expedient of more humane and considerate treatment, especially by affording them cover at night.

During my residence in Ceylon an incident occurred at Neuera-ellia, which invested one of these pretty animals with an heroic interest. A little cow, belonging to an English gentleman, was housed, together with her calf, near the dwelling of her owner, and being aroused during the night by her furious bellowing, the servants, on hastening to the stall, found her goring a leopard, which had stolen in to attack the calf. She had got it into a corner, and whilst lowing incessantly to call for help, she continued to pound it with her horns. The wild animal, apparently stupified by her unexpected violence, was detained by her till despatched by a bullet.

The number of bullock-carts encountered between Colombo and Kandy, laden with coffee from the interior, or carrying up rice and stores for the supply of the plantations in the hill-country, is quite surprising. The oxen thus employed on this single road, about seventy miles long, are estimated at upwards of twenty thousand. The bandy to which they are yoked is a barbarous two-wheeled waggon, with a covering of plaited coco-nut leaves, in which a pair of strong bullocks will draw from five to ten hundred weight, according to the nature of the country; and with this load on a level they will perform a journey of twenty miles a day.

A few of the large humped cattle of India are annually imported for draught; but the vast majority of those in use are small and dark-coloured, with a graceful head and neck, and elevated hump, a deep silky dewlap, and limbs as slender as a deer. They appear to have neither the strength nor weight requisite for this service; and yet the entire coffee crop of Ceylon, amounting annually to upwards of half a million hundred weight, is year after year brought down from the mountains to the coast by these indefatigable little creatures, which, on returning, carry up proportionally heavy loads of rice and implements for the estates.[1] There are two varieties of the native bullock; one a somewhat coarser animal, of a deep red colour; the other, the high-bred black one I have just described. So rare was a white one of this species, under the native kings, that the Kandyans were compelled to set them apart for the royal herd.[2]

Although bullocks may be said to be the only animals of draught and burden in Ceylon (horses being rarely used except in spring carriages), no attempt has been made to improve the breed, or even to better the condition and treatment of those in use. Their food is indifferent, pasture in all parts of the island being rare, and cattle are seldom housed under any vicissitudes of weather.

The labour for which they are best adapted, and in which, before the opening of roads, these cattle were formerly employed, is in traversing the jungle paths of

[1] A pair of these little bullocks carry up about twenty bushels of rice to the hills, and bring down from fifty to sixty bushels of coffee to Colombo.

[2] WOLF says that, in the year 1763, he saw in Ceylon two white oxen, each of which measured upwards of eight feet high. They were sent as a present from the King of Atchin.—*Life and Adventures*, p. 172.

the interior, carrying light loads as pack-oxen in what is called a "*tavalam*,"—a term which, substituting bullocks for camels, is equivalent to a "caravan."[1] The class of persons engaged in this traffic in Ceylon resemble in their occupations the "Banjarees" of Hindustan, who bring down to the coast corn, cotton, and oil, and take back to the interior cloths and iron and copper utensils. In the unopened parts of the island, and especially in the eastern provinces, this primitive practice still continues. When travelling in these districts I have often encountered long files of pack-bullocks toiling along the mountain paths, their bells tinkling musically as they moved; or halting during the noonday heat beside some stream in the forests, their burdens piled in heaps near the drivers, who had lighted their cooking fires, whilst the bullocks were permitted to bathe and browse.

The persons engaged in this wandering trade are chiefly Moors, and the business carried on by them consists in bringing up salt from the government depôts on the coast to be bartered with the Kandyans in the hills for "native coffee," which is grown in small quantities round every house, but without systematic cultivation. This they carry down to the maritime towns, and the proceeds are invested in cotton cloths and brass utensils, dried fish, and other commodities, with which the *tavalams* supply the secluded villages of the interior.

[1] Attempts have been made to domesticate the camel in Ceylon; but, I am told, they died of ulcers in the feet, attributed to the too great moisture of the roads at certain seasons. This explanation seems insufficient if taken in connection with the fact of the camel living in perfect health in climates equally, if not more, exposed to rain. I apprehend that sufficient justice has not been done to the experiment.

*The Buffalo.*—Buffaloes abound in all parts of Ceylon, but they are only to be seen in their native wildness in the vast solitudes of the northern and eastern provinces, where rivers, lagoons, and dilapidated tanks abound. In these they delight to immerse themselves, till only their heads appear above the surface; or, enveloped in mud to protect themselves from the assaults of insects, they luxuriate in the long sedges by the water margins. When the buffalo is browsing, a crow will frequently be seen stationed on its back, engaged in freeing it from the ticks and other pests which attach themselves to its leathery hide, the smooth brown surface of which, unprotected by hair, shines with an unpleasant polish in the sunlight. When in motion a buffalo throws back its clumsy head till the huge horns rest on its shoulders, and the nose is presented in a line with the eyes.

The temper of the wild buffalo is morose and uncertain, and such is its strength and courage that in the Hindu epic of the Ramayana its onslaught is compared to that of the tiger.[1] It is never quite safe to approach them, if disturbed in their pasture or alarmed from their repose in the shallow lakes. On such occasions they hurry into line, draw up in defensive array, with a few of the oldest bulls in advance; and, wheeling in circles, their horns clashing with a loud sound as they clank them together in their rapid evolutions, they prepare for attack; but generally, after a menacing display the herd betake themselves to flight; then forming again at a safer distance, they halt as before, elevating their nostrils, and throwing back their heads to take a defiant survey of the intruders. The true sportsman

[1] CAREY and MARSHMAN'S Transl. vol. i. p. 430, 447.

rarely molests them, so huge a creature affording no worthy mark for his skill, and their wanton slaughter adds nothing to the supply of food for their assailant.

In the Hambangtotte country, where the Singhalese domesticate buffaloes, and use them to assist in the labour of the rice lands, the villagers are much annoyed by the wild ones, that mingle with the tame when sent out to the woods to pasture; and it constantly happens that a savage stranger, placing himself at the head of the tame herd, resists the attempts of the owners to drive them homewards at sunset. In the districts of Putlam and the Seven Corles, buffaloes are generally used for draught; and in carrying heavy loads of salt from the coast towards the interior, they drag a cart over roads which would defy the weaker strength of bullocks.

In one place between Batticaloa and Trincomalie I found the natives making an ingenious use of them when engaged in shooting water-fowl in the vast salt marshes and muddy lakes. Being an object to which the birds are accustomed, the Singhalese train the buffalo to the sport, and, concealed behind, the animal browsing listlessly along, they guide it by ropes attached to its horns, and thus creep undiscovered within shot of the flock. The same practice prevails, I believe, in some of the northern parts of India, where they are similarly trained to assist the sportsman in approaching deer. One of these "sporting buffaloes" sells for a considerable sum.

In the thick forests which cover the Passdun Corle, to the east and south of Caltura, the natives use the sporting buffalo in another way, to assist in hunting deer and wild hogs. A bell is attached to its neck, and a box or basket with one side open is securely strapped on its back. This at nightfall is lighted by flambeaux of wax, and the buffalo bearing it, is driven slowly into the jungle. The huntsmen, with their fowling pieces, keep close under the darkened side, and as it moves slowly onwards, the wild animals, startled by the sound, and bewildered by the light, steal cautiously towards it in stupified fascination. Even the snakes, I am assured, will be attracted by this extraordinary object; and the leopard too falls a victim to curiosity.

There is a peculiarity in the formation of the buffalo's foot, which, though it must have attracted attention, I have never seen mentioned by naturalists. It is equivalent to the arrangement which distinguishes the foot of the reindeer from that of the stag and the antelope. In the latter, the hoofs, being constructed for lightness and flight, are compact and vertical; but, in the reindeer, the joints of the tarsal bones admit of lateral expansion, and the front hoofs curve upwards, while the two secondary ones behind (which are but slightly developed in the fallow deer and others of the same family) are prolonged vertically till, in certain positions, they are capable of being applied to the ground, thus adding to the circumference and sustaining power of the foot. It has been usually suggested as the probable design of this structure, that it is to enable the reindeer to shovel away the snow in order to reach the lichens beneath it; but I apprehend that another use of it has been overlooked, that of facilitating its movements in search of food by increasing the difficulty of its sinking in the snow.

A formation precisely analogous in the buffalo seems to point to a corresponding design. The ox, whose life is spent on firm ground, has the bones of the foot so constructed as to afford the most solid support to an animal of its great weight; but in the buffalo, which delights in the morasses on the margins of pools and rivers, the construction of the foot resembles that of the reindeer. The tarsi in front extend almost horizontally from the upright bones of the leg, and spread apart widely on touching the ground; the hoofs are flattened and broad, with the extremities turned upwards; and the false hoofs behind descend till they make a clattering sound as the animal walks. In traversing the marshes, this combination of abnormal incidents serves to give extraordinary breadth to the foot, and not only prevents the buffalo from sinking inconveniently in soft ground [1], but at the same time presents no obstacle to the withdrawal of its foot from the mud.

The buffalo, like the elk, is sometimes found in Ceylon as an albino, with purely white hair and a pink iris.

*Deer.* — "Deer," says the truthful old chronicler, Robert Knox, "are in great abundance in the woods, from the largeness of a cow to the smallness of a hare, for here is a creature in this land no bigger than the latter, though every part rightly resembleth a deer: it is called *meminna*, of a grey colour, with white spots and good meat." [2] The little creature which thus dwelt in the recollection of the old man, as one of the memo-

[1] PROFESSOR OWEN has noticed a similar fact regarding the rudiments of the second and fifth digits in the instance of the elk and bison, which have them largely expanded where they inhabit swampy ground; whilst they are nearly obliterated in the camel and dromedary, that traverse arid deserts. — OWEN *on Limbs*, p. 34; see also BELL *on the Hand*, ch. iii.

[2] KNOX'S *Relation*, *&c.*, book i. c. 6.

rials of his long captivity, is the small "musk deer"[1] so called in India, although neither sex is provided with a musk-bag. The Europeans in Ceylon know it by the name of the "moose deer;" and in all probability the terms *musk* and *moose* are both corruptions of the Dutch word "*muis*," or "mouse" deer, a name particularly applicable to the timid and crouching attitudes

"MOOSE" DEER (MOSCHUS MEMINNA).

and aspect of this beautiful little creature. Its extreme length never reaches two feet; and of those which were domesticated about my house, few exceeded ten inches in height, their graceful limbs being of proportionate delicacy. It possesses long and extremely large tusks, with which it can inflict a severe bite. The interpreter moodliar of Negombo had a *milk white* meminna in 1847, which he designed to send home as an acceptable

[1] Moschus meminna.

present to Her Majesty, but it was unfortunately killed by an accident.[1]

*Ceylon Elk.*—In the mountains, the Ceylon elk[2], which reminds one of the red deer of Scotland, attains the height of four or five feet; it abounds in all shady places that are intersected by rivers; where, though its chase affords an endless resource to the sportsman, its venison scarcely equals in quality the inferior beef of the lowland ox. In the glades and park-like openings that diversify the great forests of the interior, the spotted Axis troops in herds as numerous as the fallow deer in England; but, in journeys through the jungle, when often dependent on the guns of our party for the precarious supply of the table, we found the flesh of the Axis[3] and the Muntjac[4] a sorry substitute for that of the pea-fowl, the jungle-cock, and flamingo. The occurrence of albinos is very frequent in troops of the axis. Deer's horns are an article of export from Ceylon, and considerable quantities are annually sent to the United Kingdom.

VII. PACHYDERMATA.—*The Elephant.*—The elephant and the wild boar, the Singhalese "waloora,"[5] are the only representatives of the *pachydermatous* order. The latter, which differs somewhat from the wild boar of

[1] When the English took possession of Kandy, in 1803, they found "five beautiful milk-white deer in the palace, which was noted as a very extraordinary thing."—*Letter* in Appendix to PERCIVAL'S *Ceylon*, p. 428. The writer does not say of what species they were.

[2] Rusa Aristotelis. Dr. GRAY has lately shown that this is the great *axis* of Cuvier.—*Oss. Foss.* 502, t. 39, f. 10. The Singhalese, on following the elk, frequently effect their approaches by so imitating the call of the animal as to induce them to respond. An instance occurred during my residence in Ceylon, in which two natives, whose mimicry had mutually deceived them, crept so close together in the jungle that one shot the other, supposing the cry to proceed from the game.

[3] Axis maculata, *H. Smith.*

[4] Stylocerus muntjac, *Horsf.*

[5] Mr. BLYTH of Calcutta has distinguished, from the hog, common in India, a specimen sent to him from Ceylon, the skull of which approaches in form, that of a species from Borneo, the *sus barbatus* of S. Müller.

India, is found in droves in all parts of the island where vegetation and water are abundant.

The elephant, the lord paramount of the Ceylon forests, is to be met with in every district, on the confines of the woods, in the depths of which he finds concealment and shade during the hours when the sun is high, and from which he emerges only at twilight to wend his way towards the rivers and tanks, where he luxuriates till dawn, when he again seeks the retirement of the deep forests. This noble animal fills so dignified a place both in the zoology and œconomy of Ceylon, and his habits in a state of nature have been so much misunderstood, that I shall devote a separate section to his defence from misrepresentation, and to an exposition of what, from observation and experience, I believe to be his genuine character when free in his native domains. But this seems the proper place to allude to a recent discovery in connexion with the elephant, which strikingly confirms a conjecture which I ventured to make elsewhere [1], relative to the isolation of Ceylon, and its distinctness, in many remarkable particulars, from the great continent of India. Every writer who previously treated of the island, including the accomplished Dr. Davy and the erudite Lassen, was contented, by a glance at its outline and a reference to its position on the map, to assume that Ceylon was a fragment, which in a very remote age had been torn from the adjacent mainland, by some convulsion of nature. Hence it was taken for granted that the vegetation which covers and the races of animals which inhabit it, must be identical with those of Hindustan; to which

[1] *Ceylon, &c.*, by Sir J. Emerson Tennent, vol. i. pp. 7, 13, 85, 160, 183, n., 205, 270, &c.

Ceylon was alleged to bear the same relation as Sicily presents to the peninsula of Italy. MALTE BRUN[1] and the geographers generally, declared the larger animals of either to be common to both. I was led to question the soundness of this dictum;—and from a closer examination of its geological conformation and of its botanical and zoological characteristics I came to the conclusion that not only is there an absence of sameness between the formations of the two localities; but that plants and animals, mammals, birds, reptiles, and insects exist in Ceylon, which are not to be found in the flora and fauna of the Dekkan; but which present a striking affinity, and occasionally an actual identity, with those of the Malayan countries and some of the islands of the Eastern Archipelago. Startling as this conclusion appeared to be, it was strangely in unison with the legends of the Singhalese themselves, that at an infinitely remote period Ceylon formed an integral portion of a vast continent, known in the mythical epics of the Brahmans by the designation of "*Lanka;*" so immense that its southern extremity fell below the equator, whilst in breadth it was prolonged till its western and eastern boundaries touch at once upon the shores of Africa and China.

Dim as is this ancient tradition, it is in consistency with the conclusions of modern geology, that at the commencement of the tertiary period northern Asia and a considerable part of India were in all probability covered by the sea—but that south of India land extended eastward and westward connecting Malacca with Arabia. PROFESSOR ANSTED has propounded this view. His opinion is, that the Himalayas then existed only as a chain of islands, and did not till a much later age be-

[1] MALTE BRUN, *Geogr. Univ.*, l. xlix.

come elevated into mountain ranges,—a change which took place during the same revolution that raised the great plains of Siberia and Tartary and many parts of north-western Europe. At the same time the great continent whose position between the tropics has been alluded to, and whose previous existence is still indicated by the Coral islands, the Laccadives, the Maldives, and the Chagos group, underwent simultaneous depression by a counteracting movement.[1]

But divested of oriental mystery and geologic conjecture, and brought to the test of "geographical distribution," this once prodigious continent would appear to have connected the distant Islands of Ceylon and Sumatra and possibly to have united both to the Malay peninsula, from which the latter is now severed by the Straits of Malacca. The proofs of physical affinity between these scattered localities are exceedingly curious.

A striking dissimilarity presents itself between some of the Mammalia of Ceylon and those of the continent of India. In its general outline and feature, this branch of the island fauna, no doubt, exhibits a general resemblance to that of the mainland, although many of the larger animals of the latter are unknown in Ceylon; but, on the other hand, some species discovered there are peculiar to the island. A deer[2] as large as the Axis, but differing from it in the number and arrangement of its spots, has been described by Dr. Kelaart, to whose vigilance the natural history of Ceylon is indebted, amongst others, for the identification of two new species of monkeys[3], a number of curious shrews[4],

[1] *The Ancient World*, by D. T. ANSTED, M.A., &c., pp. 322—324,

[2] Cervus orizus, KELAART, *Prod. F. Zeyl.*, p, 83.

[3] Presbytes ursinus, *Blyth*, and P. Thersites, *Elliot*.

[4] Sorex montanus, S. ferrugineus, and Feroculus macropus.

and an orange-coloured ichneumon[1], before unknown. There are also two squirrels[2] that have not as yet been discovered elsewhere, (one of them belonging to those equipped with a parachute[3],) as well as some local varieties of the palm squirrel (Sciurus penicillatus, *Leach*).[4]

But the Ceylon Mammalia, besides wanting a number of minor animals found in the Indian peninsula, cannot boast such a ruminant as the majestic Gaur[5], which inhabits the great forests from Cape Comorin to the Himalaya; and, providentially, the island is equally free of the formidable tiger and the ferocious wolf of Hindustan. The Hyena and Cheetah[6], common in Southern India, are unknown in Ceylon; and though abundant in deer, the island possesses no example of the Antelope or the Gazelle.

Amongst the Birds of Ceylon, the same abnormity is apparent. About thirty-eight species will be presently particularised[7], which, although some of them may hereafter be discovered to have a wider geographical range, are at present believed to be unknown in continental India. I might further extend this enumeration, by including the Cheela eagle of Ceylon, which, although I have placed it in my list as identical with the *Hematornis cheela* of the Dekkan, is, I have since been assured, a different bird, and is most probably the *Falco bido* of

[1] Herpestes fulvescens, KELAART, *Prod. Faun. Zeylan.*, App. p. 42.

[2] Sciurus Tennentii, *Layard*.

[3] Sciuropterus Layardi, *Kelaart*.

[4] There is a rat found only in the Cinnamon Gardens at Colombo, Mus Ceylonus, *Kelaart;* and a mouse which Dr. Kelaart discovered at Trincomalie, M. fulvidiventris, *Blyth*, both peculiar to Ceylon. Dr. TEMPLETON has noticed a little shrew (Corsira purpurascens, *Mag. Nat. Hist.* 1855, p. 238) at Neuera-ellia, not as yet observed elsewhere.

[5] Bos cavifrons, *Hodgs.;* B. frontalis, *Lamb.*

[6] Felis jubata, *Schreb.*

[7] See Chapter on the Birds of Ceylon.

Horsfield, known to us by specimens obtained from Java and Sumatra.

As to the Fishes of Ceylon, they are of course less distinct; and besides they have hitherto been very imperfectly compared. But the Insects afford a remarkable confirmation of the view I have ventured to propound; so much so that Mr. Walker, by whom the elaborate lists appended to this work have been prepared, asserts that some of the families have a less affinity to the entomology of India than to that of Australia.[1]

But more conclusive than all, is the discovery to which I have alluded, in relation to the elephant of Ceylon. Down to a very recent period it was universally believed that only two species of the elephant are now in existence, the African and the Asiatic; distinguished by certain peculiarities in the shape of the cranium, the size of the ears, the ridges of the teeth, the number of vertebræ, and, according to Cuvier, in the number of nails on the hind feet. The elephant of Ceylon was believed to be identical with the elephant of India. But some few years back, TEMMINCK, in his survey of the Dutch possessions in the Indian Archipelago[2], announced the fact that the elephant which abounds in Sumatra (although unknown in the adjacent island of Java), and which had theretofore been regarded as the same species with the Indian one, has been recently found to possess peculiarities, in which it differs as much from the elephant of India, as the latter from its African congener. On this new species of elephant, to which the natives give the name of *gadjah*, TEMMINCK has conferred the scientific designation of the *Elephas Sumatranus*.

[1] See Chapter on the Insects of Ceylon.

[2] *Coup d'Œil Général sur les Possessions Néerlandaises dans l'Inde Archipélagique.*

The points which entitle it to this distinction he enumerated minutely in the work[1] before alluded to, but they have been summarized as follows by Prince Lucien Bonaparte.

"This species is perfectly intermediate between the Indian and African, especially in the shape of the skull, and will certainly put an end to the distinction between *Elephas* and *Loxodon*, with those who admit that anatomical genus; since although the crowns of the teeth of *E. Sumatranus* are more like the Asiatic animal, still the less numerous undulated ribbons of enamel are nearly quite as wide as those forming the lozenges of the African. The number of pairs of false ribs (which alone vary, the true ones being always six) is fourteen, one less than in the *Africanus*, *one* more than in the *Indicus*; and so it is with the dorsal vertebræ, which are twenty in the *Sumatranus* (*twenty-one* and *nineteen*, in the others), whilst the new species agrees with *Africanus* in the number of sacral vertebræ (*four*), and with *Indicus* in that of the caudal ones, which are *thirty-four*."[2]

[1] TEMMINCK, *Coup-d'œil, &c.*, t. i. c. iv. p. 328.; t. ii. c. iii. p. 91.

[2] *Proceed. Zool. Soc. London*, 1849, p. 144, *note*. The original description of TEMMINCK is as follows:

"Elephas Sumatranus, *Nob.* ressemble, par la forme générale du crâne à l'éléphant du continent de l'Asie; mais la partie libre des intermaxillaires est beaucoup plus courte et plus étroite; les cavités nasales sont beaucoup moins larges; l'espace entre les orbites des yeux est plus étroit; la partie postérieur du crâne au contraire est plus large que dans l'espèce du continent.

"Les machelières se rapprochent, par la forme de leur couronne, plutôt de l'espèce Asiatique que de celle qui est propre à l'Afrique; c'est-à-dire que leur couronne offre la forme de rubans ondoyés et non pas en losange; mais ces rubans sont de la largeur de ceux qu'on voit à la couronne des dents de l'éléphant d'Afrique; ils sont conséquemment moins nombreux que dans celui du continent de l'Asie. Les dimensions de ces rubans, dans la direction d'avant en arrière, comparées à celle prises dans la direction transversale et latérale, sont en raison de 3 ou 4 à 1; tandis que dans l'éléphant du continent elles sont comme 4 ou 6 à 1. La longueur totale de six de ces rubans, dans l'espèce nouvelle de Sumatra, ainsi que dans celle

PROFESSOR SCHLEGEL of Leyden, in a paper lately submitted by him to the Royal Academy of Sciences of Holland, (the substance of which he has obligingly communicated to me, through Baron Bentinck the Netherlands Minister at this Court), has confirmed the identity of the Ceylon elephant with that found in the Lampongs of Sumatra. The osteological comparison of which TEMMINCK has given the results was, he says, conducted by himself with access to four skeletons of the latter. And the more recent opportunity of comparing a living Sumatran elephant with one from Bengal, has served to establish other though minor points of divergence. The Indian species is more robust and powerful; the proboscis longer and more slender; and the extremity, (a point, in which the elephant of Sumatra resembles that of Africa,) is more flattened and provided with coarser and longer hair than that of India.

PROFESSOR SCHLEGEL, adverting to the large export of elephants from Ceylon to the Indian continent, which has been carried on from time immemorial, suggests the caution with which naturalists, in investigating this question, should first satisfy themselves whether the elephants they examine are really natives of the mainland,

d'Afrique, est d'environ 12 centimètres, tandis que cette longueur n'est que de 8 à 10 centimètres dans l'espèce du continent de l' Asie.

"Les autres formes ostéologiques sont à peu près les mêmes dans les trois espèces; mais il y a différence dans le nombre des os dont le squelette se compose, ainsi que le tableau comparatif ci-joint l'éprouve.

"*L'elephas Africanus* a 7 vertèbres du cou, 21 vert. dorsales, 3 lombaires, 4 sacrées, et 26 caudales; 21 paires de côtes, dont 6 vraies, et 15 fausses. *L'elephas Indicus* a 7 vertèbres du cou, 19 dorsales, 3 lombaires, 5 sacrées, et 34 caudales, 19 paires de côtes, dont 6 vraies, et 3 fausses. *L'elephas Sumatranus* a 7 vertèbres du cou, 20 dorsales, 3 lombaires, 4 sacrées, et 34 caudales; 20 paires du côtes, dont 6 vraies, et 14 fausses.

"Ces caractères ont été constatés sur trois squelettes de l'espèce nouvelle, un mâle et une femelle adultes et un jeune mâle. Nous n'avons pas encore été à même de nous procurer la dépouille de cette espèce."

or whether they have been brought to it from the islands.[1] "The extraordinary fact," he observes in his letter to me, "of the identity thus established between the elephants of Ceylon and Sumatra; and the points in which they are found to differ from that of Bengal, leads to the question whether all the elephants of the Asiatic continent belong to one single species; or whether these vast regions may not produce in some quarter as yet unexplored the one hitherto found only in the two islands referred to? It is highly desirable that naturalists who have the means and opportunity, should exert themselves to discover, whether any traces are to be found of the Ceylon elephant in the Dekkan; or of that of Sumatra in Cochin China or Siam."

To me the establishment of a fact so conclusively confirmatory of the theory I had ventured to broach, is productive of great satisfaction. But it is not a little remarkable that the distinction should not long before have been discovered between the elephant of India and that of Ceylon. Nor can it be regarded otherwise than as a singular illustration of "geographical distribution" that two remote islands should be thus shown to possess in common a species unknown in any other quarter of the globe. As bearing on the ancient myth which represents both countries as forming parts of a submerged continent, the discovery is curious—and it is equally interesting in connection with the circumstance alluded to by Gibbon, that amongst the early geographers and even down to a comparatively modern date, Sumatra and Ceylon were confounded; and grave doubts were entertained as to

[1] A further inquiry suggests itself, how far the intermixture of the breed may have served to confound specific differences, in the case of elephants bred on the continent of India, from stock partially imported from Ceylon?

which of the two was the "Taprobane" of antiquity. GEMMA FRISIUS, SEBASTIAN MUNSTER, JULIUS SCALIGER, ORTELIUS and MERCATOR contended for the former; SALMASIUS, BOCHART, CLUVERIUS, and VOSSIUS for Ceylon: and the controversy did not cease till it was terminated by DELISLE about the beginning of the last century.

VIII. CETACEA.—Whales are so frequently seen that they have been captured within sight of Colombo, and more than once their carcases, after having been flinched by the whalers, have floated on shore near the light-house, tainting the atmosphere within the fort by their rapid decomposition.

Of this family, one of the most remarkable animals on the coast is the dugong [1], a phytophagous cetacean, numbers of which are attracted to the inlets, from the bay of Calpentyn to Adam's Bridge, by the still water and the abundance of marine algæ in these parts of the gulf. One which was killed at Manaar and sent to me to Colombo [2] in 1847, measured upwards of seven feet in length; but specimens considerably larger have been taken at Calpentyn, and their flesh is represented as closely resembling veal.

The rude approach to the human outline, observed in the shape of the head of this creature, and the attitude of the mother when suckling her young, clasping it to her breast with one flipper, while swimming with the other, holding the heads of both above water; and when disturbed, suddenly diving and displaying her fish-like tail,—these, together with her habitual demonstrations of strong maternal affection, probably gave rise to the fable of the "mermaid;" and thus that earliest invention

[1] *Halicore dugung*, F. Cuv.

[2] The skeleton is now in the Museum of the Natural History Society of Belfast.

THE DUGONG

of mythical physiology may be traced to the Arab seamen and the Greeks, who had watched the movements of the dugong in the waters of Manaar.

Megasthenes records the existence of a creature in the ocean, near Taprobane, with the aspect of a woman[1]; and Ælian, adopting and enlarging on his information, peoples the seas of Ceylon with fishes having the heads of lions, panthers, and rams, and, stranger still, *cetaceans in the form of satyrs.* Statements such as these must have had their origin in the hairs, which are set round the mouth of the dugong, somewhat resembling a beard, which Ælian and Megasthenes both particularise, from their resemblance to the hair of a woman; "*καὶ γυναικῶν ὄπσιν ἔχουσιν αἶσπερ ἀντὶ πλοκάμων ἄκανθαι προσηρτήνται.*"[2]

The Portuguese cherished the belief in the mermaid,

[1] MEGASTHENES, *Indica*, fragm. lix. 34.

[2] ÆLIAN, *Nat. Hist.*, lib. xvi. ch. xviii.

and the annalist of the exploits of the Jesuits in India, gravely records that seven of these monsters, male and female, were captured at Manaar in 1560, and carried to Goa, where they were dissected by Demas Bosquez, physician to the Viceroy, and "their internal structure found to be in all respects conformable to the human."[1]

The Dutch were no less inclined to the marvellous, and they propagated the belief in the mermaid with earnestness and particularity. VALENTYN, one of their chaplains, in his account of the Natural History of Amboina, embodied in his great work on the Netherlands' Possessions in India, published so late as 1727[2], has devoted the first section of his chapter on the Fishes of that island to a minute description of the "Zee-Menschen," Zee-Wyven," and mermaids. As to the dugong he admits its resemblance to the mermaid, but repudiates the idea of its having given rise to the fable, by being mistaken for one. This error he imagines must have arisen at a time when observations on such matters were made with culpable laxity; but now more recent and minute attention has established the truth beyond cavil.

For instance, he states that in 1653, when a lieutenant in the Dutch service was leading a party of soldiers along the sea-shore in Amboina, he and all his company saw the mermen swimming at a short distance from the beach with long and flowing hair, of a colour between gray and green — and six weeks afterwards, the

[1] *Hist. de la Compagnie de Jèsus*, quoted in the *Asiat. Journ.* vol. xiv. p. 461; and in FORBES' *Orient. Memoirs*, vol. i. p. 421.

[2] FRAN. VALENTYN, *Beschryving van Oud en Nieuw Oost-Indien*, &c. 5 vol. fol. Dordrecht and Amsterdam, MDCCXXVII. vol. iii. p. 330.

creatures were again seen by him and more than fifty witnesses, at the same place, by clear daylight.[1]

"If any narrative in the world," adds VALENTYN, "deserves credit, it is this; since *not only one but two mermen* together were seen by so many eye-witnesses. Should the stubborn world, however, hesitate to believe it, it matters nothing; as there are people who would even deny that such cities as Rome, Constantinople or Cairo, exist, merely because they themselves have not happened to see them."

But what are such incredulous persons, he continues, to make of the circumstance recorded by Albert Herport in his account of India[2], that a sea-man was seen in the water near the Church of Taquan, on the morning of the 29th of April 1661, and a mermaid at the same spot the same afternoon? — or what do they say to the fact that in 1714, a mermaid was not only seen but captured near the island of Booro? "five feet Rhineland measure "in height, which lived four days and seven hours, but "refusing all food, died without leaving any intelligible "account of herself."

Valentyn, in support of his own faith in the mermaid, cites numerous other instances in which both "sea-men and women" were seen and taken at Amboina; especially one by an office-bearer in the Church of Holland[3], by whom it was surrendered to the Governor Vanderstel.

Of this well-authenticated specimen he gives an elaborate engraving amongst those of the authentic fishes of the island—together with a minute ichthyological

[1] VALENTYN, *Beschryving, &c.,* vol. iii. p. 331.

[2] Probably the *Itinerarium Indicum* of ALBRECHT HERPORT. Berne, 1669.

[3] A "krank-bezoeker" or visitant of the sick.

description of each for the satisfaction of men of science.

THE MERMAID (From VALENTYN).

The fame of this creature having reached Europe, the British Minister in Holland wrote to Valentyn on the 28th December 1716, whilst the Emperor, Peter the Great of Russia, was his guest at Amsterdam ; to communicate the desire of the Czar, that the mermaid should be brought home from Amboina for his Imperial inspection.

To complete his proofs of the existence of mermen and women, Valentyn points triumphantly to the historical fact, that in Holland in the year 1404, a mermaid was driven during a tempest, through a breach in the dyke of Edam, and was taken alive in the lake of Purmer. Thence she was carried to Harlem, where the Dutch women taught her to spin; and where, several years after, she died in the Roman Catholic faith;—"but this," says the pious Calvinistic chaplain, "in no way militates against the truth of her story."[1]

Finally Valentyn winds up his proofs, by the accumulated testimony of Pliny[2], Theodore Gaza, George of Trebisond, and Alexander ab Alexandro, to show that mermaids had in all ages been known in Gaul, Naples, Epirus, and the Morea. From these and a multitude of more modern instances he comes to the conclusion, that as there are "sea-cows," "sea-horses," and "sea-dogs;" as well as "sea-trees" and "sea-flowers" which he himself had seen, what grounds in reason are there to doubt that there may also be "sea-maidens" and "sea-men!"

## *List of Ceylon Mammalia.*

A list of the Mammalia of Ceylon is subjoined. In framing it, as well as the lists appended to the other chapters on the Fauna of the island, the principal object in view has been to exhibit the extent to which the Natural History of the island had been investigated, and collections made up to the period of my leaving the colony in 1850. It has been considered expedient to exclude a few individuals which have not had the advantage of a direct comparison with authentic specimens, either at Calcutta or in England. This will account for the omission of a number that have appeared in other catalogues, but of which many, though ascertained to exist, have not been submitted to this rigorous process of identification.

The greater portion of the species of mammals and birds contained in these lists will be found, with suitable

[1] VALENTYN, *Beschryving, &c.,* p. 333.

[2] *Nat. Hist.* l. ix. c. 5, where Pliny speaks of the Nereids.

references to the most accurate descriptions, in the admirable catalogue of the collection at the India House, published under the care of the late Dr. Horsfield. This work cannot be too highly extolled, not alone for the scrupulous fidelity with which the description of each species is referred to its first discoverer, but also for the pains which have been taken to elaborate synonymes and to collate from local periodicals and other sources, (little accessible to ordinary inquirers,) such incidents and traits as are calculated to illustrate characteristics and habits.

QUADRUMANA.

Presbytes
cephalopterus, *Zimm.*
ursinus, *Blyth.*
Priamus, *Elliot & Blyth.*
Thersites, *Blyth.*
Macacus pileatus, *Shaw & Desm.*
Loris gracilis, *Geoff.*

CHEIROPTERA.

Pteropus Edwardsii, *Geoff.*
Leschenaultii, *Dum.*
Cynopterus
marginatus, *Ham.*
Megaderma spasma, *Linn.*
lyra, *Geoff.*
Rhinolophus *affinis, Horsf.*
Hipposideros
murinus, *Elliot.*
speoris, *Elliot.*
armiger, *Hodgs.*
vulgaris, *Horsf.*
Kerivoula picta, *Pall.*
Taphozous
longimanus, *Har.*
Scotophilus Coromandelicus, *F. Cuv.*
*adversus, Horsf.*
Temminkii, *Horsf.*
Tickelli, *Blyth.*
Heathii.

CARNIVORA.

Sorex cœrulescens, *Shaw.*
ferrugineus, *Kelaart.*
serpentarius, *Is. Geoff.*
montanus, *Kelaart.*
Feroculus macropus, *Kel.*
Ursus labiatus, *Blainv.*
Lutra nair, *F. Cuv.*
Canis aureus, *Linn.*
Viverra Indica, *Geoff., Hod.*
Herpestes vitticollis, *Benn.*
griseus, *Gm.*
Smithii, *Gray.*
fulvescens, *Kelaart.*
Paradoxurus typus, *F. Cuv.*
Ceylonicus, *Pall.*
Felis pardus, *Linn.*
chaus, *Guldens.*
viverrinus, *Benn.*

RODENTIA.

Sciurus macrurus, *Forst.*
Tennentii, *Layard.*
penicillatus, *Leach.*
trilineatus, *Waterh.*
Sciuropterus Layardi, *Kel.*
Pteromys petaurista, *Pall.*
Mus bandicota, *Bechst.*
Kok, *Gray.*
Mus rufescens, *Gray.*
nemoralis, *Blyth.*
Indicus, *Geoff.*
fulvidiventris, *Blyth.*
Nesoki *Hardwickii, Gray.*
Golunda Neuera, *Kelaart.*
Ellioti, *Gray.*
Gerbillus Indicus, *Hardw.*
Lepus nigricollis, *F. Cuv.*
Hystrix leucurus, *Sykes.*

EDENTATA.

Manis pentadactyla, *Linn.*

PACHYDERMATA.

Elephas Sumatranus, *Linn.*
Sus Indicus, *Gray.*
*Zeylonicus, Blyth.*

RUMINANTIA.

Moschus meminna, *Erxl.*
Stylocerus muntjac, *Horsf.*
Axis maculata, *H. Smith.*
Rusa Aristotelis, *Cuv.*

CETACEA.

Halicore dugung, *F. Cuv.*

## CHAP. II.

### THE ELEPHANT.

*Structure and Functions.*

DURING my residence at Kandy, I had twice the opportunity of witnessing the operation on a grand scale, of capturing wild elephants, intended to be trained for the public service in the establishment of the Civil Engineer; — and in the course of my frequent journeys through the interior of the island, I succeeded in collecting so many facts relative to the habits of these interesting animals in a state of nature, as enable me not only to add to the information previously possessed, but to correct many fallacies popularly received regarding their instincts and disposition. These particulars I am anxious to place on record before proceeding to describe the scenes of which I was a spectator, during the progress of the elephant hunts in the district of the Seven Korles, at which I was present in 1846, and again in 1847.

With the exception of the narrow but densely inhabited belt of cultivated land, that extends along the seaborde of the island from Chilaw on the western coast to Tangalle on the south-east, there is no part of Ceylon in which elephants may not be said to abound; even close to the environs of the most populous localities of the interior. They frequent both the open plains and the deep forests; and their footsteps are to be seen wherever food and shade, vegetation and water[1], allure

[1] M. AD. PICTET has availed himself of the love of the elephant for water, to found on it a solution of the long-contested question as to the etymology of the word "elephant,"—a term which, whilst it has passed into almost every dialect of the West, is scarcely to be traced in any language of Asia. The Greek ἐλέφας, to which we are immediately indebted for it, did not originally mean the animal, but, as early as the time of Homer, was applied only to its tusks, and signified *ivory*. BOCHART has sought for a Semitic origin, and seizing on the Arabic *fil*, and prefixing the article *al*, suggests *alfil*, akin to ἐλεφ; but rejecting this, BOCHART himself resorts to the Hebrew *eleph*, an "ox"—and this conjecture derives a certain degree of countenance from the fact that the Romans, when they obtained their first sight of the elephant in the army of Pyrrhus, in Lucania, called it the *Luca bos*. But the αντος is still unaccounted for; and POTT has sought to remove the difficulty by introducing the Arabic *hindi*, Indian, thus making *eleph-hindi*, "*bos Indicus*." The conversion of *hindi* into αντος is an obstacle, but here the example of "tamarind" comes to aid; *tamar hindi*, the "Indian date," which in mediæval Greek forms ταμάρεντι. A theory of BENARY, that ἐλέφας might be compounded of the Arabic *al*, and *ibha*, a Sanskrit name for the elephant, is exposed to still greater etymological exception. PICTET's solution is, that in the Sanskrit epics "the King of Elephants," who has the distinction of carrying the god Indra, is called *airavata* or *airavana*, a modification of *airavanta*, "son of the ocean," which again comes from *iravat*, "abounding in water." "Nous aurions donc ainsi, comme corrélatif du grec ἐλέφαντο, une ancienne forme. *âirâvanta* ou *âilâvanta*, affaiblie plus tard en *âirâvata* ou *âirâvana*. . . . . On connaît la prédilection de l'éléphant pour le voisinage des fleuves, et son amour pour l'eau, dont l'abondance est nécessaire à son bien-être." This Sanskrit name, PICTET supposes, may have been carried to the West by the Phœnicians, who were the purveyors of ivory from India; and, from the Greek, the Latins derived *elephas*, which passed into the modern languages of Italy, Germany, and France. But it is curious that the Spaniards acquired from the Moors their Arabic term for ivory, *marfil*, and the Portuguese *marfim;* and that the Scandinavians, probably from their early expeditions to the Mediterranean, adopted *fill* as their name for the elephant itself, and *fil-bein* for ivory; in Danish, *fils-ben*. (See *Journ. Asiat.* 1843, t. xliii. p. 133.) The Spaniards of South America call the palm which produces the vegetable ivory (*Phytelephas macrocarpa*) *Palma de marfil*, and the nut itself, *marfil vegetal*.

Since the above was written Gooneratné Modliar, the Singhalese Interpreter to the Supreme Court at Colombo, has supplied me with

them, alike on the summits of the loftiest mountains, and on the borders of the tanks and lowland streams.

From time immemorial the natives have been taught to capture and tame them, and the export of elephants from Ceylon to India has been going on without interruption from the period of the first Punic War.[1] In later times all elephants were the property of the Kandyan crown; and their capture or slaughter without the royal permission was classed amongst the gravest offences in the criminal code.

In recent years there is reason to believe that their numbers have become considerably reduced. They have entirely disappeared from localities in which they were formerly numerous[2]; smaller herds have been taken in the periodical captures for the government service, and hunters returning from the chase report them to be growing scarce. In consequence of this diminution the peasantry in some parts of the island have even suspended the ancient practice of keeping watchers and fires by night to drive away the elephants from their growing crops.[3] The opening of roads and the clearing of the mountain forests of Kandy for the cultivation of coffee,

another conjecture, that the word elephant may possibly be traced to the Singhalese name of the animal, *alia*, which means literally, "the huge one." *Alia*, he adds, is not a derivation from Sanskrit or Pali, but belongs to a dialect more ancient than either.

[1] ÆLIAN, *de Nat. Anim.* lib. xvi. c. 18; COSMAS INDICOPL. p. 128.

[2] LE BRUN, who visited Ceylon A.D. 1705, says that in the district round Colombo, where elephants are now never seen, they were then so abundant, that 160 had been taken in a single corral. (*Voyage, &c.*, tom. ii. ch. lxiii. p. 331.)

[3] In some parts of Bengal, where elephants were formerly troublesome (especially near the wilds of Ramgur), the natives got rid of them by mixing a preparation of the poisonous Nepal root called *dakra* in balls of grain, and other materials, of which the animal is fond. In Cuttack, above fifty years ago, mineral poison was laid for them in the same way, and the carcases of eighty were found which had been killed by it. (*Asiat. Res.*, xv. 183.)

have forced the animals to retire to the low country, where again they have been followed by large parties of European sportsmen; and the Singhalese themselves, being more freely provided with arms than in former times, have assisted in swelling the annual slaughter.[1]

Had the motive that incites to the destruction of the elephant in Africa and India prevailed in Ceylon, that is, had the elephants there been provided with tusks, they would long since have been annihilated for the sake of their ivory.[2] But it is a curious fact that, whilst in Africa and India both sexes have tusks[3], with some slight disproportion in the size of those of the females; not one elephant in a hundred is found with tusks in Ceylon, and the few that possess them are exclusively males. Nearly all, however, have those stunted processes called *tushes*, about ten or twelve inches in length and one or two in diameter. These I have observed them to use in loosening earth, stripping off bark, and snapping asunder small branches and climbing

[1] The number of elephants has been similarly reduced throughout the south of India.

[2] The annual importation of ivory into Great Britain alone, for the last few years, has been about *one million* pounds; which, taking the average weight of a tusk at sixty pounds, would require the slaughter of 8,333 male elephants.

But of this quantity the importation from Ceylon has generally averaged only five or six hundred weight; which, making allowance for the lightness of the tusks, would not involve the destruction of more than seven or eight in each year. At the same time, this does not fairly represent the annual number of tuskers shot in Ceylon, not only because a portion of the ivory finds its way to China and to other places, but because the chiefs and Buddhist priests have a passion for collecting tusks, and the finest and largest are to be found ornamenting their temples and private dwellings. The Chinese profess that for their exquisite carvings the ivory of Ceylon excels all other, both in density of texture and in delicacy of tint; but in the European market, the ivory of Africa, from its more distinct graining and other causes, obtains a higher price.

[3] A writer in the *India Sporting Review* for October 1857 says, "In Malabar a tuskless male elephant is rare; I have seen but two."—p. 157.

plants; and hence tushes are seldom seen without a groove worn into them near their extremities.[1]

Amongst other surmises more ingenious than sound, the general absence of tusks in the elephant of Ceylon has been associated with the profusion of rivers and streams in the island; whilst it has been thrown out as a possibility that in Africa, where water is comparatively scarce, the animal is equipped with these implements in order to assist it in digging wells in the sand and in raising the juicy roots of the mimosas and succulent plants for the sake of their moisture. In support of this hypothesis, it has been observed, that whilst the tusks of the Ceylon species, which are never required for such uses, are slender, graceful and curved, seldom exceeding fifty or sixty pounds' weight, those of the African elephant are straight and thick, weighing occasionally one hundred and fifty, and even three hundred pounds.[2]

[1] The old fallacy is still renewed, that the elephant sheds his tusks. ÆLIAN says he drops them once in ten years (lib. xiv. c. 5); and PLINY repeats the story, adding that, when dropped, the elephants hide them under ground (lib. viii.) whence SHAW says, in his *Zoology*, "they are frequently found in the woods," and exported from Africa (vol. i. p. 213); and Sir W. JARDINE in the *Naturalist's Library* (vol. ix. p. 110), says, "the tusks are shed about the twelfth or thirteenth year." This is erroneous: after losing the first pair, or, as they are called, the "milk tusks," which drop in consequence of the absorption of their roots, when the animal is extremely young, the second pair acquire their full size, and become the "permanent tusks," which are never shed.

[2] Notwithstanding the inferiority in weight of the Ceylon tusks, as compared with those of the elephant of India, it would, I think, be precipitate to draw the inference that the size of the former was uniformly and naturally less than that of the latter. The truth, I believe to be, that if permitted to grow to maturity, the tusks of the one would, in all probability, equal those of the other; but, so eager is the search for ivory in Ceylon, that a tusker, when once observed in a herd, is followed up with such vigilant impatience, that he is almost invariably shot before attaining his full growth. General DE LIMA, when returning from the

But it is manifestly inconsistent with the idea that tusks were given to the elephant to assist him in digging for his food, to find that the females are less bountifully supplied with them than the males, whilst the necessity for their use extends equally to both sexes. The same argument serves to demonstrate the fallacy of the conjecture, that the tusks of the elephant were given to him as weapons of offence, for if such were the case the vast majority in Ceylon, males as well as females, would be left helpless in presence of an assailant. But although in their conflicts with one another, those which are provided with tusks may occasionally push with them clumsily at their opponents; it is a misapprehension to imagine that tusks are designed specially to serve "in warding off the attacks of the wily tiger and the furious rhinoceros, often securing the victory by one blow which transfixes the assailant to the earth."[1]

governorship of the Portuguese settlements at Mozambique, told me, in 1848, that he had been requested to procure two tusks of the largest size, and straightest possible shape, which were to be formed into a cross to surmount the high altar of the cathedral at Goa: he succeeded in his commission, and sent two, one of which was 180 pounds, and the other 170 pounds' weight, with the slightest possible curve. In a periodical, entitled *The Friend*, published in Ceylon, it is stated in the volume for 1837 that the officers belonging to the ships Quorrah and Alburhak, engaged in the Niger Expedition, were shown by a native king two tusks, each two feet and a half in circumference at the base, eight feet long, and weighing upwards of 200 pounds. (Vol. i. p. 225.) BRODERIP, in his *Zoological Recreations*, p. 255, says a tusk of 350 pounds' weight was sold at Amsterdam, but he does not quote his authority.

[1] *Menageries, &c.*, published by the Society for the Diffusion of Useful Knowledge, vol. i. p. 68: "The Elephant," ch. iii. It will be seen that I have quoted repeatedly from this volume, because it is the most compendious and careful compilation with which I am acquainted of the information previously existing regarding the elephant. The author incorporates no speculations of his own, but has most diligently and agreeably arranged all the facts collected by his predecessors. The story of antipathy between the elephant and rhinoceros is probably borrowed from ÆLIAN *de Nat.*, lib. xvii. c. 44.

So harmless and peaceful is the life of the elephant, that nature appears to have left it unprovided with any weapon of offence: its trunk is too delicate an organ to be rudely employed in a conflict with other animals, and although on an emergency it may push or gore with its tusks (to which the French have hastily given the term "*défenses*"), their almost vertical position, added to the difficulty of raising its head above the level of the shoulder, is inconsistent with the idea of their being designed for attack, since it is impossible for the elephant to strike an effectual blow, or to "wield" its tusks as the deer and the buffalo can direct their horns. Nor is it easy to conceive under what circumstances an elephant could have a hostile encounter with either a rhinoceros or a tiger, with whose pursuits in a state of nature its own can in no way conflict.

Towards man elephants evince shyness, arising from their love of solitude and dislike of intrusion; any alarm they exhibit at his appearance may be reasonably traced to the slaughter which has reduced their numbers; and as some evidence of this, it has always been observed that an elephant exhibits greater impatience of the presence of a white man than of a native. Were its instincts to carry it further, or were it influenced by any feeling of animosity or cruelty, it must be apparent that, as against the prodigious numbers that inhabit the forests of Ceylon, man would wage an unequal contest, and that of the two one or other must long since have been reduced to a helpless minority.

Official testimony is not wanting in confirmation of this view;—in the returns of 108 coroners' inquests in Ceylon, during five years, from 1849 to 1855 inclusive, held in cases of death occasioned by wild animals; 16

are recorded as having been caused by elephants, 15 by buffaloes, 6 by crocodiles, 2 by boars, 1 by a bear, and 68 by serpents (the great majority of the last class of sufferers being women and children, who had been bitten during the night). Little more than *three* fatal accidents occurring annually on the average of five years, is certainly a very small proportion in a population estimated at a million and a half, in an island abounding with elephants, with which, independently of casual encounters, voluntary conflicts are daily stimulated by the love of sport or the hope of gain. Were the elephants instinctively vicious or even highly irritable in their temperament, the destruction of human life under the circumstances must have been infinitely greater. It must also be taken into account, that some of the accidents recorded may have occurred in the rutting season, when elephants are subject to fits of temporary fury, known in India by the term *must*, in Ceylon *mudda*,—a paroxysm which speedily passes away, but during the fury of which it is dangerous even for the mahout to approach those ordinarily the gentlest and most familiar.

But, then, the elephant is said to "entertain an extraordinary dislike to all quadrupeds; that dogs running near him produce annoyance; that he is alarmed if a hare start from her form;" and from Pliny to Buffon every naturalist has recorded its supposed aversion to swine.[1] These alleged antipathies are in a great degree, if not entirely, imaginary. The habits of the elephant are essentially harmless, its wants lead to no rivalry with other animals, and the food to which it is

[1] *Menageries, &c.*, "The Elephant." ch. iii.

most attached flourishes in such abundance that it is obtained without an effort. In the quiet solitudes of Ceylon, elephants may constantly be seen browsing peacefully in the immediate vicinity of other animals, and in close contact with them. I have seen groups of deer and wild buffaloes reclining in the sandy bed of a river in the dry season, and elephants plucking the branches close beside them. They show no impatience in the company of the elk, the bear, and the wild hog; and on the other hand, I have never discovered an instance in which these animals have evinced any apprehension of elephants. The elephant's natural timidity, however, is such that it becomes alarmed on the appearance in the jungle of any animal with which it is not familiar. It is said to be afraid of the horse; but from my own experience, I should say it is the horse that is alarmed at the aspect of the elephant. In the same way, from some unaccountable impulse, the horse has an antipathy to the camel, and evinces extreme impatience, both of the sight and the smell of that animal.[1] When enraged, an elephant will not hesitate to charge a rider on horseback; but it is against the man, not against the horse, that his fury is directed; and no instance has been ever known of his wantonly assailing a horse. A horse, belonging to the late Major

[1] This peculiarity was noticed by the ancients, and is recorded by Herodotus: "*κάμηλον ἵππος φοβέεται, καὶ οὐκ ἀνέχεται οὔτε τὴν ἰδέην αὐτῆς ὁρέων οὔτε τὴν ὀδμὴν ὀσφραινόμενος*" (Herod. ch. 80). Camels have long been bred by the Grand Duke of Tuscany, at his establishment near Pisa, and even there the same instinctive dislike to them is manifested by the horse, which it is necessary to train and accustom to their presence in order to avoid accidents. Mr. BRODERIP mentions, that, "when the precaution of such training has not been adopted, the sudden and dangerous terror with which a horse is seized in coming unexpectedly upon one of them is excessive."—*Note-book of a Naturalist*, ch. iv. p. 113.

Rogers[1], had run away from his groom, and was found some considerable time afterwards grazing quietly with a herd of elephants. In DE BRY's splendid collection of travels, however, there is included "*The voyage of a Certain Englishman to Cambay;*" in which the author asserts that at Agra, in the year 1607, he was present at a spectacle given by the Viceregent of the great Mogul, in the course of which he saw an elephant destroy two horses, by seizing them in its trunk, and crushing them under foot.[2] But the display was avowedly an artificial one, and the creature must have been cruelly tutored for the occasion.

Pigs are constantly to be seen feeding about the stables of the tame elephants, which manifest no repugnance to them. As to the smaller animals, the elephant undoubtedly evinces uneasiness at the presence of a dog, but this is referable to the same cause as its impatience of a horse, namely, that neither is habitually seen by it in the forest; but it would be idle to suppose that this feeling could amount to hostility against a creature incapable of inflicting on it the slightest injury.[3] The truth I apprehend to be that, when they meet, the impudence and impertinences of the dog are offensive to

[1] Major ROGERS was many years the chief civil officer of Government in the district of Oovah, where he was killed by lightning, 1845.

[2] "Quidam etiam cum equis silvestribus pugnant. Sæpe unus elephas cum sex equis committitur; atque ipse adeo interfui cum unus elephas duos equos cum primo impetu protinus prosternerit;—injecta ènim jugulis ipsorum longa proboscide, ad se protractos, dentibus porro comminuit ac protrivit." *Angli Cujusdam in Cambayam Navigatio.* DE BRY, *Coll., &c.*, vol. iii. ch. xvi. p. 31.

[3] To account for the impatience manifested by the elephant at the presence of a dog, it has been suggested that he is alarmed lest the latter should attack *his feet*, a portion of his body of which the elephant is peculiarly careful. A tame elephant has been observed to regard with indifference a spear directed towards his head, but to shrink timidly from the same weapon when pointed at his foot.

the gravity of the elephant, and incompatible with his love of solitude and ease. Or may it be assumed as an evidence of the sagacity of the elephant, that the only two animals to which it manifests an antipathy, are the two which it has seen only in the company of its enemy, man? One instance has certainly been attested to me by an eye-witness, in which the trunk of an elephant was seized in the teeth of a Scotch terrier, and such was the alarm of the huge creature that it came at once to its knees. The dog repeated the attack, and on every renewal of it the elephant retreated in terror, holding its trunk above its head, and kicking at the terrier with its fore feet. It would have turned to flight, but for the interference of its keeper.

Major Skinner, formerly commissioner of roads in Ceylon, whose official duties in constructing highways involved the necessity of his being in the jungle for months together, always found that, by night or by day, the barking of a dog which accompanied him, was sufficient to put a herd to flight. On the whole, therefore, I am of opinion that the elephant lives on terms of amity with every quadruped in the forest, that it neither regards them as its foes, nor provokes their hostility by its acts; and that, with the exception of man, *its greatest enemy is a fly!*

The current statements as to the supposed animosity of the elephant to minor animals originated with Ælian and Pliny, who had probably an opportunity of seeing, what may at any time be observed, that when a captive elephant is picketed beside a post, the domestic animals, goats, sheep, and cattle, will annoy and irritate him by their audacity in making free with his provender; but this is an evidence in itself of the little instinctive dread which such comparatively puny creatures entertain of one so powerful and yet so gentle.

Amongst elephants themselves, jealousy and other causes of irritation frequently occasion contentions between individuals of the same herd; but on such occasions it is their habit to strike with their trunks, and to bear down their opponents with their heads. It is doubtless correct that an elephant, when prostrated by the force and fury of an antagonist of its own species, is often wounded by the downward pressure of the tusks, which in any other position it would be almost impossible to use offensively.[1]

Mr. Mercer, who in 1846 was the principal civil officer of Government at Badulla, sent me a jagged fragment of an elephant's tusk, about five inches in diameter, and weighing between twenty and thirty pounds, which had been brought to him by some natives, who, being attracted by a noise in the jungle, witnessed a combat between a tusker and one without tusks, and saw the latter with his trunk seize one of the tusks of his antagonist and wrench from it the portion in question, which measured two feet in length.

Here the trunk was shown to be the more powerful offensive weapon of the two; but I apprehend that the chief reliance of the elephant for defence is on its ponderous weight, the pressure of its foot being sufficient to crush any minor assailant after being prostrated by means of its trunk. Besides, in using its feet for this purpose, it derives a wonderful facility from the peculiar formation of the knee-joint in the hind leg, which, en-

[1] A writer in the *India Sporting Review* for October 1857 says a male elephant was killed by two others close to his camp: "the head was completely smashed in; there was a large hole in the side, and the abdomen was ripped open. The latter wound was given probably after it had fallen."—P. 175.

abling it to swing the hind feet forward close to the ground, assists it to toss the body alternately from foot to foot, till deprived of life.[1]

A sportsman who had partially undergone this operation, having been seized by a wounded elephant but rescued from its fury, described to me his sufferings as he was thus flung back and forward between the hind and fore feet of the animal, which ineffectually attempted to trample him at each concussion, and abandoned him without inflicting serious injury.

KNOX, in describing the execution of criminals by the state elephants of the former kings of Kandy, says, "they will run their teeth (*tusks*) through the body, and then tear it in pieces and throw it limb from limb;" but a Kandyan chief, who was witness to such scenes, has assured me that the elephant never once applied its tusks, but, placing its foot on the prostrate victim, plucked off his limbs in succession by a sudden movement of the trunk. If the tusks were designed to be employed offensively, some alertness would naturally be exhibited in using them; but in numerous instances where sportsmen have fallen into the power of a wounded elephant, they have escaped through the failure of the enraged animal to strike them with its tusks, even when stretched upon the ground.[2]

[1] In the Third Book of Maccabees, which is not printed in our Apocrypha, but appears in the series in the Greek Septuagint, the author, in describing the persecution of the Jews by Ptolemy Philopater, B.C. 210, states that the king swore vehemently that he would send them into the other world, "foully trampled to death by the knees and feet of elephants" (πέμψειν εἰς ᾅδην ἐν γόνασι καὶ ποσὶ θηρίων ᾐκισμένους. 3 Mac. v. 42). ÆLIAN makes the remark, that elephants on such occasions use their *knees* as well as their feet to crush their victims.—*Hist Anim.* viii. 10.

[2] The *Hastisilpe*, a Singhalese work which treats of the "Science of Elephants," enumerates amongst those which it is not desirable to

Placed as the elephant is in Ceylon, in the midst of the most luxuriant profusion of its favourite food, in close proximity at all times to abundant supplies of water, and with no enemies against whom to protect itself, it is difficult to conjecture any probable utility which it could derive from such appendages. Their absence is unaccompanied by any inconvenience to the individuals in whom they are wanting; and as regards the few who possess them, the only operations in which I am aware of their tusks being employed in relation to the œconomy of the animal, is to assist in ripping open the stem of the jaggery palms and young palmyras to extract the farinaceous core; and in splitting the juicy shaft of the plantain. Whilst the tuskless elephant crushes the latter under foot, thereby soiling it and wasting its moisture; the other, by opening it with the point of his tusk, performs the operation with delicacy and apparent ease.

These, however, are trivial and almost accidental advantages: on the other hand, owing to irregularities in their growth, the tusks are sometimes an impediment in feeding[1]; and in more than one instance in the Government studs, tusks which had so grown as to approach and cross one another at the extremities, have had to be removed by the saw; the contraction of space between them so impeding the free action of the trunk as to prevent the animal from conveying branches to its mouth.[2]

possess, "the elephant which will fight with a stone or a stick in his trunk."

[1] Among other eccentric forms, an elephant was seen in 1844, in the district of Bintenne, near Friar's-Hood Mountain, one of whose tusks was so bent that it took what sailors term a "round turn," and then resumed its curved direction as before. In the Museum of the College of Surgeons, London, there is a specimen, No. 2757, of a *spira* tusk.

[2] Since the foregoing remarks were written relative to the undefined use of tusks to the elephant, I have seen a speculation on the same subject in Dr. HOLLAND's "*Constitution of the Animal Crea-*

It is true that in captivity, and after a due course of training, the elephant discovers a new use for its tusks when employed in moving stones and piling timber; so much so that a powerful one will raise and carry on them a log of half a ton weight or more. One evening, whilst riding in the vicinity of Kandy, towards the scene of the massacre of Major Davie's party in 1803, my horse evinced some excitement at a noise which approached us in the thick jungle, and which consisted of a repetition of the ejaculation *urmph! urmph!* in a hoarse and dissatisfied tone. A turn in the forest explained the mystery, by bringing me face to face with a tame elephant, unaccompanied by any attendant. He was labouring painfully to carry a heavy beam of timber, which he balanced across his tusks, but the pathway being narrow, he was forced to bend his head to one side to permit it to pass endways; and the exertion and this inconvenience combined led him to utter the dissatisfied sounds which disturbed the composure of my horse. On seeing us halt, the elephant raised his head, reconnoitred us for a moment, then flung down the timber, and voluntarily forced himself backwards among the brushwood so as to leave a passage, of which he expected us to avail

*tion, as expressed in structural Appendages;*" but the conjecture of the author leaves the problem scarcely less obscure than before. Struck with the mere *supplemental* presence of the tusks, the absence of all apparent use serving to distinguish them from the *essential* organs of the creature, Dr. HOLLAND concludes that their production is a process incident, but not ancillary, to other important ends, especially connected with the vital functions of the trunk and the marvellous motive powers inherent to it; his conjecture is, that they are "a species of safety valve of the animal œconomy,"—and that "they owe their development to the predominance of the senses of touch and smell, conjointly with the muscular motions of which the exercise of these is accompanied." "Had there been no proboscis," he thinks, "there would have been no supplementary appendages, — the former creates the latter." — Pp. 246, 271.

ourselves. My horse hesitated: the elephant observed it, and impatiently thrust himself deeper into the jungle, repeating his cry of *urmph!* but in a voice evidently meant to encourage us to advance. Still the horse trembled; and anxious to observe the instinct of the two sagacious animals, I forbore any interference: again the elephant of his own accord wedged himself further in amongst the trees, and manifested some impatience that we did not pass him. At length the horse moved forward; and when we were fairly past, I saw the wise creature stoop and take up its heavy burthen, trim and balance it on its tusks, and resume its route as before, hoarsely snorting its discontented remonstrance.

Between the African elephant and that of Ceylon, with the exception of the striking peculiarity of the infrequency of tusks in the latter, the distinctions are less apparent to a casual observer than to a scientific naturalist. In the Ceylon species the forehead is higher and more hollow, the ears are smaller, and, in a section of the teeth, the grinding ridges, instead of being lozenge-shaped, are transverse bars of uniform breadth.

The Indian elephant is stated by Cuvier to have four nails on the hind foot, the African variety having only three: but amongst the perfections of a high-bred elephant of Ceylon, is always enumerated the possession of *twenty* nails, whilst those of a secondary class have but eighteen in all.[1]

So conversant are the natives with the structure and "points" of the elephant, that they divide them readily into castes, and describe with particularity their distinctive excellences and defects. In the *Hastisilpe*, a

[1] See Chapter on Mammalia, p. 60.

Singhalese work which treats of their management, the marks of inferior breeding are said to be "eyes restless like those of a crow, the hair of the head of mixed shades; the face wrinkled; the tongue curved and black; the nails short and green; the ears small; the neck thin, the skin freckled; the tail without a tuft, and the fore-quarter lean and low:" whilst the perfection of form and beauty is supposed to consist in the "softness of the skin, the red colour of the mouth and tongue, the forehead expanded and hollow, the ears broad and rectangular, the trunk broad at the root and blotched with pink in front; the eyes bright and kindly, the cheeks large, the neck full, the back level, the chest square, the fore legs short and convex in front, the hind quarter plump, and five nails on each foot, all smooth, polished, and round.[1] An elephant with these perfections," says the author of the *Hastisilpe*, "will impart glory and magnificence to the king; but he cannot be discovered amongst thousands, yea, there shall never be found an elephant clothed at once with *all* the excellences herein described." The "points" of an elephant are to be studied with the greatest advantage in those attached to the temples, which are always of the highest caste, and exhibit the most perfect breeding.

The colour of the animal's skin in a state of nature is generally of a lighter brown than that of those in captivity; a distinction which arises, in all probability, not so much from the wild animal's propensity to cover itself with mud and dust, as from the superior care which is taken in repeatedly bathing the tame ones, and in rub-

[1] A native of rank informed me, that "the tail of a high-caste elephant will sometimes touch the ground, but such are very rare."

bing their skins with a soft stone, a lump of burnt clay, or the coarse husk of a coco-nut. This kind of attention, together with the occasional application of oil, gives rise to the deeper black which the hides of the latter present.

Amongst the native Singhalese, however, a singular preference is evinced for elephants that exhibit those flesh-coloured blotches which occasionally mottle the skin of an elephant, chiefly about the head and extremities. The front of the trunk, the tips of the ears, the forehead, and occasionally the legs, are thus diversified with stains of a yellowish tint, inclining to pink. These are not natural; nor are they hereditary, for they are seldom exhibited by the younger individuals in a herd, but appear to be the result of some eruptive affection, the irritation of which has induced the animal in its uneasiness to rub itself against the rough bark of trees, and thus to destroy the outer cuticle.[1]

To a European these spots appear blemishes, and the taste that leads the natives to admire them is probably akin to the feeling that has at all times rendered *a white elephant* an object of wonder to Asiatics. The rarity of the latter is accounted for by regarding this peculiar appearance as the result of albinism; and notwithstanding the exaggeration of Oriental historians, who compare the fairness of such creatures to the whiteness of snow, even in its utmost perfection, I apprehend that the tint of a white elephant is little else than a flesh-colour, rendered somewhat more conspicuous by the blanching of the skin, and the lightness of the colourless hairs by

[1] This is confirmed by the fact that the scar of the ancle wound, occasioned by the rope on the legs of those which have been captured by noosing, presents precisely the same tint in the healed parts.

which it is sparsely covered. A white elephant is mentioned in the *Mahawanso* as forming part of the retinue attached to the "Temple of the Tooth" at Anarajapoora, in the fifth century after Christ[1]; but it commanded no religious veneration, and like those in the stud of the kings of Siam, it was tended merely as an emblem of royalty[2]; the sovereign of Ceylon being addressed as the "Lord of Elephants."[3] In 1633 a white elephant was exhibited in Holland[4]; but as this was some years before the Dutch had established themselves firmly in Ceylon, it was probably brought from some other of their eastern possessions.

[1] *Mahawanso*, ch. xxxviii. p. 254, A.D. 433.

[2] PALLEGOIX, *Siam, &c.*, vol. i. p. 152.

[3] *Mahawanso*, ch. xviii. p. 111. The Hindu sovereigns of Orissa, in the middle ages, bore the style of *Gaja-pati*, "powerful in elephants."—*Asiat. Res.* xv. 253.

[4] ARMANDI, *Hist. Milit. des Eléphants*, lib. ii. c. x. p. 380. HORACE mentions a white elephant as having been exhibited at Rome: "Sive elephas albus vulgi converteret ora."—HOR. *Ep.* II. 196.

# CHAP. III.

## THE ELEPHANT.

### *Habits when Wild.*

ALTHOUGH found generally in warm and sunny climates, it is a mistake to suppose that the elephant is partial either to heat or to light. In Ceylon, the mountain tops, and not the sultry valleys, are its favourite resort. In Oovah, where the elevated plains are often crisp with the morning frost, and on Pedura-talla-galla, at the height of upwards of eight thousand feet, they are found in herds, whilst the hunter may search for them without success in the hot jungles of the low country. No altitude, in fact, seems too lofty or too chill for the elephant, provided it affords the luxury of water in abundance; and, contrary to the general opinion that the elephant delights in sunshine, it seems at all times impatient of glare, and spends the day in the thickest depth of the forests, devoting the night to excursions, and to the luxury of the bath, in which it also indulges occasionally by day. This partiality for shade is doubtless ascribable to the animal's love of coolness and solitude; but it is not altogether unconnected with the position of the eye, and the circumscribed use which its peculiar mode of life permits it to make of the faculty of sight.

All the elephant hunters and natives to whom I have spoken on the subject, concur in opinion that its range of vision is circumscribed, and that it relies more on its ear and sense of smell than on its sight, which is liable to be obstructed by dense foliage; besides which, from the formation of its short neck, the elephant is incapable of directing the range of the eye much above the level of the head.[1]

The elephant's small range of vision is sufficient to account for its excessive caution, its alarm at unusual noises. and the timidity and panic exhibited at trivial

[1] After writing the above, I was permitted by the late Dr. HARRISON, of Dublin, to see some accurate drawings of the brain of an elephant, which he had the opportunity of dissecting in 1847; and on looking to that of the base, I have found a remarkable verification of the information which I collected in Ceylon.

The small figure A is the ganglion of the fifth nerve, showing the small motor and large sensitive portion.

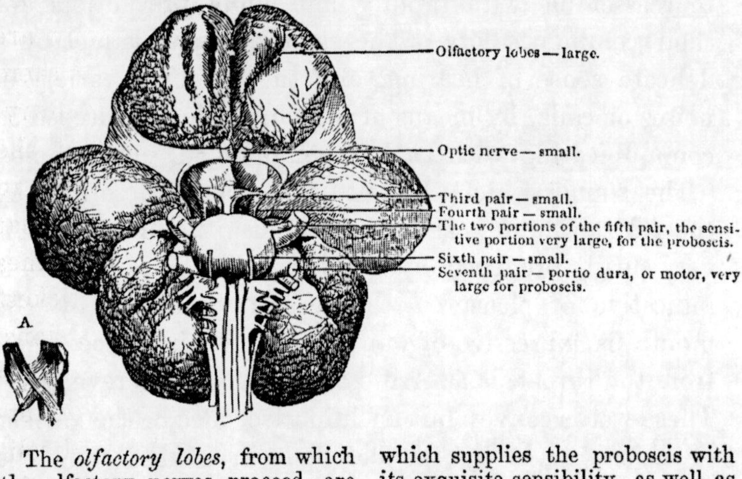


The *olfactory lobes*, from which the olfactory nerves proceed, are large, whilst the *optic and muscular nerves of the orbit are singularly small* for so vast an animal; and one is immediately struck by the prodigious size of the fifth nerve, which supplies the proboscis with its exquisite sensibility, as well as by the great size of the motor portion of the seventh, which supplies the same organ with its power of movement and action.

objects and incidents which, imperfectly discerned, excite suspicions for its safety.[1] In 1841 an officer[2] was chased by an elephant that he had slightly wounded. Seizing him near the dry bed of a river, the animal had its fore-foot already raised to crush him; but its forehead being caught at the instant by the tendrils of a climbing plant which had suspended itself from the branches above, it suddenly turned and fled; leaving him badly hurt, but with no limb broken. I have heard similar instances, equally well attested, of this peculiarity in the elephant.

On the other hand, the power of smell is so remarkable as almost to compensate for the deficiency of sight. A herd is not only apprised of the approach of danger by this means, but when scattered in the forest, and dispersed out of range of sight, they are enabled by it to reassemble with rapidity and adopt precautions for their common safety. The same necessity is met by a delicate sense of hearing, and the use of a variety of noises or calls, by means of which elephants succeed in communicating with each other upon all emergencies. "The sounds which they utter have been described by the African hunters as of three kinds: the first, which is very shrill, produced by blowing through the trunk, is indicative of pleasure; the second, produced by the mouth, is expressive of want; and the third, proceeding from the throat, is a terrific roar of anger or revenge."[3] These words convey but an imperfect idea of the variety of noises made by the elephant in Ceylon; and the shrill cry produced by blowing through his trunk, so far

[1] *Menageries, &c.*, "The Elephant," p. 27.

[2] Major ROGERS. An account of this singular adventure will be found in the *Ceylon Miscellany* for 1842, vol. i. p. 221.

[3] *Menageries, &c.*, "The Elephant," ch. iii. p. 68.

from being regarded as an indication of "pleasure," is the well-known cry of rage with which he rushes to encounter an assailant. Aristotle describes it as resembling the hoarse sound of a "trumpet." [1] The French still designate the proboscis of an elephant by the same expression "trompe," (which we have unmeaningly corrupted into *trunk*,) and hence the scream of the elephant is known as "trumpeting" by the hunters in Ceylon. Their cry when in pain, or when subjected to compulsion, is a grunt or a deep groan from the throat, with the proboscis curled upwards and the lips wide apart.

Should the attention of an individual in the herd be attracted by any unusual appearance in the forest, the intelligence is rapidly communicated by a low suppressed sound made by the lips, somewhat resembling the twittering of a bird, and described by the hunters by the word "*prut.*"

A very remarkable noise has been described to me by more than one individual, who has come unexpectedly upon a herd during the night, when the alarm of the elephants was apparently too great to be satisfied with the stealthy note of warning just described. On these occasions the sound produced resembled the hollow booming of an empty tun when struck with a wooden mallet or a muffled sledge. Major Macready, Military Secretary in Ceylon in 1836, who heard it by night amongst the wild elephants in the great forest of Bintenne, describes it as "a sort of banging noise like a

[1] Aristotle, *De Anim.*, lib. iv. c. 9. "ὅμοιον σάλπιγγι." See also Pliny, lib. x. ch. cxiii. A manuscript in the British Museum, containing the romance of "*Alexander*," which is probably of the fifteenth century, is interspersed with drawings illustrative of the strange animals of the East. Amongst them are two elephants, whose trunks are literally in the form of *trumpets with expanded mouths*. See Wright's *Archæological Album*, p. 176.

cooper hammering a cask;" and Major SKINNER is of opinion that it must be produced by the elephant striking his sides rapidly and forcibly with his trunk. Mr. CRIPPS informs me that he has more than once seen an elephant, when surprised or alarmed, produce this sound by striking the ground forcibly with the flat side of the trunk; and this movement was instantly succeeded by raising it again, and pointing it in the direction whence the alarm proceeded, as if to ascertain by the sense of smell the nature of the threatened danger. As this strange sound is generally mingled with the bellowing and ordinary trumpeting of the herd, it is in all probability a device resorted to, not alone for warning their companions of some approaching peril, but also for the additional purpose of terrifying unseen intruders.[1]

Elephants are subject to deafness; and the Singhalese regard as the most formidable of all wild animals, a "rogue"[2] afflicted with this infirmity.

Extravagant estimates are recorded of the height of the elephant. In an age when popular fallacies in relation to him were as yet uncorrected in Europe by the actual inspection of the living animal, he was supposed to grow to the height of twelve or fifteen feet. Even within the last century in popular works on natural history, the elephant, when full grown, was said to measure from seventeen to twenty feet from the ground to the shoulder.[3] At a still later period, so imperfectly had

[1] PALLEGOIX, in his *Description du Royaume Thai ou Siam*, adverts to a sound produced by the elephant when weary: "quand il est fatigué, *il frappe la terre avec sa* trompe, et en tire un son semblable à celui du cor."—Tom. i. p. 151.

[2] For an explanation of the term "rogue" as applied to an elephant, see p. 115.

[3] *Natural History of Animals.* By Sir JOHN HILL, M.D. London,

the facts been collated, that the elephant of Ceylon was believed "to excel that of Africa in size and strength." [1] But so far from equalling the size of the African species, that of Ceylon seldom exceeds the height of nine feet; even in the Hambangtotte country, where the hunters agree that the largest specimens are to be found, the tallest of ordinary herds do not average more than eight feet. WOLF, in his account of the Ceylon elephant [2], says he saw one taken near Jaffna, which measured twelve feet and one inch high. But the truth is, that the general bulk of the elephant so far exceeds that of the animals which we are accustomed to see daily, that the imagination magnifies its unusual dimensions; and I have seldom or ever met with an inexperienced spectator who did not unconsciously over-estimate the size of an elephant shown to him, whether in captivity or in a state of nature. Major DENHAM would have guessed some which he saw in Africa to be sixteen feet in height, but

1748-52, p. 565. A probable source of these false estimates is mentioned by a writer in the *Indian Sporting Review* for Oct. 1857. "Elephants were measured formerly, and even now, by natives, as to their height, by throwing a rope over them, the ends brought to the ground on each side, and half the length taken as the true height. Hence the origin of elephants fifteen and sixteen feet high. A rod held at right angles to the measuring rod, and parallel to the ground, will rarely give more than ten feet, the majority being under nine."—P. 159.

[1] SHAW'S *Zoology*. Lond. 1806. vol. i. p. 216; ARMANDI, *Hist. Milit. des Eléphans*, liv. i. ch. i. p. 2.

[2] WOLF'S *Life and Adventures*, *&c.*, p. 164. Wolf was a native of Mecklenburg, who arrived in Ceylon about 1750, as chaplain in one of the Dutch East Indiamen, and having been taken into the government employment, he served for twenty years at Jaffna, first as Secretary to the Governor, and afterwards in an office the duties of which he describes to be the examination and signature of the "writings which served to commence a suit in any of the Courts of justice." His book embodies a truthful and generally accurate account of the northern portion of the island, with which alone he was conversant, and his narrative gives a curious insight into the policy of the Dutch Government, and of the condition of the natives under their dominion.

the largest when killed was found to measure nine feet six, from the foot to the hip-bone.[1]

For a creature of such extraordinary weight it is astonishing how noiselessly and stealthily the elephant can escape from a pursuer. When suddenly disturbed in the jungle, it will burst away with a rush that seems to bear down all before it; but the noise sinks into absolute stillness so suddenly, that a novice might well be led to suppose that the fugitive had only halted within a few yards of him, when further search will disclose that it has stolen silently away, making scarcely a sound in its escape; and, stranger still, leaving the foliage almost undisturbed by its passage.

The most venerable delusion respecting the elephant, and that which held its ground with unequalled tenacity, is the ancient fallacy which is explained by SIR THOMAS BROWNE in his *Pseudodoxia Epidemica*, that "it hath no joynts; and this absurdity is seconded by another, that being unable to lye downe it sleepeth against a tree, which the hunters observing doe saw almost asunder, whereon the beast relying, by the fall of the tree falls also downe it-selfe and is able to rise no more."[2] Sir THOMAS is disposed to think that "the hint and ground of this opinion might be the grosse and somewhat cylindricall composure of the legs of the elephant, and the equality and lesse perceptible disposure of the joynts, especially in the forelegs of this animal, they

[1] DENHAM'S *Travels, &c.*, 4to p. 220. The fossil remains of the Indian elephant have been discovered at Jabalpur, showing a height of fifteen feet.—*Journ. Asiat. Soc. Beng.* vi. Professor ANSTED in his *Ancient World*, p. 197, says he was informed by Dr. Falconer "that out of eleven hundred elephants from which the tallest were selected and measured with care, on one occasion in India, there was not one whose height equalled eleven feet."

[2] *Vulgar Errors*, book iii. chap. 1.

appearing, when he standeth, like pillars of flesh;" but he overlooks the fact that PLINY has ascribed the same peculiarity to the Scandinavian beast somewhat resembling a horse, which he calls a "machlis,"[1] and that CÆSAR in describing the wild animals in the Hercynian forests, enumerates the *alce*, "in colour and configuration approaching the goat, but surpassing it in size, its head destitute of horns *and its limbs of joints*, whence it can neither lie down to rest, nor rise if by any accident it should fall, but using the trees for a resting-place, the hunters by loosening their roots bring the *alce* to the ground, so soon as it is tempted to lean on them."[2] This fallacy, as Sir THOMAS BROWNE says, is "not the daughter of latter times, but an old and grey-headed errour, even in the days of ARISTOTLE," who deals with the story as he received it from CTESIAS, by whom it

[1] Machlis (said to be derived from α, priv., and κλίνω, *cubo*, quod non cubat). "Moreover in the island of Scandinavia there is a beast called *Machlis*, that hath neither ioynt in the hough, nor pasternes in his hind legs, and therefore he never lieth down, but sleepeth leaning to a tree, wherefore the hunters that lie in wait for these beasts cut downe the trees while they are asleepe, and so take them; otherwise they should never be taken, they are so swift of foot that it is wonderful."—PLINY, *Natur. Hist.* Transl. Philemon Holland, book viii. ch. xv. p. 200.

[2] "Sunt item quæ appellantur *Alces*. Harum est consimilis capreis figura, et varietas pellium; sed magnitudine paulo antecedunt, mutilæque sunt cornibus, *et crura sine nodis articulisque habent;* neque quietis causa procumbunt; neque, si quo afflictæ casu considerunt, erigere sese aut sublevare possunt. His sunt arbores pro cubilibus; ad eas sese applicant, atque ita, paulum modo reclinatæ, quietem capiunt, quarum ex vestigiis cum est animadversum a venatoribus, quo se recipere consueverint, omnes eo loco, aut a radicibus subruunt aut accidunt arbores tantum, ut summa species earum stantium relinquatur. Huc cum se consuetudine reclinaverint, infirmas arbores pondere affligunt, atque una ipsæ concidunt."—CÆSAR, *De Bello Gall.* lib. vi. ch. xxvii.

The same fiction was extended by the early Arabian travellers to the rhinoceros, and in the MS. of the voyages of the "*Two Mahometans*," it is stated that the rhinoceros of Sumatra "n'a point d'articulation au genou ni à la main."—*Relations des Voyages, &c.*, Paris, 1845, vol. i. p. 29.

appears to have been embodied in his lost work on India. But although ARISTOTLE generally receives the credit of having exposed and demolished the fallacy of CTESIAS, it will be seen by a reference to his treatise *On the Progressive Motions of Animals,* that in reality he approached the question with some hesitation, and has not only left it doubtful in one passage whether the elephant has joints *in his knee,* although he demonstrates that it has joints in the shoulders[1]; but in another he distinctly affirms that on account of his weight the elephant cannot bend his forelegs together, but only one at a time, and reclines to sleep on that particular side.[2]

So great was the authority of ARISTOTLE, that ÆLIAN, who wrote two centuries later and borrowed many of his statements from the works of his predecessor, perpetuates this error; and, after describing the exploits of the trained elephants exhibited at Rome, adds the expression of his surprise, that an animal without joints (*ἄναρθρον*) should yet be able to dance.[3] The fiction was too agreeable to be readily abandoned by the poets

[1] "When an animal moves progressively an hypothenuse is produced, which is equal in power to the magnitude that is quiescent, and to that which is intermediate. But since the members are equal, it is necessary that the member which is quiescent should be inflected either in the knee or in the incurvation, *if the animal that walks is without knees.* It is possible, however, for the leg to be moved, when not inflected, in the same manner as infants creep; and there is an ancient report of this kind about elephants, which is not true, for such animals as these, *are moved in consequence of an inflection taking place either in their shoulders or hips.*"—ARISTOTLE, *De Ingressu Anim.*, ch. ix. Taylor's Transl.

[2] ARISTOTLE, *De Animal.*, lib. ii. ch. i. It is curious that Taylor, in his translation of this passage, was so strongly imbued with the "grey-headed errour," that in order to elucidate the somewhat obscure meaning of Aristotle, he has actually interpolated the text with the exploded fallacy of Ctesias, and after the word reclining to sleep, has inserted the words "*leaning against some wall or tree,*" which are not to be found in the original.

[3] "Ζῷον δὲ ἄναρθρον συνιέναι καὶ ῥυθμοῦ καὶ μέλους, καὶ φυλάττειν σχῆμα φύσεως δῶρα ταῦτα ἅμα καὶ ἰδιότης καθ' ἕκαστον ἐκπληκτική."—ÆLIAN, *De Nat. Anim.*, lib. ii. cap. xi.

of the Lower Empire and the Romancers of the middle ages; and PHILE, a contemporary of PETRARCH and DANTE, who in the early part of the fourteenth century, addressed his didactic poem on the elephant to the Emperor Andronicus II., untaught by the exposition of ARISTOTLE, still clung to the old delusion,

"Πόδες δὲ τούτῳ θαῦμα καὶ σαφὲς τέρας,
Οὓς, οὐ καθάπερ τἆλλα τῶν ζώων γένη,
Εἴωθε κινεῖν ἐξ ἀνάρθρων κλασμάτων·
Καὶ γὰρ στιβαροῖς συντεθέντες ὀστέοις,
Καὶ τῇ πλαδαρᾷ τῶν σφυρῶν καταστάσει,
Καὶ τῇ πρὸς ἄρθρα τῶν σκελῶν ὑποκρίσει,
Νῦν εἰς τόνους ἄγουσι, νῦν εἰς ὑφέσεις,
Τὰς παντοδαπὰς ἐκδρομὰς τοῦ θηρίου.
* * * * * *
Βραχυτέρους ὄντας δὲ τῶν ὀπισθίων
Ἀναμφιλέκτως οἶδα τοὺς ἐμπροσθίους·
Τούτοις ἐλέφας ἐνταθεὶς ὥσπερ στύλοις
Ὀρθοστάδην ἄκαμπτος ὑπνώττων μένει."

v. 106, &c.

SOLINUS introduced the same fable into his *Polyhistor;* and DICUIL, the Irish commentator of the ninth century, who had an opportunity of seeing the elephant sent by Haroun Alraschid as a present to Charlemagne[1] in the year 802, corrects the error, and attributes its perpetuation to the circumstance that the joints in the elephant's leg are not very apparent, except when he lies down.[2]

It is a strong illustration of the vitality of error, that the delusion thus exposed by Dicuil in the ninth century, was revived by MATTHEW PARIS in the thirteenth; and stranger still, that Matthew not only saw

[1] EGINHARD, *Vita Karoli*, c. xvi. and *Annales Francorum*, A.D. 810.

[2] "Sed idem Julius, unum de elephantibus mentiens, falso loquitur; dicens elephantem nunquam jacere; dum ille sicut bos certissime jacet, ut populi communiter regni Francorum elephantem, in tempore Imperatoris Karoli viderunt. Sed, forsitan, ideo hoc de elephante ficte æstimando scriptum est, eo quod genua et suffragines sui nisi quando jacet, non palam apparent."—DICUILUS, *De Mensura Orbis Terræ*, c. vii.

but made a drawing of the elephant presented to King Henry III. by the King of France in 1255, in which he nevertheless represents the legs as without joints.[1]

In the numerous mediæval treatises on natural history, known under the title of *Bestiaries*, this delusion regarding the elephant is often repeated; and it is given at length in a metrical version of the *Physiologus* of THEOBALDUS, amongst the Arundel Manuscripts in the British Museum.[2]

With the Provençal song writers, the helplessness of the fallen elephant was a favourite simile, and amongst others RICHARD DE BARBEZIEUX, in the latter half of the twelfth century, sung[3],

---

[1] *Cotton MSS.* NERO. D. 1. fol. 168, b.

[2] *Arundel MSS.* No 292, fol. 4, &c. It has been printed in the *Reliquiæ Antiquæ*, vol. i. p. 208, by Mr. WRIGHT, to whom I am indebted for the following rendering of the passage referred to:—

> in water ge sal stonden
> in water to mid side
> ðat wanne hire harde tide
> ðat ge ne falle niðer nogt
> ðat it most in hire ðogt
> for he ne haven no lið
> ðat he mugen risen wið, etc.

> "They will stand in the water,
> in water up to the middle of the side,
> that when it comes to them hard,
> they may not fall down:
> that is most in their thought,
> for they have no joint
> to enable them to rise again.
> How he resteth him this animal,
> when he walketh abroad,
> hearken how it is here told.
> For he is all unwieldy,
> forsooth he seeks out a tree,
> that is strong and stedfast,
> and leans confidently against it,
> when he is weary of walking.
> The hunter has observed this,
> who seeks to ensnare him,
> where his usual dwelling is,
> to do his will;
> saws this tree and props it
> in the manner that he best may,
> covers it well that he (the elephant) may
> not be on his guard.
> Then he makes thereby a seat,
> himself sits alone and watches
> whether his trap takes effect.
> Then cometh this unwieldy elephant,
> and leans him on his side,
> rests against the tree in the shadow,
> and so both fall together.
> If nobody be by when he falls,
> he roars ruefully and calls for help,
> roars ruefully in his manner,
> hopes he shall through help rise.
> Then cometh there one (elephant) in haste,
> hopes he shall cause him to stand up;
> labours and tries all his might,
> but he cannot succeed a bit.
> He knows then no other remedy,
> but roars with his brother,
> many and large (elephants) come there in
> search,
> thinking to make him get up,
> but for the help of them all
> he may not get up.
> Then they all roar one roar,
> like the blast of a horn or the sound of bell;
> for their great roaring
> a young one cometh running,
> stoops immediately to him,
> puts his snout under him,
> and asks the help of them all;
> this elephant they raise on his legs:
> and thus fails this hunter's trick,
> in the manner that I have told you."

[3] One of the most venerable authorities by whom the fallacy was transmitted to modern times was PHILIP de THAUN, who wrote, about

> "Atressi cum l' olifans
> Que quan chai no s' pot levar."

As elephants were but rarely seen in Europe prior to the seventeenth century, there were but few opportunities of correcting the popular fallacy by ocular demonstration. Hence SHAKSPEARE still believed that,

> "The elephant hath joints; but none for courtesy:
> His legs are for necessity, not flexure:"[1]

and DONNE sang of

> "Nature's great masterpiece, an Elephant;
> The only harmless great thing:
> Yet Nature hath given him no knee to bend:
> Himself he up-props, on himself relies;
> Still sleeping stands."[2]

Sir THOMAS BROWNE, while he argues against the delusion, does not fail to record his suspicion, that "although the opinion at present be reasonably well suppressed, yet from the strings of tradition and fruitful recurrence of errour, it was not improbable it might revive in the next generation;"[3]—an anticipation which has proved singularly correct; for the heralds still continued to explain that the elephant is the emblem of watchfulness, "*nec jacet in somno*,"[4] and poets almost of our own times paint the scene when

---

the year 1121, A.D., his *Livre des Créatures*, dedicated to Adelaide of Louvaine, Queen of Henry I. of England. In the copy of it printed by the Historical Society of Science in 1841, and edited by Mr. WRIGHT, the following passage occurs:—

> "Et Ysidres nus dit ki le elefant descrit,
> * * * * *
> Es jambes par nature nen ad que une jointure,
> Il ne pot pas gesir quant il se volt dormir,
> Ke si cuchet estait par sei nen leverait;
> Pur çeo li stot apuier, el lui del cucher,
> U à arbre u à mur, idunc dort aseur.
> E le gent de la terre, ki li volent conquere,
> Li mur enfunderunt, u le arbre enciserunt;
> Quant li elefant vendrat, ki s'i apuierat,
> La arbre u le mur carrat, e il tribucherat;
> Issi faiterement le parnent cele gent."

P. 100.

[1] *Troilus and Cressida*, act ii. sc. 3. A.D. 1609.

[2] *Progress of the Soul*, A.D. 1633.

[3] Sir T. BROWNE, *Vulgar Errors*, A.D. 1646.

[4] RANDAL HOME'S *Academy of Armory*, A.D. 1671. HOME only perpetuated the error of GUILLIM, who wrote his *Display of Heraldry*

> "Peaceful, beneath primeval trees, that cast
> Their ample shade on Niger's yellow stream,
> Or where the Ganges rolls his sacred waves,
> *Leans* the huge Elephant."[1]

It is not difficult to see whence this antiquated delusion took its origin; nor is it, as Sir THOMAS BROWNE imagined, to be traced exclusively "to the grosse and cylindricall structure" of the animal's legs. The fact is, that the elephant, returning in the early morning from his nocturnal revels in the reservoirs and water-courses, is accustomed to rub his muddy sides against a tree, and sometimes against a rock if more convenient. In my rides through the northern forests, the natives of Ceylon have often pointed out that the elephants which had preceded me must have been of considerable size, from the height at which their marks had been left on the trees against which they had been rubbing. Not unfrequently the animals themselves, overcome with drowsiness from the night's gambolling, are found dosing and resting against the trees they had so visited, and in the same manner they have been discovered by sportsmen asleep, and leaning against a rock.

It is scarcely necessary to explain that the position is accidental, and that it is taken by the elephant not from any difficulty in lying at length on the ground, but rather from the coincidence that the structure of his legs affords such support in a standing position, that reclining scarcely adds to his enjoyment of repose; and elephants in a state of captivity have been known for

in A.D. 1610; wherein he explains that the elephant is "so proud of his strength that he never bows himself to any (*neither indeed can he*), and when he is once down he cannot rise up again."—Sec. III. ch. xii. p. 147.

[1] THOMSON'S *Seasons*, A.D. 1728.

months together to sleep without lying down.[1] So distinctive is this formation, and so self-sustaining the configuration of the limbs, that an elephant shot in the brain, by Major Rogers in 1836, was killed so instantaneously that it died literally *on its knees*, and remained resting on them. About the year 1826, Captain Dawson, the engineer of the great road to Kandy, over the Kaduganava pass, shot an elephant at Hangwelle on the banks of the Kalany Ganga; *it remained on its feet*, but so motionless, that after discharging a few more balls, he was induced to go close to it, and found it dead.

The real peculiarity in the elephant in lying down is, that he extends his hind legs backwards as a man does when he kneels, instead of bringing them under him like the horse or any other quadruped. The wise purpose of this arrangement must be obvious to any one who observes the struggle with which the horse *gets up* from the ground, and the violent efforts which he makes to raise himself erect. Such an exertion in the case of the elephant, and the force requisite to apply a similar movement to raise his weight (equal to four or five tons) would be attended with a dangerous strain upon the muscles, and hence the simple arrangement, which by enabling him to draw the hind feet gradually under him, assists him to rise without a perceptible effort.

The same construction renders his gait not a "gallop,"

[1] So little is the elephant inclined to lie down in captivity, and even after hard labour, that the keepers are generally disposed to suspect illness when he betakes himself to this posture. PHILE, in his poem *De Animalium Proprietate*, attributes the propensity of the elephant to sleep on his legs, to the difficulty he experiences in rising to his feet:

'Ορθοστάδην δὲ καὶ καθεύδει παννύχως
"Οτ' οὐκ ἀναστῆσαι μὲν εὐχερῶς πέλει.

But this is a misapprehension.

as it has been somewhat loosely described[1], which would be too violent a motion for so vast a body; but a shuffle, that he can increase at pleasure to a pace as rapid as that of a man at full speed, but which he cannot maintain for any considerable distance.

It is to the structure of the knee-joint that the elephant is indebted for his singular facility in ascending and descending steep aclivities, climbing rocks and traversing precipitous ledges, where even a mule dare not

[1] *Menageries, &c.* "The elephant," ch. i.

Sir CHARLES BELL, in his essay on *The Hand and its Mechanism*, which forms one of the "Bridgewater Treatises," has exhibited the reasons deducible from organisation, which show the incapacity of the elephant to *spring* or *leap* like the horse and other animals whose structure is designed to facilitate agility and speed. In them the various bones of the shoulder and fore limbs, especially the clavicle and humerus, are set at such an angle, that the shock in descending is modified, and the joints and sockets protected from the injury occasioned by concussion. But in the elephant, where the weight of the body is immense, the bones of the leg, in order to present solidity and strength to sustain it, are built in one firm and perpendicular column; instead of being placed somewhat obliquely at their points of contact. Thus whilst the force of the weight in descending is broken and distributed by this arrangement in the case of the horse; it would be so concentrated in the elephant as to endanger every joint from the toe to the shoulder.

venture; and this again leads to the correction of another generally received error, that his legs are "formed more for strength than flexibility, and fitted to bear an enormous weight upon a level surface, without the necessity of ascending or descending great acclivities."[1] The same authority assumes that, although the elephant is found in the neighbourhood of mountainous ranges, and will even ascend rocky passes, such a service is a violation of its natural habits.

Of the elephant of Africa I am not qualified to speak, nor of the nature of the ground which it most frequents; but certainly the facts in connection with the elephant of India are all irreconcilable with the theory mentioned above. In Bengal, in the Nilgherries, in Nepal, in Burmah, in Siam, Sumatra, and Ceylon, the districts in which the elephants most abound, are all hilly and mountainous. In the latter, especially, there is not a range so elevated as to be inaccessible to them. On the very summit of Adam's Peak, at an altitude of 7,420 feet, and on a pinnacle which the pilgrims climb with difficulty, by means of steps hewn in the rock, Major Skinner, in 1840, found the spoor of an elephant.

Prior to 1840, and before coffee-plantations had been extensively opened in the Kandyan ranges, there was not a mountain or a lofty feature of land of Ceylon which they had not traversed, in their periodical migrations in search of water; and the sagacity which they display in "laying out roads" is almost incredible. They generally keep along the *backbone* of a chain of hills, avoiding steep gradients: and one curious observation was not lost upon the government surveyors, that in crossing

[1] *Menageries, &c.*, "The Elephant," ch. ii.

the valleys from ridge to ridge, through forests so dense as altogether to obstruct a distant view, the elephants invariably select the line of march which communicates most judiciously with the opposite point, by means of *the safest ford.*[1] So sure-footed are they, that there are few places where man can go that an elephant cannot follow, provided there be space to admit his bulk, and solidity to sustain his weight.

This faculty is almost entirely derived from the unusual position, as compared with other quadrupeds, of the knee joint of the hind leg; arising from the superior length of the thigh-bone, and the shortness of the metatarsus: the heel being almost where it projects in man, instead of being lifted up as a "hock." It is this which enables him, in descending declivities, to depress and adjust the weight of his hinder portions, which would otherwise overbalance and force him headlong.[2] It is by the same arrangement that he is

[1] Dr. HOOKER, in describing the ascent of the Himalayas, says, the natives in making their paths despise all zigzags, and run in straight lines up the steepest hill faces; whilst "the elephant's path is an excellent specimen of engineering — the opposite of the native track, — for it winds judiciously."—*Himalayan Journal*, vol. i. ch. iv.

[2] Since the above passage was written, I have seen in the *Journal of the Asiatic Society of Bengal*, vol. xiii. pt. ii. p. 916, a paper upon this subject, illustrated by the subjoined diagram.

The writer says, "an elephant descending a bank of too acute an angle to admit of his walking down it direct, (which, were he to attempt, his huge body, soon disarranging the centre of gravity, would certainly topple over,) proceeds thus. His first manœuvre is to kneel down close to the edge of the declivity, placing his chest to the ground: one fore-leg is then cautiously passed a short way down the slope; and if there is no natural protection to afford a firm footing, he speedily forms one by stamping into the soil if moist, or kicking out a footing if dry. This point gained, the other fore-leg is brought down in the same way; and performs the same work, a little in advance of the first; which is thus at liberty to move lower still. Then, first one and then the second of the hind legs is carefully drawn over the side, and the hind-feet in turn occupy the resting-places previously used and left by the fore ones. The course, how-

enabled, on uneven ground, to lift his feet, which are tender and sensitive, with delicacy, and plant them with such precision as to ensure his own safety as well as that of objects which it is expedient to avoid touching.

A *herd* of elephants is a family, not a group whom accident or attachment may have induced to associate together. Similarity of features and caste attest that, among the various individuals which compose it, there is a common lineage and relationship. In a herd of

ever, in such precipitous ground is not straight from top to bottom, but slopes along the face of the bank, descending till the animal

gains the level below. This an elephant has done, at an angle of 45 degrees, carrying a *howdah*, its occupant, his attendant, and sporting apparatus; and in a much less time than it takes to describe the operation." I have observed that an elephant in descending a declivity uses his knees, on the side next the bank; and his feet on the lower side only.

twenty-one elephants, captured in 1844, the trunks of each individual presented the same peculiar formation, — long, and almost of one uniform breadth throughout, instead of tapering gradually from the root to the nostril. In another instance, the eyes of thirty-five taken in one corral were of the same colour in each. The same slope of the back, the same form of the forehead, is to be detected in the majority of the same group.

In the forest several herds will browse in close contiguity, and in their expeditions in search of water they may form a body of possibly one or two hundred; but on the slightest disturbance each distinct herd hastens to re-form within its own particular circle, and to take measures on its own behalf for retreat or defence.

The natives of any place which may chance to be frequented by elephants, observe that the numbers of the same herd fluctuate very slightly; and hunters in pursuit of them, who may chance to have shot one or more, always reckon with certainty the precise number of those remaining, although a considerable interval may intervene before they again encounter them. The proportion of males is generally small, and some herds have been seen composed exclusively of females; possibly in consequence of the males having been shot. A herd usually consists of from ten to twenty individuals, though occasionally they exceed the latter number; and in their frequent migrations and nightly resort to tanks and water-courses, alliances are formed between members of associated herds, which serve to introduce new blood into the family.

In illustration of the attachment of the elephant to its young, the authority of KNOX has been quoted, that "the shees are alike tender of any one's young ones as of their own."[1] Their affection in this particular is undoubted, but I question whether it exceeds that of other animals; and the trait thus adduced of their indiscriminate kindness to all the young of the herd, — of which I have myself been an eye-witness, — so far from being an evidence of the strength of parental attachment individually, is, perhaps, somewhat inconsistent with the existence of such a passion to any extraordinary degree.[2] In fact, some individuals, who have had extensive facilities for observation, doubt whether the fondness of the female elephants for their offspring is so great as that of many other animals; as

[1] A correspondent of Buffon, M. MARCELLUS BLES, Seigneur de Moergestal, who resided eleven years in Ceylon in the time of the Dutch, says in one of his communications, that in herds of forty or fifty, enclosed in a single corral, there were frequently very young calves; and that "on ne pouvoit pas reconnaître quelles étoient les mères de chacun de ces petits éléphans, car tous ces jeunes animaux paroissent faire manse commune; ils têtent indistinctement celles des femelles de toute la troupe qui ont du lait, soit qu'elles aient elles-mêmes un petit en propre, soit qu'elles n'en aient point."—BUFFON, *Suppl. à l' Hist. des Anim.*, vol. vi. p. 25.

[2] WHITE, in his *Natural History of Selborne*, philosophising on the fact which had fallen under his own notice of this indiscriminate suckling of the young of one animal by the parent of another, is disposed to ascribe it to a selfish feeling; the pleasure and relief of having its distended teats drawn by this intervention. He notices the circumstance of a leveret having been thus nursed by a cat, whose kittens had been recently drowned: and observes, that "this strange affection was probably occasioned by that desiderium, those tender maternal feelings, which the loss of her kittens had awakened in her breast; and by the complacency and ease she derived to herself from procuring her teats to be drawn, which were too much distended with milk; till from habit she became as much delighted with this foundling as if it had been her real offspring. This incident is no bad solution of that strange circumstance which grave historians, as well as the poets, assert of exposed children being sometimes nurtured by female wild beasts that probably had lost their young. For it is not one whit more marvellous that Romulus and Remus in their infant state should be nursed by a she wolf than that a poor little suckling leveret should be fostered and cherished by a blōody Grimalkin."—WHITE'S *Selborne*, lett. xx.

instances are not wanting in Ceylon, in which, when pursued by the hunters, the herd has abandoned the young ones in their flight, notwithstanding the cries of the latter for help.

In an interesting paper on the habits of the Indian elephant, published in the *Philosophical Transactions for* 1793, Mr. CORSE says: "If a wild elephant happens to be separated from its young for only two days, though giving suck, she never after recognises or acknowledges it," although the young one evidently knows its dam, and by its plaintive cries and submissive approaches solicits her assistance.

If by any accident an elephant becomes hopelessly separated from his own herd, he is not permitted to attach himself to any other. He may browse in the vicinity, or frequent the same place to drink and to bathe; but the intercourse is only on a distant and conventional footing, and no familiarity or intimate association is under any circumstances permitted. To such a height is this exclusiveness carried, that even amidst the terror and stupefaction of an elephant corral, when an individual, detached from his own party in the *mêlée* and confusion, has been driven into the enclosure with an unbroken herd, I have seen him repulsed in every attempt to take refuge among them, and driven off by heavy blows with their trunks as often as he attempted to insinuate himself within the circle which they had formed for common security. There can be no reasonable doubt that this jealous and exclusive policy not only contributes to produce, but mainly serves to perpetuate, the class of solitary elephants which are known by the term *goondahs*, in India, and which from their vicious propensities and predatory habits are called *Hora*, or *Rogues*, in Ceylon.[1]

It is believed by the Singhalese that these are either individuals, who by accident have lost their former associates and become morose and savage from rage and solitude; or else that being naturally vicious they have become daring from the yielding habits of their milder companions, and eventually separated themselves from the rest of the herd which had refused to associate with them. Another conjecture is, that being almost universally males, the death or capture of particular females may have detached them from their former companions in search of fresh alliances.[2] It is also believed that a tame elephant escaping from captivity, unable to rejoin its former herd, and excluded from any other, becomes a "*rogue*" from necessity. In Ceylon it is generally believed that the *rogues* are all males (but of this I am not certain), and so sullen is their disposition that

[1] The term "rogue" is scarcely sufficiently accounted for by supposing it to be the English equivalent for the Singhalese word *Hora*. In that very curious book, the *Life and Adventures of* JOHN CHRISTOPHER WOLF, *late principal Secretary at Jaffnapatam in Ceylon*, the author says, when a male elephant in a quarrel about the females "is beat out of the field and obliged to go without a consort, he becomes furious and mad, killing every living creature, be it man or beast: and in this state is called *ronkedor*, an object of greater terror to a traveller than a hundred wild ones."—P. 142. In another passage, p. 164, he is called *runkedor*, and I have seen it spelt elsewhere *ronquedue*. WOLF does not give "*ronkedor*" as a term peculiar to that section of the island; but both there and elsewhere, it is obsolete at the present day, unless it be open to conjecture that the modern term "rogue" is a modification of *ronquedue*.

[2] BUCHANAN, in his *Survey of Bhagulpore*, p. 503, says that solitary males of the wild buffalo, "when driven from the herd by stronger competitors for female society, are reckoned very dangerous to meet with; for they are apt to wreak their vengeance on whatever they meet, and are said to kill annually three or four people." LIVINGSTONE relates the same of the solitary hippopotamus, which becomes soured in temper, and wantonly attacks the passing canoes.—*Travels in South Africa*, p. 231.

although two may be in the same vicinity, there is no known instance of their associating, or of a *rogue* being seen in company with another elephant.

They spend their nights in marauding, often about the dwellings of men, destroying their plantations, trampling down their gardens, and committing serious ravages in rice grounds and young coco-nut plantations. Hence from their closer contact with man and his dwellings, these outcasts become disabused of many of the terrors which render the ordinary elephant timid and needlessly cautious; they break through fences without fear; and even in the daylight a *rogue* has been known near Ambogammoa to watch a field of labourers at work in reaping rice, and boldly to walk in amongst them, seize a sheaf from the heap, and retire leisurely to the jungle. By day they generally seek concealment, but are frequently to be met with prowling about the by-roads and jungle paths, where travellers are exposed to the utmost risk from their savage assaults. It is probable that this hostility to man is the result of the enmity engendered by those measures which the natives, who have a constant dread of their visits, adopt for the protection of their growing crops. In some districts, especially in the low country of Badulla, the villagers occasionally enclose their cottages with rude walls of earth and branches to protect them from nightly assaults. In places infested by them, the visits of European sportsmen to the vicinity of their haunts are eagerly encouraged by the natives, who think themselves happy in lending their services to track the ordinary herds in consideration of the benefit conferred on the village communities by the destruction of a rogue. In 1847 one of these formidable creatures frequented for some months the Rangbodde Pass on the great mountain road leading to the sanatarium, at Neuera-ellia; and amongst other excesses, killed a Caffre belonging to the corps of Caffre pioneers, by seizing him with its trunk and beating him to death against the bank.

To return to the herd: one member of it, usually the largest and most powerful, is by common consent implicitly followed as leader. A tusker, if there be one in the party, is generally observed to be the commander; but a female, if of superior energy, is as readily obeyed as a male. In fact, in this promotion there is no reason to doubt that supremacy is almost unconsciously assumed by those endowed with superior vigour and courage rather than from the accidental possession of greater bodily strength; and the devotion and loyalty which the herd evince to their leader are very remarkable. This is more readily seen in the case of a tusker than any other, because in a herd he is generally the object of the keenest pursuit by the hunters. On such occasions the others do their utmost to protect him from danger: when driven to extremity they place their leader in the centre and crowd so eagerly in front of him that the sportsmen have to shoot a number which they might otherwise have spared. In one instance a tusker, which was badly wounded by Major ROGERS, was promptly surrounded by his companions, who supported him between their shoulders, and actually succeeded in covering his retreat to the forest.

Those who have lived much in the jungle in Ceylon, and who have had constant opportunities of watching the habits of wild elephants, have witnessed instances of the submission of herds to their leaders, that suggest an inquiry of singular interest as to the means adopted by the latter to communicate with distinctness, orders which are observed with the most implicit obedience by their followers. The following narrative of an adventure in the great central forest toward the north of the island, communicated to me by Major SKINNER, who was engaged for some time in surveying and opening roads through the thickly-wooded districts there, will serve better than any abstract description to convey an idea of the conduct of a herd on such occasions:—

"The case you refer to struck me as exhibiting something more than ordinary brute instinct, and approached nearer to reasoning powers than any other instance I can now remember. I cannot do justice to the scene, although it appeared to me at the time to be so remarkable that it left a deep impression in my mind.

"In the height of the dry season in Neuera-Kalawa, you know the streams are all dried up, and the tanks nearly so. All animals are then sorely pressed for water, and they congregate in the vicinity of those tanks in which there may remain ever so little of the precious element.

"During one of those seasons I was encamped on the bund or embankment of a very small tank, the water in which was so dried that its surface could not have exceeded an area of 500 square yards. It was the only pond within many miles, and I knew that of necessity a very large herd of elephants, which had been in the neighbourhood all day, must resort to it at night.

"On the lower side of the tank, and in a line with the embankment, was a thick forest, in which the elephants sheltered themselves during the day. On the upper side and all around the tank there was a considerable margin of open ground. It was one of those beautiful bright, clear, moonlight nights, when objects could be seen almost as distinctly as by day, and I determined to avail myself of the opportunity to observe the movements of the herd, which had already manifested some uneasiness at our presence. The locality was very favourable for my purpose, and an enormous tree projecting over the tank afforded me a secure lodgement in its branches. Having ordered the fires of my camp to be extinguished at an early hour, and all my followers to retire to rest, I took up my post of observation on the overhanging bough; but I had to remain for upwards of two hours before anything was to be seen or heard of the elephants, although I knew they were within 500 yards of me. At length, about the distance of 300 yards from the water, an unusually large elephant issued from the dense cover, and advanced cautiously across the open ground to within 100 yards of the tank, where he stood perfectly motionless. So quiet had the elephants become (although they had been roaring and breaking the jungle throughout the day and evening), that not a movement was now to be heard. The huge vidette remained in his position, still as a rock, for a few minutes, and then made three successive stealthy advances of several yards (halting for some minutes between each, with ears bent forward to catch the slightest sound), and in this way he moved slowly up to the water's edge. Still he did not venture to quench his thirst, for though his fore-feet were partially in the tank and his vast body was reflected clear in the water, he remained for some minutes listening in perfect stillness. Not a motion could be perceived in himself or his shadow. He returned cautiously and slowly to the position he had at first taken up on emerging from the forest. Here in a little while he was joined by five others, with which he again proceeded as cautiously, but less slowly than before, to within a few yards of the tank, and then posted his patrols. He then re-entered the forest and collected around him the whole herd, which must have amounted to between 80 and 100 individuals,—led them across the open ground with the most extraordinary composure and quietness, till he joined the advanced guard, when he left them for a moment and repeated his former reconnoissance at the edge of the tank. After which, having apparently satisfied himself that all was safe, he returned and obviously gave the order to advance, for in a moment the whole herd rushed into the water with a degree of unreserved confidence, so opposite to the caution and timidity which had marked their previous movements, that nothing will ever persuade me that there was not rational and preconcerted co-operation throughout the whole party, and a degree of responsible authority exercised by the patriarch leader.

"When the poor animals had gained possession of the tank (the leader being the last to enter), they seemed to abandon themselves to enjoyment without restraint or apprehension of danger. Such a mass of animal life I had never before seen huddled together in so narrow a space. It seemed to me as though they would have nearly drunk the tank dry. I watched them with great interest until they had satisfied themselves as well in bathing as in drinking, when I tried how small a noise would apprise them of the proximity of unwelcome neighbours. I had but to break a little twig, and the solid mass instantly took to flight like a herd of frightened deer, each of the smaller calves being apparently shouldered and carried along between two of the older ones."[1]

In drinking, the elephant, like the camel, although preferring water pure, shows no decided aversion to it when discoloured with mud[2]; and the eagerness with which he precipitates himself into the tanks and streams attests his exquisite enjoyment of the fresh coolness, which to him is the chief attraction. In crossing deep rivers, although his rotundity and buoyancy enable him to swim with a less immersion than other quadrupeds, he generally prefers to sink till no part of his huge body is visible except the tip of his trunk, through which he breathes, moving beneath the surface, and only now and then raising his head to look that he is keeping the proper direction.[3] In the dry season the scanty streams which, during the rains, are sufficient to convert the rivers of the low country into torrents, often entirely disappear, leaving only broad expanses of dry sand, which they have swept down with them from the hills. In this the elephants contrive to sink wells for their own use by scooping out the sand to the depth of four or five feet, and leaving a hollow for the percolation of the spring. But as the weight of the elephant would force in the side if left perpendicular, one approach is always formed with such a gradient that he can reach

[1] Letter from Major SKINNER.

[2] This peculiarity was known in the middle ages, and PHILE, writing in the fourteenth century, says, that such is his *preference* for muddy water that the elephant *stirs it* before he drinks.

"Ὕδωρ δὲ πίνει συγχυθὲν πρὶν ἂν πίνοι
Τὸ γὰρ διειδές ἀκριβῶς διαπτύει."
—PHILE *de Eleph.*, i. 144.

[3] A tame elephant, when taken by his keepers to be bathed, and to have his skin washed and rubbed, lies down on his side, pressing his head to the bottom under water, with only the top of his trunk protruded, to breathe.

the water with his trunk without disturbing the surrounding sand.

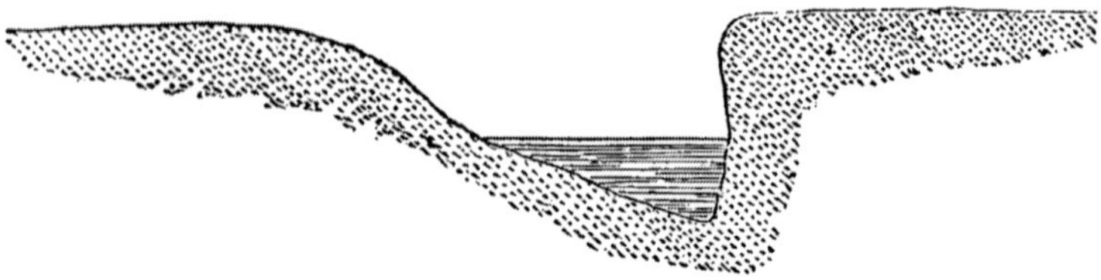

I have reason to believe, although the fact has not been authoritatively stated by naturalists, that the stomach of the elephant will be found to include a section analogous to that possessed by some of the ruminants, calculated to contain a supply of water as a provision against emergencies. The fact of his being enabled to retain a quantity of water and discharge it at pleasure has been long known to every observer of the habits of the animal; but the proboscis has always been supposed to be "his water-reservoir,"[1] and the theory of an internal receptacle has not been discussed. The truth is that the anatomy of the elephant is even yet but imperfectly understood[2], and, although some peculiarities of his

[1] BRODERIP'S *Zoological Recreations*, p. 259.

[2] For observing the osteology of the elephant, materials are of course abundant in the indestructible remains of the animal: but the study of the intestines, and the dissection of the softer parts by comparative anatomists in Europe, have been up to the present time beset by difficulties. These arise not alone from the rarity of subjects, but even in cases where elephants have died in these countries, decomposition interposes, and before the thorough examination of so vast a body can be satisfactorily completed, the great mass falls into putrefaction. The principal English authorities are *An Anatomical Account of the Elephant accidentally burnt in Dublin*, by A. MOLYNEUX, A.D. 1696; which is probably a reprint of a letter on the same subject in the library of Trinity College, Dublin, addressed by A. Moulin, to Sir William Petty, Lond. 1682. There are also some papers communicated to Sir Hans Sloane, and afterwards published in the *Philosophical Transactions* of the year 1710, by Dr. P. BLAIR, who had an opportunity of dissecting an elephant which died at Dundee in 1708. The latter writer observes that, "notwithstanding the vast interest

stomach were observed at an early period, and even their configuration described, the function of the abnormal portion remained undetermined, and has been only recently conjectured. An elephant which belonged to Louis XIV. died at Versailles in 1681 at the age of seventeen, and an account of its dissection was published in the *Mémoires pour servir à l'Histoire Naturelle*, under the authority of the Academy of Sciences, in which the unusual appendages of the stomach are pointed out with sufficient particularity, but no suggestion is made as to their probable uses."[1]

attaching to the elephant in all ages, yet has its body been hitherto very little subjected to anatomical inquiries;" and he laments that the rapid decomposition of the carcase, and other causes, had interposed obstacles to the scrutiny of the subject he was so fortunate as to find access to.

In 1723 Dr. WM. STUCKLEY published *Some Anatomical Observations made upon the Dissection of an Elephant;* but each of the above essays is necessarily unsatisfactory, and little has since been done to supply their defects. One of the latest and most valuable contributions to the subjects, is a paper read before the Royal Irish Academy, on the 18th of Feb., 1847, by Professor HARRISON, who had the opportunity of dissecting an Indian elephant which died of acute fever; but the examination, so far as he has made it public, extends only to the cranium, the brain, and the proboscis, the larynx, trachea, and œsophagus. An essential service would be rendered to science if some sportsman in Ceylon, or some of the officers connected with the elephant establishment there, would take the trouble to forward the carcase of a young one to England in a state fit for dissection.

*Postscriptum.*— I am happy to say that a young elephant, carefully preserved in spirits, has recently been obtained in Ceylon, and forwarded to Prof. Owen, of the British Museum, by the joint exertions of M. DIARD and Major SKINNER. An opportunity has thus been afforded from which science will reap advantage, of devoting a patient attention to the internal structure of this interesting animal.

[1] The passage as quoted by BUFFON from the *Mémoires* is as follows: — "L'estomac avoit peu de diamètre ; il en avoit moins que le colon, car son diamètre n'étoit que de quatorze pouces dans la partie la plus large; il avoit trois pieds et demi de longueur: l'orifice supérieur étoit à-peu-près aussi éloigné du pylore que du fond du grand cul-de-sac qui se terminoit en une pointe composée de tuniques beaucoup plus épaisses que celles du reste de l'estomac; il y avoit au fond du grand cul-de-sac plusieurs feuillets épais d'une ligne, larges d'un pouce et demi, et disposés irrégulièrement; le reste de parois intérieures étoit percé de plusieurs petits trous et

A writer in the *Quarterly Review* for December 1850, says that "CAMPER and other comparative anatomists have shown that the left, or cardiac end of the stomach in the elephant is adapted, by several wide folds of lining membrane, to serve as a receiver for water;" but this is scarcely correct, for although CAMPER has accurately figured the external form of the stomach, he disposes of the question of the interior functions with the simple remark that its folds "semblent en faire une espèce de division particulière."[1] In like manner SIR EVERARD HOME, in his *Lectures on Comparative Anatomy*, has not only carefully described the form of the elephant's stomach, and furnished a drawing of it even more accurate than CAMPER; but he has equally omitted to assign any purpose to so strange a formation, contenting himself with observing that the structure is a peculiarity, and that one of the remarkable folds nearest the orifice of the diaphragm appears to act as a valve, so that the portion beyond may be considered as an appendage similar to that of the hog and the *peccary*.[2]

par de plus grands qui correspondoient à des grains glanduleux."—BUFFON, *Hist. Nat.*, vol. xi. p. 109.

[1] "L'extrémité voisine du cardia se termine par une poche très-considérable et doublée à l'intérieure du quatorze valvules orbiculaires que semblent en faire une espèce de division particulière."—CAMPER, *Description Anatomique d'un Eléphant Mâle*, p. 37, tabl. IX.

[2] "The elephant has another peculiarity in the internal structure of the stomach. It is longer and narrower than that of most animals. The cuticular membrane of the œsophagus terminates at the orifice of the stomach. At the cardiac end, which is very narrow and pointed at the extremity, the lining is thick and glandular, and is thrown into transverse folds, of which five are broad and nine narrow. That nearest the orifice of the œsophagus is the broadest, and appears to act occasionally as a valve, so that the part beyond may be considered as an appendage similar to that of the peccary and the hog. The membrane of the cardiac portion is uniformly smooth; that of the pyloric is thicker and more vascular."—*Lectures on Comparative Anatomy*, by Sir EVERARD HOME, Bart. 4to. Lond. vol. i. p. 155. The figure of the elephant's stomach is given in his *Lectures*, vol. ii. plate xviii.

The appendage thus alluded to by Sir EVERARD HOME is the grand "cul-de-sac," noticed by the Académie des Sciences, and the "division particulière," figured by CAMPER. It is of sufficient dimensions to contain ten gallons of water, and by means of the valve above alluded to, it can be shut off from the chamber devoted to the

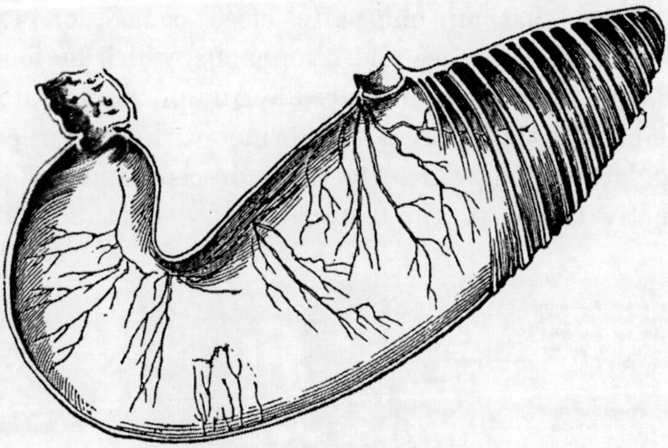

ELEPHANT'S STOMACH.

process of digestion. Professor OWEN is probably the first who, not from an autopsy, but from the mere inspection of the drawings of CAMPER and HOME, ventured to assert (in lectures hitherto unpublished), that the uses of this section of the elephant's stomach may be analogous to those ascertained to belong to a somewhat similar arrangement in the stomach of the camel, one cavity of which is exclusively employed as a reservoir for water, and performs no function in the preparation of food.[1]

[1] A similar arrangement, with some modifications, has more recently been found in the llama of the Andes, which, like the camel, is used as a beast of burden in the Cordilleras of Chili and Peru; but both these and the camel are *ruminants*, whilst the elephants belongs to the Pachydermata.

Whilst Professor OWEN was advancing this conjecture, another comparative anatomist, from the examination of another portion of the structure of the elephant, was led to a somewhat similar conclusion. Dr. HARRISON of Dublin had, in 1847, an opportunity of dissecting the body of an elephant which had suddenly died; and in the course of his examination of the thoracic viscera, he observed that an unusually close connection existed between the trachea and œsophagus, which he found to depend on a muscle unnoticed by any previous anatomist, connecting the back of the former with the forepart of the latter, along which the fibres descend and can be distinctly traced to the cardiac orifice of the stomach.

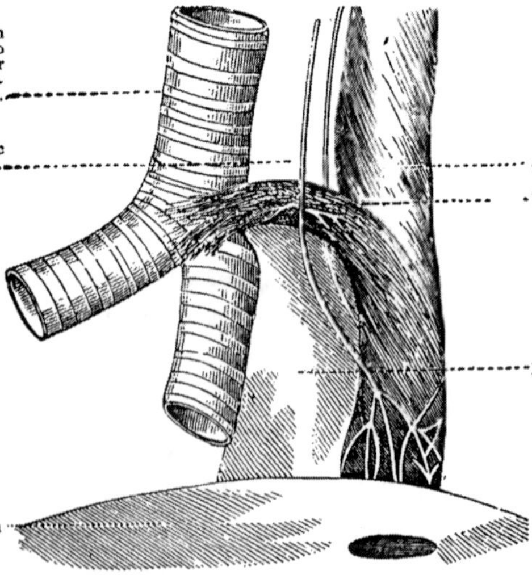


Imperfectly acquainted with the habits and functions of the elephant in a state of nature, Dr. HARRISON found it difficult to pronounce as to the use of this very peculiar structure; but looking to the intimate connection between the mechanism concerned in the functions of respiration and deglutition, and seeing that the proboscis served in a double capacity as an instrument of voice and an organ for the prehension of food, he ventured (apparently without adverting to the abnormal form of the stomach) to express the opinion that this muscle, viewing its attachment to the trachea, might either have some influence in raising the diaphragm, and thereby assisting in expiration, "*or that it might raise the cardiac orifice of the stomach, and so aid this organ to regurgitate a portion of its contents into the œsophagus.*"[1]

Dr. HARRISON, on the reflection that "we have no satisfactory evidence that the animal ever ruminates," thought it useless to speculate on the latter supposition as to the action of the newly discovered muscle, and rather inclined to the surmise that it was designed to assist the elephant in producing the remarkable sound through his proboscis known as "trumpeting;" but there is little room to doubt that of the two the rejected hypothesis was the more correct one. I have elsewhere described the occurrence to which I was myself a witness[2], of elephants inserting their proboscis in their mouths, and withdrawing gallons of water, which could only have been contained in the receptacle figured by CAMPER and HOME, and of which the true uses were discerned by the clear intellect of Professor OWEN. I was not, till very recently, aware that a similar observation as to the remarkable habit of the elephant, had been made by the author of the *Ayeen Akbery*, in his account of the *Feel*

[1] *Proceed. Roy. Irish Acad.*, vol. iv. p. 133.
[2] In the account of an elephant corral, chap. vi.

*Kaneh*, or elephant stables of the Emperor Akbar, in which he says, "an elephant frequently with his trunk takes water out of his stomach and sprinkles himself with it, and it is not in the least offensive.[1] FORBES, in his Oriental Memoirs, quotes this passage of the *Ayeen Akbery*, but without a remark; nor does any European writer with whose works I am acquainted appear to have been cognisant of the peculiarity in question.

It is to be hoped that Professor OWEN's dissection of

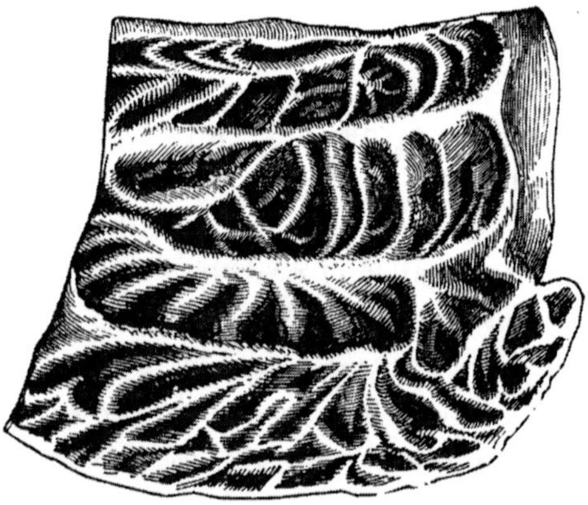

WATER-CELLS IN THE STOMACH OF THE CAMEL.

the young elephant, recently arrived, may serve to decide this highly interesting point.[2] Should scientific investigation hereafter more clearly establish the fact that, in this particular, the structure of the elephant is assimilated to that of the llama and the camel, it will be

[1] *Ayeen Akbery*, transl. by GLADWIN, vol. i. pt. i. p. 147.

[2] One of the Indian names for the elephant is *duipa*, which signifies "to drink twice" (AMANDI, p. 513). Can this have reference to the peculiarity of the stomach for retaining a supply of water? Or has it merely reference to the habit of the animal to fill his trunk before transferring the water to his mouth.

regarded as more than a common coincidence, that an apparatus, so unique in its purpose and action, should thus have been conferred by the Creator on the three animals which in sultry climates are, by this arrangement, enabled to traverse arid regions in the service of man.[1] To show this peculiar organization where it attains its fullest development, I have given a sketch of the water-cells in the stomach of the camel on the preceding page.

The *food* of the elephant is so abundant, that in feeding he never appears to be impatient or voracious, but rather to play with the leaves and branches on which he leisurely feeds. In riding by places where a herd has recently halted, I have sometimes seen the bark peeled curiously off the twigs, as though it had been done in mere dalliance. In the same way in eating grass the elephant selects a tussac which he draws from the ground by a dexterous twist of his trunk, and nothing can be more graceful than the ease with which, before conveying it to his mouth, he beats the earth from its roots by striking it gently upon his fore-leg. A coco-nut he first rolls under foot, to detach the strong outer bark, then stripping off with his trunk the thick layer of fibre within, he places the shell in his mouth, and swallows with evident relish the fresh liquid which flows as he crushes it between his grinders.

The natives of the peninsula of Jaffna always look for the periodical appearance of the elephants, at the precise

[1] The buffalo and the humped cattle of India, which are used for draught and burden, have, I believe, a development of the organisation of the reticulum which enables the ruminants generally to endure thirst, and abstain from water, somewhat more conspicuous than in the rest of their congeners; but nothing that approaches in singularity of character to the distinct cavities in the stomach exhibited by the three animals above alluded to.

time when the fruit of the palmyra palm begins to fall to the ground from ripeness. In like manner in the eastern provinces where the custom prevails of cultivating what is called *chena* land (by clearing a patch of forest for the purpose of raising a single crop, after which the ground is abandoned, and reverts to jungle again), although a single elephant may not have been seen in the neighbourhood during the early stages of the process, the Moormen, who are the principal cultivators of this class, will predict their appearance with almost unerring confidence so soon as the grains shall have begun to ripen; and although the crop comes to maturity at different periods in different districts, herds are certain to be seen at each in succession, as soon as it is ready to be cut. In these well-timed excursions, they resemble the bison of North America, which, by a similarly mysterious instinct, finds its way to portions of the distant prairies, where accidental fires have been followed by a growth of tender grass. Although the fences around these *chenas* are little more than lines of reeds loosely fastened together, they are sufficient, with the presence of a single watcher, to prevent the entrance of the elephants, who wait patiently till the rice and *coracan* have been removed, and the watcher withdrawn; and, then finding gaps in the fence, they may be seen gleaning among the leavings and the stubble; and they take their departure when these are exhausted, apparently in the direction of some other *chena*, which they have ascertained to be about to be cut.

There is something still unexplained in the dread which an elephant always exhibits on approaching a fence, and the reluctance which he displays to face the slightest artificial obstruction to his passage. In the fine old tank of Tissa-weva, close by Anarajapoora, the natives cultivate grain, during the dry season, around the margin where the ground has been left bare by the subsidence of the water. These little patches of rice they enclose with small sticks an inch in diameter and five or six feet in height, such as would scarcely serve to keep out a wild hog if he attempted to force his way through. Passages of from ten to twenty feet wide are left between each field, to permit the wild elephants, which abound in the vicinity to make their nocturnal visits to the water still remaining in the tank. Night after night these open pathways are frequented by immense herds, but the tempting corn is never touched, nor is a single fence disturbed, although the merest movement of a trunk would be sufficient to demolish the fragile structure. Yet the same spots, the fences being left open as soon as the grain has been cut and carried home, are eagerly entered by the elephants to glean amongst the stubble.

Sportsmen observe that an elephant, even when enraged by a wound, will hesitate to charge an assailant across an intervening hedge, but will hurry along it to seek for an opening. It is possible that, on the part of the elephant, there may be some instinctive consciousness, that owing to his superior bulk, he is exposed to danger from sources that might be perfectly harmless in the case of lighter animals, and hence his suspicion that every fence may conceal a snare or pitfall. Some similar apprehension is apparent in the deer, which shrinks from attempting a fence of wire, although it will clear without hesitation a solid wall of greater height.

At the same time, the caution with which the elephant is supposed to approach insecure ground and places of doubtful[1] solidity, appears to me, so far as my own observation and experience extend, to be exaggerated, and the number of temporary bridges which are annually broken down by elephants in all parts of Ceylon, is sufficient to show that, although in captivity, and when familiar with such structures, the tame ones may, and doubtless do, exhibit all the wariness attributed to them; yet, in a state of liberty, and whilst unaccustomed to such artificial appliances, their instincts are not sufficient to ensure their safety. Besides, the fact is adverted to elsewhere[2], that the chiefs of the Wanny, during the sovereignty of the Dutch, were accustomed to take in pitfalls the elephants which they rendered as tribute to government.

A fact illustrative at once of the caution and the spirit of curiosity with which an elephant regards an unaccustomed object has been frequently mentioned to me by the officers engaged in opening roads through the forest. On such occasions the wooden "tracing pegs" which they are obliged to drive into the ground to mark the levels taken during the day, will often be withdrawn by the elephants during the night, to such an extent as frequently to render it necessary to go over the work a second time, in order to replace them.[3]

Colonel HARDY, formerly Deputy Quarter-Master-General in Ceylon, when proceeding, about the year 1820, to a military out-post in the south-east of the island, imprudently landed in an uninhabited part of

[1] "One of the strongest instincts which the elephant possesses, is this which impels him to experiment upon the solidity of every surface which he is required to cross."—*Menageries, &c.* "The Elephant," vol. i. pp. 17, 19, 66.

[2] WOLF's *Life and Adventures*, p. 151. See p. 115, *note*.

[3] *Private Letter* from Dr. DAVY, author of *An Account of the Interior of Ceylon*.

the coast, intending to take a short cut through the forest, to his destination. He not only miscalculated the distance, but, on the approach of nightfall, he was chased by a vicious rogue elephant. The pursuer was nearly upon him, when, to gain time, he flung down a small dressing-case, which he happened to be carrying. The device was successful; the elephant halted and minutely examined its contents, and thus gave the colonel time to effect his escape.[1]

As regards the general sagacity of the elephant, although it has not been over-rated in the instances of those whose powers have been largely developed in captivity, an undue estimate has been formed in relation to them whilst still untamed. The difference of instincts and habits renders it difficult to institute a just comparison between them and other animals. CUVIER[2] is disposed to ascribe the exalted idea that prevails of their intellect to the feats which an elephant performs with that unique instrument, its trunk, combined with an imposing expression of countenance: but he records his own conviction that in sagacity it in no way excels the dog, and some other species of Carnivora. If there be a superiority, I am disposed to award it to the dog, not from any excess of natural capacity, but from the

[1] The *Colombo Observer* for March 1858, contains an offer of a reward of twenty-five guineas for the destruction of an elephant which infested the Rajawallé coffee plantation, in the vicinity of Kandy. Its object seemed to be less the search for food, than the satisfying of its curiosity and the gratification of its passion for mischief. Mr. TYTLER, the proprietor, states that it frequented the jungle near the estate, whence it was its custom to sally forth at night for the pleasure of pulling down buildings and trees, "and it seemed to have taken a spite at the pipes of the water-works, the pillars of which it several times broke down — its latest fancy being to wrench off the taps." This elephant has since been shot.

[2] CUVIER, *Règne Animal.* "Les Mammifères," p. 280.

higher degree of development consequent on his more intimate domestication and association with man.

One remarkable fact was called to my attention by a gentleman who resided on a coffee plantation at Rassawé, one of the loftiest mountains of the Ambogammoa range. More than once during the terrific thunder-bursts that precede the rains at the change of each monsoon, he observed that the elephants in the adjoining forest hastened from under cover of the trees and took up their station in the open ground, where I saw them on one of these occasions collected into a group; and here, he said, it was their custom to remain till the lightning had ceased, when they retired again into the jungle.[1] It must be observed; however, that showers, and especially light drizzling rain, are believed to bring the elephants from the jungle towards pathways or other openings in the forest;—and hence, in places infested by them, timid persons are afraid to travel in the afternoon during uncertain weather.

When free in its native woods the elephant evinces rather simplicity than sagacity, and its intelligence seldom exhibits itself in cunning. The rich profusion in which nature has supplied its food, and anticipated its every want, has made it independent of those devices by which carnivorous animals provide for their subsistence; and, from the absence of all rivalry between it and the other denizens of the plains, it is never required to resort to artifice for self-protection. For these reasons, in its tranquil and harmless life, it may appear to casual observers to exhibit even less than

[1] The elephant is believed by the Singhalese to express his uneasiness by his voice, on the approach of *rain;* and the Tamils have a proverb,—"*Listen to the elephant, rain is coming.*"

ordinary ability; but when danger and apprehension call for the exertion of its powers, those who have witnessed their display are seldom inclined to undervalue its sagacity.

Mr. Cripps has related to me an instance in which a recently captured elephant was either rendered senseless from fear, or, as the native attendants asserted, *feigned death* in order to regain its freedom. It was led from the corral as usual between two tame ones, and had already proceeded far towards its destination; when night closing in, and the torches being lighted, it refused to go on, and finally sank to the ground, apparently lifeless. Mr. Cripps ordered the fastenings to be removed from its legs, and when all attempts to raise it had failed, so convinced was he that it was dead, that he ordered the ropes to be taken off and the carcase abandoned. While this was being done he and a gentleman by whom he was accompanied leaned against the body to rest. They had scarcely taken their departure and proceeded a few yards, when, to their astonishment, the elephant rose with the utmost alacrity, and fled towards the jungle, screaming at the top of its voice, its cries being audible long after it had disappeared in the shades of the forest.

# APPENDIX TO CHAPTER III.

## NARRATIVES OF THE NATIVES OF CEYLON RELATIVE TO ENCOUNTERS WITH ROGUE ELEPHANTS.

THE following narratives have been taken down by a Singhalese gentleman, from the statements of the natives by whom they are recounted;—and they are here inserted, in order to show the opinion prevalent amongst the people of Ceylon as to the habits and propensities of the rogue elephant. The stories are given in words of my correspondent, who writes in English, as follows:—

1. "We," said my informant, who was a native trader of Caltura, "were on our way to Badulla, by way of Ratnapoora and Balangodde, to barter our merchandize for coffee. There were six in our party, myself, my brother-in-law, and four coolies, who carried on pingoes[1] our merchandize, which consisted of cloth and brass articles. About 4 o'clock, P. M., we were close to Idalgasinna, and our coolies were rather unwilling to go further for fear of elephants, which they said were sure to be met with at that noted place, especially as there had been a slight drizzling of rain during the whole afternoon. I was as much afraid of elephants as the coolies themselves; but I was anxious to proceed, and so, after a few words of encouragement addressed to them, and a prayer or two offered up to *Saman dewiyo*[2], we resumed our journey. I also took the

[1] Yokes borne on the shoulder, with a package at each end.

[2] The tutelary spirit of the sacred mountain, Adam's Peak.

further precaution of hanging up a few leaves.[1] As the rain was coming down fast and thick, and I was anxious to get to our halting-place before night, we moved on at a rapid pace. My brother-in-law was in the van of the party, I myself was in the rear, and the four coolies between us, all moving along on a rugged, rocky, and difficult path; as the road to Badulla till lately was on the sloping side of a hill, covered with jungle, pieces of projecting rock, and brushwood. It was about five o'clock in the evening, or a little later, and we had hardly cleared the foot of the hill and got to the plain below, when a rustling of leaves and a crackling of dry brushwood were heard on our right, followed immediately by the trumpeting of a *hora allia*[2], which was making towards us. We all fled, followed by the elephant. I, who was in the rear of the party, was the first to take to flight; the coolies threw away their pingoes, and my brother-in-law his umbrella, and all ran in different directions. I hid myself behind a large boulder of granite nearly covered by jungle: but as my place of concealment was on high ground, I could see all that was going on below. The first thing I observed was the elephant returning to the place where one of the pingoes was lying: he was carrying one of the coolies in a coil of his trunk. The body of the man was dangling with the head downward. I cannot say whether he was then alive or not; I could not perceive any marks of blood or bruises on his person: but he appeared to be lifeless. The elephant placed him down on the ground, put the pingo on his (the man's) shoulder, steadying both the man and the pingo with his trunk and fore-legs. But the man of course did not move or stand up with his pingo. Seeing this, the elephant again raised the cooly and dashed him against the ground, and then trampled

[1] The Singhalese hold the belief, that twigs taken from one bush and placed on another growing close to a pathway, ensure protection to travellers from the attacks of wild animals, and especially of elephants. Can it be that the latter avoid the path, on discovering this evidence of the proximity of recent passengers?

[2] A rogue elephant.

the body to a very jelly. This done, he took up the pingo and moved away from the spot; but at the distance of about a fathom or two, laid it down again, and ripping open one of the bundles, took out of it all the contents, *somans*[1], *cambāyas*[2], handkerchiefs, and several pieces of white cambrick cloth, all which he tore to small pieces, and flung them wildly here and there. He did the same with all the other pingoes. When this was over the elephant quietly walked away into the jungle, trumpeting all the way as far as I could hear. When danger was past I came out of my concealment, and returned to the place where we had halted that morning. Here the rest of my companions joined me soon after. The next morning we set out again on our journey, our party being now increased by some seven or eight traders from Salpity Corle: but this time we did not meet with the elephant. We found the mangled corpse of our cooly on the same spot where I had seen it the day before, together with the torn pieces of my cloths, of which we collected as fast as we could the few which were serviceable, and all the brass utensils which were quite uninjured. That elephant was a noted rogue. He had before this killed many people on that road, especially those carrying pingoes of coco-nut oil and ghee. He was afterwards killed by an Englishman. The incidents I have mentioned above, took place about twenty years ago."

The following also relates to the same locality. It was narrated to me by an old Moorman of Barberyn, who, during his earlier years, led the life of a pedlar.

2. "I and another," said he, "were on our way to Badulla, one day some twenty-five or thirty years ago. We were quietly moving along a path which wound round a hill, when all of a sudden, and without the slightest previous intimation either by the rustling of leaves or by any other sign, a huge elephant with short tusks rushed to the path. Where he had been before I can't say; I believe he must have been lying in

[1] Woman's robe. [2] The figured cloth worn by men.

wait for travellers. In a moment he rushed forward to the road, trumpeting dreadfully, and seized my companion. I, who happened to be in the rear, took to flight, pursued by the elephant, which had already killed my companion by striking him against the ground. I had not moved more than seven or eight fathoms, when the elephant seized me, and threw me up with such force, that I was carried high into the air towards a *Cahata* tree, whose branches caught me and prevented my falling to the ground. By this I received no other injury than the dislocation of one of my wrists. I do not know whether the elephant saw me after he had hurled me away through the air; but certainly he did not come to the tree to which I was then clinging: even if he had come, he couldn't have done me any more harm, as the branch on which I was was far beyond the reach of his trunk, and the tree itself too large for him to pull down. The next thing I saw was the elephant returning to the corpse of my companion, which he again threw on the ground, and placing one of his fore feet on it, he tore it with his trunk limb after limb; and dabbled in the blood that flowed from the shapeless mass of flesh which he was still holding under his foot."

3. "In 1847 or '46," said another informant, "I was a superintendent of a coco-nut estate belonging to Mr. Armitage, situated about twelve miles from Negombo. A rogue elephant did considerable injury to the estate at that time; and one day, hearing that it was then on the plantation, a Mr. Lindsay, an Englishman, who was proprietor of the adjoining property, and myself, accompanied by some seven or eight people of the neighbouring village, went out, carrying with us six rifles loaded and primed. We continued to walk along a path which, near one of its turns, had some bushes on one side. We had calculated to come up with the brute where it had been seen half an hour before; but no sooner had one of our men, who was walking foremost, seen the animal at the distance of some fifteen or twenty fathoms, than he exclaimed, 'There! there!' and immediately took to his heels, and we all

followed his example. The elephant did not see us until we had run some fifteen or twenty paces from the spot where we turned, when he gave us chase, screaming frightfully as he came on. The Englishman managed to climb a tree, and the rest of my companions did the same; as for myself I could not, although I made one or two superhuman efforts. But there was no time to be lost. The elephant was running at me with his trunk bent down in a curve towards the ground. At this critical moment Mr. Lindsay held out his foot to me, with the help of which and then of the branches of the tree, which were three or four feet above my head, I managed to scramble up to a branch. The elephant came directly to the tree and attempted to force it down, which he could not. He first coiled his trunk round the stem, and pulled it with all his might, but with no effect. He then applied his head to the tree, and pushed for several minutes, but with no better success. He then trampled with his feet all the projecting roots, moving, as he did so, several times round and round the tree. Lastly, failing in all this, and seeing a pile of timber, which I had lately cut, at a short distance from us, he removed it all (thirty-six pieces) one at a time to the root of the tree, and piled them up in a regular business-like manner; then placing his hind feet on this pile, he raised the fore part of his body, and reached out his trunk, but still he could not touch us, as we were too far above him. The Englishman then fired, and the ball took effect somewhere on the elephant's head, but did not kill him. It made him only the more furious. The next shot, however, levelled him to the ground. I afterwards brought the skull of the animal to Colombo, and it is still to be seen at the house of Mr. Armitage."

4. "One night a herd of elephants entered a village in the Four Corles. After doing considerable injury to plaintain bushes and young coco-nut trees, they retired, the villagers being unable to do anything to protect their fruit trees from destruction. But one elephant was left behind, who continued to scream the whole night through at the same spot. It was

then discovered that the elephant, on seeing a jak fruit on a tree somewhat beyond the reach of his trunk, had raised himself on his hind legs, placing his fore feet against the stem, in order to lay hold of the fruit, but unluckily for him there happened to be another tree standing so close to it that the vacant space between the two stems was only a few inches. During his attempts to take hold of the fruit one of his legs happened to get in between the two trees, where, on account of his weight and his clumsy attempts to extricate himself, it got so firmly wedged that he could not remove it, and in this awkward position he remained for some days, till he died on the spot."

# CHAP. IV.

## THE ELEPHANT.

### *Elephant Shooting.*

As the shooting of an elephant, whatever endurance and adroitness the sport may display in other respects, requires the smallest possible skill as a marksman, the numbers which are annually slain in this way may be regarded as evidence of the multitudes abounding in those parts of Ceylon to which they resort. One officer, Major ROGERS, killed upwards of 1400; another, Captain GALLWEY, has the credit of slaying more than half that number; Major SKINNER, the Commissioner of Roads, almost as many; and less persevering aspirants follow at humbler distances.[1]

[1] To persons like myself, who are not addicted to what is called "sport," the statement of these wholesale slaughters is calculated to excite surprise and curiosity as to the nature of a passion that impels men to self-exposure and privation, in a pursuit which presents nothing but the monotonous recurrence of scenes of blood and suffering. Mr. BAKER, who has recently published, under the title of "*The Rifle and the Hound in Ceylon*," an account of his exploits in the forest, gives us the assurance that "*all real sportsmen are tender-hearted men, who shun cruelty to an animal, and are easily moved by a tale of distress;*" and that although man is naturally bloodthirsty, and a beast of prey by instinct, yet that the true sportsman is distinguished from the rest of the human race by his "*love of nature and of noble scenery.*" In support of this pretension to a gentler nature than the rest of mankind, the author proceeds to attest his own abhorrence of cruelty by narrating the sufferings of an old hound, which, although "toothless," he cheered on to assail a boar at bay, but the poor dog recoiled "covered with blood, cut nearly in half, with a wound fourteen inches in length, from the lower part of the belly, passing up the flank, completely

But notwithstanding this prodigious destruction, a reward of a few shillings per head offered by the Government for taking elephants was claimed for 3500 destroyed in part of the northern province alone, in less than three years prior to 1848: and between 1851 and 1856, a similar reward was paid for 2000 in the southern province, between Galle and Hambangtotte.

Although there is little opportunity for the display of marksmanship in an elephant battue, there is one feature in the sport, as conducted in Ceylon, which contrasts favourably with the slaughterhouse details chronicled with revolting minuteness in some recent accounts of

severing the muscles of the hind leg, and extending up the spine; his hind leg having the appearance of being nearly off." In this state, forgetful of the character he had so lately given of the true sportsman, as a lover of nature and a hater of cruelty, he encouraged "the poor old dog," as he calls him, to resume the fight with the boar, which lasted for an hour, when he managed to call the dogs off; and perfectly exhausted, the mangled hound crawled out of the jungle with several additional wounds, including a severe gash in his throat. "He fell from exhaustion, and we made a litter with two poles and a horsecloth to carry him home."—P. 314. If such were the habitual enjoyments of this class of sportsmen, their motiveless massacres would admit of no manly justification. In comparison with them one is disposed to regard almost with favour the exploits of a hunter like Major ROGERS, who is said to have applied the value of the ivory obtained from his encounters towards the purchase of his successive regimental commissions, and had, therefore, an object, however disproportionate, in his slaughter of 1400 elephants.

One gentleman in Ceylon, not less distinguished for his genuine kindness of heart, than for his marvellous success in shooting elephants, avowed to me that the eagerness with which he found himself impelled to pursue them had often excited surprise in his own mind; and although he had never read the theory of Lord Kames, or the speculations of Vicesimus Knox, he had come to the conclusion that the passion thus excited within him was a remnant of the hunter's instinct, with which man was originally endowed to enable him, by the chase, to support existence in a state of nature, and which, though rendered dormant by civilisation, had not been utterly eradicated.

This theory is at least more consistent and intelligible than the "love of nature and scenery," sentimentally propounded by the author quoted above.

elephant shooting in South Africa. The practice in Ceylon is to aim invariably at the head, and the sportsman finds his safety to consist in boldly facing the animal, advancing to within fifteen paces, and lodging a bullet, either in the temple or in the hollow over the eye, or in a well-known spot immediately above the trunk, where the weaker structure of the skull affords an easy access to the brain.[1] The region of the ear is also a fatal spot, and often resorted to,—the places I have mentioned in the front of the head being only accessible when the animal is "charging." Professor HARRISON, in his communication to the Royal Irish Academy on the Anatomy of the Elephant, has rendered an intelligible explanation of this in the following passage descriptive of the cranium:—"it exhibits two remarkable facts: *first*, the small space occupied by the brain; and, *secondly*, the beautiful and curious structure of the bones of the head. The two tables of all these bones, except the occipital, are separated by rows of large cells, some from four to five inches in length, others only small, irregular, and honey-comb-like:—these all communicate with each other, and, through the frontal sinuses, with the cavity of the nose, and also with the tympanum or drum of each ear; consequently, as in some birds, these cells are filled with air, and thus while the skull attains a great size in order to afford an extensive surface

[1] The vulnerability of the elephant in this region of the head was known to the ancients, and PLINY, describing a combat of elephants in the amphitheatre at Rome, says, that one was slain by a single blow, "pilum sub oculo adactum, in vitalia capitis venerat." (Lib. viii. c. 7.) Notwithstanding the comparative facility of access to the brain afforded at this spot, an ordinary leaden bullet is not certain to penetrate, and frequently becomes flattened. The hunters, to counteract this, are accustomed to harden the ball, by the introduction of a small portion of type-metal along with the lead.

for the attachment of muscles, and a mechanical support for the tusks, it is at the same time very light and buoyant in proportion to its bulk; a property the more valuable as the animal is fond of water and bathes in deep rivers."

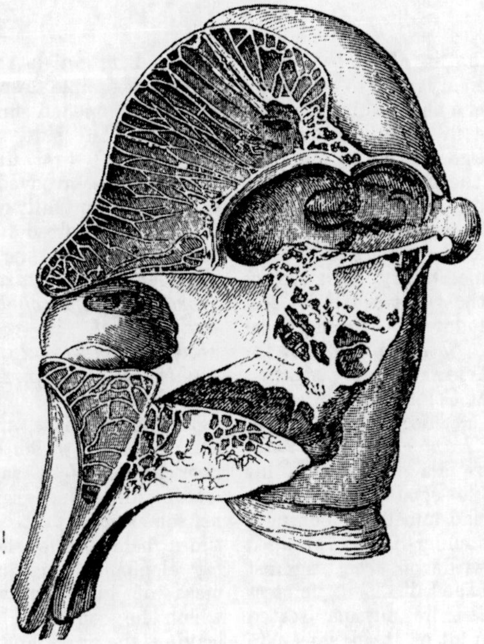

SECTION OF ELEPHANT'S HEAD.

Generally speaking, a single ball, planted in the forehead, ends the existence of the noble creature instantaneously: and expert sportsmen have been known to kill right and left, one with each barrel; but occasionally an elephant will not fall before several shots have been lodged in his head.[1]

[1] "There is a wide difference of opinion as to the most deadly shot. I think the temple the most certain, but authority in Ceylon says the

Contrasted with this, one reads with a shudder the sickening details of the African huntsman approaching *behind* the retiring animal, and of the torture inflicted by the shower of bullets which tear up its flesh and lacerate its flank and shoulders.[1]

'fronter,' that is, above the trunk. Behind the ear is said to be deadly, but that is a shot which I never fired or saw fired that I remember. If the ball go true to its mark, all shots (in the head) are certain; but the bones on either side of the honey-comb passage to the brain are so thick that there is in all a 'glorious uncertainty' which keeps a man on the *qui vive* till he sees the elephant down."—From a paper on *Elephant Shooting in Ceylon*, by Major MACREADY, late Military Secretary at Colombo.

[1] In Mr. GORDON CUMMING's account of a *Hunter's Life in South Africa*, there is a narrative of his pursuit of a wounded elephant which he had lamed by lodging a ball in its shoulder-blade. It limped slowly towards a tree, against which it leaned itself in helpless agony, whilst its pursuer seated himself in front of it, in safety, to *boil his coffee*, and observe its sufferings. The story is continued as follows: —"Having admired him for a considerable time, *I resolved to make experiments on vulnerable points;* and approaching very near I fired several bullets at different parts of his enormous skull. He only acknowledged the shots by a salaam-like movement of his trunk, with the point of which he gently touched the wounds with a striking and peculiar action. Surprised and shocked at finding that I was only prolonging the sufferings of the noble beast, which bore its trials with such dignified composure, I resolved to finish the proceeding with all possible despatch, and accordingly opened fire upon him from the left side, aiming at the shoulder. I first fired *six* shots with the two-grooved rifle, which must have eventually proved mortal. After which I fired *six* shots at the same part with the Dutch six-pounder. *Large tears now trickled from his eyes, which he slowly shut and opened, his colossal frame shivered convulsively, and falling on his side, he expired.*" (Vol. ii. p. 10.)

In another place, after detailing the manner in which he assailed a poor animal — he says, "I was loading and firing as fast as could be, sometimes at the head, sometimes behind the shoulder, until my elephant's fore-quarter was a mass of gore; notwithstanding which he continued to hold on, leaving the grass and branches of the forest scarlet in his wake. * * * Having fired *thirty-five rounds* with my two-grooved rifle, I opened upon him with the Dutch six-pounder, and when forty bullets had perforated his hide, he began for the first time, to evince signs of a dilapidated constitution." The disgusting description is closed thus: "Throughout the charge he repeatedly cooled his person with large quantities of water, which he ejected from his trunk over his sides and back, and just as the pangs of death came over him, he stood trembling violently beside a thorn tree, and kept pouring water

The shooting of elephants in Ceylon has been described with tiresome iteration in the successive journals of sporting gentlemen, but one who turns to their pages for traits of the animal and his instincts is disappointed to find little beyond graphic sketches of the daring and exploits of his pursuers, most of whom, having had no further opportunity of observation than is derived from a casual encounter with the outraged animal, have apparently tried to exalt their own prowess, by misrepresenting the ordinary character of the elephant, describing him as "savage, wary, and revengeful."[1]

These epithets may undoubtedly apply to the outcasts from the herd, the "Rogues" or *hora allia*, but so small is the proportion of these that there is not probably one *rogue* to be found for every five hundred of those in herds; and it is a manifest error, arising from imperfect information, to extend this censure to them generally, or to suppose the elephant to be an animal "thirsting for blood, lying in wait in the jungle to rush on the unwary passer-by, and knowing no greater pleasure than the act of crushing his victim to a shapeless mass beneath his feet."[2] The cruelties practised by the hunters have no doubt taught these sagacious creatures to be cautious and alert, but their precautions are simply defensive; and beyond the alarm and apprehension which they

into his bloody mouth until he died, when he pitched heavily forward with the whole weight of his forequarters resting on the points of his tusks. The strain was fair, and the tusks did not yield; but the portion of his head in which the tusks were embedded, extending a long way above the eye, yielded and burst with a muffled crash."—(*Ib.*, vol. ii. pp. 4, 5.)

[1] *The Rifle and the Hound in Ceylon*; by S. W. Baker, Esq., pp. 8, 9. "Next to a rogue," says Mr. Baker, "in ferocity, and even more persevering in the pursuit of her victim, is a female elephant." But he appends the significant qualification, "*when her young one has been killed.*"—*Ibid.*, p. 13.

[2] *Ibid.*

evince on the approach of man, they exhibit no indication of hostility or thirst for blood.

An ordinary traveller seldom comes upon elephants unless after sunset or towards daybreak, as they go to or return from their nightly visits to the tanks: but when by accident a herd is disturbed by day, they evince, if unattacked, no disposition to become assailants; and if the attitude of defence which they instinctively assume prove sufficent to check the approach of the intruder, no further demonstration is to be apprehended.

Even the hunters who go in search of them find them in positions and occupations altogether inconsistent with the idea of their being savage, wary, or revengeful. Their demeanour when undisturbed is indicative of gentleness and timidity, and their actions bespeak lassitude and indolence, induced not alone by heat, but probably ascribable in some degree to the fact that the night has been spent in watchfulness and amusement. A few are generally browsing listlessly on the trees and plants within reach, others fanning themselves with leafy branches, and a few are asleep; whilst the young run playfully among the herd, the emblems of innocence, as the older ones are of peacefulness and gravity.

Almost every elephant may be observed to exhibit some peculiar action of the limbs when standing at rest; some move the head monotonously in a circle, or from right to left; some swing their feet back and forward; others flap their ears or sway themselves from side to side, or rise and sink by alternately bending and straightening the fore knees. As the opportunities of observing this custom have been almost confined to elephants in captivity, it has been conjectured to arise from some morbid habit contracted during the length of a voyage by sea [1], or from an instinctive impulse to substitute a motion of this kind in lieu of their wonted exercise; but this supposition is erroneous; the propensity being equally displayed by those at liberty and those in captivity. When surprised by sportsmen in the depths of the jungle, individuals of a herd are always occupied in swinging their limbs in this manner; and in the several corrals which I have seen, where whole herds have been captured, the elephants in the midst of the utmost excitement, and even after the most vigorous charges, if they halted for a moment in stupor and exhaustion, manifested their wonted habit, and swung their limbs or swayed their bodies to and fro incessantly. So far from its being a substitute for exercise, those in the government employment in Ceylon are observed to practise their acquired motion, whatever it may be, with increased vigour when thoroughly fatigued after excessive work. Even the favourite practice of fanning themselves with a leafy branch seems less an enjoyment in itself than a resource when listless and at rest. The term "fidgetty" seems to describe appropriately the temperament of the elephant.

They evince the strongest love of retirement and a corresponding dislike to intrusion. The approach of a stranger is perceived less by the eye, the quickness of which is not remarkable (besides which its range is obscured by the foliage), than by sensitive smell and singular acuteness of hearing; and the whole herd is put in instant but noiseless motion towards some deeper and more secure retreat. The effectual manner in

[1] *Menageries, &c.*, "The Elephant," ch. i. p. 21.

which an animal of the prodigious size of the elephant can conceal himself, and the motionless silence which he preserves, is quite surprising; whilst beaters pass and repass within a few yards of his hiding place, he will maintain his ground till the hunter, creeping almost close to his legs, sees his little eye peering out through the leaves, when, finding himself discovered, the elephant breaks away with a crash, levelling the brushwood in his headlong career.

If surprised in open ground, where stealthy retreat is impracticable, a herd will hesitate in indecision, and, after a few meaningless movements, stand huddled together in a group, whilst one or two, more adventurous than the rest, advance a few steps to reconnoitre. Elephants are generally observed to be bolder in open ground than in cover, but, if bold at all, far more dangerous in cover than in open ground.

In searching for them, sportsmen often avail themselves of the expertness of the native trackers; and notwithstanding the demonstration of Combe that the brain of the timid Singhalese is deficient in the organ of destructiveness[1], he shows an instinct for hunting, and exhibits in the pursuit of the elephant a courage and adroitness far surpassing in interest the mere handling of the rifle, which is the principal share of the proceeding that falls to his European companions.

The beater on these occasions has the double task of finding the game and carrying the guns; and, in an animated communication to me, an experienced sportsman describes "this light and active creature, with his long glossy hair hanging down his shoulders, every

[1] *System of Phrenology*, by GEO. COMBE, vol. i. p. 256.

muscle quivering with excitement; and his countenance lighting up with intense animation, leaping from rock to rock, as nimble as a deer, tracking the gigantic game like a blood-hound, falling behind as he comes up with it, and as the elephants, baffled and irritated, make the first stand, passing one rifle into your eager hand and holding the other ready whilst right and left each barrel performs its mission, and if fortune does not flag, and the second gun is as successful as the first, three or four huge carcases are piled one on another within a space equal to the area of a dining room."[1]

It is curious that in these encounters the herd never rush forward in a body, as buffaloes or bisons do, but only one elephant at a time moves in advance of the rest to confront, or, as it is called, to "charge," the assailants. I have heard of but one instance in which *two* so advanced as champions of their companions. Sometimes, indeed, the whole herd will follow a leader, and manœuvre in his rear like a body of cavalry; but so large a party are necessarily liable to panic; and, one of them having turned in alarm, the entire body retreat with terrified precipitation.

As regards boldness and courage, a strange variety of temperament is observable amongst elephants, but it may be affirmed that they are much more generally timid than courageous. One herd may be as difficult to approach as deer, gliding away through the jungle so gently and quickly that scarcely a trace marks their passage; another, in apparent stupor, will huddle themselves together like swine, and allow their assailant to come within a few yards before they break away in

[1] Private letter from Capt. PHILIP PAYNE GALLWEY.

terror; and a third will await his approach without motion, and then advance with fury to the "charge."

In individuals the same differences are discernible; one flies on the first appearance of danger, whilst another, alone and unsupported, will face a whole host of enemies. When wounded and infuriated with pain, many of them become literally savage[1]; but, so unaccustomed are they to act as assailants, and so awkward and inexpert in using their strength, that they rarely or ever exceed in killing a pursuer who falls into their power. Although the pressure of a foot, a blow with the trunk, or a thrust with the tusk, could scarcely fail to prove fatal, three-fourths of those who have fallen into their power have escaped without serious injury. So great is this chance of impunity, that the sportsman prefers to approach within about fifteen paces of the advancing elephant, a space which gives time for a second fire should the first shot prove ineffectual, and should both fail there is still opportunity for flight.

Amongst full-grown timber, a skilful runner can escape from an elephant by "dodging" round the trees, but in cleared land, and low brushwood, the difficulty is much increased, as the small growth of underwood which obstructs the movements of man presents no obstacle to those of an elephant. On the other hand, on level and open ground the chances are rather in favour of the elephant, as his pace in full flight exceeds that of man, although as a general rule, it is unequal to that of a horse, as has been sometimes asserted.[2]

[1] Some years ago an elephant which had been wounded by a native, near Hambangtotte, pursued the man into the town, followed him along the street, trampled him to death in the bazaar before a crowd of terrified spectators, and succeeded in making good its retreat to the jungle.

[2] SHAW, in his *Zoology*, asserts that an elephant can run as swiftly as a horse can gallop. London, 1800–6, vol. i. p. 216.

The incessant slaughter of elephants by sportsmen in Ceylon, appears to be merely in subordination to the influence of the organ of destructiveness, since the carcase is never applied to any useful purpose, but left to decompose and to defile the air of the forest. The flesh is occasionally tasted as a matter of curiosity: as a steak it is coarse and tough; but the tongue is as delicate as that of an ox; and the foot is said to make palatable soup. The Caffres attached to the pioneer corps in the Kandyan province are in the habit of securing the heart of any elephant shot in their vicinity, and say it is their custom to eat it in Africa. The hide it has been found impracticable to tan in Ceylon, or to convert to any useful purpose, but the bones of those shot have of late years been collected and used for manuring coffee estates. The hair of the tail, which is extremely strong and horny, is mounted by the native goldsmith, and made into bracelets; and the teeth are sawn by the Moormen at Galle (as they used to be by the Romans during a scarcity of ivory) into plates, out of which they fashion numerous articles of ornament, knife-handles, card racks, and "presse-papiers."

## NOTE.

AMONGST extraordinary recoveries from desperate wounds, I venture to record here an instance which occurred in Ceylon to a gentleman while engaged in the chase of elephants, and which, I apprehend, has few parallels in pathological experience. Lieutenant GERARD FRETZ, of the Ceylon Rifle Regiment, whilst firing at an elephant in the vicinity of Fort MacDonald, in Oovah, was wounded in the face by the bursting of his fowling-piece, on the 22nd January, 1828. He was then about thirty-two years of age. On raising him, it was found that part of the breech of the gun and about two inches of the barrel had been driven through the frontal sinus, at the junction of the nose and forehead. It had sunk almost perpendicularly till the iron-plate called "the tail-pin," by which the barrel is made fast to the stock by a screw, had descended through the palate, carrying with it the screw, one extremity of which had forced itself into the right nostril, where it was discernible externally, whilst the headed end lay in contact with his tongue. To extract the jagged mass of iron thus sunk in the ethmoidal and sphenoidal cells was found hopelessly impracticable; but, strange to tell, after the inflammation subsided, Mr. FRETZ recovered rapidly; his general health was unimpaired, and he returned to his regiment with this singular appendage firmly embedded behind the bones of his face. He took his turn of duty as usual, attained the command of his company, participated in all the enjoyments of the mess-room, and died *eight years afterwards*, on the 1st of April, 1836, not from any consequences of this fearful wound, but from fever and inflammation brought on by other causes.

So little was he apparently inconvenienced by the presence of the strange body in his palate that he was accustomed with his finger partially to undo the screw, which but for its extreme length he might altogether have withdrawn. To enable this to be done, and possibly to assist by this means the extraction of the breech itself through the original orifice (which never entirely closed), an attempt was made in 1835 to take off a portion of the screw with a file; but, after having cut it three parts through the operation was interrupted, chiefly owing to the carelessness and indifference of Capt. FRETZ, whose death occurred before the attempt could be resumed. The piece of iron, on being removed after his decease, was found to measure $2\frac{3}{4}$ inches in length, and weighed two scruples more than two ounces and three quarters. A cast of the breech and screw now forms No. 2790 amongst the deposits in the Medical Museum of Chatham.

# CHAP. V.

## THE ELEPHANT.

---

### *An Elephant Corral.*

So long as the elephants of Ceylon were merely required in small numbers for the pageantry of the native princes, or the sacred processions of the Buddhist temples, their capture was effected either by the instrumentality of female decoys, or by the artifices and agility of the individuals and castes who devoted themselves to their pursuit and training. But after the arrival of the European conquerors of the island, and when it had become expedient to take advantage of the strength and intelligence of these creatures in clearing forests and making roads and other works, establishments were organised on a great scale by the Portuguese and Dutch, and the supply of elephants kept up by periodical battues conducted at the cost of the government, on a plan similar to that adopted on the continent of India, when herds varying in number from twenty to one hundred and upwards are driven into concealed enclosures and secured.

In both these processes, success is entirely dependent on the skill with which the captors turn to advantage the terror and inexperience of the wild elephant, since all attempts would be futile to subdue or confine by ordinary force an animal of such strength and sagacity.[1]

[1] The device of taking them by means of pitfalls still prevails in India: but in addition to the difficulty of providing against that

KNOX describes with circumstantiality the mode adopted, two centuries ago, by the servants of the King of Kandy to catch elephants for the royal stud. He says, "After discovering the retreat of such as have tusks, unto these they drive some *she elephants*, which they bring with them for the purpose, which, when once the males have got a sight of, they will never leave, but follow them wheresoever they go; and the females are so used to it that they will do whatsoever, either by word or a beck, their keepers bid them. And so they delude them along through towns and countries, and through the streets of the city, even to the very gates of the king's palace, where sometimes they seize upon them by snares, and sometimes by driving them into a kind of pound, they catch them."[1]

In Nepaul and Burmah, and throughout the Chin-Indian Peninsula, when in pursuit of single elephants, either *rogues* detached from the herd, or individuals

caution with which the elephant is supposed to reconnoitre suspicious ground, it has the further disadvantage of exposing him to injury from bruises and dislocations in his fall. Still it was the mode of capture employed by the Singhalese, and so late as 1750 WOLF relates that the native chiefs of the Wanny, when capturing elephants for the Dutch, made "pits some fathoms deep in those places whither the elephant is wont to go in search of food, across which were laid poles covered with branches and baited with the food of which he is fondest, making towards which he finds himself taken unawares. Thereafter being subdued by fright and exhaustion, he was assisted to raise himself to the surface by means of hurdles and earth, which he placed underfoot as they were thrown down to him, till he was enabled to step out on solid ground, when the noosers and decoys were in readiness to tie him up to the nearest tree."—See WOLF's *Life and Adventures*, p. 152. Shakspeare appears to have been acquainted with the plan of taking elephants in pitfalls: Decius, encouraging the conspirators, reminds them of Cæsar's taste for anecdotes of animals, by which he would undertake to lure him to his fate:

"For he loves to hear
That unicorns may be betrayed with trees,
And bears with glasses; *elephants with holes*."

JULIUS CÆSAR, Act ii. Scene I.

[1] KNOX's *Historical Relation of Ceylon*, A.D. 1681, part i. ch. vi. p. 21.

who have been marked for the beauty of their ivory, the natives avail themselves of the aid of females in order to effect their approaches and secure an opportunity of casting a noose over the foot of the destined captive. All accounts concur in expressing high admiration of their courage and address; but from what has fallen under my own observation, added to the descriptions I have heard from other eye-witnesses, I am inclined to believe that in such exploits the Moormen of Ceylon evince a daring and adroitness, surpassing all others.

These professional elephant catchers, or, as they are called, Panickeas, inhabit the Moorish villages in the north and north-east of the island, and from time immemorial have been engaged in taking elephants, which are afterwards trained by Arabs, chiefly for the use of the rajahs and native princes in the south of India, whose vakeels are periodically despatched to make purchases in Ceylon.

The ability evinced by these men in tracing elephants through the woods has almost the certainty of instinct; and hence their services are eagerly sought by the European sportsmen who go down into their country in search of game. So keen is their glance, that like hounds running "breast high" they will follow the course of an elephant, almost at the top of their speed, over glades covered with stunted grass, where the eye of a stranger would fail to discover a trace of its passage, and on through forests strewn with dry leaves, where it seems impossible to perceive a footstep. Here they are guided by a bent or broken twig, or by a leaf dropped from the animal's mouth, on which the pressure of a tooth may be detected. If at fault, they fetch a circuit like a setter, till lighting on some fresh marks, they go a-head again with renewed vigour. So delicate is the sense of smell in the elephant, and so indispensable is it to go against the wind in approaching him, that on those occasions when the wind is so still that its direction cannot be otherwise discerned, the Panickeas will suspend the film of a gossamer to determine it and shape their course accordingly.

They are enabled by the inspection of the footmarks, when impressed in soft clay, to describe the size as well as the number of a herd before it is seen; the height of an elephant at the shoulder being as nearly as possible twice the circumference of his fore foot.[1]

On overtaking the game their courage is as conspicuous as their sagacity. If they have confidence in the sportsman for whom they are finding, they will advance to the very heel of the elephant, slap him on the quarter, and convert his timidity into anger, till he turns upon his tormentor and exposes his front to receive the bullet which is awaiting him.[2]

[1] Previous to the death of the female elephant in the Zoological Gardens, in the Regent's Park, in 1851, Mr. MITCHELL, the Secretary, caused measurements to be accurately made, and found the statement of the Singhalese hunters to be strictly correct, the height at the shoulders being precisely twice the circumference of the fore foot.

[2] Major SKINNER, the Chief Officer at the head of the Commission of Roads, in Ceylon, in writing to me, mentions an anecdote illustrative of the daring of the Panickeas. "I once saw," he says, "a very beautiful example of the confidence with which these fellows, from their knowledge of the elephants, meet their worst defiance. It was in Neuera-Kalawa; I was bivouacking on the bank of a river, and had been kept out so late that I did not get to my tent until between 9 and 10 at night. On our return towards it we passed several single elephants making their way to the nearest water, but at length we came upon a large herd that had taken possession of the only road by which we could pass, and which no intimidation would induce to move off. I had some Panickeas with me; they knew the herd, and counselled extreme caution. After trying every device we could think of for a length of time, a little old Moorman of the party came to me and requested we should all retire to a distance. He then took a couple of chules (flambeaux of dried wood, or coco-nut leaves), one in

So fearless and confident are they that two men, without aid or attendants, will boldly attempt to capture the largest-sized elephant. Their only weapon is a flexible rope made of elk's or buffalo's hide, with which it is their object to secure one of the hind legs. This they effect either by following in its footsteps when in motion or by stealing close up to it when at rest, and availing themselves of its well-known propensity at such moments to swing the feet backwards and forwards, they contrive to slip a noose over the hind leg.

At other times this is achieved by spreading the noose on the ground partially concealed by roots and leaves beneath a tree on which one of the party is stationed, whose business it is to lift it suddenly by means of a cord, raising it on the elephant's leg at the moment when his companion has succeeded in provoking him to place his foot within the circle, the other end having been previously made fast to the stem of the tree. Should the noosing be effected in open ground, and no tree of sufficient strength at hand round which to wind the rope, one of the Moors, allowing himself to be pursued by the enraged elephant, entices him towards the nearest grove; where his companion, dexterously laying hold of the rope as it trails along the ground, suddenly coils it round a suitable stem, and brings the fugitive to a stand still. On finding himself thus arrested, the natural impulse of the captive is to turn on the man

each hand, and waving them above his head till they flamed out fiercely, he advanced at a deliberate pace to within a few yards of the elephant who was acting as leader of the party, and who was growling and trumpeting in his rage, and flourished the flaming torches in his face. The effect was instantaneous; the whole herd dashed away in a panic, bellowing, screaming, and crushing through the underwood, whilst we availed ourselves of the open path to make our way to our tents."

who is engaged in making fast the rope, a movement which it is the duty of his colleague to prevent by running up close to the elephant's head and provoking the animal to confront him by irritating gesticulations and taunting shouts of *dah! dah!* a monosyllable, the sound of which the elephant peculiarly dislikes. Meanwhile the first assailant, having secured one noose, comes up from behind with another, with which, amidst the vain rage and struggles of the victim, he entraps a fore leg, the rope being, as before, secured to another tree in front, and the whole four feet having been thus entangled, the capture is completed.

A shelter is then run up with branches, to protect their prisoner from the sun, and the hunters proceed to build a wigwam for themselves in front of him, kindling their fires for cooking, and making all the necessary arrangements for remaining day and night on the spot to await the process of subduing and taming his rage. In my journeys through the forest I have come unexpectedly on the halting place of adventurous hunters when thus engaged; and on one occasion, about sunrise, in ascending the steep ridge from the bed of the Malwatte river, the foremost rider of our party was suddenly driven back by a furious elephant, which we found picketed by two Panickeas on the crest of the bank. In such a position, the elephant soon ceases to struggle; and what with the exhaustion of rage and resistance, the terror of fire which he dreads, and the constant annoyance of smoke which he detests, in a very short time, a few weeks at the most, his spirit becomes subdued; and being plentifully supplied with plantains and fresh food, and indulged with water, in which he luxuriates, he grows so far reconciled to his keepers that they at length venture to remove him to their own village, or to the sea-side for shipment to India.

No part of the hunter's performances exhibits greater skill and audacity than this first forced march of the recently captured elephant from the great central forests to the sea-coast. As he is still too morose to submit to be ridden, and as it would be equally impossible to lead or to drive him by force, the ingenuity of the captors is displayed in alternately irritating and eluding him, but always so attracting his attention as to allure him along in the direction in which they want him to go. Some assistance is derived from the rope by which the original capture was effected, and which, as it serves to make him safe at night, is never removed from the leg till his taming is sufficiently advanced to permit of his being entrusted with partial liberty.

In Ceylon the principal place for exporting these animals to India is Manaar, on the western coast, to which the Arabs from the continent resort, bringing with them horses to be bartered for elephants. In order to reach the sea, open plains must be traversed, across which it requires the utmost courage, agility, and patience of the Moors to coax their reluctant charge. At Manaar the elephants are usually detained till any wound on the leg caused by the rope has been healed, when the shipment is effected in the most primitive manner. It being next to impossible to induce the still untamed creature to walk on board, and no mechanical contrivances being provided to ship him; a dhoney, or native boat, of about forty tons' burthen, and about three parts filled with the strong ribbed leaves of the Palmyra palm, is brought alongside the quay in front of the Old Dutch Fort, and lashed so that the gunwale may be as nearly as possible on a line with the level of the wharf. The elephant being placed with his back to the water is forced by goads to retreat till his hind legs go over the side of the quay, but the main contest commences when it is attempted to disengage his fore feet from the shore, and force him to entrust himself on board. The scene becomes exciting from the screams and trumpeting of the elephants, the shouts of the Arabs, the calls of the Moors, and the rushing of the crowd. Meanwhile the huge creature strains every nerve to regain the land; and the day is often consumed before his efforts are overcome, and he finds himself fairly afloat. The same dhoney will take from four to five elephants, who place themselves athwart it, and exhibit amusing adroitness in accommodating their movements to the rolling of the little vessel; and in this way they are ferried across the narrow strait which separates the continent of India from Ceylon.[1]

But the feat of ensnaring and subduing a single elephant, courageous as it is, and demonstrative of the supremacy with which man wields his "dominion over every beast of the earth," falls far short of the daring

[1] In the *Philosophical Transactions* for 1701, there is "An Account of the taking of Elephants in Ceylon, by Mr. STRACHAN, a Physician who lived seventeen years there," in which the author describes the manner in which they were shipped by the Dutch, at Matura, Galle, and Negombo. A piece of strong sail-cloth having been wrapped round the elephant's chest and stomach, he was forced into the sea between two tame ones, and there made fast to a boat. The tame ones then returned to land, and he swam after the boat to the ship, where tackle was reeved to the sail-cloth, and he was hoisted on board.

"But a better way has been invented lately," says Mr. Strachan; "a large flat-bottomed vessel is prepared, covered with planks like a floor; so that this floor is almost of a height with the key. Then the sides of the key and the vessel are adorned with green branches, so that the elephant sees no water till he is in the ship."—*Phil. Trans.*, vol. xxiii. No. 227, p. 1051.

exploit of capturing a whole herd: when from thirty to one hundred wild elephants are entrapped in one vast decoy. The mode of effecting this, as it is practised in Ceylon, is no doubt imitated, but with considerable modifications, from the methods prevalent in various parts of India. It was introduced by the Portuguese, and continued by the Dutch, the latter of whom had two elephant hunts in each year, and conducted their operations on so large a scale, that the annual export, after supplying the government establishments, was from one hundred to one hundred and fifty elephants, taken principally in the vicinity of Matura, in the southern province, and marched for shipment to Manaar.[1]

The custom in Bengal is to construct a strong enclosure (called a *keddah*), in the heart of the forest, formed of the trunks of trees firmly secured by transverse beams and buttresses, and leaving the gate for the entrance of the elephants. A second enclosure, opening from the first, contains water (if possible a rivulet); this, again, communicates with a third, which terminates in a funnel-shaped passage, too narrow to admit of an elephant turning, and within this the captives being driven in line, are secured with ropes introduced from the outside, and led away in custody of tame ones trained for the purpose.

The *keddah* being prepared, the first operation is to drive the elephants towards it, for which purpose vast bodies of men fetch a compass in the forest around the haunts of the herds, contracting it by degrees, till they complete the enclosure of a certain area, round

[1] VALENTYN, *Oud en Nieuw Oost-Indien*, ch. xv. p. 272.

which they kindle fires, and cut footpaths through the jungle, to enable the watchers to communicate and combine. All this is performed in cautious silence and by slow approaches, to avoid alarming the herd. A fresh circle nearer to the *keddah* is then formed in the same way, and into this the elephants are admitted from the first one, the hunters following from behind, and lighting new fires around the newly inclosed space. Day after day the process is repeated; till the drove having been brought sufficiently close to make the final rush, the whole party close in from all sides, and with drums, guns, shouts, and flambeaux, force the terrified animals to enter the fatal enclosure, when the passage is barred behind them, and retreat rendered impossible.

Their efforts to escape are repressed by the crowd, who drive them back from the stockade with spears and flaming torches; and at last compel them to pass on into the second enclosure. Here they are detained for a short time, and their feverish exhaustion relieved by free access to water; — until at last, being tempted by food, or otherwise induced to trust themselves in the narrow outlet, they are one after another made fast by ropes, passed in through the palisade; and picketed in the adjoining woods to enter on their course of systematic training.

These arrangements vary in different districts of Bengal; and the method adopted in Ceylon differs in many essential particulars from them all; the Keddah, or, as it is here called, the corral or *korahl* [1] (from the

[1] It is thus spelled by WOLF, in his *Life and Adventures*, p. 144. *Corral* is at the present day a household word in South America, and especially in La Plata, to designate an *enclosure for cattle.*

Portuguese *curral*, a "cattle-pen"), consists of but one enclosure instead of three. A stream or watering-place is not uniformly enclosed within it, because, although water is indispensable after the long thirst and exhaustion of the captives, it has been found that a pond or rivulet within the corral itself adds to the difficulty of leading them out, and increases their reluctance to leave it; besides which, the smaller ones are often smothered by the others in their eagerness to crowd into the water. The funnel-shaped outlet is also dispensed with, as the animals are liable to bruise and injure themselves within the narrow stockade; and should one of them die in it, as is too often the case in the midst of the struggle, the difficulty of removing so great a carcase is extreme. The noosing and securing them, therefore, takes place in Ceylon within the area of the first enclosure into which they enter, and the dexterity and daring displayed in this portion of the work far surpasses that of merely attaching the rope through the openings of the paling, as in an Indian keddah.

One result of this change in the system is manifested in the increased proportion of healthy elephants which are eventually secured and trained out of the number originally enclosed. The reason of this is obvious: under the old arrangements, months were consumed in the preparatory steps of surrounding and driving in the herds, which at last arrived so wasted by excitement and exhausted by privation that numbers died within the corral itself, and still more died during the process of training. But in later years the labour of months is reduced to weeks, and the elephants are driven in fresh and full of vigour, so that comparatively few are lost either in the enclosure or the stables. A conception of the whole operation from commencement to end will be best conveyed by describing the progress of an elephant corral as I witnessed it in 1847 in the great forest on the banks of the Alligator River, the Kimbul-oya, in the district of Kornegalle, about thirty miles north-west of Kandy.

Kornegalle, or Kurunai-galle, was one of the ancient capitals of the island, and the residence of its kings from A.D. 1319 to 1347.[1] The dwelling-house of the principal civil officer in charge of the district now occupies the site of the former palace, and the ground is strewn with fragments of columns and carved stones, the remnants of the royal buildings. The modern town consists of the bungalows of the European officials, each surrounded with its own garden; two or three streets inhabited by Dutch descendants and by Moors; and a native bazaar, with the ordinary array of rice and curry stuffs and cooking chattees of brass or burnt clay.

The charm of the village is the unusual beauty of its position. It rests within the shade of an enormous rock of gneiss upwards of 600 feet in height, nearly denuded of verdure, and so rounded and worn by time that it has acquired the form of a couchant elephant, from which it derives its name of Aetagalla, the Rock of the Tusker.[2] But Aetagalla is only the last eminence in a range of similarly-formed rocky mountains, which here terminate abruptly; and, which from the fantastic shapes into which their gigantic outlines have been

[1] See SIR J. EMERSON TENNENT'S *Ceylon*, Vol. I. Pt. III. ch. xii. p. 415.

[2] Another enormous mass of gneiss is called the Kuruminia-galla, or the Beetle-rock, from its resemblance in shape to the back of that insect, and hence is said to have been derived the name of the town, *Kuruna-galle* or Kornegalle.

wrought by the action of the atmosphere, are called by the names of the Tortoise Rock, the Eel Roçk, and the Rock of the Tusked Elephant. So impressed are the Singhalese by the aspect of these stupendous masses that in ancient grants lands are conveyed in perpetuity, or "so long as the sun and the moon, so long as Aetagalla and Andagalla shall endure."[1]

Kornegalle is the resort of Buddhists from the remotest parts of the island, who come to visit an ancient temple on the summit of the great rock, to which access is had from the valley below by means of steep paths and steps hewn out of the solid stone. Here the chief object of veneration is a copy of the sacred footstep hollowed in the granite, similar to that which confers sanctity on Adam's Peak, the towering apex of which, about forty miles distant, the pilgrims can discern from Aetagalla.

At times the heat at Kornegalle is intense, in consequence of the perpetual glow diffused from these granite cliffs. The warmth they acquire during the blaze of noon becomes almost intolerable towards evening, and the sultry night is too short to permit them to cool between the setting and the rising of the sun. The district is also liable to occasional droughts when the watercourses fail, and the tanks are dried up. One of these calamities occurred about the period of my visit, and such was the suffering of the wild animals that numbers of crocodiles and bears made their way

[1] FORBES quotes a Tamil conveyance of land, the purchaser of which is to "possess and enjoy it as long as the sun and the moon, the earth and its vegetables, the mountains and the River Cauvery exist."—*Oriental Memoirs*, vol. ii. chap. ii. It will not fail to be observed, that the same figure was employed in Hebrew literature as a type of duration—"They shall fear thee, *so long as the sun and moon endure*; throughout all generations."—Psalm lxxii. 5, 17.

into the town to drink at the wells. The soil is prolific in the extreme; rice, cotton, and dry grain are cultivated largely in the valley. Every cottage is surrounded by gardens of coco-nuts, arecas, jak-fruit and coffee; the slopes, under tillage, are covered with luxuriant vegetation, and, as far as the eye can reach on every side, there are dense forests intersected by streams, in the shade of which the deer and the elephant abound.

In 1847 arrangements were made for one of the great elephant hunts for the supply of the Civil Engineer's Department, and the spot fixed on by Mr. Morris, the Government officer who conducted the corral, was on the banks of the Kimbul river, about fifteen miles from Kornegalle. The country over which we rode to the scene of the approaching capture showed traces of the recent drought, the fields lay to a great extent untilled, owing to the want of water, and the tanks, almost reduced to dryness, were covered with the leaves of the rose-coloured lotus.

Our cavalcade was as oriental as the scenery through which it moved; the Governor and the officers of his staff and household formed a long cortége, escorted by the native attendants, horse-keepers, and foot-runners. The ladies were borne in palankins, and the younger individuals of the party carried in chairs raised on poles, and covered with cool green awnings made of the fresh leaves of the talipat palm.

After traversing the cultivated lands, the path led across open glades of park-like verdure and beauty, and at last entered the great forest under the shade of ancient trees wreathed to their crowns with climbing plants and festooned by natural garlands of convolvulus and orchids. Here silence reigned, disturbed only by the murmuring hum of glittering insects, or the shrill clamour of the plum-headed parroquet and the flute-like calls of the golden oriole.

We crossed the broad sandy beds of two rivers over-arched by tall trees, the most conspicuous of which is the Kombook [1], from the calcined bark of which the natives extract a species of lime to be used with their betel. And from the branches hung suspended over the water the gigantic pods of the huge puswael bean [2], the sheath of which measures six feet long by five or six inches broad.

On ascending the steep bank of the second stream, we found ourselves in front of the residences which had been extemporised for our party in the immediate vicinity of the corral. These cool and enjoyable structures were formed of branches and thatched with palm leaves and fragrant lemon grass; and in addition to a dining-room and suites of bedrooms fitted with tent furniture, they included kitchens, stables, and store-rooms, all run up by the natives in the course of a few days.

In former times, the work connected with these elephant hunts was performed by the "forced labour" of the natives, as part of that feudal service which under the name of Raja-kariya was extorted from the Singhalese during the rule of their native sovereigns. This system was continued by the Portuguese and Dutch, and prevailed under the British Government till its abolition by the Earl of Ripon in 1832. Under it from fifteen hundred to two thousand men superintended by their headmen, used to be occupied, in constructing the

[1] *Pentaptera paniculata.* [2] *Entada pursætha.*

corral, collecting the elephants, maintaining the cordon of watch-fires and watchers, and conducting all the laborious operations of the capture. Since the abolition of Raja-kariya, however, no difficulty has been found in obtaining the voluntary co-operation of the natives on these exciting occasions. The government defrays the expense of that portion of the preparations which involves actual cost, — for the skilled labour expended in the erection of the corral and its appurtenances, and the providing of spears, ropes, arms, flutes, drums, gunpowder, and other necessaries for the occasion.

The period of the year selected is that which least interferes with the cultivation of the rice-lands (in the interval between seed time and harvest), and the people themselves, in addition to the excitement and enjoyment of the sport, have a personal interest in reducing the number of elephants, which inflict serious injury on their gardens and growing crops. For a similar reason the priests encourage the practice, because the elephants destroy their sacred Bo-trees, of the leaves of which they are passionately fond; besides which it promotes the facility for obtaining elephants for the processions of the temples: and the Rata-mahat-mayas and headmen have a pride in exhibiting the number of retainers who follow them to the field, and the performances of the tame elephants which they lend for the business of the corral. Thus vast numbers of the peasantry are voluntarily occupied for many weeks in putting up the stockades, cutting paths through the jungle, and relieving the beaters who are engaged in surrounding and driving in the elephants.

In selecting the scene for the hunt a position is chosen which lies on some old and frequented route of the animals, in their periodical migrations in search of forage and water; and the vicinity of a stream is indispensable, not only for the supply of the elephants during the time spent in inducing them to approach the enclosure, but to enable them to bathe and cool themselves throughout the process of training after capture.

In constructing the corral itself, care is taken to avoid disturbing the trees or the brushwood within the included space, and especially on the side by which the elephants are to approach, where it is essential to conceal the stockade as much as possible by the density of the foliage. The trees used in the structure are from ten to twelve inches in diameter; and are sunk about three feet in the earth, so as to leave a length of from twelve to fifteen feet above ground; with spaces between each stanchion sufficiently wide to permit a man to glide through. The uprights are made fast by transverse beams, to which they are lashed securely by ratans and

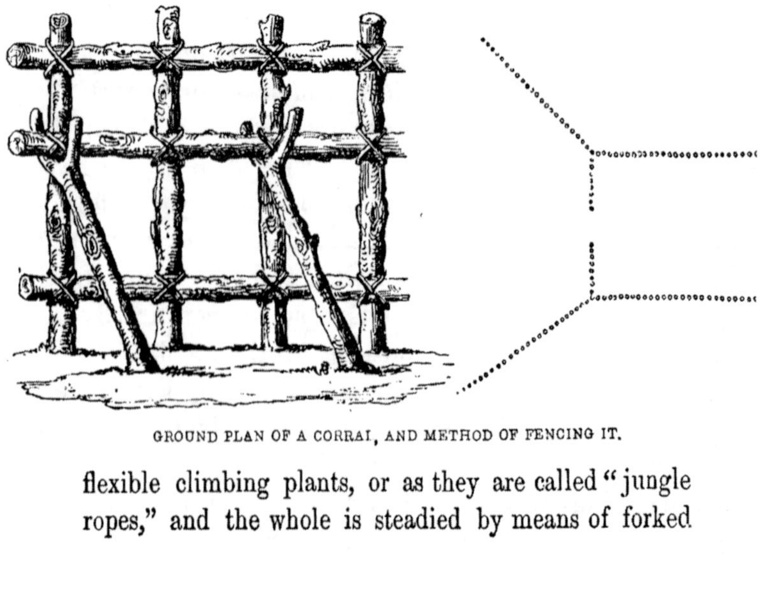

GROUND PLAN OF A CORRAL, AND METHOD OF FENCING IT.

flexible climbing plants, or as they are called "jungle ropes," and the whole is steadied by means of forked supports, which grasp the tie beams, and prevent the work from being driven outward by the rush of the wild elephants.

On the occasion I am now attempting to describe, the space thus enclosed was about 500 feet in length by 250 wide. At one end an entrance was left open, fitted with sliding bars, so prepared as to be capable of being instantly shut; — and from each angle of the end by which the elephants were to approach, two lines of the same strong fencing were continued, and cautiously concealed by the trees; so that if, instead of entering by the open passage, the herd should swerve to right, or left, they would find themselves suddenly stopped and forced to retrace their course to the gate.

The preparations were completed by placing a stage for the Governor's party on a group of the nearest trees looking down into the enclosure, so that a view could be had of the entire proceeding, from the entrance of the herd, to the leading out of the captive elephants.

It is hardly necessary to observe that the structure here described, massive as it is, would be entirely ineffectual to resist the shock, if assaulted by the full force of an enraged elephant; and accidents have sometimes happened by the breaking through of the herd; but reliance is placed not so much on the resistance of the stockade as on the timidity of the captives and their unconsciousness of their own strength, coupled with the daring of their captors and their devices for ensuring submission.

The corral being prepared, the beaters address themselves to drive in the elephants. For this purpose it is often necessary to fetch a circuit of many miles in order to surround a sufficient number, and the caution to be observed involves patience and delay; as it is essential to avoid alarming the elephants, which might otherwise escape. Their disposition being essentially peaceful, and their only impulse to browse in solitude and security, they withdraw instinctively before the slightest intrusion, and advantage is taken of this timidity and love of seclusion to cause only just such an amount of disturbance as will induce them to return slowly in the direction which it is desired they should take. Several herds are by this means concentrated within such an area as will admit of their being completely surrounded by the watchers; and day after day, by degrees, they are moved gradually onwards to the immediate confines of the corral. When their suspicions become awakened and they exhibit restlessness and alarm, bolder measures are adopted for preventing their escape. Fires are kept burning at ten paces apart, night and day, along the circumference of the area within which they are detained; a corps of from two to three thousand beaters is completed, and pathways are carefully cleared through the jungle so as to keep open a communication along the entire circuit. The headmen keep up a constant patrol, to see that their followers are alert at their posts, since neglect at any one spot might permit the escape of the herd, and undo in a moment the vigilance of weeks. By this means any attempt of the elephants to break away is generally checked, and on any point threatened a sufficient force can be promptly assembled to drive them back. At last the elephants are forced onwards so close to the enclosure, that the investing cordon is united at either end with the wings of the corral, the whole forming a circle of about two miles, within the area of which the herd is detained to await the signal for the final drive.

Two months had been spent in these preliminaries, and the preparations had been thus far completed, on the day when we arrived and took our places on the stage erected for us, overlooking the entrance to the corral. Close beneath us a group of tame elephants sent by the temples and the chiefs to assist in securing the wild ones, were picketed in the shade, and lazily fanning themselves with leaves. Three distinct herds, whose united numbers were variously represented at from forty to fifty elephants, were enclosed, and were at that moment concealed in the jungle within a short distance of the stockade. Not a sound was permitted to be made, each person spoke to his neighbour in whispers, and such was the silence observed by the multitude of the watchers at their posts, that occasionally we could hear the rustling of the branches as some of the elephants stripped off a leaf.

Suddenly the signal was made, and the stillness of the forest was broken by the shouts of the guard, the rolling of the drums and tom-toms, and the discharge of muskets; and beginning at the most distant side of the area, the elephants were urged forward at a rapid pace towards the entrance into the corral.

The watchers along the line kept silence only till the herd had passed them, and then joining the cry in their rear they drove them onward with redoubled shouts and noises. The tumult increased as the terrified rout drew near, swelling now on one side now on the other, as the herd in their panic dashed from point to point in their endeavours to force the line, but they were instantly driven back by screams, muskets, and drums.

At length the breaking of the branches and the crackling of the brushwood announced their close approach, and the leader bursting from the jungle rushed wildly forward to within twenty yards of the entrance followed by the rest of the herd. Another moment and they would have plunged into the open gate, when suddenly they wheeled round, re-entered the forest, and in spite of the hunters resumed their original position. The chief headman came forward and accounted for the freak by saying that a wild pig[1], an animal which the elephants are said to dislike, had started out of the cover and run across the leader, who would otherwise have held on direct for the corral; and intimated that as the herd was now in the highest pitch of excitement; and it was at all times much more difficult to effect a successful capture by daylight than by night when the fires and flambeaux act with double effect, it was the wish of the hunters to defer their final effort till the evening, when the darkness would greatly aid their exertions.

After sunset the scene exhibited was of extraordinary interest; the low fires, which had apparently only smouldered in the sunlight, assumed their ruddy glow amidst the darkness, and threw their tinge over the groups collected round them; while the smoke rose in eddies through the rich foliage of the trees. The crowds of spectators maintained a profound silence, and not a sound was perceptible beyond the hum of an insect. On a sudden the stillness was broken by the distant roll of a drum, fol-

[1] Fire, the sound of a horn, and the grunting of a boar are the three things which the Greeks, in the middle ages, believed the elephant specially to dislike:

Πῦρ δὲ πτοεῖται καὶ κριὸν κερασφόρον,
Καὶ τῶν μονιῶν τὴν βοὴν τὴν ἀθρόαν.

—PHILE, *Expositio de Elephante*, l. 177.

lowed by a discharge of musketry. This was the signal for the renewed assault, and the hunters entered the circle with shouts and clamour; dry leaves and sticks were flung upon the watch-fires till they blazed aloft, and formed a line of flame on every side, except in the direction of the corral, which was studiously kept dark; and thither the terrified elephants betook themselves, followed by the yells and racket of their pursuers.

The elephants approached at a rapid pace, trampling down the brushwood and crushing the dry branches; the leader emerged in front of the corral, paused for an instant, stared wildly round, and then rushed headlong through the open gate, followed by the rest of the herd. Instantly, as if by magic, the entire circuit of the corral, which up to this moment had been kept in profound darkness, blazed with thousands of lights, every hunter on the instant that the elephants entered, rushing forward to the stockade with a torch kindled at the nearest watch-fire.

The elephants first dashed to the very extremity of the enclosure, and being brought up by the fence, retreated to regain the gate, but found it closed. Their terror was sublime: they hurried round the corral at a rapid pace, but saw it now girt by fire on every side; they attempted to force the stockade, but were driven back by the guards with spears and flambeaux; and on whichever side they approached they were repulsed with shouts and volleys of musketry. Collecting into one group, they would pause for a moment in apparent bewilderment, then burst off in another direction, as if it had suddenly occurred to them to try some point which they had before overlooked; but again baffled, they slowly returned to their forlorn resting-place in the centre of the corral.

The attraction of this strange scene was not confined to the spectators; it extended to the tame elephants which were stationed outside. At the first approach of the flying herd they evinced the utmost interest. Two in particular which were picketed near the front were intensely excited, and continued tossing their heads, pawing the ground, and starting as the noise drew near. At length, when the grand rush into the corral took place, one of them fairly burst from her fastenings and rushed towards the herd, levelling a tree of considerable size which obstructed her passage.[1]

For upwards of an hour the elephants continued to traverse the corral and assail the palisade with unabated energy, trumpeting and screaming with rage after each disappointment. Again and again they attempted to force the gate, as if aware, by experience, that it ought to afford an exit as it had already served as an entrance, but they shrank back stunned and bewildered. By degrees their efforts became less and less frequent. Single ones rushed excitedly here and there, returning sullenly to their companions after each effort; and at last the whole herd, stupified and exhausted, formed themselves into a single group, drawn up in a circle with the young

[1] The other elephant, a fine tusker, which belonged to Dehigam Ratamahatmeya, continued in extreme excitement throughout all the subsequent operations of the capture, and at last, after attempting to break its way into the corral, shaking the bars with its forehead and tusks, it went off in a state of frenzy into the jungle. A few days after the Aratchy went in search of it with a female decoy, and watching its approach, sprang fairly on the infuriated beast, with a pair of sharp hooks in his hands, which he pressed into tender parts in front of the shoulder, and thus held the elephant firmly till chains were passed over its legs, and it permitted itself to be led quietly away.

in the centre, and stood motionless under the dark shade of the trees in the middle of the corral.

Preparations were now made to keep watch during the night, the guard was reinforced around the enclosure, and wood heaped on the fires to keep up a high flame till sunrise.

Three herds had been originally entrapped by the beaters outside; but with characteristic instinct they had each kept clear of the other, taking up different stations in the space invested by the watchers. When the final drive took place one herd only had entered the enclosure, the other two keeping behind; and as the gate had to be instantly shut on the first division, the last were unavoidably excluded and remained concealed in the jungle. To prevent their escape, the watchers were ordered to their former stations, the fires were replenished; and all precautions having been taken, we returned to pass the night in our bungalows by the river.

# CHAP. VI.

## THE ELEPHANT.

### *The Captives.*

As our sleeping-place was not above two hundred yards from the corral, we were frequently awakened by the din of the multitude who were bivouacking in the forest, by the merriment round the watch-fires, and now and then by the shouts with which the guards repulsed some sudden charge of the elephants in attempts to force the stockade. But at daybreak, on going down to the corral, we found all still and vigilant. The fires were allowed to die out as the sun rose, and the watchers who had been relieved were sleeping near the great fence, the enclosure on all sides being surrounded by crowds of men and boys with spears or white peeled wands about ten feet long, whilst the elephants within were huddled together in a compact group, no longer turbulent and restless, but exhausted and calm, and utterly subdued by apprehension and amazement at all that had been passing around them.

Nine only had been as yet entrapped[1], of which

[1] In some of the elephant hunts conducted in the southern provinces of Ceylon by the earlier British Governors, as many as 170 and 200 elephants were secured in a single corral, of which a portion only were taken out for the public service, and the rest shot, the motive being to rid the neighbourhood of them, and thus protect the crops from destruction. In the present instance, the object being to secure only as many as were required for the Government stud, it was not sought to entrap more than could conveniently be attended to and trained after capture.

three were very large, and two were little creatures but a few months old. One of the large ones was a "rogue," and being unassociated with the rest of the herd, he was not admitted to their circle, although permitted to stand near them.

Meanwhile, preparations were making outside to conduct the tame elephants into the corral, in order to secure the captives. Noosed ropes were in readiness; and far apart from all stood a party of the out-caste Rodiyas, the only tribe who will touch a dead carcase, to whom, therefore, the duty is assigned of preparing the fine flexible rope for noosing, which is made from the fresh hides of the deer and the buffalo.

At length, the bars which secured the entrance to the corral were cautiously withdrawn, and two trained elephants passed stealthily in, each ridden by its mahout (or *ponnekella*, as the keeper is termed in Ceylon), and one attendant; and, carrying a strong collar, formed by coils of rope made from coco-nut fibre, from which hung on either side cords of elk's hide, prepared with a ready noose. Along with these, and concealed behind them, the headman of the "*cooroowe*," or noosers, crept in, eager to secure the honour of taking the first elephant, a distinction which this class jealously contests with the mahouts of the chiefs and temples. He was a wiry little man, nearly seventy years old, who had served in the same capacity under the Kandyan king, and wore two silver bangles, which had been conferred on him in testimony of his prowess. He was accompanied by his son, named Ranghanie, equally renowned for his courage and dexterity.

On this occasion ten tame elephants were in attendance; two were the property of an adjoining temple (one of which had been caught but the year before, yet it was now ready to assist in capturing others), four belonged to the neighbouring chiefs, and the rest, including the two which first entered the corral, were part of the Government stud. Of the latter, one was of prodigious age, having been in the service of the Dutch and English Governments in succession for upwards of a century.[1] The other, called by her keeper "Siribeddi," was about fifty years old, and distinguished for gentleness and docility. She was a most accomplished decoy, and evinced the utmost relish for the sport. Having entered the corral noiselessly, carrying a mahout on her shoulders with the headman of the noosers seated behind him, she moved slowly along with a sly composure and an assumed air of easy indifference; sauntering leisurely in the direction of the captives, and halting now and then to pluck a bunch of grass or a few leaves as she passed. As she approached the herd, they put themselves in motion to meet her, and the leader, having advanced in front and passed his trunk gently over her head, turned and paced slowly back to his dejected companions. Siribeddi followed with the same listless step, and drew herself up close behind him, thus affording the nooser an opportunity to stoop under her and slip the noose over the hind foot of the wild one. The latter instantly perceived his danger, shook off the rope, and turned to attack the man. He would have suffered for his temerity had not Siribeddi protected him by raising her trunk and driving the assailant into the midst of the herd, when the old man, being slightly

[1] This elephant is since dead; she grew infirm and diseased, and died at Colombo in 1848. Her skeleton is now in the Museum of the Natural History Society at Belfast.

wounded, was helped out of the corral, and his son, Ranghanie, took his place.

The herd again collected in a circle, with their heads towards the centre. The largest male was singled out, and two tame ones pushed boldly in, one on either side of him, till the three stood nearly abreast. He made no resistance, but betrayed his uneasiness by shifting restlessly from foot to foot. Ranghanie now crept up, and, holding the rope open with both hands (its other extremity being made fast to Siribeddi's collar), and watching the instant when the wild elephant lifted its hind-foot, succeeded in passing the noose over its leg, drew it close, and fled to the rear. The two tame elephants instantly fell back, Siribeddi stretched the rope to its full length, and, whilst she dragged out the captive, her companion placed himself between her and the herd to prevent any interference.

In order to tie him to a tree he had to be drawn backwards some twenty or thirty yards, making furious resistance, bellowing in terror, plunging on all sides, and crushing the smaller timber, which bent like reeds beneath his clumsy struggles. Siribeddi drew him steadily after her, and wound the rope round the proper tree, holding it all the time at its full tension, and stepping cautiously across it when, in order to give it a second turn, it was necessary to pass between the tree and the elephant. With a coil round the stem, however, it was beyond her strength to haul the prisoner close up, which was, nevertheless, necessary in order to make him perfectly fast; but the second tame one, perceiving the difficulty, returned from the herd, confronted the struggling prisoner, pushed him shoulder to shoulder, and head to head, forcing him backwards, whilst at every step Siribeddi hauled in the slackened rope till she brought him fairly up to the foot of the tree, where he was made fast by the cooroowe people. A second noose was then passed over the other hind-leg, and secured like the first, both legs being afterwards hobbled together by ropes made from the fibre of the kitool or jaggery palm, which, being more flexible than that of the coco-nut, occasions less formidable ulcerations. The two decoys then ranged themselves, as before, abreast of

the prisoner on either side, thus enabling Ranghanie to stoop under them and noose the two fore-feet as he had already done the hind; and these ropes being made fast to a tree in front, the capture was complete, and the tame elephants and keepers withdrew to repeat the operation on another of the herd.

As long as the tame ones stood beside him the poor animal remained comparatively calm and almost passive under his distress, but the moment they moved off, and he was left utterly alone, he made the most surprising efforts to set himself free and rejoin his companions. He felt the ropes with his trunk and tried to untie the numerous knots; he drew backwards to liberate his fore-legs, then leaned forward to extricate the hind ones, till every branch of the tall tree vibrated with his struggles. He screamed in anguish, with his

proboscis raised high in the air, then falling on his side he laid his head to the ground, first his cheek and then his brow, and pressed down his doubled-in trunk as though he would force it into the earth; then suddenly rising he balanced himself on his forehead and fore-legs, holding his hind-feet fairly off the ground. This scene of distress continued some hours, with occasional pauses of apparent stupor, after which the struggle was from time to time renewed convulsively, and as if by some sudden impulse; but at last the vain strife subsided, and the poor animal remained perfectly motionless, the image of exhaustion and despair.

Meanwhile Ranghanie presented himself in front of the governor's stage to claim the accustomed largesse for tying the first elephant. He was rewarded by a shower of rupees, and retired to resume his perilous duties in the corral.

The rest of the herd were now in a state of pitiable dejection, and pressed closely together as if under a sense of common misfortune. For the most part they stood at rest in a compact body, fretful and uneasy. At intervals one more impatient than the rest would move out a few steps to reconnoitre; the others would follow at first slowly, then at a quicker pace, and at last the whole herd would rush off furiously to renew the often-baffled attempt to storm the stockade.

There was a strange combination of the sublime and the ridiculous in these abortive onsets; the appearance of prodigious power in their ponderous limbs, coupled with the almost ludicrous shuffle of their clumsy gait, and the fury of their apparently resistless charge, converted in an instant into timid retreat. They rushed madly down the enclosure, their backs arched, their tails extended, their ears spread, and their trunks raised high above their heads, trumpeting and uttering shrill screams, yet when one step further would have dashed the opposing fence into fragments, they stopped short on a few white rods being pointed at them through the paling[1]; and, on catching the derisive shouts of the

[1] The fact of the elephant exhibiting timidity, on having a long rod pointed towards him, was known to the Romans; and PLINY, quoting from the annals of PISO, relates, that in order to inculcate contempt for want of courage in the elephant, they were introduced into the circus during the triumph of METELLUS, after the conquest of

crowd, they turned in utter discomfiture, and after an objectless circle or two through the corral, they paced slowly back to their melancholy halting place in the shade.

The crowd, chiefly comprised of young men and boys, exhibited astonishing nerve and composure at such moments, rushing up to the point towards which the elephants charged, pointing their wands at their trunks, and keeping up the continual cry of *whoop! whoop!* which invariably turned them to flight.

The second victim singled out from the herd was secured in the same manner as the first. It was a female. The tame ones forced themselves in on either side as before, cutting her off from her companions, whilst Ranghanie stooped under them and attached the fatal noose, and Siribeddi dragged her out amidst unavailing struggles, when she was made fast by each leg to the nearest group of strong trees. When the noose was placed upon her fore-foot, she seized it with her trunk, and succeeded in carrying it to her mouth, where she would speedily have severed it had not a tame elephant interfered, and placing his foot on the rope pressed it downwards out of her jaws. The individuals who acted as leaders in the successive charges on the palisades were always those selected by the noosers, and the operation of tying each, from the first approaches of the decoys, till the captive was left alone by the tree, occupied on an average somewhat less than three-quarters of an hour.

It is strange that in these encounters the wild ele-

the Carthaginians in Sicily, and *driven round the area by workmen holding blunted spears*, — "Ab operariis hastas præpilatas habentibus, per circum totam actos."—Lib. viii. c. 6.

phants made no attempt to attack or dislodge the mahouts or the cooroowes, who rode on the tame ones. They moved in the very midst of the herd, any individual in which could in a moment have pulled the riders from their seats; but no effort was made to molest them.[1]

As one after another their leaders were entrapped and forced away from them, the remainder of the group

[1] "In a corral, to be on a tame elephant, seems to insure perfect immunity from the attacks of the wild ones. I once saw the old chief Mollegodde ride in amongst a herd of wild elephants, on a small elephant; so small that the Adigar's head was on a level with the back of the wild animals: I felt very nervous, but he rode right in among them, and received not the slightest molestation."—*Letter from* MAJOR SKINNER.

evinced increased emotion and excitement; but whatever may have been their sympathy for their lost companions, their alarm seemed to prevent them at first from following them to the trees to which they had been tied. In passing them afterwards they sometimes stopped, mutually entwined their trunks, lapped them round each other's limbs and neck, and exhibited the most touching distress at their detention, but made no attempt to disturb the cords that bound them.

The variety of disposition in the herd as evidenced by difference of demeanour was very remarkable: some submitted with comparatively little resistance; whilst others in their fury dashed themselves on the ground with a force sufficient to destroy any weaker animal. They vented their rage upon every tree and plant within reach; if small enough to be torn down, they levelled them with their trunks, and stripping them of their leaves and branches, they tossed them wildly over their heads on all sides. Some in their struggles made no sound, whilst others bellowed and trumpeted furiously, then uttered short convulsive screams, and at last, exhausted and hopeless, gave vent to their anguish in low and piteous moanings. Some, after a few violent efforts of this kind, lay motionless on the ground, with no other indication of suffering than the tears which suffused their eyes and flowed incessantly. Others in all the vigour of their rage exhibited the most surprising contortions; and to us who had been accustomed to associate with the unwieldy bulk of the elephant the idea that he must of necessity be stiff and inflexible, the attitudes into which they forced themselves were almost incredible. I saw one lie with the cheek pressed to the earth, and the fore-legs stretched in front, whilst the body was twisted round till the hind-legs extended in the opposite direction.

It was astonishing that their trunks were not wounded by the violence with which they flung them on all sides. One twisted his proboscis into such fantastic shapes, that it resembled the writhings of a gigantic worm; he coiled it and uncoiled it with restless rapidity, curling it up like a watch-spring, and suddenly unfolding it again to its full length. Another, which lay otherwise motionless in all the stupor of hopeless anguish, slowly beat the ground with the extremity of his trunk, as a man in despair beats his knee with the palm of his hand.

They displayed an amount of sensitiveness and delicacy of touch in the foot, which was very remarkable in a limb of such clumsy dimensions and protected by so thick a covering. The noosers could always force them to lift it from the ground by the gentlest touch of a leaf or twig, apparently applied so as to tickle; but the imposition of the rope was instantaneously perceived, and if it could not be reached by the trunk the other foot was applied to feel its position, and if possible remove it before the noose could be drawn tight.

One practice was incessant with almost the entire herd: in the interval between their struggles they beat the ground with their fore feet, and taking up the dry earth in a coil of the trunk, they flung it dexterously over every part of their body. Even when lying down, the sand within reach was thus collected and scattered over their limbs: then inserting the extremity of the trunk in their mouths, they withdrew a quantity of water, which they discharged over their backs, repeating the operation again and again, till the dust was thoroughly saturated. I was astonished at the quantity of water thus applied, which was sufficient when the elephant, as was generally the case, had worked the spot where he lay into a hollow, to convert its surface into a coating of mud. Seeing that the herd had been now twenty-four hours without access to water of any kind, surrounded by watch-fires, and exhausted by struggling and terror, the supply of moisture an elephant is capable of containing in the receptacle attached to his stomach must be very considerable.

The conduct of the tame ones during all these proceedings was truly wonderful. They displayed the most perfect conception of every movement, both of the object to be attained, and of the means to accomplish it.

They manifested the utmost enjoyment in what was going on. There was no ill-humour, no malignity in the spirit displayed, in what was otherwise a heartless proceeding, but they set about it in a way that showed a thorough relish for it, as an agreeable pastime. Their caution was as remarkable as their sagacity; there was no hurrying, no confusion, they never ran foul of the ropes, were never in the way of the animals already noosed; and amidst the most violent struggles, when the tame ones had frequently to step across the captives, they in no instance trampled on them, or occasioned the slightest accident or annoyance. So far from this, they saw intuitively a difficulty or a danger, and addressed themselves unbidden to remove it. In tying up one of the larger elephants, he contrived before he could be hauled close up to the tree, to walk once or twice round it, carrying the rope with him; the decoy, perceiving the advantage he had thus gained over the nooser, walked up of her own accord, and pushed him backwards with her head, till she made him unwind himself again; upon which the rope was hauled tight and made fast More than once, when a wild one was extending his trunk, and would have intercepted the rope about to be placed over his leg, Siribeddi, by a sudden motion of her own trunk, pushed his aside, and prevented him; and on one occasion, when successive efforts had failed to put the noose over the fore-leg of an elephant which was already secured by one foot, but which wisely put the other to the ground as often as it was attempted to pass the noose under it, I saw the decoy watch her opportunity, and when his foot was again raised, suddenly push in her own leg beneath it, and hold it up till the noose was attached and drawn tight.

One could almost fancy there was a display of dry humour in the manner in which the decoys thus played with the fears of the wild herd, and made light of their efforts at resistance. When reluctant they shoved them forward, when violent they drove them back; when the wild ones threw themselves down, the tame ones butted them with head and shoulders, and forced them up again. And when it was necessary to keep them down, they knelt upon them, and prevented them from rising, till the ropes were secured.

At every moment of leisure they fanned themselves with a bunch of leaves, and the graceful ease with which an elephant uses his trunk on such occasions is very striking. It is doubtless owing to the combination of a circular with a horizontal movement in that flexible limb; but it is impossible to see an elephant fanning himself without being struck by the singular elegance of motion which he displays. The tame ones, too, indulged in the luxury of dusting themselves with sand, by flinging it from their trunks; but it was a curious illustration of their delicate sagacity, that so long as the mahout was on their necks, they confined themselves to flinging the dust along their sides and stomach, as if aware, that to throw it over their heads and back would cause annoyance to their riders.

One of the decoys which rendered good service, and was obviously held in special awe by the wild herd, was a tusker belonging to Dehigame Rata-mahatmeya. It was not that he used his tusks for purposes of offence, but he was enabled to insinuate himself between two elephants by wedging them in where he could not force his head; besides which they assisted him in raising up the fallen and refractory with greater ease. In some instances where the intervention of the other decoys failed to reduce a wild one to order, the mere presence and approach of the tusker seemed to inspire fear, and insure submission, without more active intervention.

I do not know whether it was the surprising qualities exhibited by the tame elephants that cast the courage and dexterity of the men into the shade, but even when supported by the presence, the sagacity, and co-operation of these wonderful creatures, the part sustained by the noosers can bear no comparison with the address and daring displayed by the *picador* and *matador* in a Spanish bull-fight. They certainly possessed great quickness of eye in watching the slightest movement of the elephant, and great expertness in flinging the noose over its foot and attaching it firmly before the animal could tear it off with its trunk; but in all this they had the cover of the decoys to conceal them; and their shelter behind which to retreat. Apart from the services which, from their prodigious strength, the tame elephants are alone capable of rendering, in dragging out and securing the captives, it is perfectly obvious that without their co-operation the utmost prowess and dexterity of the hunters would not avail them, unsupported, to enter the corral and ensnare and lead out a single captive.

Of the two tiny elephants which were entrapped, one was about ten months old, the other somewhat more. The smaller one had a little bolt head covered with woolly brown hair, and was the most amusing and interesting miniature imaginable. Both kept constantly with the herd, trotting after them in every charge; when the others stood at rest they ran in and out between the legs of the older ones; and not their own mothers alone, but every female in the group caressed them in turn.

The dam of the youngest was the second elephant singled out by the noosers, and as she was dragged along by the decoys, the little creature kept by her side till she was drawn close to the fatal tree. The men at first were rather amused than otherwise by its anger; but they found that it would not permit them to place the second noose upon its mother; it ran between her and them, it tried to seize the rope, it pushed them and struck them with its little trunk, till they were forced to drive it back to the herd. It retreated slowly, shouting all the way, and pausing at every step to look back. It then attached itself to the largest female remaining in the group, and placed itself across her forelegs, whilst she hung down her trunk over its side and soothed and caressed it. Here it continued moaning and lamenting, till the noosers had left off securing its mother, when it instantly returned to her side; but as it became troublesome again, attacking every one who passed, it was at last tied up by a rope to an adjoining tree, to which the other young one was also tied. The second little one, equally with its playmate, exhibited great affection for its dam; it went willingly with its captor as far as the tree to which she was fastened, and in passing her stretched out its trunk and tried to rejoin her; but finding itself forced along, it caught at every twig and branch within its reach, and screamed with grief and disappointment.

These two little creatures were the most vociferous of the whole herd, their shouts were incessant, they struggled to attack every one within reach; and as their bodies were more lithe and pliant than those of greater growth, their contortions were quite wonderful. The most amusing thing was, that in the midst of all their agony and affliction, the little fellows seized on every article of food that was thrown to them, and ate and roared simultaneously.

Amongst the last of the elephants noosed was the *rogue*. Though far more savage than the others, he joined in none of their charges and assaults on the fences, as they uniformly drove him off and would not permit him to enter their circle. When dragged past another of his companions in misfortune, who was lying exhausted on the ground, he flew upon him and attempted to fasten his teeth in his head; this was the only instance of viciousness which occurred during the progress of the corral. When tied up and overpowered, he was at first noisy and violent, but soon lay down peacefully, a sign, according to the hunters, that his death was at hand. Their prognostication was correct; he continued for about twelve hours to cover himself with dust like the others, and to moisten it with water from his trunk; but at length he lay exhausted, and died so calmly, that having been moving but a few moment before, his death was only perceived by the myriads of black flies by which his body was almost instantly covered, although not one was visible a moment before.[1] The Rodiyas were called

[1] The surprising faculty of vultures for discovering carrion, has been a subject of much speculation, as to whether it be dependent on their power of sight or of scent. It is not, however, more mysterious than the unerring certainty and rapidity with which some of the minor animals, and more especially insects, in warm climates congregate around the offal on which they feed. Circumstanced as they are, they must be guided towards their object mainly if not exclusively by the sense of smell; but that which excites astonishment is the small degree of odour which seems to suffice for the purpose; the subtlety and rapidity with which it traverses and impregnates the air; and the keen and quick perception with which it is taken up by the organs of those creatures. The instance of the scavenger beetles has been already alluded to; the promptitude with which they discern the existence of matter suited to their purposes, and the

in to loose the ropes that bound him, from the tree, and two tame elephants being harnessed to the dead body, it was dragged to a distance without the corral.

When every wild elephant had been noosed and tied up, the scene presented was truly oriental. From one to two thousand natives, many of them in gaudy dresses and armed with spears, crowded about the enclosures. Their

speed with which they hurry to it from all directions; often from distances as extraordinary, proportionably, as those traversed by the eye of the vulture. In the instance of the dying elephant referred to above, life was barely extinct when the flies, of which not one was visible but a moment before, arrived in clouds and blackened the body by their multitude; scarcely an instant was allowed to elapse for the commencement of decomposition; no odour of putrefaction could be discerned by us who stood close by; yet some peculiar smell of mortality, simultaneously with parting breath, must have summoned them to the feast. Ants exhibit an instinct equally surprising. I have sometimes covered up a particle of refined sugar with paper on the centre of a polished table; and counted the number of minutes which would elapse before it was fastened on by the small black ants of Ceylon, and a line formed to lower it safely to the floor. Here was a substance which, to our apprehension at least, is altogether inodorous, and yet the quick sense of smell must have been the only conductor of the ants. It has been observed of those fishes which travel overland on the evaporation of the ponds in which they live, that they invariably march in the direction of the nearest water, and even when captured, and placed on the floor of a room, their efforts to escape are always made towards the same point. Is the sense of smell sufficient to account for this display of instinct in them? or is it aided by special organs in the case of the others? Dr. Mc Gee, formerly of the Royal Navy, writing to me on the subject of the instant appearance of flies in the vicinity of dead bodies, says: "In warm climates they do not wait for death to invite them to the banquet. In Jamaica I have again and again seen them settle on a patient, and hardly to be driven away by the nurse, the patient himself saying, 'Here are these flies coming to eat me ere I am dead.' At times they have enabled the doctor, when otherwise he would have been in doubt as to his prognosis, to determine whether the strange apyretic interval occasionally present in the last stage of yellow fever was the fatal lull or the lull of recovery; and 'What say the flies?' has been the settling question. Among many, many cases during a long period I have seen but one recovery after the assembling of the flies. I consider the foregoing as a confirmation of smell being the guide even to the attendants, a cadaverous smell has been perceived to arise from the body of a patient twenty-four hours before death."

families had collected to see the spectacle; women, whose children clung like little bronzed Cupids by their sides; and girls, many of them in the graceful costume of that part of the country,—a scarf, which, after having been brought round the waist, is thrown over the left shoulder, leaving the right arm and side free and uncovered.

At the foot of each tree was its captive elephant; some still struggling and writhing in feverish excitement, whilst others, in exhaustion and despair, lay motionless, except that, from time to time, they heaped fresh dust upon their heads. The mellow notes of a Kandyan flute, which was played at a distance, had a striking effect upon one or more of them; they turned their heads in the direction from which the music came, expanded their broad ears, and were evidently soothed with the plaintive sound. The two young ones alone still roared for freedom; they stamped their feet, and blew clouds of dust over their shoulders, brandishing their little trunks aloft, and attacking every one who came within their reach.

At first the older ones, when secured, spurned every offer of food, trampled it under foot, and turned haughtily away. A few, however, as they became more composed, could not resist the temptation of the juicy stems of the plantain, but rolling them under foot, till they detached the layers, they raised them in their trunks, and commenced chewing listlessly.

On the whole, whilst the sagacity, the composure, and docility of the decoys were such as to excite lively astonishment, it was not possible to withhold the highest admiration from the calm and dignified demeanour of the captives. Their entire bearing was at variance with the representation made by some of the "sportsmen" who harass them, that they are treacherous, savage, and revengeful; when tormented by the guns of their persecutors, they, no doubt, display their powers and sagacity in efforts to retaliate or escape; but here their every movement was indicative of innocence and timidity. After a struggle, in which they evinced no disposition to violence or revenge, they submitted with the calmness of despair. Their attitudes were pitiable, their grief was most touching, and their low moaning went to the heart. We could not have borne to witness their distress had their capture been effected by the needless infliction of pain, or had they been destined to ill-treatment afterwards.

It was now about two hours after noon, and the first elephants that had entered the corral having been disposed of, preparations were made to reopen the gate, and drive in the other two herds, over which the watchers were still keeping guard. The area of the enclosure was cleared; and silence was again imposed on the crowds who surrounded the corral. The bars that secured the entrance were withdrawn, and every precaution repeated as before; but as the space inside was now somewhat trodden down, especially near the entrance, by the frequent charges of the last herd, and as it was to be apprehended that the others might be earlier alarmed and retrace their steps, before the barricades could be replaced, two tame ones were stationed inside to protect the men to whom that duty was assigned.

All preliminaries being at length completed, the signal was given; the beaters on the side most distant from the corral closed in with tom-toms and discordant noises; a hedge-fire of musketry was kept up in the rear of the terrified elephants; thousands of voices urged them forward; we heard the jungle crashing as they came on, and at last they advanced through an opening amongst the trees, bearing down all before them like a charge of locomotives. They were led by a huge female, nearly nine feet high, after whom one half of the herd dashed precipitately through the narrow entrance, but the rest turning suddenly towards the left, succeeded in forcing the cordon of guards and making good their escape to the forest.

No sooner had the others passed the gate, than the two tame elephants stepped forward from either side, and before the herd could return from the further end of the enclosure, the bars were drawn, the entrance closed, and the men in charge glided outside the stockade. The elephants which had previously been made prisoners within exhibited intense excitement as the fresh din arose around them; they started to their feet, and stretched their trunks in the direction whence they winded the scent of the herd in its headlong flight; and as the latter rushed past, they renewed their struggles to get free and follow. It is not possible to imagine anything more exciting than the spectacle which the wild ones presented careering round the corral, uttering piercing screams, their heads erect and trunks aloft, the very emblems of rage and perplexity, of power and helplessness.

Along with those which entered at the second drive was one that evidently belonged to another herd, and had been separated from them in the *mêlée* when the latter effected their escape, and, as usual, his new companions in misfortune drove him off indignantly as often as he attempted to approach them.

The demeanour of those taken in the second drive differed materially from that of the preceding captives, who, having entered the corral in darkness, to find themselves girt with fire and smoke, and beset by hideous sounds and sights on every side, were speedily reduced by fear to stupor and submission — whereas, the second herd having passed into the enclosure by daylight, and its area being trodden down in many places, could clearly discover the fences, and were consequently more alarmed and enraged at their confinement. They were thus as restless as the others had been calm, and so much more vigorous in their assaults that, on one occasion, their courageous leader, undaunted by the multitude of white wands thrust towards her, was only driven back from the stockade by a hunter hurling a blazing flambeau at her head. Her attitude as she stood repulsed, but still irresolute, was a study for a painter. Her eye dilated, her ears expanded, her back arched like a tiger, and her fore-foot in air, whilst she uttered those hideous screams that are imperfectly described by the term "*trumpeting*."

Although repeatedly passing by the unfortunates from the former drove, the new herd seemed to take no friendly notice of them; they halted inquiringly for a minute, and then resumed their career round the corral, and once or twice in their headlong flight they rushed madly over the bodies of the prostrate captives as they lay in their misery on the ground.

It was evening before the new captives had grown wearied with their furious and repeated charges, and stood still in the centre of the corral collected into a terrified and motionless group. The fires were then relighted, the guard redoubled by the addition of the watchers, who were now relieved from duty in the forest, and the spectators retired to their bungalows for the night.

The business of the *third day* began by noosing and tying up the new captives, and the first sought out was their magnificent leader. Siribeddi and the tame tusker having forced themselves on either side of her, a boy in the service of the Rata-Mahatmeya succeeded in attaching a rope to her hind-foot. Siribeddi moved off, but feeling her strength insufficient to drag the reluctant prize, she went down on her fore-knees, so as to add the full weight of her body to the pull. The tusker, seeing her difficulty, placed himself in front of the prisoner, and forced her backwards, step by step, till his companion brought her fairly up to the tree, and wound the rope round the stem. Though overpowered by fear, she showed the fullest sense of the nature of the danger she had to apprehend. She kept her head turned towards the noosers, and tried to step in advance of the decoys; in spite of all their efforts, she tore off the first noose from her fore-leg, and placing it under her foot, snapped it into fathom lengths. When finally secured, her writhings were extraordinary. She doubled in her head under her chest, till she lay as round as a hedgehog, and rising again, stood on her fore-feet, and lifting her hind-feet off the ground, she wrung them from side to side, till the great tree above her quivered in every branch.

Before proceeding to catch the others, we requested that the smaller trees and jungle, which partially obstructed our view, might be broken away, being no longer essential to screen the entrance to the corral; and five of the tame elephants were brought up for the purpose. They felt the strength of each tree with their trunks, then swaying it backwards and forwards, by pushing it with their foreheads, they watched the opportunity when it was in full swing to raise their fore-feet against the stem, and bear it down to the ground. Then tearing off the festoons of climbing plants, and trampling down the smaller branches and brushwood, they pitched them with their tusks, piling them into heaps along the side of the fence.

Amongst the last that was secured was the solitary individual belonging to the fugitive herd. When they attempted to drag him backwards from the tree near

which he was noosed, he laid hold of it with his trunk and lay down on his side immoveable. The temple tusker and another were ordered up to assist, and it required the combined efforts of the three elephants to force him along. When dragged to the place at which he was to be tied up, he continued the contest with desperation, and to prevent the second noose being placed on his foot, he sat down on his haunches, almost in the attitude of the "Florentine Boar," keeping his hind-feet beneath him, and defending his fore-feet with his trunk, with which he flung back the rope as often as it was attempted to attach it.

When overpowered and made fast, his grief was most affecting; his violence sunk to utter prostration, and he

lay on the ground, uttering choking cries, with tears trickling down his cheeks.

The final operation was that of slackening the ropes, and marching each captive down to the river between two tame ones. This was effected very simply. A decoy, with a strong collar round its neck, stood on either side of the wild one, on which a similar collar was formed, by successive coils of coco-nut rope; and then, connecting the three collars together, the prisoner was effectually made safe between his two guards. During this operation, it was curious to see how the tame elephant, from time to time, used its trunk to shield the arm of its rider, and ward off the trunk of the prisoner, who resisted the placing the rope round his neck. This done, the nooses were removed from his feet, and he was marched off to the river, in which he and his companions were allowed to bathe; a privilege of which all availed themselves eagerly. Each was then made fast to a tree in the forest, and keepers being assigned to him, with a retinue of leaf-cutters, he was plentifully supplied with his favourite food, and left to the care and tuition of his new masters.

Returning from a spectacle such as I have attempted to describe, one cannot help feeling how immeasurably it exceeds in interest those royal battues where timid deer are driven in crowds to unresisting slaughter; or those vaunted "wild sports" the amusement of which appears to be in proportion to the effusion of blood. Here the only display of power was the imposition of restraint; and though considerable mortality often occurs amongst the animals caught, the infliction of pain, so far from being an incident of the operation, is most cautiously avoided from its tendency to enrage, the policy of the captor being to conciliate and soothe. The whole scene exhibits the most marvellous example of the voluntary alliance of animal sagacity and instinct in active co-operation with human intelligence and courage; and nothing else in nature, not even the chase of the whale, can afford so vivid an illustration of the sovereignty of man over brute creation even when confronted with force in its most stupendous embodiment.

Of the two young elephants which were taken in the corral, the smallest was sent down to my house at Colombo, where he became a general favourite with the servants. He attached himself especially to the coachman, who had a little shed erected for him near his own quarters at the stables. But his favourite resort was the kitchen, where he received a daily allowance of milk and plantains, and picked up several other delicacies besides. He was innocent and playful in the extreme, and when walking in the grounds he would trot up to me, twine his little trunk round my arm, and coax me to take him to the fruit-trees. In the evening the grass-cutters now and then indulged him by permitting him to carry home a load of fodder for the horses, on which occasions he assumed an air of gravity that was highly amusing, showing that he was deeply impressed with the importance and responsibility of the service entrusted to him. Being sometimes permitted to enter the dining-room, and helped to fruit at desert, he at last learned his way to the side-board; and on more than one occasion having stolen in, during the absence of the servants, he made a clear sweep of the wine-glasses and china in his endeavours to reach a basket of oranges. For these and similar pranks we were at last forced to put him away. He was sent to the Government stud, where he was affectionately received and adopted by Siribeddi, and he now takes his turn of public duty in the department of the Commissioner of Roads.

# CHAP. VII.

## THE ELEPHANT.

### *Conduct in Captivity.*

The idea prevailed in ancient times, and obtains even at the present day, that the Indian elephant surpasses that of Africa in sagacity and tractability, and consequently in capacity for training, so as to render its services more available to man. There does not appear to me to be sufficient ground for this conclusion. It originated, in all probability, in the first impressions created by the accounts of the elephant brought back by the Greeks after the Indian expedition of Alexander, and above all by the descriptions of Aristotle, whose knowledge of the animal was derived exclusively from the East. A long interval elapsed before the elephant of Africa, and its capabilities, became known in Europe. The first elephants brought to Greece by Antipater, were from India, as were also those introduced by Pyrrhus into Italy. Taught by this example, the Carthaginians undertook to employ African elephants in war. Jugurtha led them against Metellus, and Juba against Cæsar; but from inexperienced and deficient training, they proved less effective than the elephants of India[1], and the historians

[1] ARMANDI, *Hist. Milit. des Eléphants,* liv. i. ch. i. p. 2. It is an interesting fact, noticed by ARMANDI, that the elephants figured on the coins of Alexander, and the Seleucidæ invariably exhibit the characteristics of the Indian type, whilst those on Roman medals

of these times ascribed to inferiority of race, that which was but the result of insufficient education.

It must, however, be remembered that the elephants which, at a later period, astonished the Romans by their sagacity, and whose performances in the amphitheatre have been described by Ælian and Pliny, were brought from Africa, and acquired their accomplishments from European instructors[1]; a sufficient proof that under equally favourable auspices the African species are capable of developing similar docility and powers with those of India. It is one of the facts from which the inferiority of the Negro race has been inferred, that they alone, of all the nations amongst whom the elephant is found, have never manifested ability to domesticate it; and even as regards the more highly developed races who inhabited the valley of the Nile, it is observable that the elephant is nowhere to be found amongst the animals figured on the monuments of ancient Egypt, whilst the camelopard, the lion, and even the hippopotamus are represented. And although in later times the knowledge of the art of training appears to have existed under the Ptolemies, and on the southern shore of the Mediterranean, it admits of no doubt that it was communicated by the more accomplished natives of India who had settled there.[2]

can at once be pronounced African, from the peculiarities of the convex forehead and expansive ears. —*Ibid.* liv. i. cap. i. p. 3.

ARMANDI has, with infinite industry, collected from original sources a mass of curious informations relative to the employment of elephants in ancient warfare, which he has published under the title of *Histoire Militaire des Eléphants depuis les temps les plus reculés jusqu' à l'introduction des armes à feu.* Paris. 1843.

[1] ÆLIAN, lib. ii. cap. ii.

[2] See SCHLEGEL'S Essay on the

Another favourite doctrine of the earlier visitors to the East seems to me to be equally fallacious; PYRARD, BERNIER, PHILLIPE, THEVENOT, and other travellers in the sixteenth and seventeenth centuries, proclaimed the superiority of the elephant of Ceylon, in size, strength, and sagacity, above those of all other parts of India[1]; and TAVERNIER in particular is supposed to have stated that if a Ceylon elephant be introduced amongst those bred in any other place, by an instinct of nature they do him homage by laying their trunks to the ground, and raising them reverentially. This passage has been so repeatedly quoted in works on Ceylon that it has passed into an aphorism, and is always adduced as a testimony to the surpassing intelligence of the elephants of that island; although a reference to the original shows that Tavernier's observations are not only fanciful in themselves, but are restricted to the supposed excellence

Elephant and the Sphynx, *Classical Journal*, No. lx. Although the trained elephant nowhere appears upon the monuments of the Egyptians, the animal was not unknown to them, and ivory and elephants are figured on the walls of Thebes and Karnac amongst the spoils of Thothmes III., and the tribute paid to Rameses I. The Island of Elephantine, in the Nile, near Assouan (Syene) is styled in hieroglyphical writing "The Land of the Elephant;" but as it is a mere rock, it probably owes its designation to its form. See Sir GARDNER WILKINSON'S *Ancient Egyptians*, vol. i. pl. iv.; vol. v. p. 176. Above the first cataract of the Nile are two small islands, each bearing the name of Phylæ;—quære, is the derivation of this word at all connected with the Arabic term *fil?* See *ante*, p. 76, note. The elephant figured in the sculptures of Nineveh is universally as wild, not domesticated.

[1] This is merely a reiteration of the statement of ÆLIAN, who ascribes to the elephants of Taprobane a vast superiority in size, strength, and intelligence, above those of continental India,—Καὶ οἱδέ γε νησιῶται ἐλέφαντες τῶν ἠπειρωτῶν ἀλκιμώτεροί τε τὴν ῥώμην καὶ μείζους ἰδεῖν εἰσὶ, καὶ θυμοσοφώτεροι δὲ πάντα πάντῃ κρίνοιντο ἄν."—ÆLIAN, *De Nat. Anim.*, lib. xvi. cap. xviii.

ÆLIAN also, in the same chapter, states the fact of the shipment of elephants in large boats from Ceylon to the opposite continent of India, for sale to the king of Kalinga; so that the export from Manaar, described in a former passage, has been going on apparently without interruption since the time of the Romans.

of the Ceylon animal *in war*.[1] This estimate of the superiority of the elephant of Ceylon, if it ever prevailed in India, was not current there at a very early period; for in the *Ramayana*, which is probably the oldest epic in the world, the stud of Dasartha, the king of Ayodhya, was supplied with elephants from the Himalaya and the Vindhya Mountains.[2] I have had no opportunity of testing by personal observation the justice of the assumption; but from all that I have heard of the elephants of the continent, and seen of those of Ceylon, I have reason to conclude that the difference, if not imaginary, is exceptional, and must have arisen in particular and individual instances, from more judicious or elaborate instruction.

The earliest knowledge of the elephant in Europe and the West, was derived from the conspicuous position assigned to it in the wars of the East: in India, from the remotest antiquity, it formed one of the most picturesque, if not the most effective, features in the armies of the native princes.[3] It is more than

[1] The expression of TAVERNIER is to the effect that as compared with all others, the elephants of Ceylon are "plus courageux *à la guerre*." The rest of the passage is a curiosity:—

"Il faut remarquer ici une chose qu'on aura peut-être de la peine à croire mais qui est toutefois très-véritable: c'est que lorsque quelque roi ou quelque seigneur a quelqu'un de ces éléphants de Ceylan, et qu'on en amène quelqu'autre des lieux où les marchands vont les prendre, comme d'Achen, de Siam, d'Arakan, de Pegu, du royaume de Boutan, d'Assam, des terres de Cochin et de la coste du Mélinde, dès que les éléphants en voient un de Ceylan, par un instinct de nature, ils lui font la révérence, portant le bout de leur trompe à la terre et la relevant. Il est vrai que les éléphants que les grands seigneurs entretiennent, quand on les amène devant eux, pour voir s'ils sont en bon point, font trois fois une espèce de révérence avec leur trompe, *ce que j'ai vu souvent;* mais ils sont stylés à cela, et leurs maîtres le leur enseignent de bonne heure."—*Les Six Voyages de* J. B. TAVERNIER, lib. iii. ch. 20.

[2] *Ramayana*, sec. vi.; CAREY and MARSHMAN, i. 105; FAUCHE, t. i. p. 66.

[3] The only mention of the elephant in Sacred History is in the account given in *Maccabees* of the invasion of Egypt by Antiochus, who entered it 170 B.C., "with chariots and elephants, and horsemen, and a great navy."—1 Macc.

probable that the earliest attempts to take and train the elephant, were with a view to military uses, and that the art was perpetuated in later times to gratify the pride of the eastern kings, and sustain the pomp of their processions.

An impression prevails even to the present day, that the process of training is tedious and difficult, and the reduction of a full-grown elephant to obedience, slow and troublesome in the extreme.[1] In both particulars, however, the contrary is the truth. The training as it prevails in Ceylon is simple, and the conformity and obedience of the animal are developed with singular

i. 17. Frequent allusions to the use of elephants in war occur in both books; and in chap. vi. 34, it is stated that "to provoke the elephants to fight they showed them the blood of grapes and of mulberries." The term showed, "ἔδειξαν," might be thought to imply that the animals were enraged by the sight of the wine and its colour, but in the Third Book of Maccabees, in the Greek Septuagint, various other passages show that wine, on such occasions, was administered to the elephants to render them furious. — Macc. v. 2, 10, 45. PHILE mentions the same fact, *De Elephante*, i. 145.

There is a very curious account of the mode in which the Arab conquerors of Scinde, in the 9th and 10th centuries, equipped the elephant for war; which being written with all the particularity of an eye-witness, bears the impress of truth and accuracy, MASSOUDI, who was born in Bagdad at the close of the 9th century, travelled in India in the year A.D. 913, and visited the Gulf of Cambay, the coast of Malabar, and the Island of Ceylon: — from a larger account of his journeys he compiled a summary under the title of "*Moroudj al-dzeheb*," *or the* "*Golden Meadows*," the MS. of which is now in the Bibliothèque Nationale. M. REINAUD, in describing this manuscript says, on its authority, "The Prince of Mensura, whose dominions lay south of the Indus, maintained eighty elephants trained for war, each of which bore in his trunk a bent cymeter (carthel), with which he was taught to cut and thrust at all confronting him. The trunk itself was effectually protected by a coat of mail, and the rest of the body enveloped in a covering composed jointly of iron and horn. Other elephants were employed in drawing chariots, carrying baggage, and grinding forage, and the peformance of all bespoke the utmost intelligence and docility." — REINAUD, *Mémoire sur l'Inde, antérieurement au milieu du XI^e siècle, d'après les écrivains arabes, persans et chinois*. Paris, M.D.CCC. XLIX. p. 215. See SPRENGER's English Translation of Massoudi, vol. i. p. 383.

[1] BRODERIP, *Zoological Recreations*, p. 226.

rapidity. For the first three days, or till they will eat freely, which they seldom do in a less time, the newly-captured elephants are allowed to stand quiet; and, if practicable, a tame elephant is tied near to give the wild ones confidence. Where many elephants are being trained at once, it is customary to put every new captive between the stalls of half-tamed ones, when it soon takes to its food. This stage being attained, training commences by placing tame elephants on either side. The "cooroowe vidahn," or the head of the stables, stands in front of the wild elephants holding a long stick with a sharp iron point. Two men are then stationed one on either side, assisted by the tame elephants, and each holding a *hendoo* or crook[1] towards the wild one's trunk, whilst one or two others rub their hands over his back, keeping up all the while a soothing and plaintive chaunt, interlarded with endearing epithets, such as "ho! my son," or "ho! my father," or "my mother," as may be applicable to the age and sex of the captive. The elephant is at first furious, and strikes in all directions with his trunk; but the

[1] The iron goad with which the keeper directs the movements of the elephants, called a *hendoo* in Ceylon and *hawkus* in Bengal, appears to have retained the present shape from the remotest antiquity. It is figured in the medals of Caracalla in the identical form in which it is in use at the present day in India.

The Greeks called it ἅρπη, and the Romans *cuspis*.

Medal of Numidia.

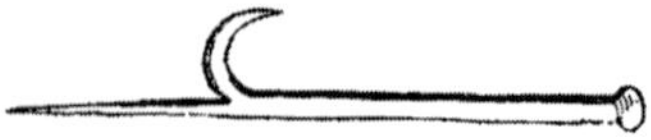

Modern Hendoo.

men in front receiving all these blows on the points of their weapons, the extremity of the trunk becomes so sore that the animal curls it up close, and seldom afterwards attempts to use it offensively. The first dread of man's power being thus established, the process of taking him to bathe between two tame elephants is greatly facilitated, and by lengthening the neck rope, and drawing the feet together as close as possible, the process of laying him down in the water is finally accomplished by the keepers pressing the sharp point of their hendoos over the backbone.

For many days the roaring and resistance which attend the operation are considerable, and it often requires the sagacious interference of the tame elephants to control the refractory wild ones. It soon, however, becomes practicable to leave the latter alone, only taking them to and from the stall by the aid of a decoy. This step lasts, under ordinary treatment, for about three weeks, when an elephant may be taken alone with his legs hobbled, and a man walking backwards in front with the point of the hendoo always presented to the elephant's head, and a keeper with an iron crook at each ear. On getting into the water, the fear of being pricked on his tender back induces him to lie down directly on the crook being only held over him *in terrorem.* Once this point has been achieved, the further process of taming is dependent upon the disposition of the creature.

The greatest care is requisite, and daily medicines are applied to heal the fearful wounds on the legs which even the softest ropes occasion. This is the great difficulty of training; for the wounds fester grievously, and months and sometimes years will elapse before an elephant will allow his feet to be touched without indications of alarm and anger.

The observation has been frequently made that the elephants most vicious and troublesome to tame, and the most worthless when tamed, are those distinguished by a thin trunk and flabby pendulous ears. The period of tuition does not appear to be influenced by the size or strength of the animals: some of the smallest give the greatest amount of trouble; whereas, in the instance of the two largest that have been taken in Ceylon within the last thirty years, both were docile in a remarkable degree. One in particular, which was caught and trained by Mr. Cripps, when Government agent, in the Seven Korles, fed from the hand the first night it was secured, and in a very few days evinced pleasure on being patted on the head.[1] There is none so obstinate, not even a *rogue*, that may not, when kindly and patiently treated, be conciliated and reconciled.

The males are generally more unmaneagable than the females, and in both an inclination to lie down to rest is regarded as a favourable symptom of approaching tractability, some of the most resolute having been known to stand for months together, even during sleep. Those which are the most obstinate and violent at first

[1] This was the largest elephant that had been tamed in Ceylon; he measured upwards of nine feet at the shoulders and belonged to the caste so highly prized for the temples. He was gentle after his first capture, but his removal from the corral to the stables, though only a distance of six miles, was a matter of the extremest difficulty; his extraordinary strength rendering him more than a match for the attendant decoys. He, on one occasion, escaped, but was recaptured in the forest; and he afterwards became so docile as to perform a variety of tricks. He was at length ordered to be removed to Colombo; but such was his terror on approaching the fort, that on coaxing him to enter the gate, he became paralysed in the extraordinary way elsewhere alluded to, and *died on the spot.*

are the soonest and most effectually subdued, and generally prove permanently docile and submissive. But those which are sullen or morose, although they may provoke no chastisement by their viciousness, are always slower in being taught, and are rarely to be trusted in after life.[1]

But whatever may be its natural gentleness and docility, the temper of an elephant is seldom to be implicitly relied on in a state of captivity and coercion. The most amenable are subject to occasional fits of stubbornness; and even after years of submission, irritability and resentment will unaccountably manifest themselves. It may be that the restraints and severer discipline of training have not been entirely forgotten; or that incidents which in ordinary health would be pro-

[1] The natives profess that the high caste elephants, such as are allotted to the temples, are of all others the most difficult to tame, and M. BLES, the Dutch correspondent of BUFFON, mentions a caste of elephants which he had heard of, as being peculiar to the Kandyan kingdom, that were not higher than a heifer (génisse), covered with hair, and insusceptible of being tamed. (BUFFON, *Supp.* vol. vi. p. 29.) Bishop HEBER, in the account of his journey from Bareilly towards the Himalayas, describes the Raja Gourman Sing, "mounted on a little female elephant, hardly bigger than a Durham ox, and almost as shaggy as a poodle."—*Journ.*, ch. xvii. It will be remembered that the mammoth discovered in 1803 embedded in icy soil in Siberia, was covered with a coat of long hair, with a sort of wool at the roots. Hence there arose the question whether that northern region had been formerly inhabited by a race of elephants, so fortified by nature against cold; or whether the individual discovered had been borne thither by currents from some more temperate latitudes. To the latter theory the presence of hair seemed a fatal objection; but so far as my own observation goes, I believe the elephants are more or less provided with hair. In some it is more developed than in others, and it is particularly observable in the young, which when captured are frequently covered with a woolly fleece, especially about the head and shoulders. In the older individuals in Ceylon, this is less apparent: and in captivity the hair appears to be altogether removed by the custom of the mahouts to rub their skin daily with oil and a rough lump of burned clay. See a paper on the subject, *Asiat. Journ.* N. S. vol. xiv. p. 182, by Mr. G. FAIRHOLME.

ductive of no demonstration whatever, may lead, in moments of temporary illness, to fretfulness and anger. The knowledge of this infirmity led to the popular belief recorded by PHILE, that the elephant had *two hearts*, under the respective influences of which it evinced ferocity or gentleness; subdued by the one to habitual tractability and obedience, but occasionally roused by the other to displays of rage and resistance.[1]

In the process of taming, the presence of the tame ones can generally be dispensed with after two months, and the captive may then be ridden by the driver alone; and after three or four months he may be entrusted with labour, so far as regards docility;—but it is undesirable, and even involves the risk of life, to work an elephant too soon; it has frequently happened that a valuable animal has lain down and died the first time it was tried in harness, from what the natives believe to be "broken heart,"—certainly without any cause inferable from injury or previous disease.[2] It is observable, that

[1] "Διπλῆς δὲ φάσιν εὐπορῆσαι καρδίας·
Καὶ τῇ μὲν εἶναι θυμικὸν τὸ θηρίον
Εἰς ἀκρατῆ κίνησιν ἠρεθισμένον,
Τῇ δὲ προσηνὲς καὶ θρασύτητος ξένον.
Καὶ πῇ μὲν αὐτῶν ἀκροᾶσθαι τῶν λόγων
Οὓς ἄν τις Ἰνδὸς εὖ τιθασεύων λέγοι,
Πῇ δὲ πρὸς αὐτοὺς τοὺς νομεῖς ἐπιτρέχειν
Εἰς τὰς παλαιὰς ἐκτραπὲν κακουργίας."

PHILE, *Expos. de Eleph.*, l. 126, &c.

[2] Captain YULE, in his *Narrative of an Embassy to Ava in* 1855, records an illustration of this tendency of the elephant to sudden death; one newly captured, the process of taming which was exhibited to the British Envoy, "made vigorous resistance to the placing of a collar on its neck, and the people were proceeding to tighten it, when the elephant, which had lain down as if quite exhausted, reared suddenly on the hind quarters, and fell on its side—*dead!*"—P. 104.

Mr. STRACHAN noticed the same liability of the elephants to sudden death from very slight causes; "of the fall," he says, "at any time, though on plain ground, they either die immediately, or languish till they die; their great weight occasioning them so much hurt by the fall."—*Phil. Trans.* A.D. 1701, vol. xxiii. p. 1052.

till a captured elephant begins to relish food, and grow fat upon it, he becomes so fretted by work, that it kills him in an incredibly short space of time.

The first employment to which an elephant is put is to tread clay in a brick-field, or to draw a waggon in double harness with a tame companion. But the work in which the display of sagacity renders his labours of the highest value, is that which involves the use of heavy materials; and hence in dragging and piling timber, or moving stones[1] for the construction of retaining walls and the approaches to bridges, his services in an unopened country are of the utmost importance. When roads are to be constructed along the face of steep declivities, and the space is so contracted that risk is incurred either of the working elephant falling over the precipice or of rocks slipping down from above, not only are the measures to which he resorts the most judicious and reasonable that could be devised, but if urged by his keeper to adopt any other, he manifests a reluctance sufficient to show that he has balanced in his own mind the comparative advantages of each. An elephant appears on all occasions to comprehend the purpose and object that he is expected to promote, and hence he voluntarily executes a variety of details without any guidance whatever from his keeper. This is one characteristic in which this animal manifests a superiority over the horse; although his strength in proportion to his weight is not so great as that of the latter.

His minute motions when engrossed by such opera-

[1] A correspondent informs me that on the Malabar coast of India, the elephant, when employed in dragging stones, moves them by means of a rope, which he either draws with his forehead, or manages by seizing it in his teeth.

tions, the activity of his eye, and the earnestness of his attitudes, can only be comprehended by being seen. In moving timber and masses of rock his trunk is the instrument on which he mainly relies, but those which have tusks turn them to good account. To get a weighty stone out of a hollow an elephant will kneel down so as to apply the pressure of his head to move it upwards, then steadying it with one foot till he can raise himself, he will apply a fold of his trunk to shift it to its place, and fit it accurately in position: this done, he will step round to view it on either side, and adjust it with due precision. He appears to gauge his task by his eye, and to form a judgment whether the weight be proportionate to his strength. If doubtful of his own power, he hesitates and halts, and if urged against his will, he roars and shows temper.

In clearing an opening through forest land, the power of the African elephant, and the strength ascribed to him by a recent traveller, as displayed in uprooting trees, have never been equalled or approached by anything I have seen of the elephant in Ceylon[1] or heard of them in India.

[1] "Here the trees were large and handsome, but not strong enough to resist the inconceivable strength of the mighty monarch of these forests; almost every tree had half its branches broken short by them and at every hundred yards I came upon entire trees, and these, *the largest in the forest*, uprooted clean out of the ground, and *broken short across their stems*."—*A Hunter's Life in South Africa.* By R. GORDON CUMMING, vol. ii. p. 305.—"Spreading out from one another, they smash and destroy all the finest trees in the forest which happen to be in their course. . . . I have rode through forests where the trees thus broken lay so thick across one another, that it was almost impossible to ride through the district."—*Ibid.*, p. 310.

Mr. Gordon Cumming does not name the trees which he saw thus "uprooted" and "broken across," nor has he given any idea of their size and weight; but Major DENHAM, who observed like traces of the elephant in Africa, saw only small trees overthrown by them; and Mr. PRINGLE, who had an opportunity of observing similar practices of the animals in the neutral territory of the Eastern frontier of the Cape of Good Hope, describes their ravages as being

Of course much must depend on the nature of the timber and the moisture of the soil; thus a strong tree on the verge of a swamp may be overthrown with greater ease than a small and low one in parched and solid ground. I have seen no "tree" deserving the name, nothing but jungle and brushwood, thrown down by the mere movement of an elephant without some special exertion of force. But he is by no means fond of gratuitously tasking his strength; and food being so abundant that he obtains it without an effort, it is not altogether apparent, even were he able to do so, why he should assail "the largest trees in the forest," and encumber his own haunts with their broken stems; especially as there is scarcely anything which an elephant dislikes more than venturing amongst fallen timber.

A tree of twelve inches in diameter resisted successfully the most strenuous struggles of the largest elephant I ever saw led to it; and when directed by their keepers to clear away jungle, the removal of even a small tree, or a healthy young coco-nut palm, is a matter both of time and exertion. Hence the services of an elephant are of much less value in clearing a forest than in dragging and piling felled timber. But in the latter occupation he manifests an intelligence and dexterity which is surprising to a stranger, because the sameness of the operation enables the animal to go on for hours disposing of log after log, almost without a hint or direction from his attendant. For example, two elephants employed

confined to the mimosas, "immense numbers of which had been torn out of the ground, and placed in an inverted position, in order to enable the animals to browse at their ease on the soft and juicy roots, which form a favourite part of their food. Many of the *larger mimosas had resisted all their efforts; and indeed it is only after heavy rain, when the soil is soft and loose, that they ever successfully attempt this operation.*"—PRINGLE'S *Sketches of South Africa.*

in piling ebony and satinwood in the yards attached to the commissariat stores at Colombo, were so accustomed to their work, that they were able to accomplish it with equal precision and with greater rapidity than if it had been done by dock-labourers. When the pile attained a certain height, and they were no longer able by their conjoint efforts to raise one of the heavy logs of ebony to the summit, they had been taught to lean two pieces against the heap, up the inclined plane of which they gently rolled the remaining logs, and placed them trimly on the top.

It has been asserted that in their occupations "elephants are to a surprising extent the creatures of habit,"[1] that their movements are altogether mechanical, and that "they are annoyed by any deviation from their accustomed practice, and resent any constrained departure from the regularity of their course." So far as my own observation goes, this is incorrect; and I am assured by officers of experience, that in regard to changing his treatment, his hours, or his occupation, an elephant evinces no more consideration than a horse, but exhibits the same pliancy and facility.

At one point, however, the utility of the elephant stops short. Such is the intelligence and earnestness he displays in work, which he seems to conduct almost without supervision, that it has been assumed[2] that he would continue his labour, and accomplish his given task, as well in the absence of his keeper as during his presence. But here his innate love of ease displays itself, and if the eye of his attendant be withdrawn, the moment he has finished the thing immediately in hand,

[1] *Menageries, &c.*, "The Elephant," vol. ii. p. 23.
[2] *Ibid.*, ch. vi. p. 138.

he will stroll away lazily, to browse or enjoy the luxury of fanning himself and blowing dust over his back.

The means of punishing so powerful an animal is a question of difficulty to his attendants. Force being almost inapplicable, they try to work on his passions and feelings, by such expedients as altering the nature of his food or withholding it altogether for a time. On such occasions the demeanour of the creature will sometimes evince a sense of humiliation as well as of discontent. In some parts of India it is customary, in dealing with offenders, to stop their allowance of sugar canes or of jaggery; or to restrain them from eating their own share of fodder and leaves till their companions shall have finished; and in such cases the consciousness of degradation betrayed by the looks and attitudes of the culprit is quite sufficient to identify him, and to excite a feeling of sympathy and pity.

The elephant's obedience to his keeper is the result of affection, as well as of fear; and although his attachment becomes so strong that an elephant in Ceylon has been known to remain out all night, without food, rather than abandon his mahout, lying intoxicated in the jungle, yet he manifests little difficulty in yielding the same submission to a new driver in the event of a change of attendants. This is opposed to the popular belief that "the elephant cherishes such an enduring remembrance of his old mahout, that he cannot easily be brought to obey a stranger."[1] In the extensive establishments of the Ceylon Government, the keepers are changed without hesitation, and the animals, when equally kindly treated, are usually found to be as tract-

[1] *Menageries, &c.*, "The Elephant," vol. i. p. 19.

able and obedient to their new driver as to the old, in fact so soon as they have become familiarised with his voice.

This is not, however, invariably the case; and Mr. CRIPPS, who had remarkable opportunities for observing the habits of the elephant in Ceylon, mentioned to me an instance in which one of a singularly stubborn disposition occasioned some inconvenience after the death of its keeper, by refusing to obey any other, till its attendants bethought them of a child about twelve years old, in a distant village, where the animal had been formerly picketed, and to whom it had displayed much attachment. The child was sent for; and on its arrival the elephant, as anticipated, manifested extreme satisfaction, and was managed with ease, till by degrees it became reconciled to the presence of a new superintendent.

It has been said that the mahouts die young, owing to some supposed injury to the spinal column from the peculiar motion of the elephant; but this remark does not apply to those in Ceylon, who are healthy, and as long lived as other men. If the motion of the elephant be thus injurious, that of the camel must be still more so; yet we never hear of early death ascribed to this cause by the Arabs.

The voice of the keeper, with a very limited vocabulary of articulate sounds, serves almost alone to guide the elephant in his domestic occupations.[1] Sir EVERARD

[1] The principal sound by which the mahouts in Ceylon direct the motions of the elephants is a repetition, with various modulations, of the words *ur-re! ur-re!* This is one of those interjections in which the sound is so expressive of the sense that persons in charge of animals of almost every description throughout the world appear to have adopted it with a concurrence that is very curious. The

HOME, from an examination of the muscular fibres in the drum of an elephant's ear, came to the conclusion, that notwithstanding the distinctness and power of his perception of sounds at a greater distance than other animals, he was insensible to their harmonious modulation and destitute of a musical ear.[1] But Professor HARRISON, in a paper read before the Royal Irish Academy in 1847, has stated that on a careful examination of the head of an elephant which he had dissected, he could "see no evidence of the muscular structure of the *membrana tympani* so accurately described by Sir E. HOME." Sir EVERARD's deduction, I may observe, is clearly inconsistent with the fact that the power of two elephants may be combined by singing to them a measured chant, somewhat resembling a sailor's capstan song; and in labour of a particular kind, such as hauling a stone with ropes, they will thus move conjointly a weight to which their divided strength would be unequal.[2]

drivers of camels in Turkey, Palestine, and Egypt encourage them to speed by shouting *ar-ré! ar-ré!* The Arabs in Algeria cry *eirich!* to their mules. The Moors seem to have carried the custom with them into Spain, where mules are still driven with cries of *arré* (whence the muleteers derive their Spanish appellation of "arrieros"). In France the Sportsman excites the hound by shouts of *hare! hare!* and the waggoner there turns his horses by his voice, and the use of the word *hurhaut!* In the North, "*Hurs* was a word used by the old Germans in urging their horses to speed;" and to the present day, the herdsmen in Ireland, and parts of Scotland, drive their pigs with shouts of *hurrish!* a sound closely resembling that used by the mahouts in Ceylon.

[1] *On the Difference between the Human Membrana Tympani and that of the Elephant.* By Sir EVERARD HOME, Bart., Philos. Trans., 1823. Paper by Prof. HARRISON, Proc. Royal Irish Academy, vol. iii. p. 386.

[2] I have already noticed the striking effect produced on the captive elephants in the corral, by the harmonious notes of an ivory flute; and on looking to the graphic description which is given, by ÆLIAN of the exploits which he witnessed as performed by the elephants exhibited at Rome, it is remarkable how very large a share

Nothing can more strongly exhibit the impulse to obedience in the elephant, than the patience with which, at the order of his keeper, he swallows the nauseous medicines of the native elephant-doctors; and it is impossible to witness the fortitude with which (without shrinking) he submits to excruciating surgical operations for the removal of tumours and ulcers to which he is subject, without conceiving a vivid impression of his gentleness and intelligence. Dr. DAVY when in Ceylon was consulted about an elephant in the government Stud, which was suffering from a deep, burrowing sore in the back, just over the back-bone, which had long resisted the treatment ordinarily employed. He recommended the use of the knife, that issue might be given to the accumulated matter, but no one of the attendants was competent to undertake the operation. "Being assured," he continues, "that the creature would behave well, I undertook it myself. The elephant was not bound, but was made to kneel down at his keeper's command — and with an amputating knife, using all my force, I made the incision required through the tough integuments. The elephant did not flinch, but rather inclined towards me when using the knife; and merely uttered a low, and as it were suppressed, groan. In short, he behaved as like a human being as possible, as if conscious (as I

of their training appears to have been ascribed to the employment of music.

PHILE, in the account which he has given of the elephant's fondness for music, would almost seem to have versified the prose narrative of ÆLIAN, as he describes its excitement at the more animated portions, its step being regulated to the time and movements of the harmony: the whole "*suprising in a creature whose limbs are without joints!*

"Καινόν τι ποιῶν ἐξ ἀνάρθρων ὀργάνων."

PHILE, *Expos. de Eleph*, l. 216.

For an account of the training and performances of the elephants at Rome, as narrated by ÆLIAN, see the appendix to this chapter.

believe he was), that the operation was for his good, and the pain unavoidable"[1]

Obedience to the orders of his keepers is not, however, to be assumed as the result of a uniform perception of the object to be attained by compliance; and we cannot but remember the touching incident which took place during the slaughter of the elephant at Exeter Change in 1846, when, after receiving ineffectually upwards of 120 balls in various parts of his body, he turned his face to his assailants on hearing the voice of his keeper, and knelt down at the accustomed word of command, so as to bring his forehead within view of the rifles.[2]

The working elephant is always a delicate animal, and requires watchfulness and care. As a beast of burden he is unsatisfactory; for although in point of mere strength there is scarcely any weight which could be conveniently placed on him that he could not carry, it is difficult to pack his load without causing abrasions that afterwards ulcerate. His skin is easily chafed by harness, especially in wet weather. During either long droughts or too much moisture, his feet become liable to sores, that render him non-effective for months. Many attempts have been made to provide him with some protection for the sole of the foot, but from his extreme weight and peculiar mode of planting the foot, they have all been unsuccessful. His eyes are also liable to frequent inflammations, and the skill of the native elephant-doctors, which has been renowned since the time of Ælian, is nowhere more strikingly displayed than in the successful treatment of such attacks.[3] In Ceylon,

[1] *The Angler in the Lake District*, p. 23.

[2] A shocking account of the death of this poor animal is given in HONE'S *Every-Day Book*, March, 1830, p. 337,

[3] ÆLIAN, lib. xiii. c. 7.

the murrain among cattle is of frequent occurrence, and carries off great numbers of animals, wild as well as tame. In such visitations the elephants suffer severely, not only those at liberty in the forest, but those carefully tended in the government stables. Out of a stud of about 40 attached to the department of the Commission of Roads, the deaths between 1841 and 1849 were on an average *four* in each year, and this was nearly doubled in those years when murrain prevailed.

Of 240 elephants, employed in the public departments of the Ceylon Government, which died in twenty-five years, from 1831 to 1856, the length of time that each lived in captivity has only been recorded in the instances of 138. Of these there died:—

| Duration of Captivity. | No. | Male. | Female. |
|---|---|---|---|
| Under 1 year | 72 | 29 | 43 |
| From 1 to 2 years | 14 | 5 | 9 |
| „ 2 „ 3 „ | 8 | 5 | 3 |
| „ 3 „ 4 „ | 8 | 3 | 5 |
| „ 4 „ 5 „ | 3 | 2 | 1 |
| „ 5 „ 6 „ | 2 | 2 | . |
| „ 6 „ 7 „ | 3 | 1 | 2 |
| „ 7 „ 8 „ | 5 | 2 | 3 |
| „ 8 „ 9 „ | 5 | 5 | . |
| „ 9 „ 10 „ | 2 | 2 | . |
| „ 10 „ 11 „ | 2 | 2 | . |
| „ 11 „ 12 „ | 3 | 1 | 2 |
| „ 12 „ 13 „ | 3 | . | 3 |
| „ 13 „ 14 „ | . | . | . |
| „ 14 „ 15 „ | 3 | 1 | 2 |
| „ 15 „ 16 „ | 1 | 1 | . |
| „ 16 „ 17 „ | 1 | . | 1 |
| „ 17 „ 18 „ | . | . | . |
| „ 18 „ 19 „ | 2 | 1 | 1 |
| „ 19 „ 20 „ | 1 | . | 1 |
| Total | 138 | 62 | 76 |

Of the 72 who died in one year's servitude, 35 expired within the first six months of their captivity. During training, many elephants die in the unaccountable manner already referred to, of what the natives designate *a broken heart*.

On being first subjected to work, the elephant is liable to severe and often fatal swellings of the jaws and abdomen.[1]

| | |
|---|---|
| From these causes there died, between 1841 and 1849 | 9 |
| Of cattle murrain | 10 |
| Sore feet | 1 |
| Colds and inflammation | 6 |
| Diarrhœa | 1 |
| Worms | 1 |
| Of diseased liver | 1 |
| Injuries from a fall | 1 |
| General debility | 1 |
| Unknown causes | 3 |

Of the entire, twenty-three were females and eleven males.

The ages of those that died could not be accurately stated, owing to the circumstance of their having been captured in corral. Two only were tuskers. Towards keeping the stud in health, nothing has been found so conducive as regularly bathing the elephants, and giving them the opportunity to stand with their feet in water, or in moistened earth.

Elephants are said to be afflicted with tooth-ache; their tushes have likewise been found with symptoms of internal perforation by some parasite, and the natives assert that, in their agony, the animals have been known

[1] The elephant which was dissected by Dr. HARRISON of Dublin, in 1847, died of a febrile attack, after four or five days' illness, which, as Dr. H. tells me in a private letter, was "very like scarlatina, at that time a prevailing disease; its skin in some places became almost scarlet."

to break them off short.[1] I have never heard of the teeth themselves being so affected, and it is just possible that the operation of shedding the subsequent decay of the milk-tushes, may have in some instances been accompanied by incidents that gave rise to this story.

At the same time the probabilities are in favour of its being true. CUVIER committed himself to the statement that the tusks of the elephant have no attachments to connect them with the pulp lodged in the cavity at their base, from which the peculiar modification of dentine, known as "ivory," is secreted[2]; and hence, by inference, that they would be devoid of sensation.

But independently of the fact that ivory is permeated by tubes so fine that at their origin from the pulpy cavity they do not exceed $\frac{1}{15000}$th part of an inch in diameter, OWEN had the tusk and pulp of the great elephant which died at the Zoological Gardens in London in 1847 longitudinally divided, and found that, "although the pulp could be easily detached from the inner surface of the cavity, it was not without a certain resistance; and when the edges of the co-adapted pulp and tusk were examined by a strong lens, the filamentary processes from the outer surface of the former could be seen stretching, as they were drawn from the dentinal tubes, before they broke. These filaments are so minute, he adds, that to the naked eye the detached surface of the pulp seems to be entire; and hence CUVIER was deceived into supposing that there was no organic

[1] See a paper entitled "*Recollections of Ceylon*," in *Fraser's Magazine* for December, 1860.

[2] *Annales du Muséum* F. viii. 1805. p. 94, and *Ossemens Fossiles*, quoted by OWEN, in the article on "Teeth," in TODD'S *Cyclop. of Anatomy, &c.*, vol. iv. p. 929.

connexion between the pulp and the ivory. But if, as there seems no reason to doubt, these delicate nervous processes traverse the tusk by means of the numerous tubes already described, if attacked by caries the pain occasioned to the elephant would be excruciating.

As to maintaining a stud of elephants for the purposes to which they are now assigned in Ceylon, there may be a question on the score of prudence and economy. In the rude and unopened parts of the country, where rivers are to be forded, and forests are only traversed by jungle paths, their labour is of value, in certain contingencies, in the conveyance of stores, and in the earlier operations for the construction of fords and rough bridges of timber. But in more highly civilised districts, and wherever macadamised roads admit of the employment of horses and oxen for draught, I apprehend that the services of elephants might, with advantage, be gradually reduced, if not altogether dispensed with.

The love of the elephant for coolness and shade renders him at all times more or less impatient of work in the sun, and every moment of leisure he can snatch is employed in covering his back with dust, or fanning himself to diminish the annoyance of the insects and heat. From the tenderness of his skin and its liability to sores, the labour in which he can most advantageously be employed is that of draught; but the reluctance of horses to meet or pass elephants renders it difficult to work the latter with safety on frequented roads. Besides, were the full load which an elephant is capable of drawing, in proportion to his muscular strength, to be placed upon waggons of corresponding dimension, the injury to the roads would be such that the wear and tear of the highways and bridges would prove too costly to be borne. On the other hand, by restricting it to a somewhat more manageable quantity, and by limiting the weight, as at present, to about *one ton and a half*, it is doubtful whether an elephant performs so much more work than could be done by a horse or by bullocks, as to compensate for the greater cost of his feeding and attendance.

Add to this, that from accidents and other causes, from ulcerations of the skin, and illnesses of many kinds, the elephant is so often invalided, that the actual cost of his labour, when at work, is very considerably enhanced. Exclusive of the salaries of higher officers attached to the government establishments, and other permanent charges, the expenses of an elephant, looking only to the wages of his attendants and the cost of his food and medicines, varies from *three shillings to four shillings and sixpence* per diem, according to his size and class.[1] Taking the average at three shillings and

[1] An ordinary-sized elephant engrosses the undivided attention of *three* men. One, as his mahout or superintendent, and two as leaf-cutters, who bring him branches and grass for his daily supplies. An animal of larger growth would probably require a third leaf-cutter. The daily consumption is two cwt. of green food with about half a bushel of grain. When in the vicinity of towns and villages, the attendants have no difficulty in procuring an abundant supply of the branches of the trees to which elephants are partial; and in journeys through the forests and unopened country, the leaf-cutters are sufficiently expert in the knowledge of those particular plants with which the elephant is satisfied. Those that would be likely to disagree with him he unerringly rejects. His favourites are the palms, especially the cluster of rich, unopened leaves, known as the "cabbage," of the coco-nut, and areca; and he delights to tear open the young trunks of the palmyra and jaggery (*Caryota urens*) in search of the farinaceous matter contained in the spongy pith. Next to these come the varieties of fig-trees, particularly the sacred *Bo* (*F. religiosa*) which is found near every temple, and the *na gaha* (*Messua ferrea*), with thick dark leaves and a scarlet flower. The leaves of the Jak-tree and bread-fruit (*Artocarpus integrifolia*, and *A. incisa*), the Wood apple (*Ægle Marmelos*), Palu (*Mimusops Indica*), and a number of

nine-pence, and calculating that hardly any individual works more than four days out of seven, the charge for each day so employed would amount to *six shillings and sixpence.* The keep per day of a powerful dray-horse, working five days in the week, would not exceed half-a-crown, and two such would unquestionably do more work than any elephant under the present system. I do not know whether it be from a comparative calculation of this kind that the strength of the elephant establishments in Ceylon has been gradually diminished of late years, but in the department of the Commissioner of Roads, the stud, which formerly numbered upwards of sixty elephants, was reduced, some years ago, to thirty-six, and is at present less than half that number.

The fallacy of the supposed reluctance of the elephant to breed in captivity has been demonstrated by many recent authorities; but with the exception of the birth of young elephants at Rome, as mentioned by ÆLIAN, the only instances that I am aware of their actually producing young under such circumstances, took place in Ceylon. Both parents had been for several years attached

others well known to their attendants, are all consumed in turn. The stems of the plaintain, the stalks of the sugar-cane, and the feathery tops of the bamboos, are irresistible luxuries. Pine-apples, water-melons, and fruits of every description, are voraciously devoured, and a coco-nut when found is first rolled under foot to detach it from the husk and fibre, and then raised in his trunk and crushed, almost without an effort, by his ponderous jaws.

The grasses are not found in sufficient quantity to be an item of daily fodder; the Mauritius or the Guinea grass is seized with avidity; lemon grass is rejected from its overpowering perfume, but rice in the straw, and every description of grain, whether growing or dry; gram (*Cicer arietinum*), Indian Corn, and millet are his natural food. Of such of these as can be found, it is the duty of the leaf-cutters, when in the jungle and on march, to provide a daily supply.

to the stud of the Commissioner of Roads, and in 1844 the female, whilst engaged in dragging a waggon, gave birth to a still-born calf. Some years before, an elephant that had been captured by Mr. Cripps, dropped a female calf, which he succeeded in rearing. As usual, the little one became the pet of the keepers; but as it increased in growth, it exhibited the utmost violence when thwarted; striking out with its hind-feet, throwing itself headlong on the ground, and pressing its trunk against any opposing object.

The duration of life in the elephant has been from the remotest times a matter of uncertainty and speculation. Aristotle says it was reputed to live from two to three hundred years[1], and modern zoologists have assigned to it an age very little less; CUVIER[2] allots two hundred and DE BLAINVILLE one hundred and twenty. The only attempt which I know of to establish a period historically or physiologically is that of FLEURENS, who has advanced an ingenious theory on the subject in his treatise "*De la Longévité Humaine.*" He assumes the sum total of life in all animals to be equivalent to five times the number of years requisite to perfect their growth and development;—and he adopts as evidence of the period at which growth ceases, the final consolidation of the bones with their *epiphyses;* which in the young consist of cartilages; but in the adult become uniformly osseous and solid. So long as the epiphyses are distinct from the bones, the growth of the animal is proceeding, but it ceases so soon as the consolidation is complete. In man, according to FLEURENS, this consummation takes place at 20 years of age, in the horse at

[1] ARISTOTELES *de Anim. l. viii.* c. 9. [2] *Menag. de Mus. Nat.* p. 107.

5, in the dog at 2; so that conformably to this theory the respective normal age for each would be 100 years for man, 25 for the horse, and 10 for a dog. As a datum for his conclusion, FLEURENS cites the instance of one young elephant in which, at 26 years old, the epiphyses were still distinct, whereas in another, which died at 31, they were firm and adherent. Hence he draws the inference that the period of completed solidification is thirty years, and consequently that the normal age of the elephant is *one hundred and fifty.*[1]

Amongst the Singhalese the ancient fable of the elephant attaining to the age of two or three hundred years still prevails; but the Europeans, and those in immediate charge of tame ones, entertain the opinion that the duration of life for about *seventy* years is common both to man and the elephant; and that before the arrival of the latter period, symptoms of debility and decay ordinarily begin to manifest themselves. Still instances are not wanting in Ceylon of trained decoys that have lived for more than double the reputed period in actual servitude. One employed by Mr. Cripps in the Seven Korles was represented by the Cooroowe people to have served the king of Kandy in the same capacity sixty years before; and amongst the papers left by Colonel Robertson (son to the historian of "Charles V."), who held a command in Ceylon in 1799, shortly after the capture of the island by the British, I have found a memorandum showing that a decoy was then attached to the elephant establishment at Matura, which the records proved to have served under the Dutch during the entire period of their occupation (extending to upwards of one hundred and forty years); and it was

[1] FLEURENS, *De la Longévité Humaine*, pp. 82, 89.

said to have been found in the stables by the Dutch on the expulsion of the Portugese in 1656.

It is perhaps from this popular belief in their almost illimitable age, that the natives generally assert that the body of a dead elephant is seldom or never to be discovered in the woods. And certain it is that frequenters of the forest with whom I have conversed, whether European or Singhalese, are consistent in their assurances that they have never found the remains of an elephant that had died a natural death. One chief, the Wannyah of the Trincomalie district, told a friend of mine, that once after a severe murrain, which had swept the province, he found the carcases of elephants that had died of the disease. On the other hand, a European gentleman, who for thirty-six years without intermission has been living in the jungle, ascending to the summits of mountains in the prosecution of the trigonometrical survey, and penetrating valleys in tracing roads and opening means of communication,—one, too, who has made the habits of the wild elephant a subject of constant observation and study,—has often expressed to me his astonishment that after seeing many thousands of living elephants in all possible situations, he had never yet found a single skeleton of a dead one, except of those which had fallen by the rifle.[1]

It has been suggested that the bones of the elephant may be so porous and spongy as to disappear in consequence of an early decomposition; but this remark would

[1] This remark regarding the elephant of Ceylon does not appear to extend to that of Africa, as I observe that BEAVER, in his *African Memoranda*, says that "the skeletons of old ones that have died in the woods are frequently found."—*African Memoranda relative to an attempt to establish British Settlements at the Island of Bulama.* Lond. 1815, p. 353.

not apply to the grinders or to the tusks; besides which, the inference is at variance with the fact, that not only the horns and teeth, but entire skeletons of deer, are frequently found in the districts inhabited by the elephant.

The natives, to account for this popular belief, declare that the survivors of the herd bury such of their companions as die a natural death.[1] It is curious that this belief was current also amongst the Greeks of the Lower Empire; and PHILE, writing early in the fourteenth century, not only describes the younger elephants as tending the wounded, but as burying the dead:

> "Ὅταν δ' ἐπιστῇ τῆς τελευτῆς ὁ χρόνος
> Κοινοῦ τέλους ἄμυναν ὁ ξένος φέρει."[2]

The Singhalese have a further superstition in relation to the close of life in the elephant: they believe that, on feeling the approach of dissolution, he repairs to a solitary valley, and there resigns himself to death. A native who accompanied Mr. Cripps, when hunting, in the forests of Anarajapoora, intimated to him that he was then in the immediate vicinity of the spot "*to which the elephants come to die,*" but that it was so mysteriously concealed, that although every one believed in its exist-

[1] A corral was organised near Putlam in 1846, by Mr. Morris, the chief officer of the district. It was constructed across one of the paths which the elephants frequent in their frequent marches, and during the course of the proceedings two of the captured elephants died. Their carcases were left of course within the enclosure, which was abandoned as soon as the capture was complete. The wild elephants resumed their path through it, and a few days afterwards the headman reported to Mr. Morris that the bodies had been removed and carried outside the corral to a spot to which nothing but the elephants could have borne them.

[2] PHILE, *Expositio de Eleph.* 1. 243.

ence, no one had ever succeeded in penetrating to it. At the corral which I have described at Korṇegalle, in 1847, Dehigame, one of the Kandyan chiefs, assured me it was the universal belief of his countrymen, that the elephants, when about to die, resorted to a valley in Saffragam, among the mountains to the east of Adam's Peak, which was reached by a narrow pass with walls of rock on either side, and that there, by the side of a lake of clear water, they took théir last repose.[1] It was not without interest that I afterwards recognised this tradition in the story of *Sinbad of the Sea*, who in his Seventh Voyage, after conveying the presents of Haroun al Raschid to the king of Serendib, is wrecked on his return from Ceylon, and sold as a slave to a master who employs him in shooting elephants for the sake of their ivory; till one day the tree on which he was stationed having been uprooted by one of the herd, he fell senseless to the ground, and the great elephant approaching wound his trunk around him and carried him away, ceasing not to proceed, until he had taken him to a place where, his terror having subsided, *he found himself amongst the bones of elephants, and knew that this was their burial place.*[2] It is curious to find this legend of Ceylon in what has, not inaptly, been described as the "Arabian Odyssey" of Sinbad; the original of which

[1] The selection by animals of a *place to die*, is not confined to the elephant. DARWIN says, that in South America "the guanacos (llamas) appear to have favourite spots for lying down to die; on the banks of the Santa Cruz river, in certain circumscribed spaces which were generally bushy and all near the water, the ground was actually white with their bones; on one such spot I counted between ten and twenty heads."—*Nat. Voy.* ch, viii. The same has been remarked in the Rio Gallegos; and at St. Jago in the Cape de Verde Islands, DARWIN saw a retired corner similarly covered with the bones of the goat, as if it were "the burial-ground of all the goats in the island."

[2] *Arabian Nights' Entertainment*, LANE's edition, vol. iii. p. 77.

evidently embodies the romantic recitals of the sailors returning from the navigation of the Indian Seas, in the middle ages[1], which were current amongst the Mussulmans, and are reproduced in various forms throughout the tales of the *Arabian Nights.*

[1] See a disquisition on the origin of the story of Sinbad, by M. REINAUD, in the introduction prefixed to his translation of the *Arabian Geography of Aboulfeda*, vol. i. p. lxxvi.

## APPENDIX TO CHAPTER VII.

As Ælian's work on *the Nature of Animals* has never, I believe, been republished in any English version, and the passage in relation to the training and performance of elephants is so pertinent to the present inquiry, I venture to subjoin a translation of the 11th Chapter of his 2nd Book.

"Of the cleverness of the elephant I have spoken elsewhere, and likewise of the manner of hunting. I have mentioned these things, a few out of the many which others have stated; but for the present I purpose to speak of their musical feeling, their tractability, and facility in learning what it is difficult for even a human being to acquire, much less a beast, hitherto so wild:—such as to dance, as is done on the stage; to walk with a measured gait; to listen to the melody of the flute and to perceive the difference of sounds, that, being pitched low lead to a slow movement, or high to a quick one: all this the elephant learns and understands, and is accurate withal, and makes no mistake. Thus has Nature formed him not only the greatest in size, but the most gentle and the most easily taught. Now if I were going to write about the tractability and aptitude to learn amongst those of India, Æthiopia, and Libya, I should probably appear to be concocting a tale and acting the braggart, or to be telling a falsehood respecting the nature of the animal founded on a mere report, all which it behoves a philosopher, and most of all one who is an ardent lover of truth, not to do. But what I have seen myself, and what others have described as having occurred at Rome, this I have chosen to relate, selecting a few facts out of many, to show the particular nature of those creatures. The elephant when tamed is an animal most gentle and most easily led to do whatever he is directed. And by way of showing honour to time, I will first narrate events of the oldest date. Cæsar Germanicus, the nephew of Tiberius, exhibited once a public show, wherein there were many full-grown elephants, male and female, and some of their breed born in this country. When their limbs were beginning to become firm, a person familiar with such animals instructed them by a strange and surpassing method of teaching; using only gentleness and kindness, and adding to his mild lessons the bait of pleasant and varied food. By this means he led them by degrees to throw off all wildness, and, as it were, to desert to a state of civilisation, conducting themselves in a manner almost human. He taught them neither to be excited on hearing the pipe, nor to be disturbed by the beat of drum, but to be soothed by the sounds of the reed, and to endure unmusical noises and the clatter of feet from persons while marching; and they were trained to feel no fear of a mass of men, nor to be enraged at the infliction of blows, not even when compelled to twist their limbs and to bend them like a stage-dancer, and this too although endowed with strength and might. And there is in this a very noble addition to nature, not to conduct themselves in a disorderly manner and disobediently towards the instructions of man; for after the dancing-master had made them expert, and they had learnt their lessons accurately, they did not belie the labour of his instruction whenever a necessity and opportunity called upon them to exhibit what they had been taught. For the whole troop came forward from this and that side of the theatre, and divided themselves into parties: they advanced walking with a mincing gait and exhibiting in their whole body and persons the manners of a beau, clothed in the flowery dresses of dancers; and on the ballet-master giving a signal with his voice, they fell into line and went round in a circle, and if it were requisite to deploy they did so. They ornamented the floor of the stage by throwing flowers upon it, and this they did in moderation and sparingly, and straightway they beat a measure with their feet and kept time together.

"Now that Damon and Spintharus and Aristoxenus and Xenophilus and Philoxenus and others should know music excellently well, and for their cleverness be ranked amongst the few, is indeed a thing of wonder, but not incredible nor contrary at all to reason. For this reason that a *man* is a rational animal, and the recipient of mind and intelligence. But that a jointless animal (ἄναρθρον) should understand rhythm and melody, and preserve a gesture, and not deviate from a measured movement, and fulfil the requirements of those who laid down instructions, these are gifts of nature, I think, and a peculiarity in every way astounding. Added to these there were things enough to drive the spectator out of his senses; when the strewn rushes and other materials for beds on the ground were placed on the sand of the theatre, and they received stuffed mattrasses such as belonged to rich houses and variegated bed coverings, and goblets were placed there very expensive, and bowls of gold and silver, and in them a great quantity of water; and tables were placed there of sweet-smelling wood and ivory very superb: and upon them flesh meats and loaves enough to fill the stomachs of animals the most voracious. When the preparations were completed and abundant, the banqueters came forward, six male and an equal number of female elephants; the former had on a male dress, and the latter a female; and on a signal being given they stretched forward their trunks in a subdued manner, and took their food in great moderation, and not one of them appeared to be gluttonous greedy, or to snatch at a greater portion, as did the Persian mentioned by Xenophon. And when it was requisite to drink, a bowl was placed by the side of each; and inhaling with their trunks they took a draught very orderly; and then they scattered the drink about in fun; but not as in insult. Many other acts of a similar kind, both clever and astonishing, have persons described, relating to the peculiarities of these animals, and I saw them writing letters on Roman tablets with their trunks, neither looking awry nor turning aside. The hand, however, of the teacher was placed so as to be a guide in the formation of the letters; and while it was writing the animal kept its eye fixed down in an accomplished and scholarlike manner."

# CHAP. VIII.

## BIRDS.

Of the *Birds* of the island, upwards of three hundred and twenty species have been indicated, for which we are indebted to the persevering labours of Dr. Templeton, Dr. Kelaart, and Mr. Layard; but many yet remain to be identified. In fact, to the eye of a stranger, their prodigious numbers, and especially the myriads of waterfowl which, notwithstanding the presence of the crocodiles, people the lakes and marshes in the eastern provinces, form one of the marvels of Ceylon.

In the glory of their plumage, the birds of the interior are surpassed by those of South America and Northern India; and the melody of their song bears no comparison with that of the warblers of Europe, but the want of brilliancy is compensated by their singular grace of form, and the absence of prolonged and modulated harmony by the rich and melodious tones of their clear and musical calls. In the elevations of the Kandyan country there are a few, such as the robin of Neuera-ellia[1] and the long-tailed thrush[2], whose song rivals that of their European namesakes; but, far beyond the attraction of their notes, the traveller rejoices in the flute-like voices of the Oriole, the Dayal-bird[3],

[1] Pratincola atrata, *Kelaart.*

[2] Kittacincla macrura, *Gm.*

[3] Copsychus saularis, *Linn.* Called by the Europeans in Ceylon the "Magpie Robin." This is not to be confounded with the other popular favourite the "Indian Robin" (Thamnobia fulicata, *Linn.*), which

and some others equally charming; when at the first dawn of day, they wake the forest with their clear *réveil.*

It is only on emerging from the dense woods and coming into the vicinity of the lakes and pasture of the low country, that birds become visible in great quantities. In the close jungle one occasionally hears the call of the copper-smith[1], or the strokes of the great orange-coloured woodpecker [2] as it beats the decaying trees in search of insects, whilst clinging to the bark with its finely-pointed claws, and leaning for support upon the short stiff feathers of its tail. And on the lofty branches of the higher trees, the hornbill[3] (the toucan of the East), with its enormous double casque, sits to watch the motions of the tiny reptiles and smaller birds on which it preys, tossing them into the air when seized, and catching them in its gigantic mandibles as they fall.[4] The remarkable excrescence on the beak of this

is "never seen in the unfrequented jungle, but, like the coco-nut palm, which the Singhalese assert will only flourish within the sound of the human voice, it is always found near the habitations of men." — E. L. LAYARD.

[1] The greater red-headed Barbet (Megalaima indica, *Lath.;* M. Philippensis, *var. A. Lath.*), the incessant din of which resembles the blows of a smith hammering a cauldron.

[2] Brachypternus aurantius, *Linn.*

[3] Buceros pica, *Scop.;* B. Malabaricus, *Jerd.* The natives assert that B. pica builds in holes in the trees, and that when incubation has fairly commenced, the female takes her seat on the eggs, and the male closes up the orifice by which she entered, leaving only a small aperture through which he feeds his partner, whilst she successfully guards their treasures from the monkey tribes; her formidable bill nearly filling the entire entrance. See a paper by Edgar L. Layard, Esq. *Mag. Nat. Hist.* March, 1853. Dr. Horsfield had previously observed the same habit in a species of Buceros in Java. (See HORSFIELD and MOORE'S *Catal. Birds,* E. I. Comp. Mus. vol. ii.) It is curious that a similar trait, though necessarily from very different instincts, is exhibited by the termites, who literally build a cell round the great progenitrix of the community, and feed her through apertures.

[4] The hornbill is also frugivorous, and the natives assert that when endeavouring to detach a fruit, if the stem is too tough to be severed by his mandibles, he flings himself off the branch so as to add the weight of his body to the pres-

extraordinary bird may serve to explain the statement of the Minorite friar Odoric, of Portenau in Friuli, who travelled in Ceylon in the fourteenth century, and

THE HORNBILL.

brought suspicion on the veracity of his narrative by asserting that he had there seen "*birds with two heads.*"[1]

The Singhalese have a belief that the hornbill never resorts to the water to drink; but that it subsists exclusively by what it catches in its prodigious bill while

sure of his beak. The hornbill abounds in Cuttack, and bears there the name of "Kuchila-Kai," or Kuchila-eater, from its partiality for the fruit of the Strychnus nux-vomica. The natives regard its flesh as a sovereign specific for rheumatic affections.—*Asiat. Res.* ch. xv. p. 184.

[1] *Itinerarius* FRATRIS ODORICI, de Foro Julii de Portu-vahonis, &c.—HAKLUYT, vol. ii. p. 39.

rain is falling. This they allege is associated with the incessant screaming which it keeps up during showers.

As we emerge from the dark shade, and approach park-like openings on the verge of the low country, quantities of pea-fowl are to be found either feeding on the seeds among the long grass or sunning themselves on the branches of the surrounding trees. Nothing to be met with in English demesnes can give an adequate idea of the size and magnificence of this matchless bird when seen in his native solitudes. Here he generally selects some projecting branch, from which his plumage may hang free of the foliage, and, if there be a dead and leafless bough, he is certain to choose it for his resting-place, whence he droops his wings and suspends his gorgeous train, or spreads it in the morning sun to drive off the damps and dews of the night.

In some of the unfrequented portions of the eastern province, to which Europeans rarely resort, and where the pea-fowl are unmolested by the natives, their number is so extraordinary that, regarded as game, it ceases to be "sport" to destroy them; and their cries at early dawn are so tumultuous and incessant as to banish sleep, and amount to an actual inconvenience. Their flesh is excellent in flavour when served up hot, though it is said to be indigestible; but, when cold, it contracts a reddish and disagreeable tinge.

The European fable of the jackdaw borrowing the plumage of the peacock, has its counterpart in Ceylon, where the popular legend runs that the pea-fowl stole the plumage of a bird called by the natives *avitchia*. I have not been able to identify the species which bears this name; but it utters a cry resembling the word *mat-kiang!* which in Singhalese means, "I *will* complain!" This they believe is addressed by the bird to the rising sun, imploring redress for its wrongs. The *avitchia* is described as somewhat less than a crow, the colours of its plumage being green, mingled with red.

But of all, the most astonishing in point of multitude, as well as the most interesting from their endless variety, are the myriads of aquatic birds and waders which frequent the lakes and watercourses; especially those along the coast near Batticaloa, between the mainland and the sand formations of the shore, and the innumerable salt marshes and lagoons to the south of Trincomalie. These, and the profusion of perching birds, fly-catchers, finches, and thrushes, that appear in the open country, afford sufficient quarry for the raptorial and predatory species—eagles, hawks, and falcons—whose daring sweeps and effortless undulations are striking objects in the cloudless sky.

I. ACCIPITRES. *Eagles.*—The Eagles, however, are small, and as compared with other countries rare; except, perhaps, the crested eagle[1], which haunts the mountain provinces and the lower hills, disquieting the peasantry by its ravages amongst their poultry; and the gloomy serpent eagle[2], which, descending from its eyrie in the lofty jungle, and uttering a loud and plaintive cry, sweeps cautiously around the lonely tanks and marshes, to feed upon the reptiles on their margin. The largest eagle is the great sea Erne[3], seen on the

[1] Spizaëtus limnaëtus, *Horsf.* The race of these birds in the Deccan and Ceylon are rather more crested, originating the Sp. Cristatellus, *Auct.*

[2] Which Gould believes to be the *Hæmatornis Bacha*, Daud.

[3] Pontoaëtus leucogaster, *Gmel.*

northern coasts and the salt lakes of the eastern provinces, particularly when the receding tide leaves bare an expanse of beach, over which it hunts, in company with the fishing eagle[1], sacred to Siva. Unlike its companions, however, the sea eagle rejects garbage for living prey, and especially for the sea snakes which abound on the northern coasts. These it seizes by descending with its wings half closed, and, suddenly darting down its talons, it soars aloft again with its writhing victim.[2]

*Hawks.*—The beautiful Peregrine Falcon[3] is rare, but the Kestrel[4] is found almost universally; and the bold and daring Goshawk[5] wherever wild crags and precipices afford safe breeding places. In the district of Anarajapoora, where it is trained for hawking, it is usual, in lieu of a hood, to darken its eyes by means of a silken thread passed through holes in the eyelids. The ignoble birds of prey, the Kites[6], keep close by the shore, and hover round the returning boats of the fishermen to feast on the fry rejected from their nets.

*Owls.*—Of the nocturnal accipitres the most remarkable is the brown owl, which, from its hideous yell, has acquired the name of the "Devil-Bird."[7] The Singha-

[1] Haliastur Indus, *Bodd.*

[2] E. L. Layard. Europeans have given this bird the name of the "Brahminy Kite," probably from observing the superstitious feeling of the natives regarding it, who believe that when two armies are about to engage, its appearance prognosticates victory to the party over whom it hovers.

[3] Falco peregrinus, *Linn.*

[4] Tinnunculus alaudarius, *Briss.*

[5] Astur trivirgatus, *Temm.*

[6] Milvus govinda, *Sykes.* Dr. Hamilton Buchanan remarks that when gorged this bird delights to sit on the entablature of buildings, exposing its back to the hottest rays of the sun, placing its breast against the wall, and stretching out its wings *exactly as the Egyptian Hawk is represented on the monuments.*

[7] Syrnium Indranee, *Sykes.* Mr. Blyth writes to me from Calcutta that there are some doubts about this bird. There would appear to be three or four distinguishable

lese regard it literally with horror, and its scream by night in the vicinity of a village is bewailed as the

THE "DEVIL BIRD."

harbinger of impending calamity.[1] There is a popula legend in connection with it, to the effect that a moros

races, the Ceylon bird approximating most nearly to that of the Malayan Peninsula.

[1] The horror of this nocturnal scream was equally prevalent in the West as in the East. Ovid introduces it in his *Fasti*, L. vi. l. 139; and Tibullus in his Elegies, L. i. El. 5. Statius says—

Nocturnæque gemunt striges, et feralia bubo
*Damna canens.* Theb. iii. l. 511.

But Pliny, l. xi. c. 93, doubts as to what bird produced the sound;—and the details of Ovid's description do not apply to an owl.

Mr. Mitford, of the Ceylon Civil Service, to whom I am indebted for many valuable notes relative to the birds of the island, regards the identification of the Singhalese Devil-Bird as open to similar

and savage husband, who suspected the fidelity of his wife, availed himself of her absence to kill her child, of whose paternity he was doubtful, and on her return placed before her a curry prepared from its flesh. Of this the unhappy woman partook, till discovering the crime by finding the finger of her infant, she fled in frenzy to the forest, and there destroyed herself. On her death she was metamorphosed, according to the Buddhist belief, into an *ulama*, or Devil-bird, which still at nightfall horrifies the villagers by repeating the frantic screams of the bereaved mother in her agony.

II. PASSERES. *Swallows.*—Within thirty-five miles of Caltura, on the western coast, are inland caves, to which the Esculent Swift[1] resorts, and there builds the "edible bird's nest," so highly prized in China. Near the spot a few Chinese immigrants have established themselves, who rent the nests as a royalty from the government, and make an annual export of the produce. But the Swifts are not confined to this district, and caves con-

doubt: he says—"The Devil-Bird is not an owl. I never heard it until I came to Kornegalle, where it haunts the rocky hill at the back of Government-house. Its ordinary note is a magnificent clear shout like that of a human being, and which can be heard at a great distance, and has a fine effect in the silence of the closing night. It has another cry like that of a hen just caught, but the sounds which have earned for it its bad name, and which I have heard but once to perfection, are indescribable, the most appalling that can be imagined, and scarcely to be heard without shuddering; I can only compare it to a boy in torture, whose screams are being stopped by being strangled. I have offered rewards for a specimen, but without success. The only European who had seen and fired at one agreed with the natives that it is of the size of a pigeon, with a long tail. I believe it is a Podargus or Night Hawk." In a subsequent note he further says—"I have since seen two birds by moonlight, one of the size and shape of a cuckoo, the other a large black bird, which I imagine to be the one which gives these calls."

[1] Collocalia brevirostris, *McClell.*; C. nidifica, *Gray.*

taining them have been found far in the interior, a fact which complicates the still unexplained mystery of the composition of their nest; and, notwithstanding the power of wing possessed by these birds, adds something to the difficulty of believing that it consists of glutinous material obtained from algæ.[1] In the nests brought to me there was no trace of organisation; and the original material, whatever it be, is so elaborated by the swallow as to present somewhat the appearance and consistency of strings of isinglass. The quantity of these nests exported from Ceylon is trifling.

*Kingfishers.* — In solitary places, where no sound breaks the silence except the gurgle of the river as it sweeps round the rocks, the lonely Kingfisher, the emblem of vigilance and patience, sits upon an overhanging branch, his turquoise plumage hardly less intense in its lustre than the deep blue of the sky above him; and so intent is his watch upon the passing fish that intrusion fails to scare him from his post.

*Sun Birds.* — In the gardens the tiny Sun Birds[2] (known as the Humming Birds of Ceylon) hover all day long, attracted to the plants, over which they hang poised on their glittering wings, and inserting their curved beaks to extract the insects that nestle in the flowers.

Perhaps the most graceful of the birds of Ceylon in form and motions, and the most chaste in colouring, is the one which Europeans call "the Bird of Paradise,"[3] and

[1] An epitome of what has been written on this subject will be found in *Dr. Horsfield's Catalogue* of the Birds in the E. I. Comp. Museum, vol. i. p. 101, &c. Mr. Morris assures me, that he has found the nests of the Esculent Swallow eighty miles distant from the sea.

[2] Nectarina Zeylanica, *Linn.*

[3] Tchitrea paradisi, *Linn.*

natives "the Cotton Thief," from the circumstance that its tail consists of two long white feathers, which stream

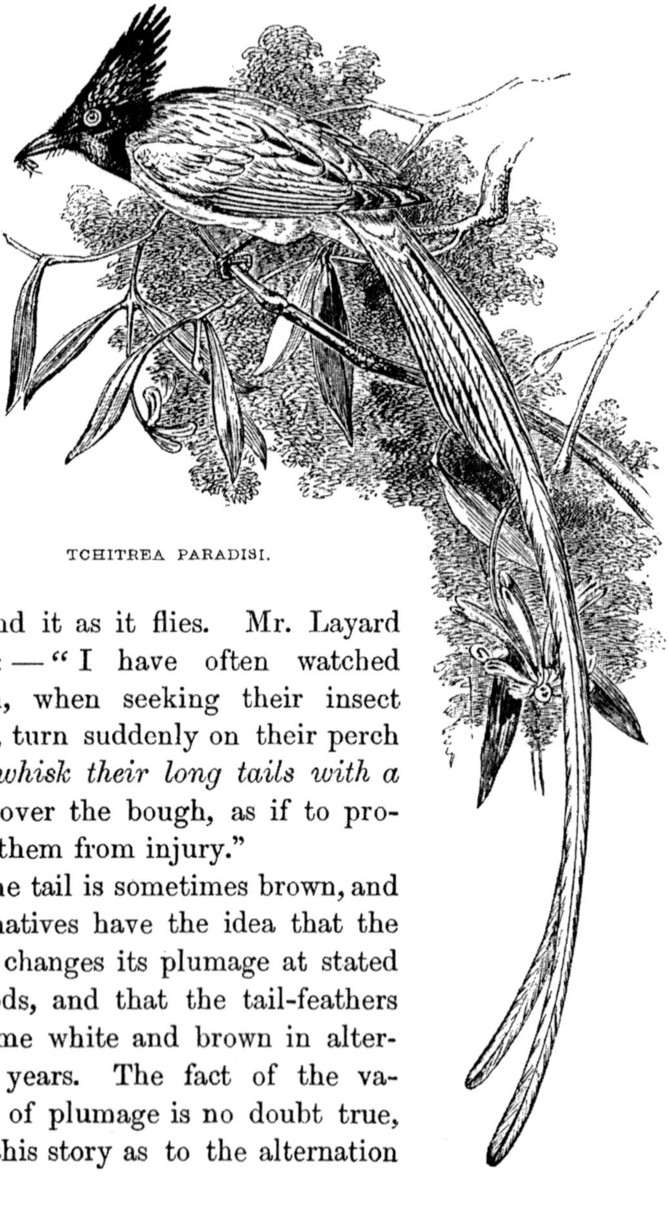

TCHITREA PARADISI.

behind it as it flies. Mr. Layard says: — "I have often watched them, when seeking their insect prey, turn suddenly on their perch and *whisk their long tails with a jerk* over the bough, as if to protect them from injury."

The tail is sometimes brown, and the natives have the idea that the bird changes its plumage at stated periods, and that the tail-feathers become white and brown in alternate years. The fact of the variety of plumage is no doubt true, but this story as to the alternation of colours in the *same* individual requires confirmation.[1]

*The Bulbul.*— The *Condatchee Bulbul*[2], which, from the crest on its head, is called by the Singhalese the "Konda Coorooła," or *Tuft bird*, is regarded by the natives as the most "*game*" of all birds; and training it to fight was one of the duties entrusted by the Kings of Kandy to the Cooroowa, or Head-man, who had charge of the King's animals and Birds. For this purpose the Bulbul is taken from the nest as soon as the sex is distinguishable by the tufted crown; and secured by a string, is taught to fly from hand to hand of its keeper. When pitted against an antagonist, such is the obstinate courage of this little creature that it will sink from exhaustion rather than release its hold. This propensity, and the ordinary character of its notes, render it impossible that the Bulbul of India could be identical with the Bulbul of Iran, the "Bird of a Thousand Songs,"[3] of which poets say that its delicate passion for the rose gives a plaintive character to its note.

*Tailor-Bird.* — *The Weaver-Bird.* — The tailor-bird[4] having completed her nest, sewing together leaves by passing through them a cotton thread twisted by herself, leaps from branch to branch to testify her happiness by

[1] The engraving of the Tchitrea given on page 244 is copied by permission from one of the splendid drawings in MR. GOULD's *Birds of India*.

[2] Pycnonotus hæmorrhous, *Gmel.*

[3] "*Hazardasitaum,*" the Persian name for the bulbul. "The Persians," according to Zakary ben Mohamed al Caswini, "say the bulbul has a passion for the rose, and laments and cries when he sees it pulled." — OUSELEY's *Oriental Collections*, vol. i. p. 16. According to Pallas it is the true nightingale of Europe, Sylvia luscinia, which the Armenians call *boulboul*, and the Crim-Tartars *byl-byl-i*.

[4] Orthotomus longicauda, *Gmel.*

a clear and merry note; and the Indian weaver[1], a still more ingenious artist, hangs its pendulous dwelling from a projecting bough; twisting it with grass into a form somewhat resembling a bottle with a prolonged neck, the entrance being inverted, so as to baffle the approaches of its enemies, the tree snakes and other reptiles. The natives assert that the male bird carries fire flies to the nest, and fastens them to its sides by a particle of soft mud;— Mr. Layard assures me that

"CISSA PUELLA."

although he has never succeeded in finding the fire fly, the nest of the male bird (for the female occupies another during incubation) invariably contains a patch

[1] Ploceus baya, *Blyth.*; P. Philippinus, *Auct.*

of mud on each side of the perch. Grass is apparently the most convenient material for the purposes of the Weaver-bird when constructing its nest, but other substances are often substituted, and some nests which I brought from Ceylon proved to be formed with delicate strips from the fronds of the dwarf date-palm, *Phœnix paludosa*, which happened to grow near the breeding place.

Amongst the birds of this order, one which, as far as I know, is peculiar to the island is *Layard's Mountain-jay* (*Cissa puella*, Blyth and Layard), is distinguished not less by the beautiful blue colour which enlivens its plumage, than by the elegance of its form and the grace of its attitudes. It frequents the hill country, and is found about the mountain streams at Neuera-ellia, and elsewhere.[1]

*Crows.* — Of all the Ceylon birds of this order the most familiar and notorious are the small glossy crows, whose shining black plumage shot with blue has suggested the title of *Corvus splendens*.[2] They frequent the towns in companies, and domesticate themselves in the close vicinity of every house; and it may possibly serve to account for the familiarity and audacity which they exhibit in their intercourse with men, that the Dutch during their sovereignty in Ceylon, enforced severe penalties against any one killing a crow, under the belief that they were instrumental in extending the

[1] The engraving above is taken by permission of Mr. Gould from one of his drawings for his *Birds of India*.

[2] There is another species, the *C. culminatus*, so called from the convexity of its bill; but though seen in the towns, it lives chiefly in the open country, and may be constantly observed wherever there are buffaloes, perched on their backs and engaged, in company with the small Minah (*Acridotheres tristis*), in freeing them from ticks.

growth of cinnamon by feeding on the fruit, and thus disseminating the undigested seed.[1]

So accustomed are the natives to their presence and exploits, that, like the Greeks and Romans, they have made the movements of crows the basis of their auguries; and there is no end to the vicissitudes of good and evil fortune which may not be predicted from the direction of their flight, the hoarse or mellow notes of their croaking, the variety of trees on which they rest, and the numbers in which they are seen to assemble.

All day long these birds are engaged in watching either the offal of the offices, or the preparation for meals in the dining-room: and as doors and windows are necessarily opened to relieve the heat, nothing is more common than the passage of a crow across the room, lifting on the wing some ill-guarded morsel from the dinner-table. No article, however unpromising its quality, provided only it be portable, can with safety be left unguarded in any apartment accessible to them. The contents of ladies' work-boxes, kid gloves, and pocket handkerchiefs vanish instantly if exposed near a window or open door. They open paper parcels to ascertain the contents; they will undo the knot on a napkin if it encloses anything eatable, and I have known a crow to extract the peg which fastened the lid of a basket in order to plunder the provender within.

On one occasion a nurse seated in a garden adjoining a regimental mess-room, was terrified by seeing a bloody clasp-knife drop from the air at her feet; but the mystery was explained on learning that a crow, which had been watching the cook chopping mince-meat, had seized

[1] WOLF'S *Life and Adventures*, p. 117.

the moment when his head was turned to carry off the knife.

One of these ingenious marauders, after vainly attitudinising in front of a chained watch-dog, that was lazily gnawing a bone, and after fruitlessly endeavouring to divert his attention by dancing before him, with head awry and eye askance, at length flew away for a moment, and returned bringing a companion which perched itself on a branch a few yards in the rear. The crow's grimaces were now actively renewed, but with no better success, till its confederate, poising itself on its wings, descended with the utmost velocity, striking the dog upon the spine with all the force of its strong beak. The *ruse* was successful; the dog started with surprise and pain, but not quickly enough to seize his assailant, whilst the bone he had been gnawing was snatched away by the first crow the instant his head was turned. Two well-authenticated instances of the recurrence of this device came within my knowledge at Colombo, and attest the sagacity and powers of communication and combination possessed by these astute and courageous birds.

On the approach of evening the crows near Colombo assemble in noisy groups along the margin of the fresh-water lake which surrounds the fort on the eastern side; and here for an hour or two they enjoy the luxury of throwing the water over their shining backs, and arranging their plumage decorously, after which they disperse, each taking the direction of his accustomed quarters for the night.[1]

[1] A similar habit has been noticed in the damask Parrots of Africa (*Palæornis fuscus*), which daily resort at the same hour to their accustomed pools to bathe.

During the storms which usher in the monsoon, it has been observed, that when coco-nut palms are destroyed by lightning, the effect frequently extends beyond a single tree, and from the contiguity and conduction of the spreading leaves, or some other peculiar cause, large groups will be affected by a single flash, a few killed instantly, and the rest doomed to rapid decay. In Belligam Bay, a little to the east of Point-de-Galle, a small island, which is covered with coco-nuts, has acquired the name of "Crow Island," from being the resort of those birds, which are seen hastening towards it in thousands towards sunset. A few years ago, during a violent storm of thunder, such was the destruction of the crows that the beach for some distance was covered with a black line of their remains, and the grove on which they had been resting was to a great extent destroyed by the same flash.[1]

III. SCANSORES. *Parroquets.*—Of the Psittacidæ the only examples are the parroquets, of which the most renowned is the *Palæornis Alexandri*, which has the historic distinction of bearing the name of the great conqueror of India, having been the first of its race introduced to the knowledge of Europe on the return of his expedition. An idea of their number may be formed from the following statement of Mr. Layard, as to the multitudes which are to be found on the western coast. "At Chilaw, I have seen such vast flights of parroquets hurrying towards the coco-nut trees which overhang the

[1] Similar instances are recorded in other countries of sudden and prodigious mortality amongst crows; but whether occasioned by lightning seems uncertain. In 1839 thirty-three thousand dead crows were found on the shores of a lake in the county Westmeath in Ireland after a storm.—THOMPSON'S *Nat. Hist. Ireland*, vol. i. p. 319. PATTERSON in his *Zoology*, p. 356, mentions other cases.

bazaar, that their noise drowned the Babel of tongues bargaining for the evening provisions. Hearing of the swarms that resorted to this spot, I posted myself on a bridge some half mile distant, and attempted to count the flocks which came from a single direction to the eastward. About four o'clock in the afternoon, straggling parties began to wend towards home, and in the course of half an hour the current fairly set in. But I soon found that I had no longer distinct flocks to count, it became one living screaming stream. Some flew high in the air till right above their homes, and dived abruptly downward with many evolutions till on a level with the trees; others kept along the ground and dashed close by my face with the rapidity of thought, their brilliant plumage shining with an exquisite lustre in the sun-light. I waited on the spot till the evening closed, when I could hear, though no longer distinguish, the birds fighting for their perches, and on firing a shot they rose with a noise like the 'rushing of a mighty wind,' but soon settled again, and such a din commenced as I shall never forget; the shrill screams of the birds, the fluttering of their innumerable wings, and the rustling of the leaves of the palm trees was almost deafening, and I was glad at last to escape to the Government Rest House."[1]

IV. COLUMBIDÆ. *Pigeons.*—Of pigeons and doves there are at least a dozen species. Some live entirely on trees[2], never alighting on the ground; others, notwithstanding the abundance of food and warmth, are

[1] *Annals of Nat. Hist.* vol. xiii. p. 263.

[2] Treron bicincta, *Jerd.*

migratory [1], allured, as the Singhalese allege, by the ripening of the cinnamon berries, and hence one species is known in the southern provinces as the "Cinnamon Dove." Others feed on the fruits of the banyan: and it is probably to their instrumentality that this marvellous tree chiefly owes its diffusion, its seeds being carried by them to remote localities. A very beautiful pigeon, peculiar to the mountain range, discovered in the lofty trees at Neuera-ellia, has, in compliment to the Viscountess Torrington, been named *Carpophaga Torringtoniæ.*

Another, called by the natives *neela-cobeya* [2], although strikingly elegant both in shape and colour, is still more remarkable for the singularly soothing effect of its low and harmonious voice. A gentleman who has spent many years in the jungle, in writing to me of this bird and of the effects of its melodious song, says, that "its soft and melancholy notes, as they came from some solitary place in the forest, were the most gentle sounds I ever listened to. Some sentimental smokers assert that the influence of the propensity is to make them feel *as if they could freely forgive all who had ever offended them;* and I can say with truth such has been the effect on my own nerves of the plaintive murmurs of the neela-cobeya, that sometimes, when irritated, and not without reason, by the perverseness of some of my native followers, the feeling has almost instantly subsided into placidity on suddenly hearing the loving tones of these beautiful birds."

[1] *Alsocomus puniceus*, the "Season Pigeon" of Ceylon, so called from its periodical arrival and departure.

[2] Chalcophaps Indicus, *Linn.*

V. GALLINÆ. *The Ceylon Jungle-fowl.*—The jungle-fowl of Ceylon[1] is shown by the peculiarity of its plumage to be not only distinct from the Indian species, but peculiar to the island. It has never yet bred or survived long in captivity, and no living specimens have been successfully transmitted to Europe. It abounds in all parts of the island, but chiefly in the lower ranges of mountains; and one of the vivid memorials which are associated with our journeys through the hills, is its clear cry, which sounds like a person calling "George Joyce,"[2] and rises at early morning amidst mist and dew, giving life to the scenery, that has scarcely yet been touched by the sun-light.

The female of this handsome bird was figured many years ago by Dr. GRAY in his illustrations of "*Indian Zoology*," under the name of *G. Stanleyi*. The cock bird subsequently received from LESSON, the name by which the species is now known: but its habitat was not discovered, until a specimen having been forwarded from Ceylon to Calcutta, Dr. BLYTH recognised it as the long-sought-for male of Dr. Gray's specimen.

Another of the Gallinæ of Ceylon, remarkable for the delicate pencillings of its plumage, as well as for the peculiarity of the double spur, from which it has acquired its trivial name, is the *Galloperdix bicalcaratus*, of which a figure is given from a drawing by Mr. Gould.

[1] Gallus Lafayetti, *Lesson.*

[2] I apprehend that in the particular of the peculiar cry the Ceylon jungle fowl differs from that of the Dekkan, where *I am told* that it crows like a bantam cock.

GALLOPERDIX BICALCARATUS.

VI. Grallæ.—On reaching the marshy plains and shallow lagoons on either side of the island, the astonishment of the stranger is excited by the endless multitudes of stilt-birds and waders which stand in long array within the wash of the water, or sweep in vast clouds above it. Ibises[1], storks[2], egrets, spoonbills[3], herons[4], and the smaller races of sand larks and plovers, are seen busily traversing the wet sand, in search of the red worm which burrows there, or peering with steady eye to watch the motions of the small fry and aquatic insects in the ripple on the shore.

VII. Anseres.—Preeminent in size and beauty, the

[1] Tantalus leucocephalus, and Ibis falcinellus.

[2] The violet-headed Stork (Ciconia leucocephala).

[3] Platalea leucorodia, *Linn.*

[4] Ardea cinerea. A. purpurea.

tall *flamingoes*[1], with rose-coloured plumage, line the beach in long files. The Singhalese have been led, from their colour and their military order, to designate them the "*English Soldier birds.*" Nothing can be more startling than the sudden flight of these splendid creatures when alarmed; their strong wings beating the air with a sound like distant thunder; and as they soar over head, the flock which appeared almost white but a moment before, is converted into crimson by the sudden display of the red lining of their wings. A peculiarity in the beak of this bird has scarcely attracted the attention it

FLAMINGO.

merits, as a striking illustration of creative wisdom in adapting the organs of animals to their local necessities.

[1] Phœnicopterus roseus, *Pallas*.

The upper mandible, which is convex in other birds, is flattened in the flamingo, whilst the lower, instead of being flat, is convex. To those who have had an opportunity of witnessing the action of the bird in its native haunts, the expediency of this arrangement is at once apparent. To counteract the extraordinary length of its legs, it is provided with a proportionately long neck, so that in feeding in shallow water the crown of the head becomes inverted and the upper mandible brought into contact with the bottom; where its flattened surface qualifies it for performing the functions of the lower one in birds of the same class; and the edges of both being laminated, it is thus enabled, like the duck, by the aid of its fleshy tongue, to sift before swallowing its food.

Floating on the surface of the deeper water, are fleets of the Anatidæ, the Coromandel teal [1], the Indian hooded gull [2], the Caspian tern, and a countless variety of ducks and smaller fowl—pintails [3], teal [4], red-crested pochards [5], shovellers [6], and terns.[7] Pelicans [8] in great numbers resort to the mouths of the rivers, taking up their position at sunrise on some projecting rock, from which to dart on the passing fish, and returning far inland at night to their retreats among the trees which overshadow some solitary river or deserted tank.

I chanced upon one occasion to come unexpectedly upon one of these remarkable breeding places during a visit which I made to the great tank of Padivil, one of those gigantic constructions by which the early kings of Ceylon have left imperishable records of their reigns.

[1] Nettapus coromandelianus, *Gm.*
[2] Larus brunnicephalus, *Jerd.*
[3] Dafila acuta, *Linn.*
[4] Querquedula crecca, *Linn.*
[5] *Fuligula rufina, Pallas.*
[6] Spatula clypeata, *Linn.*
[7] Sterna minuta, *Linn.*
[8] Pelicanus Philippensis, *Gmel.*

It is situated in the depth of the forests to the north-west of Trincomalie, and the tank is itself the basin of a broad and shallow valley, enclosed between two lines of low hills, that gradually sink into the plain as they approach towards the sea. The extreme breadth of the included space may be twelve or fourteen miles, narrowing to eleven at the spot where the retaining bund has been constructed across the valley; and when this enormous embankment was in effectual repair, and the reservoir filled by the rains, the water must have been thrown back along the basin of the valley for at least fifteen miles. It is difficult now to determine the precise distances, as the overgrowth of wood and jungle has obliterated all lines left by the original level of the lake at its junction with the forest. Even when we rode along it, the centre of the tank was deeply submerged, so that notwithstanding the partial escape, the water still covered an area of ten miles in diameter. Even now its depth when full must be very considerable, for high on the branches of the trees that grow in the area, the last flood had left quantities of driftwood and withered grass; and the rocks and banks were coated with the yeasty foam, that remains after the subsidence of an agitated flood.

The bed of the tank was difficult to ride over, being still soft and treacherous, although covered everywhere with tall and waving grass; and in every direction it was poched into deep holes by the innumerable elephants that had congregated to roll in the soft mud, to bathe in the collected water, or to luxuriate in the rich herbage, under the cool shade of the trees. The ground, too, was thrown up into hummocks like great molehills which, the natives told us, were formed by a huge earthworm, common in Ceylon, nearly two feet in length, and as thick as a small snake. Through these inequalities the water was still running off in natural drains towards the great channel in the centre, that conducts it to the broken sluice; and across these it was sometimes difficult to find a safe footing for our horses.

In a lonely spot, towards the very centre of the tank, we came unexpectedly upon an extraordinary scene. A sheet of still water, two or three hundred yards broad, and about half a mile long, was surrounded by a line of tall forest-trees, whose branches stretched above its margin. The sun had not yet risen, when we perceived some white objects in large numbers on the tops of the trees; and as we came nearer, we discovered that a vast colony of pelicans had formed their settlement and breeding-place in this solitary retreat. They literally covered the trees in hundreds; and their heavy nests, like those of the swan, constructed of large sticks, forming great platforms, were sustained by the horizontal branches. Each nest contained three eggs, rather larger than those of a goose; and the male bird stood placidly beside the female as she sat upon them.

Nor was this all; along with the pelicans prodigious numbers of other water-birds had selected this for their dwelling-place, and covered the trees in thousands, standing on the topmost branches; tall flamingoes, herons, egrets, storks, ibises, and other waders. We had disturbed them thus early, before their habitual hour for betaking themselves to their fishing-fields. By degrees, as the light increased, we saw them beginning to move upon the trees; they looked around them on every side, stretched their awkward legs behind them, extended their broad wings, gradually rose in groups, and slowly soared away in the direction of the sea-shore.

The pelicans were apparently later in their movements; they allowed us to approach as near them as the swampy nature of the soil would permit; and even when a gun was discharged amongst them, only those moved off which the particles of shot disturbed. They were in such numbers at this favourite place, that the water over which they had taken up their residence was swarming with crocodiles, attracted by the frequent fall of the young birds; and the natives refused, from fear of them, to wade in for one of the larger pelicans which had fallen, struck by a rifle ball. It was altogether a very remarkable sight.

Of the birds familiar to European sportsmen, partridges and quails are to be had at all times; the woodcock has occasionally been shot in the hills, and the ubiquitous snipe, which arrives in September from Southern India, is identified not alone by the eccentricity of its flight, but by retaining in high perfection the qualities which have endeared it to the gastronome at home. But the magnificent pheasants, which inhabit the Himalayan range and the woody hills of the Chin-Indian peninsula, have no representative amongst the tribes that people the woods of Ceylon; although a bird believed to be a pheasant has more than once been seen in the jungle, close to Rangbodde, on the road to Neuera-ellia.

---

## *List of Ceylon Birds.*

In submitting this catalogue of the birds of Ceylon, I am anxious to state that the copious mass of its contents is mainly due to the untiring energy and exertions of my friend, Mr. E. L. Layard. Nearly every bird in the list has fallen by his gun; so that the most ample facilities have been thus provided, not only for extending the limited amount of knowledge which formerly existed on this branch of the zoology of the island; but for correcting, by actual comparison with recent specimens, the errors which had previously prevailed as to imperfectly described species. The whole of Mr. Layard's fine collection is at present in England.

ACCIPITRES.

Aquila
Bonelli, *Temm.*
pennata, *Gm.*
Spizaëtus
Nipalensis, *Hodgs.*
limnæëtus, *Horsf.*
Ictinaëtus
Malayensis, *Reinw.*
Hæmatornis
Bacha, *Daud.*
spilogaster, *Blyth.*
Pontoaëtus
leucogaster, *Gm.*
ichthyaëtus, *Horsf.*
Haliastur
Indus, *Bodd.*
Falco
peregrinus, *Linn.*
peregrinator, *Sund.*
Tinnunculus
alaudarius, *Briss.*
Hypotriorchis
chicquera, *Daud.*
Baza
lophotes, *Cuv.*
Milvus
govinda, *Sykes.*
Elanus
melanopterus, *Daud.*
Astur
trivirgatus, *Temm.*
Accipiter
badius, *Gm.*
Circus
Swainsonii, *A. Smith.*
cinerascens, *Mont.*
melanoleucos, *Gm.*
*æruginosus*, *Linn.*
Athene
castonatus, *Blyth.*
scutulata, *Raffles.*
Ephialtes
scops, *Linn.*
lempijii, *Horsf.*
sunia, *Hodgs.*
Ketupa
Ceylonensis, *Gm.*
Syrnium
Indranee, *Sykes.*
Strix
Javanica, *Gm.*

PASSERES.

Batrachostomus
moniliger, *Layard.*
Caprimulgus
*Mahrattensis*, *Sykes.*
Kelaarti, *Blyth.*
Asiaticus, *Lath.*
Cypselus
batassiensis, *Gray.*
melba, *Linn.*
affinis, *Gray.*
Macropteryx
coronatus, *Tickell.*
Collocalia
brevirostris, *McClel.*
Acanthylis
caudacuta, *Lath.*
Hirundo
panayana, *Gm.*
daurica, *Linn.*
hyperythra, *Layard.*
domicola, *Jerdon.*
Coracias
Indica, *Linn.*
Harpactes
fasciatus, *Gm.*
Eurystomus
orientalis, *Linn.*
Halcyon
Capensis, *Linn.*
atricapillus, *Gm.*
Smyrnensis, *Linn.*
Ceyx
tridactyla, *Linn.*
Alcedo
Bengalensis, *Gm.*
Ceryle
rudis, *Linn.*
Merops
Philippinus, *Linn.*
viridis, *Linn.*
quincticolor, *Vieill.*
Upupa
nigripennis, *Gould.*
Nectarina
Zeylanica, *Linn.*
minima, *Sykes.*
Asiatica, *Lath.*
Lotenia, *Linn.*
Dicæum
minimum, *Tickell.*
Phyllornis
Malabarica, *Lath.*
Jerdoni, *Blyth.*
Dendrophila
frontalis, *Horsf.*
Piprisoma
agile, *Blyth.*
Orthotomus
longicauda, *Gm.*
Cisticola
cursitans, *Frankl.*
omalura, *Blyth.*
Drymoica
valida, *Blyth.*
inornata, *Sykes.*
Prinia
socialis, *Sykes.*
Acrocephalus
dumetorum, *Blyth.*
Phyllopneuste
nitidus, *Blyth.*
montanus, *Blyth.*
viridanus, *Blyth.*
Copsychus
saularis, *Linn.*
Kittacincla
macrura, *Gm.*
Pratincola
caprata, *Linn.*
atrata, *Kelaart.*
Calliope
cyanea, *Hodgs.*
Thamnobia
fulicata, *Linn.*
Cyanecula
Suecica, *Linn.*
Sylvia
affinis, *Blyth.*
Parus
cinereus, *Vieill.*
Zosterops
palpebrosus, *Temm.*

Iöra
Zeylanica, *Gm.*
typhia, *Linn.*
Motacilla
sulphurea, *Bechs.*
Indica, *Gm.*
Madraspatana, *Briss.*
Budytes
viridis, *Gm.*
Anthus
rufulus, *Vieill.*
Richardii, *Vieill.*
striolatus, *Blyth.*
Brachypteryx
Palliseri, *Kelaart.*
Alcippe
nigrifrons, *Blyth.*
Pitta
brachyura, *Jerd.*
Oreocincla
spiloptera, *Blyth.*
Merula
Wardii, *Jerd.*
Kinnisii, *Kelaart.*
Zoothera
imbricata, *Layard.*
Garrulax
cinereifrons, *Blyth.*
Pormatorhinus
melanurus, *Blyth.*
Malacocercus
rufescens, *Blyth.*
griseus, *Gm.*
striatus, *Swains.*
Pellorneum
fuscocapillum, *Blyth.*
Dumetia
albogularis, *Blyth.*
Chrysomma
Sinense, *Gm.*
Oriolus
melanocephalus, *Linn.*
*Indicus, Briss.*
Criniger
ictericus, *Stickl.*
Pycnonotus
pen cillatus, *Kelaart.*
flavirictus, *Strickl.*
hæmorrhous, *Gm.*
atricapillus, *Vieill.*
Hemipus
picatus, *Sykes.*
Hypsipetes
Nilgherriensis, *Jerd.*
Cyornis
rubeculoïdes, *Vig.*
Myiagra
azurea, *Bodd.*
Cryptolopha
cinereocapilla, *Vieill.*
Leucocerca
*compressirostris, Blyth.*
Tchitrea
paradisi, *Linn.*
Butalis
latirostris, *Raffles.*
Muttui, *Layard.*
Stoparola
melanops, *Vig.*
Pericrocotus
flammeus, *Forst.*
peregrinus, *Linn.*

Campephaga
Macei, *Less.*
Sykesii, *Strickl.*
Artamus
fuscus, *Vieill.*
Edolius
paradiseus, *Gm.*
Dicrurus
macrocercus, *Vieill.*
edoliformis, *Blyth.*
longicaudatus, *A. Hay.*
leucopygialis, *Blyth.*
*cœrulescens, Linn.*
Irena
puella, *Lath.*
Lanius
superciliosus, *Lath.*
*erythronotus, Vig.*
Tephrodornis
affinis, *Blyth*
Cissa
puella, *Blyth & Layard.*
Corvus
splendens, *Vieill.*
culminatus, *Sykes.*
Eulabes
religiosa, *Linn.*
ptilogenys, *Blyth.*
Pastor
roseus, *Linn.*
Hetærornis
pagodarum, *Gm.*
*albifrontata, Layard.*
Acridotheres
tristis, *Linn.*
Ploceus
manyar, *Horsf.*
baya, *Blyth.*
Munia
undulata, *Latr.*
*Malabarica, Linn.*
Malacca, *Linn.*
rubronigra, *Hodgs.*
striata, *Linn.*
Kelaarti, *Blyth.*
Passer
Indicus, *Jard. & Selb.*
Alauda
gulgula, *Frank.*
*Malabarica, Scop.*
Pyrrhulauda
grisea, *Scop.*
Mirafra
affinis, *Jerd.*
Buceros
gingalensis, *Shaw.*
Malabaricus, *Jerd.*

SCANSORES.

Loriculus
Asiaticus, *Lath.*
Palæornis
Alexandri, *Linn.*
torquatus, *Briss.*
cyanocephalus, *Linn.*
Calthropæ, *Layard.*
Megalaima
Indica, *Latr.*
Zeylanica, *Gmel.*
flavifrons, *Cuv.*
rubicapilla, *Gm.*

Picus
gymnophthalmus, *Blth.*
Mahrattensis, *Lath.*
*Macei, Vieill.*
Gecinus
chlorophanes, *Vieill.*
Brachypternus
aurantius, *Linn.*
Ceylonus, *Forst.*
*rubescens, Vieill.*
Stricklandi, *Layard.*
Micropternus
gularis, *Jerd.*
Centropus
rufipennis, *Illiger.*
chlororhynchos, *Blyth.*
Oxylophus
melanoleucos, *Gm.*
Coromandus, *Linn.*
Eudynamys
orientalis, *Linn.*
Cuculus
Poliocephalus, *Lath.*
striatus, *Drapiez.*
canorus, *Linn.*
Polyphasia
tenuirostris, *Gray.*
Sonneratii, *Lath.*
Hierococcyx
varius, *Vahl.*
Surniculus
dicruroïdes, *Hodgs.*
Phœnicophaus
pyrrhocephalus, *Forst.*
Zanclostomus
viridirostris, *Jerd.*

COLUMBÆ.

Treron
bicincta, *Jerd.*
flavogularis, *Blyth.*
Pompadoura, *Gm.*
chlorogaster, *Blyth.*
Carpophaga
pusilla, *Blyth.*
Torringtoniæ, *Kelaart.*
Alsocomus
puniceus, *Tickel.*
Columba
intermedia, *Strickl.*
Turtur
risorius, *Linn.*
Suratensis, *Lath.*
humilis, *Temm.*
*orientalis, Lath.*
Chalcophaps
Indicus, *Linn.*

GALLINÆ.

Pavo
cristatus, *Linn.*
Gallus
Lafayetti, *Lesson.*
Galloperdix
bicalcaratus, *Linn.*
Francolinus
Ponticerianus, *Gm.*
Perdicula
agoondah, *Sykes.*

Coturnix
Chinensis, *Linn.*
Turnix ocellatus,
*var.* Bengalensis, *Blyth.*
*var.* taigoor, *Sykes.*

GRALLÆ.

Esacus
recurvirostris, *Cuv.*
Œdicnemus
crepitans, *Temm.*
Cursorius
Coromandelicus, *Gm.*
Lobivanellus
bilobus, *Gm.*
Göensis, *Gm.*
Charadrius
virginicus, *Bechs.*
Hiaticula
Philippensis, *Scop.*
Cantiana, *Lath.*
Leschenaultii, *Less.*
Strepsilas
Interpres, *Linn.*
Ardea
purpurea, *Linn.*
cinerea, *Linn.*
asha, *Sykes.*
intermedia, *Wagler.*
garzetta, *Linn.*
*alba, Linn.*
bubulcus, *Savig.*
Ardeola
leucoptera, *Bodd.*
Ardetta
cinnamomea, *Gm.*
flavicollis, *Lath.*
Sinensis, *Gm.*
Butoroides
Javanica, *Horsf.*
Platalea
leucorodia, *Linn.*
Nycticorax
griseus, *Linn.*
Tigrisoma
melanolopha. *Raffl.*
Mycteria
australis, *Shaw.*
Leptophilus
Javanica, *Horsf.*
Ciconia
leucocephala, *Gm.*
Anastomus
oscitans, *Bodd.*

Tantalus
leucocephalus, *Gm.*
Geronticus
melanocephalus, *Lath.*
Falcinellus
igneus, *Gm.*
Numenius
arquatus, *Linn.*
phæopus, *Linn.*
Totanus
fuscus, *Linn.*
calidris, *Linn.*
glottis, *Linn.*
stagnalis, *Bechst.*
Actitis
glareola, *Gm.*
ochropus, *Linn.*
hypoleucos, *Linn.*
Tringa
minuta, *Leist.*
subarquata, *Gm.*
Limicola
platyrhyncha, *Temm.*
Limosa
ægocephala, *Linn.*
Himantopus
candidus, *Bon.*
Recurvirostra
avocetta, *Linn.*
Hæmatopus
ostralegus, *Linn.*
Rhynchœa
Bengalensis, *Linn.*
Scolopax
rusticola, *Linn.*
Gallinago
stenura, *Temm.*
*scolopacina, Bon.*
*gallinula, Linn.*
Hydrophasianus
Sinensis, *Gm.*
Ortygometra
rubiginosa, *Temm.*
Corethura
Zeylanica, *Gm.*
Rallus
striatus, *Linn.*
Indicus, *Blyth.*
Porphyrio
poliocephalus, *Lath.*
Porzana
pygmæa, *Nan.*
Gallinula
phœnicura, *Penn.*
chloropus, *Linn.*
cristata, *Lath.*

ANSERES.

Phœnicopterus
ruber, *Linn.*
Sarkidiornis
melanonotos, *Penn.*
Nettapus
Coromandelianus, *Gm.*
Anas
pœcilorhyncha, *Penn.*
Dendrocygnus
arcuatus, *Cuv.*
Dafila
acuta, *Linn.*
Querquedula
crecca, *Linn.*
circia, *Linn.*
*Fuligula*
*rufina, Pall.*
Spatula
clypeata, *Linn.*
Podiceps
Philippensis, *Gm.*
Larus
brunnicephalus, *Jerd.*
ichthyaëtus, *Pall.*
Sylochelidon
Caspius, *Lath.*
Hydrochelidon
Indicus, *Steph.*
Gelochelidon
Anglicus, *Mont.*
Onychoprion
anasthætus, *Scop.*
Sterna
Javanica, *Horsf.*
melanogaster, *Temm.*
minuta, *Linn.*
Seena
aurantia, *Gray.*
Tha'asseus
Bengalensis, *Less.*
cristata, *Steph.*
Dromas
ardeola, *Payk.*
Atagen
ariel, *Gould.*
Thalassidroma
*melanogaster, Gould.*
Plotus
melanogaster, *Gm.*
Pelicanus
Philippensis, *Gm.*
Graculus
Sinensis, *Shaw.*
pygmæus, *Pallas.*

## NOTE.

The following is a list of the birds which are, as far as is at present known, peculiar to the island; it will probably be determined at some future day that some included in it have a wider geographical range.

Hæmatornis spilogaster. The "Ceylon eagle;" was discovered by Mr. Layard in the Wanny, and by Dr. Kelaart at Trincomalie.

Athene castonotus. The chestnut-winged hawk owl. This pretty little owl was added to the list of Ceylon birds by Dr. Templeton. Mr. Blyth is at present of opinion that this bird is identical with Ath. Castanopterus, *Horsf.* of Java as figured by Temminck: *P. Col.*

Batrachostomus moniliger. The oil bird; was discovered amongst the precipitous rocks of the Adam's Peak range by Mr. Layard. Another specimen was sent about the same time to Sir James Emerson Tennent from Avisavelle. Mr. Mitford has met with it at Ratnapoora.

Caprimulgus Kelaarti. Kelaart's nightjar; swarms on the marshy plains of Neuera-ellia at dusk.

Hirundo hyperythra. The red-bellied swallow; was discovered in 1849, by Mr. Layard at Ambepusse. They build a globular nest, with a round hole at top A pair built in the ring for a hanging lamp in Dr. Gardner's study at Peradenia, and hatched their young, undisturbed by the daily trimming and lighting of the lamp.

Cisticola omalura. Layard's mountain grass warbler; is found in abundance on Horton Plain and Neuera-ellia, among the long Patena grass.

Drymoica valida. Layard's wren-warbler; frequents tufts of grass and low bushes, feeding on insects.

Pratincola atrata. The Neuera-ellia robin; a melodious songster; added to our catalogue by Dr. Kelaart.

Brachypteryx Palliseri. Ant thrush. A rare bird, added by Dr. Kelaart from Dimboola and Neuera-ellia.

Pellorneum fuscocapillum. Mr. Layard found two specimens of this rare thrush creeping about shrubs and bushes, feeding on insects.

Alcippe nigrifrons. This thrush frequents low impenetrable thickets, and seems to be widely distributed.

Oreocincla spiloptera. The spotted thrush is only found in the mountain zone about lofty trees.

Merula Kinnisii. The Neuera-ellia blackbird; was added by Dr. Kelaart.

Garrulax cinereifrons. The ashy-headed babbler; was found by Mr. Layard near Ratnapoora.

Pomatorhinus melanurus. Mr. Layard states that the mountain babbler frequents low, scraggy, impenetrable brush, along the margins of deserted cheena land. This may turn out to be little more than a local yet striking variety of P. Horsfieldii of the Indian Peninsula.

Malacocercus rufescens. The red dung thrush added by Dr. Templeton to the Singhalese Fauna, is found in thick jungle in the southern and midland districts.

Pycnonotus penicillatus. The yellow-eared bulbul; was found by Dr. Kelaart at Neuera-ellia.

Butalis Muttui. This very handsome flycatcher was procured at Point Pedro, by Mr. Layard.

Dicrurus edoliformis. Dr. Templeton found this kingcrow at the Bibloo Oya. Mr. Layard has since got it at Ambogammoa.

Dicrurus leucopygialis. The Ceylon kingcrow was sent to Mr. Blyth from the vicinity of Colombo, by Dr. Templeton. A species very closely allied to D. cœrulescens of the Indian continent.

Tephrodornis affinis. The Ceylon butcher-bird. A migatory species found in the wooded grass lands in October.

Cissa puella. Layard's mountain jay. A most lovely bird, found along mountain streams at Neuera-ellia and elsewhere.

Eulabes ptilogenys. Templeton's mynah. The largest and most beautiful of the species. It is found in flocks perching on the highest trees, feeding on berries.

Munia Kelaarti. This Grosbeak previously assumed to be M. pectoralis of Jerdon; is most probably peculiar to Ceylon.

Loriculus asiaticus. The small parroquet, abundant in various districts.

Palæornis Calthropæ. Layard's purple-headed parroquet, found at Kandy, is a very handsome bird, flying in flocks, and resting on the summits of the very highest trees. Dr. Kelaart states that it is the only parroquet of the Neuera-ellia range.

Megalaima flavifrons. The yellow-headed barbet, is not uncommon.

Megalaima rubricapilla, is found in most parts of the island.

Picus gymnophthalmus. Layard's woodpecker. The smallest of the species, was discovered near Colombo, amongst jak-trees.

Brachypternus Ceylonus. The Ceylon woodpecker, is found in abundance near Neuera-ellia.

Brachypternus rubescens. The red woodpecker.

Centropus chlororhynchus. The yellow-billed cuckoo, was detected by Mr. Layard in dense jungle near Colombo and Avisavelle.

Phœnicophaus pyrrhocephalus. The malkoha, is confined to the southern highlands.

Treron Pompadoura. The Pompadour pigeon. "The Prince of Canino has shown that this is a totally distinct bird from Tr. flavogularis, with which it was confounded: it is much smaller, with the quantity of maroon colour on the mantle greatly reduced."—Paper by Mr. BLYTH, *Mag. Nat. Hist.* p. 514 : 1857.

Carpophaga Torringtoniæ. Lady Torrington's pigeon; a very handsome pigeon discovered in the highlands by Dr. Kelaart. It flies high in long sweeps, and makes its nest on the loftiest trees. Mr. Blyth is of opinion that it is no more than a local race, barely separable from C. Elphinstonii of the Nilgiris and Malabar coast.

Carpophaga pusilla. The little-hill dove, a migratory species found by Mr. Layard in the mountain zone, only appearing with the ripened fruit of the teak, banyan, &c., on which they feed.

Gallus Lafayetti. The Ceylon jungle fowl. The female of this handsome bird was figured by Mr. GRAY (*Ill. Ind. Zool.*) under the name of G. Stanleyi. The cock bird had long been lost to naturalists, until a specimen was forwarded by Dr. Templeton to Mr. Blyth, who at once recognised it as the long-looked-for male of Mr. Gray's recently described female. It is abundant in all the uncultivated portions of Ceylon; coming out into the open spaces to feed in the mornings and evenings. Mr. Blyth states that there can be no doubt that Hardwicke's published figure refers to the hen of this species, long afterwards termed G. Lafayetti.

Galloperdix bicalcaratus. Not uncommon in suitable situations

# CHAP. IX.

## REPTILES.

LIZARDS. *Iguana.* — One of the earliest, if not the first remarkable animal to startle a stranger on arriving in Ceylon, whilst wending his way from Point-de-Galle to Colombo, is a huge lizard of from four to five feet in length, the *Talla-goyā* of the Singhalese, and Iguana [1] of the Europeans. It may be seen at noon-day searching for ants and insects in the middle of the highway and along the fences; when disturbed, but by no means alarmed, by the approach of man, it moves off to a safe distance; and, the intrusion being at an end, it returns again to the occupation in which it had been interrupted. Repulsive as it is in appearance, it is perfectly harmless, and is hunted down by dogs in the maritime provinces, and its delicate flesh, which is believed to be a specific in dysentery, is converted into curry, and its skin into shoes. When seized, it has the power of inflicting a smart blow with its tail. The Talla-goyā lives in almost any convenient hollow, such as a hole in the ground, or a deserted nest of the termites; and some small ones, which frequented my garden at Colombo, made their retreat in the heart of a decayed tree.

[1] Monitor dracæna, *Linn.* Among the barbarous nostrums of the uneducated natives, both Singhalese and Tamil, is the tongue of the iguana, which they regard as a specific for consumption, if plucked from the living animal and swallowed whole.

A still larger species, the *Kabaragoyā*[1], is partial to marshy ground, and when disturbed upon land, will take refuge in the nearest water. From the somewhat eruptive appearance of the yellow blotches on its scales, a closely allied species, similarly spotted, formerly obtained amongst naturalists the name of *Monitor exanthematicus*, and it is curious that the native appellation of this one, *kabara*[2], is suggestive of the same idea. The Singhalese, on a strictly homœopathic principle, believe that its fat, externally applied, is a cure for cutaneous disorders, but that taken inwardly it is poisonous. The skilfulness of the Singhalese in their preparation of poisons, and their addiction to using them, are unfortunately notorious traits in the character of the rural population. Amongst these preparations, the one which above all others excites the utmost dread, from the number of murders attributed to its agency, is the potent kabara-tel — a term which Europeans sometimes corrupt into *cobra-tel*, implying that the venom is obtained from the hooded-snake; whereas it professes to be extracted from the "kabara-goyā." Such is the bad renown of this formidable poison, that an individual suspected of having it in his possession, is cautiously shunned by his neighbours. Those especially who are on doubtful terms with him, suspect their own servants lest they should be suborned to mix kabara-tel in the curry. So subtle is the virus sup-

[1] Hydrosaurus salvator, *Laur.* Tail compressed; fingers long; nostrils near the extremity of the snout. A black band on each temple; round yellow spots disposed in transverse series on the back. Teeth with the crown compressed and notched.

[2] In the *Mahawanso* the hero, Tissa, is said to have been "afflicted with a cutaneous complaint which made his skin scaly like that of the *godho*."—Ch. xxiv. p. 148. "Godho" is the Pali name for the Kabara-goyā.

posed to be, that one method of administering it, is to introduce it within the midrib of a leaf of betel, and close

THE KABARA-GOYA.

the orifice with chunam; and, as it is an habitual act of courtesy for one Singhalese on meeting another to offer the compliment of a betel-leaf, which it would be rudeness to refuse, facilities are thus afforded for presenting the concealed drug. It is curious that to this latent suspicion has been traced the origin of a custom universal amongst the natives, of nipping off with the thumb nail the thick end of the stem before chewing the betel.

In the preparation of this mysterious compound, the unfortunate Kabara-goya is forced to take a painfully prominent part. The receipt, as written down by a Kandyan, was sent to me from Kornegalle, by Mr. Morris, the civil officer of that district; and in dramatic arrangement it far outdoes the cauldron of *Macbeth's* witches. The ingredients are extracted from venomous snakes, the cobra de capello, the Carawilla, and the Tic-polonga, by making incisions in the head of these reptiles and suspending them over a chattie to collect the poison as it flows. To this, arsenic and other drugs are added, and the whole is "boiled in a human skull, with the aid of the three Kabara-goyas, which are tied on three sides of the fire, with their heads directed towards it, and tormented by whips to make them hiss, so that the fire may blaze. The froth from their lips is then added to the boiling mixture, and so soon as an oily scum rises to the surface, the *kabara-tel* is complete."

It is obvious that arsenic is the main ingredient in the poison, and Mr. Morris reported to me that the mode of preparing it, described above, was actually practised in his district. This account was transmitted by him apropos to the murder of a Mohatal[1] and his wife, which had been committed with the *kabara-tel*, and

[1] A native head-man of low rank.

was then under investigation. Before commencing the operation of preparing the poison, a cock has to be sacrificed to the *yakhos* or demons.

This ugly lizard is itself regarded with such aversion by the Singhalese, that if a *kabara* enter a house or walk over the roof, it is regarded as an omen of ill fortune, sickness, or death; and in order to avert the evil, a priest is employed to go through a rhythmical incantation; one portion of which consists in the repetition of the words

Kabara goyin wan dōsey
Ada palayan e dōsey.

"These are the inflictions caused by the Kabara-goya — let them now be averted!"

It is one of the incidents that serve to indicate that Ceylon may belong to a separate circle of physical geography, that this lizard, though found to the eastward in Burmah[1], has not hitherto been discovered in the Dekkan or Hindustan,

*Blood-suckers.*—The lizards already mentioned, however, are but the stranger's introduction to innumerable varieties of others, all most attractive in their sudden movements, and some unsurpassed in the brilliancy of their colouring, which bask on banks, dart over rocks, and peer curiously out of the chinks of every ruined wall. In all their motions there is that vivid and brief energy, the rapid but restrained action associated with their

[1] In corroboration of the view propounded elsewhere (see pp. 7, 84, &c.), and opposed to the popular belief that Ceylon, at some remote period, was detached from the continent of India by the interposition of the sea, a list of reptiles will be found at p. 319, including, not only individual species, but whole genera peculiar to the island, and not to be found on the mainland. See a paper by Dr. A. GÜNTHER on *The Geog. Distribution of Reptiles*, Magaz. Nat. Hist. for March, 1859, p. 230.

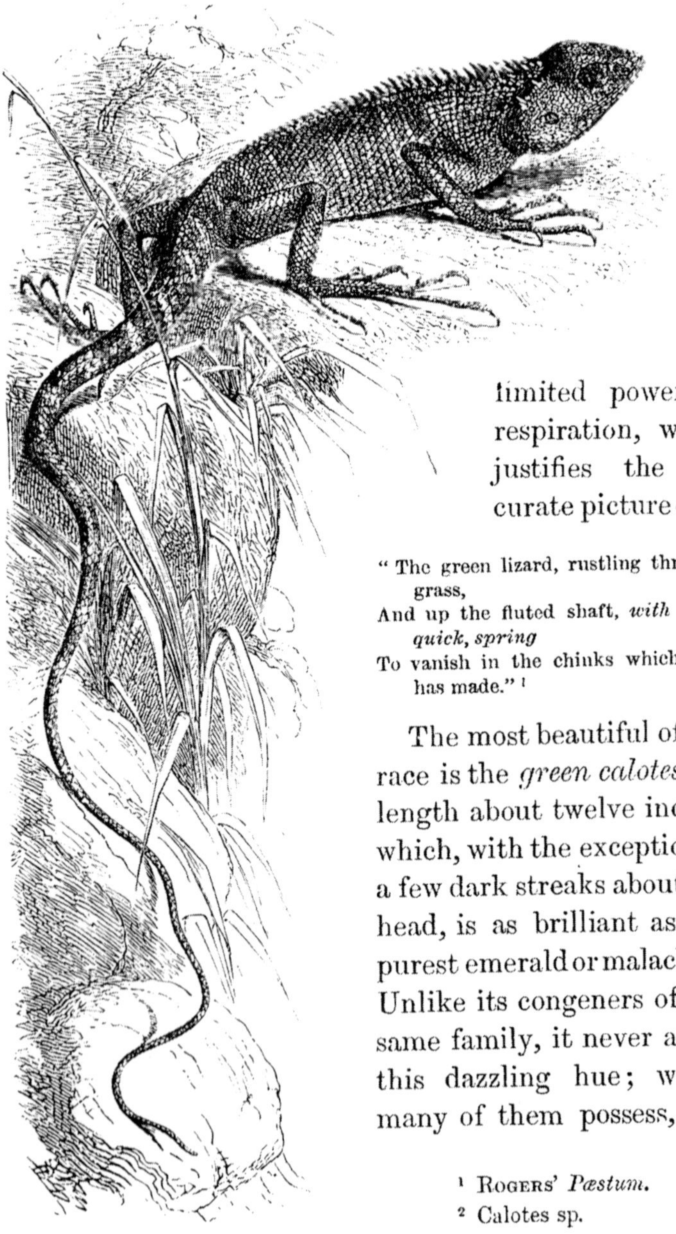

CALOTES OPHIOMACHUS

limited power of respiration, which justifies the accurate picture of—

"The green lizard, rustling thro' the grass,
And up the fluted shaft, *with short, quick, spring*
To vanish in the chinks which time has made."[1]

The most beautiful of the race is the *green calotes*[2], in length about twelve inches, which, with the exception of a few dark streaks about the head, is as brilliant as the purest emerald or malachite. Unlike its congeners of the same family, it never alters this dazzling hue; whilst many of them possess, but

[1] ROGERS' *Pæstum*.

[2] Calotes sp.

in a less degree, the power, like the chameleon, of exchanging their ordinary colours for others less conspicuous. One of the most remarkable features in the physiognomy of those lizards is the prominence of their cheeks. This results from the great development of the muscles of the jaws; the strength of which is such that they can crush the hardest integuments of the beetles on which they feed. The calotes will permit its teeth to be broken, rather than quit its hold of a stick into which it may have struck them. It is not provided, like so many other tropical lizards, with a gular sac or throat-pouch, capable of inflation when in a state of high excitement. The tail, too, is rounded, not compressed, thus clearly indicating that its habits are those of a land-animal.

The *Calotes versicolor*, and another, the *Calotes ophiomachus*, of which a figure is attached, possess in a remarkable degree the faculty, above alluded to, of changing their hue. The head and neck, when the animal is irritated or hastily swallowing its food, become of a brilliant red (whence the latter species has acquired the name of the "blood-sucker"), whilst the usual tint of the rest of the body is converted into pale yellow.[1] The *sitana*[2], and a number of others, exhibit similar phenomena.

The lyre-headed lizard[3], which is not uncommon in the woods about Kandy, is more bulky than any of the species of Calotes, and not nearly so active in its move-

[1] The characteristics by which the *Calotes ophiomachus* may be readily recognised, are a small crest formed by long spines running on each side of the neck to above the ear, coupled with a green ground-colour of the scales. Many specimens are uniform, others banded transversely with white, and others again have a black band on each side of the neck.

[2] Sitana Ponticereana, *Cuv.*

[3] Lyriocephalus scutatus, *Linn.*

ments. As usually observed it is of a dull greenish brown, but when excited its back becomes a rich olive green, leaving the head yellowish: the underside of the body is of a very pale blue, almost approaching white. The open mouth exhibits the fauces of an intense vermilion tint; so that, although extremely handsome, this lizard presents, from its extraordinarily shaped head and threatening gestures, a most malignant aspect. It is, however, perfectly harmless.

*Chameleon.*—The true chameleon[1] is found, but not in great numbers, in the dry districts to the north of Ceylon, where it frequents the trees, in slow pursuit of its insect prey; but compensated for the sluggishness of its other movements, by the electric rapidity of its extensible tongue. Apparently sluggish in its general habits, the chameleon rests motionless on a branch, from which its varied hues render it scarcely distinguishable in colour; and there patiently awaits the approach of the insects on which it feeds. Instantly on their appearance its wonderful tongue comes into play.

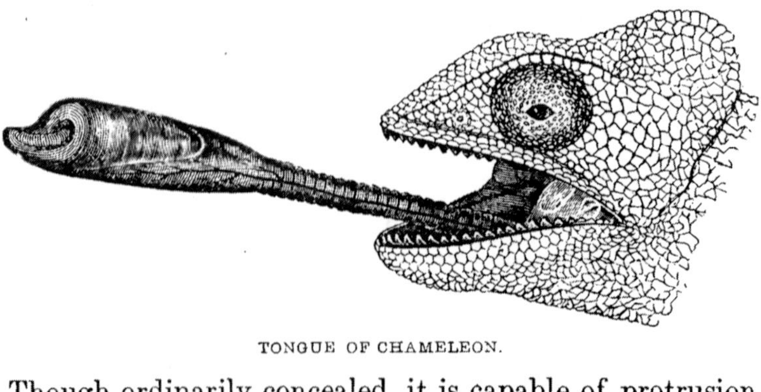

TONGUE OF CHAMELEON.

Though ordinarily concealed, it is capable of protrusion till it exceeds in length the whole body of the creature. No sooner does an incautious fly venture within reach

[1] Chameleo vulgaris, *Daud.*

than the extremity of this treacherous weapon is disclosed, broad and cuneiform, and covered with a viscid fluid; and this, extended to its full length, is darted at its prey with an unerring aim, and redrawn within the jaws with a rapidity that renders the act almost invisible.[1]

Whilst the faculty of this creature to assume all the colours of the rainbow has attracted the wonder of all ages, sufficient attention has hardly been given to the imperfect sympathy which subsists between the two lobes of its brain, and the two sets of nerves that permeate the opposite sides of its frame. Hence, not only has each of the eyes an action quite independent of the other, but one side of its body appears to be sometimes asleep whilst the other is vigilant and active; one will assume a green tinge whilst the opposite one is red; and it is said that the chameleon is utterly unable to swim, from the incapacity of the muscles of the two sides to act in concert.

*Ceratophora.*—This which till lately was an unique lizard, known by only two specimens, one in the British Museum, and another in that of Leyden, was ascertained by Dr. Kelaart, about five years ago, to be a native of the higher Kandyan hills, where it is sometimes seen in the older trees in pursuit of insect larvæ. The first specimen brought to Europe was called *Ceratophora Stoddartii,* after the name of its finder; and the recent discovery of several others in the National Collection has enabled me, by the aid of Dr. A. Günther, to add some important facts to their history.

This lizard is remarkable for having no external ear; and it has acquired its generic name from the

[1] Prof. RYMER JONES, art. *Reptilia*, in TODD'S *Cyclop. of Anat.* vol. iv. pt. i. p. 292.

curious horn-like process on the extremity of the nose. This horn, as it is found in mature males of ten inches in length, is five lines long, conical, pointed, and slightly curved; a miniature form of the formidable weapon, from which the *Rhinoceros* takes its name. But the comparison does not hold good either from an anatomical or a physiological point of view. For, whilst the horn of the rhinoceros is merely a dermal production, a conglomeration of hairs cemented into one dense mass as hard as bone, and answering the purpose of a defensive weapon, besides being used for digging up the roots on which the animal lives; the horn of the *ceratophora* is formed of a soft, spongy substance, coated by the rostral shield, which is produced into a kind of sheath. Although flexible, it always remains erect, owing to the elasticity of its substance. Not having access to a living specimen, which would afford the opportunity of testing conjecture, we are left to infer from the internal structure of this horn, that it is an erectile organ which, in moments of irritation, will swell like the comb of a cock. This opinion as to its physiological nature is confirmed by the remarkable circumstance that, like the rudimentary comb of the hen and young cocks, the female and the immature males of the *ceratophora* have the horn exceedingly small. In mature females of eight inches in length (and the females appear always to be smaller than the males), the horn is only one half or one line long; while in immature males five inches in length, it is one line and a half.

Among the specimens sent from Ceylon by Dr. Kelaart, and now in the British Museum, there is one which so remarkably differs from *C. Stoddartii*, that it attracted my attention, by the peculiar form of this rostral appendage. Dr. GÜNTHER pronounced it to be a new

CERATOPHORA TENNENTII
and

species; and Dr. Gray concurring in this opinion, they have done me the honour to call it *Ceratophora Tennentii.* Its "horn" somewhat resembles the comb of a cock not only in its internal structure, but also in its external appearance; it is nearly six lines long by two broad, slightly compressed, soft, flexile, and extensible, and covered with a corrugated, granular skin. It bears no resemblance to the depressed rostral hump of *Lyriocephalus*, and the differences of the new species from the latter lizard may be easily seen from the annexed drawing and the notes given below.[1]

*Geckoes.*—The most familiar and attractive of the lizard class are the *Geckoes*[2], that frequent the sitting-rooms, and being furnished with pads to each toe, they are enabled to ascend perpendicular walls and adhere to glass and ceilings. Being nocturnal in their habits, the pupil of the eye, instead of being circular as in the diurnal species, is linear and vertical like that of the cat. As soon as evening arrives, the geckoes are to be seen in every house in keen and crafty pursuit of their prey; emerging from the chinks and recesses where they conceal themselves

[1] The specimen in the British Museum is apparently an adult male, ten inches long, and is, with regard to the distribution of the scales and the form of the head, very similar to *C. Stoddartii.* The posterior angles of the orbit are not projecting, but there is a small tubercle behind them; and a pair of somewhat larger tubercles on the neck. The gular sac is absent. There are five longitudinal quadrangular, imbricate scales on each side of the throat; and the sides of the body present a nearly horizontal series of similar scales. The scales on the median line of the back scarcely form a crest; it is, however, more distinct on the nape of the neck. The scales on the belly, on the extremities, and on the tail are slightly keeled. Tail nearly round. This species is more uniformly coloured than *C. Stoddartii;* it is greenish, darker on the sides.

[2] Hemidactylus maculatus, *Dum.* et *Bib.*, H. Leschenaultii, *Dum.* et *Bib*; H. frenatus, *Schlegel.* Of these the last is very common in the houses of Colombo. Colour, grey; sides with small granules; thumb short; chin-shields four; tail rounded with transverse series of small spines; femoral and preanal pores in a continuous line. GRAY, *Lizards*, p. 155.

during the day, to search for insects that then retire to settle for the night. In a boudoir where the ladies of my family spent their evenings, one of these familiar and amusing little creatures had its hiding-place behind a gilt picture frame. Punctually as the candles were lighted, it made its appearance on the wall to be fed with its accustomed crumbs; and if neglected, it reiterated it sharp, quick call of *chic, chic, chit,* till attended to. It was of a delicate gray colour, tinged with pink; and having by accident fallen on a work-table, it fled, leaving part of its tail behind it, which, however, it reproduced within less than a month. This faculty of reproduction is doubtless designed to enable the creature to escape from its assailants: the detaching of the limb is evidently its own act; and it is observable, that when reproduced, the tail generally exhibits some variation from the previous form, the diverging spines being absent, the new portion covered with small square uniform scales placed in a cross series, and the scuta below being seldom so distinct as in the original member.[1] In an officer's quarters in the fort of Colombo, a geckoe had been taught to come daily to the dinner-table, and always made its appearance along with the dessert. The family were absent for some months, during which the house underwent extensive repairs, the roof having been raised, the walls stuccoed, and the ceilings whitened. It was naturally surmised that so long a suspension of its accustomed habits would have led to the disappearance of the little lizard; but on the return of its old friends, it made its entrance as usual at their first dinner the instant the cloth was removed.

*Crocodile.* — The Portuguese in India, like the Spa-

[1] *Brit. Mus. Cat.* p. 143; KELAART's *Prod. Faun. Zeylan.*, p. 183.

niards in South America, affixed the name of *lagarto* to the huge reptiles that infested the rivers and estuaries of both continents; and to the present day the Europeans in Ceylon apply the term *alligator* to what are in reality *crocodiles*, which literally swarm in the still waters and tanks in the low country, but rarely frequent rapid streams, and have never been found in the marshes among the hills. The differences, however, between the two, when once ascertained, are sufficiently marked, to prevent their being afterwards confounded. The head of the alligator is broader and the snout less prolonged, and the canine teeth of the under jaw, instead of being received into foramina in the upper, as in the crocodile, fit into furrows on each side of it. The legs of the alligator, too, are not denticulated, and the feet are only semi-palmate.

The following drawing exhibits a cranium of each.

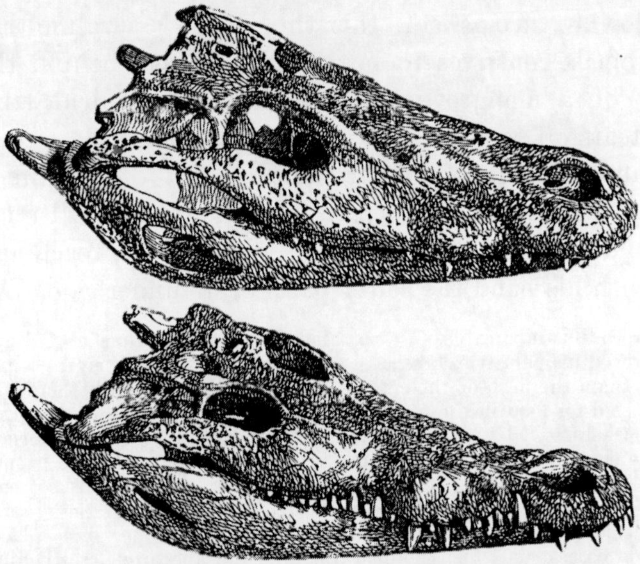

SKULLS OF ALLIGATOR AND CROCODILE

The instincts of the crocodiles in Ceylon do not lead to

any variation from the habits of those found in other countries. There would appear to be two well-distinguished species found in the island, the *Eli-kimboola*[1], the Indian crocodile, inhabiting the rivers and estuaries throughout the low countries of the coasts, attaining the length of sixteen or eighteen feet, and ready to assail man when pressed by hunger; and the marsh-crocodile[2], which lives exclusively in fresh water, frequenting the tanks in the northern and central provinces, and confining its attacks to the smaller animals: in length it seldom exceeds twelve or thirteen feet. Sportsmen complain that their dogs are constantly seized by both species; and water-fowl, when shot, frequently disappear before they can be secured by the fowler.[3] It is generally believed in Ceylon that, in the case of larger animals, the crocodile abstains from devouring them till the commencement of decomposition facilitates the operation of swallowing. To assist in this, the natives assure me that the reptile contrives to fasten the carcase behind the roots of a mangrove or some other convenient tree, and tears off each piece by a backward spring.

There is another popular belief that the crocodile is exceedingly sensitive to tickling; and that it will relax its hold of a man, if he can only contrive to reach and rub with his hand the softer parts of its under side.[4] An

[1] Crocodilus biporcatus, *Cuvier*.

[2] Crocodilus palustris, *Less.*

[3] In Siam the flesh of the crocodile is sold for food in the markets and bazaars. "Un jour je vis plus de cinquante crocodiles, petits et grands, attachés aux colonnes de leurs maisons. Ils les vendent la chair comme on vendrait de la chair de porc, mais à bien meilleur marché."—PALLEGOIX, *Siam*, vol. i. p. 174.

[4] A native gentleman who resided for a long time at Caltura, tells me that in the rivers which flow into the sea, both there and at Bentotte, crocodiles are frequently caught in corrals, formed of stakes driven into the ground in shallow water, and so constructed, that when the reptile enters to seize the bait placed within, the aperture closes behind, and secures him. A professional "crocodile charmer" then enters, muttering a spell, and with one end

incident indicative of some reality in this piece of folk-lore, once came under my own observation. One morning, about sunrise, when riding across the sandy plain near the old fort of Moeletivoe, we came suddenly upon a crocodile asleep under some bushes of the Buffalo-thorn, several hundred yards from the water. The terror of the poor wretch was extreme, when it awoke and found itself discovered and completely surrounded. It was a hideous creature, upwards of ten feet long, and evidently of prodigious strength, had it been in a condition to exert it, but consternation completely paralysed it. It started to its feet and turned round in a circle hissing and clanking its bony jaws, with its ugly green eye intently fixed upon us. On being struck with a stick, it lay perfectly quiet and apparently dead. Presently it looked cunningly round, and made a rush towards the water, but on a second blow it lay again motionless and feigning death. We tried to rouse it, but without effect, pulled its tail, slapped its back, struck its hard scales, and teased it in every way, but all in vain; nothing would induce it to move till accidentally my son, then a boy of twelve years old, tickled it gently under the arm, and in an instant it drew the limb close to its side and turned to avoid a repetition of the experiment. Again it was touched under the other arm, and the same emotion was exhibited, the great monster twisting about like an infant to avoid being tickled. The scene was highly amusing, but the sun was rising high, and we pursued our journey to Moeletivoe,

of a stick pats the creature gently on the head for a time. The operator then boldly mounts astride upon its shoulders, and continues to soothe it with his one hand, whilst with the other he contrives to pass a rope under its body, by which it is at last dragged on shore. This story serves to corroborate the narrative of Mr. Waterton and his alligator.

leaving the crocodile to make its way to the adjoining lake.

The Singhalese believe that the crocodile can only move swiftly on sand or smooth clay, its feet being too tender to tread firmly on hard or stony ground. In the dry season, when the watercourses begin to fail and the tanks become exhausted, the marsh-crocodiles have occasionally been encountered in the jungle, wandering in search of water. During a severe drought in 1844, they deserted a tank near Kornegalle and traversed the town during the night, on their way to another reservoir in the suburb; two or three fell into the wells; others, in their trepidation, laid eggs in the street, and some were found entangled in garden-fences and killed.

Generally, however, during the extreme drought, when unable to procure their ordinary food from the drying up of the watercourses, they bury themselves in the mud, and remain in a state of torpor till released by the recurrence of rains.[1] At Arne-tivoe, in the eastern province, whilst riding across the parched bed of the tank, I was shown the recess, still bearing the form and impress of a crocodile, out of which the animal had been seen to emerge the day before. A story was also related to me of an officer attached to the department of the Surveyor-General, who, having pitched his tent in a similar position, was disturbed during the night by feeling a movement of the earth below his bed, from which on the following day a crocodile emerged, making its appearance from beneath the matting.[2]

The fresh water species that inhabits the tanks is essen-

[1] HERODOTUS records the observations of the Egyptians that the crocodile of the Nile abstains from food during the four winter months. —*Euterpe*, lviii.

[2] HUMBOLDT relates a similar story as occurring at Calabazo, in Venezuela.—*Personal Narrative*, c. xvi.

tially cowardly in its instincts, and hastens to conceal itself on the appearance of man. A gentleman (who told me the circumstance), when riding in the jungle, overtook a crocodile, evidently roaming in search of water. It fled to a shallow pool almost dried by the sun, and, thrusting its head into the mud till it covered up its eyes, remained unmoved in profound confidence of perfect concealment. In 1833, during the progress of the Pearl Fishery, Sir Robert Wilmot Horton employed men to drag for crocodiles in a pond which was infested by them in the immediate vicinity of Aripo. The pool was about fifty yards in length, by ten or twelve wide, shallowing gradually to the edge, and not exceeding four or five feet at the deepest part. As the party approached the bund, from twenty to thirty reptiles, which had been basking in the sun, rose and fled to the water. A net, specially weighted so as to sink its lower edge to the bottom, was then stretched from bank to bank and swept to the further end of the pond, followed by a line of men with poles to drive the crocodiles forward: so complete was the arrangement, that no individual could have evaded the net, yet, to the astonishment of the Governor's party, not one was to be found when it was drawn on shore, and no means of escape for them was apparent or possible except by their descending into the mud at the bottom of the pond.

The lagoon of Batticaloa, and indeed all the still waters of this district, are remarkable for the numbers and prodigious size of the crocodiles which infest them. Their teeth are sometimes so large that the natives mount them with silver lids and use them for boxes to carry the powdered chunam, which they chew with the betel leaf. During one of my visits to the lake a crocodile was caught within a few yards of the government agent's residence, a hook having been laid the night before, baited with the entrails of a goat; and made fast, in the native fashion, by a bunch of fine cords, which the creature cannot gnaw asunder as it would a solid rope, since they sink into the spaces between its teeth. The one taken was small, being only about ten or eleven feet in length, whereas they are frequently killed from fifteen to nineteen feet long. As long as it was in the water, it made strong resistance to being hauled on shore, carrying the canoe out into the deep channel, and occasionally raising its head above the surface, and clashing its jaws together menacingly. This action has a horrid sound, as the crocodile has no fleshy lips, and it brings its teeth and the bones of the mouth together with a loud crash, like the clank of two pieces of hard wood. After playing it a little, the boatmen drew it to land, and when once fairly on the shore all courage and energy seemed utterly to desert it. It tried once or twice to regain the water, but at last lay motionless and perfectly helpless on the sand. It was no easy matter to kill it; a rifle ball sent diagonally through its breast had little or no effect, and even when the shot had been repeated more than once, it was as full of life as ever.[1] It

[1] A remarkable instance of the vitality of the common crocodile, *C. biporcatus*, was related to me by a gentleman at Galle: he had caught on a baited hook an unusually large one, which his coolies disembowelled, the aperture in the stomach being left expanded by a stick placed across it. On returning in the afternoon with a view to secure the head, they found that the creature had crawled for some distance, and made its escape into the water.

"A curious incident occurred some years ago on the Maguruganga, a stream which flows through the Pasdun Corle, to join the Bentolle river. A man was fishing seated on the branch of a tree that overhung the water; and to shelter himself from the drizzling rain, he covered his head and shoulders with a bag folded into a shape common with the natives. While in this attitude, a leopard sprung upon him from the jungle, but, missing its aim, seized the bag and not the man, and fell with it into the river. Here a crocodile, which had been eyeing the angler in despair, seized the leopard as it

feigned death and lay motionless, with its eye sclosed; but, on being pricked with a spear, it suddenly regained all its activity. It was at last finished by a harpoon, and then opened. Its maw contained several small tortoises, and a quantity of broken bricks and gravel, taken medicinally, to promote digestion.

During our journeys we had numerous opportunities of observing the habits of these hideous creatures, and I am far from considering them so formidable as they are usually supposed to be. They are evidently not wantonly destructive; they act only under the influence of hunger, and even then their motions on land are awkward and ungainly, their action timid, and their whole demeanour devoid of the sagacity and courage which characterise other animals of prey.

TESTUDINATA. *Tortoise.*—Land tortoises are numerous, but present no remarkable features beyond the beautiful marking of the starred variety[1], which is common in the north-western province around Putlam and Chilaw, and is distinguished by the bright yellow rays which diversify the deep black of its dorsal shield. From one of these which was kept in my garden I took a number of flat ticks (*Ixodes*), which adhere to its fleshy neck in such a position as to baffle any attempt of the animal itself to remove them; but as they are exposed to constant danger of being crushed against the plastron during the protrusion and retraction of the head, each is covered with a horny case almost as resistant as the carapace of the tortoise itself. Such an adaptation of structure is scarcely less striking than that of the

fell, and sunk with it to the bottom." — *Letter* from GOONERATNE Modliar, interpreter of the Supreme Court, 10th Jany., 1861.

[1] Testudo stellata.

parasites found on the spotted lizard of Berar by Dr. Hooker, each of which presents the distinct colour of the scale to which it adheres.[1]

The marshes and pools of the interior are frequented by *terrapins*[2], which the natives are in the habit of keeping alive in wells under the conviction that they clear them of impurities. These fresh-water tortoises, the greater number of which are included in the genus *Emys* of naturalists, are distinguished by having their toes webbed. Their shell is less convex than that of their congeners on land (but more elevated than that of the sea-turtle); and it has been observed that the more rounded the shell, the nearer does the terrapin approach to the land-tortoise both in its habits and in

THE THREE-RIDGED TORTOISE (EMYS TRIJUGA)

[1] HOOKER'S *Himalayan Journals*, vol. i. p. 37.

[2] *Cryptopus granum*, SCHÖPF. DR. KELAART, in his *Prodromus* (p. 179), refers this to the common Indian species, *C. punctata*; but it is distinct. It is generally distributed in the lower parts of Ceylon, in lakes and tanks. It is the one usually put into wells to act the part of a scavenger. By the Singhalese it is named *Kiri-ibba*.

the choice of its food. Some of them live upon animal as well as vegetable food, and those which subsist exclusively on the former, are noted as having the flattest shells.

The terrapins lay about thirty eggs in the course of several weeks, and these are round, with a calcareous shell. They thrive in captivity, provided that they have a regular supply of water and of meat, cut into small pieces and thrown to them. The tropical species, if transferred to a colder climate, should have arrangements made for enabling them to hybernate during the winter: they will die in a very short time if exposed to a temperature below the freezing point.[1]

The edible turtle[2] is found on all the coasts of the island, and sells for a few shillings or a few pence, according to its size and abundance at the moment. A very repulsive spectacle is exhibited in the markets of Jaffna by the mode in which the flesh of the turtle is sold piece-meal, whilst the animal is still alive, by the families of the Tamil fishermen. The creatures are to be seen in the market-place undergoing this frightful mutilation; the plastron and its integuments having been previously removed, and the animal thrown on its back, so as to display all the motions of the heart, viscera, and lungs. A broad knife, from twelve to eighteen inches in length, is first inserted at the left side, and the women, who are generally the operators, introduce

[1] Of the *Emys trijuga*, the fresh water tortoise figured on preceding page, the technical characteristics are;—vertical plates lozenge-shaped; shell convex and oval; with three more or less distinct longitudinal keels; shields corrugated; with areola situated in the upper posterior corner. Shell brown, with the areolæ and the keels yellowish; head brown, with a yellow streak over each eye.

[2] Chelonia virgata, *Schweig.*

one hand to scoop out the blood, which oozes slowly. The blade is next passed round, till the lower shell is detached and placed on one side, and the internal organs exposed in full action. A customer, as he applies, is served with any part selected, which is cut off as ordered, and sold by weight. Each of the fins is thus successively removed, with portions of the fat and flesh, the turtle showing, by its contortions, that each act of severance is productive of agony. In this state it lies for hours, writhing in the sun, the heart[1] and head being usually the last pieces selected, and till the latter is cut off the snapping of the mouth, and the opening and closing of the eyes, show that life is still inherent, even when the shell has been nearly divested of its contents.

At certain seasons the flesh of turtle on the south-western coast of Ceylon is avoided as poisonous, and some lamentable instances are recorded of deaths ascribed to its use. At Pantura, to the south of Colombo, twenty-eight persons who had partaken of turtle in October, 1840, were immediately seized with sickness, after which coma supervened, and eighteen died during the night. Those who survived said there was nothing unusual in the appearance of the flesh except that it was fatter than ordinary. Other similarly fatal occurrences have been attributed to turtle curry; but as they have never been proved to proceed exclusively from that source, there is room for believing that the poison may have been contained in some other ingredient.

In the Gulf of Manaar turtle is frequently found

[1] ARISTOTLE was aware of the fact that the turtle will live after the removal of the heart.—*De Vita et Morte*, ch. ii.

of such a size as to measure between four and five feet in length; and on one occasion, in riding along the sea-shore north of Putlam, I saw a man in charge of some sheep, resting under the shade of a turtle shell, which he had erected on sticks to protect him from the sun — almost verifying the statement of Ælian, that in the seas off Ceylon there are tortoises so large that several persons may find ample shelter beneath a single shell.[1]

The hawksbill-turtle[2], which supplies the tortoise-shell of commerce, was at former times taken in great numbers in the vicinity of Hambangtotte during the season when they came to deposit their eggs. This gave rise to the trade in tortoise-shell at Point de Galle, where it is still manufactured into articles of ornament by the Moors; but the shell they employ is almost entirely imported from the Maldives.

If taken from the animal after death and decomposition, the colour of the shell becomes clouded and milky, and hence the cruel expedient is resorted to of seizing the turtles as they repair to the shore to deposit their eggs, and suspending them over fires till heat makes the plates on the dorsal shields start from the bone of the carapace, after which the creature is permitted to escape to the water.[3] In illustration of the resistless influence

[1] "Τίκτονται δὲ ἄρα ἐν ταύτῃ τῇ θαλάττῃ, καὶ χελῶναι μέγισται, ὧνπερ οὖν τὰ ἔλυτρα ὄροφοι γίνονται· καὶ γάρ ἐστι καὶ πεντεκαίδεκα πηχῶν ἓν χελώνειον, ὡς ὑποικεῖν οὐκ ὀλίγους, καὶ τοὺς ἡλίους πυρωδεστάτους ἀποστέγει, καὶ σκιὰν ἀσμένοις παρέχει."—Lib. xvi. c. 17. Ælian copied this statement literatim from MEGASTHENES, *Indica Frag.* lix. 31. May not Megasthenes have referred to some tradition connected with the gigantic fossilised species discovered on the Sewalik Hills, the remains of which are now in the Museum at the East India House?

[2] Caretta imbricata, *Linn.*

[3] At Celebes, whence the finest tortoise-shell is exported to China, the natives kill the turtle by blows on the head, and immerse the shell

of instinct at the period of breeding, it may be mentioned that the identical tortoise is believed to return again and again to the same spot, notwithstanding that at each visit she may have to undergo a repetition of this torture. In the year 1826, a hawksbill turtle was taken near Hambangtotte, which bore a ring attached to one of its fins that had been placed there by a Dutch officer thirty years before, with a view to establish the fact of these recurring visits to the same beach.[1]

An opportunity is afforded on the sea-shore of Ceylon for observing a remarkable illustration of instinct in the turtle, when about to deposit its eggs. As if conscious that if she went and returned by one and the same line across the sandy beach, her hiding place would be discovered at its farthest extremity, she resorts to the expedient of curving her course, so as to regain the sea by a different track; and after depositing the eggs, burying them about eighteen inches deep, she carefully smoothes over the surface to render the precise spot indiscernible. The Singhalese, aware of this device, sound her line of march with a rod till they come upon the concealed nest.

*Snakes.*—It is perhaps owing to the aversion excited by the ferocious expression and unusual action of serpents, combined with an instinctive dread of attack[2], that exaggerated ideas prevail both as to their numbers in Ceylon, and the danger to be apprehended from encountering them. The Singhalese profess to distinguish a great many kinds, of which they say not more than

in boiling water to detach the plates. Dry heat is only resorted to by the unskilful, who frequently destroy the tortoise-shell in the operation.—*Journal Indian Archipel.* vol. iii. p. 227, 1849.

[1] BENNETT'S *Ceylon, &c.*, c. xxxiv.

[2] Genesis iii. 15.

one half have as yet been scientifically identified [1]; but so cautiously do serpents make their appearance, that the surprise of persons long resident is invariably expressed at the rarity with which they are to be seen; and from my own journeys through the jungle, often of from two to five hundred miles, I have frequently returned without observing a single snake. Mr. Bennett, who resided much in the south-east of the island, ascribes the rarity of serpents in the jungle to the abundance of the wild peafowl, whose partiality to young snakes renders them the chief destroyers of these reptiles. It is likely, too, that they are killed by the jungle-cocks; for they are frequently eaten by the common barn-door fowl in Ceylon. This is rendered the more probable by the fact, that in those districts where the extension of cultivation, and the visits of sportsmen, have reduced the numbers of the jungle-cocks and pea-fowl, snakes have perceptibly increased. The deer also are enemies of the snakes, and the natives who have had opportunities of watching their encounters assert that they have seen deer rush upon a serpent and crush it by leaping on it with all its four feet.

As to the venomous powers of snakes, DR. DAVY, whose

[1] This is not likely to be true: in a very large collection of snakes made in Ceylon by Mr. C. R. Butler, and recently examined by Dr. Günther, of the British Museum, only a single specimen proved to be new.

There is, however, one venomous snake, of the existence of which I am assured by a native correspondent in Ceylon, no mention has yet been made by European naturalists. It is called *Māpilā* by the Singhalese; it is described to me as being about four feet in length, of the diameter of the little finger, and of a uniform dark brown colour. It is said to be often seen in company with another snake called in Singhalese *Lay Medilla*, a name which implies its deep red hue. The latter is believed to be venomous. It would be well if some collector in Ceylon would send home for examination the species which respectively bear these names.

attention was carefully directed to the poisonous serpents of Ceylon[1], came to the conclusion that but *four*, out of twenty species examined by him, were venomous, and that of these only two (the *tic-polonga*[2] and *cobra de capello*[3]) were capable of inflicting a wound likely to be fatal to man. The third is the *carawala*[4], a brown snake of about two feet in length; and for the fourth, of which only a few specimens have been procured, the Singhalese have no name in their vernacular — a proof that it is neither deadly nor abundant. But Dr. Davy's estimate of the venom of the *carawala* is below the truth, as cases have been authenticated to me, in which death from its bite ensued within a few days. The effect, however, is not uniformly fatal; a circumstance which the natives explain by asserting that there are three varieties of the carawala, named the *hil-la*, the *dunu*, and the *mal*-carawala; the second being the largest and the most dreaded.

In like manner, the *tic-polonga*, particularised by Dr. Davy, is said to be but one out of seven varieties of that formidable reptile. The word "*tic*" means literally the "spotted" polonga, from the superior clearness of the markings on its scales. Another, the *nidi*, or "sleeping" polonga, is so called from the fact that a person bitten by it is soon prostrated by a lethargy from which he never awakes.[5] These formidable serpents so infested

[1] See DAVY'S *Ceylon*, ch. xiv.

[2] Daboia elegans, *Daud.*

[3] Naja tripudians, *Merr.*

[4] Trigonocephalus hypnale, *Merr.*

[5] The other varieties are the *getta*, *lay*, *alu*, *kunu*, and *nil-polongas*. I have heard of an eighth, the *palla-polonga*.

Amongst the numerous pieces of folk-lore in Ceylon in connexion with snakes, is the belief that a deadly enmity subsists between the polonga and the cobra de capello, and that the latter, which is naturally shy and retiring, is provoked to conflicts by the audacity of its rival. Hence the proverb applied to persons at enmity, that

the official residence of the District Judge of Trincomalie in 1858, as to compel his family to abandon it. In another instance, a friend of mine, going hastily to take a supply of wafers from an open tin case which stood in his office, drew back his hand, on finding the box occupied by a tic-polonga coiled within it. During my residence in Ceylon, I never heard of the death of a European which was caused by the bite of a snake; and in the returns of coroners' inquests made officially to my department, such accidents to the natives appear chiefly to have happened at night, when the animal, having been surprised or trodden on, inflicted the wound in self-defence.[1] For these reasons the Singhalese, when obliged to leave their houses in the dark, carry a stick with a loose ring, the noise[2] of which as they strike it on the ground is sufficient to warn the snakes to leave their path.

"they hate like the polonga and cobra."

The Singhalese believe the polonga to be by far the most savage and wanton of the two, and they illustrate this by a popular legend, that once upon a time a child, in the absence of its mother, was playing beside a tub of water, which a cobra, impelled by thirst during a long-continued drought, approached to drink, the unconscious child all the while striking it with its hands to prevent the intrusion. The cobra, on returning, was met by a tic-polonga, which seeing its scales dripping with delicious moisture, entreated to be told the way to the well. The cobra, knowing the vicious habits of the other snake, and anticipating that it would kill the innocent child which it had so recently spared, at first refused, and only yielded on condition that the infant was not to be molested. But the polonga, on reaching the tub, was no sooner obstructed by the little one, than it stung him to death.

[1] In a return of 112 coroners' inquests, in cases of death from wild animals, held in Ceylon in five years, from 1851 to 1855 inclusive, 68 are ascribed to the bites of serpents; and in almost every instance the assault is set down as having taken place *at night*. The majority of the sufferers were children and women.

[2] PLINY notices that the serpent has the sense of hearing more acute than that of sight; and that it is more frequently put in motion by the sound of footsteps than by the appearance of the intruder, "excitatur pede sæpius."—Lib. viii. c. 36.

*Cobra de Capello.* — The cobra de capello is the only one exhibited by the itinerant snake-charmers: and the truth of Davy's conjecture, that they control it, not by extracting its fangs, but by courageously availing themselves of its well-known timidity and extreme reluctance to use its fatal weapons, received a painful confirmation during my residence in Ceylon, by the death of one of these performers, whom his audience had provoked to attempt some unaccustomed familiarity with the cobra; it bit him on the wrist, and he expired the same evening. The hill near Kandy, on which the official residences of the Governor and Colonial Secretary are built, is covered in many places with the deserted nests of the white ants (*termites*), and these are the favourite retreats of the sluggish and spiritless cobra, which watches from their apertures the toads and lizards on which it preys. Here, when I have repeatedly come upon them, their only impulse was concealment; and on one occasion, when a cobra of considerable length could not escape, owing to the bank being nearly precipitous on both sides of the road, a few blows from my whip were sufficient to deprive it of life.[1]

A gentleman who held a civil appointment at Kornegalle, had a servant who was bitten by a snake;

[1] A Singhalese work, the *Sarpa-dosā*, enumerates four castes of the cobra; — the *raja*, or king; the *bamunu*, or Brahman; the *velanda*, or trader; and the *gori*, or agriculturist. Of these the raja, or "king of the cobras," is said to have the head and the anterior half of the body of so light a colour, that at a distance it seems like a silvery white. The work is quoted, but not correctly, in the *Ceylon Times* for January, 1857. It is more than probable, as the division represents the four castes of the Hindus, Chastriyas, Brahmans Vaisyas, and Sudras; that the insertion of the *gori* instead of the latter was a pious fraud of some copyist to confer rank upon the Vellales, the agricultural caste of Ceylon.

and he informed me that on enlarging a hole near the foot of the tree under which the accident occurred, he unearthed a cobra of upwards of three feet long, and so purely white as to induce him to believe that it was an albino. With the exception of the *rat-snake*[1], the cobra de capello is the only serpent which seems from choice to frequent the vicinity of human dwellings, doubtless attracted by the young of the domestic fowl and by the moisture of the wells and drainage.

The young cobras, it is said, in the *Sarpa-dosā*, are not venomous till after the thirteenth day, when they shed their coat for the first time.

The Singhalese remark that if one cobra be destroyed near a house, its companion is almost certain to be discovered immediately after,—a popular belief which I had an opportunity of verifying on more than one occasion. Once, when a snake of this description was

[1] *Coryphodon Blumenbachii.* There is a belief in Ceylon that the bite of the rat-snake, though harmless to man, is fatal to black cattle. The Singhalese add that it would be equally so to man were the wound to be touched by cow-dung. WOLF, in the interesting story of his *Life and Adventures in Ceylon*, mentions that rat-snakes were often so domesticated by the natives as to feed at their batle. He says: "I once saw an example of this in the house of a native. It being meal time, he called his snake, which immediately came forth from the roof under which he and I were sitting. He gave it victuals from his own dish, which the snake took of itself from off a fig-leaf that was laid for it, and ate along with its host. When it had eaten its fill, he gave it a kiss, and bade it go to its hole."

Major SKINNER, writing to me 12th Dec., 1858, mentions the still more remarkable case of the domestication of the cobra de capello in Ceylon. "Did you ever hear," he says, "of tame cobras being kept and domesticated about a house, going in and out at pleasure, and in common with the rest of the inmates? In one family, near Negombo, cobras are kept as protectors, in the place of dogs, by a wealthy man who has always large sums of money in his house. But this is not a solitary case of the kind. I heard of it only the other day, but from undoubtedly good authority. The snakes glide about the house, a terror to thieves, but never attempting to harm the inmates."

killed in a bath of the Government House at Colombo, its mate was found in the same spot the day after; and again, at my own stables, a cobra of five feet long, having fallen into the well, which was too deep to permit its escape, its companion of the same size was found the same morning in an adjoining drain.[1] On this occasion the snake, which had been several hours in the well, swam with ease, raising its head and hood above water; and instances have repeatedly occurred of the cobra de capello voluntarily taking considerable excursions by sea. When the "Wellington," a government vessel employed in the conservancy of the pearl banks, was anchored about a quarter of a mile from the land, in the bay of Koodremalé, a cobra was seen, about an hour before sunset, swimming vigorously towards the ship. It came within twelve yards, when the sailors assailed it with billets of wood and other missiles, and forced it to return to land. The following morning they discovered the track which it had left on the shore, and traced it along the sand till it was lost in the jungle. On a later occasion, in the vicinity of the same spot, when the "Wellington" was lying at some distance from the shore, a cobra was found and killed on board, where it could only have gained access by climbing up the cable. It was first discovered by a sailor, who felt the chill as it glided over his foot.

One curious tradition in Ceylon embodies the popular legend, that the stomach of the cobra de capello occasionally contains a precious stone of such unapproachable

[1] PLINY notices the affection that subsists between the male and female asp; and that if one of them happens to be killed, the other seeks to avenge its death.—Lib. viii. c. 37.

brilliancy as to surpass all known jewels. This inestimable stone is called the *nāga-mānik-kya*; but not one snake in thousands is supposed to possess such a treasure. The cobra, before eating, is believed to cast it up and conceal it for the moment; else its splendour, like a flambeau, would attract all beholders. The tales of the peasantry, in relation to it, all turn upon the devices of those in search of the gem, and the vigilance and cunning of the cobra by which they are baffled; the reptile itself being more enamoured of the priceless jewel than even its most ardent pursuers.

In BENNETT's account of "*Ceylon and its Capabilities*," there is another curious piece of Singhalese folk-lore, to the effect, that the cobra de capello every time it expends its poison *loses a joint of its tail*, and eventually acquires a head resembling that of a toad. A recent addition to zoological knowledge has thrown light on the origin of this popular fallacy. The family of "false snakes" (*pseudo typhlops*, as Schlegel names the group) have till lately consisted of but three species, of which only one was known to inhabit Ceylon. They belong to a family intermediate between the serpents and that Saurian group commonly called *Slow-worms* or *Glass-snakes*; they in fact represent the slow-worms of the temperate regions in Ceylon. They have the body of a snake, but the cleft of their mouth is very narrow, and they are unable to detach the lateral parts of the lower jaw from each other, as the true snakes do when devouring a prey. The most striking character of the group, however, is the size and form of the tail; this is very short, and according to the observations of

Professor Peters of Berlin[1], shorter in the female than in the male. It does not terminate in a point as in other snakes, but is truncated obliquely, the abrupt surface of its extremity being either entirely flat, or more or less convex, and always covered with rough

THE UROPELTIS PHILIPPINUS.

keels. The reptile assists its own movements by pressing the rough end to the ground, and from this peculiar form of the tail, the family has received the name of *Uropeltidæ*, or "Shield-tails." Within a very recent period important additions have been made to this family, which now consists of four genera and eleven species. Those occurring in Ceylon are enumerated in the List

[1] Peters, *De Serpentum familia Uropeltaceorum.* Berol. 4. 1861.

appended to this chapter. One of these, the *Uropeltis grandis* of Kelaart [1], is distinguished by its dark brown colour, shot with a bluish metallic lustre, closely approaching the ordinary shade of the cobra; and the tail is abruptly and flatly compressed as though it had been severed by a knife. The form of this singular reptile will be best understood by a reference to the accompanying figure; and there can, I think, be little doubt that to its strange and anomalous structure is to be traced the fable of the transformation of the cobra de capello. The colour alone would seem to identify the two reptiles, but the head and mouth are no longer those of a serpent, and the disappearance of the tail might readily suggest the mutilation which the tradition asserts.

The Singhalese Buddhists, in their religious abstinence from inflicting death on any creature, are accustomed, after securing a venomous snake, to enclose it in a basket woven of palm leaves, and to set it afloat on a river.

*The Python.*—The great python [2] (the "boa," as it is commonly designated by Europeans, the "anaconda" of Eastern story), which is supposed to crush the bones of an elephant, and to swallow the tiger, is found, though

[1] The *Uropeltis grandis* of Kelaart, which was at first supposed to be a new species, proves to be identical with *U. Phillippinus* of Cuvier. It is doubtful, however, whether this species be found in the Phillippine Islands, as stated by Cuvier; and it is more than probable that the typical specimen came from Ceylon — a further illustration of the affinity of the fauna of Ceylon to that of the Eastern Archipelago. The characteristics of this reptile, as given by Dr. GRAY, are as follows:— "Caudal disc subcircular, with large scattered tubercles; snout subacute, slightly produced. Dark brown, lighter below, with some of the scales dark brown in the centre near the posterior edge. GRAY, *Proceed. Zool. Soc.* 1858, p. 262.

[2] Python reticulatus, *Gray.*

not of such portentous dimensions, in the cinnamon gardens within a mile of the fort of Colombo, where it feeds on hog-deer, and other smaller animals.

The natives occasionally take it alive, and securing it to a pole expose it for sale as a curiosity. One that was brought to me tied in this way measured seventeen feet with a proportionate thickness: but one more fully grown, which crossed my path on a coffee estate on the Peacock Mountain at Pusilawa, considerably exceeded these dimensions. Another which I watched in the garden at Elie House, near Colombo, surprised me by the ease with which it erected itself almost perpendicularly in order to scale a wall upwards of ten feet high.

The Singhalese assert that when it has swallowed a deer, or any animal of similarly inconvenient bulk, the python draws itself through the narrow aperture between two trees, in order to crush the bones and assist in the process of deglutition.

It is a singular fact that the small and innocuous ground-snakes called *Calamariæ*, which abound on the continent of India and in the islands, are not to be found in Ceylon; where they would appear to be replaced by two singular genera, the *Aspidura* and *Haplocercus*. These latter have only one series of shields below the tail, whilst most other harmless snakes (*Calamaria* included) have a double series of sub-caudals. The *Aspidura* has been known to naturalists for many years[1]; the *Haplocercus* of Ceylon has only recently been described by Dr. Günther, and of it not more than three existing specimens are known: hence

[1] Boie in Isis 1827 p. 517.

its habits and the extent of its distribution over the island are still left in uncertainty.[1]

Of ten species of snakes that ascend trees in Ceylon to search for squirrels and lizards, and to rifle the nests of birds, one half, including the green *carawala*, and the deadly *tic polonga*, are believed by the natives to be venomous; but the truth of this is very dubious. I have heard of the cobra being found on the crown of a coco-nut palm, attracted, it was said, by the toddy which was flowing at the time, it being the season for drawing it. Surrounding Elie House, near Colombo, in which I resided, were a number of tall *casuarinas* and India-rubber trees, whose branches almost touched the lattices of the window of the room in which I usually sat. These were a favourite resort of the tree-snakes, and in the early morning the numbers which clung to them were sometimes quite remarkable. I had thus an opportunity of observing the action of these creatures, which seems to me one of vigilance rather than of effort, the tongue being in perpetual activity, as if it were an organ of feeling; and in those in which the nose is elongated, a similar mobility and restlessness,

[1] GÜNTH. *Col. Snakes*, p. 14. In the hope that some inquirer in Ceylon will be able to furnish such information as may fill up this blank in the history of the haplocercus, the following particulars are here appended. The largest of the specimens in the British Museum is about twenty-five inches in length; the body thin, and much elongated; the head narrow, and not distinct from the neck, the tail of moderate length. Forehead covered by three shields, one anterior and two posterior frontals; no loreal shield; one small shield before, two behind the eye; seven shields along the upper lip, the eye being above the fourth. The scales are disposed in seventeen longitudinal series; they are lanceolate and strongly keeled. The upper parts are uniform blackish or brown, with two dorsal rows of small indistinct black spots; occiput with a whitish collar, edged with darker. The lower parts uniform yellowish.

especially when alarmed, affords evidence of the same faculty.

The general characteristic of the Tree-snake is an exceedingly thin and delicate body, often adorned with colours exquisite as those of the foliage amongst which they live concealed. In some of the South American species the tints vie in brilliancy with those of the humming-birds; whilst their forms are so flexible and slender as to justify the name conferred on them of "*whip-snakes*." The Siamese, to denote these combinations of grace and splendour, call them "Sun-beams." A naturalist[1], describing a bright green species in Brazil (*Philodryas viridissimus*), writes: "I am always delighted when I find that another tree-snake has settled in my garden. You look for a bird's nest, the young ones have gone, but you find their bed occupied by one of these beautiful creatures, which will coil up its body of two feet in length within a space no larger than the hollow of your hand. They appear to be always watchful; for at the instant you discover one, the quick playing of the long, black, forked tongue will show you that you too are observed. On perceiving the slightest sign of your intention to disturb it, the snake will dart upwards through the branches and over the leaves which scarcely appear to bend beneath the weight. A moment more, and you have lost sight of it. Whenever I return to Europe, you may be sure that in my hot-house those harmless, lovely creatures shall not be missing."

Ceylon has several species of Tree-snakes, and one of the most common is the green *Passerita*, easily recog-

[1] Dr. WUCHERER of Bahia.

TREE SNAKE.

*Passerita fusca.*

nized from its bright colour and from the pointed moveable appendage, into which the snout is prolonged. The snakes of this genus being active chiefly during the night, the pupil of the eye is linear and horizontal. They never willingly descend from trees, but prey there upon nocturnal Saurians, geckoes, small birds and their young; and they are perfectly harmless, although they often try to bite. It is strange that none of the numerous specimens which it has been attempted to bring to Europe have ever fed in captivity; whilst in South America they take their food freely in confinement, provided that some green plants are placed in their cage.

In Ceylon I have never seen any specimen of a larger size than three feet; whilst they are known to attain to more than five on the Indian Continent.

The inference is obvious, that the green coloration of the majority of tree-snakes has more or less connection with their habits and mode of life. Indeed, whenever a green-coloured snake is observed, it may at once be pronounced, if slender or provided with a prehensile tail, to be of the kind which passes its life on trees· but if it be short-bodied then it lives on the prairies. There are nevertheless tree-snakes which have a very different coloration; and one of the most remarkable species is the *Passerita fusca* or *Dryinus fuscus*, of which a figure is annexed. It closely resembles the green Passerita in form, so that naturalists have considered it to be a mere variety. It is entirely of a shining brown, shot with purple, and the yellow longitudinal stripe which runs along the side of the belly of the green species, is absent in this one. It is much more rare than the green one, and does not appear to be found in Hindostan: no intermediate forms have been observed in Ceylon.

*Water-Snakes.*—The fresh-water snakes, of which several species[1] inhabit the still waters and pools, are all harmless in Ceylon. A gentleman, who found near a river an agglutinated cluster of the eggs of one variety (*Tropidophis schistosus?*), placed them under a glass shade on his drawing-room table, where one by one the young reptiles emerged from the shell to the number of twenty.

The *sea-snakes* of the Indian tropics did not escape the notice of the early Greek mariners who navigated those seas; and amongst the facts collected by them, Ælian has briefly recorded that the Indian Ocean produces serpents *with flattened tails*[2], whose bite, he adds, is to be dreaded less for its venom than the laceration of its teeth. The first statement is accurate, but the latter is incorrect, as there is an all but unanimous concurrence of opinion that every species of this family of serpents is more or less poisonous. The compression of the tail noticed by Ælian is one of the principal characteristics of these reptiles, as their motion through the water is mainly effected by its aid, coupled with the undulating movement of the rest of the body. Their scales, instead of being imbricated like those of land-snakes, form hexagons; and those on the belly, instead of being scutate and enlarged, are nearly of the same size and form as on other parts of the body.

[1] Chersydrus granulatus, *Merr.*; Cerberus cinereus, *Daud.*; Tropidophis schistosus, *Daud.*

[2] "Πλατεῖς τὰς οὐράς." ÆLIAN, L. xvi. c. 8.

Ælian speaks elsewhere of fresh-water snakes. His remark on the compression of the tail shows that his informants were aware of this speciality in those that inhabit the sea.

Sea-snakes (*Hydrophis*) are found on all the coasts of Ceylon. I have sailed through large shoals of them in the Gulf of Manaar, close to the pearl-banks of Aripo. The fishermen of Calpentyn on the west live in perpetual dread of them, and believe their bite to be fatal. In the course of an attempt which was recently made to place a lighthouse on the great rocks of the south-east coast, known by seamen as the Basses[1], or *Baxos*, the workmen who first landed found the portion of the surface liable to be covered by the tides, honeycombed, and hollowed into deep holes filled with water, in which were abundance of fishes and some molluscs. Some of these cavities also contained sea-snakes from four to five feet long, which were described as having the head "hooded like the cobra de capello, and of a light grey colour, slightly speckled. They coiled themselves like serpents on land, and darted at poles thrust in among them. The Singhalese who accompanied the party, said that they not only bit venomously, but crushed the limb of any intruder in their coils."[2]

Still, sea-snakes, though well-known to the natives, are not abundant round Ceylon, as compared with their numbers in other places. Their principal habitat is the ocean between the southern shores of China and the northern coast of New Holland; and their western limit appears to be about the longitude of Cape Comorin. It has long since been ascertained that they frequent the seas that separate the islands of the Pacific; but they have never yet been found in the Atlantic, nor even

[1] The Basses are believed to be the remnants of the great island of Giri, swallowed up by the sea.—*Mahawanso*, ch. i. p. 4. They may possibly be the *Bassæ* of Ptolemy's map of *Taprobane*.

[2] Official Report to the Governor of Ceylon.

on the western shores of tropical America. And if, as has been stated[1], they have been seen on a late occasion in considerable numbers in the Bay of Panama, the fact can only be regarded as one of the rare instances, in which a change in the primary distribution of a race of animals has occurred, either by an active or a passive immigration. Being exclusively inhabitants of the sea, they are liable to be swept along by the influence of currents; but to compensate for this they have been endowed with a wonderful power of swimming. The individuals of all the groups of terrestrial serpents are observed to be possessed of this faculty to a greater or a less degree; and they can swim for a certain distance without having any organs specially modified for the purpose; except, perhaps, the lung, which is a long sac capable of taking in a sufficient quantity of air, to keep the body of the snake above water. Nor do we find any peculiar or specially adapted organs even in the fresh-water-snakes, although they can catch frogs or fishes while swimming. But in the *hydrophids*, which are permanent inhabitants of the ocean, and which in an adult state, approach the beach only occasionally, and for very short times, the tail, which is rounded and tapering in the others, is compressed into a vertical rudder-like organ, similar to, and answering all the purposes of, the caudal fin in a fish. When these snakes are brought on shore or on the deck of a ship, they are helpless, and struggle vainly in awkward attitudes. Their food consists exclusively of such fishes as are found near the surface; a fact which affords ample proof that they do not descend to great depths, although

[1] Proc. Zool. Soc. 1858.

SEA SNAKE.

*Hydrophis sublævis.*

they can dive as well as swim. They are often found in groups during calm weather, sleeping on the sea; but owing to their extreme caution and shyness, attempts to catch them are rarely successful; on the least alarm, they suddenly expel the air from their lungs and descend below the surface; a long stream of rising air-bubbles marking the rapid course which they make below. Their poisonous nature has been questioned; but the presence of a strong perforated tooth and of a venomous gland sufficiently attest their dangerous powers, even if these had not been demonstrated by the effects of their bite. But fortunately for the fishermen, who sometimes find them unexpectedly among the contents of their nets, sea-snakes are unable, like other venomous serpents, to open the jaws widely, and in reality they rarely inflict a wound. Dr. Cantor believes, that they are blinded by the light when removed from their own element; and he adds that they become sluggish and speedily die.[1]

Those found near the coasts of Ceylon are generally small,—from one to three feet in length, and apparently immature; and it is certain that the largest specimens taken in the Pacific do not attain to greater length than eight feet. In colour they are generally of a greenish brown, in parts inclining to yellow, with occasionally cross bands of black. The species figured in the accompanying drawing is the *Hydrophis sublœvis* of Gray; or *Hydrus cyanocinctus* of Boie.[2] The specimen from

[1] *Catal. Mal. Rept.* p. 136.

[2] Its technical characteristics are as follows,—Body rather slender; ground colour yellowish with irregular black rings. Scales nearly smooth; ventral plates broad, six-sided, smooth, some divided into two, by a slight central groove. Occipital shields large, triangular, and produced, with a small central shield behind them; a series of four large temporal shields; chin-shields

which the drawing is taken, was obtained by Dr. Templeton at Colombo.

The use of the Pamboo-Kaloo, or snake-stone, as a remedy in cases of wounds by venomous serpents, has probably been communicated to the Singhalese by the itinerant snake-charmers who resort to the island from the coast of Coromandel; and more than one well-authenticated instance of its successful application has been told to me by persons who had been eye-witnesses to what they described. On one occasion, in March, 1854, a friend of mine was riding, with some other civil officers of the Government, along a jungle path in the vicinity of Bintenne, when he saw one of two Tamils, who were approaching the party, suddenly dart into the forest and return, holding in both hands a cobra de capello which he had seized by the head and tail. He called to his companion for assistance to place it in their covered basket, but, in doing this, he handled it so inexpertly that it seized him by the finger, and retained its hold for a few seconds, as if unable to retract its fangs. The blood flowed, and intense pain appeared to follow almost immediately; but, with all expedition, the friend of the sufferer undid his waistcloth, and took from it two snake-stones, each of the size of a small almond, intensely black and highly polished, though of an extremely light substance. These he applied, one to each wound inflicted by the teeth of the serpent, to which they attached themselves closely; the blood that oozed from the bites being rapidly imbibed by the porous texture of the article applied. The stones ad-

in two pairs; eyes very small, over the fourth and fifth labials; one ante- and two post-oculars; the second upper labial shield elongated.

hered tenaciously for three or four minutes, the wounded man's companion in the meanwhile rubbing his arm downwards from the shoulder towards the fingers. At length the snake-stones dropped off of their own accord; the suffering of the man appeared to subside; he twisted his fingers till the joints cracked, and went on his way without concern. Whilst this had been going on, another Indian of the party who had come up took from his bag a small piece of white wood, which resembled a root, and passed it gently near the head of the cobra, which the latter immediately inclined close to the ground; he then lifted the snake without hesitation, and coiled it into a circle at the bottom of his basket. The root by which he professed to be enabled to perform this operation with safety he called the *Naya-thalic Kalanga* (the root of the snake-plant), protected by which he professed his ability to approach any reptile with impunity.

In another instance, in 1853, Mr. Lavalliere, then District Judge of Kandy, informed me that he saw a snake-charmer in the jungle, close by the town, search for a cobra de capello, and, after disturbing one in its retreat, the man tried to secure it, but, in the attempt, he was bitten in the thigh till blood trickled from the wound. He instantly applied the *Pamboo-Kaloo*, which adhered closely for about ten minutes, during which time he passed the root which he held in his hand backwards and forwards above the stone, till the latter dropped to the ground. He assured Mr. Lavalliere that all danger was then past. That gentleman obtained from him the snake-stone he had relied on, and saw him repeatedly afterwards in perfect health.

The substances used on both these occasions are now

in my possession. The roots employed by the several parties are not identical. One appears to be a bit of the stem of an Aristolochia; the other is so dried as to render its identification difficult, but it resembles the quadrangular stem of a jungle vine. Some species of Aristolochia, such as the *A. serpentaria* of North America, are supposed to act as specifics in the cure of snake-bites; and the *A. indica* is the plant to which the ichneumon is popularly believed to resort as an antidote when bitten[1]; but it is probable that the use of any particular plant by the snake-charmers is a pretence, or rather a delusion, the reptile being overpowered by the resolute action of the operator[2], and not by the influence

[1] For an account of the encounter between the ichneumon and the venomous snakes of Ceylon, see Ch. I. p. 39.

[2] The following narrative of the operations of a snake-charmer in Ceylon is contained in a note from Mr. Reyne, of the department of public works: "A snake-charmer came to my bungalow in 1854, requesting me to allow him to show me his snakes dancing. As I had frequently seen them, I told him I would give him a rupee if he would accompany me to the jungle, and catch a cobra, that I knew frequented the place. He was willing, and as I was anxious to test the truth of the charm, I counted his tame snakes, and put a watch over them until I returned with him. Before going I examined the man, and satisfied myself he had no snake about his person. When we arrived at the spot, he played on a small pipe, and after persevering for some time out came a large cobra from an ant hill, which I knew it occupied. On seeing the man it tried to escape, but he caught it by the tail and kept swinging it round until we reached the bungalow. He then made it dance, but before long it bit him above the knee. He immediately bandaged the leg above the bite, and applied a snake-stone to the wound to extract the poison. He was in great pain for a few minutes, but after that it gradually went away, the stone falling off just before he was relieved. When he recovered he held a cloth up, which the snake flew at, and caught its fangs in it; while in that position, the man passed his hand up its back, and having seized it by the throat, he extracted the fangs in my presence and gave them to me. He then squeezed out the poison on to a leaf. It was a clear oily substance, and when rubbed on the hand produced a fine lather. I carefully watched the whole operation, which was also witnessed by my clerk and two or three other persons. *Colombo*, 13*th January*, 1860.—H. E. Reyne."

of any secondary appliance. In other words, the confidence inspired by the supposed talisman enables its possessor to address himself fearlessly to his task, and thus to effect, by determination and will, what is popularly believed to be the result of charms and stupefaction. Still it is curious that, amongst the natives of Northern Africa, who lay hold of the *Cerastes* without fear or hesitation, impunity is ascribed to the use of a plant with the juice of which they anoint themselves before touching the reptile [1]; and Bruce says of the people of Sennar, that they acquire exemption from the fatal consequences of the bite by chewing a particular root, and washing themselves with an infusion of certain plants. He adds that a portion of this root was given him, with a view to test its efficacy in his own person, but that he had not sufficient resolution to make the experiment.

As to the snake-stone itself, I submitted one, the application of which I have been describing, to Mr. Faraday, who has communicated to me, as the result of his analysis, his belief that it is "a piece of charred bone which has been filled with blood perhaps several times, and then carefully charred again. Evidence of this is afforded, as well by the apertures of cells or tubes on its surface as by the fact that it yields and breaks under pressure, and exhibits an organic structure within. When heated slightly, water rises from it, and also a little ammonia; and, if heated still more highly in the air, carbon burns away, and a bulky white ash is left, retaining the shape and size of the stone." This ash, as is evident from inspection, cannot have belonged to

[1] Hasselquist.

any vegetable substance, for it is almost entirely composed of phosphate of lime. Mr. Faraday adds that "if the piece of matter has ever been employed as a spongy absorbent, it seems hardly fit for that purpose in its present state; but who can say to what treatment it has been subjected since it was fit for use, or to what treatment the natives may submit it when expecting to have occasion to use it?"

The probability is, that the animal charcoal, when instantaneously applied, may be sufficiently porous and absorbent to extract the venom from the recent wound, together with a portion of the blood, before it has had time to be carried into the system; and that the blood which Mr. Faraday detected in the specimen submitted to him was that of the Indian on whose person the effect was exhibited on the occasion to which my informant was an eye-witness. The snake-charmers from the coast who visit Ceylon profess to prepare the snake-stones for themselves, and to preserve the composition a secret. Dr. Davy[1], on the authority of Sir Alexander Johnston, says the manufacture of them is a lucrative trade, carried on by the monks of Manilla, who supply the merchants of India — and his analysis confirms that of Mr. Faraday. Of the three different kinds which he examined — one being of partially burnt bone, and another of chalk, the third, consisting chiefly of vegetable matter, resembled bezoar,—all of them (except the first, which possessed a slight absorbent power) were quite inert, and incapable of having any effect except on the imagination of the patient. Thunberg was shown the snake-stone used by the boers at the

[1] *Account of the Interior of Ceylon*, ch. iii. p. 101.

Cape in 1772, which was imported for them "from the Indies, especially from Malabar," at so high a price that few of the farmers could afford to possess themselves of it; he describes it as convex on one side, black, and so porous that "when thrown into water, it caused bubbles to rise;" and hence, by its absorbent qualities, it served, if speedily applied, to extract the poison from the wound.[1]

*Cæcilia.*—The rocky jungle, bordering the higher coffee estates, provides a safe retreat for a very singular animal, first introduced to the notice of European naturalists about a century ago by Linnæus, who gave it the name *Cæcilia glutinosa*, to indicate two peculiarities manifest to the ordinary observer—an apparent defect of vision, from the eyes being so small and embedded as to be scarcely distinguishable; and a power of secreting from minute pores in the skin a

[1] *Thunberg*, vol. i. p. 155. Since the foregoing account was published, I have received a note from Mr. HARDY, relative to the *piedra ponsona*, the snake-stone of Mexico, in which he gives the following account of the method of preparing and applying it: "Take a piece of hart's horn of any convenient size and shape; cover it well round with grass or hay, enclose both in a thin piece of sheet copper well wrapped round them, and place the parcel in a charcoal fire till the bone is sufficiently charred.

"When cold, remove the calcined horn from its envelope, when it will be ready for immediate use. In this state it will resemble a solid black fibrous substance, of the same shape and size as before it was subjected to this treatment.

"USE.—The wound being slightly punctured, apply the bone to the opening, to which it will adhere firmly for the space of two minutes; and when it falls, it should be received into a basin of water. It should then be dried in a cloth, and again applied to the wound. But it will not adhere longer than about one minute. In like manner it may be applied a third time; but now it will fall almost immediately, and nothing will cause it to adhere any more.

"These effects I witnessed in the case of a bite of a rattle-snake at Oposura, a town in the province of Sonora, in Mexico, from whence I obtained my recipe; and I have given other particulars respecting it in my Travels in the Interior of Mexico, published in 1830. R. W. H. HARDY. *Bath, 30th January*, 1860."

viscous fluid, resembling that of snails, eels, and some salamanders. Specimens are rare in Europe owing to the readiness with which it decomposes, breaking down into a flaky mass in the spirits in which it is attempted to preserve it.

The creature is about the length and thickness of an ordinary round desk ruler, a little flattened before and rounded behind. It is brownish, with a pale stripe along either side. The skin is furrowed into 350 circular folds, in which are imbedded minute scales. The head is tolerably distinct, with a double row of fine curved teeth for seizing the insects and worms on which it is supposed to live.

Naturalists are most desirous that the habits and metamorphoses of this creature should be carefully ascertained, for great doubts have been entertained as to the position it is entitled to occupy in the chain of creation.

*Batrachians.*—In the numerous marshes formed by the overflowing of the rivers in the plains of the low country, there are many varieties of frogs, which, both by their colours and by their extraordinary size, are calculated to excite the surprise of a stranger. In the lakes around Colombo and the still water near Trincomalie, there are huge creatures of this family, from six to eight inches in length [1], of an olive hue, deepening into brown on the back and yellow on the under side. A Kandyan species, recently described, is of much smaller dimensions, but distinguished by its brilliant colouring, a beautiful grass green above and deep orange underneath.[2]

[1] A Singhalese variety of the *Rana cutipora?* and the Malabar bull-frog, *Hylarana Malabarica.* A frog named by BLYTH *Rana robusta*, proves to be a Ceylon specimen of the *R. cutipora.*

[2] *R. Kandiana*, Kelaart.

In the shrubberies around my house at Colombo the graceful little tree-frogs [1] were to be found in great numbers, sheltered under broad leaves to protect them from the scorching sun;—some of them utter a sharp metallic sound at night, similar to that produced by smacking the lips.

In the gardens and grounds toads [2] crouch in the shade, and pursue the flies and minute coleoptera. In Ceylon, as in Europe, these creatures suffer from the bad renown of injecting a poison into the wound inflicted by their bite.[3] The main calumny is confuted by the fact that no toad has yet been discovered furnished with any teeth whatsoever; but the obnoxious repute still attaches to the milky exudation sometimes perceptible from glands situated on either side behind the head; nevertheless experiments have shown, that though acrid, the secretions of the toad are incapable of exciting more than a slight erythema on the most delicate skins. The smell is, however, fetid and offensive, and hence toads are less exposed to the attacks of carnivorous animals and of birds than frogs, in which such glands do not exist.

In the class of Reptiles, those only are included in the order of Batrachians which undergo a metamorphosis before attaining maturity; and as t ey offer the only example amongst Vertebrate animals of this marvellous transformation, they are justly considered as the lowest in the scale, with the exception of fishes, which remain during life in that stage of development which is only the commencement of existence to a frog.

[1] *Polypedates maculatus*, Gray.

[2] *Bufo melanostictus*, Schneid.

[3] In Ceylon this error is as old as the third century, B. C., when, as the *Mahawanso* tells us, the wife of "King Asoka attempted to destroy the great bo-tree (at Magadha) *with the poisoned fang of a toad*."—Ch. xx. p. 122.

In undergoing this change, it is chiefly the organs of respiration that manifest alteration. In its earliest form the young batrachian, living in the water, breathes as a fish does by *gills*, either free and projecting as in the water-newt, or partially covered by integument as in the tadpole. But the gills disappear as the lungs gradually become developed: the duration of the process being on an average one hundred days from the time the eggs were first deposited. After this important change, the true batrachian is incapable any longer of living continuously in water, and either betakes itself altogether to the land, or seeks the surface from time to time to replenish its exhausted lungs.[1]

The change in the digestive functions during metamorphosis is scarcely less extraordinary; frogs, for example, which feed on animal substances at maturity, subsist entirely upon vegetable when in the condition of larvæ, and the subsidiary organs undergo remarkable development, the intestinal canal in the earlier stage being five times its length in the later one.

Of the family of tailed batrachians, Ceylon does not furnish a single example; but of those without this appendage, the island, as above remarked, affords many varieties; seven distinguishable species pertaining to the genus *rana*, or true frogs with webs to the hind feet; two to the genus *bufo*, or true toads, and five to the *Polypedates*, or East Indian "tree-frogs;" besides a few others in allied genera. The "tree-frog," whose

[1] A few Batrachians, such as the *Siren* of Carolina, the *Proteus* of Illyria, the *Axolotl* of Mexico, and the *Menobranchus* of the North American Lakes, retain their gills during life; but although provided with lungs in mature age, they are not capable of living out of the water. Such batrachians form an intermediate link between reptiles and fishes.

toes are terminated by rounded discs which assist it in climbing, possesses, in a high degree, the faculty of changing its hues; and one as green as a leaf to-day, will be found grey and spotted like the bark to-morrow. One of these beautiful little creatures, which had seated itself on the gilt pillar of a lamp on my dinner-table, became in a few minutes scarcely distinguishable in colour from the or-molu ornament to which it clung.

---

## *List of Ceylon Reptiles.*

I am indebted to Dr. Gray and Dr. Günther, of the British Museum, for a list of the reptiles of Ceylon; but many of those new to Europeans have been carefully described by the late Dr. Kelaart in his *Prodromus Faunæ Zeylanicæ* and its appendices, as well as in the 13th vol. *Magaz. Nat. Hist.* (1854).

SAURA.

Hydrosaurus
 salvator, *Wagler.*
Monitor
 dracæna, *Linn.*
Riopa
 punctata, *Linn.*
 Hardwickii, *Gray.*
Brachymeles
 Bonitæ, *Dum. & Bib.*
Tiliqua
 rufescens, *Shaw.*
Eumeces
 Taprobanius, *Kel.*
Nessia
 Burtoni, *Gray.*
Acontias
 Layardi, *Kelaart.*
Argyrophis
 bramicus, *Daud.*
Lygosoma
 fallax, *Peters.*
Rhinophis
 oxyrhynchus, *Schn.*
 punctatus, *J. Müll.*
 philippinus, *J. Müll.*
 homolepis, *Hempr.*
 planiceps. *Peters*
 Blythii, *Kelaart.*
 melanogaster, *Gray.*
Uropeltis
 grandis, *Kelaart.*
 *saffragamus, Kelaart.*
Silybura
 Ceylonica, *Cuv.*
Hemidactylus
 frenatus, *Schleg.*
 Leschenaultii, *Dum. & Bib.*
 trihedrus, *Daud.*
 maculatus, *Dum. & Bib.*
 Piresii, *Kelaart.*
 Coctœi, *Dum. & Bib.*
 pustulatus, *Dum.*
 sublævis, *Cantor.*
Peripia
 Peronii, *Dum. & Bib.*
Gymnodactylus
 Kandianus, *Kelaart.*
Sitana
 Ponticereana, *Cuv.*
Lyriocephalus
 scutatus, *Linn.*
Ceratophora
 Stoddartii, *Gray.*
 Tennentii, *Günther.*
Otocryptis
 bivittata, *Wiegm.*
*Salea Jerdoni, Gray.*
Calotes
 ophiomachus, *Merr.*
 nigrilabris, *Peters.*
 versicolor, *Daud.*
 Rouxii, *Dum. & Bib.*
 mystaceus, *Dum.*
Chameleo
 vulgaris, *Daud.*

OPHIDIA.

Megæra
 trigonocephala, *Latr.*
Trigonocephalus
 hypnalis, *Merr.*
Daboia
 elegans, *Daud.*
*Pelamys*
 *bicolor, Daud.*
*Aturia*
 *lapemoides, Gray.*
Hydrophis
 sublævis, *Gray,*
 cyanocinctus, *Daud.*
Chersydrus
 granulatus, *Schneid.*
Cerberus
 cinereus, *Daud.*
Tropidophis
 schistosus, *Daud.*
Python
 reticulatus, *Gray.*
Cylindrophis
 rufa, *Schneid.*
 maculata, *Linn.*
Aspidura
 brachyorrhos, *Boie.*
 trachyprocta, *Cope.*
Haplocercus
 Ceylonensis, *Günth.*
Oligodon
 subquadratus, *Dum. & Bib.*

subgriseus, *Dum. & Bib.*
sublineatus, *Dum. & Bib.*
Simotes
Russellii, *Daud.*
purpurascens, *Schleg.*
Ablabes
collaris, *Gray.*
Tropidonotus
quincunciatus, *Schleg.*
var. funebris.
var. carinatus.
stolatus, *Linn.*
chrysargus, *Boie.*
Cynophis
Helena, *Daud.*
Coryphodon
Blumenbachii, *Merr.*
Cyclophis
calamaria, *Günth.*
Chrysopelea
ornata, *Shaw.*
Dendrophis
picta, *Gm.*
Passerita
mycterizans, *Linn.*
fusca.
Dipsadomorphus
Ceylonensis, *Günth.*
Lycodon
aulicus, *Linn.*
Cercaspis
carinata, *Kuhl.*
Bungarus
fasciatus, *Schneid.*
var. Ceylonensis, *Gthr.*
Naja
tripudians, *Merr.*

CHELONIA.

Testudo
stellata, *Schweig.*
Emys
Sebæ, *Gray.*
trijuga, *Schweigg.*
Caretta
imbricata, *Linn.*
Chelonia
virgata, *Schweigg.*

EMYDOSAURI.

Crocodilus
biporcatus, *Cuv.*
palustris, *Less.*

BATRACHIA.

Rana
hexadactyla, *Less.*
Kuhlii, *Schleg.*
cutipora, *Dum. & Bib.*
tigrina, *Daud.*
vittigera, *Wiegm.*
Malabarica, *Dum. & Bib.*
Kandiana, *Kelaart.*
Neuera-elliana, *Kel.*
Bufo
melanostictus, *Schneid.*
Kelaartii, *Günth.*
Ixalus
variabilis, *Günth.*
leucorhinus, *Martens.*
poecilopleurus, *Mart.*
aurifasciatus, *Schleg.*
schmardanus, *Kelaart.*
Polypedates
maculatus, *Gray.*
microtympanum, *Gth.*
eques, *Günth.*
Limnodytes
lividus, *Blyth.*
macularis, *Blyth.*
mutabilis, *Kelaart.*
maculatus, *Kelaart.*
Kaloula
pulchra, *Gray.*
balteata, var. *Günth.*
stellata, *Kelaart.*
Adenomus
badioflavus, *Cope.*
Pyxicephalus
fodiens, *Jerd.*
Engystoma
rubrum, *Jerd.*

PSEUDOPHIDIA.

Cæcilia
glutinosa, *Linn.*

NOTE.—The following species are peculiar to Ceylon (and the genera Ceratophora, Otocryptis, Uropeltis, Aspidura, Cercaspis, and Haplocercus would appear to be similarly restricted); — Lygosoma fallax; Trimesurus Ceylonensis, T. nigromarginatus; Megæra Trigonocephala; Trigonocephalus hypnalis; Daboia elegans; Rhinophis punctatus, Rh. homolepis, Rh. planiceps, Rh. Blythii, Rh. melanogaster; Uropeltis grandis; Silybura Ceylonica; Cylindrophis maculata; Aspidura brachyorrhos; Haplocercus Ceylonensis; Oligodon sublineatus; Cynophis Helena; Cyclophis calamaria; Dipsadomorphus Ceylonensis; Cercaspis carinata; Ixalus variabilis, I. leucorhinus, I. poecilopleurus; Polypedates microtympanum, P. eques.

## CHAP. X.

### FISHES.

HITHERTO no branch of the zoology of Ceylon has been so imperfectly investigated as its Ichthyology. Little has been done in the examination and description of its fishes, especially those which frequent the rivers and inland waters. Mr. BENNETT, who was for some years employed in the Civil Service, directed his attention to the subject, and published in 1830 some portions of a projected work on the marine fishes of the island [1], but it never proceeded beyond the description of thirty individuals. The great work of Cuvier and Valenciennes [2] particularises about one hundred species, specimens of which were procured from Ceylon by Reynard, Leschenault and other correspondents; but of these not more than half a dozen belong to fresh water.

The fishes of the coast, so far as they have been examined, present few that are not in all probability common to the seas of Ceylon and India. A series of drawings, including upwards of six hundred species and varieties of Ceylon fish, all made from recently-captured specimens, has been submitted to Professor Huxley, and

[1] *A Selection of the most Remarkable and Interesting Fishes found on the Coast of Ceylon.* By J. W. BENNETT, Esq. London, 1830.

[2] *Histoire Naturelle des Poissons.*

a notice of their general characteristics forms an interesting appendix to the present chapter.[1]

Of those in ordinary use for the table the finest by far is the Seir-fish [2], a species of Scomberoids, which is called *Tora-malu* by the natives. It is in size and form very similar to the salmon, to which the flesh of the female fish, notwithstanding its white colour, bears a very close resemblance both in firmness and flavour.

Mackerel, carp, whitings, mullet both red and striped, perches and soles are abundant, and a sardine (*Sardinella Neohowii*, Val.) frequents the southern and eastern coast in such profusion that in one instance in 1839, a gentleman who was present saw upwards of four hundred thousand taken in a haul of the nets in the little bay of Goyapanna, east of Point-de-Galle. As this vast shoal approached the shore the broken water became as smooth as if a sheet of ice had been floating below the surface.[3]

*Poisonous Fishes.* — The sardine has the reputation of being poisonous at certain seasons, and accidents ascribed to eating it are recorded in all parts of the island. Whole families of fishermen who have partaken of it have died. Twelve persons in the jail of Chilaw were thus poisoned, about the year 1829; and the deaths of soldiers have repeatedly been ascribed to the same cause. It is difficult in such instances to say with certainty whether the fish were in fault; whether there

[1] See note B appended to this chapter.

[2] *Cybium* (*Scomber*, Linn.) *guttatum.*

[3] These facts serve to explain the story told by the friar ODORIC of Friuli, who visited Ceylon about the year 1320 A.D., and says there are "fishes in those seas that come swimming towards the said country in such abundance that for a great distance into the sea nothing can be seen but the backs of fishes, which casting themselves on the shore, do suffer men for the space of three daies to come and to take as many of them as they please, and then they return again into the sea."—*Hakluyt*, vol. ii. p. 57.

was not a peculiar susceptibility in the condition of the recipients; or whether the mischief may not have been occasioned by the wilful administration of poison, or its accidental occurrence in the brass cooking vessels used by the natives. The popular belief was, however, deferred to by an order passed by the Governor in Council in February, 1824, which, after reciting that "Whereas it appears by information conveyed to the Government that at three several periods at Trincomalie, death has been the consequence to several persons from eating the fish called Sardinia during the months of January and December," enacts that it shall not be lawful in that district to catch sardines during these months, under pain of fine and imprisonment. This order is still in force, but the fishing continues notwithstanding.[1]

*Sharks.*—Sharks appear on all parts of the coast, and instances continually occur of persons being seized by them whilst bathing even in the harbours of Trincomalie and Colombo. In the Gulf of Manaar they are taken for the sake of their oil, of which they yield such a quantity that "shark's oil" is a recognised export. A trade also exists in drying their fins, for which, owing to the gelatine contained in them, a ready market is found in China; whither the skin of the basking shark is also sent, to be converted, it is said, into shagreen.

*Saw Fish.*—The huge *Pristis antiquorum*[2] infests

[1] There are other species of Sardine found at Ceylon besides the *S. Neohowii;* such as the *S. lineolata*, Cuv. and Val. and the *S. leiogaster*, Cuv. and Val. xx. 270, which was found by M. Reynaud at Trincomalie. It occurs also off the coast of Java. Another Ceylon fish of the same group, a Clupea, is known as the "poisonous sprat;" the bonito (*Thynnus affinis*, Cang.), the kangewena, or unicorn fish (*Balistes?*), and a number of others, are more or less in bad repute from the same imputation.

[2] Two other species are found in the Ceylon waters, *P. cuspidatus* and *P. pectinatus*.

the eastern coast of the island, where it attains a length of from twelve to fifteen feet, including the serrated rostrum from which its name is derived. This

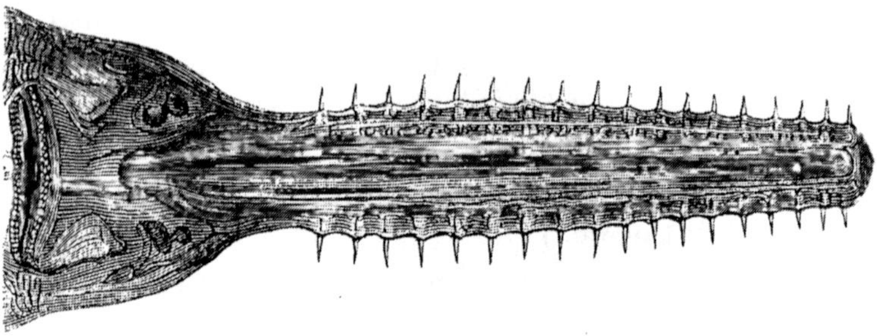

HEAD OF THE SAW-FISH (PRISTIS ANTIQUORUM)

powerful weapon seems designed to compensate for the inadequacy of the ordinary maxillary teeth which are unusually small, obtuse, and insufficient to capture and kill the animals which form the food of this predatory shark. To remedy this, the fore part of the head and its cartilages are prolonged into a flattened plate, the length of which is nearly equal to one third of the whole body; its edges being armed with formidable teeth, that are never shed or renewed, but increase in size with the growth of the creature.

The *Rays* form a large tribe of cartilaginous fishes in which, although the skeleton is not osseous, the development of organs is so advanced that they would appear to be the highest of the class, approaching nearest to amphibians. They are easily distinguished from the sharks by their broad and flat body, the pectoral fins being expanded like wings on each side of the trunk. They are all inhabitants of the ocean, and some grow to a prodigious size. Specimens have been caught of twenty feet in breadth. These, however, are of rare occurrence, as such huge monsters usually retreat into the depths of the sea, where they are secure from the

THE RAY (AËTOBATES NARINARI).

molestation of man. It is, generally speaking, only the young and the smaller species that approach the coasts, where they find a greater supply of those marine animals which form their food. The Rays have been divided into several generic groups, and the one of which a drawing (*Aëtobates narinari*[1]) is given, has very marked characteristics in its produced snout, pointed and winged-like pectoral fins, and exceedingly long, flagelliform tail. The latter is armed with a strong, serrated spine, which is always broken off by the fishermen immediately on capture, under the impression that wounds inflicted by it are poisonous. Their fears, however, are utterly ground-

[1] *Raja narinari*, Bl. Schn. p. 361. Henle., Plagiost. p. 179. *Aëtobates narinari*, Müll. und

less, as the ray has no gland for secreting any venomous fluid. The apprehension may, however, have originated in the fact that a lacerated wound such as would be produced by a serrated spine, is not unlikely to assume a serious character, under the influence of a tropical climate. The species figured on the last page is brownish-olive on the upper surface, with numerous greenish-white round spots, darkening towards the edges. The anterior annulations of the tail are black and white, the posterior entirely black. Its mouth is transverse and paved with a band of flattened teeth calculated to crush the hard shells of the animals on which it feeds. It moves slowly along the bottom in search of its food, which consists of crustacea and mollusca, and seems to be unable to catch fishes or other quickly moving animals. Specimens have been taken near Ceylon, of six feet in width. Like most deep-sea fishes, the ray has a wide geographical range, and occurs not only in all the Indian Ocean, but also in the tropical tracts of the Atlantic.

Another armed fish, renowned since the times of Ælian and Pliny for its courage in attacking the whale, and even a ship, is the sword-fish (*Xiphias gladius*).[1] Like the thunny and bonito, it is an inhabitant of the deeper seas, and, though known in the Mediterranean, is chiefly confined to the tropics. The dangerous weapon with which nature has equipped it is formed by the prolongation and intertexture of the bones of the upper jaw into an exceedingly compact cylindrical protuberance,

[1] Ælian tells a story of a ship in the Black Sea, the bottom of which was penetrated by the sword of a *Xiphias* (L. xiv. c. 23); and Pliny (L. xxxii. c. 8) speaks of a similar accident on the coast of Mauritania. In the British Museum there is a specimen of a plank of oak, pierced by a sword-fish, and still retaining the broken weapon.

somewhat flattened at the base, but tapering to a sharp point. In strange inconsistence with its possession of so formidable an armature, the general disposition of the sword-fish is represented to be gentle and inoffensive; and although the fact of its assaults upon the whale has been incontestably established, yet the motive for such conflicts, and the causes of its enmity, are beyond conjecture. Competition for food is out of the question, as the Xiphias can find its own supplies without rivalry on the part of its gigantic antagonist; and as to converting the whale itself into food, the sword-fish, from the construction of its mouth and the small size of its teeth, is quite incapable of feeding on animals of such dimensions.

In the seas around Ceylon sword-fishes sometimes attain to the length of twenty feet, and are distinguished by the unusual height of the dorsal fin. Those both of the Atlantic and Mediterranean possess this fin in its full proportions, only during the earlier stages of their growth. Its dimensions even then are much smaller than in the Indian species; and it is a curious fact that it gradually decreases as the fish approaches to maturity; whereas in the seas around Ceylon, it retains its full size throughout the entire period of life. They raise it above the water, whilst dashing along the surface in their rapid course; and there is no reason to doubt that it occasionally acts as a sail.

The Indian species (which are provided with two long and filamentous ventral fins) have been formed into the genus *Histiophorus;* to which belongs the individual figured on the next page. It is distinguished from others most closely allied to it, by having the immense dorsal fin of one uniform dark violet colour; whilst in its congeners, it is spotted with blue. The fish from which the engraving has been made, was procured by Dr. Tem-

THE SWORD-FISH (HISTIOPHORUS IMMACULATUS).

pleton, near Colombo. The species was previously known only by a single specimen captured in the Red Sea, by Rüppell, who conferred upon it the specific designation of "*immaculatus.*"[1]

ÆLIAN, in his graphic account of the strange forms presented by the fishes inhabiting the seas around Ceylon, says that one in particular is so grotesque in its configuration, that no painter would venture to depict it; its main peculiarity being that it has feet or claws rather than fins.[2] The annexed drawing[3] may

[1] Trans. Zool. Soc. ii. p. 71. Pl. 15.

[2] Πόδας γε μὴν χηλὰς ἢ πτερύγια. —Lib. xvi. c. 18.

[3] The fish from which this drawing of the *Cheironectes* was made, was taken near Colombo, and from the peculiarities which it presents it is in all probability a new and undescribed species. Dr. GÜNTHER has remarked, that in it, whilst the first and second dorsal spines are situated as usual over the eye (and form, one the angling bait of the fish, the other the crest above the nose), the third is at an unusual distance from the second, and is not separated, as in the other species, from the soft fin by a notch.

probably represent the creature to which the informants of Ælian referred. It is a cheironectes; one of a group in which the bones of the carpus form arms that support the pectoral fins, and enable these fishes to walk along the moist ground, almost like quadrupeds.

They belong to the family of *Lophiads* or "anglers," not unfrequent on the English coast; which conceal

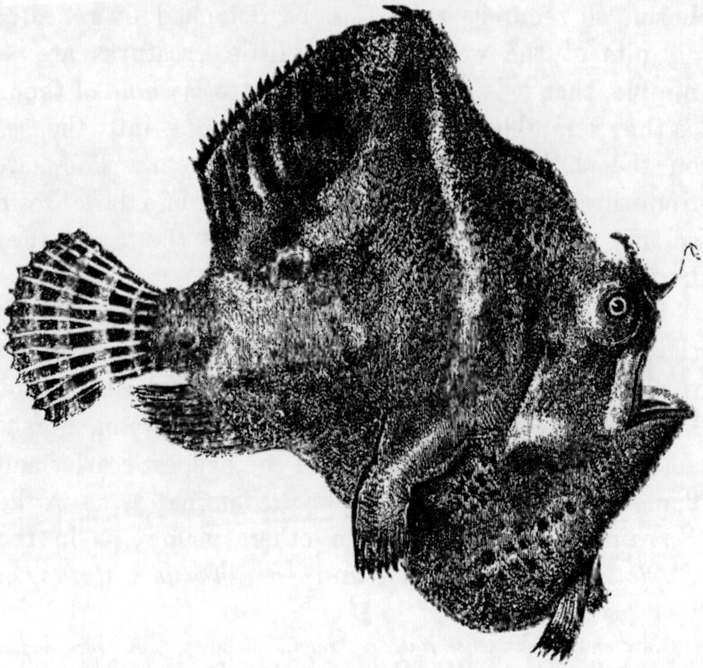

CHEIRONECTES.

themselves in the mud, displaying only the erectile ray, situated on the head, which bears an excrescence on its extremity resembling a worm; by agitating which, they attract the smaller fishes, that thus become an easy prey.

On the rocks in Ceylon which are washed by the surf

there are quantities of the curious little fish, *Salarias alticus*[1], which possesses the faculty of darting along the surface of the water, and running up the wet stones, with the utmost ease and rapidity. By aid of the pectoral and ventral fins and gill-cases, they move across the damp sand, ascend the roots of the mangroves, and climb up the smooth face of the rocks in search of flies; adhering so securely as not to be detached by repeated assaults of the waves. These little creatures are so nimble, that it is almost impossible to lay hold of them, as they scramble to the edge, and plunge into the sea on the slightest attempt to molest them. They are from three to four inches in length, and of a dark brown colour, almost undistinguishable from the rocks they frequent.

But the most striking to the eye of a stranger are those fishes whose brilliancy of colouring has won for them the wonder even of the listless Singhalese. Some, like the Red Sea Perch (*Holocentrum rubrum*, Forsk) and the Great Fire Fish[2], are of the deepest scarlet and flame colour; in others purple predominates, as in the *Serranus flavo-cœruleus;* in others yellow, as in the *Chætodon Brownriggii*[3], and *Acanthurus vittatus*, of

[1] CUV. and VALEN., *Hist. Nat. des Poissons*, tom. xi. p. 249. It is identical with *S. tridactylus*, Schn.

[2] *Pterois muricata*, Cuv. and Val. iv. 363. *Scorpæna miles*, Bennett; named by the Singhalese, "*Maharata-gini*," the Great Red Fire, a very brilliant red species spotted with black. It is very voracious, and is regarded on some parts of the coast as edible, while on others it is rejected.

[3] *Glyphisodon Brownriggii*, Cuv. and Val. v. 484; *Chætodon Brownriggii*, Bennett. A very small fish about two inches long, called *Kaha bartikyha* by the natives. It is distinct from Chœtodon, in which BENNETT placed it. Numerous species of this genus are scattered throughout the Indian Ocean. It derives its name from the fine hair-like character of its teeth. They are found chiefly among coral reefs, and, though eaten, are not much esteemed. In the French colonies they are called "Chauffe-soleil." One species is found on

Bennett[1], and numbers, from the lustrous green of their scales, have obtained from the natives the appropriate name of *Giraway*, or *parrots*, of which one, the *Sparus Hardwickii* of Bennett, is called the "Flower Parrot," from its exquisite colouring, being barred with irregular bands of blue, crimson, and purple, green, yellow, and grey, and crossed by perpendicular stripes of black.

Of these richly coloured fishes the most familiar in the Indian seas are the *Pteroids*. They are well known on the coast of Africa, and thence eastward to Polynesia; but they do not extend to the west coast of America, and are utterly absent from the Atlantic. The rays of the dorsal and pectoral fins are so elongated, that when specimens were first brought to Europe it was conjectured that these fishes have the faculty of flight, and hence the specific name of "*volitans*." But this is an error, for, owing to the deep incisions between the pectoral rays, the pteroids are wholly unable to sustain themselves in the air. They are not even bold swimmers, living close to the shore and never venturing into the deep sea. Their head is ornamented with a number of filaments and cutaneous appendages, of which one over

the shores of the New World (*G. saxatalis*), and it is curious that Messrs. QUOY and GAIMARD found this fish at the Cape de Verde Islands in 1827.

[1] This fish has a sharp round spine on the side of the body near the tail; a formidable weapon, which is generally partially concealed within a scabbard-like incision. It raises or depresses this spine at pleasure. The fish is yellow, with several nearly parallel blue stripes on the back and sides; the belly is white, the tail and fins brownish green, edged with blue.

It is found in rocky places; and according to BENNETT, who has figured it in his second plate, it is named *Seweya*. It has been known, however, to all the old ichthyologists, Valentyn, Renard, Seba, Artedi, and has been named *Chætodon lineatus*, by Linné. It is scarce on the southern coast of Ceylon.

each eye and another at the angles of the mouth are the most conspicuous. Sharp spines project on the crown and on the side of the gill-apparatus, as in the other sea-perches, *Scorpæna*, *Serranus*, &c., of which these are

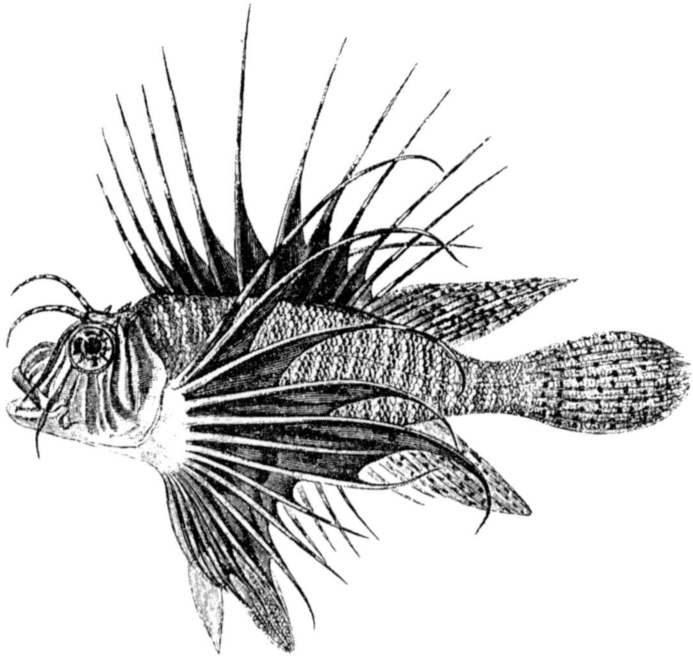

PTEROIS VOLITANS.

only a modified and ornate form. The extraordinary expansion of their fins is not, however, accompanied by a similar development of the bones to which they are attached, simply because they appear to have no peculiar function, as in flying fishes, or in those where the spines of the fins are weapons of offence. They attain to the length of twelve inches, and to a weight of about two pounds; they live on small marine animals, and by the Singhalese the flesh (of some at least) is considered good for table. Nine or ten species are known to occur in the East Indian Seas, and of these the one figured above is, perhaps, the most common.

Another species known to occur on the coasts of Ceylon, is the *Scorpæna miles*, Bennett, or *Pterois miles*, Günther[1], of which Bennett has given a figure[2], but it is not altogether correct in some particulars.

In the fishes of Ceylon, however, beauty is not confined to the brilliancy of their tints. In some, as in the *Scarus harid*, Forsk[3], the arrangement of the scales is so graceful, and the effect is so heightened by modifications of colour, as to present the appearance of tessellation, or mosaic work.

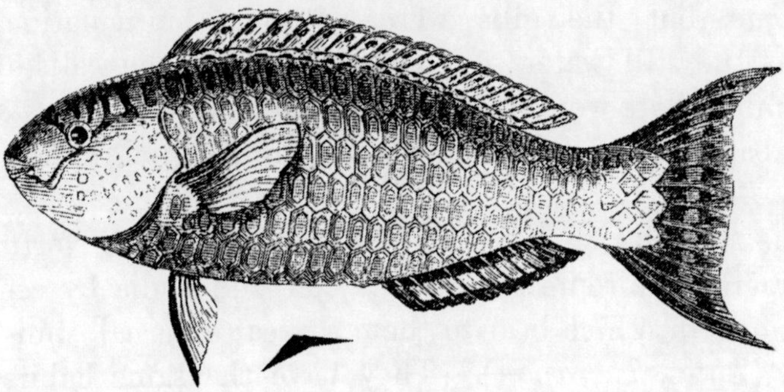

SCARUS HARID.
After Bennett.

*Fresh-water Fishes.*—Of the fresh-water fish, which inhabit the rivers and tanks, so very little has hitherto been known to naturalists[4], that of nineteen drawings

[1] The fish from the Sea of Pinang, described by Dr. CANTOR with this name (Catal. Mal. Fish. p. 42), is again different, and belongs to a third species.

[2] *Fishes of Ceylon*, Pl. ix.

[3] This is the fish figured by BENNETT as *Sparus pepo*. *Fishes of Ceylon*, Plate xxviii.

[4] In extenuation of the little that is known of the fresh-water fishes of Ceylon, it may be observed that very few of them are used at table by Europeans, and there is therefore no stimulus on the part of the natives to catch

sent home by Major Skinner in 1852, although specimens of well-known genera, Colonel Hamilton Smith pronounced nearly the whole to be new and undescribed species.

Of eight of these, which were from the Mahawelliganga, and caught in the vicinity of Kandy, five were carps; two were *Leucisci*, and one a *Mastacembelus* (*M. armatus*, Lacep); one was an *Ophiocephalus*, and one a *Polyacanthus*, with no serræ on the gills. Six were from the Kalanyganga, close to Colombo, of which two were *Helostoma*, in shape approaching the Chætodon; two *Ophiocephali*, one a *Silurus*, and one an *Anabas*, but the gills were without denticulation. From the still water of the lake, close to the walls of Colombo, there were two species of *Eleotris*, one *Silurus* with barbels, and two *Malacopterygians*, which appear to be *Bagri*.

The *fresh-water Perches* of Europe and of the North of America are represented in Ceylon and India by several genera, which bear to them a great external similarity (*Lates*, *Therapon*). They have the same habits as their European allies, and their flesh is considered equally wholesome, but they appear to enter salt-water, or at least brackish water, more freely. It is, however,

them. The burbot and grey mullet are occasionally eaten, but they taste of mud, and are not in request.

Some years ago the experiment was made, with success, of introducing into Mauritius the *Osphromenus olfax* of Java, which has also been taken to French Guiana. In both places it is now highly esteemed as a fish for table. As it belongs to a family which possesses the faculty, hereafter alluded to, of surviving in the damp soil after the subsidence of the water in the tanks and rivers, it might with equal advantage be acclimated in Ceylon. It grows to 20 lbs. weight and upwards.

in their internal organisation that they differ most from the perches of Europe; their skeletons are composed of

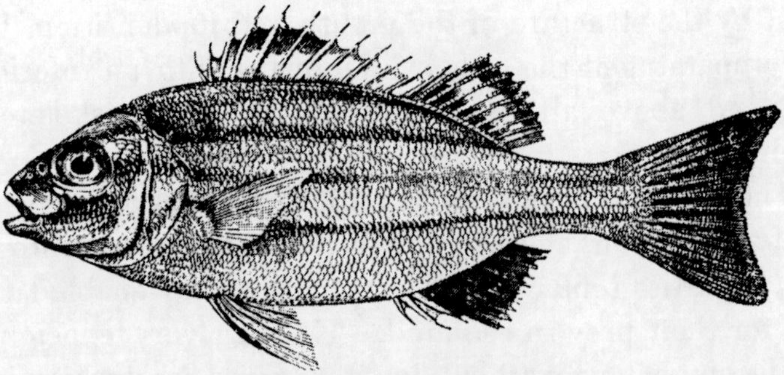

THERAPON QUADRILINEATUS.

fewer vertebræ, and the air bladder of the *Therapon* is divided into two portions, as in the carps. Four species at least of this genus inhabit the lakes and rivers of Ceylon, and one of them, of which a figure is given above, has been but imperfectly described in any ichthyological work[1]; it attains to the length of seven inches.

In addition to marine eels, in which the Indian coasts abound, Ceylon has some true fresh-water eels, which never enter the sea. These are known to the natives under the name of *Theliya*, and to naturalists by that of *Mastacembelus*. They have sometimes in ichthyological systems been referred to the Scombridæ and other marine families, from the circumstance that the dorsal fin anteriorly is composed of spines. But, in addition to the

[1] Holocentrus quadrilineatus, *Bloch*. It is allied to *Helotes polytœnia*, Bleek., from Halmaheira, from which it can be readily distinguished by having only five or six blackish longitudinal bands, the black humeral spot being between the first and second; another blackish blotch is in the spinous dorsal fin. There are two specimens in the British Museum collection, one of which has recently arrived from Amoy; of the other the locality is unknown. See GÜNTHER, *Acanthopt. Fishes*, vol. i. p. 282, where mention of the black humeral spot has been omitted.

general shape of the body, their affinity to the eel is attested, by their confluent fins, by the absence of ventral fins, by the structure of the mouth and its dentition, by the apparatus of the gills, which opens with an inferior slit, and above all by the formation of the skeleton itself.[1]

Their skin is covered with minute scales, coated by a slimy exudation, and the upper jaw is produced into a soft tripartite tentacle, with which they are enabled to feel for their prey in the mud. They are very tenacious of life, and belong, without doubt, to those fishes which in Ceylon descend during the drought into the muddy soil.[2] Their flesh very much resembles that of the eel, and is highly esteemed.[3] They were first made known to European naturalists by Russell[4], who brought to Europe from the rivers round Aleppo specimens, some of which are still preserved in the collection of the British Museum. Aleppo is the most western point of their geographical range, the group being mainly confined to the East-Indian continent and its islands.

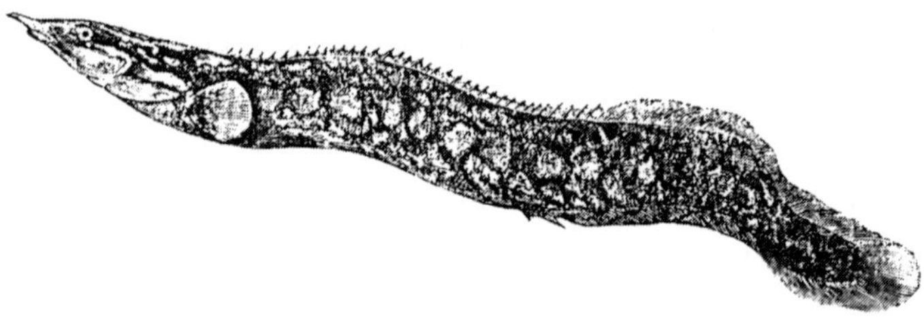

MASTACEMBELUS ARMATUS.

In Ceylon only one species appears to occur, the

[1] See GÜNTHER'S *Acanthopt. Fishes*, vol. iii. (Family Mastacembelidæ).

[2] See post, p. 351.

[3] CUV. and VAL., *Hist. Poiss.* vol. iii. p. 459.

[4] *Nat. Hist. Aleppo*, 2nd edit. Lond. 1794, vol. ii. p. 208, pl. vi.

*Mastacembelus armatus.*[1] The back is armed with from thirty-five to thirty-nine short, stout spines; there being three others before the anal fin. The ground colour of the fish is brown, and the head has two rather irregular longitudinal black bands; deep-brown spots run along the back as well as along the dorsal and anal fins; and the sides are ornamented with irregular and reticulated brown lines. This eel attains to the length of two feet. The old females do not show any markings, being of a uniform brown colour.

In the collection of Major Skinner, before alluded to, brought together without premeditation, the naturalist will be struck by the preponderance of those genera which are adapted by nature to endure a temporary privation of moisture; and this, taken in connection with the vicissitudes affecting the waters they inhabit, exhibits a surprising illustration of the wisdom of the Creator in adapting the organisation of his creatures to the peculiar circumstances under which they are destined to exist.

So abundant are fish in all parts of the island, that Knox says, not the running streams alone, but the reservoirs and ponds, "nay, every ditch and little plash of water but ankle deep hath fish in it."[2] But many of these reservoirs and tanks are, twice in each year, liable

[1] Macrognathus armatus, *Lacép.*; Mastacembelus armatus, *Cuv.*, *Val.*

[2] KNOX's *Historical Relation of Ceylon*, Part I. ch. vii. The occurrence of fish in the most unlooked-for situations, is one of the mysteries of other eastern countries as well as Ceylon and India. In Persia irrigation is carried on to a great extent by means of wells sunk in line in the direction in which it is desired to lead a supply of water, and these are connected by channels, which are carefully arched over to protect them from evaporation. These *kanats*, as they are called, are full of fish, although neither they nor the wells they unite have any connection with streams or lakes.

to be evaporated to dryness till the mud of the bottom is converted into dust, and the clay cleft by the heat into gaping apertures; yet within a very few days after the change of the monsoon, the natives are busily engaged in fishing in those very spots and in the hollows contiguous to them, although the latter are entirely unconnected with any pool or running streams. Here they fish in the same way which Knox described nearly 200 years ago, with a funnel-shaped basket, open at bottom and top, "which," as he says, "they jibb down, and the end sticks in the mud, which often happens upon a fish; which, when they feel beating itself against the sides, they put in their hands and take it out, and reive a ratan through their gills, and so let them drag after them."[1]

FROM KNOX'S CEYLON, A. D. 1681

This operation may be seen in the lowlands, traversed

[1] KNOX, *Historical Relation of Ceylon*, Part I. ch. vi.

by the high road leading from Colombo to Kandy. Before the change of the monsoon, the hollows on either side of the highway are covered with dust or stunted grass; but when flooded by the rains, they are immediately resorted to by the peasants with baskets, constructed precisely as Knox has stated, in which the fish are entrapped and taken out by the hand.[1]

So singular a phenomenon as the sudden re-appearance of full-grown fishes in places that a few days before had been encrusted with hardened clay, has not failed to attract attention; but the European residents have been content to explain it by hazarding conjectures, either that the spawn must have lain imbedded in the dried earth till released by the rains, or that the fish, so unexpectedly discovered, fall from the clouds during the deluge of the monsoon.

As to the latter conjecture; the fall of fish during showers, even were it not so problematical in theory, is too rare an event to account for the punctual appearance of those found in the rice-fields, at stated periods of the year. Both at Galle and Colombo in the south-west monsoon, fish are popularly believed to have fallen from the clouds during violent showers, but those found on the occasions that give rise to this belief, consist of the smallest fry, such as could be caught up by water-spouts, and vortices analogous to them, or otherwise blown on shore from the surf; whereas those which

[1] As anglers, the native Singhalese exhibit little expertness; but for fishing the rivers, they construct with singular ingenuity fences formed of strong stakes, protected by screens of ratan, that stretch diagonally across the current; and along these the fish are conducted into a series of enclosures from which retreat is impracticable. Mr. Layard, in the *Magazine of Natural History* for May, 1853, has given a diagram of one of these fish "corrals," as they are called, of which a copy is shown on the next page.

suddenly appear in the replenished tanks and in the hollows which they overflow, are mature and well-grown fish.[1] Besides, the latter are found, under the circumstances I have described, in all parts of the interior, whilst the prodigy of a supposed fall of fish from the sky has been noticed, I apprehend, only in the vicinity of the sea, or of some inland water.

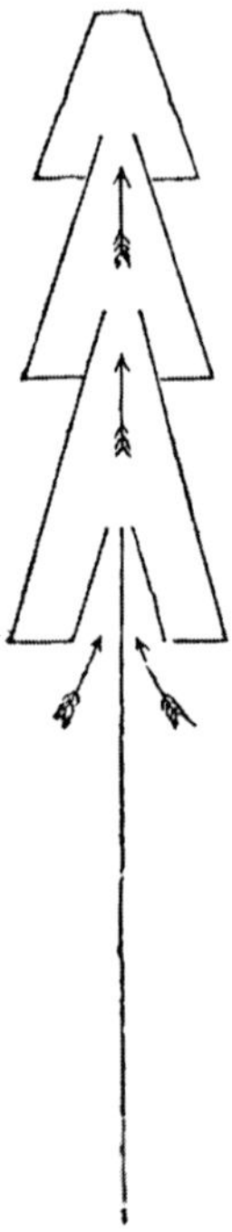

FISH CORRAL.

The surmise of the buried spawn is one sanctioned by the very highest authority. Mr. YARRELL in his "*History of British Fishes*," adverting to the fact that ponds (in India) which had been previously converted into hardened mud, are replenished with small fish in a very few days after the commencement of each rainy season, offers this solution of the problem as probably the true one: "The impregnated ova of the fish of one rainy season are left unhatched in the mud through the dry season, and from their low state of organisation as ova, the vitality is preserved till the recurrence, and contact

[1] I had an opportunity, on one occasion only, of witnessing the phenomenon which gives rise to this popular belief. I was driving in the cinnamon gardens near the fort of Colombo, and saw a violent but partial shower descend at no great distance before me. On coming to the spot I found a multitude of small silvery fish from one and a half to two inches in length, leaping on the gravel of the high road, numbers of which I collected and brought away in my palankin. The spot was about half a mile from the sea, and entirely unconnected with any watercourse or pool.

Mr. WHITING, who was many years resident in Trincomalie, writes me that he "had often been told by the natives on that side of the island that it sometimes rained fishes; and on one occasion" (he adds) "I was taken by them, in 1849, to a field at the village of Karrancotta-tivo, near Batticaloa, which was dry when I passed over it in the morning, but had been covered in two hours by sudden rain to the depth of three inches, in which there was then a quantity of small

of the rain and oxygen in the next wet season, when vivification takes place from their joint influence."[1]

This hypothesis, however, appears to have been advanced upon imperfect data; for although some fish, like the salmon, scrape grooves in the sand and place their spawn in inequalities and fissures; yet as a general rule spawn is deposited not beneath but on the surface of the ground or sand over which the water flows, the adhesive nature of each egg supplying the means of attachment. But in the Ceylon tanks not only is the surface of the soil dried to dust after the evaporation of the water, but earth itself, twelve or eighteen inches deep, is converted into sun-burnt clay, in which, although the eggs of mollusca, in their calcareous covering, are in some instances preserved, it would appear to be as impossible for the ova of fish to be kept from decomposition as for the fish themselves to sustain life. Besides, moisture in such situations is only to be found at a depth to which spawn could not be conveyed by the parent fish, by any means with which we are yet acquainted.

fish. The water had no connection with any pond or stream whatsoever." Mr. CRIPPS, in like manner, in speaking of Galle, says: "I have seen in the vicinity of the fort, fish taken from rain-water that had accumulated in the hollow parts of land that in the hot season are perfectly dry and parched. The place is accessible to no running stream or tank; and either the fish, or the spawn from which they were produced, must of necessity have fallen with the rain."

Mr. J. PRINSEP, the eminent secretary to the Asiatic Society of Bengal, found a fish in the pulviometer at Calcutta, in 1838.—*Journ. Asiat. Soc. Bengal*, vol. vi. p. 465.

A series of instances in which fishes have been found on the continent of India under circumstances which lead to the conclusion that they must have fallen from the clouds, have been collected by the late Dr. BUIST of Bombay, and will be found in the appendix to this chapter.

[1] YARRELL, *History of British Fishes*, introd. vol. i. p. xxvi. This too was the opinion of Aristotle, *De Respiratione*, c. ix.

But supposing it possible to carry the spawn sufficiently deep, and to deposit it safely in the mud below, which is still damp, whence it could be liberated on the return of the rains, a considerable interval would still be necessary after the replenishing of the ponds with water to admit of vivification and growth. Yet so far from this interval being allowed to elapse, the rains have no sooner fallen than the taking of the fish commences, and those captured by the natives in wicker cages are mature and full grown instead of being "small fish" or fry, as supposed by Mr. Yarrell.

Even admitting the soundness of his theory, and the probability that, under favourable circumstances, the spawn in the tanks might be preserved during the dry season so as to contribute to the perpetuation of their breed, the fact is no longer doubtful, that adult fish in Ceylon, like some of those that inhabit similar waters both in the New and Old World, have been endowed by the Creator with the singular faculty of providing against the periodical droughts either by journeying overland in search of still unexhausted water, or, on its utter disappearance, by burying themselves in the mud to await the return of the rains.

It is an illustration of the eagerness with which, after the expedition of Alexander the Great, particulars connected with the natural history of India were sought for and arranged by the Greeks, that in the works both of ARISTOTLE and THEOPHRASTUS facts are recorded of the fishes in the Indian rivers migrating in search of water, of their burying themselves in the mud on its failure, of their being dug out thence alive during the dry season, and of their spontaneous reappearance on the return of the rains. The earliest notice is in ARISTOTLE's treatise *De Respiratione*[1], where he mentions the strange discovery of living fish found beneath the surface of the soil, "*τῶν ἰχθύων οἱ πολλοὶ ζῶσιν ἐν τῇ γῇ, ἀκινητίζοντες μέντοι, καὶ εὑρίσκονται ὀρυττόμενοι*;" and in his History of Animals he conjectures that in ponds periodically dried the ova of the fish so buried become vivified at the change of the season.[2] HERODOTUS had previously hazarded a similar theory to account for the sudden appearance of fry in the Egyptian marshes on the rising of the Nile; but the cases are not parallel. THEOPHRASTUS, the friend and pupil of Aristotle, gave importance to the subject by devoting to it his essay Περὶ *τῆς τῶν ἰχθύων ἐν ξηρῷ διαμονῆς*, *De Piscibus in sicco degentibus*. In this, after adverting to the fish called *exocœtus*, from its habit of going on shore to sleep, "*ἀπὸ τῆς κοιτῆς*," he instances the small fish (*ἰχθύδια*), that leave the rivers of India to wander like frogs on the land; and likewise a species found near Babylon, which, when the Euphrates runs low, leave the dry channels in search of food, "moving themselves along by means of their fins and tail." He proceeds to state that at Heraclea Pontica there are places in which fish are dug out of the earth, "*ὀρυκτοὶ τῶν ἰχθύων*," and he accounts for their being found under such circumstances by the subsidence of the rivers, "when the water being evaporated the fish gradually descend beneath the soil in search of moisture; and the surface becoming hard they are preserved in the damp clay below it, in a state of torpor, but are capable of vigorous movements when disturbed." "In this manner, too," adds Theophrastus, "the buried fish

[1] Chap. ix. [2] Lib. vi. ch. 15, 16, 17.

propagate, leaving behind them their spawn, which becomes vivified on the return of the waters to their accustomed bed." This work of Theophrastus became the great authority for all subsequent writers on this question. ATHENÆUS quotes it [1], and adds the further testimony of POLYBIUS, that in Gallia Narbonensis fish are similarly dug out of the ground.[2] STRABO repeats the story [3], and the Greek naturalists one and all received the statement as founded on reliable authority.

Not so the Romans. LIVY mentions it as one of the prodigies which were to be "expiated" on the approach of a rupture with Macedon, that "in Gallico agro qua induceretur aratrum sub glebis pisces emersisse," [4] thus taking it out of the category of natural occurrences. POMPONIUS MELA, obliged to notice the matter in his account of Narbon Gaul, accompanies it with the intimation that although asserted by both Greek and Roman authorities, the story was either a delusion or a fraud. JUVENAL has a sneer for the rustic —

> "miranti sub aratro
> Piscibus inventis."—*Sat.* xiii. 63.

And SENECA, whilst he quotes Theophrastus, adds ironically, that now we must go to fish with a *hatchet* instead of a hook; "non cum hamis, sed cum dolabra ire piscatum." PLINY, who devotes the 35th chapter of his 9th book to this subject, uses the narrative of Theophrastus, but with obvious caution, and universally the Latin writers treated the story as a fable.

In later times the subject received more enlightened attention, and Beckman, who in 1736 published his

[1] Lib. viii. ch. 2.
[2] *Ib.* ch. 4.
[3] Lib. iv. and xii.
[4] Lib. xlii. ch. 2.

commentary on the collection Περὶ Θαυμασίων ἀκουσμάτων, ascribed to Aristotle, has given a list of the authorities about his own times,—GEORGIUS AGRICOLA, GESNER, RONDELET, DALECHAMP, BOMARE, and GRONOVIUS, who not only gave credence to the assertions of Theophrastus, but adduced modern instances in corroboration of his Indian authorities.

As regards the fresh-water fishes of India and Ceylon, the fact is now established that certain of them possess the power of leaving the rivers and returning to them again after long migrations on dry land, and modern observation has fully confirmed their statements. They leave the pools and nullahs in the dry season, and led by an instinct as yet unexplained, shape their course through the grass towards the nearest pool of water. A similar phenomenon is observable in countries similarly circumstanced. The Doras of Guiana [1] have been seen travelling over land during the dry season in search of their natural element [2], in such droves that the negroes fill baskets with them during these terrestrial excursions. PALLEGOIX in his account of Siam, enumerates three species of fishes which leave the tanks and channels

[1] *D. Hancockii*, CUV. et VAL.

[2] Sir R. Schomburgk's *Fishes of Guiana*, vol. i. pp. 113, 151, 160. Another migratory fish was found by Bosc very numerous in the fresh waters of Carolina and in ponds liable to become dry in summer. When captured and placed on the ground, "they *always directed themselves towards the nearest water*, *which they could not possibly see*, and which they must have discovered by some internal index. They belong to the genus *Hydrargyra*, and are called Swampines.—KIRBY, *Bridgewater Treatise*, vol. i. p. 143.

Eels kept in a garden, when August arrived (the period at which instinct impels them to go to the sea to spawn) were in the habit of leaving the pond, and were invariably found moving eastward *in the direction of the sea*.—YARRELL, vol. ii. p. 384. Anglers observe that fish newly caught, when placed out of sight of water, always struggle towards it to escape.

and traverse the damp grass[1]; and SIR JOHN BOWRING, in his account of his embassy to the Siamese kings in 1855, states, that in ascending and descending the river Meinam to Bankok, he was amused with the novel sight of fish leaving the river, gliding over the wet banks, and losing themselves amongst the trees of the jungle.[2]

The class of fishes endowed with this power are chiefly those with labyrinthiform pharyngeal bones, so disposed in plates and cells as to retain a supply of moisture, which, whilst they are crawling on land, gradually exudes so as to keep the gills damp.[3]

The individual most frequently seen in these excursions in Ceylon is a perch called by the Singhalese *Kavaya* or *Kawhy-ya*, and by the Tamils *Pannei-eri*, or *Sennal*. It is closely allied to the *Anabas scandens* of Cuvier, the *Perca scandens* of Daldorf. It grows to about six inches in length, the head round and covered with scales, and the edges of the gill-covers strongly denticulated. Aided by the apparatus already adverted to in its head, this little creature issues boldly from its native pools and addresses itself to its toilsome march generally at night or in the early morning, whilst the grass is still damp with the dew; but in its distress it is sometimes compelled to move by day, and Mr. E. L. Layard on one occasion encountered a number of them travelling along a hot and dusty road under the midday sun.[4]

[1] PALLEGOIX, vol. i. p. 144.

[2] Sir J. BOWRING'S *Siam, &c.*, vol. i. p. 10.

[3] CUVIER and VALENCIENNES, *Hist. Nat. des Poissons*, tom. vii. p. 246.

[4] *Annals and Mag. of Nat. Hist.*, May, 1853, p. 390. Mr. Morris, the government-agent of Trincomalie, writing to me on this subject in 1856, says—"I was lately on duty inspecting the bund of a large tank at Nade-cadua, which, being out of repair, the remaining water was confined in a small hollow in the otherwise dry bed.

Referring to the *Anabas scandens*, DR. HAMILTON BUCHANAN says, that of all the fish with which he was acquainted it is the most tenacious of life; and he has known boatmen on the Ganges to keep them for five or six days in an earthen pot without water, and daily to use what they wanted, finding them as lively and fresh as when caught.[1] Two Danish naturalists residing at

Whilst there heavy rain came on, and, as we stood on the high ground, we observed a pelican on the margin of the shallow pool gorging himself; our people went towards him and raised a cry of fish! fish! We hurried down, and found numbers of fish struggling upwards through the grass in the rills formed by the trickling of the rain. There was scarcely water enough to cover them, but nevertheless they made rapid progress up the bank, on which our followers collected about two bushels of them at a distance of forty yards from the tank. They were forcing their way up the knoll, and, had they not been intercepted first by the pelican and afterwards by ourselves, they would in a few minutes have gained the highest point and descended on the other side into a pool which formed another portion of the tank. They were chub, the same as are found in the mud after the tanks dry up." In a subsequent communication in July, 1857, the same gentleman says—"As the tanks dry up the fish congregate in the little pools till at last you find them in thousands in the moistest parts of the beds, rolling in the blue mud which is at that time about the consistence of thick gruel."

"As the moisture further evaporates the surface fish are left uncovered, and they crawl away in search of fresh pools. In one place I saw hundreds diverging in every direction, from the tank they had just abandoned to a distance of fifty or sixty yards, and still travelling onwards. In going this distance, however, they must have used muscular exertion sufficient to have taken them half a mile on level ground, for at these places all the cattle and wild animals of the neighbourhood had latterly come to drink; so that the surface was everywhere indented with footmarks in addition to the cracks in the surrounding baked mud, into which the fish tumbled in their progress. In those holes which were deep and the sides perpendicular they remained to die, and were carried off by kites and crows."

"My impression is that this migration takes place at night or before sunrise, for it was only early in the morning that I have seen them progressing, and I found that those I brought away with me in chatties appeared quiet by day, but a large proportion managed to get out of the chatties at night—some escaped altogether, others were trodden on and killed."

"One peculiarity is the large size of the vertebral column, quite disproportioned to the bulk of the fish. I particularly noticed that all in the act of migrating had their gills expanded."

[1] *Fishes of the Ganges*, 4to. 1822.

Tranquebar, have contributed their authority to the fact of this fish ascending trees on the coast of Coromandel, an exploit from which it acquired its epithet of *Perca scandens* DALDORF, who was a lieutenant in the Danish East India Company's service, communicated to Sir Joseph Banks, that in the year 1791 he had taken this fish from a moist cavity in the stem of a Palmyra palm, that grew near a lake. He saw it when already five feet above the ground struggling to ascend still higher; —" suspending itself by its gill-covers, and bending its tail to the left, it fixed its anal fin in the cavity of the bark, and sought by expanding its body to urge its way upwards, and its march was only arrested by the hand with which he seized it."[1]

There is considerable obscurity about the story of this ascent, although corroborated by M. JOHN. Its motive for climbing is not apparent, since water being close at hand it could not have gone for sake of the moisture contained in the fissures of the palm; nor could it be in search of food, as it lives not on fruit but on aquatic insects.[2] The descent, too, is a question of difficulty.

[1] *Transactions Linn. Soc.* vol. iii. p. 63. It is remarkable, however, that this discovery of Daldorf, which excited so great an interest in 1791, had been anticipated by an Arabian voyager a thousand years before. Abou-zeyd, the compiler of the remarkable MS. known since Renaudot's translation by the title of the *Travels of the Two Mahometans*, states that Suleyman, one of his informants, who visited India at the close of the ninth century, was told there of a fish which, issuing from the waters, ascended the coco-nut palms to drink their sap, and returned to the sea. "On parle d'un poisson de mer qui, sortant de l'eau, monte sur la cocotier et boit le suc de la plante; ensuite il retourne à la mer." See REINAUD, *Rélations des Voyages faits par les Arabes et Persans dans le neuvième siècle*, tom. i. p. 21, tom. ii. p. 93.

[2] Kirby says that it is "in pursuit of certain crustaceans that form its food" (*Bridgewater Treatise*, vol i. p. 144); but I am not aware of any crustaceans in the island which ascend the palmyra or feed upon its fruit. The *Birgus latro*, which inhabits Mauritius, and is said to climb the coco-nut

The position of its fins, and the spines on its gill-covers, might assist its journey upwards, but the same apparatus would prove anything but a facility in steadying its journey down. The probability is, as suggested by Buchanan, that the ascent which was witnessed by Daldorf was accidental, and ought not to be regarded as the habit of the animal. In Ceylon I heard of no instance of the perch ascending trees[1], but the fact is well established that both it, the *pullata* (a species of *polyacanthus*), and others, are capable of long journeys on the level ground.[2]

*Burying Fishes.*—But a still more remarkable power possessed by some of the Ceylon fishes, is that already alluded to, of secreting themselves in the earth in the dry season, at the bottom of the exhausted ponds, and there awaiting the renewal of the water at the change of the monsoon. The instinct of the crocodile to resort to the same expedient has been already referred to[3], and in like manner the fish, when distressed by the evaporation of the tanks, seek relief by immersing first their heads,

for this purpose, has not been observed in Ceylon.

[1] This assertion must be qualified by a fact stated by Mr. E. A. Layard, who mentions that on visiting one of the fishing stations on a Singhalese river, where the fish are caught in staked enclosures, as described at p. 342, and observing that the chambers were covered with netting, he asked the reason, and was told "*that some of the fish climbed up the sticks and got over.*"—*Mag. Nat. Hist.* for May 1823, p. 390-1.

[2] Strange accidents have more than once occurred at Ceylon arising from the habit of the native anglers; who, having neither baskets nor pockets in which to place what they catch, will seize a fish in their teeth whilst putting fresh bait on their hook. In August, 1853, a man was carried into the Pettah hospital at Colombo, having a climbing perch, which he thus attempted to hold, firmly imbedded in his throat. The spines of its dorsal fin prevented its descent, whilst those of the gill-covers equally forbade its return. It was eventually extracted by the forceps through an incision in the œsophagus, and the patient recovered. Other similar cases have proved fatal.

[3] See *ante*, p. 285.

and by degrees their whole bodies, in the mud; sinking to a depth at which they find sufficient moisture to preserve life in a state of lethargy long after the bed of the tank has been consolidated by the intense heat of the sun. It is possible, too, that the cracks which reticulate the surface may admit air to some extent to sustain their faint respiration.

The same thing takes place in other tropical regions, subject to vicissitudes of drought and moisture. The Protopterus[1], which inhabits the Gambia (and which though demonstrated by Professor Owen to possess all the essential organisation of fishes, is nevertheless provided with true lungs), is accustomed in the dry season, when the river retires into its channel, to bury itself to the depth of twelve or sixteen inches in the indurated mud of the banks, and to remain in a state of torpor till the rising of the stream after the rains enables it to resume its active habits. At this period the natives of the Gambia, like those of Ceylon, resort to the river, and secure the fish in considerable numbers as they flounder in the still shallow water. A parallel instance occurs in Abyssinia in relation to the fish of the Mareb, one of the sources of the Nile, the waters of which are partially absorbed in traversing the plains of Taka. During the summer its bed is dry, and in the slime at the depth of more than six feet is found a species of fish without scales, different from any known to inhabit the Nile.[2]

[1] *Lepidosiren annectans*, Owen. See *Linn. Trans.* 1839.

[2] This statement will be found in QUATREMERE'S *Mémoires sur l'Egypte*, tom. i. p. 17, on the authority of Abdullah ben Ahmed ben Solaim Assouany, in his *History of Nubia*, "Simon, héritier présomptif du royaume d'Alouah, m'a assuré que l'on trouve, dans la vase qui couvre le fond de cette rivière, un grand poisson sans écailles, qui ne ressemble en rien aux poissons du Nil, et que, pour l'avoir, il faut creuser à une toise et plus de pro-

In South America the "round-headed hassar" of Guiana, *Callicthys littoralis,* and the "yarrow," a species of the family Esocidæ, although they possess no specially modified respiratory organs, are accustomed to bury themselves in the mud on the subsidence of water in the pools during the dry season.[1] The *Loricaria* of Surinam, another Siluridan, exhibits a similar instinct, and resorts to the same expedient. Sir R. Schomburgk, in his account of the fishes of Guiana, confirms this account of the Callicthys, and says "they can exist in muddy lakes without any water whatever, and great numbers of them are sometimes dug up from such situations."[2]

In those portions of Ceylon where the country is flat, and small tanks are extremely numerous, the natives are accustomed in the hot season to dig in the mud for

fondeur." To this passage there is appended this note:—"Le patriarche Mendes, cité par Legrand (*Relation Hist. d'Abyssinie,* du P. LOBO, p. 212-3) rapporte que, le fleuve Mareb, après avoir arrosé une étendue de pays considérable, se perd sous terre; et que quand les Portugais faisaient la guerre dans ce pays, ils fouilloient dans le sable, et y trouvoient de la bonne eau et du bon poisson. Au rapport de l'auteur de *l'Ayin Akbery* (tom. ii. p. 146, ed. 1800), dans le Soubah de Caschmir, près du lieu nommé Tilahmoulah, est une grande pièce de terre qui est inondée pendant la saison des pluies. Lorsque les eaux se sont évaporées, et que la vase est presque sèche, les habitans prennent des bâtons d'environ une aune de long, qu'ils enfoncent dans la vase, et ils y trouvent quantité de grands et petits poissons." In the library of the British Museum there is an unique MS. of MANOEL DE ALMEIDA, written in the sixteenth century, from which Balthasar Tellec compiled his *Historia General de Ethiopia alta,* printed at Coimbra in 1660, and in it the above statement of Mendes is corroborated by Almeida, who says that he was told by João Gabriel, a Creole Portuguese, born in Abyssinia, who had visited the Mareb, and who said that the "fish were to be found everywhere eight or ten palms down, and that he had eaten of them."

[1] See Paper "*on some Species of Fishes and Reptiles in Demerara,*" by J. HANDCOCK, Esq., M.D., *Zoological Journal,* vol. iv. p. 243.

[2] A curious account of the *borachung* or "ground fish" of Bhootan, will be found in Note (C.) appended to this chapter.

fish. Mr. Whiting, the chief civil officer of the eastern province, informs me that, on two occasions, he was present accidentally when the villagers were so engaged, once at the tank of Malliativoe, within a few miles of Kottiar, near the bay of Trincomalie, and again at a tank between Ellendetorre and Arnitivoe, on the bank of the Vergel river. The clay was firm, but moist, and as the men flung out lumps of it with a spade, it fell to pieces, disclosing fish from nine to twelve inches long, which were full grown and healthy, and jumped on the bank when exposed to the sun light.

Being desirous of obtaining a specimen of fish so exhumed, I received from the Moodliar of Matura, A.B. Wickremeratne, a fish taken along with others of the same kind from a tank in which the water had dried up ; it was found at a depth of a foot and a half where the mud was still moist, whilst the surface was dry and hard. The fish which the moodliar sent to me is an Anabas, closely resembling the *Perca scandens* of Daldorf; but on minute examination it proves to be a

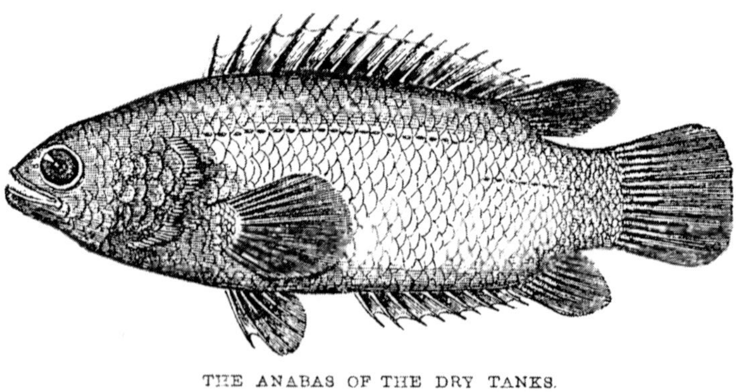

THE ANABAS OF THE DRY TANKS.

species unknown in India, and hitherto found only in Borneo and China. It is the *A. oligolepis* of Bleek.

But the faculty of becoming torpid at such periods is not confined in Ceylon to the crocodile sand fishes;—it is also possessed by some of the fresh-water mollusca and aquatic coleoptera. One of the former, the *Ampullaria glauca*, is found in still water in all parts of the island, not alone in the tanks, but in rice-fields and the watercourses by which they are irrigated. When, during the dry season, the water is about to evaporate, it burrows and conceals itself[1] till the returning rains restore it to activity, and reproduce its accustomed food. There, at a considerable depth in the soft mud, it deposits a bundle of eggs with a white calcareous shell, to the number of one hundred or more in each group. The *Melania Paludina* in the same way retires during the droughts into the muddy soil of the rice lands; and it can only be by such an instinct that this and other mollusca are preserved when the tanks evaporate, to re-appear in full growth and vigour immediately on the return of the rains.[2]

[1] A knowledge of this fact was turned to prompt account by Mr. Edgar S. Layard, when holding a judicial office at Point Pedro in 1849. A native who had been defrauded of his land complained before him of his neighbour, who, during his absence, had removed their common landmark, diverting the original watercourse and obliterating its traces by filling it up to a level with the rest of the field. Mr. Layard directed a trench to be sunk at the contested spot, and discovering numbers of the Ampullaria, the remains of the eggs, and the living animal which had been buried for months, the evidence was so resistless as to confound the wrong-doer, and terminate the suit.

[2] For a similar fact relative to the shells and water beetles in the pools near Rio Janeiro, see DARWIN'S *Nat. Journal*, ch. v. p. 99. BENSON, in the first vol. of *Gleanings of Science*, published at Calcutta in 1829, describes a species of *Paludina* found in pools, which are periodically dried up in the hot season but reappear with the rains, p. 363. And in the *Journal of the Asiatic Society of Bengal* for Sept. 1832, Lieut HUTTON, in a singularly interesting paper, has followed up the same subject by a narrative of his own observations at Mirzapore, where in June, 1832, after a few heavy showers of rain, that formed pools on the surface of the ground near a mango grove, he saw the *Paludinæ* issuing from

Dr. John Hunter[1] has advanced an opinion that hybernation, although a result of cold, is not its immediate consequence, but is attributable to that deprivation of food and other essentials which extreme cold occasions, and against the recurrence of which nature makes a timely provision by a suspension of her functions. Excessive heat in the tropics produces an effect upon animals and vegetables analogous to that of excessive cold in northern regions, and hence it is reasonable to suppose that the torpor induced by the one may be but the counterpart of the hybernation which results from the other. The frost that imprisons the alligator in the Mississippi as effectually cuts it off from food and action as the drought which incarcerates the crocodile in the sun-burnt clay of a Ceylon tank. The hedgehog of Europe enters on a period of absolute torpidity as soon as the inclemency of winter deprives it of its ordinary supply of slugs and insects; and the *tenrec*[2] of Madagascar, its tropical representative, exhibits the same tendency during the period when excessive heat produces in that climate a like result.

the ground, "pushing aside the moistened earth and coming forth from their retreats; but on the disappearance of the water not one of them was to be seen above ground. Wishing to ascertain what had become of them he turned up the earth at the base of several trees, and invariably found the shells buried from an inch to two inches below the surface." Lieut. Hutton adds that the *Ampullariæ* and *Planorbes*, as well as the *Paludinæ* are found in similar situations during the heats of the dry season. The British *Pisidea* exhibit the same faculty (see a monograph in the *Camb. Phil. Trans.* vol. iv.). The fact is elsewhere alluded to in the present work of the power possessed by the land leech of Ceylon of retaining vitality even after being parched to hardness during the heat of the rainless season. LYELL mentions the instance of some snails in Italy which, when they hybernate, descend to the depth of five feet and more below the surface. *Princip. of Geology, &c.* p. 373.

[1] HUNTER'S *Observations on parts of the Animal Œconomy*, p. 88.

[2] *Centetes ecaudatus*, Illiger.

The descent of the *Ampullaria*, and other fresh-water molluscs, into the mud of the tanks, has its parallel in the conduct of the *Bulimi* and *Helices* on land. The European snail, in the beginning of winter, either buries itself in the earth or withdraws to some crevice or overarching stone to await the returning vegetation of spring. So, in the season of intense heat, the *Helix Waltoni* of Ceylon, and others of the same family, before retiring under cover, close the aperture of their shells with an impervious epiphragm, which effectually protects their moisture and juices from evaporation during the period of their æstivation. The Bulimi of Chili have been found alive in England in a box packed in cotton after an interval of two years, and the animal inhabiting a land-shell from Suez, which was attached to a tablet and deposited in the British Museum in 1846, was found in 1850 to have formed a fresh epiphragm, and on being immersed in tepid water, it emerged from its shell. It became torpid again on the 15th November, 1851, and was found dead and dried up in March, 1852.[1] But exceptions serve to prove the accuracy of Hunter's opinion almost as strikingly as accordances, since the same genera of animals that hybernate in Europe, where extreme cold disarranges their œconomy, evince no symptoms of lethargy in the tropics, provided their food be not diminished by the heat. Ants, which are torpid in Europe during winter, work all the year round in India, where sustenance is uniform.[2] The shrews of Ceylon (*Sorex montanus* and *S. ferrugineus* of Kelaart), like

[1] *Annals of Natural History*, 1850. See DR. BAIRD'S *Account of Helix desertorum; Excelsior, &c.*, ch. i. p. 345.

[2] Colonel SKYES has described in the *Entomological Trans.* the operations of an ant in India which lays up a store of hay against the rainy season.

those at home, subsist upon insects, but as they inhabit a region where the equable temperature admits of the pursuit of their prey at all seasons of the year, unlike those of Europe, they never hybernate. A similar observation applies to bats, which are dormant during a northern winter when insects are rare, but never become torpid in any part of the tropics. The bear, in like manner, is nowhere deprived of its activity except when the rigour of severe frost cuts off its access to its accustomed food. On the other hand, the tortoise, which in Venezuela immerses itself in indurated mud during the hot months shows no tendency to torpor in Ceylon, where its food is permanent; and yet it is subject to hybernation when carried to the colder regions of Europe.

To the fish in the detached tanks and pools when the heat, by exhausting the water, deprives them at once of motion and sustenance, the practical effect must be the same as when the frost of a northern winter encases them in ice. Nor is it difficult to believe that they can successfully undergo the one crisis when we know beyond question that they may survive the other.[1]

*Hot-water Fishes.* — Another incident is striking in connection with the fresh-water fishes of Ceylon. I have described elsewhere the hot springs of Kannea[2], in the

[1] YARRELL, vol. i. p. 364, quotes the authority of Dr. J. Hunter in his *Animal Œconomy*, that fish, "after being frozen still retain so much of life as when thawed to resume their vital actions;" and in the same volume (*Introd.* vol. i. p. xvii.) he relates from JESSE's *Gleanings in Natural History*, the story of a gold fish (*Cyprinus auratus*), which, together with the water in a marble basin, was frozen into one solid lump of ice, yet, on the water being thawed, the fish became as lively as usual. Dr. RICHARDSON, in the third vol. of his *Fauna Borealis Americana*, says the grey sucking carp, found in the fur countries of North America, may be frozen and thawed again without being killed in the process.

[2] See SIR J. EMERSON TENNENT's *Ceylon*, &c., vol. ii. p. 496.

vicinity of Trincomalie, the water in which flows at a temperature varying at different seasons from 85° to 115°. In the stream formed by these wells M. Reynaud found and forwarded to Cuvier two fishes which he took from the water at a time when his thermometer indicated a temperature of 37° Reaumur, equal to 115° of Fahrenheit. The one was an Apogon, the other an Ambassis, and to each, from the heat of its habitat, he assigned the specific name of "thermalis."[1]

---

## *List of Ceylon Fishes.*

In the following list, the Acanthopterygian fishes of Ceylon has been prepared for me by Dr. GÜNTHER, and will be found the most complete which has appeared of this order. I am also indebted to him for the correction of the list of Malacopterygians, which I hope ere long to render still more extended, as well as that of the Cartilaginous fishes.

[1] CUV. and VAL., vol. iii. p. 363. In addition to the two fishes above named, a loche *Cobitis thermalis*, and a carp, *Nuria thermoicos*, were found in the hot-springs of Kannea, at a heat 40° Cent., 114° Fahr., and a roach, *Leuciscus thermalis*, when the thermometer indicated 50° Cent., 122° Fahr.—*Ib.* xviii. p. 59, xvi. p. 182, xvii. p. 94. Fish have been taken from a hot spring at Pooree when the thermometer stood at 112° Fahr., and as they belonged to a carnivorous genus, they must have found prey living in the same high temperature.—*Journ. Asiatic Soc. of Beng.* vol. vi. p. 465. Fishes have been observed in a hot spring at Manila which raises the thermometer to 187°, and in another in Barbary, the usual temperature of which is 172°; and Humboldt and Bonpland, when travelling in South America, saw fishes thrown up alive from a volcano, in water that raised the temperature to 210°, being two degrees below the boiling point. PATTERSON'S *Zoology*, Pt. ii. p. 211; YARRELL'S *History of British Fishes*, vol. i. In. p. xvi.

## I. OSSEOUS.

### ACANTHOPTERYGII.

BERYCIDÆ, *Lowe.*
Myripristis murdjan, *Forsk.*
Holocentrum rubrum, *Forsk.*
spiniferum, *Forsk.*
diadema, *Lacép.*

PERCIDÆ, *Günther.*
* Lates calcarifer, *Bl.*
Serranus louti, *Forsk.*
pachycentrum, *C. & V.*
guttatus, *Bl.*
Sonneratii, *C. & V.*
angularis, *C. & V.*
marginalis, *Bl.*
hexagonatus, *Forsk.*
flavocœruleus, *Lacép.*
biguttatus, *C. & V.*
lemniscatus, *C. & V.*
Amboinensis, *Bleek.*
bœnak, *C. & V.*
Grammistes orientalis, *Bl.*
Genyoroge Sebæ, *C. & V.*
Bengalensis, *C. & V.*
marginata, *C. & V.*
rivulata, *C. & V.*
gibba, *Forsk.*
spilura, *Benn.*
Mesoprion aurolineatus, *C. & V.*
rangus, *C. & V.*
quinquelineatus, *Rüpp.*
Johnii, *Bl.*
annularis, *C. & V.*
? Priacanthus Blochii, *Bleek.*
Ambassis n. sp., *Günth.*
Commersonii, *C. & V.*
thermalis, *C. & V.*
Apogon Ceylonicus, *C. & V.*
thermalis, *C. & V.*
annularis, *Rüpp.* var. roseipinnis.
Chilodipterus quinquelineatus, *C. & V.*

PRISTIPOMATIDÆ, *Günther.*
Dules Bennettii, *Bleek.*
* Therapon servus, *Bloch.*
* trivittatus, *Buch. Ham.*
quadrilineatus, *Bl.*
* Helotes polytænia, *Bleek.*
Pristipoma hasta, *Bloch.*
maculatum, *Bl.*
Diagramma punctatum, *Ehrenb.*
orientale, *Bl.*
pœcilopterum, *C. & V.*
Blochii, *C. & V.*
lineatum, *Gm.*
Radja, *Bleek.*
Lobotes auctorum, *Günth.*
Gerres oblongus, *C & V.*
Scolopsis Japonicus, *Bl.*
bimaculatus, *Rüpp.*
monogramma, *k. & v. H.*
Synagris furcosus, *C. & V.*
Pentapus aurolineatus, *Lacép.*
Smaris balteatus, *C. & V.*
Cæsio cœrulaureus, *Lacép.*

MULLIDÆ, *Gray.*
Upeneus tæniopterus, *C. & V.*
Indicus, *Shaw.*
cyclostoma *Lacép.*
Upe. trifasciatus, *Lacép.*
cinnabarinus, *C. & V.*
Upeneoides vittatus, *Forsk.*
tragula.
sulphureus, *C. & V.*
Mulloides flavolineatus, *Lacép.*
Ceylonicus, *C. & V.*

SPARIDÆ, *Günther.*
Lethrinus frenatus, *C. & V.*
cinereus, *C. & V.*
fasciatus, *C. & V.*
? ramak, *Forsk.*
opercularis, *C. & V.*
erythrurus, *C. & V.*
Pagrus spinifer, *Forsk.*
Crysophrys hasta, *Bl.*
? Pimelepterus Ternatensis, *Bleek.*

SQUAMIPINNES, *Günther.*
Chætodon Layardi, *Blyth.*
oligacanthus, *Bleek.*
setifer, *Bl.*
vagabundus, *L.*
guttatissimus, *Benn.*
pictus, *Forsk.*
xanthocephalus, *Benn.*
Sebæ, *C. & V.*
Heniochus macrolepidotus, *Artedi.*
Holacanthus annularis, *Bl.*
xanthurus, *Benn.*
imperator, *Bl.*
Scatophagus argus, *Gm.*
Ephippus orbis, *Bl.*
Drepane punctata, *Gm.*

CIRRHITIDÆ, *Gray.*
Cirrhites Forsteri, *Schn.*

CATAPHRACTI, *Cuv.*
Scorpæna polyprion, *Bleek.*
Pterois volitans, *L.*
miles, *Benn.*
Tetraroge longispinis, *C. & V.*
Platycephalus insidiator, *Forsk.*
punctatus, *C. & V.*
serratus, *C. & V.*
tuberculatus, *C. & V.*
suppositus, *Trosch.*
Dactylopterus orientalis, *C. & V.*

TRACHINIDÆ, *Günther.*
? Uranoscopus guttatus, *C. & V.*
Percis millepunctata, *Günth.*
Sillago sihama, *Forsk.*

SCIÆNIDÆ, *Günther.*
Sciæna diacantha, *Lacép.*
maculata, *Schn.*
Dussumieri, *C & V.*
Corvina miles, *C. & V.*
Otolithus argenteus, *k. & v. H.*

POLYNEMIDÆ, *Günther.*
Polynemus heptadactylus, *C. & V.*
hexanemus, *C. & V.*
Indicus, *Shaw.*
plebeius, *Gm.*
tetradactylus, *Shaw.*

SPHYRÆNIDÆ, *Agass.*
Sphyræna jello, *C. & V.*
obtusata, *C. & V.*

TRICHIURIDÆ, *Günther.*
Trichiurus savala, *Cuv.*

SCOMBRIDÆ, *Günther*.
?. Thynnus affinis, *Cant*.
Cybium Commersonii, *Lacép*.
guttatum, *Schn*.
Naucrates ductor, *L*.
Elacate nigra, *Bl*.
? n. sp.
Echeneis remora, *L*.
scutata, *Günth*.
naucrates, *L*.
Stromateus cinereus, *Bl*.
niger, *Bl*.
Coryphæna hippurus, *L*.
Mene maculata, *Schn*.

CARANGIDÆ, *Günther*.
Caranx Heberi, *Benn*.
Rottleri, *Bl*.
calla, *C. & V*.
xanthurus, *K. & v. H*.
talamparoides, *Bleek*.
Malabaricus, *Schn*.
speciosus, *Forsk*.
carangus, *Bl*.
hippos, *L*.
armatus, *Forsk*.
ciliaris, *Bl*.
gallus, *L*.
Micropteryx chrysurus, *L*.
Seriola nigro-fasciata, *Rüpp*.
Chorinemus lysan, *Forsk*.
Sancti Petri, *C. & V*.
Trachynotus oblongus, *C. & V*.
ovatus, *L*.
Psettus argenteus, *L*.
Platax vespertilio, *Bl*.
Raynaldi, *C. & V*.
Zanclus sp. n.
Lactarius delicatulus, *C. & V*.
Equula fasciata, *Lacép*.
edentula, *Bl*.
daura, *Cuv*.
interrupta.
Gazza minuta, *Bl*.
equulæformis, *Rüpp*.
Pempheris sp.

XIPHIIDÆ, *Agass*.
Histiophorus immaculatus, *Rüpp*.

THEUTYIDÆ, *Günther*.
Theutys Javus, *L*.
stellata, *Forsk*.
nebulosa, *A. & G*.

ACRONURIDÆ, *Günther*.
Acanthurus triostegus, *L*.
nigrofuscus, *Forsk*.
lineatus, *L*.
Tennentii, *Gthr*.
leucosternon, *Bennett*.
ctenodon, *C. & V*.
rhombeus, *Kittl*.
xanthurus, *Blyth*.
Acronurus melas, *C. & V*.
melanurus, *C. & V*.
Naseus unicornis, *Forsk*.
brevirostris, *C. & V*.
tuberosus, *Lacép*.
lituratus, *Forster*.

AULOSTOMATA, *Cuvier*.
Fistularia serrata, *Bl*.

BLENNIIDÆ, *Müll*.
Salarias fasciatus, *Bl*.
Sal. marmoratus, *Benn*.
tridactylus, *Schn*.
quadricornis, *C. & V*.

GOBIIDÆ, *Müll*.
Gobius ornatus, *Rüpp*.
giuris, *Buch. Ham*.
albopunctatus, *C. & V*.
grammepomus, *Bleek*.
Apocryptes lanceolatus, *Bl*.
Periophthalmus Koelreuteri, *Pall*.
Eleotris ophiocephalus, *K. & v. H*.
fusca, *Bl*.
sexguttata, *C. & V*.
muralis, *A. & G*.

MASTACEMBELIDÆ, *Günther*.
Mastacembelus armatus, *Lacép*.

PEDICULATI, *Cuv*.
Antennarius marmoratus, *Günth*.
hispidus, *Schn*.
pinniceps, *Commers*.
Commersonii, *Lacép*.
multiocellatus. *Günth*.
bigibbus, *Lacép*.

ATHERINIDÆ, *Günther*.
Atherina Forskalii, *Rüpp*.
duodecimalis, *C. & V*.

MUGILIDÆ, *Günther*.
Mugil planiceps, *C. & V*.
Waigiensis, *A. G*.
Ceylonensis, *Günth*.

OPHIOCEPHALIDÆ, *Günther*.
Ophiocephalus punctatus, *Bl*.
Kelaartii, *Günth*.
striatus, *Bl*.
marulius, *Ham. Buch*.
Channa orientalis, *Schn*.

LABYRINTHICI, *Cuv*.
Anabas oligolepis, *Bleek*.
Polyacanthus signatus, *Günth*.

PHARYNGOGNATHI.

Amphiprion Clarkii, *J. Benn*.
Dascyllus aruanus, *C. & V*.
trimaculatus, *Rüpp*.
Glyphisodon septem-fasciatus, *C. & V*.
Brownrigii, *Benn*.
cœlestinus, *Sol*.
Etroplus Suratensis, *Bl*.
Julis lunaris *Linn*.
decussatus, *W Benn*.
formosus, *C. & V*.
quadricolor, *Lesson*.
dorsalis, *Quoy & Gaim*.
aureomaculatus, *W. Benn*.
Ceilanicus, *E. Benn*.
Finlaysoni, *C. & V*.
purpureo-lineatus, *C. & V*.
cingulum, *C. & V*.
Gomphosus fuscus, *C. & V*.
cœruleus, *Comm*.
viridis, *W. Benn*.
Scarus pepo, *W. Benn*.
harid, *Forsk*.
Tautoga fasciata, *Thunb*.
Hemirhamphus Reynaldi, *C. & V*.
Georgii *C. & V*.
Exocœtus evolans, *Linn*.
Belone annulata, *C. & V*.

MALACOPTERYGII (ABDOMINALES).

Bagrus gulio, *Buch.*
albilabris, *C. & V.*
Plotosus lineatus, *C. & V.*
Barbus tor, *C. & V.*
Nuria thermoicos, *C. & V.*
Leuciscus dandia, *C. & V.*
scalpellus, *C. & V.*
Ceylonicus, *E. Benn.*
thermalis, *C. & V.*
Cobitis thermalis, *C. & V.*
Chirocentrus dorab, *Forsk.*
Elops saurus, *L.*
Megalops cundinga, *Buch.*
Engraulis Brownii, *Gm.*
Sardinella leiogaster, *C. & V.*
lineolata, *C. & V.*
Neohowii.
Saurus myops, *Val.*
Saurida tombil, *Bl.*

MALACOPTERYGII (SUB-BRANCHIATI).

Pleuronectes, *L.*

MALACOPTERYGII (APODA).

Muræna.

LOPHOBRANCHI.

Syngnathus, *L.*

PLECTOGNATHII.

Tetraodon ocellatus, *W. Benn.*
tepa, *Buch.*
argyropleura, *E. Bennett.*
argentatus, *Blyth.*
Balistes biaculeatus, *W. Benn.*
lineatus, *Bl.*
Triacanthus biaculeatus, *W. Benn.*
Alutarius lævis, *Bl.*

## II. CARTILAGINOUS.

Pristis antiquorum, *Lath.*
cuspidatus, *Lath.*
pectinatus, *Lath.*
Chiloscyllium plagiosum, *Benn.*
Stegostoma fasciatum, *Bl.*
Carcharias acutus, *Rüpp.*
Sphyrna zygæna, *L.*
Rhynchobatus lævis, *Bl.*
Trygon uarnak, *Forsk.*
Pteroplatea micrura, *Bl.*
Tæniura lymna, *Forsk.*
Myliobatis Nieuhofii, *Bl.*
Aëtobates narinari, *Bl.*

---

## NOTE (A.)

### INSTANCES OF FISHES FALLING FROM THE CLOUDS IN INDIA.

(*From the Bombay Times*, 1856.)

See Page 343.

The late Dr. Buist, after enumerating cases in which fishes were said to have been thrown out from volcanoes in South America and precipitated from clouds in various parts of the world, adduced the following instances of similar occurrences in India. "In 1824," he says, "fishes fell at Meerut, on the men of Her Majesty's 14th Regiment, then out at drill, and were caught in numbers. In July, 1826, live fish were seen to fall on the grass at Moradabad during a storm. They were the common cyprinus, so prevalent in our Indian waters. On the 19th of February, 1830, at noon, a heavy fall of fish occurred at the Nokulhatty factory, in the Daccah zillah;

depositions on the subject were obtained from nine different parties. The fish were all dead; most of them were large; some were fresh, others were rotten and mutilated. They were seen at first in the sky, like a flock of birds, descending rapidly to the ground; there was rain drizzling, but no storm. On the 16th and 17th of May, 1833, a fall of fish occurred in the zillah of Futtehpoor, about three miles north of the Jumna, after a violent storm of wind and rain. The fish were from a pound and a half to three pounds in weight, and of the same species as those found in the tanks in the neighbourhood. They were all dead and dry. A fall of fish occurred at Allahabad, during a storm in May, 1835; they were of the chowla species, and were found dead and dry after the storm had passed over the district. On the 20th of September, 1839, after a smart shower of rain, a quantity of live fish, about three inches in length and all of the same kind, fell at the Sunderbunds, about twenty miles south of Calcutta. On this occasion it was remarked that the fish did not fall here and there irregularly over the ground, but in a continuous straight line, not more than a span in breadth. The vast multitudes of fish, with which the low grounds round Bombay are covered, about a week or ten days after the first burst of the monsoon, appear to be derived from the adjoining pools or rivulets, and not to descend from the sky. They are not, so far as I know, found in the higher parts of the island. I have never seen them, (though I have watched carefully,) in casks collecting water from the roofs of buildings, or heard of them on the decks or awnings of vessels in the harbour, where they must have appeared had they descended from the sky. One of the most remarkable phenomena of this kind occurred during a tremendous deluge of rain at Kattywar, on the 25th of July, 1850, when the ground around Rajkote was found literally covered with fish; some of them were found on the tops of haystacks, where probably they had been drifted by the storm. In the course of twenty-four successive hours twenty-seven inches of rain fell, thirty-five fell in twenty-six hours, seven inches within one hour and a half, being the heaviest fall on record. At Poonah, on the 3rd of August, 1852, after a very heavy fall of rain, multitudes of fish were caught on the ground in the cantonments, full half a mile from the nearest stream. If showers of fish are to be explained on the assumption that they are carried up by squalls or violent winds, from rivers or spaces of water not far away from where they fall, it would be nothing wonderful were they seen to descend from the air during the furious squalls which occasionally occur in June."

---

## NOTE (B.)

### CEYLON FISHES.

(*Memorandum by Professor Huxley.*)

See Page 324.

The large series of beautifully coloured drawings of the fishes of Ceylon, which has been submitted to my inspection, possesses an unusual value for several reasons.

The fishes, it appears, were all captured at Colombo, and even had those from other parts of Ceylon been added, the geographical area would not have been very extended. Nevertheless there are more than 600 drawings, and though it is possible that some of these represent varieties in different stages of growth of the same species, I have not been able to find definite evidence of the fact in any of those groups which I have particularly tested. If, however, these drawings represent *six hundred* distinct species of fish, they constitute, so far as I know, the largest collection of fish from one locality in existence.

The number of known British fishes may be safely assumed to be less than 250, and Mr. Yarrell enumerates only 226, Dr. Cantor's valuable work on Malayan fishes enumerates not more than 238, while Dr. Russell has figured only 200 from

Coromandel. Even the enormous area of the Chinese and Japanese seas has as yet not yielded 800 species of fishes.

The large extent of the collection alone, then, renders it of great importance: but its value is immeasurably enhanced by the two circumstances,—*first*, that every drawing was made while the fish retained all that vividness of colouring which becomes lost so soon after its removal from its native element; and *secondly*, that when the sketch was finished its subject was carefully labelled, preserved in spirits, and forwarded to England, so that at the present moment the original of every drawing can be subjected to anatomical examination, and compared with already named species.

Under these circumstances, I do not hesitate to say that the collection is one of the most valuable in existence, and might, if properly worked out, become a large and secure foundation for all future investigation into the ichthyology of the Indian Ocean.

It would be very hazardous to express an opinion as to the novelty or otherwise of the species and genera figured without the study of the specimens themselves, as the specific distinctions of fish are for the most part based upon character—the fin-rays, teeth, the operculum, &c., which can only be made out by close and careful examination of the object, and cannot be represented in ordinary drawings however accurate.

There are certain groups of fish, however, whose family traits are so marked as to render it almost impossible to mistake even their portraits, and hence I may venture, without fear of being far wrong, upon a few remarks as to the general features of the ichthyological fauna of Ceylon.

In our own seas rather less than a tenth of the species of fishes belong to the cod tribe. I have not found one represented in these drawings, nor do either Russell or Cantor mention any in the surrounding seas, and the result is in general harmony with the known laws of distribution of these most useful of fishes.

On the other hand, the mackerel family, including the tunnies, the bonitas, the dories, the horse-mackerels, &c., which form not more than one sixteenth of our own fish fauna, but which are known to increase their proportion in hot climates, appear in wonderful variety of form and colour, and constitute not less than one fifth of the whole of the species of Ceylon fish. In Russell's catalogue they form less than one fifth, in Cantor's less than one sixth.

Marine and other siluroid fishes, a group represented on the continent of Europe, but doubtfully, if at all, in this country, constitute one twentieth of the Ceylon fishes. In Russell's and Cantor's lists they form about one thirtieth of the whole.

The sharks and rays form about one seventh of our own fish fauna. They constitute about one tenth or one eleventh of Russell's and Cantor's lists, while among these Ceylon drawings I find not more than twenty, or about one thirtieth of the whole, which can be referred to this group of fishes. It must be extremely interesting to know whether this circumstance is owing to accident, or to the local peculiarities of Colombo, or whether the fauna of Ceylon really is deficient in such fishes.

The like exceptional character is to be noticed in the proportion of the tribe of flat fishes, or *Pleuronectidæ*. Soles, turbots, and the like, form nearly one twelfth of our own fishes. Both Cantor and Russell give the flat fishes as making one twenty-second part of their collection, while in the whole 600 Ceylon drawings I can find but five *Pleuronectidæ*.

When this great collection has been carefully studied, I doubt not that many more interesting distributional facts will be evolved.

---

Since receiving this note from Professor Huxley, the drawings in question have been submitted to Dr. Gray, of the British Museum. That eminent naturalist, after a careful analysis, has favoured me with the following memorandum of the fishes they represent, numerically contrasting them with those of China and Japan, so far as we are acquainted with the ichthyology of those seas:—

| | Ceylon. | China and Japan. |
|---|---|---|
| **CARTILAGINEA.** | | |
| Squali | 12 | 15 |
| Raiæ | 19 | 20 |
| Sturiones | 0 | 1 |
| **OSTINOPTERYGII.** | | |
| Plectognathi. | | |
| tetraodontidæ | 10 | 21 |
| balistidæ | 9 | 19 |
| Lophobranchii. | | |
| syngnathidæ | 2 | 2 |
| pegasidæ | 0 | 3 |
| Ctenobranchii. | | |
| lophidæ | 1 | 3 |
| Cyclopodi. | | |
| echeneidæ | 0 | 1 |
| cyclopteridæ | 0 | 1 |
| gobidæ | 7 | 35 |
| Percini. | | |
| callionymidæ | 0 | 7 |
| uranoscopidæ | 0 | 7 |
| cottidæ | 0 | 13 |
| triglidæ | 11 | 37 |
| polynemidæ | 12 | 3 |
| mullidæ | 1 | 7 |
| percidæ | 26 | 12 |
| berycidæ | 0 | 5 |
| sillaginidæ | 3 | 1 |
| sciænidæ | 19 | 13 |
| hæmulinidæ | 6 | 12 |
| serranidæ | 31 | 38 |
| theraponidæ | 8 | 20 |
| Pe. cirrhitidæ | 0 | 2 |
| mænidiæ | 37 | 25 |
| sparidæ | 16 | 17 |
| acanthuridæ | 14 | 6 |
| chætodontidæ | 25 | 21 |
| fistularidæ | 2 | 3 |
| Periodopharyngi. | | |
| mugilidæ | 5 | 7 |
| anabantidæ | 6 | 15 |
| pomacentridæ | 10 | 11 |
| Pharyngognathi. | | |
| labridæ | 16 | 35 |
| scomberesocidæ | 13 | 6 |
| blenniidæ | 3 | 8 |
| Scomberina. | | |
| zeidæ | 0 | 2 |
| sphyrænidæ | 5 | 4 |
| scomberidæ | 118 | 62 |
| xiphiidæ | 0 | 1 |
| cepolidæ | 0 | 5 |
| Heterosomata. | | |
| platessoideæ | 5 | 22 |
| siluridæ | 31 | 24 |
| cyprinidæ | 19 | 52 |
| scopelinidæ | 2 | 7 |
| salmonidæ | 0 | 1 |
| clupeidæ | 43 | 22 |
| gadidæ | 0 | 12 |
| macruridæ | 1 | 0 |
| Apodes. | | |
| anguillidæ | 8 | 12 |
| murænidæ | 8 | 6 |
| sphagebranchidæ | 8 | 10 |

---

## NOTE (C).

### ON THE BORA-CHUNG, OR "GROUND-FISH" OF BHOOTAN.

See P. 353.

In Bhootan, at the south-eastern extremity of the Himalayas, a fish is found, the scientific name of which is unknown to me, but it is called by the natives the *Bora-chung*, and by European residents the "ground-fish of Bhootan." It is described in the *Journal of the Asiatic Society of Bengal for* 1839, by a writer (who had seen it alive), as being about two feet in length, and cylindrical, with a thick body, somewhat shaped like a pike, but rounder, the nose curved upwards, the colour olive-green, with orange stripes, and the head speckled with crimson.[1] This fish, according to the native story, is caught not in the rivers in whose vicinity it is found, but "in perfectly dry places in the middle of grassy jungle, sometimes as far as two miles from the banks." Here, on finding a hole four or five inches in diameter, they commence to dig, and continue till they come to water; and presently the *bora-chung* rises to the surface, sometimes from a depth of nineteen feet. In these extemporised wells these fishes are found always in pairs, and when brought to the surface they glide rapidly over the ground with a serpentine motion. This account appeared in 1839; but some years later, Mr. Campbell, the Superintendent of Darjeeling, in a communication to the same journal[2], divested the story of much of its exaggeration, by stating, as the result of personal inquiry in Bhootan, that the *bora-chung* inhabits the jheels and slow-running streams near the hills, but lives principally on the banks, into which it penetrates from one to five or six feet. The entrance to these retreats leading from the river into the bank is generally a few inches below the surface, so that the fish can return to the water at pleasure. The mode of catching them is by introducing the hand into these holes; and the *bora-chungs* are found generally two in each chamber, coiled concentrically like snakes. It is not believed that they bore their own burrows, but that they take possession of those made by land-crabs. Mr. Campbell denies that they are more capable than other fish of moving on dry ground. From the particulars given, the *bora-chung* would appear to be an *Ophiocephalus*, probably the *O. barka* described by Buchanan, as inhabiting holes in the banks of rivers tributary to the Ganges.

[1] Paper by Mr. J. T. PEARSON, *Journ. Asiat. Soc. Beng.*, vol. viii. p. 551.

[2] *Journ. Asiat. Soc. Beng.*, vol. xi. p. 963.

# CHAP. XI.

## SHELLS.

*Mollusca.—Radiata, &c.*

CEYLON has long been renowned for the beauty and variety of the shells which abound in its seas and inland waters, and in which an active trade has been organised by the industrious Moors, who clean them with great expertness, arrange them in satin-wood boxes, and send them to Colombo and all parts of the island for sale. In general, however, these specimens are more prized for their beauty than valued for their rarity, though some of the "Argus" cowries [1] have been sold as high as *four guineas* a pair.

One of the principal sources whence their supplies are derived is the beautiful Bay of Venloos, to the north of Batticaloa, formed by the embouchure of the Natoor river. The scenery at this spot is enchanting. The sea is overhung by gentle acclivities wooded to the summit; and in an opening between two of these eminences the river flows through a cluster of little islands covered with mangroves and acacias. A bar of rocks projects across it, at a short distance from the shore; and these are frequented all day long by pelicans, that come at

[1] *Cypræa Argus.*

sunrise to fish, and at evening return to their solitary breeding-places remote from the beach. The strand is literally covered with beautiful shells in rich profusion, and the dealers from Trincomalie know the proper season to visit the bay for each particular description. The entire coast, however, as far north as the Elephant Pass, is indented by little rocky inlets, where shells of endless variety may be collected in great abundance.[1] During the north-east monsoon a formidable surf bursts upon the shore, which is here piled high with mounds of yellow sand; and the remains of shells upon the water mark show how rich the sea is in mollusca. Amongst them are prodigious numbers of the ubiquitous violet-coloured *Ianthina*[2], which rises when the ocean is calm, and by means of its inflated vesicles floats lightly on the surface.

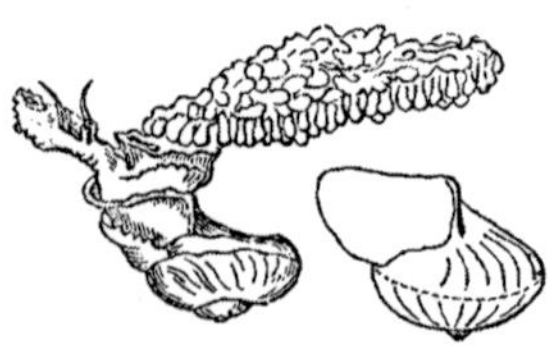

IANTHINA.

The trade in shells is one of extreme antiquity in Ceylon. The Gulf of Manaar has been fished from the earliest times for the large chank shell, *Turbinella*

[1] In one of these beautiful little bays near Catchavelly, between Trincomalie and Batticaloa, I found the sand within the wash of the sea literally covered with mollusca and shells, and amongst others a species of *Bullia* (B. vittata, I think), the inhabitant of which has the faculty of mooring itself firmly by sending down its membranous foot into the wet sand, where, imbibing the water, this organ expands horizontally into a broad fleshy disc, by which the animal anchors itself, and thus secured, collects its food in the ripple of the waves. On the slightest alarm, the water is discharged, the disc collapses into its original dimensions, and the shell and its inhabitant disappear together beneath the sand.

BULLIA VITTATA.

[2] *Ianthina communis*, Krauss, and *I. prolongata*, Blainv.

*rapa*, to be exported to India, where it is still sawn into rings and worn as anklets and bracelets by the women of Hindustan. Another use for these shells is their conversion into wind instruments, which are sounded in the temples on all occasions of ceremony. A chank, in which the whorls, instead of running from left to right, as in the ordinary shell, are reversed, and run from right to left, is regarded with such reverence that a specimen formerly sold for its weight in gold, but one may now be had for four or five pounds. COSMAS INDICO-PLEUSTES, writing in the fifth century, describes a place on the west coast of Ceylon, which he calls Marallo, and says it produced "κοχλίους," which THEVENOT translates "oysters;" in which case Marallo might be conjectured to be Bentotte, near Colombo, which yields the best edible "oysters" in Ceylon.[1] But the shell in question was most probably the chank, and Marallo was Mantotte, off which it is found in great numbers.[2] In fact, two centuries later Abouzeyd, an Arab, who wrote an account of the trade and productions of India, speaks of these shells by the name they still bear, which he states to be *schenek*[3]; but "schenek" is not an Arabic word, and is merely an attempt to spell the local term, *chank*, in Arabic characters.

[1] COSMAS INDICO-PLEUSTES, in Thevenot's ed. t. i. p. 21.

[2] At Kottiar, near Trincomalie, I was struck with the prodigious size of the edible oysters, which were brought to us at the rest-house. The shell of one of these measured a little more than eleven inches in length, by half as many broad: thus unexpectedly attesting the correctness of one of the stories related by the historians of Alexander's expedition, that in India they had found oysters a foot long. PLINY says: "In Indico mari Alexandri rerum auctores pedalia inveniri prodidere."—*Nat. Hist.* lib. xxxii. ch. 31. DARWIN says, that amongst the fossils of Patagonia, he found "a massive gigantic oyster, sometimes even a foot in diameter."—*Nat. Voy.*, ch. viii.

[3] ABOUZEYD, *Voyages Arabes, &c.*, t. i. p. 6; REINAUD, *Mémoire sur l'Inde, &c.* p. 222.

BERTOLACCI mentions a curious local peculiarity[1] observed by the fishermen in the natural history of the chank. "All shells," he says, "found to the northward of a line drawn from a point about midway from Manaar to the opposite coast (of India) are of the kind called *patty*, and are distinguished by a short flat head; and all those found to the southward of that line are of the kind called *pajel*, and are known from having a longer and more pointed head than the former. Nor is there ever an instance of deviation from this singular law of nature. The *Wallampory*, or 'right-hand chanks,' are found of both kinds."

This tendency of particular localities to re-produce certain specialities of form and colour is not confined to the sea or to the instance of the chank shell. In the gardens which line the suburbs of Galle in the direction of Matura the stems of the coco-nut and jak trees are profusely covered with the shells of the beautiful striped *Helix hæmastoma*. Stopping frequently to collect them, I was led to observe that each separate garden seemed to possess a variety almost peculiar to itself; in one the mouth of every individual shell was *red*; in another, separated from the first only by a wall, *black*; and in others (but less frequently) *pure white*; whilst the varieties of external colouring were equally local. In one enclosure they were nearly all red, and in an adjoining one brown.[2]

[1] See also the *Asiatic Journal for* 1827, p. 469.

[2] DARWIN, in his *Naturalist's Voyage*, mentions a parallel instance of the localised propagation of colours amongst the cattle which range the pasturage of East Falkland Island: "Round Mount Osborne about half of some of the herds were mouse-coloured, a tint not common anywhere else,—near Mount Pleasant dark-brown prevailed; whereas south of Choiseul Sound white beasts with black heads and feet were common."—Ch. ix. p. 192.

A trade more ancient by far than that carried on in chanks, and infinitely more renowned, is the fishery of pearls on the west coast of Ceylon, bordering the Gulf of Manaar. No scene in Ceylon presents so dreary an aspect as the long sweep of desolate shore to which, from time immemorial, adventurers have resorted from the uttermost ends of the earth in search of the precious pearls for which this gulf is renowned. On approaching it from sea the only perceptible landmark is a building erected by Lord Guildford, as a temporary residence for the Governor, and known by the name of the "Doric," from the style of its architecture. A few coco-nut palms appear next above the low sandy beach, and presently are discovered the scattered houses which form the villages of Aripo and Condatchy.

Between these two places, or rather between the Kalaar and Arrive river, the shore is raised to a height of many feet, by enormous mounds of shells, the accumulations of ages, the millions of oysters[1], robbed of their pearls, having been year after year flung into heaps, that extend for a distance of many miles.

During the progress of a pearl-fishery, this singular and dreary expanse becomes suddenly enlivened by the crowds who congregate from distant parts of India; a town is improvised by the construction of temporary dwellings, huts of timber and cajans[2], with tents of palm leaves or canvas; and bazaars spring up, to feed the multitude on land, as well as the seamen and divers in the fleets of boats that cover the bay.

[1] It is almost unnecessary to say that the shell fish which produces the true Oriental pearls is not an oyster, but belongs to the genus Avicula, or more correctly, Meleagrina. It is the *Meleagrina Margaritifera* of Lamarck.

[2] *Cajan* is the local term for the plaited fronds of a coco-nut.

I visited the pearl banks officially in 1848 in company with Capt. Steuart, the official inspector. My immediate object was to inquire into the causes of the suspension of the fisheries, and to ascertain the probability of reviving a source of revenue, the gross receipts from which had failed for several years to defray the cost of conservancy. In fact, between 1837 and 1854, the pearl banks were an annual charge, instead of producing an annual income, to the colony. The conjecture, hastily adopted, to account for the disappearance of mature shells, had reference to mechanical causes; the received hypothesis being that the young broods had been swept off their accustomed feeding grounds, by the establishment of unusual currents, occasioned by deepening the narrow passage between Ceylon and India at Paumbam. It was also suggested, that a previous Governor, in his eagerness to replenish the colonial treasury, had so "scraped" and impoverished the beds as to exterminate the oysters. To me, neither of these suppositions appeared worthy of acceptance; for, in the frequent disruptions of Adam's Bridge, there was ample evidence that the currents in the Gulf of Manaar had been changed at former times without destroying the pearl beds: and moreover the oysters had disappeared on many former occasions, without any imputation of improper management on the part of the conservators; and returned after much longer intervals of absence than that which fell under my own notice, and which was then creating serious apprehension in the colony.

A similar interruption had been experienced between 1820 and 1828: the Dutch had had no fishing for twenty-seven years, from 1768 till 1796[1]; and they had been equally unsuccessful from 1732 till 1746. The Arabs were well acquainted with similar vicissitudes, and Albyrouni (a contemporary of Avicenna), who served under Mahmoud of Ghuznee, and wrote in the eleventh century, says that the pearl fishery, which formerly existed in the Gulf of Serendib, had become exhausted in his time, simultaneously with the appearance of a fishery at Sofala, in the country of the Zends, where pearls were unknown before; and hence, he says, arose the conjecture that the pearl oyster of Serendib had migrated to Sofala.[2]

It appeared to me that the explanation of the phenomenon was to be sought, not merely in external causes, but also in the instincts and faculties of the animals themselves, and, on my return to Colombo, I ventured to renew a recommendation, which had been made years before, that a scientific inspector should be appointed to study the habits and the natural history of the pearl-oyster, and that his investigations should be facilitated by the means at the disposal of the Government.

Dr. Kelaart was appointed to this office, by Sir H. G. Ward, in 1857, and his researches speedily developed results of great interest. In opposition to the received opinion that the pearl-oyster is incapable of voluntary

[1] This suspension was in some degree attributable to disputes with the Nabob of Arcot and other chiefs, and the proprietors of temples on the opposite coast of India, who claimed a right to participate in the fisheries of the Gulf of Manaar.

[2] "Il y avait autrefois dans le Golfe de Serendyb, une pêcherie de perles qui s'est épuisée de notre temps. D'un autre côté il s'est formé une pêcherie à Sofala dans le pays des Zends, là où il n'en existait pas auparavant—on dit que c'est la pêcherie de Serendyb qui s'est transportée à Sofala."—ALBYROUNI, *in* REINAUD'S *Fragmens Arabes, &c.*, p. 125; see also REINAUD'S *Mémoire sur l'Inde*, p. 228.

movement, and unable of itself to quit the place to which it is originally attached[1], he demonstrated, not only that it possesses locomotive powers, but also that their exercise is indispensable to its œconomy when obliged to search for food, or compelled to escape from local impurities. He showed that, for this purpose, it can sever its byssus, and re-form it at pleasure, so as to migrate and moor itself in favourable situations.[2] The establishment of this important fact may tend to solve the mystery of the occasional disappearances of the oyster; and if coupled with the further discovery that it is susceptible of translation from place to place, and even from salt to brackish water, it seems reasonable to expect that beds may be formed with advantage in positions suitable for its growth and protection. Thus, like the edible oyster of our own shores, the pearl-oyster may be brought within the domain of pisciculture, and banks may be created in suitable places, just as the southern shores of France are now being colonised with oysters, under the direction of M. Coste.[3] The operation of sowing the sea with pearl, should the experiment succeed, would be as gorgeous in reality, as it is grand in conception; and the wealth of Ceylon, in her "treasures of the deep," might eclipse the renown of her gems when she merited the title of the "Island of Rubies."

On my arrival at Aripo, the pearl-divers, under the orders of their Adapanaar, put to sea, and commenced

[1] STEUART'S *Pearl Fisheries of Ceylon*, p. 27; CORDINER'S *Ceylon, &c.*, vol. ii. p. 45.

[2] See Dr. KELAART'S Report on the Pearl Oyster in the *Ceylon Calendar for* 1858.—*Appendix*, p. 14.

[3] *Rapport de* M. COSTE, Professeur d'Embryogénie, &c., Paris, 1858,

the examination of the banks.[1] The persons engaged in this calling are chiefly Tamils and Moors, who are trained for the service by diving for chanks. The pieces of apparatus employed to assist the diver in his operations are exceedingly simple in their character: they consist merely of a stone, about thirty pounds' weight, (to accelerate the rapidity of his descent,) which is suspended over the side of the boat, with a loop attached to it for receiving the foot; and of a net-work basket, which he takes down to the bottom and fills with the oysters as he collects them. MASSOUDI, one of the earliest Arabian geographers, describing, in the ninth century, the habits of the pearl-divers in the Persian Gulf, says that, before descending, each filled his ears with cotton steeped in oil, and compressed his nostrils by a piece of tortoise-shell.[2] This practice continues there to the present day[3]; but the diver of Ceylon rejects all such expedients; he inserts his foot in the "sinking stone" and inhales a full breath; presses his nostrils with his left hand; raises his body as high

[1] Detailed accounts of the pearl fishery of Ceylon and the conduct of the divers, will be found in PERCIVAL's *Ceylon*, ch. iii.; and in CORDINER's *Ceylon*, vol. ii. ch. xvi. There is also a valuable paper on the same subject by Mr. LE BECK, in the *Asiatic Researches*, vol. v. p. 993; but by far the most able and intelligent description is contained in the *Account of the Pearl Fisheries of Ceylon*, by JAMES STEUART, Esq., Inspector of the Pearl Banks, 4to. Colombo, 1843.

[2] MASSOUDI says that the Persian divers, as they could not breathe through their nostrils, *cleft the root of the ear* for that purpose: "*Ils se fendaient la racine de l'oreille pour respirer;* en effet, ils ne peuvent se servir pour cet objet des narines, vu qu'ils se les bouchent avec des morceaux d'écailles de tortue marine ou bien avec des morceaux de corne ayant la forme d'un fer de lance. En même temps ils se mettent dans l'oreille du coton trempé dans de l'huile."—*Moroudj-al-Dzeheb, &c.*, REINAUD. *Mémoire sur l'Inde*, p. 228.

[3] Colonel WILSON says they compress the nose with horn, and close the ears with beeswax. See *Memorandum on the Pearl Fisheries in Persian Gulf.—Journ. Geogr. Soc.* 1833, vol. iii. p. 283.

as possible above water, to give force to his descent; and, liberating the stone from its fastenings, he sinks rapidly below the surface. As soon as he has reached the bottom, the stone is drawn up, and the diver, throwing himself on his face, commences with alacrity to fill his basket with oysters. This, on a concerted signal, is hauled rapidly to the surface; the diver assisting his own ascent by springing on the rope as it rises.

Improbable tales have been told of the capacity which these men acquire of remaining for prolonged periods under water. The divers who attended on this occasion were amongst the most expert on the coast, yet not one of them was able to complete a full minute below. Captain Steuart, who filled for many years the office of Inspector of the Pearl Banks, assured me that he had never known a diver to continue at the bottom longer than eighty-seven seconds, nor to attain a greater depth than thirteen fathoms; and on ordinary occasions they seldom exceeded fifty-five seconds in nine fathom water.[1]

The only precaution to which the Ceylon diver devotedly resorts, is the mystic ceremony of the shark-charmer, whose exorcism is an indispensable preliminary to every fishery. His power is believed to be hereditary; nor is it supposed that the value of his incantations is at all dependent upon the religious faith professed by the operator, for the present head of the family happens to

[1] RIBEYRO says that a diver could remain below whilst two *credos* were being repeated: "Il s'y tient l'espace de deux *credo*." — Lib. i. ch. xxii. p. 169. PERCIVAL says the usual time for them to be under water was two minutes, but that some divers stayed *four* or *five*, and one *six* minutes. — *Ceylon*, p. 91; LE BECK says that in 1797 he saw a Caffre boy from Karical, remain down for the space of seven minutes. — *Asiat. Res.* vol. v. p. 402.

be a Roman Catholic. At the time of our visit this mysterious functionary was ill and unable to attend; but he sent an accredited substitute, who assured me that although he himself was ignorant of the grand and mystic secret, the mere fact of his presence, as a representative of the higher authority, would be recognised and respected by the sharks.

Strange to say, though the Gulf of Manaar abounds with these hideous creatures, not more than one well authenticated accident[1] is known to have occurred from this source during any pearl fishery since the British have had possession of Ceylon. In all probability the reason is that the sharks are alarmed by the unusual number of boats, the multitude of divers, the noise of the crews, the incessant plunging of the sinking stones, and the descent and ascent of the baskets filled with shells. The dark colour of the divers themselves may also be a protection; whiter skins might not experience an equal impunity. Massoudi relates that the divers of the Persian Gulf were so conscious of this advantage of colour, that they were accustomed to blacken their limbs, in order to baffle the sea monsters.[2]

The result of our examination of the pearl banks, on this occasion, was such as to discourage the hope of an early fishery. The oysters in point of number were abundant, but in size they were little more than "spat," the largest being barely a fourth of an inch in diameter. As at least seven years are required to furnish the growth at which pearls may be sought with advantage[3],

[1] CORDINER'S *Ceylon*, vol. ii. p. 52.

[2] "Ils s'enduisaient les pieds et les jambes d'une substance noirâtre, afin de faire peur aux monstres marins, que, sans cela, seraient tentés de les dévorer." —*Moroudj-al-Dzeheb*, REINAUD, *Mém. sur l'Inde*, p. 228.

[3] Along with this two plates are

the inspection served only to suggest the prospect (which has since been realised) that in time the income from this source might be expected to revive;—and, forced to content ourselves with this anticipation, we weighed anchor from Condatchy, on the 30th March, and arrived on the following day at Colombo.

The banks of Aripo are not the only localities, nor is the *avicula* the only mollusc, by which pearls are furnished. The Bay of Tamblegam, connected with the magnificent harbour of Trincomalie, is the seat of another pearl fishery, and the shell which produces them is the thin transparent oyster (*Placuna placenta*), whose clear white shells are used, in China and elsewhere, as a substitute for window glass. They are also collected annually for the sake of the diminutive pearls contained in them. These are exported to the coast of India, to be calcined for lime, which the luxurious affect to chew with their betel. These pearls are also burned in the mouths of the dead. So prolific are the mollusca of the *Placuna*, that the quantity of shells taken by the licensed renter in the three years prior to 1858, could not have been less than eighteen millions.[1] They delight in brackish water, and on more than one recent occasion, an excess of either salt water or fresh has proved fatal to great numbers of them.

On the occasion of a visit which I made to Batticaloa, in September, 1848, I made some inquiries relative to a story which had reached me of musical sounds, said to be

given from drawings made for the Official Inspector, and exhibiting the ascertained size of the pearl oyster at every period of its growth, from the "spat" to the mature shell. The young "brood" are shown at Nos. 1 and 2. The shell at four months old, No. 3. No. 4, six months. No. 5, one year. No. 6, two years. The second plate exhibits the shell at its full growth.

[1] *Report of* Dr. KELAART, Oct. 1857.

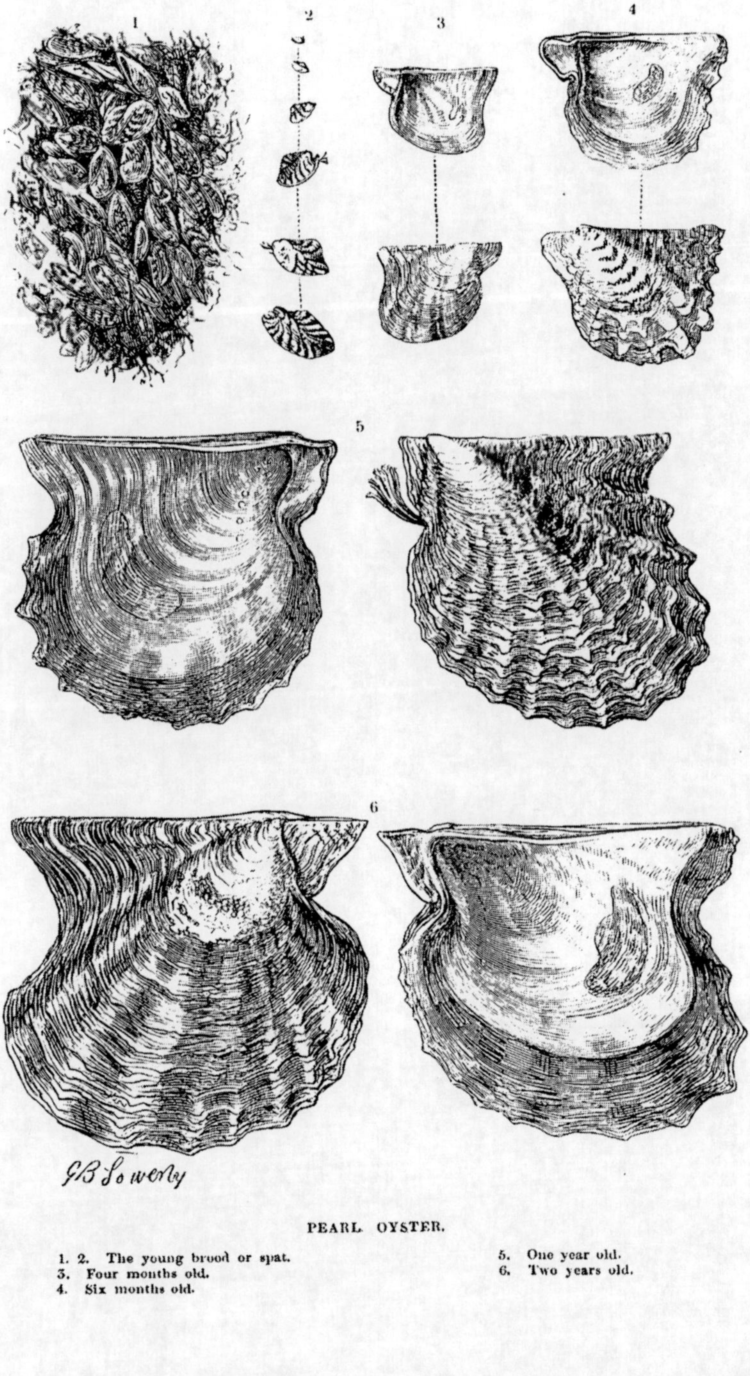


PEARL OYSTER.

1. 2. The young brood or spat.
3. Four months old.
4. Six months old.
5. One year old.
6. Two years old.

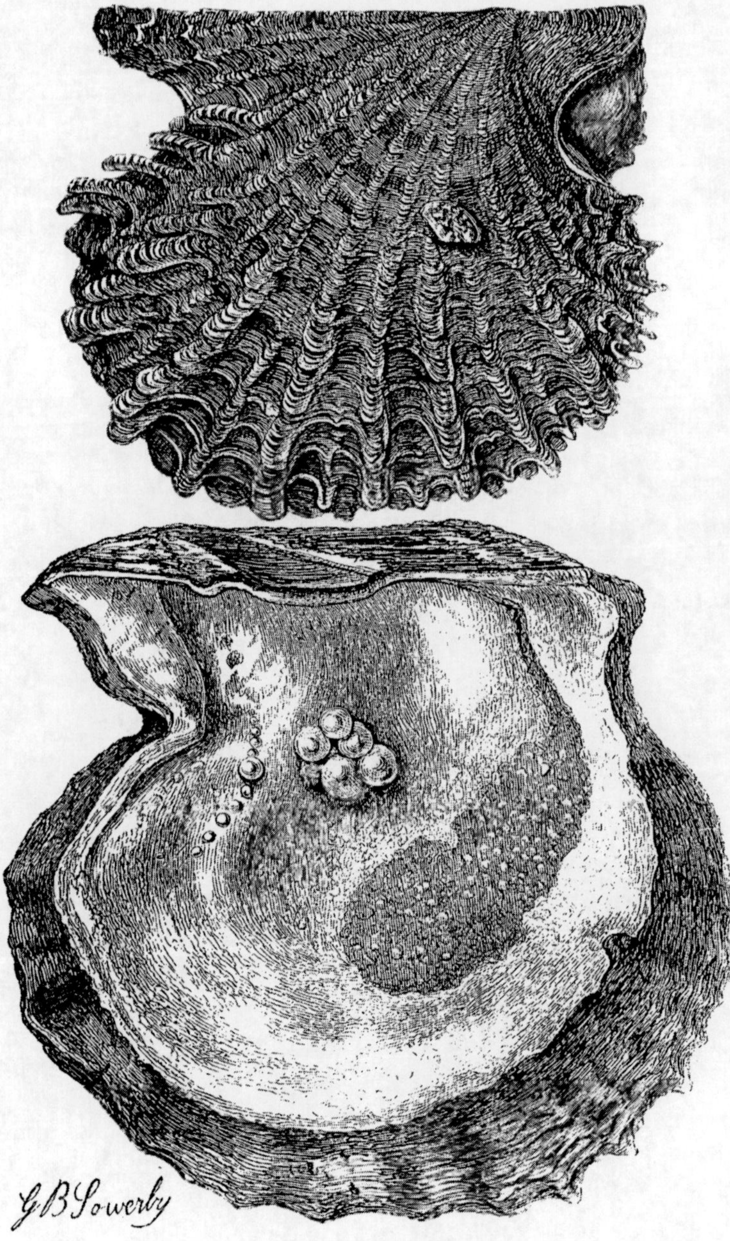


THE PEARL OYSTER.

Full Growth.

often heard issuing from the bottom of the lake, at several places, both above and below the ferry opposite the old Dutch Fort; and which the natives suppose to proceed from some fish peculiar to the locality. The report was confirmed in all its particulars, and one of the spots whence the sounds proceed was pointed out between the pier and a rock that intersects the channel, two or three hundred yards to the eastward. They were said to be heard at night, and most distinctly when the moon was nearest the full, and they were described as resembling the faint sweet notes of an Æolian harp. I sent for some of the fishermen, who said they were perfectly aware of the fact, and that their fathers had always known of the existence of the musical sounds, heard, they said, at the spot alluded to, but only during the dry season, as they cease when the lake is swollen by the freshes after the rain. They believed them to proceed not from a fish, but from a shell, which is known by the Tamil name of (*oorie cooleeroo cradoo,* or) the "crying shell," a name in which the sound seems to have been adopted as an echo to the sense. I sent them in search of the shell, and they returned bringing me some living specimens of different shells, chiefly *littorina* and *cerithium.*[1]

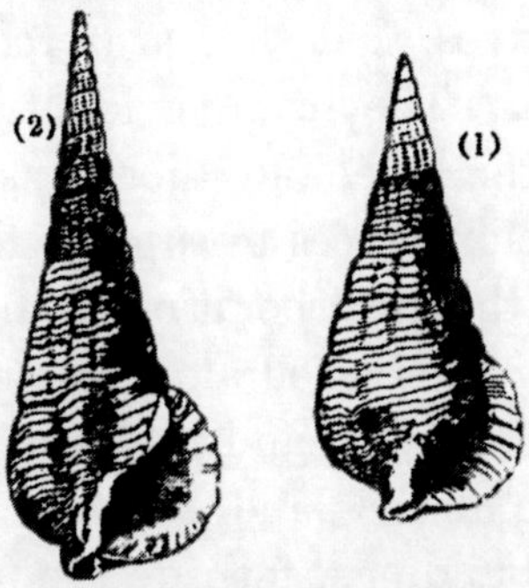

CERITHIUM PALUSTRE.

[1] *Littorina lævis. Cerithium palustre.* Of the latter the specimens brought to me were dwarfed and solid, exhibiting in this particular the usual peculiarities that distinguish (1) shells inhabiting a rocky locality from (2) their congeners in a sandy bottom. Their longitudinal development was less, with greater breadth, and increased strength and weight.

In the evening when the moon rose, I took a boat and accompanied the fishermen to the spot. We rowed about two hundred yards north-east of the jetty by the fort gate; there was not a breath of wind, nor a ripple except those caused by the dip of our oars. On coming to the point mentioned, I distinctly heard the sounds in question. They came up from the water like the gentle thrills of a musical chord, or the faint vibrations of a wine-glass when its rim is rubbed by a moistened finger. It was not one sustained note, but a multitude of tiny sounds, each clear and distinct in itself; the sweetest treble mingling with the lowest bass. On applying the ear to the woodwork of the boat, the vibration was greatly increased in volume. The sounds varied considerably at different points, as we moved across the lake, as if the number of the animals from which they proceeded was greatest in particular spots; and occasionally we rowed out of hearing of them altogether, until on returning to the original locality the sounds were at once renewed.

This fact seems to indicate that the causes of the sounds, whatever they may be, are stationary at several points; and this agrees with the statement of the natives, that they are produced by mollusca, and not by fish. They came evidently and sensibly from the depth of the lake, and there was nothing in the surrounding circumstances to support the conjecture that they could be the reverberation of noises made by insects on the shore conveyed along the surface of the water; for they were loudest and most distinct at points where the nature of the land, and the intervention of the fort and its buildings, forbade the possibility of this kind of conduction.

Sounds somewhat similar are heard under water at some places on the western coast of India, especially in the harbour of Bombay.[1] At Caldera, in Chili, musical cadences are stated to issue from the sea near the landing-place; they are described as rising and falling fully four notes, resembling the tones of harp strings, and mingling like those at Batticaloa, till they produce a musical discord of great delicacy and sweetness. The

[1] These sounds are thus described by Dr. BUIST in the *Bombay Times* of January 1847:

"A party lately crossing from the promontory in Salsette called the 'Neat's Tongue,' to near Sewree, were, about sunset, struck by hearing long distinct sounds like the protracted booming of a distant bell, the dying cadence of an Æolian harp, the note of a pitch-pipe or pitch-fork, or any other long-drawn-out musical note. It was, at first, supposed to be music from Parell floating at intervals on the breeze; then it was perceived to come from all directions, almost in equal strength, and to arise from the surface of the water all around the vessel. The boatmen at once intimated that the sounds were produced by fish, abounding in the muddy creeks and shoals around Bombay and Salsette; they were perfectly well known, and very often heard. Accordingly, on inclining the ear towards the surface of the water; or, better still, by placing it close to the planks of the vessel, the notes appeared loud and distinct, and followed each other in constant succession. The boatmen next day produced specimens of the fish—a creature closely resembling in size and shape the fresh-water perch of the north of Europe—and spoke of them as plentiful and perfectly well known. It is hoped they may be procured alive, and the means afforded of determining how the musical sounds are produced and emitted, with other particulars of interest supposed new in Ichthyology. We shall be thankful to receive from our readers any information they can give us in regard to a phenomenon which does not appear to have been heretofore noticed, and which cannot fail to attract the attention of the naturalist. Of the perfect accuracy with which the singular facts above related have been given, no doubt will be entertained when it is mentioned that the writer was one of a party of five intelligent persons, by all of whom they were most carefully observed, and the impressions of all of whom in regard to them were uniform. It is supposed that the fish are confined to particular localities—shallows, estuaries, and muddy creeks, rarely visited by Europeans; and that this is the reason why hitherto no mention, so far as we know, has been made of the peculiarity in any work on Natural History."

This communication elicited one from Vizagapatam, relative to "musical sounds like the prolonged notes on the harp" heard to proceed from under water at that station. It appeared in the *Bombay Times* of Feb. 13, 1849.

same interesting phenomenon has been observed at the mouth of the Pascagoula, in the State of Mississippi, and of another river called the "Bayon coq del Inde," on the northern shore of the Gulf of Mexico. The animals from which they proceed have not been identified at either of these places, and the mystery remains unsolved, whether the sounds at Batticaloa are given forth by fishes or by molluscs.

Certain fishes are known to utter sounds when removed from the water[1], and some are capable of making noises when under it[2]; but all the circumstances connected with the sounds which I heard at Batticaloa are unfavourable to the conjecture that they were produced by either.

Organs of hearing have been clearly ascertained to

[1] The Cuckoo Gurnard (*Triglia cuculus*) and the maigre (*Sciæna aquila*) utter sounds when taken out of the water (YARRELL, vol. i. p. 44, 107); and herrings when the net has just been drawn have been observed to do the same. This effect has been attributed to the escape of air from the air bladder, but no air bladder has been found in the *Cottus*, which makes a similar noise.

[2] The fishermen assert that a fish about five inches in length, found in the lake at Colombo, and called by them "*magoora*," makes a grunt when disturbed under water. PALLEGOIX, in his account of Siam, speaks of a fish resembling a sole, but of brilliant colouring with black spots, which the natives call the "dog's tongue," that attaches itself to the bottom of a boat, "et fait entendre un bruit très-sonore et même harmonieux." —Tom. i. p. 194. A *Silurus*, found in the Rio Parana, and called the "armado," is remarkable for making a harsh grating noise when caught by hook or line, which can be distinctly heard when the fish is beneath the water. DARWIN, *Nat. Journ.* ch. vii. Aristotle and Ælian were aware of the existence of this faculty in some of the fishes of the Mediterranean. ARISTOTLE, *De Anim.*, lib. iv. ch. ix.; ÆLIAN, *De Nat. Anim.*, lib. x. ch. xi.; see also PLINY, lib. ix. ch. vii., lib. xi. ch. cxiii.; ATHENÆUS, lib. vii. ch. iii. vi. I have heard of sounds produced under water at Baltimore, and supposed to be produced by the "cat-fish;" and at Swan River, in Australia, where they are ascribed to the "trumpeter." A similar noise heard in the Tagus is attributed by the Lisbon fishermen to the "*Corvina*"—but what fish is meant by that name, I am unable to tell.

exist, not only in fishes[1], but in mollusca. In the oyster the presence of an acoustic apparatus of the simplest possible construction has been established by the discoveries of Siebold[2], and from our knowledge of the reciprocal relations existing between the faculties of hearing and of producing sounds, the ascertained existence of the one affords legitimate grounds for inferring the co-existence of the other in animals of the same class.[3]

Besides, it has been clearly established, that one at least of the gasteropoda is furnished with the power of producing sounds. Dr. Grant, in 1826, communicated to the Edinburgh Philosophical Society the fact, that on placing some specimens of the *Tritonia arborescens* in a glass vessel filled with sea water, his attention was attracted by a noise which he ascertained to proceed from these mollusca. It resembled the "clink" of a steel wire on the side of the jar, one stroke only being given at a time, and repeated at short intervals.[4]

The affinity of structure between the *Tritonia* and the mollusca inhabiting the shells brought to me at Batticaloa, might justify the belief of the natives of Ceylon, that the latter are the authors of the sounds I heard; and the description of those emitted by the former as given by Dr. Grant, so nearly resemble them, that I have always regretted my inability, on the occa-

[1] AGASSIZ, *Comparative Physiology*, sec. ii. 158.

[2] It consists of two round vesicles containing fluid, and crystalline or elliptical calcareous particles or otolites, remarkable for their oscillatory action in the living or recently killed animal. OWEN'S *Lectures on the Comparative Anatomy and Physiology of the Invertebrate Animals*, 1855, p. 511-552.

[3] I am informed that Professor MÜLLER read a paper on "Musical fishes" before the Academy of Berlin, in 1856. It will probably be found in the volume of MÜLLER'S *Archiv. für Physiologie* for that year; but I have not had an opportunity of reading it.

[4] *Edinburgh Philosophical Journ.*, vol. xiv. p. 188. See also the Appendix to this chapter.

sion of my visits to Batticaloa, to investigate the subject more narrowly. At subsequent periods I have since renewed my efforts, but without success, to obtain specimens or observations of the habits of the living mollusca. The only species afterwards sent to me were *Cerithia;* but no vigilance sufficed to catch the desired sounds, and I still hesitate to accept the dictum of the fishermen, as the same mollusc abounds in all the other brackish estuaries on the coast; and it would be singular, if true, that the phenomenon of its uttering a musical note should be confined to a single spot in the lagoon of Batticaloa.[1]

Although naturalists have long been familiar with the marine testacea of Ceylon, no successful attempt has yet been made to form a classified catalogue of the species; and I am indebted to the eminent conchologist, Mr. Sylvanus Hanley, for the list which accompanies this notice.

In drawing it up, Mr. Hanley observes that he found it a task of more difficulty than would at first be surmised, owing to the almost total absence of reliable data from which to construct it. Three sources were available: collections formed by resident naturalists, the contents of the well-known satin-wood boxes prepared at Trincomalie, and the laborious elimination of locality from the habitats ascribed to all the known species in the multitude of works on conchology in general.

But, unfortunately, the first resource proved fallacious. There is no large collection in this country composed exclusively of Ceylon shells;—and as the very few cabinets

[1] The letter which I received from Dr. Grant on this subject, I have placed in a note to the present chapter, in the hope that it may stimulate some other inquirer in Ceylon to prosecute the investigation which I was unable to carry out successfully.

rich in the marine treasures of the island have been filled as much by purchase as by personal exertion, there is an absence of the requisite confidence that all professing to be Singhalese have been actually captured in the island and its waters.

The cabinets arranged by the native dealers, though professing to contain the productions of Ceylon, include shells which have been obtained from other islands in the Indian seas; and the information contained in books, probably from these very circumstances, is either obscure or deceptive. The old writers content themselves with assigning to any particular shell the too-comprehensive habitat of "the Indian Ocean," and seldom discriminate between a specimen from Ceylon and one from the Eastern Archipelago or Hindustan. In a very few instances, Ceylon has been indicated with precision as the habitat of particular shells, but even here the views of specific essentials adopted by modern conchologists, and the subdivisions established in consequence, leave us in doubt for which of the described forms the collective locality should be retained.

Valuable notices of Ceylon shells are to be found in detached papers, in periodicals, and in the scientific surveys of exploring voyages. The authentic facts embodied in the monographs of REEVE, KUSTER, SOWERBY, and KIENER, have greatly enlarged our knowledge of the marine testacea; and the land and fresh-water mollusca have been similarly illustrated by the contributions of BENSON and LAYARD to the *Annals of Natural History*.

The dredge has been used, but only in a few insulated spots along the coasts of Ceylon; European explorers have been rare; and the natives, anxious only to secure the showy and saleable shells of the sea, have neglected the less attractive ones of the land and the lakes. Hence Mr. Hanley finds it necessary to premise that the list appended, although the result of infinite labour and research, is less satisfactory than could have been wished. "It is offered," he says, "with diffidence, not pretending to the merit of completeness as a shell-fauna of the island, but rather as a form, which the zeal of other collectors may hereafter elaborate and fill up."

Looking at the little that has yet been done, compared with the vast and almost untried field which invites explorers, an assiduous collector may quadruple the species hitherto described. The minute shells especially may be said to be unknown; a vigilant examination of the corals and excrescences upon the spondyli and pearl-oysters would signally increase our knowledge of the Rissoæ, Chemnitziæ, and other perforating testacea, whilst the dredge from the deep water will astonish the amateur by the wholly new forms it can scarcely fail to display.

---

## *List of Ceylon Shells.*

The arrangement here adopted is a modified Lamarckian one, very similar to that used by Reeve and Sowerby, and by Mr. HANLEY, in his *Illustrated Catalogue of Recent Shells.*[1]

[1] Below will be found a general reference to the Works or Papers in which are given descriptive notices of the shells contained in the following list; the names of the authors (in full or abbreviated) being, as usual, annexed to each species.

ADAMS, *Proceed. Zool. Soc.* 1853, 54, 56; *Thesaur. Conch.* ALBERS, *Zeitsch. Malakoz.* 1853. ANTON, *Wiegm. Arch. Nat.* 1837; *Verzeichn. Conch.* BECK in *Pfeiffer, Symbol. Helic.* BENSON, *Ann. Nat. Hist.* vii. 1851; xii. 1853; xviii. 1856. BLAINVILLE, *Dict. Sc. Nat.; Nouv. Ann. Mus. His. Nat.* i. BOLTEN, *Mus.* BORN, *Test. Mus. Cæs. Vind.* BRODERIP, *Zool. Journ.* i. iii. BRUGUIERE, *Encyc.*

Aspergillum Javanum. *Brug.* Enc. Mét.
sparsum, *Sowerby.* Gen. Shells.[1]
clavatum, *Chenu,* Illust. Conch.
Teredo nucivorus. *Sp.* Skr. Nat. Sels.[2]
Solen truncatus, *Wood,* Gen. Conch.
linearis, *Wood,* Gen. Conch.
cultellus, *Linn.* Syst. Nat.
radiatus, *Linn.* Syst. Nat.
Anatina subrostrata, *Lam.* Ani. s. Vert.
Anatinella Nicobarica, *Gm.* Syst. Nat.
Lutraria Egyptiaca, *Chemn.* Conch. Cab.
Blainvillea vitrea, *Chemn.* Conch. Cab.[3]
Scrobicularia angulata, *Chem.* Con. Cab.[4]
Mactra complanata, *Desh.* Proc. Zl. Soc.[5]
tumida, *Chemn.* Conch. Cab.
antiquata, *Reeve* (as of *Spengl.*), C. Icon.
cygnea, *Chemn.* Conch. Cab.
Corbiculoides, *Deshayes,* Pr. Zl. S. 1854.
Mesodesma
Layardi, *Deshayes,* Pr. Zool. Soc. 1854.
striata, *Chemn.* Conch. Cab.[6]
Crassatella rostrata, *Lam.* Anim. s. Vert.
sulcata, *Lam.* Anim. s. Vert.
Amphidesma
duplicatum, *Sowerby.* Species Conch.
Pandora Ceylanica, *Sowerby,* Conch. Mis.
Galeomma Layardi, *Desh.* Pr. Zl. S. 1856.
Kellia peculiaris, *Adams,* Pr. Zl. S. 1856.
Petricola cultellus, *Desh.* Pr. Zl. S. 1853.
Sanguinolaria rosea, *Lam.* Anim. s. Vert.
Psammobia rostrata, *Lam.* Anim. s. Vert.
occidens, *Gm.* Systema Naturæ.
Skinneri, *Reeve,* Conch. Icon.[7]
Layardi, *Desh.* P. Z. Soc. 1854.

---

[1] A. dichotomum, *Chenu.*
[2] Fistulana gregata, *Lam.*
[3] Blainvillea, *Hupé.*
[4] Latraria tellinoides, *Lam.*
[5] I have also seen M. hians of Philippi in a Ceylon collection.
[6] M. Taprobanensis, *Index Test. Suppl.*
[7] Psammotella Skinneri, *Reeve.*

*Méthod. Vers.* CARPENTER, *Proc. Zool. Soc.* 1856. CHEMNITZ, *Conch. Cab.* CHENU, *Illus. Conch.* DESHAYES, *Encyc. Méth. Vers.*; *Mag. Zool.* 1831; *Voy. Belanger*; *Edit. Lam. An. s. Vert.*; *Proceed. Zool. Soc.* 1853, 54, 55. DILLWYN, *Descr. Cat. Shells.* DOHRN, *Proc. Zool. Soc.* 1857, 58; *Malak. Blätter*; *Land and Fluviatile Shells of Ceylon.* DUCLOS, *Monog of Oliva.* FABRICIUS, *in Pfeiffer Monog. Helic.*; *in Dohrn's MSS.* FÉRUSSAC, *Hist. Mollusques.* FORSKÄL, *Anim. Orient.* GMELIN, *Syst. Nat.* GRAY, *Proc. Zool. Soc.* 1834, 52; *Index Testaceologicus Suppl.*; *Spicilegia Zool.*; *Zool. Journ.* i.; *Zool. Beechey Voy.* GRATELOUP, *Act. Linn. Bordeaux*, xi. GUERIN, *Rev. Zool.* 1847. HANLEY, *Thesaur. Conch.* i.; *Recent Bivalves*; *Proc. Zool. Soc.* 1858. HINDS, *Zool. Voy. Sulphur*; *Proc. Zool. Soc.* HUTTON, *Journ. As. Soc.* KARSTEN, *Mus. Lesk.* KIENER, *Coquilles Vivantes.* KRAUSS, *Sud-Afrik Mollusk.* LAMARCK, *An. sans Vertéb.* LAYARD, *Proc. Zool. Soc.* 1854. LEA, *Proceed. Zool. Soc.* 1850. LINNÆUS, *Syst. Nat.* MARTINI, *Conch. Cab.* MAWE, *Introd. Linn. Conch.*; *Index Test. Suppl.* MEUSCHEN, in *Gronov. Zoophylac.* MENKE, *Synop. Mollus.* MULLER, *Hist. Verm. Terrest.* PETIT, *Pro. Zool. Soc.* 1842. PFEIFFER, *Monog. Helic.*; *Monog. Pneumon.*; *Proceed. Zool. Soc.* 1852, 53, 54, 55, 56; *Zeitschr. Malacoz.* 1853. PHILIPPI, *Zeitsch. Mal.* 1846, 47; *Abbild. Neuer Conch.* POTIEZ et MICHAUD, *Galerie Douai.* RANG, *Mag. Zool.* ser. i. p. 100. RÉCLUZ, *Proceed. Zool. Soc.* 1845; *Revue Zool. Cuv.* 1841; *Mag. Conch.* REEVE, *Conch. Icon.*; *Proc. Zool. Soc.* 1842, 52. SCHUMACHER, *Syst.* SHUTTLEWORTH. SOLANDER, in *Dillwyn's Desc. Cat. Shells*; SOWERBY, *Genera Shells*; *Species Conch.*; *Conch. Misc.*; *Thesaur. Conch.*; *Conch. Illus.*; *Proc. Zool. Soc.*; *App. to Tankerville Cat.* SPENGLER, *Skrivt. Nat. Selsk. Kiobenhav.* 1792. SWAINSON, *Zool. Illust.* ser. ii. TEMPLETON, *Ann. Nat. Hist.* 1858. TROSCHEL, in *Pfeiffer, Mon. Pneum*; *Zeitschr. Malak.* 1847; *Wiegm. Arch. Nat.* 1837. WOOD, *General Conch.*

lunulata, *Desh.* P. Z. Soc. 1854.
amethystus, *Wood*, Gen. Conch.[1]
rugosa, *Lam.* Anim. s. Vert.[2]
Tellina virgata, *Linn.* Syst. Nat.[3]
rugosa, *Born*, Test. Mus. Cæs. Vind.
ostracea, *Lam.* Anim. s. Vert.
ala, *Hanley*, Thesaur. Conch. i.
inæqualis, *Hanley*, Thesaur, Conch. i.
Layardi, *Deshayes*, P. Z. Soc. 1854.
callosa, *Deshayes.* P. Z. Soc. 1854.
rubra, *Deshayes*, P. Z. Soc. 1854.
abbreviata, *Deshayes*, P. Z. Soc. 1854.
foliacea, *Linn.* Systema Naturæ.
lingua-felis, *Linn.* Systema Naturæ.
vulsella, *Chemn.* Conch. Cab.[4]
Lucina interrupta, *Lam.* Anim. s. Vert.[5]
Layardi, *Deshayes*, Pr. Zool. Soc. 1855.
Donax scortum, *Linn.* Syst. Nat.
cuneata, *Linn.* Syst. Nat.
faba, *Chem.* Conch. Cab.
spinosa, *Gm.* Syst. Nat.
paxillus, *Reeve*, Conch. Icon.
Cyrena Ceylanica, *Chemn.* Conch. Cab.
Tennentii, *Hanley*, P. Z. Soc. 1858.
Cytherea Erycina, *Linn.* Syst. Nat.[6]
meretrix, *Linn.* Syst. Nat.[7]
castanea, *Lam.* Anim. s. Vert.
castrensis, *Linn.* Syst. Nat.
casta, *Gm.* Syst. Nat.
rostata, *Chemn.* Conch. Cab.
læta, *Gm.* Syst. Nat.
trimaculata, *Lam.* Anim. s. Vert.
Hebræa, *Lam.* Anim. s. Vert.
rugifera, *Lam.* Anim. s. Vert.
scripta, *Linn*, Syst. Nat.
gibbia, *Lam.* Anim. s. Vert.
Meroe, *Linn.* Syst. Nat.
testudinalis, *Lam.* Anim. s. Vert.
seminuda, *Anton.* Wiegm. A. Nat. 1837.[8]
Venus reticulata, *Linn.* Syst. Nat.[9]
pinguis, *Chemn.* Conch. Cab.
recens, *Philippi*, Abbild. Neuer Conch.
thiara, *Dillw.* Descriptive Cat. Shells.
Malabarica, *Chemn.* Conch. Cab.
Bruguieri, *Hanley*, Recent Bivalves.
papilionacea, *Lam.* Anim. s. Vert.
Indica, *Sowerby*, Thesaur. Conch. ii.
inflata, *Deshayes*, Proc. Zool. Soc. 1853.[10]
Ceylonensis. *Sowerby*, Thes. Conch. ii.
literata, *Linn.* Systema Naturæ.
textrix, *Chemn.* Conch. Cab.[11]
Cardium unedo, *Linn.* Syst. Nat.
maculosum, *Wood*, Gen. Con.
leucostomum, *Born*, Tt. M. Cæs. Vind.
rugosum, *Lam.* Anim. s. Vert.
biradiatum, *Bruguiere*, En. Méth. Vers.
attenuatum, *Sowerby*, Conch. Illust.
enode, *Sowerby*, Conch. Illust.
papyraceum, *Chemn.* Conch. Cab.
ringiculum, *Sowerby*, Conch. Illust.
subrugosum, *Sowerby*, Conch. Illust.
latum, *Born*, Test. Mus. Cæs. Vind.
Asiaticum, *Chemn* Conch. Cab.
Cardita variegata, *Brug.* Enc. Méth. Vers.
bicolor, *Lam.* Anim. s. Vert.
Arca rhombea, *Born*, Test. Mus.
vellicata, *Reeve*, Conch. Icon.
cruciata, *Philippi*, Ab. Neur Conch.
decussata, *Reeve* (as of Sowerby), C. I.[12]
scapha, *Meuschen*, in Gronov. Zoo.
Pectunculus nodosus, *Reeve*, Conch. Icon.
pectiniformis, *Lam.* Anim. s. Vert.
Nucula mitralis, *Hinds*, Zool. voy. Sul.
Layardi, *Adams*, Proc. Zool. Soc. 1856.
Mauritii (*Hanley* as of *Hinds*), Rec. Biv.
Unio
corrugatus, *Müller*, Hist. Verm. Ter.[13]
marginalis, *Lam.* Anim. s. Vert.
Lithodomus
cinnamoneus, *Lam.* Anim. s. Vert.
Mytilus viridis, *Linn.* Syst. Nat.[14]
bilocularis, *Linn.* Syst. Nat.
Pinna inflata, *Chemn.* Conch. Cab.
cancellata, *Mawe*, Intr. Lin. Conch.
Malleus vulgaris, *Lam.* Anim. s. Vert.
albus, *Lam.* Anim. s. Vert.
Meleagrina margaritifera, *Linn.* Syst. Nat.
vexillum, *Reeve*, Conch. Icon.[15]
Avicula macroptera, *Reeve*, Conch. Icon.
Lima squamosa, *Lam.* Anim. s. Vert.
Pecten plica, *Linn.* Syst. Nat.
radula, *Linn.* Syst. Nat.
pleuronectes, *Linn.* Syst. Nat.
pallium, *Linn.* Syst. Nat.
senator, *Gm.* Syst. Nat.
histrionicus, *Gm.* Syst. Nat.
Indicus, *Deshayes*, Voyage Belanger.
Layardi, *Reeve*, Conch, Icon.
Spondylus Layardi, *Reeve*, Conch. Icon.
candidus, *Reeve* (as of *Lam.*) C. Icon.
Ostrea hyotis, *Linn.* Syst. Nat.
glaucina, *Lam* Anim. s. Vert.
Mytiloides, *Lam.* Anim. s. Vert.
cucullata? var. *Born* Test. M. Vind.[16]
Vulsella
Pholadiformis, *Reeve*, C. Icn. (immat.)
Placuna placenta, *Linn.* Syst. Nat.
Lingula anatina, *Lam.* Anim. s. Vert.

---

[1] P. cærulescens, *Lam.*
[2] Sanguinolaria rugosa, *Lam.*
[3] T. striatula of Lamarck is also supposed to be indigenous to Ceylon.
[4] T. rostrata, *Lam.*
[5] L. divaricata is found, also, in mixed Ceylon collections.
[6] C. dispar of Chemnitz is occasionally found in Ceylon collections.
[7] C. impudica, *Lam.*
[8] As Donax.
[9] V. corbis, *Lam.*
[10] As Tapes.
[11] V. textile, *Lam.*
[12] ? Arca Helblingii, *Chemn.*
[13] Mr. Cuming informs me that he has forwarded no less than six distinct *Uniones* from Ceylon to Isaac Lea, of Philadelphia, for determination or description.
[14] M. smaragdinus, *Chemn.*
[15] As Avicula.
[16] The specimens are not in a fitting state for positive determination. They are strong, extremely narrow, with the beak of the lower valve much produced, and the inner edge of the upper valve denticulated throughout. The muscular impressions are dusky brown.

Hyalæa tridentata, *For.* Anim. Orient.[1]
Chiton, 2 species (*Layard*).
Patella Reynaudii, *Deshayes*, Voy. Be.
testudinaria, *Linn.* Syst. Nat.
Emarginula fissurata, *Ch.* C. Cab.[2] *Lam.*
Calyptræa (Crucibulum) violascens, *Carpenter*, Proc. Zool. Soc. 1856.
Dentalium
octogonum, *Lam.* Anim. s. Vert.
aprinum, *Linn.* Syst. Nat.
Bulla soluta, *Chemn.* Conch. Cab.[3]
vexillum, *Chemn.* Conch. Cab.
Bruguieri, *Adams*, Thes. Conch.
elongata, *Adams*, Thes. Conch.
ampulla, *Linn.* Syst. Nat.
Lamellaria (as Marsenia Indica, *Leach.* in Brit. Mus.) allied to L. Mauritiana, if not it.
Vaginula maculata, *Templ.* An. Nat.
Limax, 2 sp.
Parmacella Tennentii, *Templ.*[4]
Vitrina irradians, *Pfeiffer*, Mon. Helic.
Edgariana, *Ben.* Ann. N. H. 1853 (xii.)
membranacea, *Ben.* A. N. H. 1853 (xii.)
Helix hæmastoma, *Linn.* Syst. Nat.
vittata, *Müller*, Vermium Terrestrium.
bistrialis, *Beck*, in Pfeiff. Symb. Helic.
Tranquebarica, *Fabricius*, in *Pfeiff.* Monog. Helic.
Juliana, *Gray*, Proc. Zool. Soc. 1834.
Waltoni, *Reeve*, Proc. Zool. Soc. 1842.
Skinneri, *Reeve*, Conch. Icon. vii.
corylus, *Reeve*, Conch. Icon. vii.
umbrina (*Reeve*, as of *Pfeiff.*), C. Ic. vii.
fallaciosa, *Férussac*, Hist. Mollus.
Rivolii, *Deshayes*, Enc. Méth. Vers. ii.
Charpentieri, *Pfeiff.* Monog. Helic.
erronea, *Albers.* *Zeitschr.* Mal. 1853.
carneola, *Pfeiff.* Monog. Helic.
convexiuscula, *Pfeiff.* Monog. Helic.
gnoma, *Pfeiff.* Monog. Helic.
Chenui, *Pfeiff.* Monog. Helic.
semidecussata, *Pfeiff.* Monog. Helic.
phœnix, *Pfeiff.* Monog. Helic.
superba, *Pfeiff.* Monog. Helic.
Ceylanica, *Pfeiff.* Monog. Helic.
Gardnerii, *Pfeiff.* Monog. Helic.
coriaria, *Pfeiff.* Monog. Helic.
Layardi, *Pfeiff.* Monog. Helic.
concavospira, *Pfeiff.* Monog. Helic.
novella, *Pfeiff.* Monog. Helic.
verrucula, *Pfeiff.* Monog. Helic.
hyphasma, *Pfeiff.* Monog. Helic.
Emiliana, *Pfeiff.* Monog. Helic.
Woodiana, *Pfeiff.* Monog. Helic.
partita, *Pfeiff.* Monog. Helic.
biciliata, *Pfeiff.* Monog. Helic.
Isabellina, *Pfeiff.* Proc. Zool. Soc.
trifilosa, *Pfeiff.* Proc. Zool. Soc. 1854.
politissima, *Pfeiff.* Proc. Zool. Sc. 1854.
Thwaitesii, *Pfeiff.* Proc. Zool. Soc. 1854.
nepos, *Pfeiff.* Proc. Zool. Soc. 1855.
subopaca, *Pfeiff.* Proc. Zool. Soc. 1853.
subconoidea, *Pfeiff.* Proc. Zool. S. 1854.
ceraria, *Benson*, An. Nat. H. 1853 (xii.)
vilipensa, *Benson*, An. N. H. 1853 (xii.)
perfucata, *Benson*, A. N. H. 1853 (xii.)
puteolus, *Benson*, An. N. H. 1853 (xii.)
mononema, *Benson*, A. N. H. 1853 (xii.)
marcida, *Benson*, An. N. H. 1853 (xii.)
galerus, *Benson*, A. N. H. 1856 (xviii.)
albizonata, *Dohrn*, Proc. Zoo. Soc. 1858.
Nietneri, *Dohrn*, MS.[5]
Grevillei, *Pfeiff.* Proc. Zool. Soc. 1856.
Streptaxis Layardi, *Pfeiff.* Mon. Helic.
Cingalensis, *Pfeiff.* Monog. Helic.
Pupa
muscerda, *Benson*, A. N. H. 1853 (xii.)
mimula, *Benson*, A. N. H. 1856 (xviii.)
Ceylanica, *Pfeiff.* Monog. Helic.
Bulimus
trifasciatus, *Brug.* Encycl. Méth. Vers.
pullus, *Gray*, Proc. Zool. Soc. 1834.
gracilis, *Hutton*, Journ. Asiat. Soc. iii.
punctatus, *Anton*, Verzeichn. Conch.
Ceylanicus, *Pfeiff.* (? Blævis, *Gray*, in Index Testaceologicus.)
adumbratus, *Pfeiff.* Monog. Helic.
intermedius, *Pfeiff.* Monog. Helic.
proletarius, *Pfeiff.* Monog. Helic.
albizonatus, *Reeve*, Conch. Icon.
Mavortius, *Reeve*, Conch. Icon.
fuscoventris, *Ben.* A. N. H. 1856 (xviii.)
rufopictus, *Ben.* A. N H. 1856 (xviii.)
panos, *Benson*, Ann. Nat. H. 1853 (xii.)
Achatina nitens, *Gray*, Spicilegia Zool.
inornata, *Pfeiff.* Monog. Helic.
capillacea, *Pfeiff.* Monog. Helic.
Ceylanica, *Pfeiff.* Monog. Helic.
Punctogallana, *Pfeiff.* Monog. Helic.
pachycheila, *Benson.*
veruina, *Bens.* A. Nat. Hist. 1853 (xii.)
parabilis, *Bens.* A. N. Hist. 1856 (xviii.)
Succinea Ceylanica, *Pfeiff.* Monog. Helic.
Auricula
Ceylanica, *Adams*, Pr. Zool. Soc. 1854.[6]
Ceylanica, *Petit*, Proc. Zool. Soc. 1842.[7]
Layardi, *Adams*, Proc. Zool. Soc. 1854.[8]
pellucens, *Menke*, Synopsis Moll.
Pythia
Ceylanica, *Pfeiff.* Zeits. Malacoz. 1853.
ovata, *Pfeiff.* Proc. Zool. Soc. 1854.
Truncatella
Ceylanica, *Pfeiff.* Proc. Zool. Soc. 1856.
Cyclostoma (*Cyclophorus*) Ceylanicum, *Sowerby*, Thes. Conch.
involvulum, *Müller*, Verm. Terrest.
Menkeanum, *Philippi*, Zeit. Mal. 1847.
punctatum, *Gratel.* A.L. Bordeaux (xi.)
loxostoma, *Pfeiff.* Monog. Pneumon.

---

1 As Anomia.

2 The fissurata of Humphreys and Dacosta, pl. 4. — E. rubra, *Lamarck.*

3 B. Ceylanica, *Brug.*

4 P. Tennentii. " Greyish brown, with longitudinal rows of rufous spots, forming interrupted bands along the sides. A singularly handsome species, having similar habits to *Limax.* Found in the valleys of the Kalany Ganga, near Ruanwellé." — *Templeton* MSS.

5 Not far from bistrialis and Ceylanica. The manuscript species of Mr. Dohrn will shortly appear in his intended work upon the land and fluviatile shells of Ceylon.

6 As Ellobium.

7 As Melampus.

8 As Ophicardelis.

alabastrum, *Pfeiff.* Monog. Pneumon.
Bairdii, *Pfeiff.* Monog. Pneumon.
Thwaitesii, *Pfeiff.* Monog. Pneumon.
annulatum, *Trosch.* in Pfeiff. M. Pneum.
parapsis, *Bens.* An. Nat. Hist. 1853 (xii.)
parma, *Bens.* An. Nat. His. 1856 (xviii.)
cratera, *Bens.* An. N. Hist. 1856 (xviii.)
(*Leptopoma*) halophilum, *Benson*, Ann. Nat. Hist. (ser. 2 vii.) 1851.
orophilum, *Bens.* A. N. H. (ser. 2. xi.)
apicatum, *Bens.* A. N. H. 1856 (xviii.)
conulus, *Pfeiff.* Proc. Zool. Soc. 1854.
flammeum, *Pfeiff.* Monog. Pneumon.
semiclausum, *Pfeiff.* Monog. Pneumon.
pœcilum, *Pfeiff.* Monog. Pneumon.
elatum, *Pfeiff.* Monog. Pneumon.
Cyclostoma (*Aulopoma*).
Iteri, *Guérin*, Rev. Zool. 1847.
helicinum, *Chemn.* Conch. Cab.
Hoffmeisteri, *Troschel*, Zeit. Mal. 1847.
grande, *Pfeiff.* Monog. Pneumon.
spheroideum, *Dohrn*, Malak. Blätter.
(?) gradatum, *Pfeiff.* Monog. Pneumon.
Cyclostoma (*Pterocyclos*).
Cingalense, *Bens.* A. N. H. (ser. 2. xi.)
Troscheli, *Bens.* Ann. Nat. Hist. 1851.
Cumingii, *Pfeiff.* Monog. Pneumon.
bifrons, *Pfeiff.* Monog. Pneumon.
Cataulus Templemani, *Pfeiff.* Mon. Pneu.
eurytrema, *Pfeiff.* Proc. Zool. Soc. 1852.
marginatus, *Pfeiff.* Proc. Zool. Soc. 1853.
duplicatus, *Pfeiff.* Proc. Zool. Soc. 1854.
aureus, *Pfeiff.* Proc. Zool. Soc. 1855.
Layardi, *Gray*, Proc. Zool. Soc. 1852.
Austenianus, *Bens.* A. N. H. 1853 (xii.)
Thwaitesii, *Pfeiff.* Proc. Zo. Soc. 1852.
Cumingii, *Pfeiff.* Proc. Zool. Soc. 1856.
decorus, *Bens.* Ann. Nat. Hist. 1853.
hæmastoma, *Pfeiff.* Proc. Zo. Soc. 1856.
Planorbis
Coromandelianus, *Fab.* in *Dorhn's* MS.
Stelzeneri, *Dohrn*, Proc. Zool. Soc. 1858.
elegantulus, *Dohrn*, Proc. Z. Soc. 1858.
Limnæa
tigrina, *Dohrn*, Proc. Zool. Soc. 1858.
pinguis, *Dohrn*, Proc. Zool. Soc. 1858.
Melania
tuberculata, *Müller*, Verm. Ter.[1]
spinulosa, *Lam.* Anim. s. Vert.
corrugata, *Lam.* Anim. s. Vert.
rudis, *Lea*, Proc. Zool. Soc. 1850.
acanthica, *Lea*, Proc. Zool. Soc. 1850.
Zeylanica, *Lea*, Proc. Zool. Soc. 1850.
confusa, *Dohrn*, Proc. Zool. Soc. 1858.
datura, *Dohrn*, Proc. Zool. Soc. 1858.
Layardi, *Dohrn*, Proc. Zool. Soc. 1858.
Paludomus
abbreviatus, *Reeve*, Pr. Zool. Soc. 1852.
clavatus, *Reeve*, Proc. Zool. Soc. 1852.
dilatatus, *Reeve*, Proc. Zool. Soc. 1852.
globulosus, *Reeve*, Conch. Icon.
decussatus, *Reeve*, Proc Zool. Soc. 1852.
nigricans, *Reeve*, Conch. Icon.
constrictus, *Reeve*, Proc. Zo. Soc. 1852.
bicinctus, *Reeve*, Proc. Zool. Soc. 1852.
phasianinus, *Reeve*, Proc. Zo Soc. 1852.
lævis, *Layard*, Proc. Zool. Soc. 1854.
palustris, *Layard*, Proc. Zool. Soc. 1854.
fulguratus, *Dohrn*, Proc. Zo. Soc. 1857.
nasutus, *Dohrn*, Proc. Zool. Soc. 1857.
sphæricus, *Dohrn*, Proc. Zo. Soc. 1857.
solidus, *Dohrn*, Proc. Zool. Soc. 1857.
distinguendus, *Dohrn*, Proc. Z. S. 1857.
Cumingianus, *Dohrn*, Proc. Z. S. 1857.
dromedarius, *Dohrn*, Proc. Z. S. 1857.
Skinneri, *Dohrn*, Proc. Zool. Soc. 1857.
Swainsoni, *Dohrn*, Proc. Zo. Soc. 1857.
nodulosus, *Dohrn*, Proc. Zo. Soc. 1857.
Paludomus (*Tanalia*).
loricatus, *Reeve*, Conch. Icon.
erinaceus, *Reeve*, Proc. Zool. Soc. 1852.
æreus, *Reeve*, Proc. Zool. Soc. 1852.
Layardi, *Reeve*, Proc. Zool. Soc. 1852.
undatus, *Reeve*, Conch. Icon.
Gardneri, *Reeve*, Conch. Icon.
Tennentii, *Reeve*, Conch. Icon.
Reevei, *Layard*, Proc. Zool. Soc. 1854.
violaceus, *Layard*, Proc. Zool. Soc. 1854.
similis, *Layard*. Proc. Zool. Soc. 1854.
funiculatus, *Layard*, Pr. Z. Soc. 1854.
Paludomus (*Philopotamis*).
sulcatus, *Reeve*, Conch. Icon.
regalis, *Layard*, Proc. Zool. Soc. 1854.
Thwaitesii, *Layard*, P. Zool. Soc. 1854.
Pirena atra, *Linn.* Systema Naturæ.
Paludina melanostoma, *Bens.*
Ceylanica, *Dohrn*, Pr. Zool. Soc. 1857.
Bythinia stenothyroides, *Dohrn*, Proc. Zool. Soc. 1857.
modesta, *Dohrn*, MS.
inconspicua, *Dohrn*, Pr. Zool. Soc. 1857.
Ampullaria Layardi, *Reeve*, Conch. Icon.
mœsta, *Reeve*, Conch. Icon.
cinerea, *Reeve*, Conch. Icon.
Woodwardi, *Dohrn*, Pr. Zool. Soc. 1858.
Tischbeini, *Dohrn*, Proc. Zool. Soc. 1858.
carinata, *Swainson*, Zool. Illus. ser. 2.
paludinoides, Cat. *Cristofori & Jan.*[2]
Malabarica, *Philippi*, monog. Ampul.[2]
Luzonica, *Reeve*, Conch. Icon.[2]
Sumatrensis, *Philippi*, monog. Ampul.[2]
Navicella eximia, *Reeve*, Conch. Icon.
reticulata, *Reeve*, Conch. Icon.
Livesayi, *Dohrn*, Proc. Zool. Soc. 1858.
squamata, *Dohrn*, Proc. Zool. Soc. 1858.
depressa, *Lam.* Anim. s. Vert.
Neritina
crepidularia, *Lam.* Anim. s. Vert.
melanostoma, *Trosch.* W. A. Nat. 1837.
triserialis, *Sowerby*, Conch. Illustr.
Colombaria, *Recluz*, Pr. Zool. Soc. 1845.
Perottetiana, *Recluz*, Rev. Z. Cuv. 1841.
Ceylanensis, *Recluz*, Mag. Conch. 1851.
Layardi, *Reeve*, Conch. Icon.
rostrata, *Reeve*, Conch. Icon.
reticulata, *Sowerby*, Conch. Illustr.
Nerita plicata, *Linn.* Systema Naturæ.
costata, *Chemn.* Conch. Cab.
plexa, *Chemn.* Conch. Cab.[3]
Natica aurantia, *Lam.* Anim. s. Vert.
mammilla, *Linn.* Systema Naturæ.
picta, *Reeve* (as of *Recluz*), C. Icon.
arachnoidea, *Gm.* Systema Naturæ.
lineata, *Lam.* Anim. s. Vert.

---

1 M. fasciolata, *Olivier*.
2 These four species are included on the authority of Mr. Dohrn.
3 N. exuvia, *Lam.* not *Linn.*

adusta, *Ch.* C. C. f. 1926-7, & *Karsten.*[1]
pellis-tigrina, *Karsten*, Mus. Lesk.[2]
didyma, *Bolten*, Mus.[3]
Ianthina prolongata, *Blainv.* D. S. N. xxiv.
communis, *Kr.* (as of *L.* in part) S. A. M.
Sigaretus, sp.[4]
Stomatella
calliostoma, *Adams*, Thesaur. Conch.
Haliotis varia, *Linn.* Systema Naturæ.
striata, *Martini* (as of *Linn.*), C. Cab. i.
semistriata, *Reeve*, Conch. Icon.
Tornatella solidula, *Linn.* Systema Nat.
Pyramidella
maculosa, *Lam.* Anim. s. Vert.
Eulima Martini, *Adams*, Thes. Conch. ii.
Siliquaria
muricata, *Born.* Test. Mus. Cæs. Vind.
Scalaria raricostata, *Lam.* Anim. s. Vert.
Delphinula laciniata, *Lam.* Anim. s. Vert.
distorta, *Linn.* Syst. Nat.[5]
Solarium perdix, *Hinds.* Proc. Zool. Soc.
Layardi, *Adams*, Proc. Zool. Soc. 1854.[6]
Rotella vestiaria, *Linn.* Syst. Nat.
Phorus pallidulus, *Reeve*, Conch. Icon. i.
Trochus
elegantulus, *Gray*, Index Tes. Suppl.
Niloticus, *Linn.* Syst. Nat.
Monodonta labio, *Linn.* Syst. Nat.
canaliculata, *Lam.* Anim. s. Vert.
Turbo versicolor, *Gm.* Syst. Nat.
princeps, *Philippi.*[7]
Planaxis undulatus, *Lam.* Anim. s. Vert.[8]
Littorina angulifera, *Lam.* Anim. s. Vert.
melanostoma, *Gray*, Zool., *Beech.* Voy.[9]
Chemnitzia
trilineata, *Adams*, Proc. Zool. Soc. 1853.
lirata, *Adams*, Proc. Zool. Soc. 1853.
Phasianella
lineolata, *Gray*, Index Test. Suppl.
Turritella
bacillum, *Kiener*, Coquilles Vivantes.
columnaris, *Kiener*, Coquilles Vivantes.
duplicata, *Linn.* Syst. Nat.
attenuata, *Reeve*, Syst. Nat.
Cerithium fluviatile, *Potiez & Michaud*, Galerie Douai.
Layardi (Cerithidea), *Adams*, Proc. Zool. Soc. 1854.
palustre, *Linn.* Syst. Nat.
aluco, *Linn.* Syst. Nat.
asperum, *Linn.* Syst. Nat.
telescopium, *Linn.* Syst. Nat.
palustre obeliscus, *Linn.* Syst. Nat.
fasciatum, *Brug.* Encycl. Méth. Vers.
rubus, *Sower.* (as of *Mart.*), Thes. C. ii.
Sowerbyi, *Kiener*, Coquilles Vivantes (teste Sir E. Tennent).
Pleurotoma Indica, *Deshayes*, Voyage Belanger.
virgo, *Lam.* Anim. s. Vert.
Turbinella pyrum, *Linn.* Syst. Nat.
rapa, *Lam.* Anim. s. Vert. (the Chank.)
cornigera, *Lam.* Anim. s. Vert.
spirillus, *Linn.* Syst. Nat.
Cancellaria
trigonostoma, *Lam.* Anim. s. Vert.[10]
scalata, *Sowerby*, Thesaur. Conch.
articularis, *Sowerby*, Thesaur. Conch.
Littoriniformis, *Sowerby*, Thes. Conch.
contabulata, *Sowerby*, Thes. Conch.
Fasciolaria
filamentosa, *Lam.* Anim. s. Vert.
trapezium, *Linn.* Syst. Nat.
Fusus longissimus, *Lam.* Anim. s. Vert.
colus, *Linn.* Mus. Lud. Ulricæ.
toreuma, *Deshayes* (as Mur. t. *Martyn*).[11]
laticostatus, *Deshayes*, Mag. Zool. 1831.
Blosvillei, *Deshayes*, E. Méth. Vers., ii.
Pyrula rapa, *Linn.* Syst. Nat.[12]
citrina, *Lam.* Anim. s. Vert.
pugilina, *Born*, Test. Mus. Vind.[13]
ficus, *Linn.* Syst. Nat.
ficoides, *Lam.* Anim. s. Vert.
Ranella crumena, *Lam.* Anim. s. Vert.
spinosa, *Lam.* Anim. s. Vert.
rana, *Linn.* Syst. Nat.[14]
margaritula, *Deshayes*, Voy. Belanger.
Murex haustellum, *Linn.* Syst. Nat.
adustus, *Lam.* Anim. s. Vert.
microphyllus, *Lam.* Anim. s. Vert.
anguliferus, *Lam.* Anim. s. Vert.
palmarosæ, *Lam.* Anim. s. Vert.
ternispina, *Kiener* (as of *Lam.*), Coquilles Vivantes.
tenuispina, *Lam.* Anim. s. Vert.
ferrugo, *Mawe*, Index. Test. Suppl.[15]
Reeveanus, *Shuttleworth* (teste *Cuming*)
Triton anus, *Linn.* Syst. Nat.[16]
mulus, *Dillwyn*, Descript. Cat. Shells.
retusus, *Lam.* Anim. s. Vert.
pyrum, *Linn.* Syst. Nat.
clavator, *Chemn.* Conch. Cab.
Ceylonensis, *Sowerby*, Proc. Zool. Soc.
lotorium, *Lam.* (not *Linn.*) An. s. Vert.
lampas, *Linn.* Syst. Nat.
Pterocera lambis, *Linn.* Syst. Nat.
millepeda, *Linn.* Syst. Nat.
Strombus canarium, *Linn.* Syst. Nat.[17]
succinctus, *Linn.* Syst. Nat.
fasciatus, *Born*, Test. Mus. Cæs. Vind.

---

[1] Conch. Cab. f. 1926-7, and N. melanostoma, *Lam.* in part.
[2] Chemn. Conch. Cab. 1892-3.
[3] N. glaucina, *Lam.* not *Linn.*
[4] A species (possibly Javanicus) is known to have been collected. I have not seen it.
[5] Not of *Lamarck.* D. atrata, *Reeve.*
[6] Philippia L.
[7] Zeit. Mal. 1846 for T. argyrostoma, *Lam* not *Linn.*
[8] Buccinum pyramidatum, *Gm.* in part: B. sulcatum, var. C. of *Brug.*
[9] Teste Cuming.
[10] As Delphinulat.
[11] Ed. *Lam.* Anim. s. Vert.
[12] P. papyracea, *Lam.* In mixed collections I have seen the Chinese P. bezoar of *Lamarck* as from Ceylon.
[13] P. vespertilio, *Gm.*
[14] R. albivaricosa, *Reeve.*
[15] M. anguliferus var. *Lam.*
[16] T. cynocephalus of *Lamarck* is also met with in Ceylon collections.
[17] S. incisus of the Index Testaceologicus (urceus, var. *Sow.* Thesaur.) is found in mixed Ceylon collections.

Sibbaldii, *Sowerby*, Thesaur. Conch. t.
lentiginosus, *Linn.* Syst. Nat.
marginatus, *Linn.* Syst. Nat.
Lamarckii, *Sowerby*, Thesaur. Conch.
Cassis glauca, *Linn.* Syst. Nat.[1]
canaliculata, *Lam.* Anim. s. Vert.
Zeylanica, *Lam.* Anim. s. Vert.
areola, *Linn.* Syst. Nat.
Ricinula albolabris, *Blainv.* Nouv. Ann. Mus. H. N. i.[2]
horrida, *Lam.* Anim. s. Vert.
morus, *Lam.* Anim. s. Vert.
Purpura fiscella, *Chemn.* Conch. Cab.
Persica, *Linn.* Syst. Nat.
hystrix. *Lam.* (not *Linn.*) An. s. Vert.
granatina, *Deshayes*, Voy. Belanger.
mancinella, *Lam.* (as of *Linn.*) An. s. V.
bufo, *Lam.* Anim. s. Vert.
carinifera, *Lam.* Anim. s. Vert.
Harpa conoidalis, *Lam.* Anim, s. Vert.
minor, *Lam.* Anim. s. Vert.
Dolium pomum, *Linn.* Syst. Nat.
olearium, *Linn.* Syst. Nat.
perdix, *Linn.* Syst. Nat.
maculatum, *Lam.* Anim. s. Vert.
Nassa ornata, *Kiener*, Coq. Vivantes.[3]
verrucosa, *Brug.* Encycl. Méth. Vers.
crenulata, *Brug.* Encycl. Méth. Vers.
olivacea, *Brug.* Encycl. Méth. Vers.
glans, *Linn.* Syst. Nat.
arcularia, *Linn.* Syst. Nat.
papillosa, *Linn.* Syst. Nat.
Phos virgatus, *Hinds*, Zool. Sul. Moll.
retecosus, *Hinds*, Zool. Sulphur, Moll.
senticosus, *Linn.* Syst. Nat.
Buccinum melanostoma, *Sowerby*, App. to Tankerv. Cat.
erythrostoma, *Reeve*, Conch. Icon.
Proteus, *Reeve*, Conch. Icon.
rubiginosum, *Reeve*, Conch. Icon.
Eburna spirata, *Linn.* Syst. Nat.[4]
canaliculata, *Schumacher*, S. A. s. V.[5]
Ceylanica, *Bruguiere*, En. Méth. Vers.
Bullia vittata, *Linn.* Syst. Nat.
lineolata, *Sowerby*, Tankerv. Cat.[6]
Melanoides, *Deshayes*, Voy. Belan.
Terebra chlorata, *Lam.* Anim. s. Vert.
muscaria, *Lam.* Anim. s. Vert.
lævigata, *Gray*, Proc. Zool. Soc. 1834.
maculata, *Linn.* Syst. Nat.
subulata, *Linn.* Syst. Nat.
concinna, *Deshayes*, ed. *Lam.* A. s.V.
myurus, *Lam.* Anim. s. Vert.
tigrina, *Gm.* Syst. Nat.
cerithina, *Lam.* Anim. s. Vert.
Columbella flavida, *Lam.* Anim. s. Vert.
fulgurans, *Lam.* Anim. s. Vert.
mendicaria, *Linn.* Syst. Nat.
scripta, *Lam.* Anim. s. Vert. (Teste *Jay*).
Mitra
episcopalis, *Dillwyn*, Des. Cat. Shells.
cardinalis, *Lam.* Anim. s. Vert.
crebrilirata, *Reeve*, Conch. Icon.
punctostriata, *Adams*, Proc. Zool. So. 1854.
insculpta, *Adams*, Proc. Zool. Soc. 1854.
Layardi, *Adams*, Proc. Zool. Soc. 1854.[7]
Voluta vexillum, *Chemn.* Conch. Cab.
Lapponica, *Linn.* Syst. Nat.
Melo Indicus, *Gm.* Syst. Nat.
Marginella Sarda, *Kiener*, Coq. Vivantes.
Ovulum ovum, *Linn.* Syst. Nat.
verrucosum, *Linn.* Syst. Nat.
pudicum, *Adams*, Proc. Zool. Soc. 1854.
Cypræa Argus, *Linn.* Syst. Nat.
Arabica, *Linn.* Syst. Nat.
Mauritiana, *Linn.* Syst. Nat.
hirundo, *Linn.* Syst. Nat.
Lynx, *Linn.* Syst. Nat.
asellus, *Linn.* Syst. Nat.
erosa, *Linn.* Syst. Nat.
vitellus, *Linn.* Syst. Nat.
stolida, *Linn.* Syst. Nat.
mappa, *Linn.* Syst. Nat.
helvola, *Linn.* Syst. Nat.
errones, *Linn.* Syst. Nat.
cribraria, *Linn.* Syst. Nat.
globulus, *Linn.* Syst. Nat.
clandestina, *Linn.* Syst. Nat.
ocellata, *Linn.* Syst. Nat.
caurica, *Linn.* Syst. Nat.
tabescens, *Soland.* in Dillwyn Des. C. Sh.
gangrenosa, *Soland.* in Dillw. D. C. Sh.
interrupta, *Gray*, Zool. Journ. i.
lentiginosa, *Gray*, Zool. Journ. i.
pyriformis, *Gray*, Zool. Journ. i.
nivosa, *Broderip*, Zool. Journ. iii.
poraria, *Linn.* Syst. Nat.
testudinaria, *Linn.* Syst. Nat.
Terebellum
subulatum, *Lam.* Anim. s. Vert.
Ancillaria glabrata, *Linn.* Syst. Nat.
candida, *Lam.* Anim. s. Vert.
Oliva Maura, *Lam.* Anim. s. Vert.
erythrostoma, *Lam.* Anim. s. Vert.
gibbosa, *Born*, Test. Mus. Cæs.[8]
nebulosa, *Lam.* Anim. s. Vert.
Macleayana, *Duclos*, Monogr. of Oliva.
episcopalis, *Lam.* Anim. s. Vert.
elegans, *Lam.* Anim. s. Vert.
ispidula, *Linn.* Syst. Nat. (partly).[9]
Zeilanica, *Lam.* Anim. s. Vert.
undata, *Lam.* Anim. s. Vert.
irisans, *Lam.* Anim. s. Vert. (teste *Duclos*).
Conus miles, *Linn.* Syst. Nat.
generalis, *Linn.* Syst. Nat.
betulinus, *Linn.* Syst. Nat.
stercus-muscarum, *Linn.* Syst. Nat.
Hebræus, *Linn.* Syst. Nat.
virgo, *Linn.* Syst. Nat.
geographicus, *Linn.* Syst. Nat.
aulicus, *Linn.* Syst. Nat.
figulinus, *Linn.* Syst. Nat.
striatus, *Linn.* Syst. Nat.
senator, *Linn.* Syst. Nat.[10]
literatus, *Linn.* Syst. Nat.

---

1 C. plicaria of *Lamarck*, and C. coronulata of *Sowerby*, are also said to be found in Ceylon.

2 As Purpura.

3 N. suturalis, *Reeve* (as of *Lam.*), is met with in mixed Ceylon collections.

4 E. areolata, *Lam.*

5 E. spirata, *Lam.* not *Linn.*

6 B. Belangeri, *Kiener.*

7 As Turricula L.

8 O. utriculus, *Dillwyn.*

9 C. planorbis, *Born*; C. vulpinus, *Lam.*

10 Conus ermineus, *Born*, in part.

imperialis, *Linn.* Syst. Nat.
textile, *Linn.* Syst. Nat.
terebra, *Born*, Test. Must. Cæs. Vind.
tessellatus, *Born*, Test. Mus. Cæs. Vind.
augur, *Bruguiere*, Encycl. Méth. Vers.
obesus, *Bruguiere*, Encycl. Méth. Vers.
araneosus, *Brug.* Encycl. Méth. Vers.
gubernator, *Brug.* Encycl. Méth. Vers.
monile, *Brug.* Encycl. Méth. Vers.
nimbosus, *Brug.* Encycl. Méth. Vers.
eburneus, *Brug.* Encycl. Méth. Vers.
vitulinus, *Brug.* Encycl. Méth. Vers.
quercinus, *Brug.* Encycl. Méth. Vers.
lividus, *Brug.* Encycl. Méth. Vers.
Omaria, *Brug.* Encycl. Méth. Vers.
Maldivus, *Brug.* Encycl. Méth. Vers.
nocturnus, *Brug.* Encycl. Méth. Vers.
Ceylonensis, *Brug.* Encycl. Méth. Vers.
arenatus, *Brug.* Encycl. Méth. Vers.
Nicobaricus, *Brug.* Encycl. Méth. Vers.
glans, *Brug.* Encycl. Méth. Vers.
Amadis, *Chemn.* Conch. Cab.
punctatus, *Chemn.* Conch. Cab.
minimus, *Reeve* (as of *Linn.*), C. Icon.
terminus, *Lam.* Anim. s. Vert.
lineatus, *Chemn.* Conch. Cab.
episcopus, *Brug.* Encycl. Méth. Vers.
verriculum, *Reeve*, Conch. Cab.
zonatus, *Brug.* Encycl. Méth. Vers.
rattus, *Brug.* En. Mth. V. (teste *Chemn.*)
pertusus, *Brug.* Encycl. Méth. Vers.
Nussatella, *Linn.* Syst. Nat.
lithoglyphus, *Brug.* En. Méth. Vers.[4]
tulipa, *Linn.* Syst. Nat.
Ammiralis, var. *Linn.* teste *Brug.*
Spirula Peronii, *Lam.* Anim. s. Vert.
Sepia Hieredda, *Rang.* M. Z. ser. i. p. 100.
Sepioteuthis, *Sp.*
Loligo, *Sp.*

A conclusion not unworthy of observation may be deduced from this catalogue; namely, that Ceylon was the unknown, and hence unacknowledged, source of almost every extra-European shell which has been described by Linnæus without a recorded habitat. This fact gives to Ceylon specimens an importance which can only be appreciated by collectors and the students of Mollusca.

## 2. RADIATA.

The eastern seas are profusely stocked with radiated animals, but it is to be regretted that they have as yet received but little attention from English naturalists. Recently, however, Dr. Kelaart has devoted himself to the investigation of some of the Singhalese species, and has published his discoveries in the Journal of the Ceylon Branch of the Asiatic Society for 1856–8. Our information respecting the radiata on the confines of the island is, therefore, very scanty; with the exception of the genera[1] examined by him. Hence the notice of this extensive class of animals must be limited to indicating

[1] Actinia, 9 sp.; Anthea, 4 sp.; Actinodendron, 3 sp.; Dioscosoma, 1 sp.; Peechea, 1 sp.; Zoanthura, 1 sp.

a few of those which exhibit striking peculiarities, or which admit of the most common observation.

*Star Fish.*—Very large species of *Ophiuridæ* are to be met with at Trincomalie, crawling busily about, and insinuating their long serpentine arms into the irregularities and perforations in the rocks. To these they attach themselves with such a firm grasp, especially when they perceive that they have attracted attention, that it is almost impossible to procure unmutilated specimens without previously depriving them of life, or at least modifying their muscular tenacity. The upper surface is of a dark purple colour, and coarsely spined; the arms of the largest specimens are more than a foot in length, and very fragile.

The star fishes, with immovable rays [1], are by no means rare; many kinds are brought up in the nets, or may be extracted from the stomachs of the larger market fish. One very large species [2], figured by Joinville in the manuscript volume in the library at the India House, is not uncommon; it has thick arms, from which and the disc numerous large fleshy cirrhi of a bright crimson colour project downwards, giving the creature a remarkable aspect. No description of it, so far as I am aware, has appeared in any systematic work on zoology.

*Sea Slugs.*—There are a few species of *Holothuriæ*, of which the trepang is the best known example. It is largely collected in the Gulf of Mânaar, and dried in the sun to prepare it for export to China. A good description and figures of its varieties are still desiderata.

*Parasitic Worms.*—Of these entozoa, the *Filaria medinensis*, or Guinea-worm, which burrows in the

[1] *Asterias*, Linn.

[2] *Pentaceros?*

cellular tissue under the skin, is well known in the north of the island, but rarely found in the damper districts of the south and west. In Ceylon, as elsewhere, the natives attribute its occurrence to drinking the waters of particular wells; but this belief is inconsistent with the fact that its lodgment in the human body is almost always effected just above the ankle. This shows that the minute parasites are transferred to the skin of the leg from the moist vegetation bordering the footpaths leading to wells. At this period the creatures are very small, and the process of insinuation is painless and imperceptible. It is only when they attain to considerable size, a foot or more in length, that the operation of extracting them is resorted to, when exercise may have given rise to inconvenience and inflammation.

These pests in all probability received their popular name of *Guinea-worms*, from the narrative of Bruno or Braun, a citizen and surgeon of Basle, who about the year 1611 made several voyages to that part of the African coast, and on his return published, amongst other things, an account of the local diseases.[1] But Linschoten, the Dutch navigator, had previously observed the same worms at Ormus in 1584, and they are thus described, together with the method of removing them, in the English version of his voyage.

"There is in Ormus a sickenesse or co amon plague of wormes, which growe in their legges, it is thought that they proceede of the water that they drink. These wormes are like unto lute strings, and about two or three fadomes longe, which they must plucke out and winde them aboute a straw or a feather, everie day some

[1] In DE BRY'S *Collect.*, vol. i. p. 49.

part thereof, so longe as they feele them creepe; and when they hold still, letting it rest in that sort till the next daye, they bind it fast and annoynt the hole, and the swelling from whence it commeth foorth, with fresh butter, and so in ten or twelve dayes, they winde them out without any let, in the meanetime they must sit still with their legges, for if it should breake, they should not without great paine get it out of their legge, as I have seen some men doe."[1]

The worm is of a whitish colour, sometimes inclining to brown. Its thickness is from a half to two-thirds of a line, and its length has sometimes reached to ten or twelve feet. Small specimens have been found beneath the tunica conjunctiva of the eye; and one species of the same genus of *Nematoidea* infests the cavity of the eye itself.[2]

*Planaria.*—In the journal already mentioned, Dr. Kelaart has given descriptions of fifteen species of planaria, and four of a new genus, instituted by him for the reception of those differing from the normal kinds by some peculiarities which they exhibit in common. At Point Pedro, Mr. Edgar Layard met with one on the bark of trees, after heavy rain, which would appear to belong to the subgenus *geoplana.*[3]

*Acalephæ.*—Acalephæ[4] are plentiful, so much so, indeed, that they occasionally tempt the larger cetacea into the Gulf of Manaar. In the calmer months of the year, when the sea is glassy, and for hours together

[1] JOHN HUIGHEN VAN LINSCHOTEN *his Discours of Voyages into the Easte and West Indies.* London, 1599, p. 16.

[2] OWEN'S *Lectures on the Invertebrata*, p. 96.

[3] "A curious species, which is of a light brown above, white underneath; very broad and thin, and has a peculiarly shaped tail, half-moon-shaped in fact, like a grocer's cheese knife."

[4] Jelly-fish.

undisturbed by a ripple, the minute descriptions are rendered perceptible by their beautiful prismatic tinting. So great is their transparency that they are only to be distinguished from the water by the return to the eye of the reflected light that glances from their delicate and polished surfaces. Less frequently they are traced by the faint hues of their tiny peduncles, arms, or tentaculæ; and it has been well observed that they often give the seas in which they abound the appearance of being crowded with flakes of half-melted snow. The larger kinds, when undisturbed in their native haunts,

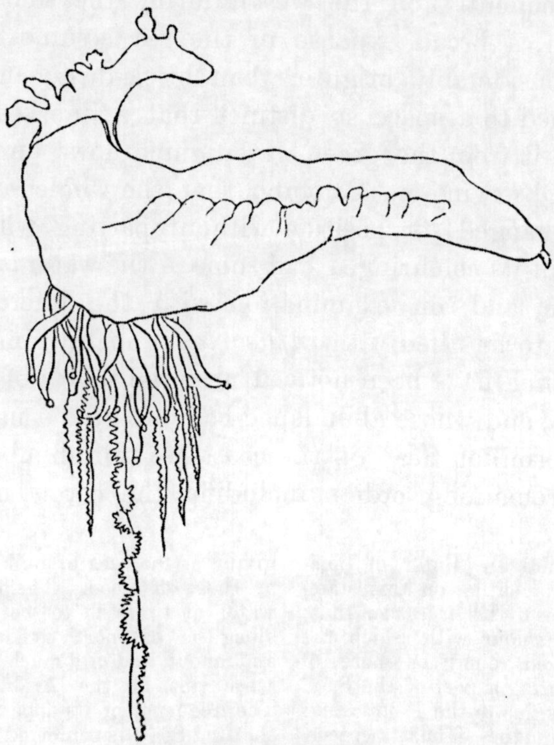

PHYSALUS URTICULUS.

attain to considerable size. A faintly blue medusa,

nearly a foot across, may be seen in the Gulf of Manaar, where, no doubt, others of still larger growth are to be found.

Occasionally after storms, the beach at Colombo is strewn with the thin transparent globes of the "Portuguese Man of War," *Physalus urticulus*, which are piled upon the lines left by the waves, like globules of glass delicately tinted with purple and blue. They sting, as their trivial name indicates, like a nettle when incautiously touched.

*Red infusoria.*—On both sides of the island (but most frequently on the west), during the south-west monsoon, a broad expanse of the sea assumes a red tinge, considerably brighter than brick-dust; and this is confined to a space so distinct that a line seems to separate it from the green water which flows on either side. Observing at Colombo that the whole area so tinged changed its position without parting with any portion of its colouring, I had some of the water brought on shore, and, on examination with the microscope, found it to be filled with *infusoria*, probably similar to those which have been noticed near the shores of South America, and whose abundance has imparted a name to the "Vermilion Sea" off the coast of California.[1]

The remaining orders, including the corals, madre-

[1] The late Dr. BUIST, of Bombay, in commenting on this statement, writes to the *Athenæum* that: "The red colour with which the sea is tinged, round the shores of Ceylon, during a part of the S.W. monsoon is due to the *Proto-coccus nivalis*, or the Himatta-coccus, which presents different colours at different periods of the year—giving us the seas of milk as well as those of blood. The coloured water at times is to be seen all along the coast north to Kurrachee, and far out, and of a much more intense tint in the Arabian Sea. The frequency of its appearance in the Red Sea has conferred on it its name."

pores, and other polypi, have yet to find a naturalist to undertake their investigation, but in all probability the new species are not very numerous.

---

## NOTE.

## TRITONIA ARBORESCENS.

THE following is the letter of Dr. Grant, referred to at page 385:—

Sir,—I have perused, with much interest, your remarkable communication received yesterday, respecting the musical sounds which you heard proceeding from under water, on the east coast of Ceylon. I cannot parallel the phenomenon you witnessed at Batticaloa, as produced by marine animals, with anything with which my past experience has made me acquainted in marine zoology. Excepting the faint clink of the *Tritonia arborescens*, repeated only once every minute or two, and apparently produced by the mouth armed with two dense horny laminæ, I am not aware of any sounds produced in the sea by branchiated invertebrata. It is to be regretted that in the memorandum you have not mentioned your observations on the living specimens brought you by the sailors as the animals which produced the sounds. Your authentication of the hitherto unknown fact, would probably lead to the discovery of the same phenomenon in other common accessible paludinæ, and other allied branchiated animals, and to the solution of a problem, which is still to me a mystery, even regarding the *tritonia.*

My two living *tritonia*, contained in a large clear colourless glass cylinder, filled with pure sea water, and placed on the central table of the Wernerian Natural History Society of Edinburgh, around which many members were sitting, continued to clink audibly within the distance of twelve feet during the whole meeting. These small animals were individually not half the size of the last joint of my little finger. What effect the mellow sounds of millions of these, covering the shallow bottom of a tranquil estuary, in the silence of night, might produce, I can scarcely conjecture.

In the absence of your authentication, and of all geological explanation of the continuous sounds, and of all source of fallacy from the hum and buzz of living creatures in the air or on the land, or swimming on the waters, I must say that I should be inclined to seek for the source of sounds so audible as those you describe rather among the pulmonated vertebrata, which swarm in the depths of these seas—as fishes, serpents (of which my friend Dr. Cantor has described about twelve species he found in the Bay of Bengal), turtles, palmated birds, pinnipedous and cetaceous mammalia, &c.

The publication of your memorandum in its present form, though not quite satisfactory, will, I think, be eminently calculated to excite useful inquiry into a neglected and curious part of the economy of nature.

I remain, Sir,

Yours most respectfully,

ROBERT E. GRANT.

*Sir J. Emerson Tennent, &c. &c.*

# CHAP. XII.

## INSECTS.

Owing to the favourable combination of heat, moisture, and vegetation, the myriads of insects in Ceylon form one of the characteristic features of the island. In the solitude of the forests there is a perpetual music from their soothing and melodious hum, which frequently swells to a startling sound as the cicada trills his sonorous drum on the sunny bark of some tall tree. At morning the dew hangs in diamond drops on the threads and gossamer which the spiders suspend across every pathway; and above the pool dragon-flies, of more than metallic lustre, flash in the early sunbeams. The earth teems with countless ants, which emerge from beneath its surface, or make their devious highways to ascend to their nests in the trees. Lustrous beetles, with their golden elytra, bask on the leaves, whilst minuter species dash through the air in circles, which the ear can follow by the booming of their tiny wings. Butterflies of large size and gorgeous colouring, flutter over the endless expanse of flowers, and at times the extraordinary sight presents itself of flights of these delicate creatures, generally of a white or pale yellow hue, apparently miles in breadth, and of such prodigious extension as to occupy hours, and even days, uninterruptedly in their passage — whence coming no one knows; whither going no one can tell.[1] As day declines, the moths issue from their retreats, the crickets add their shrill voices to swell the din; and when darkness descends, the eye is charmed with the millions of emerald lamps lighted up by the fire-flies amidst the surrounding gloom.

As yet no attempt has been made to describe the insects of Ceylon systematically, much less to enumerate the prodigous number of species that abound in every locality. Occasional observers have, from time to time, contributed notices of particular families to the Scientific Associations of Europe, but their papers remain undigested, and the time has not yet arrived for the preparation of an Entomology of the island.

What DARWIN remarks of the Coleoptera of Brazil is nearly as applicable to the same order of insects in Ceylon: "The number of minute and obscurely coloured beetles is exceedingly great; the cabinets of Europe can as yet, with partial exceptions, boast only of the larger species from tropical climates, and it is sufficient to disturb the composure of an entomologist to look forward to the future dimensions of a catalogue with any pretensions to completeness."[2] M. Nietner, a German entomologist, who has spent some years in Ceylon, has recently published, in one of the local

[1] The butterflies I have seen in these wonderful migrations in Ceylon were mostly *Callidryas Hilariæ*, *C. Alcmeone*, and *C. Pyranthe*, with straggling individuals of the genus *Euplœa*, *E. Coras*, and *E. Prothoe*. Their passage took place in April and May, generally in a north-easterly direction. The natives have a superstitious belief that their flight is ultimately directed to Adam's Peak, and that their pilgrimage ends on reaching the sacred mountain. A friend of mine travelling from Kandy to Kornegalle, drove for nine miles through a cloud of white butterflies, which were passing across the road by which he went.

[2] *Nat. Journal*, p. 39.

periodicals, a series of papers on the Coleoptera of the island, in which every species introduced is stated to be previously undescribed.[1]

COLEOPTERA.—*Buprestidæ; Golden Beetles.*—In the morning the herbaceous plants, especially on the eastern side of the island, are studded with these gorgeous beetles, whose golden wing-cases[2] are used to enrich the embroidery of the Indian zenana, whilst the lustrous joints of the legs are strung on silken threads, and form necklaces and bracelets of singular brilliancy.

These exquisite colours are not confined to one order, and some of the Elateridæ[3] and Lamellicorns exhibit hues of green and blue, that rival the deepest tints of the emerald and sapphire.

*Scavenger Beetles.*—Scavenger beetles[4] are to be seen wherever the presence of putrescent and offensive matter affords opportunity for the display of their repulsive but most curious instincts; fastening on it with eagerness, severing it into lumps proportionate to their strength, and rolling it along in search of some place sufficiently soft in which to bury it, after having deposited their eggs in the centre. I had frequent opportunities, especially in traversing the sandy jungles in the level plains to the north of the island, of observing the unfailing appearance of these creatures instantly on the dropping of horse dung, or any other substance

[1] Republished in the *Ann. Nat. Hist.*

[2] *Sternocera Chrysis; S. sternicornis.*

[3] Of the family of *Elateridæ*, one of the finest is a Singhalese species, the *Campsosternus Templetonii*, of an exquisite golden green colour, with blue reflections (described and figured by Mr. WESTWOOD in his *Cabinet of Oriental Entomology*, pl. 35, f. 1). In the same work is figured another species of large size, also from Ceylon, this is the *Alaus sordidus.*—WESTWOOD, l. c. pl. 35, f. 9.

[4] *Ateuchus sacer; Copris sagax; C. capucinus*, &c. &c.

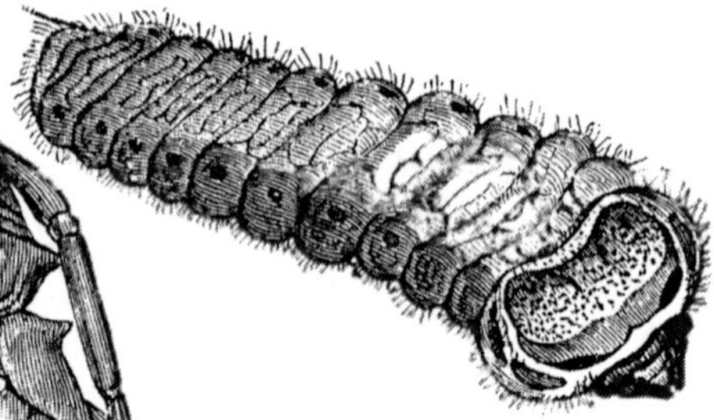

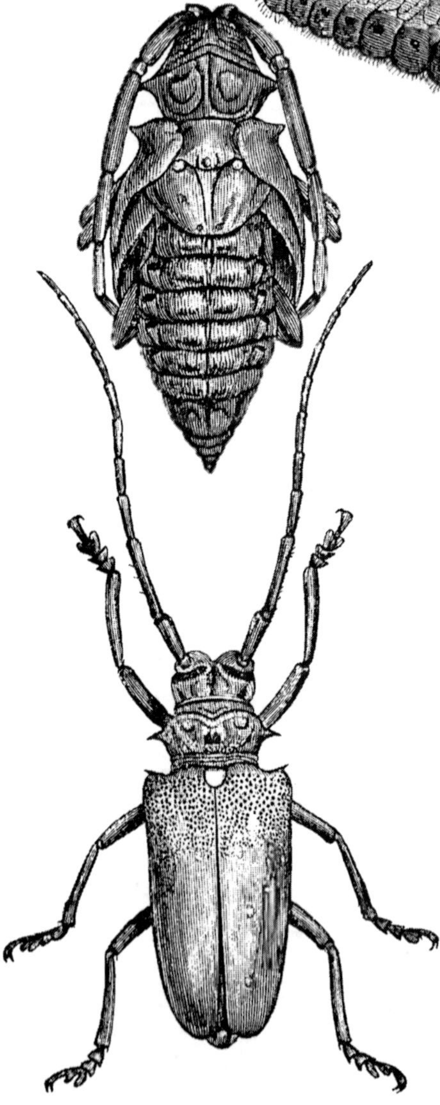

LONGICORN BEETLE (BATOCERA RUBUS).

suitable for their purpose; although not one was visible but a moment before. Their approach on the wing is announced by a loud and joyous booming sound, as they dash in rapid circles in search of the desired object, led by their sense of smell, and evidently little assisted by the eye in shaping their course towards it. In these excursions they exhibit a strength of wing and sustained power of flight, such as is possessed by no other class of beetles with which I am acquainted, but which is obviously indispensable for the due performance of the useful functions they discharge.

*The Coco-nut Beetle.*—In the luxuriant forests of Ceylon the extensive family of *Longicorns*[1] and *Passalidæ* live in destructive abundance. To the coco-nut planters the ravages committed by beetles are painfully familiar.[2] The larva of one species *of Dynastidæ*, the *Oryctes rhinoceros*, called by the Singhalese "*Gascooroominiya*," makes its way into the younger trees, descending from the top, and after perforating them in all directions, forms a cocoon of the gnawed wood and sawdust, in which it reposes during its sleep as a pupa, till the arrival of the period when it emerges as a perfect beetle. Notwithstanding the repulsive aspect of the large pulpy larvæ of these beetles, they are esteemed a luxury by the Malabar coolies, who so far avail themselves of the privilege accorded by the Levitical law, which permitted the Hebrews to eat "the beetle after his kind."[3]

Amongst the superstitions of the Singhalese arising out of their belief in demonology, one remarkable one is connected with the appearance of a beetle when observed on the floor of a dwelling-house after nightfall. The popular belief is that in obedience to a certain form of incantation (called *cooroominiya-pilli*) a demon

[1] The engraving on the preceding page represents in its various transformations one of the most familiar and graceful of the longicorn beetles of Ceylon, the *Batocera rubus*.

[2] There is a paper in the *Journ. of the Asiat. Society of Ceylon*, May, 1845, by Mr. CAPPER, on the ravages perpetrated by these beetles. The writer had recently passed through several coco-nut plantations, "varying in extent from 20 to 150 acres, and about two to three years old; and in these he did not discover a single young tree untouched by the cooroominiya."—P. 49.

[3] Leviticus, xi. 22.

in the shape of a beetle is sent to the house of some person or family whose destruction it is intended to compass, and who presently falls sick and dies. The only means of averting this catastrophe is, that some one, himself an adept in necromancy, should perform a counter-charm, the effect of which is to send back the disguised beetle to destroy his original employer; for in such a conjuncture the death of one or the other is essential to appease the demon whose intervention has been invoked. Hence the discomfort of a Singhalese on finding a beetle in his house after sunset, and his anxiety to expel but not to kill it.

*Tortoise Beetles.*—There is one family of insects, the members of which cannot fail to strike the traveller by their singular beauty, the *Cassididæ* or tortoise beetles, in which the outer shell overlaps the body, and the limbs are susceptible of being drawn entirely within it. The rim is frequently of a different tint from the centre, and one species which I have seen is quite startling from the brilliancy of its colouring, which gives it the appearance of a ruby enclosed in a frame of pearl; but this wonderful effect disappears immediately on the death of the insect.

ORTHOPTERA. *Leaf-insects.*—But in relation to the insects of Ceylon the admiration of their colours is still less exciting than the astonishment created by the forms in which some of the families present themselves; especially the "soothsayers" (*Mantidæ*) and "walking leaves." The latter[1], exhibiting the most cunning of all nature's devices for the preservation of her creatures, are found in the jungle in all varieties of hues, from the pale yellow of an opening bud to the rich green of

[1] *Phyllium siccifolium.*

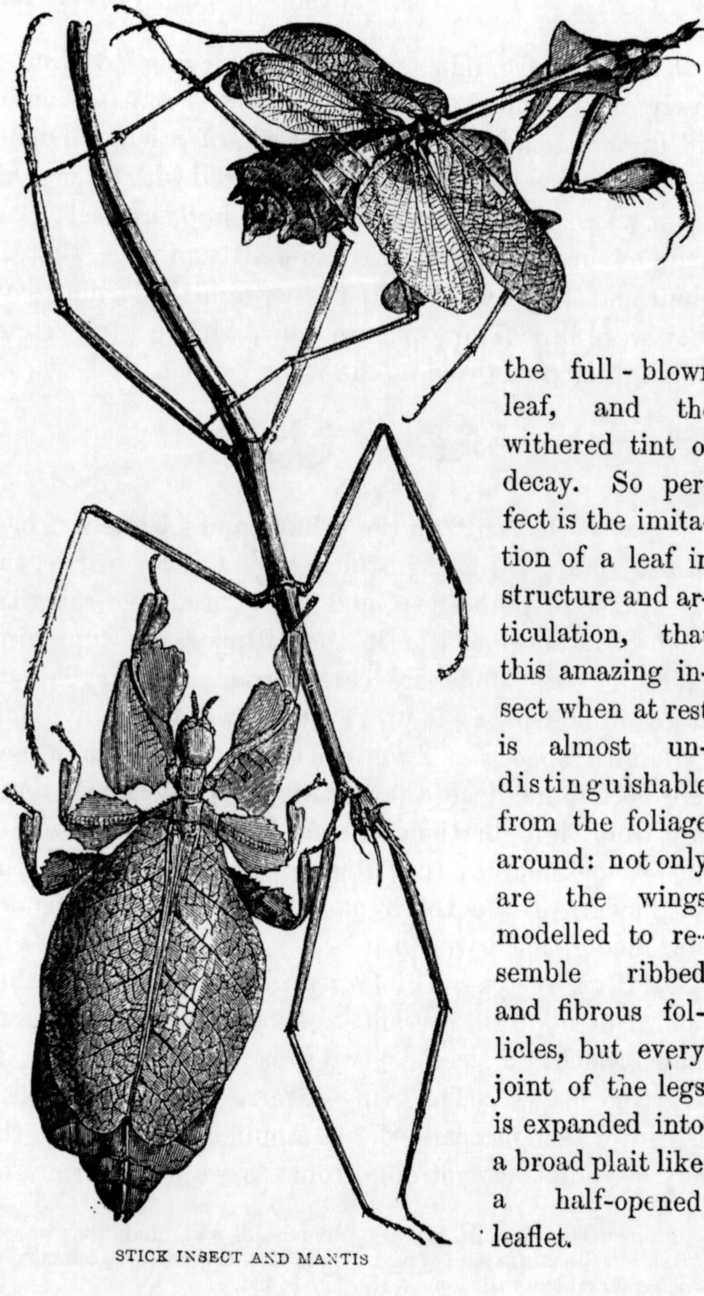

STICK INSECT AND MANTIS

the full-blown leaf, and the withered tint of decay. So perfect is the imitation of a leaf in structure and articulation, that this amazing insect when at rest is almost undistinguishable from the foliage around: not only are the wings modelled to resemble ribbed and fibrous follicles, but every joint of the legs is expanded into a broad plait like a half-opened leaflet.

It rests on its abdomen, the legs serving to drag it slowly along, and thus the flatness of its attitude serves still further to add to the appearance of a leaf. One of the most marvellous incidents connected with its organisation was exhibited by one which I kept under a glass shade on my table, it laid a quantity of eggs, that, in colour and shape, were not to be distinguished from *seeds*. They were brown and pentangular, with a short stem, and slightly punctured at the intersections.

EGGS OF THE LEAF-INSECT.

The "soothsayer," on the other hand (*Mantis superstitiosa*, Fab.[1]), little justifies by its propensities the appearance of gentleness, and the attitudes of sanctity, which have obtained for it the title of the "praying mantis." Its habits are carnivorous, and degenerate into cannibalism, as it preys on the weaker individuals of its own species. Two which I enclosed in a box were both found dead a few hours after, literally severed limb from limb in their encounter. The formation of the foreleg enables the tibia to be so closed on the sharp edge of the thigh as to amputate any slender substance grasped within it.

*The Stick-insect.*—The *Phasmidæ* or spectres, another class of orthoptera, present as close a resemblance to small branches or leafless twigs as their congeners do to green leaves. The wing-covers, where they exist, instead of being expanded, are applied so closely to the body as to detract nothing from its rounded form, and

[1] *M. aridifolia* and *M. extensicollis*, as well as *Empusa gongylodes*, remarkable for the long leaf-like head, and dilatations on the posterior thighs, are common in the island.

hence the name which they have acquired of "*walking-sticks.*" Like the *Phyllium*, the *Phasma* lives exclusively on vegetables, and some attain the length of several inches.

Of all the other tribes of the *Orthoptera* Ceylon possesses many representatives; in swarms of cockroaches, grasshoppers, locusts, and crickets.

NEUROPTERA. *Dragon-flies.*—Of the *Neuroptera*, some of the dragon-flies are pre-eminently beautiful; one species, with rich brown-coloured spots upon its gauzy wings, is to be seen near every pool.[1] Another[2], which dances above the mountain streams in Oovah, and amongst the hills descending towards Kandy, gleams in the sun as if each of its green enamelled wings had been sliced from an emerald.

*The Ant-lion.*—Of the ant-lion, whose larvæ have earned a bad renown from their predaceous ingenuity, Ceylon has, at least, four species, which seem peculiar to the island.[3] This singular creature, preparatory to its pupal transformation, contrives to excavate a conical pitfall in the dust to the depth of about an inch, in the bottom of which it conceals itself, exposing only its open mandibles above the surface; and here every ant and soft-bodied insect which curiosity tempts to descend, or accident may precipitate into the trap, is ruthlessly seized and devoured by its ambushed inhabitant.

*The White Ant.*—But of the insects of this order the most noted are the *white ants* or termites (which are ants only by a misnomer). They are, unfortunately, at once ubiquitous and innumerable in every spot where

[1] *Libellula pulchella.*

[2] *Euphœa splendens.*

[3] *Palpares contrarius*, Walker; *Myrmeleon gravis*, Walker; *M. dirus*, Walker; *M. barbarus*, Walker.

the climate is not too chilly, or the soil too sandy, for them to construct their domed edifices.

These they raise from a considerable depth under ground, excavating the clay with their mandibles, and moistening it with tenacious saliva[1] until it assume the appearance, and almost the consistency, of sandstone. So delicate is the trituration to which they subject this material, that the goldsmiths of Ceylon employ the powdered clay of the ant hills in preference to all other substances in the preparation of crucibles and moulds for their finer castings; and KNOX says, "the people use this finer clay to make their earthen gods of, it is so pure and fine."[2] These structures the termites erect with such perseverance and durability that they frequently rise to the height of ten or twelve feet from

[1] It becomes an interesting question whence the termites derive the large supplies of moisture with which they not only temper the clay for the construction of their long covered-ways above ground, but for keeping their passages uniformly damp and cool below the surface. Yet their habits in this particular are unvarying, in the seasons of droughts as well as after rain; in the driest and least promising positions, in situations inaccessible to drainage from above, and cut off by rocks and impervious strata from springs from below. Dr. Livingstone, struck with this phenomenon in Southern Africa, asks: "Can the white ants possess the power of combining the oxygen and hydrogen of their vegetable food by vital force so as to form water?"—*Travels*, p. 22. And he describes at Angola, an insect* resembling the *Aphrophora spumaria;* seven or eight individuals of which distil several pints of water every night.—P. 414. It is highly probable that the termites are endowed with some such faculty: nor is it more remarkable that an insect should combine the gases of its food to produce water, than that a fish thould decompose water in order to provide itself with gas. FOURCROIX found the contents of the air-bladder in a carp to be pure nitrogen.—*Yarrell*, vol. i. p. 42. And the aquatic larva of the dragon-fly extracts air for its respiration from the water in which it is submerged. A similar mystery pervades the inquiry whence plants under peculiar circumstances derive the water essential to vegetation.

[2] KNOX's *Ceylon*, Part I. ch. vi. p. 24.

* *A. goudotti?* Bennett.

the ground, with a corresponding diameter. They are so firm in their texture that the weight of a horse makes no apparent indentation on their solidity; and even the intense rains of the monsoon, which no cement or mortar can long resist, fail to penetrate the surface or substance of an ant hill.[1] In their earlier stages the termites proceed with such energetic rapidity, that I have seen a pinnacle of moist clay, six inches in height and twice as large in diameter, constructed underneath a table between sitting down to dinner and the removal of the cloth.

As these lofty mounds of earth have all been carried up from beneath the surface, a cave of corresponding dimensions is necessarily scooped out below, and here, under the multitude of miniature cupolas and pinnacles which canopy it above, the termites hollow out the royal chamber for their queen, with spacious nurseries surrounding it on all sides; and all are connected by arched galleries, long passages, and doorways of the most intricate and elaborate construction. In the centre and underneath the spacious dome is the recess for the queen — a hideous creature, with the head and thorax of an ordinary termite, but a body swollen to a hundred

[1] Dr. HOOKER, in his *Himalayan Journal* (vol. i. p. 20) is of opinion that the nests of the termites are not independent structures, but that their nucleus is "the debris of clumps of bamboos or the trunks of large trees which these insects have destroyed." He supposes that the dead tree falls leaving the stump coated with sand, *which the action of the weather soon fashions into a cone.* But independently of the fact that the "action of the weather" produces little or no effect on the closely cemented clay of the white ants' nest, they may be daily seen constructing their edifices in the very form of a cone, which they ever after retain. Besides which, they appear in the midst of terraces and fields where no trees are to be seen; and Dr. Hooker seems to overlook the fact that the termites rarely attack a living tree; and although their nests may be built against one, it continues to flourish not the less for their presence.

times its usual and proportionate bulk, and presenting the appearance of a mass of shapeless pulp. From this great progenitrix proceed the myriads that people the subterranean hive, consisting, like the communities of the genuine ants, of labourers and soldiers, which are destined never to acquire a fuller development than that of larvæ, and the perfect insects which in due time become invested with wings and take their departing flight from the cave. But their new equipment seems only destined to facilitate their dispersion from the parent nest, which takes place at dusk; and almost as quickly as they leave it they divest themselves of their ineffectual wings, waving them impatiently and twisting them in every direction till they become detached and drop off, and the swarm, within a few hours of their emancipation, become a prey to the night-jars and bats, which are instantly attracted to them as they issue in a cloud from the ground. I am not prepared to say that the other insectivorous birds would not gladly make a meal of the termites, but, seeing that in Ceylon their numbers are chiefly kept in check by the crepuscular birds, it is observable, at least as a coincidence, that the dispersion of the swarm generally takes place at *twilight*. Those that escape the *caprimulgi* fall a prey to the crows, on the morning succeeding their flight.

The strange peculiarity of the omnivorous ravages of the white ants is that they shrink from the light; in all their expeditions for providing food they construct a covered pathway of moistened clay, and their galleries above ground extend to an incredible distance from the central nest. No timber, except ebony and ironwood, which are too hard, and those which are strongly impregnated with camphor or aromatic oils, which they dislike, presents any obstacle to their ingress. I have had a case of wine filled, in the course of two days, with almost solid clay, and only discovered the presence of the white ants by the escape from the corks. I have had a portmanteau in my tent so peopled with them in the course of a single night that the contents were found worthless in the morning. In an incredibly short time a detachment of these pests will destroy a press full of records, reducing the paper to fragments; and a shelf of books will be tunnelled into a gallery if it happen to be in their line of march. The timbers of a house when fairly attacked are eaten from within till the beams are reduced to an absolute shell, so thin that it may be punched through with the point of the finger: and even kyanized wood, unless impregnated with an extra quantity of corrosive sublimate, appears to occasion them no inconvenience. The only effectual precaution for the protection of furniture is incessant vigilance—the constant watching of every article, and its daily removal from place to place, in order to baffle their assaults.

They do not appear in the hills above the elevation of 4000 or 5000 feet. One species of white ant, the *Termes Taprobanes*, was at one time believed by Mr. Walker to be peculiar to the island, but it has recently been found in Sumatra and Borneo, and in some parts of Hindustan.

There is a species of Termes in Ceylon (*T. monoceros*), which always builds its nest in the hollow of an old tree; and, unlike the others, carries on its labours without the secrecy and protection of a covered way. A marching column of these creatures may be observed at early morning in the vicinity of their nest, returning laden with the spoils collected during their foraging excursions. These consist of comminuted vegetable matter, derived, it may be, from a thatched roof, if one happens to be within reach, or from the decaying leaves of a coco-nut. Each little worker in the column carries its tiny load in its jaws; and the number of individuals in one of these lines of march must be immense, for the column is generally about two inches in width, and very densely crowded. One was measured which had most likely been in motion for hours, moving in the direction of the nest, and was found to be upwards of sixty paces in length. If attention be directed to the mass in motion, it will be observed that flanking it on each side throughout its whole length are stationed a number of horned soldier termites, whose duty it is to protect the labourers, and to give notice of any danger threatening them. This latter duty they perform by a peculiar quivering motion of the whole body, which is rapidly communicated from one to the other for a considerable distance; a portion of the column is then thrown into confusion for a short time, but confidence soon returns, and the progress of the little creatures goes on with steadiness and order as before. The nest is of a black colour, and resembles a mass of scoriæ; the insects themselves are of a pitchy brown.[1]

HYMENOPTERA. *Mason Wasp.*—In Ceylon as in all other countries, the order of hymenopterous insects arrests us less by the beauty of their forms than the marvels of their sagacity and the achievements of their

[1] For these particulars of the *termes monoceros*, I am indebted to Mr. Thwaites, of the Roy. Botanic Garden at Kandy.

instinct. A fossorial wasp of the family of *Sphegidæ*[1], which is distinguished by its metallic lustre, enters by the open windows, and converts irritation at its movements into admiration of the graceful industry with which it stops up the keyholes and similar apertures with clay in order to build in them a cell. Into this it thrusts the pupa of some other insect, within whose body it has previously introduced its own eggs. The whole is surrounded with moistened earth, through which the young parasite, after undergoing its transformations, gnaws its way into light, to emerge as a four-winged fly.[2]

A formidable species (*Sphex ferruginea* of St. Fargeau), which is common to India and most of the eastern islands, is regarded with the utmost dread by the unclad natives, who fly precipitately on finding them-

[1] It belongs to the genus *Pelopæus*, *P. Spinolæ*, of St. Fargeau. The *Ampulex compressa*, which drags about the larvæ of cockroaches into which it has implanted its eggs, belongs to the same family.

[2] Mr. E. L. Layard has given an interesting account of this Mason wasp in the *Annals and Magazine of Nat. History* for May, 1853.

"I have frequently," he says, "selected one of these flies for observation, and have seen their labours extend over a period of a fortnight or twenty days; sometimes only half a cell was completed in a day, at others as much as two. I never saw more than twenty cells in one nest, seldom indeed that number, and whence the caterpillars were procured was always to me a mystery. I have seen thirty or forty brought in of a species which I knew to be very rare in the perfect state, and which I had sought for in vain, although I knew on what plant they fed.

"Then again how are they disabled by the wasp, and yet not injured so as to cause their immediate death? Die they all do, at least all that I have ever tried to rear, after taking them from the nest.

"The perfected fly never effects its egress from the closed aperture, through which the caterpillars were inserted, and when cells are placed end to end, as they are in many instances, the outward end of each is always selected. I cannot detect any difference in the thickness in the crust of the cell to cause this uniformity of practice. It is often as much as half an inch through, of great hardness, and as far as I can see impervious to air and light. How then does the enclosed fly always select the right end, and with what secretion is it supplied to decompose this mortar?"

selves in the vicinity[1] of its nests. These are of such ample dimensions, that when suspended from a branch, they often measure upwards of six feet in length.[2]

*Bees.*—Bees of several species and genera, some unprovided with stings, and some in size scarcely exceeding a house-fly, deposit their honey in hollow trees, or suspend their combs from a branch. The spoils of their industry form one of the chief resources of the uncivilised Veddahs, who collect the wax in the upland forests, to be bartered for arrow points and clothes in the lowlands.[3] I have never heard of an instance of persons being attacked by the bees of Ceylon, and hence the natives assert, that those most productive of honey are destitute of stings.

*The Carpenter Bee.*—The operations of one of the most interesting of the tribe, the Carpenter bee[4], I have watched with admiration from the window of the Colo-

[1] It ought to be remembered in travelling in the forests of Ceylon that sal volatile applied immediately is a specific for the sting of a wasp.

[2] At the January (1839) meeting of the Entomological Society, Mr. Whitehouse exhibited portions of a wasps' nest from Ceylon, between seven and eight feet long and two feet in diameter, and showed that the construction of the cells was perfectly analogous to those of the hive bee, and that when connected each has a tendency to assume a circular outline. In one specimen where there were three cells united the outer part was circular, whilst the portions common to the three formed straight walls. From this Singhalese nest Mr. Whitehouse demonstrated that the wasps at the commencement of their comb proceed slowly, forming the bases of several together, whereby they assume the hexagonal shape, whereas, if constructed separately, he thought each single cell would be circular. See *Proc. Ent. Soc.* vol. iii. p. 16.

[3] A gentleman connected with the department of the Surveyor-General writes to me that he measured a honey-comb which he found fastened to the overhanging branch of a small tree in the forest near Adam's Peak, and found it nine links of his chain or about six feet in length and a foot in breadth where it was attached to the branch, but tapering towards the other extremity. "It was a single comb with a layer of cells on either side, but so weighty that the branch broke by the strain."

[4] *Xylocopa tenuiscapa*, Westw.; Another species found in Ceylon is the *X. latipes*, Drury.

nial Secretary's official residence at Kandy. So soon as the day grew warm, these active creatures were at work perforating the wooden columns which supported the verandah. They poised themselves on their shining purple wings, as they made the first lodgment in the

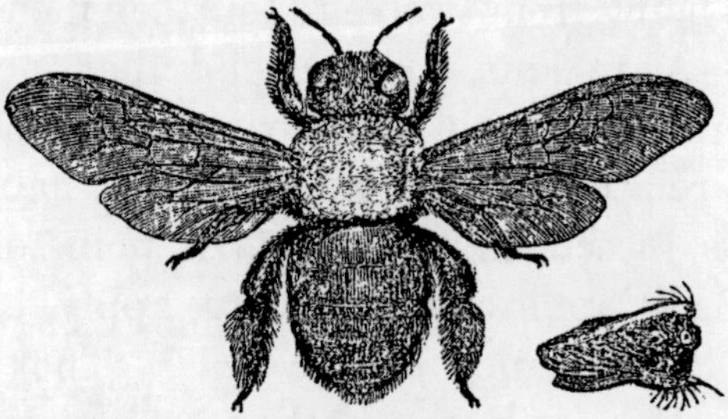

THE CARPENTER BEE.

wood, enlivening the work with an uninterrupted hum of delight, which was audible to a considerable distance. When the excavation had proceeded so far that the insect could descend into it, the music was suspended, but renewed from time to time, as the little creature came to the orifice to throw out the chips, to rest, or to enjoy the fresh air. By degrees, a mound of saw-dust was formed at the base of the pillar, consisting of particles abraded by the mandibles of the bee. These, when the hollow was completed to the depth of several inches, were partially replaced in the excavation after being agglutinated to form partitions between the eggs, as they were deposited within. The mandibles [1] of these bees are admirably formed for the purpose of working out the tunnels required, being short, stout, and usually furnished at the tip with two teeth which are rounded somewhat into the form of cheese-cutters.

[1] See figure above.

These when brought into operation cut out the wood in the same way as a carpenter's double gouge, the teeth being more or less hollowed out within. The female alone is furnished with these powerful instruments. In the males the mandibles are slender as compared with those of the females. The bores of some of these bees are described as being from twelve to fourteen inches in length.

*Ants.*—As to ants, I apprehend that, notwithstanding their numbers and familiarity, information is very imperfect relative to the varieties and habits of these marvellous insects in Ceylon.[1] In point of multitude it is scarcely an exaggeration to apply to them the figure of "the sands of the sea." They are everywhere; in the earth, in the houses, and on the trees; they are to be seen in every room and cupboard, and almost on every plant in the jungle. To some of the latter they are, perhaps, attracted by the sweet juices secreted by the aphides and coccidæ.[2] Such is the pas-

[1] Mr. Jerdan, in a series of papers in the thirteenth volume of the *Annals of Natural History*, has described forty-seven species of ants in Southern India. But M. Nietner has recently forwarded to the Berlin Museum upwards of seventy species taken by him in Ceylon, chiefly in the western province and the vicinity of Colombo. Of these many are identical with those noted by Mr. Jerdan as belonging to the Indian continent. One (probably *Drepanognathus saltator* of Jerdan) is described by M. Nietner as occasionally "moving by jumps of several inches at a spring."

[2] Dr. DAVY, in a paper on Tropical Plants, has introduced the following passage relative to the purification of sugar by ants:

"If the juice of the sugar-cane—the common syrup as expressed by the mill—be exposed to the air, it gradually evaporates, yielding a light-brown residue, like the ordinary muscovado sugar of the best quality. If not protected, it is presently attacked by ants, and in a short time is, as it were, converted into white crystalline sugar, the ants having refined it by removing the darker portion, probably preferring that part from its containing azotized matter. The negroes, I may remark, prefer brown sugar to white; they say its sweetening power is greater; no doubt its nourishing quality is greater, and therefore as an article of diet deserving of preference. In refining sugar as in refining salt (coarse bay salt containing a little iodine), an error may be committed in abstracting matter designed by nature for a useful purpose."

sion of the ants for sugar, and their wonderful faculty of discovering it, that the smallest particle of a substance containing it is quickly covered with them, though placed in the least conspicuous position, where not a single one may have been visible a moment before. But it is not sweet substances alone that they attack; no animal or vegetable matter comes amiss to them; no aperture appears too small to admit them; it is necessary to place everything which it may be desirable to keep free from their invasion, under the closest cover, or on tables with cups of water under every foot. As scavengers, they are invaluable; and as ants never sleep, but work without cessation during the night as well as by day, every particle of decaying vegetable or putrid animal matter is removed with inconceiveable speed and certainty. In collecting shells, I have been able to turn this propensity to good account; by placing them within their reach, the ants in a few days removed every vestige of the mollusc from the innermost and otherwise inaccessible whorls; thus avoiding all risk of injuring the enamel by any mechanical process.

But the assaults of the ants are not confined to dead animals alone, they attack equally such small insects as they can overcome, or find disabled by accidents or wounds; and it is not unusual to see some hundreds of them surrounding a maimed beetle, or a bruised cockroach, and hurrying it along in spite of its struggles. I have, on more than one occasion, seen a contest between them and one of the viscous ophidians, *Cœcilia glutinosa*[1], a reptile resembling an enormous earthworm, common in the Kandyan hills, of an inch in diameter,

[1] See *ante*, p. 317.

and nearly two feet in length. On these occasions it would seem as if the whole community had been summoned and turned out for such a prodigious effort; they surround their victim literally in tens of thousands, inflicting wounds on all parts, and forcing it along towards their nest in spite of resistance. In one instance to which I was a witness, the conflict lasted for the latter part of a day, but towards evening the Cœcilia was completely exhausted, and in the morning it had totally disappeared, having been carried away either whole or piecemeal by its assailants.

The species I here allude to is a very small ant, which the Singhalese call by the generic name of *Koombiya*. There is a species still more minute, and evidently distinct, which frequents the caraffes and toilet vessels. A third, probably the *Formica nidificans* of Jerdan, is black, of the same size as that last mentioned, and, from its colour, called the *Kalu koombiya* by the natives. In the houses its propensities and habits are the same as those of the others; but I have observed that it frequents the trees more profusely, forming small paper cells for its young, like miniature wasps' nests, in which it deposits its eggs, suspending them from a twig.

The most formidable of all is the great red ant or Dimiya.[1] It is particularly abundant in gardens, and on fruit trees; it constructs its dwellings by glueing the leaves of such species as are suitable from their shape and pliancy into hollow balls, and these it lines with a kind of transparent paper, like that manufactured by the wasp. I have watched them at the interesting operation of forming these dwellings;—a line of ants standing on the edge of one leaf bring another into contact

[1] *Formica smaragdina*, Fab.

with it, and hold both together with their mandibles till their companions within attach them firmly by means of their adhesive paper, the assistants outside moving along as the work proceeds. If it be necessary to draw closer a leaf too distant to be laid hold of by the immediate workers, they form a chain by depending one from the other till the object is reached, when it is at length brought into contact, and made fast by cement.

Like all their race, these ants are in perpetual motion, forming lines on the ground along which they pass, in continual procession to and from the trees on which they reside. They are the most irritable of the whole order in Ceylon, biting with such intense ferocity as to render it difficult for the unclad natives to collect the fruit from the mango trees, which the red ants especially frequent. They drop from the branches upon travellers in the jungle, attacking them with venom and fury, and inflicting intolerable pain both upon animals and man. On examining the structure of the head through a microscope, I found that the mandibles, instead of merely meeting in contact, are so hooked as to cross each other at the points, whilst the inner line is sharply serrated throughout its entire length; thus occasioning the intense pain of their bite, as compared with that of the ordinary ant.

To check the ravages of the coffee bug[1] (*Lecanium coffeæ*, Walker), which for some years past has devastated some of the plantations in Ceylon, the experiment was made of introducing the red ants, who feed greedily on the Coccus. But the remedy threatened to be attended with some inconvenience, for the Malabar Coolies, with bare and oiled skins, were so frequently

[1] For an account of this pest, see p. 437.

and fiercely assaulted by the ants as to endanger their stay on the estates.

The ants which burrow in the ground in Ceylon are generally, but not invariably, black, and some of them are of considerable size. One species, about the third of an inch in length, is abundant in the hills, and especially about the roots of trees, where they pile up the earth in circular heaps round the entrance to their nests, and in doing this I have observed a singular illustration of their instinct. To carry up each particle of sand by itself would be an endless waste of labour, and to carry two or more loose ones securely would be to them embarrassing, if not impossible. To overcome the difficulty they glue together with their saliva so much earth or sand as is sufficient for a burden, and each ant may be seen hurrying up from below with his load, carrying it to the top of the circular heap outside, and throwing it over, the mass being so strongly attached as to roll to the bottom without breaking asunder.

The ants I have been here describing are inoffensive, differing in this particular from the Dimiya and another of similar size and ferocity, which is called by the Singhalese *Kaddiya*. They have a legend illustrative of their alarm for the bites of the latter, to the effect that the cobra de capello invested the Kaddiya with her own venom in admiration of the singular courage displayed by these little creatures.[1]

LEPIDOPTERA. *Butterflies.*—In the interior of the island butterflies are comparatively rare, and, contrary to the ordinary belief, they are seldom to be seen in the sunshine. They frequent the neighbourhood of the jungle, and especially the vicinity of the rivers and

[1] KNOX'S *Historical Relation of Ceylon*, pt. i. ch. vi. p. 23.

waterfalls, living mainly in the shade of the moist foliage, and returning to it in haste after the shortest flights, as if their slender bodies were speedily dried up and exhausted by exposure to the intense heat.

Among the largest and most gaudy of the Ceylon Lepidoptera is the great black and yellow butterfly (*Ornithoptera darsius*, Gray); the upper wings of which measure six inches across, and are of deep velvet black, the lower ornamented by large particles of satiny yellow, through which the sunlight passes. Few insects can compare with it in beauty, as it hovers over the flowers of the heliotrope, which furnish the favourite food of the perfect fly, although the caterpillar feeds on the aristolochia and the *betel leaf*, and suspends its chrysalis from its drooping tendrils.

Next in size as to expanse of wing, though often exceeding it in breadth, is the black and blue *Papilio Polymnestor*, which darts rapidly through the air, alighting on the ruddy flowers of the hibiscus, or the dark green foliage of the citrus, on which it deposits its eggs. The larvæ of this species are green with white bands, and have a hump on the fourth or fifth segment. From this hump the caterpillar, on being irritated, protrudes a singular horn of an orange colour, bifurcate at the extremity, and covered with a pungent mucilaginous secretion. This is evidently intended as a weapon of defence against the attack of the ichneumon flies, that deposit their eggs in its soft body, for when the grub is pricked, either by the ovipositor of the ichneumon, or by any other sharp instrument, the horn is at once protruded, and struck upon the offending object with unerring aim.

Amongst the more common of the larger butterflies

is the *P. Hector*, with gorgeous crimson spots set in the black velvet of the inferior wings; these, when fresh, are shot with a purple blush, equalling in splendour the azure of the European "*Emperor.*"

*The Spectre Butterfly.*—Another butterfly, but belonging to a widely different group, is the "sylph" (*Hestia Jasonia*), called by the Europeans by the various names of *Floater*, *Spectre*, and *Silver-paper-fly*, as indicative of its graceful flight. It is found only in the deep shade of the damp forest, usually frequenting the vicinity of pools of water and cascades, about which it sails heedless of the spray, the moisture of which may even be beneficial in preserving the elasticity of its thin and delicate wings, that bend and undulate in the act of flight.

The *Lycænidæ*[1], a particularly attractive group, abound near the enclosures of cultivated grounds, and amongst the low shrubs edging the patenas, flitting from flower to flower, inspecting each in turn, as if attracted by their beauty, in the full blaze of sun-light; and shunning exposure less sedulously than the other diurnals. Some of the more robust kinds[2] are magnificent in the bright light, from the splendour of their metallic blues and glowing purples, but they yield in elegance of form and variety to their tinier and more delicately-coloured congeners.

Short as is the eastern twilight, it has its own peculiar forms, and the naturalist marks with interest the small, but strong, *Hesperidæ*[3], hurrying, by abrupt and jerking flights, to the scented blossoms of the champac or

[1] *Lycæna polyommatus, &c.*

[2] *Amblypodia pseudocentaurus, &c.*

[3] *Pamphila hesperia, &c.*

the sweet night-blowing moon-flower; and, when darkness gathers around, we can hear, though hardly distinguish amid the gloom, the humming of the powerful wings of innumerable hawk moths, which hover with their long proboscides inserted into the starry petals of the periwinkle.

Conspicuous amidst these nocturnal moths is the richly-coloured *Acherontia Satanas*, one of the Singhalese representatives of our Death's-head moth, which utters a sharp and stridulous cry when seized. This sound has been conjectured to be produced by the friction of its thorax against the abdomen;—Reaumur believed it to be caused by the rubbing of the palpi against the tongue. I have never been able to observe either motion, and Mr. E. L. Layard is of opinion that the sound is emitted from two apertures concealed by tufts of wiry bristles thrown out from each side of the inferior portion of the thorax.[1]

*Moths.*—Among the strictly nocturnal *Lepidoptera* are some gigantic species. Of these the cinnamon-eating *Atlas*, often attains the dimensions of nearly a foot in the stretch of its superior wings. It is very common in the gardens about Colombo, and its size, and the transparent talc-like spots in its wings, cannot fail to strike even the most careless saunterer. But little inferior to it in size is the famed Tusseh silk moth[2], which feeds on the country almond (*Terminalia catappa*) and the palma Christi or Castor-oil plant; it

[1] There is another variety of the same moth in Ceylon which closely resembles it in its markings, but in which I have never detected the uttering of this curious cry. It is smaller than the *A. Satanas*, and, like it, often enters dwellings at night, attracted by the lights; but I have not found its larvæ, although that of the other species is common on several widely different plants.

[2] *Antheræa mylitta*, Drury.

is easily distinguishable from the Atlas, which has a triangular wing, whilst its is falcated, and the transparent spots are covered with a curious thread-like division drawn across them.

Towards the northern portions of the island this valuable species entirely displaces the other, owing to the fact that the almond and *palma Christi* abound there. The latter plant springs up spontaneously on every manure-heap or neglected spot of ground; and might be cultivated, as in India, with great advantage, the leaf to be used as food for the caterpillar, the stalk as fodder for cattle, and the seed for the expression of castor-oil. The Dutch took advantage of this facility, and gave every encouragement to the cultivation of silk at Jaffna[1], but it never attained such a development as to become an article of commercial importance. Ceylon now cultivates no silkworms whatever, notwithstanding this abundance of the favourite food of one species; and the rich silken robes sometimes worn by the Buddhist priesthood are imported from China and the continent of India.

In addition to the Atlas moth and the Mylitta, there are many other *Bombycidæ* in Ceylon; and, though the

[1] The Portuguese had made the attempt previous to the arrival of the Dutch, and a strip of land on the banks of the Kalany river near Colombo, still bears the name of Orta Seda, the silk garden. The attempt of the Dutch to introduce the true silkworm, the *Bombyx mori*, took place under the governorship of Ryklof Van Goens, who, on handing over the administration to his successor in A.D. 1663, thus apprises him of the initiation of the experiment:—"At Jaffna Palace a trial has been undertaken to feed silkworms, and to ascertain whether silk may be reared at that station. I have planted a quantity of mulberry trees, which grow well there, and they ought to be planted in other directions."—VALENTYN, chap. xiii. The growth of the mulberry trees is noticed the year after in a report to the governor-general of India, but the subject afterwards ceased to be attended to.

silk of some of them, were it susceptible of being unwound from the cocoon, would not bear a comparison with that of the *Bombyx mori*, or even of the Tusseh moth, it might still prove to be valuable when carded and spun. If the European residents in the colony would rear the larvæ of these Lepidoptera, and make drawings of their various changes, they would render a possible service to commerce, and a certain one to entomological knowledge.

*Stinging Caterpillars.*—The Dutch carried to their Eastern settlements two of their home propensities, which distinguish and embellish the towns of the Low Countries; they indulged in the excavation of canals, and they planted long lines of trees to diffuse shade over the sultry passages in their Indian fortresses. For the latter purpose they employed the Suriya (*Hibiscus populneus*), whose broad umbrageous leaves and delicate yellow flowers impart a delicious coolness, and give to the streets of Galle and Colombo the fresh and enlivening aspect of walks in a garden.

In the towns, however, the suriya trees are productive of one serious inconvenience. They are the resort of a hairy greenish caterpillar[1], longitudinally striped, great numbers of which frequent them, and at a certain stage of growth descend by a silken thread to the ground and hurry away, probably in search of a suitable spot in which to pass through their metamorphoses. Should they happen to alight, as they often do, upon some lounger below, and find their way to his unprotected skin, they inflict, if molested, a sting as pungent, but far more lasting, than that of a nettle or a star-fish.

[1] The species of moth with which it is identified has not yet been determined, but it most probably belongs to a section of Boisduval's genus *Bombyx* allied to *Cnethocampa*, Stephens.

Attention being thus directed to the quarter whence an assailant has lowered himself down, the caterpillars above will be found in clusters, sometimes amounting to hundreds, clinging to the branches and the bark, with a few straggling over the leaves or suspended from them by lines. These pests are so annoying to children as well as destructive to the foliage, that it is often necessary to singe them off the trees by a flambeau fixed on the extremity of a pole; and as they fall to the ground they are eagerly devoured by the crows and domestic fowls.[1]

*The Wood-carrying Moth.*—There is another family of insects, the singular habits of which will not fail to attract the traveller in the cultivated tracts of Ceylon—these are moths of the genus *Oiketicus*[2], of which the females are devoid of wings, and some possess no articulated feet. Their larvæ construct for themselves cases, which they suspend to a branch frequently of the pomegranate[3], surrounding them with the stems of leaves, and thorns or pieces of twigs bound together by threads, till the whole presents the appearance of a bundle of rods about an inch and a half long; and, from the resemblance of this to a Roman fasces, one

[1] Another caterpillar which feeds on the jasmine flowering Carissa, stings with such fury that I have known a gentleman to shed tears while the pain was at its height. It is short and broad, of a pale green, with fleshy spines on the upper surface, each of which seems to be charged with the venom that occasions this acute suffering. The moth which this caterpillar produces, *Neæra lepida*, Cramer; *Limacodes graciosa*, Westw., has dark brown wings, the primary traversed by a broad green band. It is common in the western side of Ceylon. The larvæ of the genus *Adolia* are also hairy, and sting with virulence.

[2] *Eumeta*, Wlk.

[3] The singular instincts of a species of Thecla, *Dipsas Isocrates*, Fab., in connection with the fruit of the pomegranate, were fully described by Mr. Westwood, in a paper read before the Entomological Society of London in 1835.

African species has obtained the name of "Lictor." The German entomologists denominated the group *Sackträger*, the Singhalese call them *Dara-kattea* or "billets of firewood," and regard the inmates as human beings, who, as a punishment for stealing wood in some former state of existence, have been condemned to undergo a metempsychosis under the form of these insects.

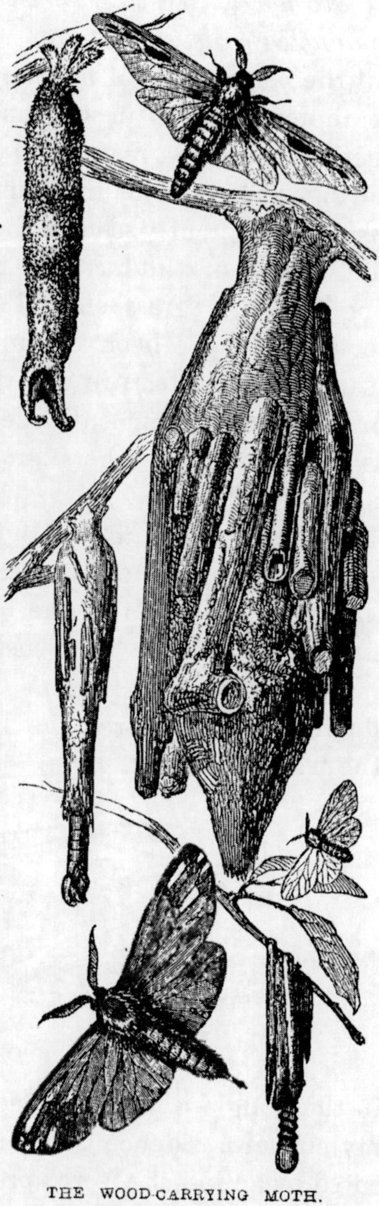
THE WOOD-CARRYING MOTH.

The male, at the close of the pupal rest, escapes from one end of this singular covering, but the female makes it her dwelling for life; moving about with it at pleasure, and entrenching herself within it, when alarmed, by drawing together the purse-like aperture at the open end. Of these remarkable creatures there are five ascertained species in Ceylon: *Psyche Doubledaii*, Westw.; *Metisa plana*, Walker; *Eu-*

*meta Cramerii*, Westw.; *E. Templetonii*, Westw.; and *Cryptothelea consorta*, Temp.

All the other tribes of minute *Lepitoptera* have abundant representatives in Ceylon; some of them most attractive from the great beauty of their markings and colouring. The curious little split-winged moth (*Pterophorus*) is frequently seen in the cinnamon gardens and in the vicinity of the fort, hid from the noon-day heat among the cool grass shaded by the coco-nut topes. Three species have been captured, all characterised by the same singular feature of having the wings fan-like, separated nearly their entire length into detached sections, resembling feathers in the pinions of a bird expanded for flight.

HOMOPTERA. *Cicada.*—Of the *Homoptera*, the one which will most frequently arrest attention is the cicada, which, resting high up on the bark of a tree, makes the forest re-echo with a long-sustained noise so curiously resembling that of a cutler's wheel that the creature producing it has acquired the highly-appropriate name of the "knife-grinder."

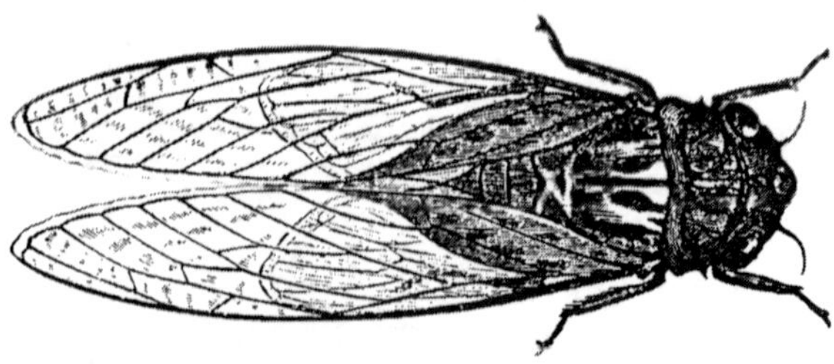

CICADA—"THE KNIFE-GRINDER."

In the jungle which adjoined the grounds attached to my official residence at Kandy, the shrubs were frequented by an insect covered profusely with a snow-white powder, arranged in delicate filaments that curl like a head of dressed celery. These it moves without dispersing the powder: but when dead they fall rapidly to dust. I regret that I did not preserve specimens, but I have reason to think that they are the larvæ of the *Flata limbata*, or of some other closely allied species[1], though I have not seen in Ceylon any of the wax produced by the *flata*.

HEMIPTERA. *Bugs.*—On the shrubs in his compound the newly-arrived traveller will be attracted by an insect of a pale green hue and delicately-thin configuration, which, resting from its recent flight, composes its scanty wings, and moves languidly along the leaf. But experience will teach him to limit his examination to a respectful view of its attitudes; it is one of a numerous family of bugs, (some of them most attractive[2] in their colouring,) which are inoffensive if unmolested, but if touched or irritated, exhale an odour that, once endured, is never afterwards forgotten.

APHANIPTERA. *Fleas.*—Fleas are equally numerous, and may be seen in myriads in the dust of the streets or skipping in the sunbeams which fall on the clay floors of the cottages. The dogs, to escape them, select for their sleeping places spots where a wood fire has been previously kindled; and here prone on the white ashes,

FŒCILOPTERA TENNENTINA.

ELIDIPTERA EMERSONIANA.

[1] Amongst the specimens of this order which I brought from Ceylon, two proved to be new and undescribed, and have been named by Mr. A. WHITE *Elidiptera Emersoniana* and *Pœciloptera Tennentina.*

[2] Such as *Cantuo ocellatus, Leptoscelis Marginalis, Callidea Stockerius,* &c. &c. Of the aquatic species, the gigantic *Belostoma Indicum* cannot escape notice, attaining a size of nearly three inches.

their stomachs close to the earth, and their hind legs extended behind, they repose in comparative coolness, and bid defiance to their persecutors.

DIPTERA. *Mosquitoes.*—But of all the insect pests that beset an unseasoned European the most provoking by far is the truculent mosquito.[1] Next to the torture which it inflicts, its most annoying peculiarities are the booming hum of its approach, its cunning, its audacity, and the perseverance with which it renews its attacks however frequently repulsed. These characteristics are so remarkable as fully to justify the conjecture that the mosquito, and not the ordinary fly, constituted the plague inflicted upon Pharaoh and the Egyptians.[2]

[1] *Culex laniger?* Wied. In Kandy Mr. Thwaites finds *C. fuscanus*, *C. circumvolens*, &c., and one with a most formidable hooked proboscis, to which he has assigned the appropriate name *C. Regius*.

[2] The precise species of insect by means of which the Almighty signalised the plague of flies, remains uncertain, as the Hebrew term *arob* or *orov*, which has been rendered in one place, "Divers sorts of flies," Ps. cv. 31; and in another, "swarms of flies," Exod. viii. 21, &c., means merely "an assemblage," a "mixture," or a "swarm," and the expletive "*of flies*" is an interpolation of the translators. This, however, serves to show that the fly implied was one easily recognisable by its habit of *swarming*; and the further fact that it *bites*, or rather stings, is elicited from the expression of the Psalmist, Ps. lxxviii. 45, that the insects by which the Egyptians were tormented "devoured them," so that here are two peculiarities inapplicable to the domestic fly, but strongly characteristic of gnats and mosquitoes.

Bruce thought that the fly of the fourth plague was the "zimb" of Abyssinia which he so graphically describes; and WESTWOOD, in an ingenious passage in his *Entomologist's Text-book*, p. 17, combats the strange idea of one of the bishops, that it was a cockroach! and argues in favour of the mosquito. This view he sustains by a reference to the habits of the creature, the swarms in which it invades a locality, and the audacity with which it enters the houses; and he accounts for the exemption of "the land of Goshen in which the Israelites dwelt," by the fact of its being sandy pasture above the level of the river; whilst the mosquitoes were produced freely in the rest of Egypt, the soil of which was submerged by the rising of the Nile.

In all the passages in the Old Testament in which flies are alluded to, otherwise than in connection with the Egyptian infliction, the word used in the Hebrew is *zevov*, which the Septuagint renders by the ordinary generic term for flies in general, μυῖα, "*musca*" (Eccles. x. 1, Isaiah vii. 10); but in every

Even in the midst of endurance from their onslaughts one cannot but be amused by the ingenuity of their movements; as if aware of the risk incident to an open assault, a favourite mode of attack is, when concealed by a table, to assail the ankles through the meshes of the stocking, or the knees which are ineffectually protected by a fold of Russian duck. When you are reading, a mosquito will rarely settle on that portion of your hand which is within range of your eyes, but cunningly stealing by the underside of the book fastens on the wrist or little finger, and noiselessly inserts his proboscis there. I have tested the classical expedient recorded by Herodotus, who states that the fishermen inhabiting the fens of Egypt, cover their beds with their nets, knowing that the mosquitoes, although they bite through linen robes, will not venture through a net.[1] But, notwithstanding the opinion of Spence[2], that nets with meshes an inch square will effectually exclude them, I have been satisfied by painful experience that (if the theory be not altogether fallacious) at least the modern mosquitoes of Ceylon are uninfluenced by the

instance in which mention is made of the miracle of Moses, the Septuagint says that the fly produced was the *κυνομυία*, the "dog-fly." What insect was meant by this name it is not now easy to determine, but ÆLIAN intimates that the dog-fly both inflicts a wound and emits a booming sound, in both of which particulars it accords with the mosquito (lib. iv. 51); and PHILO-JUDÆUS, in his *Vita Mosis*, lib. i. ch. xxiii., descanting on the plague of flies, and using the term of the Septuagint, *κυνομυῖα*, describes it as combining the characteristic of "the most impudent of all animals, the fly and the dog, exhibiting the courage and the cunning of both, and fastening on its victim with the noise and rapidity of an arrow" — *μετὰ ῥοῖζου καθάπερ βέλος*. This seems to identify the dog-fly of the Septuagint with the description of the Psalmist, Ps. lxxviii. 45, and to vindicate the conjecture that the tormenting mosquito, and not the house-fly, was commissioned by the Lord to humble the obstinacy of the Egyptian tyrant.

[1] HERODOTUS, *Euterpe*, xcv.

[2] KIRBY and SPENCE'S *Entomology*, letter iv.

same considerations which restrained those of the Nile under the successors of Cambyses.

*The Coffee-Bug.*—Allusion has been made in a previous passage to the coccus known in Ceylon as the "Coffee-Bug (*Lecanium Caffeæ*, Wlk.), which of late years has made such destructive ravages in the plantations in the Mountain Zone.[1] The first thing that attracts attention on looking at a coffee tree infested by it, is the number of brownish wart-like bodies that stud the young shoots and occasionally the margins on the underside of the leaves.[2] Each of these warts or scales is a transformed female, containing a large number of eggs which are hatched within it.

When the young ones come out from their nest, they run about over the plant like diminutive wood-lice, and at this period there is no apparent distinction between male and female. Shortly after being hatched the males seek the underside of the leaves, while the females prefer the young shoots as a place of abode. If the under surface of a leaf be examined, it will be found to be studded, particularly on its basil half, with minute yellowish-white specks of an oblong form.[3] These are the larvæ of the males undergoing transformation into pupæ, beneath their own skins; some of these specks are always in a more advanced state than the others, the full-grown ones being whitish and scarcely a line

[1] The following notice of the "coffee-bug," and of the singularly destructive effects produced by it on the plants, has been prepared chiefly from a memoir presented to the Ceylon Government by the late Dr. Gardner, in which he traces the history of the insect from its first appearance in the coffee districts, until it had established itself more or less permanently in all the estates in full cultivation throughout the island.

[2] See the annexed drawing, Fig. 1.

[3] Figs. 2, and 3 and 5 in the engraving, where these and all the other figures are considerably enlarged.

THE COFFEE BUG.

*Lecanium Caffeæ.*

long. Some of this size are translucent, the insect having escaped; the darker ones still retain it within, of an oblong form, with the rudiment of a wing on each side attached to the lower part of the thorax and closely applied to the sides; the legs are six in number, the four hind ones being directed backwards, the anterior forwards (a peculiarity not common in other insects); the two antennæ are also inclined backwards, and from the tail protrude three short bristles, the middle one thinner and longer than the rest.

When the transformation is complete, the mature insect makes its way from beneath the pellucid case [1], all its organs having then attained their full size: the head is sub-globular, with two rather prominent black eyes, and two antennæ, each with eleven joints, hairy throughout, and a tuft of rather longer hairs at the apices; the legs are also covered with hairs, the wings are horizontal, of an obovate oblong shape, membranous, and extending a little farther than the bristles of the tail. They have only two nerves, neither of which reaches so far as the tips; one of them runs close to the costal margin, and is much thicker than the other, which branches off from its base and skirts along the inner margin; behind the wings is attached a pair of minute halteres of peculiar form. The possession of wings would appear to be the cause why the full-grown male is more rarely seen on the coffee bushes than the female.

The female, like the male, attaches herself to the surface of the plant, the place selected being usually

[1] Fig. 4. Mr. WESTWOOD, who observed the operation in one species, states that they escape backwards, the wings being extended flatly over the head.

the young shoots; but she is also to be met with on the margins of the undersides of the leaves (on the upper surface neither the male nor female ever attach themselves); but, unlike the male, which derives no nourishment from the juices of the tree (the mouth being obsolete in the perfect state), she punctures the cuticle with a proboscis (a very short three-jointed *promuscis*), springing as it were from the breast, but capable of being greatly porrected, and inserted in the cuticle of the plant, and through this she abstracts her nutriment. In the early pupa state the female is easily distinguishable from the male, by being more elliptical and much more convex. As she increases in size her skin distends and she becomes smooth and dry; the rings of the body become effaced; and losing entirely the form of an insect, she presents, for some time, a yellowish pustular shape, but ultimately assumes a roundish conical form, of a dark brown colour.[1]

Until she has nearly reached her full size, she still possesses the power of locomotion, and her six legs are easily distinguishable in the under surface of her corpulent body; but at no period of her existence has she wings. It is about the time of her obtaining full size that impregnation takes place[2]; after which the scale becomes somewhat more conical, assumes a darker

[1] Figs. 6 and 7. There are many other species of the Coccus tribe in Ceylon, some (Pseudococcus?) never appearing as a scale, the female wrapping herself up in a white cottony exudation; many species nearly allied to the true Coccus infest common plants about gardens, such as the Nerium Oleander, Plumeria Acuminata, and others with milky juices: another subgenus (Ceroplastes?), the female of which produces a protecting waxy material, infests the Gendurassa Vulgaris, the Furrcæa Gigantea, the Jak tree, Mango, and other common trees.

[2] Reaumur has described the singular manner in which this occurs. *Mem.* tom. iv.

colour, and at length is permanently fixed to the surface of the plant, by means of a cottony substance interposed between it and the vegetable cuticle to which it adheres. The scale, when full grown, exactly resembles in miniature the hat of a Cornish miner[1], there being a narrow rim at the base, which gives increased surface of attachment. It is about $\frac{1}{8}$ inch in diameter, by about $\frac{1}{12}$ deep, and it appears perfectly smooth to the naked eye; but it is in reality studded over with a multitude of very minute warts, giving it a dotted appearance. Except the margin, which is ciliated, it is entirely destitute of hairs. The number of eggs contained in one of the scales is enormous, amounting in a single one to 691. The eggs are of an oblong shape, of a pale flesh colour, and perfectly smooth.[2] In some of the scales, the eggs when laid on the field of the microscope resemble those masses of life sometimes seen in decayed cheese.[3] A few small yellowish maggots are sometimes found with them, and these are the larvæ[4] of insects, the eggs of which have been deposited in the female while the scale was soft. They escape when mature by cutting a small round hole in the dorsum of the scale.

It is not till after this pest has been on an estate for two or three years that it shows itself to an alarming extent. During the first year a few only of the ripe scales are seen scattered over the bushes, generally on the younger shoots; but that year's crop does not suffer much, and the appearance of the tree is little altered.

[1] Fig. 8.
[2] Fig. 9.
[3] Figs. 10, 11.
[4] Of the parasitic Chalcididiæ, many genera of which are well known to deposit their eggs in the soft Coccus, viz.: Encystus, Coccophagus, Pteromalus, Mesosela, Agonioneurus; besides Aphidius, a minutely sized genus of Ichneumonidæ. Most, if not all, of these genera are Singhalese.

The second year, however, brings a change for the worse; if the young shoots and the underside of the leaves be now examined, the scales will be found to have become much more numerous, and with them appear a multitude of white specks, which are the young scales in a more or less forward state. The clusters of berries now assume a black sooty look, and a great number of them fall off before coming to maturity; the general health of the tree also begins to fail, and it acquires a blighted appearance. A loss of crop is this year sustained, but to no great extent.

The third year brings about a more serious change, the whole plant acquires a black hue, appearing as if soot had been thrown over it in great quantities; this is caused by the growth of a parasitic fungus[1] over the shoots and the upper surface of the leaves, forming a fibrous coating, somewhat resembling velvet or felt. This never makes its appearance till the insect has been a considerable time on the bush, and probably owes its existence there to an unhealthy condition of the juices of the leaf, consequent on the irritation produced by the coccus, since it never visits the upper surface of the leaf until the latter has fully established itself on the lower. At this period the young shoots have an exceedingly disgusting look from the dense mass of yellow pustular bodies forming on them, the leaves get shrivelled, and the infected trees become conspicuous in the row. The black ants are assiduous in their visits to

[1] *Racodium?* Species of this genus are not confined to the coffee plant alone in Ceylon, but follow the "bugs" in their attacks on other bushes. It appears like a dense interlaced mesh of fibres, each made up of a single series of minute oblong vesicles applied end to end.

them. Two-thirds of the crop is lost, and on many trees not a single berry forms.

This *Lecanium*, or a very closely allied species, has been observed in the Botanic Garden at Peradenia, on the *Citrus acida, Psidium pomiferum, Myrtus Zeylanica, Rosa Indica, Careya arborea, Vitex Negundo*, and other plants. The coffee coccus has generally been first observed in moist, hollow places sheltered from the wind; and thence it has spread itself even over the driest and most exposed parts of the island. On some estates, after attaining a maximum, it has generally declined, but has shown a liability to reappear, especially in low sheltered situations, and it is believed to prevail most extensively in wet seasons. While in its earlier stages, it is easily transmitted from one estate to another, on the clothes of human beings, and in various other ways, which will readily suggest themselves. Dr. Gardner, after a careful consideration and minute examination of estates, arrived at the conclusion, that all remedies suggested up to that time had utterly failed, and that none at once cheap and effectual was likely to be discovered. He seems also to have been of opinion that the insect was not under human control; and that even if it should disappear, it would only be when it should have worn itself out as other blights have been known to do in some mysterious way. Whether this may prove to be the case or not, is still very uncertain, but every thing observed by Dr. Gardner tends to indicate the permanency of the pest.

## *List of Ceylon Insects.*

For the following list of the insects of the island, and the remarks prefixed to it, I am indebted to Mr. F. Walker, by whom it has been prepared after a careful inspection of the collections made by Dr. Templeton, Mr. E. L. Layard, and others; as well as of those in the British Museum and in the Museum of the East India Company.[1]

"A short notice of the aspect of the island will afford the best means of accounting, in some degree, for its entomological Fauna: first, as it is an island, and has a mountainous central region, the tropical character of its productions, as in most other cases, rather diminishes, and somewhat approaches that of higher latitudes.

"The coast-region of Ceylon, and fully one-third of its northern part, have a much drier atmosphere than that of the rest of its surface; and their climate and vegetation are nearly similar to those of the Carnatic, with which this island may have been connected at no very remote period.[2] But if, on the contrary, the land in Ceylon is gradually rising, the difference of its Fauna from that of Central Hindustan is less remarkable. The peninsula of the Dekkan might then be conjectured to have been nearly or wholly separated from the central part of Hindustan, and confined to the range of mountains along the eastern coast; the insect-fauna of which is as yet almost unknown, but will probably be found to have more resemblance to that of Ceylon than to the insects of

[1] The entire of the new species contained in this list have been described in a series of papers by Mr. WALKER in successive numbers of the *Annals of Natural History* (1858—61): those from Dr. TEMPLETON's collection of which descriptions have been taken, have been at his desire transferred to the British Museum for future reference and comparison.

[2] On the subject of this conjecture see *ante*, p. 60.

northern and western India — just as the insect-fauna of Malaya appears more to resemble the similar productions of Australasia than those of the more northern continent.

" Mr. Layard's collection was partly formed in the dry northern province of Ceylon; and among them more Hindustan insects are to be observed than among those collected by Dr. Templeton, and found wholly in the district between Colombo and Kandy. According to this view the faunas of the Nilgherry Mountains, of Central Ceylon, of the peninsula of Malacca, and of Australasia would be found to form one group; — while those of Northern Ceylon, of the western Dekkan, and of the level parts of Central Hindustan would form another of more recent origin. The insect-fauna of the Carnatic is also probably similar to that of the lowlands of Ceylon; but it is still unexplored. The regions of Hindustan in which species have been chiefly collected, such as Bengal, Silhet, and the Punjaub, are at the distance of from 1300 to 1600 miles from Ceylon, and therefore the insects of the latter are fully as different from those of the above regions as they are from those of Australasia, to which Ceylon is as near in point of distance, and agrees more with regard to latitude.

" Dr. Hagen has remarked that he believes the fauna of the mountains of Ceylon to be quite different from that of the plains and of the shores. The south and west districts have a very moist climate, and as their vegetation is like that of Malabar, their insect-fauna will probably also resemble that of the latter region.

" The insects mentioned in the following list are thus distributed: —

" Order COLEOPTERA.

" The recorded species of *Cicindelidæ* inhabit the plains or the coast country of Ceylon, and several of them are also found in Hindustan.

" Many of the species of *Carabidæ* and of *Staphylinidæ*, especially those collected by Mr. Thwaites, near Kandy, and by M. Nietner at Colombo, have much resemblance to the insects of these two families in North Europe; in the *Scydmœnidæ*, *Ptiliadæ*, *Phalacridæ*, *Nitidulidæ*, *Colydiadæ*, and *Lathridiadæ* the northern form is still more striking, and strongly contrasts with the tropical forms of the gigantic *Copridæ*, *Buprestidæ*, and *Cerambycidæ*, and with the *Elateridæ*, *Lampyridæ*, *Tenebrionidæ*, *Helopidæ*, *Meloidæ*, *Curculionidæ*, *Prionidæ*, *Cerambycidæ*, *Lamiidæ*, and *Endomychidæ*.

"The *Copridæ*, *Dynastidæ*, *Melolonthidæ*, *Cetoniadæ*, and *Passalidæ* are well represented on the plains and on the coast, and the species are mostly of a tropical character.

"The *Hydrophilidæ* have a more northern aspect, as is generally the case with aquatic species.

"The order *Strepsiptera* is here considered as belonging to the *Mordellidæ*, and is represented by the genus *Myrmecolax*, which is peculiar, as yet, to Ceylon.

"In the *Curculionidæ* the single species of *Apion* will recall to mind the great abundance of that genus in North Europe.

"The *Prionidæ* and the two following families have been investigated by Mr. Pascoe, and the *Hispidæ*, with the five following families, by Mr. Baly; these two gentlemen are well acquainted with the above tribes of beetles, and kindly supplied me with the names of the Ceylon species.

## Order ORTHOPTERA.

"These insects in Ceylon have mostly a tropical aspect. The *Physapoda*, which will probably be soon incorporated with them, are likely to be numerous, though only one species has as yet been noticed.

## Order NEUROPTERA.

"The list here given is chiefly taken from the catalogue published by Dr. Hagen, and containing descriptions of the species named by him or by M. Nietner. They were found in the most elevated parts of the island, near Rangbodde, and Dr. Hagen informs me that not less than 500 species have been noticed in Ceylon, but that they are not yet recorded, with the exception of the species here enumerated. It has been remarked that the *Trichoptera* and other aquatic *Neuroptera* are less local than the land species, owing to the more equable temperature of the habitation of their larvæ, and on account of their being often conveyed along the whole length of rivers. The species of *Psocus* in the list are far more numerous than those yet observed in any other country, with the exception of Europe.

### Order HYMENOPTERA.

"In this order the *Formicidæ* and the *Poneridæ* are very numerous, as they are in other damp and woody tropical countries. Seventy species of ants have been observed, but as yet few of them have been named. The various other families of aculeate *Hymenoptera* are doubtless more abundant than the species recorded indicate, and it may be safely reckoned that the parasitic *Hymenoptera* in Ceylon far exceed one thousand species in number, though they are yet only known by means of about two dozen kinds collected at Kandy by Mr. Thwaites.

### Order LEPIDOPTERA.

"The fauna of Ceylon is much better known in this order than in any other of the insect tribes, but as yet the *Lepidoptera* alone in their class afford materials for a comparison of the productions of Ceylon with those of Hindustan and of Australasia; nine hundred and thirty-two species have been collected by Dr. Templeton and by Mr. Layard in the central, western, and northern parts of the island. All the families, from the *Papilionidæ* to the *Tineidæ*, abound, and numerous species and several genera appear, as yet, to be peculiar to the island. As Ceylon is situate at the entrance to the eastern regions, the list in this volume will suitably precede the descriptive catalogues of the heterocerous *Lepidoptera* of Hindustan, Java, Borneo, and of other parts of Australasia, which are being prepared for publication. In some of the heterocerous families several species are common to Ceylon and to Australasia, and in various cases the faunas of Ceylon and of

Australasia seem to be more similar than those of Ceylon and of Hindustan. The long intercourse between those two regions may have been the means of conveying some species from one to the other. Among the *Pyralites*, *Hymenia recurvalis* inhabits also the West Indies, South America, West Africa, Hindustan, China, Australasia, Australia, and New Zealand; and its food-plant is probably some vegetable which is cultivated in all those regions; so also *Desmia afflictalis* is found in Sierra Leone, Abyssinia, Ceylon, and China.

### Order DIPTERA.

" About fifty species were observed by Dr. Templeton, but most of those here recorded were collected by Mr. Thwaites at Kandy, and have a great likeness to North European species. The mosquitoes are very annoying on account of their numbers, as might be expected from the moisture and heat of the climate. *Culex laniger* is the coast species, and the other kinds here mentioned are from Kandy. Humboldt observed that in some parts of South America each stream had its peculiar mosquitoes, and it yet remains to be seen whether the gnats in Ceylon are also thus restricted in their habitation. The genera *Sciara*, *Cecidomyia*, and *Simulium*, which abound so exceedingly in temperate countries, have each one representative species in the collection made by Mr. Thwaites. Thus an almost new field remains for the Entomologist in the study of the yet unknown Singhalese Diptera, which must be very numerous.

### Order HEMIPTERA.

" The species of this order in the list are too few and too similar to those of Hindustan to need any particular mention. *Lecanium coffeæ* may be noticed, on account of its infesting the coffee plant, as its name indicates, and the ravages of other species of the genus will be remembered, from the fact that one of them, in other regions, has put a stop to the cultivation of the orange as an article of commerce.

"In conclusion, it may be observed that the species of insects in Ceylon may be estimated as exceeding 10,000 in number, of which about 2000 are enumerated in this volume.

### Class ARACHNIDA.

"Four or five species of spiders, of which the specimens cannot be satisfactorily described; one *Ixodes* and one *Chelifer* have been forwarded to England from Ceylon by Mr. Thwaites."

---

**NOTE.**—The asterisk prefixed denotes the species discovered in Ceylon since Sir J. E. Tennent's departure from the Island in 1849.

Order COLEOPTERA, *Linn.*

Fam. CICINDELIDÆ, *Steph.*

Cicindela, *Linn.*
flavopunctata, *Aud.*
discrepans, *Wlk.*
aurofasciaca, *Guér.*
quadrilineata, *Fabr.*
biramosa. *Fabr.*
catena, *Fabr.*
*insignificans, *Dohrn.*
Tricondyla, *Latr.*
femorata, *Wlk.*
*tumidula, *Wlk.*
*scitiscabra, *Wlk.*
*concinna, *Dohrn.*

Fam. CARABIDÆ, *Leach.*

Casnonia, *Latr.*
*punctata, *Niet.*
*pilifera, *Niet.*
Ophionea, *Klug.*
*cyanocephala, *Fabr.*
Euplynes, *Niet.*
Dohrnii, *Niet.*
Heteroglossa, *Niet.*
*elegans, *Niet.*
*ruficollis. *Niet.*
*bimaculata, *Niet.*
Zuphium, *Latr.*
*pubescens, *Niet.*
Pheropsophus, *Solier.*
Catoirei, *Dej.*
bimaculatus, *Fabr.*
Cymindis, *Latr.*
rufiventris, *Wlk.*
Anchista, *Niet.*
*modesta, *Niet.*
Dromius, *Bon.*
marginifer, *Wlk.*
repandens, *Wlk.*
Lebia, *Latr.*
bipars, *Wlk.*
Creagris, *Niet.*
labrosa, *Niet.*
Elliotia, *Niet.*
paliipes, *Niet.*
Maraga. *Wlk.*
planigera. *Wlk.*
Catascopus, *Kirby.*
facialis, *Wied.*
reductus, *Wlk.*
Scarites. *Fabr.*
obliterans, *Wlk.*
subsignans, *Wlk.*
designans, *Wlk.*
*minor, *Niet.*
Clivina, *Latr.*
*rugosifrons, *Niet.*
*elongatula. *Niet.*
*maculata, *Niet.*
recta, *Wlk.*
Leistus, *Fræhl.*
linearis, *Wlk.*
Isotarsus, *Laferté.*
quadrimaculatus, *Oliv.*
Panagæus, *Latr.*
retractus, *Wlk.*
Chlænius, *Bon.*
bimaculatus, *Dej.*
diffinis *Reiche.*
*Ceylanicus, *Niet.*
*quinque-maculatus, *Niet.*
pulcher, *Niet.*
cupricollis, *Niet.*
rugulosus, *Niet.*
Anchomenus, *Bon.*
illocatus, *Wlk.*
Agonum, *Bon.*
placidulum, *Wlk.*
Colpodes? *Macl.*
marginicollis, *Wlk.*
Argutor, *Meg.*
degener, *Wlk.*
relinquens, *Wlk.*
Simphyus, *Niet.*
*unicolor, *Niet.*
Bradytus, *Steph.*
stolidus, *Wlk.*
Curtonotus, *Steph.*
compositus, *Wlk.*
Harpalus, *Latr.*
*advolans, *Niet.*
dispellens. *Wlk.*
Calodromus, *Niet.*
*exornatus, *Niet.*
Megaristerus, *Niet.*
*mandibularis. *Niet.*
*stenolophoides, *Niet.*
*Indicus. *Niet.*
Platysma. *Bon.*
retinens, *Wlk.*
Morio. *Latr.*
trogositoides, *Wlk.*
cucujoides, *Wlk.*
Barysomus, *Dej.*
*Gyllenhalii, *Dej.*
Oodes, *Bon.*
*piceus, *Niet.*
Selenophorus, *Dej.*
infixus, *Wlk.*
Orthogonius, *Dej.*
femoratus, *Dej.*
Helluodes, *Westw.*
Taprobanæ, *Westw.*
Physocrotaphus, *Parry.*
Ceylonicus. *Parry.*
*minax, *West.*
Physodera, *Esch.*
Eschscholtzii, *Parry.*
Omphra, *Latr.*
*ovipennis, *Reiche.*
Planetes, *Macl.*
bimaculatus, *Macleay.*
Cardiaderus. *Dej.*
scitus, *Wlk.*
Distrigus, *Dej.*
*costatus, *Niet.*
*submetallicus, *Niet.*
rufopiceus, *Niet.*
*æneus, *Niet.*
*Dejeani, *Niet.*
Drimostoma, *Dej.*
*Ceylanicum, *Niet.*

*marginale, *Wlk.*
Cyclosomus, *Latr.*
flexuosus, *Fabr.*
Ochthephilus, *Niet.*
*Ceylanicus, *Niet.*
Spathinus, *Niet.*
*nigriceps, *Niet.*
Acupalpus, *Latr.*
derogatus, *Wlk.*
extremus, *Wlk.*
Bembidium, *Latr.*
finitimum, *Wlk.*
*opulentum, *Niet.*
*truncatum, *Niet.*
*tropicum, *Niet.*
*triangulare, *Niet.*
*Ceylanicum, *Niet.*
Klugii, *Niet.*
*ebeninum, *Niet.*
*orientale, *Niet.*
*emarginatum, *Niet.*
*ornatum, *Niet.*
*scydmænoides, *Niet.*

Fam. PAUSSIDÆ, *Westw.*

Cerapterus, *Swed.*
latipes, *Swed.*
Pleuropterus, *West.*
Westermanni, *West.*
Paussus, *Linn.*
pacificus, *West.*

Fam. DYTISCIDÆ, *Macl.*

Cybister, *Curt.*
limbatus, *Fabr.*
Dytiscus, *Linn.*
extenuans, *Wlk.*
Eunectes, *Erich.*
griseus, *Fabr.*
Hydaticus, *Leach.*
festivus, *Ill.*
vittatus, *Fabr.*
dislocans, *Wlk.*
fractifer, *Wlk.*
Colymbetes, *Clairv.*
interclusus, *Wlk.*
Hydroporus, *Clairv.*
interpulsus, *Wlk.*
intermixtus, *Wlk.*
lætabilis, *Wlk.*
*inefficiens, *Wlk.*

Fam. GYRINIDÆ, *Leach.*

Dineutes, *Macl.*
spinosus, *Fabr.*
Porrorhynchus, *Lap.*
indicans, *Wlk.*
Gyretes, *Brullé.*
discifer, *Wlk.*
Gyrinus, *Linn.*
nitidulus, *Fabr.*
obliquus, *Wlk.*
Orectochilus, *Esch.*
*lenocinium, *Dohrn.*

Fam. STAPHILINIDÆ, *Leach.*

Ocypus, *Kirby.*
longipennis, *Wlk.*
congruus, *Wlk.*
punctilinea, *Wlk.*
*lineatus *Wlk.*
Philonthus, *Leach.*
*pedestris, *Wlk.*
Xantholinus, *Dahl.*
cinctus, *Wlk.*
*inclinans, *Wlk.*
Sunius, *Leach.*
*obliquus, *Wlk.*
Œdichirus, *Erich.*
*alatus, *Niet.*
Pœderus, *Fabr.*
alternans, *Wlk.*
Stenus, *Latr.*
*barbatus, *Niet.*
*lacertoides, *Niet.*
Osorius ? *Leach.*
*compactus, *Wlk.*
Prognatha, *Latr.*
decisa, *Wlk.*
*tenuis, *Wlk.*
Leptochirus, *Perty.*
*bispinus, *Erich.*
Oxytelus, *Grav.*
rudis, *Wlk.*
productus, *Wlk.*
*bicolor, *Wlk.*
Trogophlœus, *Mann.*
*Taprobanæ, *Wlk.*
Omalium, *Grav.*
filiforme, *Wlk.*
Aleochara, *Grav.*
postica, *Wlk.*
*translata, *Wlk.*
*subjecta. *Wlk.*
Dinarda, *Leach.*
serricornis, *Wlk.*'

Fam. PSELAPHIDÆ, *Leach.*

Pselaphanax, *Wlk.*
setosus, *Wlk.*

Fam. SCYDMÆNIDÆ, *Leach.*

Erineus, *Wlk.*
monstrosus, *Wlk.*
Scydmænus, *Latr.*
*megamelas, *Wlk.*
*alatus, *Niet.*
*femoralis, *Niet.*
*Ceylanicus, *Niet.*
*intermedius, *Niet.*
*pselaphoides, *Niet.*
*advolans, *Niet.*
*pubescens, *Niet.*
*pygmæus, *Niet.*
*glanduliferus, *Niet.*
*graminicola, *Niet.*
*pyriformis, *Niet.*
*angusticeps, *Niet.*
*ovatus, *Niet.*

Fam. PTILIADÆ, *Wo.*

Trichopteryx, *Kirby.*
*cursitans, *Niet.*
*immatura, *Niet.*
*invisibilis, *Niet.*
Ptilium, *Schüpp.*
*subquadratum, *Niet.*
Ptenidium, *Erich.*
*macrocephalum, *Niet.*

Fam. PHALACRIDÆ, *Leach.*

Phalacrus, *Payk.*
conjiciens, *Wlk.*
confectus, *Wlk.*

Fam. NITIDULIDÆ, *Leach.*

Nitidula, *Fabr.*
contigens, *Wlk.*
intendens, *Wlk.*
significans, *Wlk.*
tomentifera, *Wlk.*
*submaculata, *Wlk.*
*glabricula, *Dohrn.*
Nitidulopsis, *Wlk.*
æqualis, *Wlk.*
Meligethes, *Kirby.*
*orientalis, *Niet.*
*respondens, *Wlk.*
Rhizophagus, *Herbst.*
parallelus, *Wlk.*

Fam. COLYDIADÆ, *Woll.*

Lyctus, *Fabr.*
retractus, *Wlk.*
disputans, *Wlk.*
Ditoma, *Illig.*
rugicollis, *Wlk.*

Fam. TROGOSITIDÆ, *Kirby.*

Trogosita, *Oliv.*
insinuans, *Wlk.*
*rhyzophagoides, *Wlk.*

Fam. CUCUJIDÆ, *Steph.*

Lœmophlœus, *Dej.*
ferrugineus, *Wlk.*
Cucujus ? *Fabr.*
*incommodus, *Wlk.*
Silvanus, *Latr.*
retrahens, *Wlk.*
*scuticollis, *Wlk.*
*porrectus, *Wlk.*
Brontes, *Fabr.*
*orientalis, *Dej.*

Fam. LATHRIDIANÆ, *Woll.*

Lathridius, *Herbst.*
perpusillus, *Wlk.*
Corticaria, *Marsh.*
resecta, *Wlk.*
Monotoma, *Herbst.*
concinnula, *Wlk.*

Fam. DERMESTIDÆ, *Leach.*

Dermestes, *Linn.*
vulpinus, *Fabr.*
Attagenus, *Latr.*
defectus, *Wlk.*
rufipes, *Wlk.*
Trinodes, *Meg.*
hirtellus, *Wlk.*

Fam. BYRRHIDÆ, *Leach.*

Inclica, *Wlk.*
solida, *Wlk.*

Fam. HISTERIDÆ, *Leach.*

Hister, *Linn.*
Bengalensis, *Weid.*

encaustus, *Mars.*
orientalis, *Payk.*
bipustulatus, *Fabr.*
*mundissimus, *Wlk.*
Saprinus, *Erich.*
semipunctatus, *Fabr.*
Platysoma, *Leach.*
atratum ? *Erichs.*
desinens, *Wlk.*
restoratum, *Wlk.*
Dendrophilus, *Leach.*
finitimus, *Wlk.*

Fam. APHODIADÆ, *Macl.*

Aphodius, *Illig.*
robustus, *Wlk.*
dynastoides, *Wlk.*
pallidicornis, *Wlk.*
mutans, *Wlk.*
sequens, *Wlk.*
Psammodius, *Gyll.*
inscitus, *Wlk.*

Fam. TROGIDÆ, *Macl.*

Trox, *Fabr.*
inclusus, *Wlk.*
cornutus, *Fabr.*

Fam. COPRIDÆ, *Leach.*

Ateuchus, *Weber.*
sacer, *Linn.*
Gymnopleurus, *Illig.*
smaragdifer, *Wlk.*
Kœnigii, *Fabr.*
Sisyphus, *Latr.*
setosulus, *Wlk.*
subsidens, *Wlk.*
prominens, *Wlk.*
Orepanocerus, *Kirby.*
Taprobanæ, *West.*
Copris, *Geoffr.*
Pirmal, *Fabr.*
sagax, *Quens.*
capucinus, *Fabr.*
cribricollis, *Wlk.*
repertus, *Wlk.*
sodalis, *Wlk.*
signatus, *Wlk.*
diminutivus, *Wlk.*
Onthophagus, *Latr.*
Bonassus, *Fabr.*
cervicornis, *Fabr.*
prolixus, *Wlk.*
gravis, *Wlk.*
difficilis, *Wlk.*
lucens, *Wlk.*
negligens, *Wlk.*
mœrens, *Wlk.*
turbatus, *Wlk.*
Onitis, *Fabr.*
Philemon, *Fabr.*

Fam. DYNASTIDÆ, *Macl.*

Oryctes, *Illig.*
rhinoceros, *Linn.*
Xylotrupes, *Hope.*
Gideon, *Linn.*
reductus, *Wlk.*
solidipes, *Wlk.*
Phileurus, *Latr.*
detractus, *Wlk.*
Orphnus, *Macl.*
detegens, *Wlk.*
scitissimus, *Wlk.*

Fam. GECTRUPIDÆ, *Leach.*

Bolboceras, *Kirby.*
lineatus, *Westw.*

Fam. MELOLONTHIDÆ, *Macl.*

Melolontha, *Fabr.*
nummicudens, *Newm.*
rubiginosa, *Wlk.*
ferruginosa, *Wlk.*
seriata, *Hope.*
pinguis, *Wlk.*
setosa, *Wlk.*
Rhizotrogus, *Latr.*
hirtipectus, *Wlk.*
æqualis, *Wlk.*
costatus, *Wlk.*
inductus, *Wlk.*
exactus, *Wlk.*
sulcifer, *Wlk.*
Phyllopertha, *Kirby.*
transversa, *Burm.*
Silphodes, *Westw.*
Indica, *Westw.*
Trigonostoma, *Dej.*
assimile, *Hope.*
compressum ? *Weid.*
nanum, *Wlk.*
Serica, *Macl.*
pruinosa, *Hope.*
Popilia, *Leach.*
marginicollis, *Newm.*
cyanella, *Hope.*
discalis, *Wlk.*
Sericesthis, *Dej.*
rotundata, *Wlk.*
subsignata, *Wlk.*
mollis, *Wlk.*
confirmata, *Wlk.*
Plectris, *Lep. & Serv.*
solida, *Wlk.*
punctigera, *Wlk.*
glabrilinea, *Wlk.*
Isonychus, *Mann.*
ventralis, *Wlk.*
pectoralis, *Wlk.*
Omaloplia, *Meg.*
fracta, *Wlk.*
interrupta, *Wlk.*
semicincta, *Wlk.*
*hamifera, *Wlk.*
*picta, *Dohrn.*
*nana, *Dohrn.*
Apogonia, *Kirby.*
nigricans, *Hope.*
Phytalus, *Erich.*
eurystomus, *Burm.*
Ancylonycha, *Dej.*
Reynaudii, *Blanch.*
Leucopholis, *Dej.*
Mellei, *Guer.*
pinguis, *Burm.*
Anomala, *Meg.*
elata, *Fabr.*
humeralis, *Wlk.*
discalis, *Wlk.*
varicolor, *Sch.*
conformis, *Wlk.*
similis, *Hope.*
punctatissima, *Wlk.*
infixa, *Wlk.*
Mimela, *Kirby.*
variegata, *Wlk.*
mundissima, *Wlk.*
Parastasia, *Westw.*
rufopicta, *Westw.*
Euchlora, *Macl.*
viridis, *Fabr.*
perplexa, *Hope.*

Fam. CETONIADÆ, *Kirby.*

Glycyphana, *Burm.*
versicolor, *Fabr.*
luctuosa, *Gory.*
variegata, *Fabr.*
marginicollis, *Gory.*
Clinteria, *Burm.*
imperalis, *Schaum.*
incerta, *Parry.*
chloronota, *Blanch.*
Tæniodera, *Burm.*
Malabariensis, *Gory.*
quadrivittata, *White.*
alboguttata, *Vigors.*
Protætia, *Burm.*
maculata, *Fabr.*
Whitehousii, *Parry.*
Agestrata, *Erich.*
nigrita, *Fabr.*
orichalcea, *Linn.*
Coryphocera, *Burm.*
elegans, *Fabr.*
Nacronota, *Hoffm.*
quadrivittata, *Sch.*

Fam. TRICHIADÆ, *Leach.*

Valgus, *Scriba.*
addendus, *Wlk.*

Fam. LUCANIDÆ, *Leach.*

Odontolabis, *Burm.*
Bengalensis, *Parry.*
emarginatus, *Dej.*
Ægus, *Macl.*
acuminatus, *Fabr.*
lunatus, *Fabr.*
Singhala, *Blanch.*
tenella, *Blanch.*

Fam. PASSALIDÆ, *Macl.*

Passalus, *Fabr.*
transversus, *Dohrn.*
interstitialis, *Perch.*
punctiger ? *Lefeb.*
bicolor, *Fabr.*

Fam. SPHÆRIDIADÆ, *Leach*

Sphæridium, *Fabr.*
tricolor, *Wlk.*
Cercyon, *Leach.*
*vicinale, *Wlk.*

Fam. HYDROPHILIDÆ, *Leach.*

Hydrous, *Leach.*
*rufiventris, *Niet.*

*inconspicuus, *Niet.*
Hydrobius, *Leach.*
stultus, *Wlk.*
Philydrus, *Solier.*
esuriens, *Wlk.*
Berosus, *Leach.*
*decrescens, *Wlk.*
Hydrochus, *Germ.*
*lacustris, *Niet.*
Georyssus, *Latr.*
*gemma, *Niet.*
*insularis, *Dohrn.*
Dastarcus, *Wlk.*
porosus, *Wlk.*

Fam. BUPRESTIDÆ, *Steph.*

Sternocera, *Esch.*
chrysis, *Linn.*
sternicornis, *Linn.*
Chrysochroa, *Solier.*
ignita, *Linn.*
Chinensis, *Lap.*
Rajah, *Lap.*
*cyaneocephala, *Fabr.*
Chrysodema, *Lap.*
sulcata, *Thunb.*
Belionota, *Esch.*
scutellaris, *Fabr.*
*Petiti, *Gory.*
Chrysobothris, *Esch.*
suturalis, *Wlk.*
Agrilus, *Meg.*
sulcicollis, *Wlk.*
*cupreiceps, *Wlk.*
*cupreicollis, *Wlk.*
*armatus, *Fabr.*

Fam. ELATERIDÆ, *Leach.*

Campsosternos, *Latr.*
Templetonii, *Westw.*
aureolus, *Hope.*
Bohemannii, *Cand.*
venustulus, *Cand.*
pallidipes, *Cand.*
Agrypnus, *Esch.*
fuscipes, *Fabr.*
Alaus, *Esch.*
speciosus, *Linn.*
sordidus, *Westw.*
Cardiophorus, *Esch.*
humerifer, *Wlk.*
Corymbites, *Latr.*
dividens, *Wlk.*
divisa, *Wlk.*
*bivittava, *Wlk.*
Lacon, *Lap.*
*obesus, *Cand.*
Athous, *Esch.*
punctosus, *Wlk.*
inapertus, *Wlk.*
decretus, *Wlk.*
inefficiens, *Wlk.*
Ampedus, *Meg.*
*acutifer, *Wlk.*
*discicollis, *Wlk.*
Legna, *Wlk.*
idonea, *Wlk.*

Fam. LAMPYRIDÆ, *Leach.*

Lycus, *Fabr.*
triangularis, *Hope.*
geminus, *Wlk*
astutus, *Wlk.*
fallax, *Wlk.*
planicornis, *Wlk.*
melanopterus, *Wlk.*
pubicornis, *Wlk.*
duplex, *Wlk.*
costifer, *Wlk.*
revocans, *Wlk.*
dispellens, *Wlk.*
*pubipennis, *Wlk.*
*humerifer, *Wlk.*
expansicornis, *Wlk.*
divisus, *Wlk.*
Dictyopterus, *Latr.*
internexus, *Wlk.*
Lampyris, *Geoff.*
tenebrosa, *Wlk.*
diffinis, *Wlk.*
lutescens, *Wlk.*
*vitrifera, *Wlk.*
Colophotia, *Dej.*
humeralis, *Wlk.*
[vespertina, *Fabr.*
perplexa, *Wlk.* ?]
intricata, *Wlk.*
extricans, *Wlk.*
promelas, *Wlk.*
Harmatelia, *Wlk.*
discalis, *Wlk.*
bilinea, *Wlk.*

Fam. TELEPHORIDÆ, *Leach.*

Telephorus, *Schäff.*
dimidiatus, *Fabr.*
malthinoides, *Wlk.*
Eugeusis, *Westw.*
palpator, *Westw.*
gryphus, *Hope.*
olivaceus, *Hope.*

Fam. CEBRIONIDÆ, *Steph.*

Callirhipis, *Latr.*
Templetonii, *Westw.*
Championii, *Westw.*

Fam. MELYRIDÆ, *Leach.*

Malachius, *Fabr.*
plagiatus, *Wlk.*
Malthinus, *Latr.*
*forticornis, *Wlk.*
*retractus, *Wlk.*
fragilis, *Dohrn.*
Enicopus, *Steph.*
proficiens, *Wlk.*
Honosca, *Wlk.*
necrobioides, *Wlk.*

Fam. CLERIDÆ, *Kirby.*

Cylidrus, *Lap.*
sobrinus, *Dohrn.*
Stigmatium, *Gray.*
elaphroides, *Westw.*
Necrobia, *Latr.*
rufipes, *Fabr.*
aspera, *Wlk.*

Fam. PTINIDÆ, *Leach.*

Ptinus, *Linn.*
*nigerrimus, *Boield.*

Fam. DIAPERIDÆ, *Leach.*

Diaperis, *Geoff.*
velutina, *Wlk.*
fragilis, *Dohrn.*

Fam. TENEBRIONIDÆ, *Leach.*

Zophobas, *Dej.*
errans ? *Dej.*
clavipes, *Wlk.*
? solidus, *Wlk.*
Pseudoblaps, *Guer.*
nigrita, *Fabr.*
Tenebrio, *Linn.*
rubripes, *Hope.*
retenta, *Wlk.*
Trachyscelis, *Latr.*
brunnea, *Dohrn.*

Fam. OPATRIDÆ, *Shuck.*

Opatrum, *Fabr.*
contrahens, *Wlk.*
bilineatum, *Wlk.*
planatum, *Wlk.*
serricolle, *Wlk.*
Asida, *Latr.*
horrida, *Wlk.*
Crypticus, *Latr.*
detersus, *Wlk.*
longipennis, *Wlk.*
Phaleria, *Latr.*
rufipes, *Wlk.*
Toxicum, *Latr.*
oppugnans, *Wlk.*
biluna, *Wlk.*
Boletophagus, *Ill.*
*morosus, *Dohrn.*
*exasperatus, *Dohrn.*
Uloma, *Meg.*
scita, *Wlk.*
Alphitophagus, *Steph.*
subfascia, *Wlk.*

Fam. HELOPIDÆ, *Steph.*

Osdara, *Wlk.*
picipes, *Wlk.*
Cholipus, *Dej.*
brevicornis, *Dej.*
parabolicus, *Wlk.*
læviusculus, *Wlk.*
Helops, *Fabr.*
ebeninus, *Wlk.*
Camaria, *Lep. & Serv.*
amethystina, *L. & S.*
Amarygmus, *Dalm.*
chrysomeloides, *Dej.*

Fam. MELOIDÆ, *Woll.*

Epicauta, *Dej.*
nigrifinis, *Wlk.*
Cissites, *Latr.*
testaceus, *Fabr.*
Mylabris, *Fabr.*
humeralis, *Wlk.*
alterna, *Wlk.*
*recognita, *Wlk.*
Atractocerus, *Pal., Bv.*
debilis, *Wlk.*
reversus, *Wlk.*

Fam. ŒDEMERIDÆ, *Steph.*
Cistela, *Fabr.*
congrua, *Wlk.*
*falsifica, *Wlk.*
Allecula, *Fabr.*
fusiformis, *Wlk.*
elegans, *Wlk.*
*flavifemur, *Wlk.*
Sora, *Wlk.*
*marginata, *Wlk.*
Thaccona, *Wlk.*
dimelas, *Wlk.*

Fam. MORDELLIDÆ, *Steph.*
Acosmus, *Dej.*
languidus, *Wlk.*
Rhipiphorus, *Fabr.*
*tropicus, *Niet.*
Mordella, *Linn.*
composita, *Wlk.*
*defectiva, *Wlk.*
Myrmecolax, *Westw.*
*Nietneri, *Westw.*

Fam. ANTHICIDÆ, *Wlk.*
Anthicus, *Payk.*
*quisquilarius, *Niet.*
*insularius, *Niet.*
*sticticollis, *Wlk.*

Fam. CISSIDÆ, *Leach.*
Cis, *Latr.*
contendens, *Wlk.*

Fam. TOMICIDÆ, *Shuck.*
Apate, *Fabr.*
submedia, *Wlk.*
Bostrichus, *Geoff.*
mutilatus, *Wlk.*
*vertens, *Wlk.*
*moderatus, *Wlk.*
*testaceus, *Wlk.*
*exiguus, *Wlk.*
Platypus, *Herbst.*
minax, *Wlk.*
solidus, *Wlk.*
*latifinis, *Wlk.*
Hylurgus, *Latr.*
determinans, *Wlk.*
*concinnulus, *Wlk.*
Hylesinus, *Fabr.*
curvifer, *Wlk.*
despectus, *Wlk.*
irresolutus, *Wlk.*

Fam. CURCULIONIDÆ, *Leach.*
Bruchus, *Linn.*
scutellaris, *Fabr.*
Spermophagus, *Steven.*
convolvuli, *Thunb.*
figuratus, *Wlk.*
Cisti, *Fabr.*
incertus, *Wlk.*
decretus, *Wlk.*
Dendropemon, *Schön.*
*melancholicus, *Dohrn.*
Dendrotrogus, *Jek.*
Dohrnii, *Jek.*
discrepans, *Dohrn.*
Eucorynus, *Schön.*
colligendus, *Wlk.*
colligens, *Wlk.*
Basitropis, *Jek.*
*disconotatus, *Jek.*
Litocerus, *Schön.*
punctulatus, *Dohrn.*
Tropideres, *Sch.*
punctulifer, *Dohrn.*
fragilis, *Wlk.*
Cedus, *Waterh.*
*cancellatus, *Dohrn.*
Xylinades, *Latr.*
sobrinulus, *Dohrn.*
indignus, *Wlk.*
Xenocerus, *Germ.*
anguliferus, *Wlk.*
revocans, *Wlk.*
*anchoralis, *Dohrn.*
Callistocerus, *Dohrn.*
*Nietneri, *Dohrn.*
Anthribus, *Geoff.*
longicornis, *Fabr.*
apicalis, *Wlk.*
facilis, *Wlk.*
Aræcerus, *Schön.*
coffeæ, *Fabr.*
*insidiosus, *Fabr.*
*musculus, *Dohrn.*
*intangens, *Wlk.*
*bifovea, *Wlk.*
Dipieza, *Pasc.*
*insignis, *Dohrn.*
Apolecta, *Pasc.*
*Nietneri, *Dohrn.*
*musculus, *Dohrn.*
Arrhenodes, *Steven.*
miles, *Sch.*
pilicornis, *Sch.*
dentirostris, *Jek.*
approximans, *Wlk.*
Veneris, *Dohrn.*
Cerobates, *Schön.*
thrasco, *Dohrn.*
aciculatus, *Wlk.*
Ceocephalus, *Schön.*
cavus, *Wlk.*
*reticulatus, *Fabr.*
Nemocephalus, *Latr.*
sulcirostris, *De Haan.*
planicollis, *Wlk.*
spinirostris, *Wlk.*
Apoderus, *Oliv.*
longicollis ? *Fabr.*
Tranquebaricus, *Fabr.*
cygneus, *Fabr.* ?
scitulus, *Wlk.*
*triangularis, *Fabr.*
*echinatus, *Sch.*
Rhynchites, *Herbst.*
suffundens, *Wlk.*
*restituens, *Wlk.*
Apion, *Herbst.*
*Cingalense, *Wlk.*
Strophosomus, *Bilbug.*
*suturalis, *Wlk.*
Piazomias, *Schön.*
æqualis, *Wlk.*
Astycus, *Schön.*
lateralis, *Fabr.* ?
ebeninus, *Wlk.*
*immunis, *Wlk.*
Cleonus, *Schön.*
inducens, *Wlk.*
Myllocerus, *Schön.*
transmarinus, *Herbst.* ?
spurcatus, *Wlk.*
*retrahens, *Wlk.*
*posticus, *Wlk.*
Phyllobius, *Schön.*
*mimicus, *Wlk.*
Episomus, *Schön.*
pauperatus, *Fabr.*
Lixus, *Fabr.*
nebulifascia, *Wlk.*
Aclees, *Schön.*
cribratus, *Dej.*
Alcides, *Dalm.*
signatus, *Boh.*
obliquus, *Wlk.*
transversus, *Wlk.*
*clausus, *Wlk.*
Acicnemis, *Fairm.*
Ceylonicus, *Jek.*
Apotomorhinus, *Schön.*
signatus, *Wlk.*
alboater, *Wlk.*
Cryptorhynchus, *Illig.*
ineffectus, *Wlk.*
assimilans, *Wlk.*
declaratus, *Wlk.*
notabilis, *Wlk.*
vexatus, *Wlk.*
Camptorhinus, *Schön.* ?
reversus, *Wlk.*
*indiscretus, *Wlk.*
Desmidophorus, *Chevr.*
hebes, *Fabr.*
communicans, *Wlk.*
strenuus, *Wlk.*
*discriminans, *Wlk.*
inexpertus, *Wlk.*
fasciculicollis, *Wlk.*
Sipalus, *Schön.*
granulatus, *Fabr.*
porosus, *Wlk.*
tinctus, *Wlk.*
Mecopus, *Dalm.*
*Waterhousei, *Dohrn.*
Rhynchophorus, *Herbst.*
ferrugineus, *Fabr.*
introducens, *Wlk.*
Protocerus, *Schön.*
molossus ? *Oliv.*
Sphænophorus, *Schön.*
glabridiscus, *Wlk.*
exquisitus, *Wlk.*
Dehaani ? *Jek.*
cribricollis, *Wlk.*
? panops, *Wlk.*
Cossonus, *Clairv.*
*quadrimacula, *Wlk.*
? hebes, *Wlk.*
ambiguus, *Sch.* ?
Scitophilus, *Schön.*
orizæ, *Linn.*
disciferus, *Wlk.*
Mecinus, *Germ.*
* ? relictus, *Wlk.*

Fam. PRIONIDÆ, *Leach.*
Trictenotoma, *G. R. Gray.*

Templetoni, *Westw.*
Prionomma, *White.*
orientalis, *Oliv.*
Acanthophorus, *Serv.*
serraticornis, *Oliv.*
Cnemoplites, *Newm.*
Rhesus, *Motch.*
Ægosoma, *Serv.*
Cingalense, *White.*

Fam. Cerambycidæ, *Kirby.*

Cerambyx, *Linn.*
indutus, *Newm.*
vernicosus, *Pasc.*
consocius, *Pasc.*
versutus, *Pasc.*
nitidus, *Pasc.*
macilentus, *Pasc.*
venustus, *Pasc.*
torticollis, *Dohrn.*
Sebasmia, *Pasc.*
Templetoni, *Pasc.*
Callichroma, *Latr.*
trogoninum, *Pasc.*
telephoroides, *Westw.*
Homalomelas, *White.*
gracilipes, *Parry.*
zonatus, *Pasc.*
Colobus, *Serv.*
Cingalensis, *White.*
Thranius, *Pasc.*
gibbosus, *Pasc.*
Deuteromma, *Pasc.*
mutica, *Pasc.*
Obrium, *Meg.*
laterale, *Pasc.*
mœstum, *Pasc.*
Psilomerus, *Blanch.*
macilentus, *Pasc.*
Clytus, *Fabr.*
vicinus, *Hope.*
ascendens, *Pasc.*
Walkeri, *Pasc.*
annularis, *Fabr.*
*aurilinea, *Dohrn.*
Rhaphuma, *Pasc.*
leucoscutellata, *Hope.*
Ceresium, *Newm.*
cretatum, *White.*
Zeylanicum, *White.*
Stromatium, *Serv.*
barbatum, *Fabr.*
maculatum, *White.*
Hespherophanes, *Muls.*
simplex, *Gyll.*

Fam. Lamiidæ, *Kirby.*

Nyphona, *Muls.*
cylindracea, *White.*
Mesosa, *Serv.*
columba, *Pasc.*
Coptops, *Serv.*
bidens, *Fabr.*
Xylorhiza, *Dej.*
adusta, *Wied.*
Cacia, *Newm.*
triloba, *Pasc.*
Batocera, *Blanch.*
rubus, *Fabr.*
ferruginea, *Blanch.*
Monohammus, *Meg.*
fistulator, *Germ.*
crucifer, *Fabr.*
nivosus, *White.*
commixtus, *Pasc.*
Cereopsius, *Dup.*
patronus, *Pasc.*
Pelargoderus, *Serv.*
tigrinus, *Chevr.*
Olenocamptus, *Chevr.*
bilobus, *Fabr.*
Praonetha, *Dej.*
annulata, *Chevr.*
posticalis, *Pasc.*
Apomecyna, *Serv.*
histrio, *Fabr.* var. ?
Ropica, *Pasc.*
præusta, *Pasc.*
Hathlia, *Serv.*
procera, *Pasc.*
Iolea, *Pasc.*
proxima, *Pasc.*
histrio, *Pasc.*
Glenea, *Newm.*
sulphurella, *White.*
commissa, *Pasc.*
scapifera, *Pasc.*
vexator, *Pasc.*
Stibara, *Hope.*
nigricornis, *Fabr.*

Fam. Hispidæ, *Kirby.*

Oncocephala, *Dohrn.*
deltoides, *Dohrn.*
Leptispa, *Baly.*
pygmæa, *Baly.*
Amplisba, *Baly.*
Döhrnii, *Baly.*
Estigmena, *Hope.*
Chinensis, *Hope.*
Hispa, *Linn.*
hystrix, *Fabr.*
erinacea, *Fabr.*
nigrina, *Dohrn.*
*Walkeri, *Baly.*
Platypria, *Guér.*
echidna, *Guér.*

Fam. Cassididæ, *Westw.*

Episticta, *Boh.*
matronula, *Boh.*
Hoplionota, *Hope.*
tetraspilota, *Baly.*
rubromarginata, *Boh.*
horrifica, *Boh.*
Aspidomorpha, *Hope.*
St. crucis, *Fabr.*
miliaris, *Fabr.*
pallidimarginata, *Baly.*
dorsata, *Fabr.*
calligera, *Boh.*
micans, *Fabr.*
Cassida, *Linn.*
clathrata, *Fabr.*
timefacta, *Boh.*
farinosa, *Boh.*
Laccoptera, *Boh.*
14-notata, *Boh.*
Coptcycla, *Chevr.*
sex-notata, *Fabr.*
13-signata, *Boh.*
13-notata, *Boh.*
ornata, *Fabr.*
Ceylonica, *Boh.*
Balyi, *Boh.*
trivittata, *Fabr.*
15-punctuata, *Boh.*
catenata, *Dej.*

Fam. Sagridæ, *Kirby.*

Sagra, *Fabr.*
nigrita, *Oliv.*

Fam. Donacidæ, *Lacord.*

Donacia, *Fabr.*
Delesserti, *Guér.*
Coptocephala, *Chev.*
Templetoni, *Baly.*

Fam. Eumolpidæ, *Baly.*

Corynodes, *Hope.*
cyaneus, *Hope.*
æneus, *Baly.*
Glyptoscelis, *Chevr.*
Templetoni, *Baly.*
pyrospilotus, *Baly.*
micans, *Baly.*
cupreus, *Baly.*
Eumolpus, *Fabr.*
lemoides, *Wlk.*

Fam. Cryptocephalidæ, *Kirby.*

Cryptocephalus, *Geoff.*
sex-punctatus, *Fabr.*
Walkeri, *Baly.*
Diapromorpha, *Lac.*
Turcica, *Fabr.*

Fam. Chrysomelidæ, *Leach.*

Chalcolampa, *Baly.*
Templetoni, *Baly.*
Lina, *Meg.*
convexa, *Baly.*
Chrysomela, *Linn.*
Templetoni, *Baly.*

Fam. Galerucidæ, *Steph.*

Galeruca, *Geoff.*
*pectinata, *Dohrn.*
Graptodera, *Chevr.*
cyanea, *Fabr.*
Monolepta, *Chevr.*
pulchella, *Baly.*
Thyamis, *Steph.*
Ceylonicus, *Baly.*

Fam. Coccinellidæ, *Latr.*

Epilachna, *Chevr.*
28-punctata, *Fabr.*
Delessortii, *Guér.*
pubescens, *Hope.*
innuba, *Oliv.*
Coccinella, *Linn.*
tricincta, *Fabr.*
*repanda, *Muls.*
tenuilinea, *Wlk.*
rejiciens, *Wlk.*
interrumpens, *Wlk.*

quinqueplaga, *Wlk.*
simplex, *Wlk.*
antica, *Wlk.*
flaviceps, *Wlk.*
Neda, *Muls.*
tricolor, *Fabr.*
Coelophora, *Muls.*
9-maculata, *Fabr.*?
Chilocorus, *Leach.*
opponens, *Wlk.*
Scymnus, *Kug.*
variabilis, *Wlk.*

Fam. EROTYLIDÆ, *Leach.*

Fatua, *Dej.*
Nepalensis, *Hope.*
Triplax, *Payk.*
decorus, *Wlk.*
Tritoma, *Fabr.*
*bifacies, *Wlk.*
*preposita, *Wlk.*
Ischyrus, *Cherz.*
grandis, *Fabr.*

Fam. ENDOMYCHIDÆ, *Leach.*

Eugonius, *Gerst.*
annularis, *Gerst.*
lunulatus, *Gerst.*
Eumorphus, *Weber.*
pulchripes, *Gerst.*
*tener, *Dohrn.*
Stenotarsus, *Perty.*
Nietneri, *Gerst.*
*castaneus, *Gerst.*
*tomentosus, *Gerst.*
*vallatus, *Gerst.*
Lycoperdina, *Latr.*
glabrata, *Wlk.*
Ancylopus, *Gerst.*
melanocephalus, *Oliv.*
Saula, *Gerst.*
*nigripes, *Gerst.*
*ferruginea, *Gerst.*
Mycetina, *Gerst.*
castanea, *Gerst.*

## Order ORTHOPTERA, *Linn.*

Fam. FORFICULIDÆ, *Steph.*

Forficula, *Linn.*
——— ?

Fam BLATTIDÆ, *Steph.*

Panesthia, *Serv.*
Javanica, *Serv.*
plagiata, *Wlk.*
Polyzosteria, *Burm.*
larva.
Corydia, *Serv.*
Petiveriana, *Linn.*

Fam. MANTIDÆ, *Leach.*

Empusa, *Illig.*
gongylodes, *Linn.*
Harpax, *Serv.*
signifer, *Wlk.*
Schizocephala, *Serv.*
bicornis, *Linn.*
Mantis, *Linn.*
superstitiosa, *Fabr.*
aridifolia, *Stoll.*
extensicollis ? *Serv.*

Fam. PHASMIDÆ, *Serv.*

Acrophylla, *Gray.*
systropedon, *Westw.*
Phasma, *Licht.*
sordidum, *De Haan.*
Phyllium, *Illig.*
siccifolium, *Linn.*

Fam. GRYLLIDÆ, *Steph.*

Acheta, *Linn.*
bimaculata, *Deg.*
supplicans, *Wlk.*
æqualis, *Wlk.*
confirmata, *Wlk.*
Platydactylus, *Brull.*
crassipes, *Wlk.*
Steirodon, *Serv.*
lanceolatum, *Wlk.*
Phyllophora, *Thunb.*
falsifolia, *Wlk.*
Acanthodis, *Serv.*
rugosa, *Wlk.*
Phaneroptera, *Serv.*
attenuata, *Wlk.*
Phymateus, *Thunb.*
miliaris, *Linn.*
Truxalis, *Linn.*
exaltata, *Wlk.*
porrecta, *Wlk.*
Acridium, *Geoffr.*
extensum, *Wlk.*
deponens, *Wlk.*
rufitibia, *Wlk.*
cinctifemur, *Wlk.*
respondens, *Wlk.*
nigrifascia, *Wlk.*

## Order PHYSAPODA, *Dum.*

Thrips, *Linn.*
stenomelas, *Wlk.*

## Order NEUROPTERA, *Linn.*

Fam. SERICOSTOMIDÆ, *Steph.*

Mormonia, *Curt.*
*ursina, *Hagen.*

Fam. LEPTOCERIDÆ, *Leach.*

Macronema, *Pict.*
multifarium, *Wlk.*
*splendidum, *Hagen.*
*nebulosum, *Hagen.*
*obliquum, *Hagen.*
*Ceylanicum, *Niet.*
*annulicorne, *Niet.*
Molanna, *Curt.*
mixta, *Hagen.*
Setodes, *Ramb.*
*Iris, *Hagen.*
*Ino, *Hagen.*

Fam. PSYCHOMIDÆ, *Curt.*

Chimarra, *Leach.*
*auriceps, *Hagen.*
*funesta, *Hagen.*
*sepulcralis, *Hagen.*

Fam. HYDROPSYCHIDÆ, *Curt.*

Hydropsyche, *Pict.*
*Taprobanes, *Hagen.*
*mitis, *Hagen.*

Fam. RHYACOPHILIDÆ, *Steph.*

Rhyacophila, *Pict.*
*castanea, *Hagen.*

Fam. PERLIDÆ, *Leach.*

Perla, *Geoffr.*
angulata, *Wlk.*
*testacea, *Hagen.*
*limosa, *Hagen.*

Fam. SIALIDÆ, *Westw.*

Dilar, *Ramb.*
*Nietneri, *Hagen.*

Fam. HEMEROBIDÆ, *Leach.*

Mantispa, *Illig.*
*Indica, *Westw.*
mutata, *Wlk.*
Chrysopa, *Leach.*
invaria, *Wlk.*
*tropica, *Hagen.*
aurifera, *Wlk.*
*punctata, *Hagen.*
Micromerus, *Ramb.*
*linearis, *Hagen.*
*australis, *Hagen.*
Hemerobius, *Linn.*
*frontalis, *Hagen.*
Coniopteryx, *Hal.*
*cerata, *Hagen.*

Fam. MYRMELEONIDÆ, *Leach.*

Palpares, *Ramb.*
contrarius, *Wlk.*
Acanthoclisis, *Ramb.*
*—n. s. *Hagen.*
*molestus, *Wlk.*
Myrmeleon, *Linn.*
gravis, *Wlk.*
dirus, *Wlk.*
barbarus, *Wlk.*
Ascalaphus, *Fabr.*
nugax, *Wlk.*
incusans, *Wlk.*
*cervinus, *Niet.*

Fam. PSOCIDÆ, *Leach.*

Psocus, *Latr.*

*Taprobanes, *Hagen.*
*oblitus, *Hagen.*
*consitus, *Hagen.*
*trimaculatus, *Hagen.*
*obtusus, *Hagen.*
*elongatus, *Hagen.*
*chloroticus, *Hagen.*
*aridus, *Hagen.*
*coleoptratus, *Hagen.*
*dolabratus, *Hagen.*
*infelix, *Hagen.*

Fam. TERMITIDÆ, *Leach.*

Termes, *Linn.*
Taprobanes, *Wlk.*
fatalis, *Kœn.*
monoceros, *Kœn.*
*umbilicatus, *Hagen.*
*n. s. *Jouv.*
*n. s. *Jouv.*

Fam. EMBIDÆ, *Hagen.*

Oligotoma, *Westw.*
*Saundersii, *Westw.*

Fam. EPHEMERIDÆ, *Leach.*

Bætis, *Leach.*
Taprobanes, *Wlk.*
Potamanthus, *Pict.*
*fasciatus, *Hagen.*
*annulatus, *Hagen.*
*femoralis, *Hagen.*
Cloe, *Burm.*
*tristis, *Hagen.*
*consucta, *Hagen.*
*solida, *Hagen.*
*sigmata, *Hagen.*
*marginalis, *Hagen.*
Cænis, *Steph.*
perpusilla, *Wlk.*

Fam. LIBELLULIDÆ.

Calopteryx, *Leach.*
Chinensis, *Linn.*
Euphœa, *Selys.*
splendens, *Hagen.*
Micromerus, *Ramb.*
lineatus, *Burm.*
Trichocnemys, *Selys.*
*serapica, *Hagen.*
Lestes, *Leach.*
*elata, *Hagen.*
*gracilis, *Hagen.*
Agrion, *Fabr.*
*Coromandelianum, *F.*
*tenax, *Hagen.*
*hilare, *Hagen.*
*velare, *Hagen.*
*delicatum, *Hagen.*
Gynacantha, *Ramb.*
subinterrupta, *Ramb.*
Epophthalmia, *Burm.*
vittata, *Burm.*
Zyxomma, *Ramb.*
petiolatum, *Ramb.*
Acisoma, *Ramb.*
panorpoides, *Ramb.*
Libellula, *Linn.*
Marcia, *Drury.*
Tillarga, *Fabr.*
variegata, *Linn.*
flavescens, *Fabr.*
Sabina, *Drury.*
viridula, *Pal. Beauv.*
congener, *Ramb.*
soror, *Ramb.*
Aurora, *Burm.*
violacea, *Niet.*
perla, *Hagen.*
sanguinea, *Burm.*
trivialis, *Ramb.*
contaminata, *Fabr.*
equestris, *Fabr.*
nebulosa, *Fabr.*

## Order HYMENOPTERA, *Linn.*

Fam. FORMICIDÆ, *Leach.*

Formica, *Linn.*
smaragdina, *Fabr.*
mitis, *Smith.*
*Taprobane, *Smith.*
*variegata, *Smith.*
*exercita, *Wlk.*
*exundans, *Wlk.*
*meritans, *Wlk.*
*latebrosa, *Wlk.*
*pangens, *Wlk.*
*ingruens, *Wlk.*
*detorquens, *Wlk.*
*diffidens, *Wlk.*
*obscurans, *Wlk.*
*indeflexa, *Wlk.*
consultans, *Wlk.*
Polyrhachis, *Smith.*
*illaudatus, *Wlk.*

Fam. PONERIDÆ, *Smith.*

Odontomachus, *Latr.*
simillimus, *Smith.*
Typhlopone, *Westw.*
Curtisii, *Shuck.*
Myrmica, *Latr.*
basalis, *Smith.*
contigua, *Smith.*
glyciphila, *Smith.*
*consternens, *Wlk.*
Crematogaster, *Lund.*
*pellens, *Wlk.*
*deponens, *Wlk.*
*forticulus, *Wlk.*
Pseudomyrma, *Guré.*
*atrata, *Smith.*
allaborans, *Wlk.*
Atta, *St. Farg.*
didita, *Wlk.*
Pheidole, *Westw.*
Janus, *Smith.*
*Taprobanæ, *Smith.*
*rugosa, *Smith.*
Meranoplus, *Smith.*
*dimicans, *Wlk.*
Cataulacus, *Smith.*
Taprobanæ, *Smith.*

Fam. MUTILLIDÆ, *Leach.*

Mutilla, *Linn.*
*Sibylla, *Smith.*
Tiphia, *Fabr.*
*decrescens, *Wlk.*

Fam. EUMENIDÆ, *Westw.*

Odynerus, *Latr.*
*tinctipennis, *Wlk.*
*intendens, *Wlk.*
*intendens, *Wlk.*
Scolia, *Fabr.*
auricollis, *St. Farg.*

Fam. CRABRONIDÆ, *Leach.*

Philanthus, *Fabr.*
basalis, *Smith.*
Stigmus, *Jur.*
*congruus, *Wilk.*

Fam. SPHEGIDÆ, *Steph.*

Ammophila, *Kirby.*
atripes, *Smith.*
Pelopæus, *Latr.*
Spinolæ, *St. Farg.*
Sphex, *Fabr.*
ferruginea, *St. Farg.*
Ampulex, *Jur.*
compressa, *Fabr.*

Fam. LARRIDÆ, *Steph.*

Larrada, *Smith.*
*extensa, *Wlk.*

Fam. POMPILIDÆ, *Leach.*

Pompilus, *Fabr.*
analis, *Fabr.*

Fam. APIDÆ, *Leach.*

Andrena, *Fabr.*
*exagens, *Wlk.*
Nomia, *Latr.*
rustica, *Westw.*
*vincta, *Wlk.*
Allodaps, *Smith.*
*marginata, *Smith.*
Ceratina, *Latr.*
viridis, *Guér.*
picta, *Smith.*
*simillima, *Smith.*
Cœlioxys, *Latr.*
capitata, *Smith.*
Croeisa, *Jur.*
*ramosa, *St. Farg.*
Stelis, *Panz.*
carbonaria, *Smith.*
Anthophora, *Latr.*
zonata, *Smith.*
Xylocopa, *Latr.*
tenuiscapa, *Westw.*
latipes, *Drury.*
Apis, *Linn.*
Indica, *Smith.*
Trigona, *Jur.*
iridipennis, *Smith.*
*præterita, *Wlk.*

Fam. CHRYSIDÆ, *Wlk.*

Stilbum, *Spin.*
splendidum, *Dahl.*

Fam. DORYLIDÆ, *Shuck.*

Enictus, *Shuck.*
porizonoides, *Wlk.*

Fam. ICHNEUMONIDÆ *Leach.*

Cryptus, *Fabr.*
 *onustus, *Wlk.*
Hemiteles? *Grav.*
 *varius, *Wlk.*
Porizon, *Fall.*
 *dominans, *Wlk.*
Pimpla, *Fabr.*
 albopicta, *Wlk.*

Fam. BRACONIDÆ, *Hal.*

Microgaster, *Latr.*
 *recusans, *Wlk.*
 *significans, *Wlk.*
 *subducens, *Wlk.*
 *detracta, *Wlk.*
Spathius, *Nees.*
 *bisignatus, *Wlk.*
 *signipennis, *Wlk.*
Heratemis, *Wlk.*
 *filosa, *Wlk.*
Nebartha, *Wlk.*
 *macropoides, *Wlk.*
Psyttalia, *Wlk.*
 *testacea, *Wlk.*

Fam. CHALCIDIÆ, *Spin.*

Chalcis, *Fabr.*
 *dividens, *Wlk.*
 *pandens, *Wlk.*
Halticella, *Spin.*
 *rufimanus, *Wlk.*
 *inficiens, *Wlk.*
Dirrhinus, *Dalm.*
 *anthracia, *Wlk.*
Eurytoma, *Ill.*
 *contraria, *Wlk.*
 indefensa, *Wlk.*
Eucharis, *Latr.*
 *convergens, *Wlk.*
 *deprivata, *Wlk.*
Pteromalus, *Swed.*
 *magniceps, *Wlk.*
Encyrtus, *Latr.*
 *obstructus, *Wlk.*

Fam. DIAPRIDÆ, *Hal.*

Diapria, *Latr.*
 apicalis, *Wlk.*

## Order LEPIDOPTERA, *Linn.*

Fam. PAPILIONIDÆ, *Leach.*

Ornithoptera, *Boisd.*
 Darsius, *G. R. Gray.*
Papilio, *Linn.*
 Diphilus, *Esp.*
 Jophon, *G. R. Gray.*
 Hector, *Linn.*
 Romulus, *Cram.*
 Polymnestor, *Cram.*
 Crino, *Fabr.*
 Helenus, *Linn.*
 Pammon, *Linn.*
 Polytes, *Linn.*
 Erithonius, *Cram.*
 Antipathis, *Cram.*
 Agamemnon, *Linn.*
 Eurypilus, *Linn.*
 Bathycles, *Zinck-Som.*
 Sarpedon, *Linn.*
 dissimilis, *Linn.*
Pontia, *Fabr.*
 Nina, *Fabr.*
Pieris, *Schr.*
 Eucharis, *Drury.*
 Coronis, *Cram.*
 Epicharis, *Godt.*
 Nama, *Doubl.*
 Remba, *Moore.*
 Mesentina, *Godt.*
 Severina, *Cram.*
 Namouna, *Doubl.*
 Phryne, *Fabr.*
 Paulina, *Godt.*
 Thestylis, *Doubl.*
Callosune, *Doubl.*
 Eucharis, *Fabr.*
 Danaë, *Fabr.*
 Etrida, *Boisd.*
Idmais, *Boisd.*
 Calais, *Cram.*
Thestias, *Boisd.*
 Mariamne, *Cram.*
 Pirene, *Linn.*
Hebomoia, *Hübn.*
 Glaucippe, *Linn.*
Eronia, *Hübn.*
 Valeria, *Cram.*
Callidryas, *Boisd.*
 Philippina, *Boisd.*
 Pyranthe, *Linn.*
 Hilaria, *Cram.*
 Alcmeone, *Cram.*
 Thisorella, *Boisd.*
Terias, *Swain.*
 Drona, *Horsf.*
 Hecabe, *Linn.*

Fam. NYMPHALIDÆ, *Swain.*

Euplœa, *Fabr.*
 Prothoe, *Godt.*
 Core, *Cram.*
 Alcathoë, *Godt.*
Danais, *Latr.*
 Chrysippus, *Linn.*
 Plexippus, *Linn.*
 Aglae, *Cram.*
 Melissa, *Cram.*
 Limniacæ, *Cram.*
 Juventa, *Cram.*
Hestia, *Hübn.*
 Jasonia, *Westw.*
Telchinia, *Hübn.*
 violæ, *Fabr.*
Cethosia, *Fabr.*
 Cyane, *Fabr.*
Messarus, *Doubl.*
 Erymanthis, *Drury.*
Atella, *Doubl.*
 Phalanta, *Drury.*
Argynnis, *Fabr.*
 Niphe, *Linn.*
 Clagia, *Godt.*
Ergolis, *Boisd.*
 Taprobana, *West.*
Vanessa, *Fabr.*
 Charonia, *Drury.*
Libythea, *Fabr.*
 Medhavina, *Wlk.*
 Pushcara, *Wlk.*
Pyrameis, *Hübn.*
 Charonia, *Drury.*
 Cardui, *Linn.*
 Callirhoë, *Hübn.*
Junonia, *Hübn.*
 Limonias, *Linn.*
 Œnone, *Linn.*
 Orithyia, *Linn.*
 Laomedia, *Linn.*
 Asterie, *Linn.*
Precis, *Hübn.*
 Iphita, *Cram.*
Cynthia, *Fabr.*
 Arsinoe, *Cram.*
Parthenos, *Hübn.*
 Gambrisius, *Fabr.*
Limenitis, *Fabr.*
 Calidusa, *Moore.*
Neptis, *Fabr.*
 Heliodore, *Fabr.*
 Columella, *Cram.*
 aceris, *Fabr.*
 Jumbah, *Moore.*
 Hordonia, *Stoll.*
Diadema, *Boisd.*
 Auge, *Cram.*
 Bolina, *Linn.*
Symphædra, *Hübn.*
 Thyelia, *Fabr.*
Adolias, *Boisd.*
 Evelina, *Stoll.*
 Lubentina, *Fabr.*
 Vasanta, *Moore.*
 Garuda, *Moore.*
Nymphalis, *Latr.*
 Psaphon, *Westw.*
 Bernardus, *Fabr.*
 Athamas, *Cram.*
 Fabius, *Fabr.*
 Kallima, *Doubl.*
 Philarchus, *Westw.*
 Melanitis, *Fabr.*
 Banksia, *Fabr.*
 Leda, *Linn.*
 Casiphone, *G. R. Gray.*
 undularis, *Boisd.*
Ypththima, *Hübn.*
 Lysandra, *Cram.*
 Parthalis, *Wlk.*
Cyllo, *Boisd.*
 Gorya, *Wlk.*
 Cathæna, *Wlk.*
 Embolima, *Wlk.*
 Neilgherriensis, *Guér.*
 Purimata, *Wlk.*
 Pushpamitra, *Wlk.*
Mycalesis, *Hübn.*
 Patnia, *Moore.*
 Gamaliba, *Wlk.*
 Dosaron, *Wlk.*
 Samba, *Moore.*
Cænonympha, *Hübn.*
 Euaspla, *Wlk.*
Emesis, *Fabr.*
 Echerius, *Stoll.*

Fam. LYCÆNIDÆ, *Leach.*

Anops, *Boisd.*

Bulis, *Boisd.*
Thetys, *Drury.*
Loxura, *Horsf.*
Atymnus, *Cram.*
Myrina, *Godt.*
Selimnus, *Doubled.*
Triopas, *Cram.*
Amblypodia, *Horsf.*
Longinus, *Fabr.*
Narada, *Horsf.*
pseudocentaurus, *Do.*
quercetorum, *Boisd.*
Aphnæus, *Hübn.*
Pindarus, *Fabr.*
Etolus, *Cram.*
Hephæstos, *Doubled.*
Crotus, *Doubled.*
Dipsas, *Doubled.*
chrysomallus, *Hübn.*
Isocrates, *Fabr.*
Lycæna, *Fabr.*
Alexis, *Stoll.*
Bœtica, *Linn.*
Cnejus, *Horsf.*
Rosimon, *Fabr.*
Theophrastus, *Fabr.*
Pluto, *Fabr.*
Parana, *Horsf.*
Nyseus, *Guér.*
Ethion, *Boisd.*
Celeno, *Cram.*
Kandarpa, *Horsf.*
Elpis, *Godt.*
Chimonas, *Wlk.*
Gandara, *Wlk.*
Chorienis, *Wlk.*
Geria, *Wlk.*
Doanas, *Wlk.*
Sunya, *Wlk.*
Audhra, *Wlk.*
Polyommatus, *Latr.*
Akasa, *Horsf.*
Puspa, *Horsf.*
Laius, *Cram.*
Ethion, *Boisd.*
Cattigara, *Wlk.*
Gorgippia, *Wlk.*
Lucia, *Westw.*
Epius, *Westw.*
Pithecops, *Horsf.*
Hylax, *Fabr.*

Fam. HESPERIDÆ, *Steph.*

Goniloba, *Westw.*
Iapetus, *Cram.*
Pyrgus, *Hübn.*
Superna, *Moore.*
Danna, *Moore.*
Genta, *Wlk.*
Sydrus, *Wlk.*
Nisoniades, *Hübn.*
Diocles, *Boisd.*
Salsala, *Moore.*
Toides, *Wlk.*
Pamphila, *Fabr.*
Augias, *Linn.*
Achylodes, *Hübn.*
Temala, *Wlk.*
Hesperia, *Fabr.*
Indrani, *Moore.*
Chaya, *Moore.*
Cinnara, *Moore.*
gremius, *Latr.*
Cendochates, *Wlk.*
Tiagara, *Wlk.*
Cotiaris, *Wlk.*
Sigala, *Wlk.*

Fam. SPHINGIDÆ, *Leach.*

Sesia, *Fabr.*
Hylas, *Linn.*
Macroglossa, *Ochs.*
Stellatarum, *Linn.*
gyrans, *Boisd.*
Corythus, *Boisd.*
divergens, *Wlk.*
Calymnia, *Boisd.*
Panopus, *Cram.*
Chœrocampa, *Dup.*
Thyelia, *Linn.*
Nyssus, *Drury.*
Clotho, *Drury.*
Oldenlandiæ, *Fabr.*
Lycetus, *Cram.*
Silhetensis, *Boisd.*
Pergesa, *Wlk.*
Acteus, *Cram.*
Panacra, *Wlk.*
vigil, *Guér.*
Daphnis, *Hübn.*
Nerii, *Linn.*
Zonilia, *Boisd.*
Morpheus, *Cram.*
Macrosila, *Boisd.*
obliqua, *Wlk.*
discistriga, *Wlk.*
Sphinx, *Linn.*
convolvuli, *Linn.*
Acherontia, *Ochs.*
Satanas, *Boisd.*
Smerinthus, *Latr.*
Dryas, *Boisd.*

Fam. CASTNIIDÆ, *Wlk.*

Eusemia, *Dalm.*
bellatrix, *Westw.*
Ægocera, *Latr.*
Venulia, *Cram.*
bimacula, *Wlk.*

Fam. ZYGÆNIDÆ, *Leach.*

Syntomis, *Ochs.*
Schœnherri, *Boisd.*
Creusa, *Linn.*
Imaon, *Cram.*
Glaucopis, *Fabr.*
subaurata, *Wlk.*
Enchromia, *Hübn.*
Polymena, *Cram.*
diminuta, *Wlk.*

Fam. LITHOSIIDÆ, *Steph.*

Scaptesyle, *Wlk.*
bicolor, *Wlk.*
Nyctemera, *Hübn.*
lacticinia, *Cram.*
latistriga, *Wlk.*
Coleta, *Cram.*
Euschema, *Hübn.*
subrepleta, *Wlk.*
transversa, *Wlk.*
vilis, *Wlk.*
Chalcosia, *Hübn.*
Tiberina, *Cram.*
venosa, *Anon.*
Eterusia, *Hope.*
Ædea, *Linn.*
Trypanophora, *Koll.*
Taprobanes, *Wlk.*
Heteropan, *Wlk.*
scintillans, *Wlk.*
Hypsa, *Hübn.*
plana, *Wlk.*
caricæ, *Fabr.*
ficus, *Fabr.*
Vitessa, *Moor.*
Zemire, *Cram.*
Lithosia, *Fabr.*
antica, *Wlk.*
brevipennis, *Wlk.*
Setina, *Schr.*
semifascia, *Wlk.*
solita, *Wlk.*
Doliche, *Wlk.*
hilaris, *Wlk.*
Pitane, *Wlk.*
conserta, *Wlk.*
Æmene, *Wlk.*
Taprobanes, *Wlk.*
Dirades, *Wlk.*
attacoides, *Wlk.*
Cyllene, *Wlk.*
transversa, *Wlk.*
*spoliata, *Wlk.*
Bizone, *Wlk.*
subornata, *Wlk.*
peregrina, *Wlk.*
Deiopeia, *Steph.*
pulcella, *Linn.*
Astrea, *Drury.*
Argus, *Kollar.*

Fam. ARCTIIDÆ, *Leach.*

Alope, *Wlk.*
ocellifera, *Wlk.*
Sangaiida, *Cram.*
Tinolius, *Wlk.*
eburneigutta, *Wlk.*
Creatonotos, *Hübn.*
interrupta, *Linn.*
emittens, *Wlk.*
Acmonia, *Wlk.*
lithosioides, *Wlk.*
Spilosoma, *Steph.*
subfascia, *Wlk.*
Cycnia, *Hübn.*
rubida, *Wlk.*
sparsigutta, *Wlk.*
Antheua, *Wlk.*
discalis, *Wlk.*
Aloa, *Wlk.*
lactinea, *Cram.*
candidula, *Wlk.*
erosa, *Wlk.*
Amerila, *Wlk.*
Melanthus, *Cram.*
Ammatho, *Wlk.*
cunionotatus, *Wlk.*

Fam. LIPARIDÆ, *Wlk.*

Artaxa, *Wlk.*
guttata, *Wlk.*

*varians, *Wlk.*
atomaria, *Wlk.*
Acyphas, *Wlk.*
viridescens, *Wlk.*
Lacida, *Wlk.*
rotundata, *Wlk.*
antica, *Wlk.*
subnotata, *Wlk.*
complens, *Wlk.*
promittens, *Wlk.*
strigulifera, *Wlk.*
Amsacta ? *Wlk.*
tenebrosa, *Wlk.*
Antipha, *Wlk.*
costalis, *Wlk.*
Anaxila, *Wlk.*
notata, *Wlk.*
Procodeca, *Wlk.*
angulifera, *Wlk.*
Redoa, *Wlk.*
submarginata, *Wlk.*
Euproctis, *Hübn.*
virguncula, *Wlk.*
bimaculata, *Wlk.*
lunata, *Wlk.*
tinctifera, *Wlk.*
Cispia, *Wlk.*
plagiata, *Wlk.*
Dasychira, *Hübn.*
pudibunda, *Linn.*
Lymantria, *Hübn.*
grandis, *Wlk.*
marginata, *Wlk.*
Enome, *Wlk.*
ampla, *Wlk.*
Dreata, *Wlk.*
plumipes, *Wlk.*
geminata, *Wlk.*
mutans, *Wlk.*
mollifera, *Wlk.*
Pandala, *Wlk.*
dolosa, *Wlk.*
Charnidas, *Wlk.*
junctifera, *Wlk.*

Fam. PSYCHIDÆ, *Bru.*

Psyche, *Schr.*
Doubledaii, *Westw.*
Metisa, *Wlk.*
plana, *Wlk.*
Eumeta, *Wlk.*
Cramerii, *Westw.*
Templetonii, *Westw.*
Cryptothelea, *Templ.*
consorta, *Templ.*

Fam. NOTODONTIDÆ, *St.*

Cerura, *Schr.*
liturata, *Wlk.*
Stauropus, *Germ.*
alternans, *Wlk.*
Nioda, *Wlk.*
fusiformis, *Wlk.*
transversa, *Wlk.*
Rilia, *Wlk.*
lanceolata, *Wlk.*
basivitta, *Wlk.*
Ptilomacra, *Wlk.*
juvenis, *Wlk.*
Elavia, *Wlk.*
metaphæa, *Wlk.*
Notodonta, *Ochs.*
ejecta, *Wlk.*
Ichthyura, *Hübn.*
restituens, *Wlk.*

Fam. LIMACODIDÆ, *Dup.*

Scopelodes, *Westw.*
unicolor, *Westw.*
Messata, *Wlk.*
rubiginosa, *Wlk.*
Miresa, *Wlk.*
argentifera, *Wlk.*
aperiens, *Wlk.*
Nyssia, *Herr. Sch.*
læta, *Westw.*
Neæra, *Herr. Sch.*
graciosa, *Westw.*
Narosa, *Wlk.*
conspersa, *Wlk.*
Naprepa, *Wlk.*
varians, *Wlk.*

Fam. DREPANULIDÆ, *Wlk.*

Oreta, *Wlk.*
suffusa, *Wlk.*
extensa, *Wlk.*
Arna, *Wlk.*
apicalis, *Wlk.*
Ganisa, *Wlk.*
postica, *Wlk.*

Fam. SATURNIIDÆ, *Wlk.*

Attacus, *Linn.*
Atlas, *Linn.*
lunula, *Anon.*
Antheræa, *Hübn.*
Mylitta, *Drury.*
Assama, *Westw.*
Tropæa, *Hübn.*
Selene, *Hübn.*

Fam. BOMBYCIDÆ, *Steph.*

Trabala, *Wlk.*
basalis, *Wlk.*
prasina, *Wlk.*
Lasiocampa, *Schr.*
trifascia, *Wlk.*
Megasoma, *Boisd.*
venustum, *Wlk.*
Lebeda, *Wlk.*
repanda, *Wlk.*
plagiata, *Wlk.*
bimaculata, *Wlk.*
scriptiplaga, *Wlk.*

Fam. COSSIDÆ, *Newm.*

Cossus, *Fabr.*
quadrinotatus, *Wlk.*
Zeuzera, *Latr.*
leuconota, *Steph.*
pusilla, *Wlk.*

Fam. HEPIALIDÆ, *Steph.*

Phassus, *Steph.*
signifer, *Wlk.*

Fam. CYMATOPHORIDÆ, *Herr. Sch.*

Thyatira, *Ochs.*
repugnans, *Wlk.*

Fam. BRYOPHILIDÆ, *Guén.*

Bryophila, *Treit.*
semipars, *Wlk.*

Fam. BOMBYCOIDÆ, *Guén.*

Diphtera, *Ochs.*
deceptura, *Wlk.*

Fam. LEUCANIDÆ, *Guén.*

Leucania, *Ochs.*
confusa, *Wlk.*
exempta, *Wlk.*
inferens, *Wlk.*
collecta, *Wlk.*
Brada, *Wlk.*
truncata, *Wlk.*
Crambopsis, *Wlk.*
excludens, *Wlk.*

Fam. GLOTTULIDÆ, *Guén.*

Polytela, *Guén.*
gloriosa, *Fabr.* }
Glottula, *Guén.*
Dominica, *Cram.*
Chasmina, *Wlk.*
pavo, *Wlk.*
cygnus, *Wlk.*

Fam. APAMIDÆ, *Guén.*

Laphygma, *Guén.*
obstans, *Wlk.*
trajiciens, *Wlk.*
Prodenia, *Guén.*
retina, *Friv.*
glaucistriga, *Wlk.*
apertura, *Wlk.*
Calogramma, *Wlk.*
festiva, *Don.*
Heliophobus, *Boisd.*
discrepans, *Wlk.*
Hydræcia, *Guén.*
lampadifera, *Wlk.*
Apamea, *Ochs.*
undecilia, *Wlk.*
Celæna, *Steph.*
serva, *Wlk.*

Fam. CARADRINIDÆ, *Guén.*

Amyna, *Guén.*
selenampha, *Guén.*

Fam. NOCTUIDÆ, *Guén.*

Agrotis, *Ochs.*
aristifera, *Guén.*
congrua, *Wlk.*
punctipes, *Wlk.*
mundata, *Wlk.*
transducta, *Wlk.*
plagiata, *Wlk.*
plagifera, *Wlk.*

Fam. HADENIDÆ, *Guén.*

Eurois, *Hübn.*
auriplena, *Wlk.*
inclusa, *Wlk.*
Epiceia, *Wlk.*
subsignata, *Wlk.*
Hadena, *Treit.*
subcurva, *Wlk.*
postica, *Wlk.*

retrahens, *Wlk.*
confundens, *Wlk.*
congressa, *Wlk.*
ruptistriga, *Wlk.*
Ansa, *Wlk.*
filipalpis, *Wlk.*

Fam. XYLINIDÆ, *Guén.*

Ragada, *Wlk.*
pyrorchroma, *Wlk.*
Cryassa, *Wlk.*
bifacies, *Wlk.*
Egelista, *Wlk.*
rudivitta, *Wlk.*
Xylina, *Ochs.*
deflexa, *Wlk.*
inchoans, *Wlk.*

Fam. HELIOTHIDÆ, *Guén.*

Heliothis, *Ochs.*
armigera, *Hübn.*

Fam. HÆMEROSIDÆ, *Guén.*

Ariola, *Wlk.*
cœlisigna, *Wlk.*
dilectissima, *Wlk.*
saturata, *Wlk.*

Fam. ACONTIDÆ, *Guén.*

Xanthodes, *Guén.*
intersepta, *Guén.*
Acontia, *Ochs.*
tropica, *Guén.*
olivacea, *Wlk.*
fasciculosa, *Wlk.*
signifera, *Wlk.*
turpis, *Wlk.*
mlanöides, *Wlk.*
approximans, *Wlk.*
divulsa, *Wlk.*
*egens, *Wlk.*
plenicosta, *Wlk.*
determinata, *Wlk.*
hypætroides, *Wlk.*
Chlumetia, *Wlk.*
multilinea, *Wlk.*

Fam. ANTHOPHILIDÆ, *Guén.*

Micra, *Guén.*
destituta, *Wlk.*
derogata, *Wlk.*
simplex, *Wlk.*

Fam. ERIOPIDÆ, *Guén.*

Callopistria, *Hübn.*
exotica, *Guén.*
rivularis, *Wlk.*
duplicans, *Wlk.*

Fam. EURHIPIDÆ, *Guén.*

Penicillaria, *Guén.*
nugatrix, *Guén.*
resoluta, *Wlk.*
solida, *Wlk.*
ludatrix, *Wlk.*
Rhesala, *Wlk.*
imparata, *Wlk.*
Eutelia, *Hübn.*
favillatrix, *Wlk.*
thermesiides, *Wlk.*

Fam. PLUSIIDÆ, *Boisd.*

Abrostola, *Ochs.*
transfixa, *Wlk.*
Plusia, *Ochs.*
aurifera, *Hübn.*
verticillata, *Guén.*
agramma, *Guén.*
obtusisigna, *Wlk.*
nigriluna, *Wlk.*
signata, *Wlk.*
dispellens, *Wlk.*
propulsa, *Wlk.*

Fam. CALPIDÆ, *Guén.*

Calpe, *Treit.*
minuticornis, *Guén.*
Orœsia, *Guén.*
emarginata, *Fabr.*
Deva, *Wlk.*
conducens, *Wlk.*

Fam. HEMICERIDÆ, *Guén.*

Westermannia, *Hübn.*
superba, *Hübn.*

Fam. HYBLÆIDÆ, *Guén.*

Hyblæa, *Guén.*
Puera, *Cram.*
constellata, *Guén.*
Nolasena, *Wlk.*
ferrifervens, *Wlk.*

Fam. GONOPTERIDÆ, *Guén.*

Cosmophila, *Boisd.*
Indica, *Guén.*
xanthindyma, *Boisd.*
Anomis, *Hübn.*
fulvida, *Guén.*
iconica, *Wlk.*
Gonitis, *Guén.*
combinans, *Wlk.*
albitibia, *Wlk.*
mesogona, *Wlk.*
guttanivis, *Wlk.*
involuta, *Wlk.*
basalis, *Wlk.*
Eporedia, *Wlk.*
damnipennis, *Wlk.*
Rusicada, *Wlk.*
nigritarsis, *Wlk.*
Pasipeda, *Wlk.*
rufipalpis, *Wlk.*

Fam. TOXOCAMPIDÆ, *Guén.*

Toxocampa, *Guén.*
metaspila, *Wlk.*
sexlinea, *Wlk.*
quinquelina, *Wlk.*
Albonica, *Wlk.*
reversa, *Wlk.*

Fam. POLYDESMIDÆ, *Guén.*

Polydesma, *Boisd.*
boarmoides, *Wlk.*
erubescens, *Wlk.*

Fam. HOMOPTERIDÆ, *Bois.*

Alamis, *Guén.*
spoliata, *Wlk.*
Homoptera, *Boisd.*
basipallens, *Wlk.*
retrahens, *Wlk.*
costifera, *Wlk.*
divisistriga, *Wlk.*
procumbens, *Wlk.*
Diacuista, *Wlk.*
homopteroides, *Wlk.*
Daxata, *Wlk.*
bijungens, *Wlk.*

Fam. HYPOGRAMMIDÆ, *Guén.*

Briarda, *Wlk.*
precedens, *Wlk.*
Brana, *Wlk.*
calopasa, *Wlk.*
Corsa, *Wlk.*
lignicolor, *Wlk.*
Avatha, *Wlk.*
includens, *Wlk.*
Gadirtha, *Wlk.*
decrescens, *Wlk.*
impingens, *Wlk.*
spurcata, *Wlk.*
rectifera, *Wlk.*
duplicans, *Wlk.*
intrusa, *Wlk.*
Ercheia, *Wlk.*
diversipennis, *Wlk.*
Plotheia, *Wlk.*
frontalis, *Wlk.*
Diomea, *Wlk.*
rotundata, *Wlk.*
chloromela, *Wlk.*
orbicularis, *Wlk.*
muscosa, *Wlk.*
Dinumma, *Wlk.*
placens, *Wlk.*
Lusia, *Wlk.*
geometroides, *Wlk.*
perficita, *Wlk.*
repulsa, *Wlk.*
Abunis, *Wlk.*
trimesa, *Wlk.*

Fam. CATEPHIDÆ, *Guén.*

Cocytodes, *Guén.*
cœrula, *Guén.*
modesta, *Wlk.*
Catephia, *Ochs.*
linteola, *Guén.*
Anophia, *Guén.*
acronyctoides, *Guén.*
Steiria, *Wlk.*
subobliqua, *Wlk.*
trajiciens, *Wlk.*
Aucha, *Wlk.*
velans, *Wlk.*
Ægilia, *Wlk.*
describens, *Wlk.*
Maceda, *Wlk.*
mansueta, *Wlk.*

Fam. HYPOCALIDÆ, *Guén.*

Hypocala, *Guén.*
efflorescens, *Guén.*
subsatura, *Guén.*

Fam. CATOCALIDÆ, *Boisd.*

Blenina, *Wlk.*

donans, *Wlk.*
accipiens, *Wlk.*

Fam. OPHIDERIDÆ, *Guén.*

Ophideres, *Boisd.*
Materna, *Linn.*
fullonica, *Linn.*
Cajeta, *Cram.*
Ancilla, *Cram.*
Salaminia, *Cram.*
Hypermnestra, *Cram.*
multiscripta, *Wlk.*
bilineosa, *Wlk.*
Potamophera, *Guén.*
Manlia, *Cram.*
Lygniodes, *Guén.*
reducens, *Wlk.*
disparans, *Wlk.*
hypoleuca, *Guén.*

Fam. EREBIDÆ, *Guén.*

Oxyodes, *Guén.*
Clytia, *Cram.*

Fam. OMMATOPHORIDÆ, *Guén.*

Speiredonia, *Hübn.*
retrahens, *Wlk.*
Sericia, *Guén.*
anops, *Guén.*
parvipennis, *Wlk.*
Patula, *Guén.*
macrops, *Linn.*
Argiva, *Hübn.*
hieroglyphica, *Drury.*
Beregra, *Wlk.*
replenens, *Wlk.*

Fam. HYPOPYRIDÆ, *Guén.*

Spiramia, *Guén.*
Heliconia, *Hübn.*
triloba, *Guén.*
Hypopyra, *Guén.*
vespertil o, *Fabr.*
Ortospana, *Wlk.*
connectens. *Wlk.*
Entomogramma, *Guén.*
fautrix, *Guén.*

Fam. BENDIDÆ, *Guén.*

Homæa, *Guén.*
clathrum, *Guén.*
Hulodes, *Guén.*
caranea, *Cram.*
palumba, *Guén.*

Fam. OPHIUSIDÆ, *Guén.*

Sphingomorpha, *Guén.*
Chlorea, *Cram.*
Lagoptera, *Guén.*
honesta, *Hübn.*
magica, *Hübn.*
dotata, *Fabr.*
Ophiodes, *Guén.*
discriminans, *Wlk.*
basistigma, *Wlk.*
Cerbia, *Wlk.*
fugitiva, *Wlk.*
Ophisma, *Guén.*
lætabilis, *Guen.*
deficiens, *Wlk.*
gravata, *Wlk.*
circumferens, *Wlk.*
terminans, *Wlk.*
Achæa, *Hübn.*
Melicerta, *Drury.*
Mezentia, *Cram.*
Cyllota, *Guén.*
Cyllaria, *Cram.*
fusifera, *Wlk.*
signivitta, *Wlk.*
reversa, *Wlk.*
combinans, *Wlk.*
expectans, *Wlk.*
Serrodes, *Guén.*
campana, *Guén.*
Naxia, *Guén.*
absentimacula, *Guén.*
Onelia, *Guén.*
calefaciens, *Wlk.*
calorifica, *Wlk.*
Calesia, *Guén.*
hœmorrhoda, *Guén.*
Hypætra, *Guén.*
trigonifera, *Wlk.*
curvifera, *Wlk.*
condita, *Wlk.*
complacens, *Wlk.*
divisa, *Wlk.*
Ophiusa, *Ochs.*
myops, *Guén.*
albivitta, *Guén.*
Achatina, *Sulz.*
fulvotænia, *Guén.*
simillima, *Guén.*
festinata, *Wlk.*
pallidilinea, *Wlk.*
luteipalpis, *Wlk.*
Fodina, *Guén.*
stola, *Guén.*
Grammodes, *Guén.*
Ammonia, *Cram.*
Mygdon, *Cram.*
stolida, *Fabr.*
mundicolor, *Wlk.*

Fam. EUCLIDIDÆ, *Guén.*

Trigonodes, *Guén.*
Hippasia, *Cram.*

Fam. REMIGIDÆ, *Guén.*

Remigia, *Guén.*
Archesia, *Cram.*
frugalis, *Fabr.*
pertendens, *Wlk.*
congregata, *Wlk.*
opturata, *Wlk.*

Fam. FOCILLIDÆ, *Guén.*

Focilla, *Guén.*
submemorans, *Wlk.*

Fam. AMPHIGANIDÆ, *Guén.*

Lacera, *Guén.*
capella, *Guén.*
Amphigonia, *Guén.*
hepatizans, *Guén.*

Fam. THERMISIDÆ, *Guén.*

Sympis, *Guén.*
rufibasis, *Guén.*
Thermesia, *Hübn.*
finipalpis, *Wlk.*
soluta, *Wlk.*
Azazia, *Wlk.*
rubricans, *Boisd.*
Selenis, *Guén.*
nivisapex, *Wlk.*
multiguttata, *Wlk.*
semilux, *Wlk.*
Ephyrodes, *Guén.*
excipiens, *Wlk.*
cristisfera, *Wlk.*
lineifera, *Wlk.*
Capnodes, *Guén.*
*maculicosta, *Wlk.*
Ballatha, *Wlk.*
atrotumens, *Wlk.*
Daranissa, *Wlk.*
digramma, *Wlk.*
Darsa, *Wlk.*
defectissima, *Wlk.*

Fam. URAPTERYDÆ, *Guén.*

Lagyra, *Wlk.*
Talaca, *Wlk.*

Fam. ENNOMIDÆ, *Guén.*

Hyperythra, *Guén.*
limbolaria, *Guén.*
Orsonoba, *Wlk.*
Rajaca, *Wlk.*
Fascellina, *Wlk.*
chromataria, *Wlk.*
Laginia, *Wlk.*
bractiaria, *Wlk.*

Fam. BOARMIDÆ, *Guén.*

Amblychia, *Guén.*
angeronia, *Guén.*
poststrigaria, *Wlk.*
Boarmia, *Treit.*
sublavaria, *Guén.*
admissaria, *Guén.*
raptaria, *Wlk.*
Medasina, *Wlk.*
Bhurmitra, *Wlk.*
Suiasasa, *Wlk.*
diffluaria, *Wlk.*
caritaria, *Wlk.*
exclusaria, *Wlk.*
Hypochroma, *Guén.*
minimaria, *Guén.*
Gnophos, *Treit.*
Pulinda, *Wlk.*
Culataria, *Wlk.*
Hemerophila, *Steph.*
vidhisara, *Wlk.*
Agathia, *Guén.*
blandiaria, *Wlk.*
Bulonga, *Wlk.*
Ajaia, *Wlk.*
Chacoraca, *Wlk.*
Chandubija, *Wlk.*

Fam. GEOMETRIDÆ, *Guén.*

Geometra, *Linn.*

specularia, *Guén.*
Nanda, *Wlk.*
Nemoria, *Hübn.*
caudularia, *Guén.*
solidaria, *Guén.*
Thalassodes, *Guén.*
quadraria, *Guén.*
catenaria, *Wlk.*
immissaria, *Wlk.*
Sisunaga, *Wlk.*
adornataria, *Wlk.*
meritaria, *Wlk.*
cœlataria, *Wlk.*
gratularia, *Wlk.*
chlorozonaria, *Wlk.*
læsaria, *Wlk.*
simpliciaria, *Wlk.*
immissaria, *Wlk.*
Comibæna, *Wlk.*
Divapala, *Wlk.*
impulsaria, *Wlk.*
Celenna, *Wlk.*
saturaturia, *Wlk.*
Pseudoterpna, *Wlk.*
Vivilaca, *Wlk.*
Amaurinia, *Guén.*
rubrolimbaria, *Wlk.*

Fam. PALYADÆ, *Guén.*

Eumelea, *Dunc.*
ludovicata, *Guén.*
aureliata, *Guén.*
carnearia, *Wlk.*

Fam. EPHYRIDÆ, *Guén.*

Ephyra, *Dup.*
obrinaria, *Wlk.*
decursaria, *Wlk.*
Cacavena, *Wlk.*
abhadraca, *Wlk.*
Vasudeva, *Wlk.*
Susarmana, *Wlk.*
Vutumana, *Wlk.*
inæquata, *Wlk.*

Fam. ACIDALIDÆ, *Guén.*

Drapetodes, *Guén.*
mitaria, *Guén.*
Pomasia, *Guén.*
Psylaria, *Guén.*
Sunandaria, *Wlk.*
Acidalia, *Treit.*
obliviaria, *Wlk.*
adeptaria, *Wlk.*
nexiaria, *Wlk.*
addictaria, *Wlk.*
actiosaria, *Wlk.*
defamataria, *Wlk.*
negataria, *Wlk.*
actuaria, *Wlk.*
cæsaria, *Wlk.*
Cabera, *Steph.*
falsaria, *Wlk.*
decussaria, *Wlk.*
famularia, *Wlk.*
nigrarenaria, *Wlk.*
Hyria, *Steph.*
elataria, *Wlk.*
marcidaria, *Wlk.*
oblataria, *Wlk.*

grataria, *Wlk.*
rhodinaria, *Wlk.*
Timandra, *Dup.*
Ajuia, *Wlk.*
Vijuia, *Wlk.*
Agyris, *Guén.*
deliaria, *Guén.*
Zanclopteryx, *Herr. Sch.*
saponaria, *Herr. Sch.*

Fam. MICRONIDÆ, *Guén.*

Micronia, *Guén.*
caudata, *Fabr.*
aculeata, *Guén.*

Fam. MACARIDÆ, *Guén.*

Macaria, *Curt.*
Eleonora, *Cram.*
Varisara, *Wlk.*
Rhagivata, *Wlk.*
Palaca, *Wlk.*
honestaria, *Wlk.*
Sangata, *Wlk.*
honoraria, *Wlk.*
cessaria, *Wlk.*
subcaudaria, *Wlk.*
Doava, *Wlk.*
adjutaria, *Wlk.*
figuraria, *Wlk.*

Fam. LARENTIDÆ, *Guén.*

Sauris, *Guén.*
hirudinata, *Guén.*
Camptogramma, *Steph.*
baccata, *Guén.*
Blemyia, *Wlk.*
Bataca, *Wlk.*
blitiaria, *Wlk.*
Coremia, *Guén.*
Gomatina, *Wlk.*
Lobophora, *Curt.*
Salisuca, *Wlk.*
Ghosha, *Wlk.*
contributaria, *Wlk.*
Mesogramma, *Steph.*
lactularia, *Wlk.*
scitaria, *Wlk.*
Eupithecia, *Curt.*
recensitaria, *Wlk.*
admixtaria, *Wlk.*
immixtaria, *Wlk.*
Gathynia, *Wlk.*
miraria, *Wlk.*

Fam. PLATYDIDÆ, *Guén.*

Trigonia, *Guén.*
Cydonialis, *Cram.*

Fam. HYPENIDÆ, *Herr.*

Dichromia, *Guén.*
Orosialis, *Cram.*
Hypena, *Schr.*
rhombalis, *Guén.*
jocosalis, *Wlk.*
mandatalis, *Wlk.*
quæsitalis, *Wlk.*
laceratalis, *Wlk.*
iconicalis, *Wlk.*
labatalis, *Wlk.*

obacerralis, *Wlk.*
pactalis, *Wlk.*
raralis, *Wlk.*
paritalis, *Wlk.*
surreptalis, *Wlk.*
detersalis, *Wlk.*
ineffectalis, *Wlk.*
incongrualis, *Wlk.*
rubripunctum, *Wlk.*
Gesonia, *Wlk.*
*obeditalis, *Wlk.*
duplex, *Wlk.*

Fam. HERMINIDÆ, *Dup.*

Herminia, *Latr.*
Timonalis, *Wlk.*
diffusalis, *Wlk.*
interstans, *Wlk.*
Adrapsa, *Wlk.*
ablualis, *Wlk.*
Bertula, *Wlk.*
abjudicalis, *Wlk.*
raptatalis, *Wlk.*
contigens, *Wlk.*
Bocana, *Wlk.*
jutalis, *Wlk.*
manifestalis, *Wlk.*
ophiusalis, *Wlk.*
vagalis, *Wlk.*
turpatalis, *Wlk.*
hypernalis, *Wlk.*
gravatalis, *Wlk.*
tumidalis, *Wlk.*
Orthaga, *Wlk.*
Euadrusalis, *Wlk.*
Hipoepa, *Wlk.*
lapsalis, *Wlk.*
Lamura, *Wlk.*
oberratalis, *Wlk.*
Echana, *Wlk.*
abavalis, *Wlk.*
Dragana, *Wlk.*
pansalis, *Wlk.*
Pingrasa, *Wlk.*
accuralis, *Wlk.*
Egnasia, *Wlk.*
ephyradalis, *Wlk.*
accingalis, *Wlk.*
participalis, *Wlk.*
usurpatalis, *Wlk.*
Berresa, *Wlk.*
natalis, *Wlk.*
Imma, *Wlk.*
rugosalis, *Wlk.*
Chusaris, *Wlk.*
retatalis, *Wlk.*
Corgatha, *Wlk.*
zonalis, *Wlk.*
Catada, *Wlk.*
glomeralis, *Wlk.*
captiosalis, *Wlk.*

Fam. PYRALIDÆ, *Guén.*

Pyralis, *Linn.*
ignifualis, *Wlk.*
Palesalis, *Wlk.*
reconditalis, *Wlk.*
Idalialis, *Wlk.*
Janassalis, *Wlk.*
Aglossa, *Latr.*
Gnidusalis, *Wlk.*

Labanda, *Wlk.*
herbealis, *Wlk.*

Fam. ENNYCHIDÆ, *Dup.*

Pyrausta, *Schr.*
*absistalis, *Wlk.*

Fam. ASOPIDÆ, *Guén.*

Desmia, *Westw.*
afflictalis, *Guén.*
concisalis, *Wlk.*
Ædiodes, *Guén.*
flavibasalis. *Guén.*
effertalis, *Wlk.*
Samea, *Guén.*
gratiosalis, *Wlk.*
Asopia, *Guén.*
vulgalis, *Guén.*
falsidicalis, *Wlk.*
abruptalis, *Wlk.*
latimarginalis, *Wlk.*
præteritalis, *Wlk.*
Eryxalis, *Wlk.*
roridalis, *Wlk.*
Agathodes, *Guén.*
ostentalis, *Geyer.*
Leucinades, *Guén.*
orbonalis, *Guén.*
Hymenia, *Hübn.*
recurvalis, *Fabr.*
Agrotera, *Schr.*
suffusalis, *Wlk.*
decessalis, *Wlk.*
Isopteryx, *Guén.*
*melaleucalis, *Wlk.*
*impulsalis, *Wlk*
*spilomelalis. *Wlk.*
acclaralis, *Wlk.*
abnegatalis, *Wlk.*

Fam. HYDROCAMPIDÆ, *Guén.*

Oligostigma, *Guén.*
obitalis, *Wlk.*
votalis, *Wlk.*
Cataclysta, *Herr. Sch.*
dilucidalis, *Guér.*
bisectalis, *Wlk.*
blandialis, *Wlk.*
elutalis, *Wlk.*

Fam. SPILOMELIDÆ, *Guén.*

Lepyrodes, *Guén.*
geometralis, *Guén.*
lepidalis, *Wlk.*
peritalis, *Wlk.*
Phalangiodes, *Guén.*
Neptisalis, *Cram.*
Spilomela, *Guén.*
meritalis, *Wlk.*
abdicalis, *Wlk.*
decussalis, *Wlk.*
aurolinealis, *Wlk.*
Nistra, *Wlk.*
cœlatalis, *Wlk.*
Pagyda, *Wlk.*
salvalis, *Wlk.*
Massepha, *Wlk.*
absolutalis, *Wlk.*

Fam. MARGARODIDÆ, *Guén.*

Glyphodes, *Guén.*
diurnalis, *Guén.*
decretalis, *Guén.*
cœsalis, *Wlk.*
univocalis, *Wlk.*
Phakellura, *L. Guild.*
gazorialis, *Guén.*
Margarodes, *Guén.*
psittacalis, *Hübn.*
pomonalis, *Guén.*
hilaralis, *Wlk.*
Pygospila, *Guén.*
Tyresalis, *Cram.*
Neurina, *Guén.*
Procopialis, *Cram.*
ignibasalis, *Wlk.*
Ilurgia, *Wlk.*
defamalis, *Wlk.*
Maruca, *Wlk.*
ruptalis, *Wlk.*
caritalis, *Wlk.*

Fam. BOTYDÆ, *Guén.*

Botys, *Latr.*
marginalis, *Cram.*
sellalis, *Guén.*
multilinealis, *Guén.*
admensalis, *Wlk.*
abjungalis, *Wlk.*
rutilalis, *Wlk.*
admixtalis. *Wlk.*
cœlatalis, *Wlk.*
deductalis, *Wlk.*
celsalis, *Wlk.*
vulsalis, *Wlk.*
ultimalis, *Wlk.*
tropicalis, *Wlk.*
abstrusalis, *Wlk.*
ruralis, *Wlk.*
adhœsalis, *Wlk.*
illisalis, *Wlk.*
stultalis, *Wlk.*
adductalis, *Wlk.*
histricalis, *Wlk.*
illectalis, *Wlk.*
suspicalis, *Wlk.*
Janassalis, *Wlk.*
Nephealis, *Wlk.*
Cynaralis. *Wlk.*
Dialis, *Wlk.*
Thaisalis, *Wlk.*
Dryopealis, *Wlk.*
Myrinalis, *Wlk.*
phycidalis, *Wlk.*
annulalis, *Wlk.*
brevilinealis, *Wlk.*
plagiatalis, *Wlk.*
Ebulea, *Guén.*
aberratalis, *Wlk.*
Camillalis, *Wlk.*
Pionea, *Guén.*
actualis, *Wlk*
Optiletalis, *Wlk.*
Jubesalis, *Wlk.*
brevialis, *Wlk.*
suffusalis, *Wlk.*
Scopula, *Schr.*
revocatalis, *Wlk.*
turgidalis, *Wlk.*
volutatalis, *Wlk.*

Godara, *Wlk.*
pervasalis, *Wlk.*
Herculia, *Wlk.*
bractialis, *Wlk.*
Mecyna, *Guén.*
deprivalis, *Wlk.*

Fam. SCOPARIDÆ, *Guén.*

Scoparia, *Haw.*
murificalis, *Wlk.*
congestalis, *Wlk.*
Alconalis, *Wlk.*
Davana, *Wlk.*
Phalantalis, *Wlk.*
Darsania, *Wlk.*
Niobesalis, *Wlk.*
Dosara, *Wlk.*
cœlatella. *Wlk.*
lapsalis, *Wlk.*
immeritalis, *Wlk.*

Fam. CHOREUTIDÆ, *Staint.*

Niaccaba, *Wlk.*
sumptialis, *Wlk.*
Simæthis, *Leach*
Clatella, *Wlk.*
Damonella, *Wlk.*
Bathusella, *Wlk.*

Fam. PHYCIDÆ, *Staint.*

Myelois, *Hübn.*
actiosella, *Wlk.*
bractiatella, *Wlk.*
cautella, *Wlk.*
adaptella, *Wlk.*
illusella, *Wlk.*
basifuscella, *Wlk.*
Ligeralis, *Wlk.*
Marsyasalis, *Wlk.*
Dascusa, *Wlk.*
Valensalis, *Wlk.*
Daroma, *Wlk.*
Zeuxoalis, *Wlk.*
Epulusalis, *Wlk.*
Timeusalis. *Wlk.*
Homœsoma, *Curt.*
gratella, *Wlk.*
Getusella, *Wlk.*
Nephopteryx, *Hübn.*
Etolusalis, *Wlk.*
Cyllusalis, *Wlk.*
Hylasalis. *Wlk.*
Acisalis, *Wlk.*
Harpaxalis, *Wlk.*
Æolusalis, *Wlk.*
Argiadesalis, *Wlk.*
Philiasalis, *Wlk.*
Pempelia, *Hübn.*
laudatella, *Wlk.*
Prionapteryx, *Steph.*
Lincusalis, *Wlk.*
Pindicitora, *Wlk.*
Acreonalis, *Wlk.*
Annusalis, *Wlk.*
Thysbesalis, *Wlk.*
Linceusalis, *Wlk.*
Lacipea, *Wlk.*
muscosella, *Wlk.*
Araxes, *Steph.*

admotella, *Wlk.*
decusella, *Wlk.*
celsella, *Wlk.*
admigratella, *Wlk.*
cœsella, *Wlk.*
candidatella, *Wlk.*
Catagela, *Wlk.*
adjurella, *Wlk.*
acricuella, *Wlk.*
lunulella, *Wlk.*

Fam. CRAMBIDÆ, *Dup.*

Crambus, *Fabr.*
concinellus, *Wlk.*
Darbhaca, *Wlk.*
inceptella, *Wlk.*
Jartheza, *Wlk.*
honorella, *Wlk.*
Bulina, *Wlk.*
solitella, *Wlk.*
Bembina, *Wlk.*
Cyanusalis, *Wlk.*
Chilo, *Zinck.*
dodatella, *Wlk.*
gratiosella, *Wlk.*
aditella, *Wlk.*
blitella, *Wlk.*
Dariausa, *Wlk.*
Eubusalis, *Wlk.*
Arrhade, *Wlk.*
Ematheonalis, *Wlk.*
Darnensis, *Wlk.*
Strephonella, *Wlk.*

Fam. CHLŒPHORIDÆ, *Staint.*

Thagora, *Wlk.*
figurans, *Wlk.*
Earias, *Hübn.*
chromatana, *Wlk.*

Fam. TORTRICIDÆ, *Steph.*

Lozotænia, *Steph.*
retractana, *Wlk.*
Peronea, *Curt.*
divisana, *Wlk.*
Lithogramma, *Steph.*
flexilineana, *Wlk.*
Dictyopteryx, *Steph.*
punctana, *Wlk.*
Homona, *Wlk.*
fasciculana, *Wlk.*
Hemonia, *Wlk.*
obiferana, *Wlk.*
Achroia, *Hübn.*
tricingulana, *Wlk.*

Fam. YPONOMEUTIDÆ, *Steph.*

Atteva, *Wlk.*
niveigutta, *Wlk.*

Fam. GELICHIDÆ, *Staint.*

Depressaria, *Haw.*
obligatella, *Wlk.*
fimbriella, *Wlk.*
Decuaria, *Wlk.*
mendicella, *Wlk.*
Gelechia, *Hübn.*
nugatella, *Wlk.*
calatella, *Wlk.*
deductella, *Wlk.*
Perionella, *Wlk.*
Gizama, *Wlk.*
blandiella, *Wlk.*
Enisipia, *Wlk.*
falsella, *Wlk.*
Gapharia, *Wlk.*
recitatella, *Wlk.*
Goesa, *Wlk.*
decusella, *Wlk.*
Cimitra, *Wlk.*
seclusella, *Wlk.*
Ficulea, *Wlk.*
blandulella, *Wlk.*
Fresilia, *Wlk.*
nesciatella, *Wlk.*
Gesontha, *Wlk.*
captiosella, *Wlk.*
Aginis, *Wlk.*
hilariella, *Wlk.*
Cadra, *Wlk.*
defectella, *Wlk.*

Fam. GLYPHYPTIDÆ, *Staint.*

Glyphyteryx, *Hübn.*
scitulella, *Wlk.*
Hybele, *Wlk.*
mansuetella, *Wlk.*

Fam. TINEIDÆ, *Leach.*

Tinea, *Linn.*
tapetzella, *Linn.*
receptella, *Wlk.*
pelionella, *Linn.*
plagiferella, *Wlk.*

Fam. LYONETIDÆ, *Staint.*

Cachura, *Wlk.*
objectella, *Wlk.*

Fam. PTEROPHORIDÆ, *Zell.*

Pterophorus, *Geoffr.*
leucadactylus, *Wlk.*
oxydactylus, *Wlk.*
anisodactylus, *Wlk.*

## Order DIPTERA, *Linn.*

Fam. MYCETOPHILIDÆ, *Hal.*

Sciara, *Meig.*
*valida, *Wlk.*

Fam. CECIDOMYZIDÆ, *Hal.*

Cecidomyia, *Latr.*
*primaria, *Wlk.*

Fam. SIMULIDÆ, *Hal.*

Simulium, *Latr.*
*destinatum, *Wlk.*

Fam. CHIRONOMIDÆ, *Hal.*

Ceratopogon, *Meig.*
*albocinctus, *Wlk.*

Fam. CULICIDÆ, *Steph.*

Culex, *Linn.*
regius, *Thwaites.*
fuscanus, *Wied.*
circumvolans, *Wlk.*
contrahens, *Wlk.*

Fam. TIPULIDÆ, *Hal.*

Ctenophora, *Fabr.*
Taprobanes, *Wlk.*
Gymnoplistia ? *Westw.*
hebes, *Wlk.*

Fam. STRATIOMIDÆ, *Latr.*

Ptilocera, *Wied.*
quadridentata, *Fabr.*
fastuosa, *Geist.*
Pachygaster, *Meig.*
rufitarsis, *Macq.*
Acanthina, *Wied.*
azurea, *Geist.*

Fam. TABANIDÆ, *Leach.*

Pangonia, *Latr.*
Taprobanes, *Wlk.*

Fam. ASILIDÆ, *Leach.*

Trupanea, *Macq.*
Ceylanica, *Macq.*
Asilus, *Linn.*
flavicornis, *Macq.*
Barium, *Wlk.*

Fam. DOLICHOPIDÆ, *Leach.*

Psilopus, *Meig.*
*procuratus, *Wlk.*

Fam. MUSCIDÆ, *Latr.*

Tachina ? *Fabr.*
*tenebrosa, *Wlk.*
Musca, *Linn.*
domestica, *Linn.*
Dacus, *Fabr.*
*interclusus, *Wlk.*
*nigroæneus, *Wlk.*
*detentus, *Wlk.*
Ortalis, *Fall.*
*confundens, *Wlk.*
Sciomyza, *Fall.*
*leucotelus, *Wlk.*
Drosophila, *Fall.*
*restituens, *Wlk.*

Fam. NYCTERIBIDÆ, *Leach.*

Nycteribia, *Latr.*
———? a species parasitic on Scatophilus Coromandelicus, *Bligh.*

## Order HEMIPTERA, *Linn.*

Fam. PACHYCORIDÆ, *Dall.*

Cantuo, *Amyot & Serv.*
ocellatus, *Thunb.*
Callidea, *Lap.*
superba, *Dall.*
Stockerus, *Linn.*

Fam. EURYGASTERIDÆ, *Dall.*

Trigonosoma, *Lap.*
Desfontainii, *Fabr.*

Fam. PLATASPIDÆ, *Dall.*

Coptosoma, *Lap.*
laticeps, *Dall.*

Fam. HALYDIDÆ, *Dall.*

Halys, *Fabr.*
dentata, *Fabr.*

Fam. PENTATOMIDÆ, *Steph.*

Pentatoma, *Oliv.*
Timorensis, *Hope.*
Taprobanensis, *Dall.*
Catacanthus, *Spin.*
incarnatus, *Drury.*
Rhaphigaster, *Lap.*
congrua, *Wlk.*

Fam. EDESSIDÆ, *Dall.*

Aspongopus, *Lap.*
anus, *Fabr.*
Tesseratoma, *Lep. & Serv.*
papillosa, *Drury.*
Cyclopelta, *Am. & Serv.*
siccifolia, *Hope.*

Fam. PHYLLOCEPHALIDÆ, *Dall.*

Phyllocephala, *Lap.*
Ægyptiaca, *Lefeb.*

Fam. MICTIDÆ, *Dall.*

Mictis, *Leach.*
castanea, *Dall.*
valida, *Dall.*
punctum, *Hope.*
Crinocerus, *Burm.*
ponderosus, *Wlk.*

Fam. ANISOSCELIDÆ, *Dall.*

Leptoscelis, *Lap.*
ventralis, *Dall.*
turpis, *Wlk.*
marginalis, *Wlk.*
Serinetha, *Spin.*
Taprobanensis, *Dall.*
abdominalis, *Fabr.*

Fam. ALYDIDÆ, *Dall.*

Alydus, *Fabr.*
linearis, *Fabr.*

Fam. STENOCEPHALIDÆ, *Dall.*

Leptocorisa, *Latr.*
Chinensis, *Dall.*

Fam. COREIDÆ, *Steph.*

Rhopalus, *Schill.*
interruptus, *Wlk.*

Fam. LYGÆIDÆ, *Westw.*

Lygæus, *Fabr.*
lutescens, *Wlk.*
figuratus, *Wlk.*
discifer, *Wlk.*
Rhyparochromus, *Curt.*
testaceipes, *Wlk.*

Fam. ARADIDÆ, *Wlk.*

Piestosoma, *Lap.*
picipes, *Wlk.*

Fam. TINGIDÆ, *Wlk.*

Calloniana, *Wlk.*
*elegans, *Wlk.*

Fam. CIMICIDÆ, *Wlk.*

Cimex, *Linn.*
lectularius, *Linn.?*

Fam. REDUVIIDÆ, *Steph.*

Pirates, *Burm.*
marginatus, *Wlk.*
Acanthaspis, *Am. & Serv.*
sanguinipes, *Wlk.*
fulvispina, *Wlk.*

Fam. HYDROMETRIDÆ, *Leach.*

Ptilomera, *Am. & Serv.*
laticauda, *Hardw.*

Fam. NEPIDÆ, *Leach.*

Belostoma, *Latr.*
Indicum, *St. Farg.*
Nepa, *Linn.*
minor, *Wlk.*

Fam. NOTONECTIDÆ, *Steph.*

Notonecta, *Linn.*
abbreviata, *Wlk.*
simplex, *Wlk.*
Corixa, *Geoff.*
*subjacens, *Wlk.*

## Order HOMOPTERA, *Latr.*

Fam. CICADIDÆ, *Westw.*

Dundubia, *Am. & Serv.*
stipata, *Wlk.*
Clonia, *Wlk.*
Larus, *Wlk.*
Cicada, *Linn.*
limitaris, *Wlk.*
nubifurca, *Wlk.*

Fam. FULGORIDÆ, *Schaum.*

Hotinus, *Am. & Serv.*
maculatus, *Oliv.*
fulvirostris, *Wlk.*
coccineus, *Wlk.*
Pyrops, *Spin.*
punctata, *Oliv.*
Aphæna, *Guér.*
sanguinalis, *Westw.*
Elidiptera, *Spin.*
Emersoniana, *White.*

Fam. CIXIIDÆ, *Wlk.*

Eurybrachys, *Guér.*
tomentosa, *Fabr.*
dilatata, *Wlk.*
crudelis, *Westw.*
Cixius, *Latr.*
*nubilus, *Wlk.*

Fam. ISSIDÆ, *Wlk.*

Hemisphærius, *Schaum.*
*Schaumi, *Stal.*
*bipustulatus, *Wlk.*

Fam. DERBIDÆ, *Schaum.*

Thracia, *Westw.*
pterophorides, *Westw.*
Derbe, *Fabr.*
*furcato-vittata, *Stal.*

Fam. FLATTIDÆ, *Schaum.*

Flatoides, *Guér.*
hyalinus, *Fabr.*
tenebrosus, *Wlk.*
Ricania, *Germ.*
Hemerobii, *Wlk.*
Pœciloptera, *Latr.*
pulverulenta, *Guér.*
stellaris, *Wlk.*
Tennentina, *White.*

Fam. MEMBRACIDÆ, *Wlk.*

Oxyrhachis, *Germ.*
*indicans, *Wlk.*
Centrotus, *Fabr.*
*reponens, *Wlk.*
*malleus, *Wlk.*
substitutus, *Wlk.*
*decipiens, *Wlk.*
*relinquens, *Wlk.*
*imitator, *Wlk.*
*repressus, *Wlk.*
*terminalis, *Wlk.*

Fam. CERCOPIDÆ, *Leach.*

Cercopis, *Fabr.*
inclusa, *Wlk.*
Ptyelus, *Lep. & Serv.*
costalis, *Wlk.*

Fam. TETTIGONIIDÆ, *Wlk.*

Tettigonia, *Latr.*
paulula, *Wlk.*

Fam. SCARIDÆ, *Wlk.*

Ledra, *Fabr.*
rugosa, *Wlk.*
conica, *Wlk.*
Gypona, *Germ.*
prasina, *Wlk.*

Fam. IASSIDÆ, *Wlk.*

Acocephalus, *Germ.*
porrectus, *Wlk.*

Fam. PSYLLIDÆ, *Latr.*

Psylla, *Goff.*
*marginalis, *Wlk.*

Fam. COCCIDÆ, *Leach.*

Lecanium, *Illig.*
Coffeæ, *Wlk.*

# CHAP. XIII.

## ARTICULATA.

---

*Arachnida — Myriopoda — Crustacea, etc.*

WITH a few striking exceptions, the true *spiders* of Ceylon resemble in œconomy and appearance those we are accustomed to see at home;—they frequent the houses, the gardens, the rocks and the stems of trees, and along the sunny paths, where the forest meets the open country, the *Epeira* and her congeners, the true net-weaving spiders, extend their lacework, the grace of the designs being even less attractive than the beauty of the creatures that elaborate them.

Such of them as live in the woods select with singular sagacity the bridle-paths and narrow passages for expanding their nets; perceiving no doubt that the larger insects frequent these openings for facility of movement through the jungle; and that the smaller ones are carried towards them by currents of air. Their nets are stretched across the path from four to eight feet above the ground, suspended from projecting shoots, and attached, if possible, to thorny shrubs; and they sometimes exhibit the most remarkable scenes of carnage and destruction. I have taken down a ball as large as a man's head consisting of successive layers rolled together, in the heart of which was the original den of the family,

SPIDER

*Mygale fasciata.*

whilst the envelope was formed, sheet after sheet, by coils of the old web filled with the wings and limbs of insects of all descriptions, from large moths and butterflies to mosquitoes and minute coleoptera. Each layer appeared to have been originally hung across the passage to intercept the expected prey; and, when it had become surcharged with carcases, to have been loosened, tossed over by the wind or its own weight, and wrapped round the nucleus in the centre, the spider replacing it by a fresh sheet, to be in turn detached and added to the mass within.

Separated by marked peculiarities both of structure and instinct, from the spiders which live in the open air, and busy themselves in providing food during the day, the *Mygale fasciata* is not only sluggish in its habits, but disgusting in its form and dimensions. Its colour is a gloomy brown, interrupted by irregular blotches and faint bands (whence its trivial name); it is sparingly sprinkled with hairs, and its limbs, when expanded, stretch over an area of six to eight inches in diameter. It is familiar to Europeans in Ceylon, who have given it the name, and ascribed to it the fabulous propensities, of the Tarentula.[1]

The Mygale is found abundantly in the northern and eastern parts of the island, and occasionally in dark unfrequented apartments in the western province; but its inclinations are solitary, and it shuns the busy traffic of towns.

The largest specimens I have seen were at Gampola, in the vicinity of Kandy, and one taken in the store-

[1] Species of the true *Tarentula* are not uncommon in Ceylon; they are all of very small size, and perfectly harmless.

room of the rest-house there, nearly covered with its legs an ordinary-sized breakfast plate.[1]

This hideous creature does not weave a broad web or spin a net like other spiders, but nevertheless it forms a comfortable mansion in the wall of a neglected building, the hollow of a tree, or under the eave of an overhanging stone. This it lines throughout with a tapestry of silk of a tubular form; and of a texture so exquisitely fine and closely woven, that no moisture can penetrate it. The extremity of the tube is carried out to the entrance, where it expands into a little platform, stayed by braces to the nearest objects that afford a firm hold. In particular situations, where the entrance is exposed to the wind, the mygale, on the approach of the monsoon, extends the strong tissue above it so as to serve as an awning to prevent the access of rain.

The construction of this silken dwelling is exclusively designed for the domestic luxury of the spider; it serves no purpose in trapping or securing prey, and no external disturbance of the web tempts the creature to sally out to surprise an intruder, as the epeira and its congeners would.

By day it remains concealed in its den, whence it issues at night to feed on larvæ and worms, devouring cockroaches and their pupæ, and attacking the milleped, gryllotalpæ, and other fleshy insects.

Mr. EDGAR L. LAYARD has described[2] an encounter between a Mygale and a cockroach, which he witnessed in the madua of a temple at Alittane, between Anarajapoora and Dambool. When about a yard apart, each

[1] See Plate opposite,

[2] *Ann. and Mag. Nat. Hist.* May, 1853.

discerned the other and stood still, the spider with his legs slightly bent and his body raised, the cockroach confronting him and directing his antennæ with a restless undulation towards his enemy. The spider, by stealthy movements, approached to within a few inches and paused, both parties eyeing each other intently; then suddenly a rush, a scuffle, and both fell to the ground, when the blatta's wings closed, the spider seized it under the throat with his claws, and dragged it into a corner, when the action of his jaws was distinctly audible. Next morning Mr. Layard found that the soft parts of the body had been eaten, nothing but the head, thorax, and elytra remaining.

But, in addition to minor and ignoble prey, the Mygale rests under the imputation of seizing small birds and feasting on their blood. The author who first gave popular currency to this story was Madame MERIAN, a zoological artist of the last century, many of whose drawings are still preserved in the Museums of St. Petersburg, Holland, and England. In a work on the Insects of Surinam, published in 1705[1], she figured the *Mygale avicularia*, in the act of devouring a humming bird. The accuracy of her statement has since been impugned[2] by a correspondent of the Zoological Society of London, on the ground that the mygale makes no net, but lives in recesses, to which no humming-bird would resort; and hence, the writer somewhat illogically declares, that he "disbelieves the existence of any bird-catching spider."

[1] *Dissertatio de Generatione et Metamorphosibus Insectorum Surinamensium*, Amst. 1701. Fol.

[2] By Mr. MACLEAY in a paper communicated to the Zoological Society of London, *Proc.* 1834, p. 12.

Some years later, however, the same writer felt it incumbent on him to qualify this hasty conclusion [1], in consequence of having seen at Sydney an enormous spider, the *Epeira diadema*, in the act of sucking the juices of a bird (the *Zosterops dorsalis* of Vigors and Horsfield), which it had caught in the meshes of its geometrical net. This circumstance, however, did not in his opinion affect the case of the *Mygale;* and even as regards the *Epeira*, Mr. MacLeay, who witnessed the occurrence, was inclined to believe the instance to be accidental and exceptional; "an exception indeed so rare, that no other person had ever witnessed the fact."

Subsequent observation has, however, served to sustain the story of Madame Merian.[2] Baron Walckenaer and Latreille both corroborated it by other authorities; and M. Moreau da Jonnès, who studied the habits of the Mygale in Martinique, says it hunts far and wide in search of its prey, conceals itself beneath leaves for the purpose of surprising them, and climbs the branches of trees to devour the young of the humming bird, and of the *Certhia flaveola*. As to its mode of attack, M. Jonnès says that when it throws itself on its victim it clings to it by the double hooks of its tarsi, and strives to reach the back of the head, to insert its jaws between the skull and the vertebræ.[3]

[1] See *Ann. and Mag. of Nat. Hist.* for 1842, vol. viii. p. 324.

[2] See authorities quoted by Mr. SHUCKARD in the *Ann. and Mag. of Nat. Hist.* 1842, vol. viii. p. 436, &c.

[3] At a meeting of the Entomological Society, July 20, 1855, a paper was read by Mr. H. W. BATES, who stated that in 1849 at Cameta in Brazil, he "was attracted by a curious movement of the large grayish brown Mygale on the trunk of a vast tree: it was close beneath a deep crevice or chink in the tree, across which this species weaves a dense web, at one end open for its exit and entrance. In the present instance the lower part of the web was broken, and two small finches were entangled in its folds. The finch was about

For my own part, no instance came to my knowledge in Ceylon of a mygale attacking a bird; but PERCIVAL, who wrote his account of the island in 1805, describes an enormous spider (possibly an Epeirid) thinly covered with hair which "makes webs strong enough to entangle and hold even small birds that form its usual food." [1]

The fact of its living on millepeds, blattæ, and crickets, is universally known; and a lady who lived at Marandahn, near Colombo, told me that she had, on one occasion, seen a little house-lizard (*gecko*) seized and devoured by one of these ugly spiders.

Walckenaer has described a spider of large size, under the name of *Olios Taprobanius*, which is very common in Ceylon, and conspicuous from the fiery hue of the under surface, the remainder being covered with gray hair so short and fine that the body seems almost denuded. It spins a moderate-sized web, hung vertically between two sets of strong lines, stretched one above the other athwart the pathways. Some of the threads thus carried horizontally from tree to tree at a considerable height from the ground are so strong as to cause a painful check across the face when moving quickly against them; and more than once in riding I have had my hat lifted off my head by one of these cords.[2]

the size of the common Siskin of Europe, and he judged the two to be male and female; one of them was quite dead, but secured in the broken web; the other was under the body of the spider, not quite dead, and was covered in parts with a filthy liquor or saliva exuded by the monster. "The species of spider," Mr. Bates says, "I cannot name; it is wholly of a gray brown colour, and clothed with coarse pile." "If the Mygales," he adds, "did not prey upon vertebrated animals, I do not see how they could find sufficient subsistence."—*The Zoologist*, vol. xiii. p. 480.

[1] PERCIVAL's *Ceylon*, p. 313.

[2] Over the country generally are scattered species of *Gasteracantha*, remarkable for their firm shell-

An officer in the East India Company's Service[1], in a communication to the Asiatic Society of Bengal, describes the gigantic web of a black and red spider six inches in diameter, (his description of which, both in colour and size, seems to point to some species closely allied to the *Olios Taprobanius*,) which he saw near Monghyr on the Ganges; in this web "a bird was entangled, and the young spiders, eight in number, and entirely of a brick red colour, were feeding on the carcase.[2]

The voracious *Galeodes* has not yet been noticed in Ceylon; but its carnivorous propensities are well known in those parts of Hindustan, where it is found, and where it lives upon crickets, coleoptera, and other insects, as well as small lizards and birds. This "tiger of the insect world," as it has aptly been designated by a gentleman who was a witness to its ferocity[3], was seen to attack a young sparrow half grown, and seize it by the thigh, *which it sawed through.* The "savage then caught the bird by the throat, and put an end to its sufferings by cutting off its head." "On another occasion," says the same authority, "Dr. Baddeley confined one of these spiders under a glass wall-shade with two young musk-rats (*Sorex Indicus*), both of which it destroyed." It must be added, however, that neither in the instance of the bird, of the lizard, or the rats, did the galeodes devour its prey after killing it.

covered bodies, with projecting knobs arranged in pairs. In habit these anomalous-looking *Epeiridæ* appear to differ in no respect from the rest of the family, waylaying their prey in similar situations and in the same manner.

Another very singular subgenus, met with in Ceylon, is distinguished by the abdomen being dilated behind, and armed with two long spines, arching obliquely backwards. These abnormal kinds are not so handsomely coloured as the smaller species of typical form.

[1] Capt. Sherwill.

[2] *Jour. Asiat. Soc. Bengal*, 1850, vol. xix. p. 475.

[3] Capt. Hutton. See a paper on the *Galeodes vorax* in the *Journal of the Asiatic Society of Bengal*, vol. xi. Part II. p. 860.

In the hills around Pusilawa, I have seen the haunts of a curious species of long-legged spiders[1], popularly called "harvest-men," which congregate in hollow trees and in holes in the banks by the roadside, in groups of from fifty to a hundred, that to a casual observer look like bunches of horse-hair. This appearance is produced by the long and slender legs of these creatures, which are of a shining black, whilst their bodies, so small as to be mere specks, are concealed beneath them. The same spider is found in the low country near Galle, but there it shows no tendency to become gregarious. Can it be that they thus assemble in groups in the hills for the sake of accumulated warmth at the cool altitude of 4000 feet?

*Ticks.* — Ticks are to be classed among the intolerable nuisances to the Ceylon traveller. They live in immense numbers in the jungle[2], and attaching themselves to the

[1] *Phalangium bisignatum.*

[2] Dr. HOOKER, in his *Himalayan Journal*, vol. i. p. 279, in speaking of the multitude of these creatures in the mountains of Nepal, wonders what they find to feed on, as in these humid forests in which they literally swarmed, there was neither pathway nor animal life. In Ceylon they abound everywhere in the plains on the low brushwood; and in the very driest seasons they are quite as numerous as at other times. In the mountain zone, which is more humid, they are less prevalent. Dogs are tormented by them: and they display something closely allied to cunning in always fastening on an animal in those parts where they cannot be torn off by his paws; on his eye-brows, the tips of his ears, and the back of his neck. With a corresponding instinct I have always observed in the gambols of the Pariah dogs, that they invariably commence their attentions by mutually gnawing each other's ears and necks, as if in pursuit of ticks from places from which each is unable to expel them for himself. Horses have a similar instinct; and when they meet, they apply their teeth to the roots of the ears of their companions, to the neck and the crown of the head. The buffaloes and oxen are relieved of ticks by the crows which rest on their backs as they browse, and free them from these pests. In the low country the same acceptable office is performed by the "cattle-keeper heron" (*Ardea bubulcus*), which is "sure to be found in attendance on them while grazing; and the animals seem to know their

plants by the two forelegs, lie in wait to catch at unwary animals as they pass. A shower of these diminutive vermin will sometimes drop from a branch, if unluckily shaken, and disperse themselves over the body, each fastening on the neck, the ears, and eyelids, and inserting a barbed proboscis. They burrow, with their heads pressed as far as practicable under the skin, causing a sensation of smarting, as if particles of red hot sand had been scattered over the flesh. If torn from their hold, the suckers remain behind and form an ulcer. The only safe expedient is to tolerate the agony of their penetration till a drop of coco-nut oil or the juice of a lime can be applied, when these little furies drop off without further ill consequences. One very large species, dappled with grey, attaches itself to the buffaloes.

*Mites.* — The *Trombidium tinctorum* of Hermann is found about Aripo, and generally over the northern provinces, — where after a shower of rain or heavy night's dew, they appear in countless myriads. It is about half an inch long, like a tuft of crimson velvet, and imparts its colouring matter readily to any fluid in which it may be immersed. It feeds on vegetable juices, and is perfectly innocuous. Its European representative, similarly tinted, and found in garden mould, is commonly called the "Little red pillion."

MYRIAPODS. — The certainty with which an accidental pressure or unguarded touch is resented and retorted by a bite, makes the centipede, when it has taken up its temporary abode within a sleeve or the fold of a dress, by far the most unwelcome of all the Singhalese assailants. The great size, too (little short of a foot in length),

benefactors, and stand quietly, while the birds peck their tormentors from their flanks."—*Mag. Nat. Hist.* p. 111, 1844.

to which it sometimes attains, renders it formidable, and, apart from the apprehension of unpleasant consequences from a wound, one shudders at the bare idea of such a hideous creature crawling over the skin, beneath the innermost folds of one's garments.

At the head of the *Myriapods*, and pre-eminent from a superiorly-developed organisation, stands the genus *Cermatia:* singular-looking objects; mounted upon

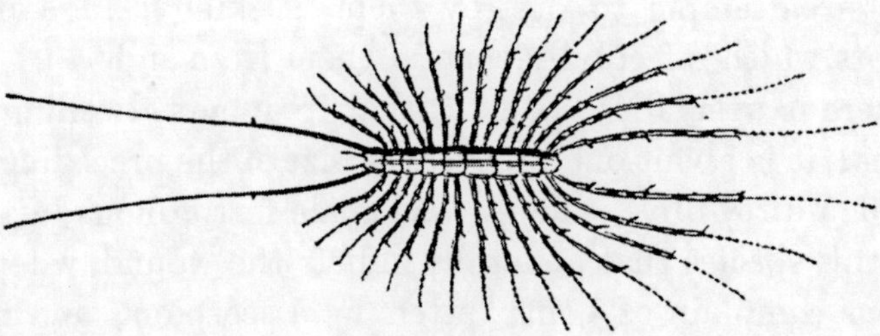

CERMATIA.

slender legs, of gradually increasing length from front to rear, the hind ones in some species being amazingly prolonged, and all handsomely marked with brown annuli in concentric arches. These myriapods are harmless, excepting to woodlice, spiders, and young cockroaches, which form their ordinary prey. They are rarely to be seen; but occasionally at daybreak, after a more than usually abundant repast, they may be observed motionless, and resting with their regularly extended limbs nearly flat against the walls. On being disturbed they dart away with a surprising velocity, to conceal themselves in chinks until the return of night.

But the species to be really dreaded are the true *Scolopendræ*, which are active and carnivorous, living in holes in old walls and other gloomy dens. One species[1] attains to nearly the length of a foot, with corresponding breadth; it is of a dark purple colour, approaching black, with yellowish legs and antennæ, and in its whole aspect repulsive and frightful. It is strong and active, and evinces an eager disposition to fight when molested. The *Scolopendræ* are gifted by nature with a rigid coriaceous armour, which does not yield to common pressure, or even to a moderate blow; so that they often escape the most well-deserved and well-directed attempts to destroy them, seeking refuge in retreats which effectually conceal them from sight.

There is a smaller species[2], that frequents dwelling-houses; it is about one quarter the size of the preceding, and of a dirty olive colour, with pale ferruginous legs. It is this species that generally inflicts the wound, when persons complain of being bitten by a scorpion; and it has a mischievous propensity for insinuating itself into the folds of dress. The bite at first does not occasion more suffering than would arise from the penetration of two coarsely-pointed needles; but after a little time the wound swells, becomes acutely painful, and if it be over a bone or any other resisting part, the sensation is so intolerable as to produce fever. The agony subsides after a few hours' duration. In some cases the bite is unattended by any particular degree of annoyance, and in these instances it is to be supposed that the contents of the poison gland had become exhausted by previous efforts, since, if much tasked, the organ requires rest to enable it to resume its accustomed functions and to secrete a supply of venom.

*The Fish-insect.*—The chief inconvenience of a

[1] *Scolopendra crassa*, Temp. [2] *Scolopendra pallipes.*

residence in Ceylon, both on the coast and in the mountains, is the prevalence of damp, and the difficulty of protecting articles liable to injury from this cause. Books, papers, and manuscripts rapidly decay; especially during the south-west monsoon, when the atmosphere is saturated with moisture. Unless great precautions are taken, the binding fades and yields, the leaves grow mouldy and stained, and letter-paper, in an incredibly short time, becomes so spotted and spongy as to be unfit for use. After a very few seasons of neglect, a book falls to pieces, and its decomposition attracts hordes of minute insects, that swarm to assist in the work of destruction. The concealment of these tiny creatures during daylight renders it difficult to watch their proceedings, or to discriminate the precise species most actively engaged; but there is every reason to believe that the larvæ of the death-watch and numerous acari are amongst the most active. As nature seldom peoples a region supplied with abundance of suitable food, without, at the same time, taking measures of precaution against the disproportionate increase of individuals; so have these vegetable depredators been provided with foes who pursue and feed greedily upon them. These are of widely different genera; but instead of their services being gratefully recognised, they are popularly branded as accomplices in the work of destruction. One of these ill-used creatures is a tiny, tail-less scorpion (*Chelifer*[1]), and another is the pretty

[1] Of the first of these, three species have been noticed in Ceylon, all with the common characteristics of being nocturnal, very active, very minute, of a pale chesnut colour, and each armed with a crab-like claw. They are

*Chelifer Librorum*, Temp.
" *oblongus*, Temp.
" *acaroides*, Hermann.

Dr. Templeton appears to have been puzzled to account for the

little silvery creature (*Lepisma*), called by Europeans the "fish-insect."[1]

The latter, which is a familiar genus, comprises several species, of which only two have as yet been described; one is of a large size, most graceful in its movements, and singularly beautiful in appearance, owing to the whiteness of the pearly scales from which its name is derived. These, contrasted with the dark hue of the other parts, and its tri-partite tail, attract the eye as the insect darts rapidly along. Like the chelifer, it shuns the light, hiding in chinks till sunset, but is actively engaged throughout the night feasting on the acari and soft-bodied insects which assail books and papers.

*Millepeds.*—In the hot dry season, and more especially in the northern portions of the island, the eye is attracted along the edges of the sandy roads by fragments of the dislocated rings of a huge species of millepede[2], lying in short curved tubes, the cavity admitting the tip of the little finger. When perfect the creature is two-thirds of a foot long, of a brilliant jet black, and with above a hundred yellow legs, which, when moving onward, present the appearance of a series of undulations from rear to front, bearing the

appearance of the latter species in Ceylon, so far from its native country, but it has most certainly been introduced from Europe, in Dutch or Portuguese books.

[1] *Lepisma niveo-fasciata*, Templeton, and *L. niger*, Temp. It was called "Lepisma" by Fabricius, from its fish-like scales. It has six legs, filiform antennæ, and the abdomen terminated by three elongated setæ, two of which are placed nearly at right angles to the central one. LINNÆUS states that the European species, with which book collectors are familiar, was first brought in sugar ships from America. Hence, possibly, these are more common in seaport towns in the South of England and elsewhere, and it is almost certain that, like the chelifer, one of the species found on book-shelves in Ceylon, has been brought thither from Europe.

[2] *Julus ater*.

animal gently forwards. This *Julus* is harmless, and may be handled with perfect impunity. Its food consists chiefly of fruits and the roots and stems of succulent vegetables, its jaws not being framed for any more formidable purpose. Another and a very pretty species [1], quite as black, but with a bright crimson band down the back, and the legs similarly tinted, is common in the gardens about Colombo and throughout the western province.

CRUSTACEA.—The seas around Ceylon abound with marine articulata; but a knowledge of the crustacea of the island is at present a desideratum; and with the exception of the few commoner species that frequent the shores, or are offered in the markets, we are literally without information, excepting the little that can be gleaned from already published systematic works.

In the bazaars several species of edible crabs are exposed for sale; and amongst the delicacies at the tables of Europeans, curries made from prawns and lobsters are the triumphs of the Ceylon cuisine. Of these latter the fishermen sometimes exhibit specimens [2] of extraordinary dimensions and of a beautiful purple hue, variegated with white. Along the level shore north and south of Colombo, and in no less profusion elsewhere, the nimble little

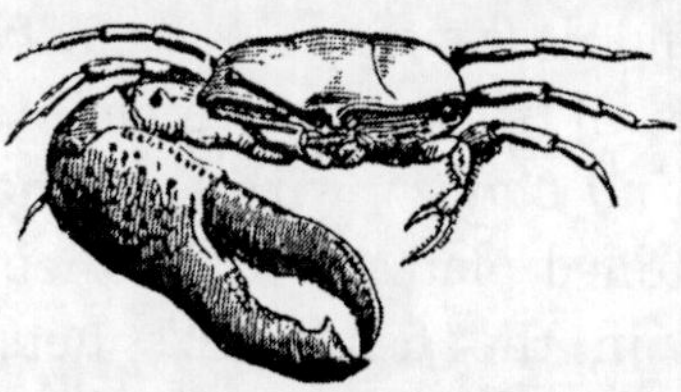

CALLING CRAB OF CEYLON.

Calling Crabs [3] scamper over the moist sands, carrying aloft the enormous hand (sometimes larger than the

[1] *Julus carnifex*, Fab.

[2] *Palinurus ornatus*, Fab.



[3] *Gelasimus tetragonon?* Edw.; *G. annulipes?* Edw.; *G. Dussumieri?* Edw.

rest of the body), which is their peculiar characteristic, and which, from its beckoning gesture has suggested their popular name. They hurry to conceal themselves in the deep retreats which they hollow out in the banks that border the sea.

*Sand Crabs.*—In the same localities, or a little farther inland, the *Ocypode* [1] burrows in the dry soil, making deep excavations, bringing up literally armfulls of sand; which with a spring in the air, and employing its other limbs, it jerks far from its burrows, distributing it in a circle to the distance of several feet.[2] So inconvenient are the operations of these industrious pests that men are kept regularly employed at Colombo in filling up the holes formed by them on the surface of the Galle face. This, the only equestrian promenade of the capital, is so infested by these active little creatures that accidents often occur through horses stumbling in their troublesome excavations.

*Painted Crabs.*—On the reef of rocks which lies to the south of the harbour at Colombo, the beautiful little painted crabs[3], distinguished by dark red markings on a yellow ground, may be seen all day long running nimbly in the spray, and ascending and descending in security the almost perpendicular sides of the rocks which are washed by the waves. *Paddling Crabs*[4], with the hind pair of legs terminated by flattened plates to assist them in swimming, are brought up in the fishermen's nets. *Hermit Crabs* take possession of the deserted shells of the univalves, and crawl in pursuit of garbage along the moist beach. Prawns and shrimps furnish deli-

[1] *Ocypode ceratophthalmus*, Pall.

[2] *Ann. Nat. Hist.* April, 1852. Paper by Mr. EDGAR L. LAYARD.

[3] *Grapsus strigosus*, Herbst.

[4] *Neptunus pelagicus*, Linn.; *N. sanguinolentus*, Herbst, &c. &c.

cacies for the breakfast table; and the delicate little pea crab, *Pontonia inflata*[1], recalls its Mediterranean congener[2], which attracted the attention of Aristotle, from taking up its habitation in the shell of the living pinna.

ANNELIDÆ. — The marine *Annelides* of the island have not as yet been investigated; a cursory glance, however, amongst the stones, on the beach at Trincomalie and in the pools that afford convenient basins for examining them, would lead to the belief that the marine species are not numerous; tubicole genera, as well as some nereids, are found, but there seems to be little diversity, though it is not impossible that a closer scrutiny might be repaid by the discovery of some interesting forms.

*Leeches.*—Of all the plagues which beset the traveller in the rising grounds of Ceylon, the most detested are the land leeches.[3] They are not frequent in the plains,

[1] MILNE EDW., *Hist. Nat. Crust.*, vol. ii. p. 360.

[2] *Pinnotheres veterum.*

[3] *Hæmadipsa Ceylanica*, Bosc. Blainv. These pests are not, however, confined to Ceylon; they infest the lower ranges of the Himalaya.—HOOKER, vol. i. p. 107; vol. ii. p. 54. THUNBERG, who records (*Travels*, vol. iv. p. 232) having seen them in Ceylon, likewise met with them in the forests and slopes of Batavia. MARSDEN (*Hist.* p. 311) complains of them dropping on travellers in Sumatra. KNORR found them at Japan; and it is affirmed that they abound in islands farther to the eastward. M. GAY encountered them in Chili.—(MOQUIN-TANDON, *Hirudinées*, p. 211, 346). It is very doubtful, however, whether all these are to be referred to one species. M. DE BLAINVILLE, under *H. Ceylanica*, in the *Dict. de Scien. Nat.* vol. xlvii. p. 271, quotes M. Bosc as authority for the kind which that naturalist describes being "rouges et tachetées;" which is scarcely applicable to the Singhalese species. It is more than probable therefore, considering the period at which M. Bosc wrote, that he obtained his information from travellers to the further east, and has connected with the habitat universally ascribed to them from old KNOX's work (Part I. chap. vi.) a meagre description, more properly belonging to the land leech of Batavia or Japan. In all likelihood, therefore, there

which are too hot and dry for them; but amongst the rank vegetation in the lower ranges of the hill country, may be a *H. Boscii*, distinct from the *H. Ceylanica*. That which is found in Ceylon is round,

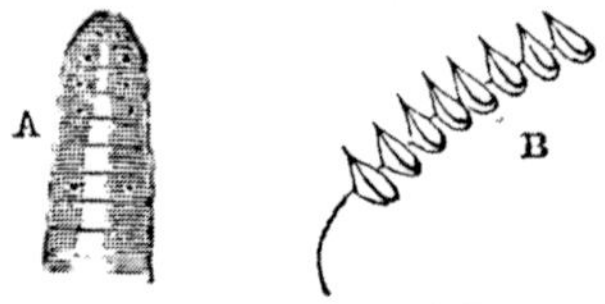


EYES AND TEETH OF THE LAND LEECH OF CEYLON.

a little flattened on the inferior surface, largest at the anal extremity, thence gradually tapering forward, and with the anal sucker composed of four rings, and wider in proportion than in other species. It is of a clear brown colour, with a yellow stripe the entire length of each side, and a greenish dorsal one. The body is formed of 100 rings; the eyes, of which there are five pairs, are placed in an arch on the dorsal surface; the first four pairs occupying contiguous rings (thus differing from the water-leeches, which have an unoccupied ring betwixt the third and fourth); the fifth pair are located on the seventh ring, two vacant rings intervening. To Mr. Thwaites, Director of the Botanic Garden at Peradenia, who at my request examined their structure minutely, I am indebted for the following most interesting particulars respecting them. "I have been giving a little time to the examination of the land leech. I find it to have five pairs of ocelli, the first four seated on corresponding segments, and the posterior pair on the seventh segment or ring, the fifth and sixth rings being eyeless (*fig.* A). The mouth is very retractile, and the aperture is shaped as in ordinary leeches. The serratures of the teeth, or rather the teeth themselves, are very beautiful. Each of the three 'teeth,' or cutting instruments, is principally muscular, the muscular body being very clearly seen. The rounded edge in which the teeth are set appears to be cartilaginous in structure; the teeth are very numerous, (*fig.* B); but some near the base have a curious appendage, apparently (I have not yet made this out quite satisfactorily) set upon one side. I have not yet been able to detect the anal or sexual pores. The anal sucker seems to be formed of four rings, and on each side above is a sort of crenated flesh-like appendage. The tint of the common species is yellowish-brown or snuff-coloured, streaked with black, with a yellow-greenish dorsal, and another lateral line along its whole length. There is a larger species to be found in this garden with a broad green dorsal fascia; but I have not been able to procure one although I have offered a small reward to any coolie who will bring me one." In a subsequent communication Mr. Thwaites remarks "that the dorsal longitudinal fascia is of the same width as the lateral ones, and differs only in being perhaps slightly more green; the colour of the three fasciæ varies from brownish-yellow to bright green." He likewise states "that the rings which compose the body are just 100, and the teeth 70 to 80 in each set, in a single row, except to one end, where they are in a double row."

which is kept damp by frequent showers, they are found in tormenting profusion. They are terrestrial, never visiting ponds or streams. In size they are about an inch in length, and as fine as a common knitting needle; but they are capable of distension till they equal a quill in thickness, and attain a length of nearly two inches. Their structure is so flexible that they can insinuate themselves through the meshes of the finest stocking, not only seizing on the feet and ankles, but ascending to the back and throat and fastening on the tenderest parts of the body. In order to exclude them, the coffee planters, who live amongst these pests, are obliged to

LAND LEECHES IN PURSUIT.

envelope their legs in "leech gaiters" made of closely woven cloth. The natives smear their bodies with oil, tobacco ashes, or lemon juice[1]; the latter serving not only to stop the flow of blood, but to expedite the healing of the wounds. In moving, the land leeches have the power of planting one extremity on the earth and raising the other perpendicularly to watch for their victim. Such is their vigilance and instinct, that on

[1] The Minorite friar, ODORIC of Portenau, writing in A.D. 1320, says that the gem-finders who sought the jewels around Adam's Peak, "take lemons which they peel, anointing themselves with the juice thereof, so that the leeches may not be able to hurt them."—HAKLUYT, *Voy.* vol. ii. p. 58.

the approach of a passer-by to a spot which they infest, they may be seen amongst the grass and fallen leaves on the edge of a native path, poised erect, and preparing for their attack on man and horse. On descrying their prey they advance rapidly by semi-circular strides, fixing one end firmly and arching the other forwards, till by successive advances they can lay hold of the traveller's foot, when they disengage themselves from the ground and ascend his dress in search of an aperture to enter. In these encounters the individuals in the rear of a party of travellers in the jungle invariably fare worst, as the leeches, once warned of their approach, congregate with singular celerity. Their size is so insignificant, and the wound they make is so skilfully punctured, that both are generally imperceptible, and the first intimation of their onslaught is the trickling of the blood or a chill feeling of the leech when it begins to hang heavily on the skin from being distended by its repast. Horses are driven wild by them, and stamp the ground in fury to shake them from their fetlocks, to which they hang in bloody tassels. The bare legs of the palankin bearers and coolies are a favourite resort; and, as their hands are too much engaged to be spared to pull them off, the leeches hang like bunches of grapes round their ankles; and I have seen the blood literally flowing over the edge of a European's shoe from their innumerable bites. In healthy constitutions the wounds, if not irritated, generally heal, occasioning no other inconvenience than a slight inflammation and itching; but in those with a bad state of body, the punctures, if rubbed, are liable to degenerate into ulcers, which may lead to the loss of limb or even of life. Both Marshall and Davy mention, that during the march of troops in the mountains, when the Kandyans were in rebellion, in 1818, the soldiers, and especially the Madras sepoys, with the pioneers and coolies, suffered so severely from this cause that numbers perished.[1]

One circumstance regarding these land leeches is remarkable and unexplained; they are helpless without moisture, and in the hills where they abound at all other times, they entirely disappear during long droughts;—yet re-appear instantaneously on the very first fall of rain; and in spots previously parched, where not one was visible an hour before, a single shower is sufficient to reproduce them in thousands, lurking beneath the decaying leaves, or striding with rapid movements across the gravel. Whence do they re-appear? Do they, too, take a "summer sleep," like the reptiles, molluscs, and tank fishes? or may they, like the *Rotifera*, be dried up and preserved for an indefinite period, resuming their vital activity on the mere recurrence of moisture? [2]

Besides a species of the medicinal leech, which [3] is

[1] DAVY'S *Ceylon*, p. 104; MARSHALL'S *Ceylon*, p. 15.

[2] See an account of the *Rotifera* and their faculty of repeated vivifaction, in the note appended to this chapter.

[3] *Hirudo sanguisorba.* The paddi-field leech of Ceylon, used for surgical purposes, has the dorsal surface of blackish olive, with several longitudinal striæ, more or less defined; the crenated margin yellow. The ventral surface is fulvous, bordered laterally with olive; the extreme margin yellow. The eyes are ranged as in the common medicinal leech of Europe; the four anterior ones rather larger than the others. The teeth are 140 in each series, appearing as a single row; in size

DORSAL.

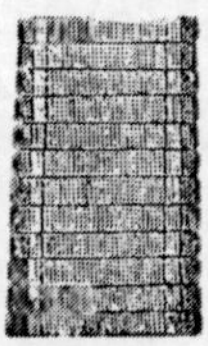
VENTRAL.

diminishing gradually from one end, very close set, and about half the width of a tooth apart. When full grown, these leeches are about

found in Ceylon, nearly double the size of the European one, and with a prodigious faculty of engorging blood, there is another pest in the low country, which is a source of considerable annoyance, and often of loss, to the husbandman. This is the cattle leech[1], which infests the stagnant pools, chiefly in the alluvial lands around the base of the mountain zone, whither the cattle resort by day, and the wild animals by night, to quench their thirst and to bathe. Lurking amongst the rank vegetation that fringes these deep pools, and hid by the broad leaves, or concealed among the stems and roots covered by the water, there are quantities of these pests in wait to attack the animals on their approach to drink. Their natural food consists of the juices of lumbrici and other invertebrata; but they

two inches long, but reaching to six inches when extended. Mr. Thwaites, to whom I am indebted for these particulars, adds that he saw in a tank at Kolona Korle leeches which appeared to him flatter and of a darker colour than those described above, but that he had not an opportunity of examining them particularly.

Mr. Thwaites states that there is a smaller tank leech of an olive-green colour, with some indistinct longitudinal striæ on the upper surface; the crenated margin of a pale yellowish-green; ocelli as in the paddi-field leech; length, one inch at rest, three inches when extended.

Mr. E. L. LAYARD informs us, *Mag. Nat. Hist.* p. 225, 1853, that a bubbling spring at the village of Tonniotoo, three miles S. W. of Moeletivoe, supplies most of the leeches used in the island. Those in use at Colombo are obtained in the immediate vicinity.

[1] *Hæmopsis paludum.* In size the cattle leech of Ceylon is somewhat larger than the medicinal leech of Europe; in colour it is of a uniform brown without bands, unless a rufous margin may be so considered. It has dark striæ. The body is somewhat rounded, flat when swimming, and composed of rather more than ninety rings. The greatest dimension is a little in advance of the anal sucker; the body thence tapers to the other extremity, which ends in an upper lip projecting considerably beyond the mouth. The eyes, ten in number, are disposed as in the common leech. The mouth is oval, the biting apparatus with difficulty seen, and the teeth not very numerous. The bite is so little acute that the moment of attachment, and the incision of the membrane is scarcely perceived by the sufferer from its attack.

generally avail themselves of the opportunity afforded by the dipping of the muzzles of the animals in the water to fasten on their nostrils, and by degrees to make their way to the deeper recesses of the nasal passages, and the mucous membranes of the throat and gullet. As many as a dozen have been found attached to the epiglottis and pharynx of a bullock, producing such irritation and submucous effusion that death has eventually ensued; and so tenacious are the leeches that even after death they retain their hold for some hours.[1]

---

## ARTICULATA.

### *APTERA.*

#### THYSANURA.

Podura *albicollis.*
*atricollis.*
*viduata.*
*pilosa.*
Archoreutes *coccinea.*
Lepisma nigrofasciata, *Temp.*
*nigra.*

#### ARACHNIDA.

Buthus afer, *Linn.*
Ceylonicus, *Koch.*
Scorpio *linearis.*
Chelifer librorum.
*oblongus.*
Obisium *crassifemur.*
Phrynus lunatus, *Pall.*
Thelyphonus caudatus, *Linn.*
Phalangium *bisignatum.*
Mygale fasciata, *Walck.*
Olios taprobanius, *Walck.*
Nephila . . . . . ?
Trombidium tinctorum, *Herm.*
Oribata . . . . . ?
Ixodes . . . . . ?

#### MYRIAPODA.

Cermatia *dispar.*
Lithobius *umbratilis.*
Scolopendra *crassa.*
spinosa, *Newp.*
*pallipes.*
*Grayii? Newp.*
tuberculidens, *Newp.*
Ceylonensis, *Newp.*
flava, *Newp.*
*olivacea.*
*abdominalis.*
Cryptops *sordidus.*
*assimilis.*
Geophilus *tegularius.*
*speciosus.*
Julus *ater.*
carnifex, *Fabr.*
*pallipes.*
*flaviceps.*
*pallidus.*

[1] Even men, when stooping to drink at a pool, are not safe from the assault of the cattle leeches. They cannot penetrate the human skin, but the delicate membrane of the mucous passages is easily ruptured by their serrated jaws. Instances have come to my knowledge of Europeans into whose nostrils they had gained admission and caused serious disturbance.

Craspedosoma *juloides*.
*præusta*.
Polydesmus *granulatus*.
Cambala *catenulata*.
Zephronia *conspicua*.

## *CRUSTACEA.*

DECAPODA BRACHYURA.

*Polybius*.
Neptunus pelagicus, *Linn*.
sanguinolentus, *Herbst*.
Thalamita . . . . . ?
Thelphusa *Indica*, *Latr*.
*Cardisoma* . . . . . ?
Ocypoda ceratophthalmus, *Pall*.
*macrocera*. *Edw*.
Gelasimus *tetragonon*, *Edw*.
*annulipes*, *Edw*.
Macrophthalmus *carinimanus*, *Latr*.
Grapsus *messor*, *Forsk*.
strigosus, *Herbst*.
Plagusia depressa, *Fabr*.
Calappa philargus, *Linn*.
*tuberculata*, *Fabr*.
Matuta victor, *Fabr*.
Leucosia *fugax*, *Fabr*.
*Dorippe*.

DECAPODA ANOMURA.

*Dromia* . . . . ?
Hippa Asiatica, *Edw*.
Pagurus affinis, *Edw*.
*punctulatus*, *Oliv*.
*Porcellana* . . . . ?

DECAPODA MACRURA.

Scyllarus *orientalis*, *Fabr*.
Palinurus ornatus, *Fabr*.
*affinis*, *N.S.*
*Crangon* . . . . ?
*Alpheus* . . . . ?
Pontonia inflata, *Edw*.
Palæmon carcinus, *Fabr*.
Stenopus . . . . ?
Peneus . . . . ?

STOMATOPODA.

*Squilla* . . . . ?
Gonodactylus chiragra, *Fabr*.

## *CIRRHIPEDIA.*

*Lepas*.
*Balanus*.

## *ANNELIDA.*

Tubicolæ.
Dorsibranchiata.
Abranchia.
Hirudo *sanguisorba*.
*Thwaitesii*.
Hæmopsis *paludum*.
Hæmadipsa Ceylana, *Blainv*.
Lumbricus . . . . ?

---

# NOTE

## ON THE FACULTY OF REPEATED RE-VIVIFICATION POSSESSED BY THE *ROTIFERA*, ETC.

The *Rotifer*, a singular creature, although it can only truly live in water, inhabits the moss on house-tops, dying each time the sun dries up its place of retreat, to revive as often as a shower of rain supplies it with the moisture essential to its existence; thus employing several years to exhaust the eighteen days of life which nature has allotted to it. These creatures were discovered by LEUWENHOECK, and have become the types of a class already numerous, which undergo the same conditions of life, and possess the same faculty. Besides the *Rotifera*, the *Tardigrades*, (which belong to the *Acari*,) and certain paste-eels, all exhibit a similar phenomenon.

But although these different species may die and be resuscitated several times in succession, this power has its limits, and each successive experiment generally proves fatal to one or more individuals. SPALLANZANI, in his experiments on the *Rotifera*, did not find that any survived after the sixteenth alternation of desiccation and damping, but paste-eels bore seventeen of these vicissitudes.

SPALLANZANI, after thoroughly drying sand rich in *Rotifera*, kept it for more than three years, moistening portions taken from it every five or six months. BAKER went further still in his experiments on paste-eels, for he kept the paste from which they had been taken, without moistening it in any way, for twenty-seven years, and at the end of that time the eels revived on being immersed in a drop of water. *If they had exhausted their lives all at once and without these intermissions, these Rotifera and paste-eels would not have lived beyond sixteen or eighteen consecutive days.*

To remove all doubt as to the complete desiccation of the animalcules experimented on by SPALLANZANI and BAKER, M. DOYÈRE has published, in the *Annales des Sciences Naturales* for 1842, the results of his own observation, in cases in which the mosses containing the insects were dried under the receiver of an air-pump and left there for a week; after which they were placed in a stove heated to 267° Fahr., and yet, when again immersed in water, a number of the *Rotifera* became as lively as ever.

Further particulars of these experiments will be found in the Appendix to the *Rambles of a Naturalist*, &c., by M. QUARTREFAGE.

# INDEX.

THE END.